The Writer's Workplace
with Readings

NINTH EDITION

The Writer's Workplace

with Readings

Building College Writing Skills

SANDRA SCARRY

Formerly with the Office of Academic Affairs
City University of New York

JOHN SCARRY

Formerly Senior Professor of English
Hostos Community College
City University of New York

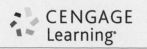

CENGAGE
Learning·

Australia • Brazil • Mexico • Singapore • United Kingdom • United States

CENGAGE
Learning

The Writer's Workplace with Readings: Building College Writing Skills, Ninth Edition
Scarry and Scarry

Content Developer: Rachel Kerns

Associate Content Developer: Jacob Schott

Senior Content Developer: Brooke Foged

Product Assistant: Katy Werring

Marketing Manager: Erica Messenger

Content Project Manager: Aimee Bear

Art Director: Diana Graham

Manufacturing Planner: Betsy Donaghey

IP Analyst: Ann Hoffman

IP Project Manager: Kathryn Kucharek

Production Service/ Compositor: Lumina Datamatics

Text and Cover Designer: Diana Graham

For product information and technology assistance, contact us at
Cengage Learning Customer & Sales Support, 1-800-354-9706

For permission to use material from this text or product, submit all requests online at **www.cengage.com/permissions**. Further permissions questions can be emailed to **permissionrequest@cengage.com**.

Library of Congress Control Number: 2016951207

Student Edition:
ISBN: 978-1-305-96095-4

Loose-leaf Edition:
ISBN: 978-1-305-95099-3

Cengage Learning
20 Channel Center Street
Boston, MA 02210
USA

Cengage Learning is a leading provider of customized learning solutions with employees residing in nearly 40 different countries and sales in more than 125 countries around the world. Find your local representative at **www.cengage.com**.

Cengage Learning products are represented in Canada by Nelson Education, Ltd.

To learn more about Cengage Learning Solutions, visit **www.cengage.com**.

Purchase any of our products at your local college store or at our preferred online store **www.cengagebrain.com**.

Printed in the United States of America
Print Number: 02   Print Year: 2017

FOR OUR STUDENTS

What shall I do this year? What shall I become? What shall I learn—truly learn and know that I have learned by the time I look at these pages next year?

Lorraine Hansberry
Journal entry of August 23, 1962

CONTENTS

PART 3   UNDERSTANDING THE POWER OF WORDS   261

14   Choosing Words That Work   263

15   Paying Attention to Look-Alikes and Sound-Alikes   281

PART 4   CREATING EFFECTIVE PARAGRAPHS   307

16   Working with Paragraphs: Topic Sentences and Controlling Ideas   309

20 Developing Paragraphs: Description 381

21 Developing Paragraphs: Process Analysis 405

22 Developing Paragraphs: Comparison/Contrast 421

PART 6   SUMMARIZING SHORT TEXTS ACROSS THE DISCIPLINES   617

PART 7   FURTHER READINGS FOR THE COLLEGE WRITER   637

The goal of this course is to guide students toward effective writing. When students master basic grammar and usage, they are on their way to academic success. Students need to acquaint themselves with professional writers whose work will broaden their understanding of what constitutes good writing. *The Writer's Workplace with Readings* will help fill any gaps in the fundamentals and will demonstrate that one of the best ways to raise the level of a student's writing is to study professional models, absorb the best they have to offer, and then respond with writing practice.

The Writer's Workplace with Readings contains a **foundational plan** that instructors and their students can follow to produce more powerful writing. This textbook is the product of more than twenty-five years of classroom teaching and has led to adoptions nationwide in two- and four-year colleges. This proven approach to the learning of sentence skills and the development of effective paragraphs and essays has served more than **half a million** students in the United States and Canada, and has established *The Writer's Workplace with Readings* as a leader in the field. The programs have helped students not only in their English classes but also in the work of many of their other courses. Because of the deliberate inclusion of many topics related to college issues and the world of work, even in grammar exercises, *The Writer's Workplace with Readings* engages users with topics relevant to the concerns of today's college students.

One of the central goals of *The Writer's Workplace with Readings* is to provide **flexibility** for both teacher and student. As a result, we organized the book so that it works equally well in the classroom, in the writing lab, in collaborative groups, with a tutor, or at home. In fact, when we consider the completeness of the book itself and the wealth of resources available online, the result is a system of total support for any and all developmental needs.

New to This Edition

1. **Revised emphasis on relevance and student engagement.** New practice activities and exercises have been added to every chapter. New examples provide a richer context to each writing lesson. The scope and diversity of themes and topics reflect the evolving engagements and concerns of the writer's workshop user:
   - improved examples and revised activities with an eye on relevance, student interest, and relatability
   - improved design for clarity and ease of use

2. **Updated ESL coverage.** We have restructured Appendix A, "Reference Guide for the ESOL Student," to provide the most complete learning experience for the ESOL learner. Our reference guide now includes an improved design layout of charts and tables, enriched examples for clarity and student comprehension, an Idiomatic Expressions table, even more gerunds and infinitives, solutions for confusing prepositions (*in* and *on*), and enhanced treatment of verbs with stative meanings.

3. **Part 6, "Summarizing Short Texts across the Disciplines," is revised with new readings.** The skill of summarizing is as important as ever for the college student, and this section includes short readings carefully curated to help develop this skill. Including a series of activities directly related to other

college courses, these ten short texts are excerpted from a variety of disciplines, such as education, psychology, and anthropology.

4. **Part 7, "Further Readings for the College Writer" is improved with deeper coverage.** The completely rewritten "Strategies for the Active Reader" includes an opening paragraph to contextualize Scarry and Scarry's already comprehensive reading strategies. Increased attention is devoted to evolving technologies and the adaptive techniques students must learn in order to engage positively with the digital educational environment.

   - The thoroughly rewritten "Strategies for the Active Reader" includes:
     - screen and digital reading strategies
     - context clues
     - vocabulary instructions and how to use a dictionary
     - revised and expanded vocabulary instruction to improve reading skills

   - Six new readings broaden the range of topics and styles for greater relevance to the student. New readings in the "Further Readings for the College Writer" section of *The Writer's Workplace with Readings* include the informative science essay "Space Food" by Scott M. Smith et al.; the outlandish and highly entertaining essay "The Huge, Bee-Decapitating Hornet That Can't Survive Group Hugs" by Matt Simon; the nonconformist call to arms "If I Feel Uncomfortable I must be Doing Something Right" by Elliot Begoun; the deeply personal "The Perils of Being Too Nice" by Jen Kim; the confrontational "Ban Computers and Cell Phones from Classrooms" by Dr. Ira Hyman; and an examination of self and society in "Why I Decided to Buy a Handgun" by Trevor Hughes.

5. **"Working Together" and "Portfolio Suggestions" include freshly cultivated readings and improved activities to ensure that the content is relevant and relatable.** Several new topics for the "Working Together" feature call for the discussion of and written response to current issues of interest to today's college students: career-related writing, college sports and money, and the challenges facing many veterans.

6. **Chapter 33 includes updated MLA citation instruction.** New material features updated criteria based on the newly released *MLA Handbook*, Eighth Edition.

Special Features of *The Writer's Workplace with Readings*

The Process Writing Approach

The first two chapters of *The Writer's Workplace with Readings* introduce the idea that writing is a process. From the very start, students engage in short skill-building activities that give them opportunities to practice all the actual techniques and concepts taught in these chapters. Whether the skill is freewriting, brainstorming, or revising for coherence and unity, students participate directly in these important stages of the writing process.

The Comprehensiveness of a Grammar Handbook

Students come to college writing classes from a wide range of backgrounds. Many students expect that their developmental English class will address any gaps in their knowledge of grammar. This textbook more than satisfies those expectations.

Unrivaled by other writing textbooks, *The Writer's Workplace with Readings* contains an exceptionally comprehensive language development section. Carefully crafted definitions, charts, and rules provide visual aids for students as they learn the underlying elements of sentence structure and punctuation. A careful sequencing of topics builds from less complex to more complex concepts as the students proceed from nouns and verbs, to phrases and fragments, to coordination and subordination. After having absorbed this material, students will be able to discuss, analyze, and edit their own writing, as well as better understand the comments made by instructors on papers they return. Instructors who have concentrated on this sentence-building section of the book report that our easy-to-follow presentation leads to better outcomes and student engagement.

Carefully Constructed Practices, Exercises, and Mastery Tests to Address Different Rates of Learning

Because all students learn at different rates, some students need more practice opportunities than others in order to absorb a particular concept fully. Whether the concept is subordination or parallel structure, our textbook offers multiple opportunities to address students' needs. The quality and quantity of these exercises is unsurpassed. Students benefit from these additional practice opportunities, and with the aid of the answer key to selected exercises, they can manage their progress.

Continuous Discourse

Exercises teaching grammar skills use continuous discourse. Building a foundation in sentence skills and reading fresh and stimulating information that contains humor and human interest will make grammar exercises all the more appealing.

Editing Tests

The Editing Student Writing feature appears in Chapters 4 through 13 and serves as a cumulative review. Each of these exercises asks students to analyze student writing by identifying and correcting errors using editing symbols. When students become familiar with these symbols, they find it easier to interpret corrections that instructors or peers make when evaluating their work. Finally, we have included these exercises to remind students of the importance of editing their own papers before they hand them in; the errors they find in these exercises are the types of errors they must learn to find in their own writing.

Focus on Word Choice

All writing is made stronger when the writer pays careful attention to word choice. Word choices can range from deciding on the correct form of *its* and *it's,* to understanding why the word *kid* is not appropriate in formal writing. The two chapters that make up this section contain lessons that demonstrate the need for precise and appropriate language.

Patterns of Rhetorical Development

Strong paragraphs are the solid blocks of any good piece of writing, and students need to build on such foundations to produce successful college essays. The organization of the chapters in Part 4 follows the classical rhetorical modes, the most commonly accepted method of introducing developmental students to the discipline of college writing. Each explains the basic elements needed to develop a paragraph using a particular rhetorical pattern. Students study and then practice the specific elements of each mode. A step-by-step method then guides them to the constructions of basic paragraphs or essays. Finally, accessible professional models precede a list of writing topics. These models encourage students to compose their own creative paragraphs that demonstrate their skill with each rhetorical mode. Many instructors who have used previous editions of the text consider this section to be the heart of the book.

Step-by-Step Approach

Following the study and practice of the elements of each particular mode, students will follow a step-by-step guide to construct their own paragraphs. This ensures a focus on each element, whether it is the topic sentence, a supporting detail, or a transitional expression. This section keeps developmental students on task and builds confidence.

Professional Writing Models with Inspiring Content

While the professional models in each chapter have the primary goal of demonstrating a rhetorical mode, each example serves to enrich our students' lives and increase their love of reading. Mature individuals deserve to be challenged by stimulating and sometimes provocative content. With the confidence gained from the study and practice of each modal element, students will be inspired by these short professional paragraphs to produce thoughtful and creative writing pieces of their own. A list of related writing topics accompanies each model paragraph for student-writers' consideration.

Write for Success

In each chapter, a topic is presented to engage students in discussion and writing on an issue directly related to factors that determine a person's success in college.

Collaborative Work

Developing writers benefit from the input of their peers and instructors, so the book encourages students to collaborate whenever possible. In the prewriting stages, in-class brainstorming and discussion of ideas for specific writing topics are especially productive to help students get started. Collaborative work is again useful during the stages of editing and revision.

Following the Progress of a Student Essay

This feature gives students a unique opportunity to develop an essay of their own as they follow each part of a model student essay on the same topic. This activity's structure provides one important advantage over other approaches. Students can compare the quality of their own work at each stage with the work of the model student.

A Focus on the Thesis Statement

The Writer's Workplace with Readings focuses on writing a strong thesis statement, which is critical for student success. For the student who finds it difficult to narrow a topic, find the controlling idea, or indicate the strategy of development, "Focus on the Thesis Statement" offers very valuable strategies.

Model Introductions and Conclusions

Because of the challenges that accompany constructing introductory and concluding paragraphs, this text presents a variety of introductory and concluding strategies used by professional writers. Students can study these examples and use these strategies in their own writing.

Development of the Classic Argument

Developing an essay centered on argument or persuasion challenges even the most experienced of writers. This type of writing demands logical and critical thinking. Instructors will find several short arguments that are accessible to students because they are close to students' experiences and provide opportunities for debate. These models will help students grasp the classic elements of argumentative writing before composing an argument of their own.

The Research Paper

The goal of this feature is to teach the skills of quoting, paraphrasing, and summarizing. Students at this level need these skills before they can hope to be successful at writing a research paper. The importance of avoiding plagiarism is stressed, and up-to-date MLA documentation examples are provided.

The Essay Exam

Students have the opportunity to analyze typical essay exam questions and develop strategies for writing the answers under the pressures of a time constraint.

Summarizing Short Texts Across the Disciplines

Ten brief texts from a variety of disciplines offer opportunities for students to learn how to summarize college textbook material, an essential skill for academic work.

Active Reading Approach

The Writer's Workplace with Readings depends heavily on student participation in the process of writing, but no successful writing is produced without significant attention to reading and study skills. The section called "Strategies for the Active Reader" begins Part 7, and it emphasizes the importance of active reading for the developmental writing student. One of the essays, the classic "How to Mark a Book" by Mortimer Adler, makes the case for active reading. Students are encouraged to become more engaged in the texts they are reading and to place more emphasis on their critical thinking skills, which will take students far beyond the experience of a particular writing class and will enrich many other parts of their lives.

Further Readings Illustrating Rhetorical Modes

In addition to the carefully chosen professional models used throughout the first five parts of *The Writer's Workplace with Readings*, twenty-one high-interest essays support the work of the book, with each reading giving the student additional opportunities for study and enjoyment. Each reading illustrates a particular rhetorical mode, thus reinforcing the work of previous chapters. Brief introductory notes help students understand and appreciate the background and context of each reading. Finally, two sets of questions guide the instructor through classroom work. The first set, "Questions for Critical Thinking," concentrates on the structure of each piece, while the second set, "Writing in Response," stimulates critical reaction to the themes and leads to a number of challenging writing opportunities.

Other Features

End-of-Activities

The "Working Together" activity appears at the end of every and provides the instructor with an additional or alternative lesson plan that encourages critical thinking and collaborative learning. These activities tend to stress college issues (e.g., hazing) and job-related issues (e.g., sexual harassment). Portfolio Suggestions complement the "Working Together" feature and encourage students to gather and save all their writing efforts for evaluation purposes and also for ongoing and future writing projects.

Five Appendices

The five appendices offer a wealth of pertinent and useful reference material. This section is an especially valuable resource for speakers of English as a Second Language. The first appendix deals with specific issues for ESOL, while the other appendices include material on parts of speech, irregular verbs, spelling, and transitions. Together, all these sections serve as a resource for students who find themselves in other courses that require coherent writing.

An Answer Key to Practices and Selected Exercises

The answer key at the end of the book provides answers to all the practices and approximately one-third of the exercises in the book. For instance, where three exercises are given on a topic, the answers to the first exercise are always included. This answer key allows students to work independently. Of course, answers to the Mastery and Editing Tests are given only in the Annotated Instructor's Edition.

Hundreds of Suggestions for Writing Topics

Throughout the text, numerous writing topics are suggested. These topics are always related to and suggested by the content at hand. We repeatedly incorporate discussion and collaboration in the brainstorming stages so students can expand their thinking and learn to question their assumptions. Students are encouraged to take notes during discussions and save their own paragraphs, other classmates' ideas, and any other material they may have gathered for future writing assignments.

Additional Resources

The Writer's Workplace with Readings is supported by a wide range of instructional materials, each one designed to aid the teacher's classroom work:

Annotated Instructor's Edition

This book provides answers to the practices and exercises for the student edition.

Instructor Companion Site

The Instructor Companion Site offers instructors a wide array of helpful teaching tools, specially designed by the authors to address the needs of a variety of instructors and course structures, including additional resources, helpful tips, and sample syllabi for a variety of courses.

Instructor's Resource Manual with Exercises and Test Bank

The variety of materials in this manual enhances, reinforces, and complements the material presented in the primary text. The revised Instructor's Resource Manual supports the new edition of *The Writer's Workplace with Readings* with a view toward integrating materials more closely with the objectives, chapter content, and readings in the textbook. Instructors will find comprehensive support for planning and organizing their courses including specific sample syllabi, additional assignments, sample student writings, and a compendium of assignments presented in the manual. The Test Bank includes diagnostic, exercise, and mastery tests, which in turn include multiple-choice, identify, fill-in-the-blank, correction, and revision questions.

MindTap is a customizable, easy-to-use learning platform that supports both skills assessment and personalized learning. Based on content from *The Writer's Workplace with Readings*, MindTap includes an interactive eBook, Aplia follow-up assignments for practice and review, additional readings, related writing assignments, pre-made digital flash cards, and multimedia activities that connect directly to what students are learning. Instructors who use MindTap will find it easy to sequence, individualize, and customize.

Aplia for *The Writer's Workplace with Readings* (www.aplia.com/developmentalenglish)

Aplia offers instruction, practice, and immediate feedback to help developmental students master their writing and grammar skills. Add, drop, mix, and match chapters and lessons. Aplia for *The Writer's Workplace with Readings* is a student resource that provides developmental writing students with clear, succinct, and engaging writing instruction and practice to help students master basic writing and grammar skills. Aplia for *The Writer's Workplace with Readings* features ongoing individualized practice, immediate feedback, and grades that can be automatically uploaded so instructors can see where students are having difficulty.

Cognero

Cognero is Cengage Learning's flexible, online system that gives instructors the freedom to author, edit, and manage test-bank content from multiple Cengage Learning solutions.

Acknowledgments

The latest edition of our book finds us once more indebted to a host of people, including those who have inspired us and those who have worked with us to make certain our initial vision of the book was realized. First of all, we thank some wonderful colleagues at Hostos Community College (Professors Vermell Blanding, Sue Dicker, and Cynthia Jones chief among them) and all the amazing students we have taught there. Their inspiration has been a constant source of energy and creativity to us. First and foremost, it is the hard work and courage of our students, and indeed of all the students who have used our textbook, that motivate us to refine the text. We have come to realize that the skills taught in this book have the ability to empower people and change their lives.

We would not achieve the degree of success we do with each new edition without the invaluable insights of our professional reviewers. The fruits of their many years of collective experience, and their individual perceptions for the needs of this latest revised manuscript, have made our efforts for this new edition possible. To each of them, our sincerest gratitude:

Adam Carlberg, *Tallahassee Community College*

Johanna Enger, *Wood Tobé-Coburn School*

Carolyn McCargish, *Oklahoma Panhandle State University*

Suzanne McDonald, *Fox Valley Technical College*

Aydasara Ortega, *New York Career Institute*

Nick Pratt, *Garret College*

Megan Uberti, *State College of Florida, Bradenton*

David Valladares, *Tallahassee Community College*

ellyy/Shutterstock.com

An Invitation to Writing

Appreciate That You Are Unique

No two people think exactly alike. Even identical twins grow up to develop many individual qualities. Appreciate your uniqueness. You have valuable life experiences, ideas, and perceptions that are worth writing about. You already know more than you think you know, and writing will help you learn more about yourself. In college, we celebrate the diversity of ideas.

- In what ways are you different from your family and friends?
- What three qualities make you a unique person?

Gathering Ideas for Writing

1

CHAPTER OBJECTIVES — In this first chapter, you will practice several **prewriting techniques** used by professional writers as well as student writers as they generate ideas and gather material for writing.

- journal writing

- focused freewriting

- brainstorming, clustering, and outlining

- paragraph development preview

- essay development preview

- conducting interviews and surveys

Overview of the Writing Process

The following chart shows the stages a writer goes through to produce a finished piece of writing. Writers may differ slightly in how they approach a task, but for most of us the following steps are necessary.

THE WRITING PROCESS

PREWRITING STAGES

1. Choose the topic and consider what aspect of that topic interests you.

2. Gather ideas using prewriting techniques.

WRITING AND REVISING

3. Compose a first draft and then set it aside for a time.

4. Reread your first draft and, if possible, ask the instructor or classmates for input.

5. Revise the first draft by adding, cutting, and moving material. Continue to revise, correcting grammar errors and producing new drafts, until you are satisfied.

PROOFREADING

6. Proofread the final copy, looking especially for typographical errors (typos), misspellings, and omitted words.

Christopher Futcher/Getty Images

Beginning to Write: Caring about Your Topic

Whether you are writing a college paper or a report at work, your belief in the importance of your topic and confidence in your own ideas will be major factors in your success as a writer. Sometimes a college writing assignment can seem to have little or no relevance beyond a requirement for a passing grade. In this course, however, you should consider each assignment as an opportunity to do the following:

- discover that you have ideas worth expressing
- explore topics that you care about
- incorporate the ideas of others into your own work

Prewriting Techniques: The First Step in the Writing Process

Prewriting, the earliest stage of the writing process, uses techniques such as brainstorming, clustering, and outlining to transform thoughts into words.

Very few writers ever sit down and start writing immediately. To produce effective work, most writers begin by using a variety of strategies called *prewriting techniques.* These techniques help writers generate ideas and gather material about topics that are of interest to them or that they are required to write about for their work. Prewriting techniques are a way to explore and give some order to what might otherwise be a confusing hodgepodge of different thoughts on a topic. These techniques reassure every writer who feels the stress of looking at a blank page or an empty computer screen, knowing it has to be filled. Not only will the writer have needed material but he or she can also plan how to develop that material: what the major ideas will be, what the order of those ideas will be, and what specific details will be used. The rest of this chapter will describe these prewriting techniques and provide opportunities to practice them.

Journal Writing

Journal writing is the written record of a person's observations, thoughts, reactions, or opinions. Kept daily, or nearly every day, the journal usually draws on the writer's experiences.

At some point in their lives, many people keep a diary or a journal. They may keep a simple record of day-to-day events, or they may want to explore thoughts and opinions about a variety of topics. If the journal is a personal one, the writer does not have to worry about making a mistake or being misunderstood. Furthermore, the journal writer need not worry about handwriting or the organization of ideas. The writer is the only person who will be reading the pages of that journal. Personal journals allow us to be totally honest and to write about anything we wish.

If you keep a personal journal, you might want to record events that happen around you, focus on problems you are trying to solve, or note your personal reactions to the people you know. Until you actually put your thoughts into words, you may not be fully aware of all your feelings and opinions. Most writers are surprised and pleased with the results of their personal explorations in writing.

For some people, a journal is a kind of scrapbook of meaningful written expressions they find around them. These journals could include drawings, quotations from books and articles, snippets of overheard conversations, or information heard on the radio or television. Over time, journals help students grow as writers and add to their overall success in college.

Another type of journal is the one that will definitely have an audience, even if that audience is only a single instructor. In many writing classes, instructors require students to keep a more public journal as part of a semester's work. In this more public journal, handwriting will be important and some topics might be considered inappropriate. Sometimes this journal contributes to the final grade for a course. Instructors who make a journal part of their semester's assignments understand how such writing, done frequently, gives students valuable practice in setting thoughts down on paper.

Entry from *The Diary of Latoya Hunter*

Keeping a journal is especially popular during adolescence, partly because these years are usually a time of uncertainty when young people are trying to discover themselves as individuals. The following selection is from the published diary of a junior high school student, Latoya Hunter, who began to keep a journal when she was only twelve years old. The diary reports on her growing need for independence and her changing perceptions of the world around her.

> Today my friend Isabelle had a fit in her house. It was because of her mother. She's never home and she expects Isabelle to stay by herself. Today she was extra late because she was out with her boyfriend. Isabelle was really mad. She called her father and told him she wanted to live with him because her mother only cared about one person—her boyfriend. She was so upset. She was throwing things all over the place and crying. I never saw her like that before. It was really sad to see. I felt bad when I had to leave her all by herself. I hope she and her mother work it out but all mothers are the same. They think that you're young and shouldn't have an opinion. It's really hard to communicate with my parents. They'll listen to me but that's about it. They hardly take me seriously and it's because of my age. It's like discrimination! If you do speak your mind, you end up getting beaten. The real pain doesn't come from the belt though, it comes from inside. That's the worst pain you could ever feel.

ACTIVITY **1** **Writing a Journal Entry of Your Own**

In the selection you have just read, Latoya Hunter sadly observes a friend going through an emotional crisis. Latoya uses her journal to explore her own feelings about parent–child relationships and to express what she thinks are some of the common failings of parents.

Write a journal entry of your own. Report an incident in which you were successful or unsuccessful in communicating with someone you know. The person could be a family member or someone from outside your family. Looking back on the incident, what contributed to the success or failure of that communication? What part did each person play that led to the final outcome?

_____

_____

_____

_____

_____

_____

_____

_____

_____

_____

_____

_____

_____

_____

_____

_____

_____

_____

_____

_____

Focused Freewriting

Focused freewriting offers another way to explore writing topics. With this technique, the writer keeps on writing for a predetermined amount of time and does not stop, no matter what. The goal of this technique is to put words on paper; even if nothing new comes to mind, the writer keeps going by repeating a particular idea. This approach is one way to free a writer from what is often called "writer's block," that moment in the writing process when a person runs out of words and becomes paralyzed by the blank page or computer screen.

> **Focused freewriting** is a prewriting technique in which the writer explores a topic by writing for a predetermined amount of time without stopping, even if it means repeating the same ideas.

Here, for example, is what one young man wrote when he was asked to write for five minutes on the topic of *keeping a journal:*

I'm supposed to write about journal writing. I've never kept a journal so how can I say anything about it? But I broke into my younger sister's diary once and found out about a boy she had kissed. It was one of those diaries with those little keys and I ruined the lock. She didn't speak to me for over a month and my parents were mad at me. I thought it was funny at the time. After that she didn't keep a diary anymore. So now what should I say? Now what should I say? I don't really know. I guess I might keep a journal to keep track of important things that happen to me, like the day my dad came home with a used car for me—now that was really cool. Of course, it had a lot of problems that we had to fix over the next year little by little, but that was really an awesome day.

ACTIVITY 2 **Focused Freewriting**

For this exercise, consider the topic *My Attitude toward Writing* as an opportunity to practice focused freewriting. Write for at least five minutes without stopping, making sure that you keep going even if you have to repeat some thoughts.

_____

_____

_____

_____

_____

_____

_____

_____

_____

_____

Brainstorming, Clustering, and Outlining

Brainstorming

Of all the prewriting techniques, brainstorming is perhaps the most widely used. Brainstorming is an exercise in free association. You allow a thought or phrase to lead you from one idea to the next until you feel you have fully explored your topic. Many writers find brainstorming liberating because item order is unimportant and no special connection is needed between items. The main goal is to jot down everything while your mind explores different paths. Later, you can sort the items, grouping some and eliminating others. Unless you are doing outside research, brainstorming is probably the best way to discover ideas for writing.

Brainstorming is a prewriting technique in which the writer uses free association to create a list of whatever words, phrases, or ideas come to mind on a given topic. It can be done alone or in a group.

The following list shows a college student's initial brainstorming on the topic of *parent–teen communication*.

Problems talking with my father
> Called me immature sometimes
> Occasionally shouted
> Too tense
> Seemed overly critical

Stacy's father
> Seemed to have a sense of humor about everything, not so serious, easygoing

Guidance counselor
> Always calm, no hurry, always listened

What prevents a good conversation with a parent?
> person's voice—loud, soft, angry, calm
> namecalling, putdowns
> words that hurt
> bad language
> body language—no eye contact, frowning, glaring
> authoritarian or controlling
> monopolizing the conversation
> tense
> withdrawal or the silent treatment
> disrespectful and rude
> rushed, not listening
> rigid, won't consider any other viewpoint
> sarcastic

Below is a revised brainstorming list showing how the student has reorganized the initial list.

Advice to Parents: How to Communicate with Your Teens
Choose your words carefully
> do not call people names
> do not belittle them—use example of my father
> do not use bad language
> do not be disrespectful
> do not be mean or sarcastic
> do not use the silent treatment or monopolize the talk

(continued on next page)

Listen to the way you sound, your tone, your attitude

    watch the volume of your voice—use example of Stacy's father

    wait until you have calmed down so you do not sound angry and tense

    don't sound rushed and hurried, as if you have no time to listen

    don't sound too controlling

Take a look at your body language

    work at being calm and relaxed

    do not withdraw; if possible give the person a hug or a pat on the shoulder

    no physical abuse—pushing, shoving, slapping

    what is your facial expression (frowning, glaring, smirking, no eye contact)?

Clustering

Clustering is another method of gathering ideas during the prewriting stage. Clustering is very similar to brainstorming, except that when you cluster, you produce a visual map of your ideas rather than a list. Begin by placing a key idea (usually a single word or phrase) in the center of the page. Then jot down other words and phrases that come to mind as you think about this key idea. As you work, draw lines or branches to connect the items.

Here is how the writer might have explored the topic *Parent–Teen Communication* using a clustering technique:

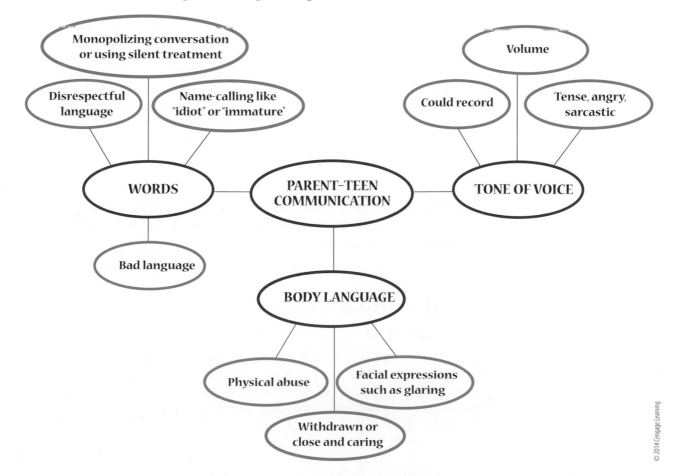

Clustering is a prewriting technique that emphasizes the connections among items on a brainstorming list. The topic is written in the middle of the page and has a circle drawn around it. As details or ideas are generated, they are circled and then lines are drawn to connect them to related details or ideas. This process continues until the topic has been fully explored. Variations of clustering are known as *mapping, webbing,* and *branching.*

ACTIVITY **3** **Using Brainstorming or Clustering to Develop a Topic of Your Own**

Use either brainstorming or clustering to develop your ideas on one of the following topics:

- communicating with teachers
- communicating on a cell phone
- communicating on the Internet (e-mail and chat rooms)

Create your brainstorming list or cluster on a separate sheet of paper.

Outlining

After generating ideas on a subject using these prewriting techniques, it is now important to put your thoughts into a logical order before presenting them to your audience. This is where the outlining begins. Outlining is the most formal method of organizing ideas at the prewriting stage. It is more difficult than the other prewriting techniques and usually comes after considerable brainstorming and rearranging of ideas. In a formal outline you must distinguish between major headings and subheadings and list these points in the order in which you will present them. Because organization and order are so important in outlining, we follow a conventional system of numbers and letters. In the sample outline that follows, notice the use of roman capital numerals (I, II, III) for major headings, indented capital letters (A, B, C) for subheadings, and arabic numbers (1, 2, 3) to show the next level of subheadings.

Outlining, the most formal method of organizing prewriting ideas, uses numerals and letters to distinguish between major headings and subheadings of a planned piece of writing.

Developing a Paragraph from an Outline

The outline is absolutely essential for keeping you on track and well-organized when crafting a piece of writing. In part 4 of this book, a more thorough approach to paragraph development will be considered. As a preview of the process, consider first the example of paragraph development below. Here, the student is developing a paragraph that advises parents to choose their words carefully when communicating with their children.

Each line in the draft paragraph on the right is matched in color with the corresponding points pre-written on the outline. The topic sentence and concluding sentence appear in red font.

I.　When parents talk to their teens, they should avoid harmful forms of communication.
　　A.　Namecalling
　　　　1.　My dad called me immature.
　　　　2.　Parents use words like "idiot."
　　B.　Bad language
　　　　1.　Swear words and insults
　　C.　The silent treatment

When parents talk to their teens, they should avoid harmful forms of communication. In the heat of the moment, some parents use namecalling when dealing with their children. My father, for example, has often used the word "immature" to describe me when I've made a mistake. The only effect his words had on me was to make me feel bad about myself. I have heard some of my friends' parents call them "idiots" or worse. Sometimes, parents of teenagers become so frustrated that they resort to using bad language. They swear and make insulting comments. When they calm down, it is too late to take back their words. The damage has been done. Finally, there is the complete opposite of the wrong words, and that is no words at all. When parents use the silent treatment, they refuse to discuss issues with their teenagers. As a result, nothing gets resolved. Instead of calling their children names, using bad language, and refusing to talk, parents should approach their teenagers respectfully when problems arise.

Developing an Essay from an Outline

The only difference between a paragraph outline and an essay outline is the length. Since an essay contains an introduction, multiple body paragraphs, and a conclusion, the outline you create will be considerably longer. However, the formatting will be the same: roman capital numerals (I, II, III) for major headings, indented capital letters (A, B, C) for subheadings, and arabic numbers (1, 2, 3) to show the next level of subheadings. (Essay development will be covered in part 5 of this book.)

Review the cluster diagram on the topic of *Parent-Teen Communication*. Here is how the student's outline of the material might have developed:

ADVICE TO PARENTS: How to Communicate with Your Teens

I　Introduction
　　Topic Sentence: Parents need to consider their words, tone, and body-language when they talk to their teens.
II　Choose your words carefully.
　　A.　Do not call people names.
　　　　1.　My father called me immature.
　　　　2.　Parents sometimes use words like "idiot."

(continued on next page)

    B. Do not use bad language.

    C. Do not be disrespectful.

    D. Do not monopolize the conversation.

    E. Do not use the silent treatment.

III Listen to your tone.

    A. Wait until you have calmed down so you do not sound angry and tense.

    B. Watch the volume of your voice.

        1. Stacy's father speaks softly.

        2. Stacy's father speaks reassuringly.

    C. Recording a conversation would reveal tone.

IV Observe your body language.

    A. Notice your facial expression.

        1. Are you glaring?

        2. Are you full of rage?

    B. Make eye contact.

    C. Do not withdraw; if possible, give the person a hug or hold that person's hand.

    D. Physical abuse is never appropriate.

V Conclusion

Parents who think about these three factors of communication will be able to avoid a lot of pain and heartache.

ACTIVITY **4**   **Making an Outline**

Using the title "Communication in the Twenty-First Century," make an outline for an essay that would describe modern forms of communication. You may want to consider the following items: Internet, e-mail, instant messaging, Skype, online courses, blogs, Facebook, fax machines, printers, digital cameras, smartphones, iPods, and iPads.

_____

_____

_____

_____

_____

_____

_____

_____

_____

_____

Student Essay

Now we are ready to look at the student essay that evolved from the initial brain-storming list. Notice that the writer is not bound to follow the brainstorming list or the outline word for word. As the student wrote, a certain creative flow occurred.

ADVICE TO PARENTS

How to Communicate with Your Teens

INTRODUCTION

When parents and teens cannot sit down and talk together, parents should take a long hard look at themselves to see if part of the blame might lie with them. Parents need to consider three factors: the words they choose, the tone of voice they use, and the message their body language gives.

PARAGRAPH 1 OF DEVELOPMENT

One usually thinks of words as being at the center of communication and, of course, words are important. The wrong words can unintentionally put people in a bad mood. Parents very often belittle their children or call them names. My father, for example, sometimes used the word "immature" to describe me when I made a mistake. I felt put down. It would probably have been better if he had talked with me about the situation and explained why he thought I had made a bad choice. I have heard parents call their children "idiots" and even worse. Namecalling only makes teens angry and defensive. It is hard after being attacked to feel open to any discussion at all. I have heard teens and parents use bad language and speak disrespectfully to each other. Speaking in the heat of the moment, people often say things they really do not mean, but when they calm down, it is too late to take back the words. The harm is done. Then there is the parent who monopolizes the discussion, giving the teen no opportunity to explain his or her position. Finally, there is the complete opposite of the wrong words, and that is no words at all. Have you ever experienced the silent treatment? With this approach, everyone feels terrible and there is no chance to work out a problem.

PARAGRAPH 2 OF DEVELOPMENT

A parent's tone of voice is a second factor in communicating with a teenager. Something said in a tense, harsh, or angry voice creates unnecessary bad feelings. The same words said with a firm but soft and reassuring voice can make for a completely different conversation. Even the volume of a person's voice can make a tremendous difference when people talk. My friend Stacy, for example, has a lot of disagreements with her father, but I have never heard their disagreements turn into angry arguments. Her father is from another country where people speak very softly. His voice is so calm and soft that I suppose this is one reason why Stacy never seems to get angry with him. He also uses a lot of humor, and they can laugh about her occasional outrageous behavior. It might be a good idea if some parents would record themselves when they are talking with their teenagers. They might be very surprised to hear their tone. This might give them a better understanding of why their teenagers suddenly become upset or withdrawn.

(continued on next page)

PARAGRAPH 3 OF DEVELOPMENT

Also, I wish some parents could see themselves when they are talking to their teens. Their body language really communicates, "I am angry at you!" Facial expressions can be glaring or even full of rage. To communicate with your teen, you need to make eye contact and, if possible, even give an affectionate hug or hold the teen's hand; in other words, let your body language say that you care about him or her even though you are upset about your teen's behavior. Obviously, any kind of physical abuse is never appropriate. Slapping, hitting, or punching is absolutely unacceptable. If you cannot control your teen without physical restraint, you need to seek outside help.

CONCLUSION

If only parents would understand the importance of words, tone, and body language the next time they faced a conflict with their teens, much needless pain and heartache could be avoided.

Conducting Interviews and Surveys

Journal writing, focused freewriting, brainstorming, and outlining are all techniques that you can use to explore your thoughts and ideas. Often, however, a writer needs to go further and obtain information from outside sources. An excellent way to obtain such information is to conduct an interview or prepare and distribute a survey or questionnaire. News reporters, marketers, social workers, and government employees are only a few of the people who use these techniques in their everyday work.

Interviews

Interviews are useful in many situations. Speaking to a single individual can provide information that you might not be able to get any other way. For example, you might want to interview an older family member to preserve the stories of your family's past. You might want to talk to someone who is working in a career that interests you. If you were considering a career in law, for example, speaking to a lawyer in your community might be more revealing than reading a book about the legal profession. An interview is also an excellent way to find information on very current topics, material you might have trouble finding in the library or even on the Internet.

The secret of a good interview lies in what happens before the interview. You must prepare properly. First of all, make an appointment with the person you want to interview. Let that person know how long the interview will take. If you intend to bring a recorder, be sure to ask for permission in advance. It is important for the person being interviewed to know what to expect so he or she can be relaxed and in a receptive frame of mind. Most important, the interviewer should always have a number of questions prepared beforehand. Few interviews go well without some structure and a sense of direction. This is not to say that every question must be asked in the order or with the exact wording as in the original plan; an interviewer is not restricted to a fixed set of questions. An interview can often take an interesting and unexpected turn with a single good question that leads to a surprising exploration of a subject.

When you prepare your questions, compose them so that the answers require some thought. You do not want to ask questions that can be answered with a simple yes or no; such replies are not useful because they do not encourage any in-depth discussion of the answer.

ACTIVITY 5 **Preparing Questions for an Interview**

The following five pairs of sentences could have been used in an interview in which a person was trying to learn about a lawyer's work. In each case, check which question would more likely lead to a thoughtful interview response.

_____ 1. What is a typical day at work like?

_____   How many hours a day do you work?

_____ 2. How much do you earn in a year?

_____   What is the range of salaries that a person could expect to earn as a lawyer?

_____ 3. What kind of law do you practice?

_____   What are the different areas of law practice, and how did you choose which one you wanted to pursue?

_____ 4. What is the most interesting case you have ever had?

_____   Have you ever had an interesting case?

_____ 5. Do you ever have a bad day?

_____   What are some of your greatest challenges, and how do you handle them?

Surveys

Taking a survey is an especially helpful prewriting technique when you want to write about a certain group's attitudes, practices, or experiences. For instance, you could do a survey on your classmates' attitudes toward binge drinking, your family's attitudes about how to share the household chores, or your community's attitudes about the need for a teen center. A survey is somewhat like an interview in that the person conducting it prepares a set of questions. However, an interview is conducted one on one, and the conversation has great flexibility. A survey, on the other hand, is usually written in advance. A number of participants agree to answer a set of questions. If they write their answers, the survey takes the form of a questionnaire. They may or may not complete the survey in your presence. What you will get will be the briefest answers to your questions—no more, no less. Obviously, you will run into difficulty if you realize later that you should have asked different questions. Therefore, in a survey, most of the work lies in the preparation of the questions and in experimenting with different ways of presenting questions to get the best answers. Unlike the interview, the survey may include questions that can be answered with a yes or a no. You may also want to ask questions that call for precise facts and figures. Here are a few other considerations:

1. Will people give their names, or will they be anonymous?
2. How will the surveys be returned? Most surveys can be completed online using free software. However you may choose to have the surveys emailed to your personal email account.

3. Do not be surprised if some people fail to answer the survey's questions at all. If the survey is too long or too complicated, people may decide they do not have time to fill it out. After all, most people volunteer to answer a survey, and they will be completing it as a favor to you.

4. The more responses there are to a survey, the more valid are the results. For example, if you want to know the attitudes of your classmates toward journal writing, the closer you come to having a 100 percent response, the more valid the survey will be.

5. How will you tally the answers? Will the results be presented as a chart, or will you write a report in which you explain the results?

ACTIVITY 6   **Composing Questions for a Survey**

Several serious problems on college campuses today relate to the use of alcohol. Underage drinking, binge drinking, drunken fights, and vandalism of property are some of the problems college administrations face. Compose five questions that could be included in a survey of your classmates to determine their drinking habits. Construct each question so that it asks for personal experience, not a person's opinion about what other students are doing. Here is an example:

Which of the following best describes how often you have an alcoholic drink?

a. never

b. only on holidays and other special occasions

c. two or three times a month

d. once or twice a week

e. three or more times a week

f. every day

1. _____

_____

_____

_____

_____

2. _____

_____

_____

_____

_____

3. _____

_____

_____

_____

_____

4. _____

_____

_____

_____

_____

5. _____

_____

_____

_____

_____

WRITE FOR SUCCESS

Now that you are in college, what are some of the issues that could prevent you from making school your priority? Write a response that considers the issues that personally affect you: an outside job, family responsibilities, competing pastimes such as watching television or spending time on your computer or smartphone.

Working Together

Carlina Teteris/Moment/Getty Images

Taking a Survey: Student Attitudes about Writing

Writers gather material for their work in a number of ways. One way is to conduct a survey, drawing on the experiences of people who have something in common. For this prewriting exercise, you will participate in a survey with all the students in your class. The survey asks students about their experiences with writing and their attitudes toward writing. As a class, you may add to or change the questions suggested here, but everyone should answer exactly the same questions.

Use the following procedure:

1. Refer to the survey in Activity 6.
2. Put your name or an assigned number in the top right corner of the survey for purposes of identification.
3. Answer the survey questions as completely and honestly as possible.
4. Select two people who will collect all the surveys and lead the class in tallying the information. One person can read off the responses; the other person can put the information on a blackboard where everyone can view the information and take notes.

PORTFOLIO SUGGESTION

A **portfolio** is a collection of materials representing a person's best work and is intended to help in the evaluation of that work, often for a grade in a course. A writer may also include materials to use in future work.

To start building your portfolio, take back your own page of responses to the survey and add it to any notes you took about the results of the class survey. Jot down any other ideas that might have come to you as you thought about the topic. Place all these in your portfolio and keep them for possible use in future writing assignments.

Consider using the interview and the survey as techniques for gathering material that can be transformed quite easily into an essay. Remember that people who write for a living—newspaper and magazine writers, for example—depend heavily on these techniques as they work on their material.

Student Survey

1. How would you describe the ideal place for a writer to work?

_____

_____

_____

_____

2. Where do you do your best writing—in the library, at home, or someplace else?

_____

_____

3. Is a certain time of day better for you than other times? When do you concentrate best?

_____

4. How long can you write with concentration before you need a break?

_____

5. What concerns do you have when you write?

_____

6. Have you ever kept a journal?

_____

7. Do you prefer composing on a computer or writing by hand?

_____

8. In high school, how many of your classes included writing opportunities? How often were you required to write?

_____

9. Keeping in mind that most people today use a telephone or e-mail to keep in touch, how often do you find yourself writing a letter?

   a. never   **b.** almost never   **c.** sometimes   **d.** often

10. At this point in your school career, which of the following best describes your attitude about writing?

   _____ I enjoy writing most of the time.

   _____ I occasionally like to write.

   _____ I usually do not like to write.

   _____ I don't have any opinion about writing at all.

Recognizing the Elements of Good Writing 2

CHAPTER OBJECTIVES

In this chapter, you will learn how a number of elements help to create effective writing.

- a carefully chosen **subject**
- a clear **purpose**
- a targeted **audience**
- a consistent and appropriate **voice**
- an overall **unity**
- a basic **coherence**

The Subject: What the Writing Is about

The *subject* of a piece of writing is also called the *topic* or the *central theme*. The subject can be chosen by the writer or assigned by someone else. We've all heard the student who complains, "I don't have anything to say." Not true! It may be that the student hasn't yet developed the skill to put ideas into writing, but we all know more than we think we do. We all know about our families, our homes, our friends, our opinions, and our experiences. We have childhood memories, interests, activities we participate in, and dreams. When we write, we need to tap into these life experiences and life lessons to find topics that interest us. We also need to remember that, if necessary, we can gather more information by consulting others.

Even with an assigned topic, a writer can often find an interesting aspect or approach to the subject. For example, on the subject of *paying for higher education*, a writer might choose one of the following approaches:

Topic: paying for higher education

Approaches	Examples
Tell a personal story:	The story of the debt that eternally stalks me
Discuss the effects:	The effects of free higher education on a society
Explain how to do something:	How to pay off college debt in five years
Show contrasts:	College student life in Sweden contrasted with college student life in America
Take a stand on an issue:	Higher education should be free and available to everyone

ACTIVITY ① **Providing Examples for Different Approaches to a Subject**

Below are five possible approaches a writer might take, given the topic of *working while going to school*. Provide a possible example for each approach.

1. personal story

   _____

2. effects

   _____

3. how to do something

   _____

4. comparison/contrast

   _____

   _____

5. persuasion

   _____

Purpose: The Writer's Intention

In school, when a student hands in a writing assignment, that student's primary purpose is usually to get a good grade. At work, an employee may produce a written document with the purpose of getting ahead in a job. These examples are not what we mean by *purpose*. In writing, *purpose* is what the piece of writing itself is intended to accomplish, apart from any other personal aims of the writer. The main purposes for writing are entertainment, information, and persuasion.

Sean Drakes/CON/Getty Images

Entertainment

A writer may want to entertain an audience. One way to do this is by telling a good story. We all remember, as children, how much fun it was when someone read us a story. We were being entertained. Most of the stories we see on television are shown for the purpose of entertainment. The novels we read were written to entertain us. What we call *narrative writing* (the telling of stories) is mostly in this category.

Information—Presentation of Facts

Most of the writing you will do in school and in your future career will be informational in nature. In school, you will take written tests and write papers to explain what you know about a subject; at work, you might find yourself explaining why your company's profits have diminished or increased. In formal writing, these explanations can be developed in more than one way, depending on the type of information required. The methods of development that you will learn in this book include the following:

- illustration (giving examples)
- narration (telling a story)

- description (using sensory images)
- process (explaining how to do something)
- comparison or contrast (examining similarities or differences)
- cause and effect (showing the relationship between two actions)
- definition and analysis (exploring the meaning of a term)
- classification (putting material into mutually exclusive groups)

Persuasion or Argumentation

Persuasive writing, or argumentation, tries to persuade the reader to agree with the writer's point of view on a topic. In our daily lives, the newspaper editorial is the most common example of persuasive writing. Such writing entails the use of logical reasoning along with facts and examples to support the writer's claims. An argument seeks to change the reader's mind or confirm a belief already held. Finally, the conclusion often pleads for a plan of action.

ACTIVITY **2**   **Understanding Purpose in Writing**

If your instructor told you that your assignment was to write an essay on some aspect of technology, each person in the class would most likely choose a slightly different topic. Below are five different topics concerned with some aspect of technology. For each topic, indicate what the writer's possible purpose (entertainment, information, or persuasion) could be.

Topic   *Purpose*

1. the cost of iPads   _____

2. my cell phone nightmare   _____

3. why everyone needs e-mail   _____

4. how to send a text message   _____

5. why our company should upgrade now   _____

Audience: The Writer's Intended Readers

If a writer is to be effective, he or she must understand who the audience is. Several important questions need to be asked. For example, what do the readers already know about the subject? What are their present attitudes toward the subject? Are they likely to agree with the writer's point of view? What are their ages? What is their level of education? Will they have similar interests, tastes, or political points of view?

Any number of factors could be important in determining how a writer chooses words and presents ideas. For example, if the readers are small children, the choice of vocabulary and ideas will have to be age appropriate. On the other hand, if the readers are adult professionals (perhaps a group of nurses or a team of engineers), the writer will be expected to know and use the terminology of that field. Sometimes the subject is a very sensitive one. In that case, the writer will need to treat the subject with appropriate seriousness.

ACTIVITY **3**   Identifying an Audience and a Purpose

Five possible writing subjects follow. In each case, choose a specific audience and imagine what the writer's purpose could be. An example has been done for you.

Subject	Audience	Purpose
Description of two history courses	College students	Information

Subject	Audience	Purpose
1. Protecting against identity theft	_____	_____
2. My first heartbreak	_____	_____
3. A letter asking for stronger laws against animal cruelty	_____	_____
4. A proposal requesting that video game design be taught in schools	_____	_____
5. How to create a successful fashion blog	_____	_____

Voice: How the Writer's Attitude Is Revealed

It is very difficult for a writer to be objective; writing almost always reveals conscious and unconscious attitudes. The voice of the writer comes through the text in the words chosen and the strategies used. In general, we can think of *voice* as revealing two different attitudes:

1. **Voice reveals an attitude toward the subject matter.** A politician might write *passionately* about his or her views; a comic writer would have a *humorous* or *ironic* voice; and a music critic might reveal an *admiring* or *judgmental* attitude.

2. **Voice reveals an attitude toward the audience.** The writer's attitude toward the audience ranges from very formal (such as the attitude of a scientist submitting a research study to an academic journal) to less formal (such as the attitude of a student writing a friendly e-mail to a classmate).

The experienced writer knows how to choose an appropriate voice, one that fits the purpose of the writing. For example, the cooking instructions on a box of rice are unlikely to carry any indication of a voice, which would give some feeling of the writer's personality. When an event is reported in a magazine or a newspaper, it should be presented without any obvious voice, although at times the writer's attitude becomes apparent by the choice of some words that carry positive or negative connotations. In other cases, an attitude is revealed by the choice of facts that are either included or excluded. In general, writing that informs is more objective than writing that seeks to entertain or persuade.

Another way a writer uses voice is by the choice of a personal pronoun. For example, in a diary or a memoir the obvious choice of pronoun would be the first person singular (*I* and *me*); in an article on car repair, the writer might well choose to address readers in the informal second person (*you*), a common choice for writing that includes directions or advice. For a business proposal to market a new product, the third person (*he, she, it,* or *they*), the most formal or objective, would be the most appropriate. This is the voice to use for academic and professional writing. In short, the appropriate level of formality between writer and audience is what determines the choice of personal pronoun used.

Two further points about *voice* should be kept in mind. First is the importance of remaining consistent. Unless you have a clear reason for changing your writing voice, do not make a change. In other words, when you begin to address your readers as *you*, do not change to *we* later in the same piece of writing. The second point is always to be *sincere*. Do not try to be someone you are not. For instance, using unfamiliar words from a thesaurus is not a good idea because the use of such words could easily sound a little out of place compared to the rest of your writing. You should be especially careful about this if English is your second language. Before you use more sophisticated words in your own writing, you should fully understand the meanings of the words and how they are used in different contexts.

Formal Writing in the Third Person
(*he, him, she, her, it,* or *they, them*)

In formal writing, where there is a distance between the writer and the reader, the *third person* is generally used. This is the voice you would use for most college-level work as well as job-related work. Read the paragraph that follows and study the writer's use of the third person. (Each use of a third person pronoun has been highlighted, along with the noun to which each pronoun refers.)

Young families today can be overwhelmed by the vast amount of information available on the Internet. They often find themselves helping their younger children find information for a variety of school projects, perhaps searching for a picture of an Indian longhouse or an experiment that could be used for a science fair. For families with teenagers, the problems can be much more frustrating. What are their children finding on the Internet and with whom are they chatting behind the closed doors of their bedrooms? It can be daunting for parents to Google an item and find there are 19,000 entries for that item. Undoubtedly they will be frightened to know that it will be nearly impossible to keep ahead of their children's ability to navigate all the new ways of communicating.

Less Formal Writing in the Second Person (*you, your*)

Here is the same material, but rewritten in a less formal voice, using the second person (*you*). Notice the passage uses more casual language. This choice is effective when the writer is giving instructions or speaking directly to the reader. (Each use of the second person has been highlighted.)

> Are you a parent who is overwhelmed by the vast amount of information available on the Internet? Do you find yourself trying to help your young child find appropriate information for a school project, such a picture of an Indian longhouse or an experiment that he or she could use for a science fair? If you have teenagers, your problems can be much more frustrating. What are your children finding on the Internet, and with whom are your children chatting behind the closed doors of their bedrooms? You may be daunted when you Google an item and find there are 19,000 entries for that item. You will undoubtedly be frightened to know that it will be nearly impossible for you to keep ahead of your children's ability to navigate all the new ways of communicating.

ACTIVITY 4   **Voice: Rewriting a Paragraph Using First Person Singular (*I*)**

Compose a new paragraph using the same content as in the two paragraphs you have just read, but now use the first person singular (*I*). Remember that using the first person singular results in the most informal voice in writing. The result is a more personal and casual tone, such as used in a diary or a memoir.

_____

_____

_____

_____

_____

ACTIVITY 5   **Voice: Rewriting a Paragraph to Avoid the Second Person (*You*)**

In many college courses, one important objective is for students to learn the proper standards for writing academic and work-related assignments. This involves the use of the more formal voice (not the second person *you*) in written work. Rewrite the following paragraph to avoid the use of the second person *you*. For instance, the opening words "Your world" could be rewritten as "The world," "This world," or "Our world."

> Your world is becoming ever smaller, and the rate of change is ever faster. When you graduate, statistics show that you will change jobs as many as ten times during your working years. You may even change from one field

(continued on next page)

to another. You will most likely work at a job that is unrelated to what you imagine yourself doing now while you are attending college. The work environment will be increasingly composed of people from many cultures and countries. What will be important is whether or not you are able to think broadly. Therefore, you should consider taking courses in college that will give you a wide range of opportunities. In a world that is much more global than ever before, nearly all fields (e.g., health, economics, and business) will not operate just within their own country's borders. You will need an international perspective in order to deal with all the issues of our day. If you understand other cultures, you will be much more successful in the global society that will be your world.

Your rewrite:

_____

_____

_____

_____

_____

Unity: All Parts Relating to the Central Theme

In good writing, every sentence connects to the subject, with every detail directly related to the main idea. All of the parts go together to make up a whole. The result is a sense of oneness, so that by the end of the piece, the writing feels complete. The reader should have no trouble grasping the writer's main idea.

ACTIVITY **6** **Editing Student Writing for Unity**

The following paragraph lacks unity because some sentences do not contribute to the main idea. As you read the paragraph, find and cross out four sentences that do not support the unity of the piece.

Often a new technology that starts out being very useful can prove to have a serious downside. Facebook is just such a technology. It started in a Harvard dorm room by Mark Zuckerberg and fellow students, who began the site to create a Harvard Facebook. Zuckerberg had been captain of his high school fencing team. Now just about everyone uses Facebook. According to *Business Insider*, about 1.3 billion Americans are registered as users. People enthusiastically post their personal thoughts and photos, as well as maintain ongoing conversations with their "friends." Facebook makes its money through advertisement. It turns out that many people have posted their thoughts and photos a little too freely. Thank goodness our country enjoys freedom of the press. Unfortunately for some, ideas and photos posted on Facebook do not go away. Many live to regret material they have posted. Young people looking for jobs should be concerned. Employers do not hesitate to look up a prospective hire on Facebook. If they do not like what they see, the person may not get hired. What happened to one young teacher should be a lesson for all. She had accompanied a student group to Europe. Wanting to show family and friends back home a scene from her trip, she posted a picture of herself smiling and holding up a glass of German beer. Germany is famous for its tasty beers. The administrators in the school where she taught viewed the photo and decided to fire her for being a bad influence on her students. The moral to this story seems to be that one should realize the consequences of making personal information public.

Coherence: Clear and Logical Progression of Thought

A piece of writing needs careful organization of all its parts so that one idea leads logically to the next. To help all the parts relate to one another, writers use three important techniques: *repetition of key words, use of synonyms and pronouns to refer to key words*, and *careful choice of transitional expressions*.

All writers must continually work to achieve coherence. Even professional writers write more than one draft because they see room for improvement as they move from one idea, one sentence, or one paragraph to the next. If something is unclear or lacks logical sequence, they revise. You too will be working on coherence in many of the chapters of this book.

The following paragraph is taken from a December 2000 article in the *Harvard Business Review*. The piece was intended to show people in business how to create "buzz" about a new fashion trend and thereby increase the sales of a product. The hot product in this case was a shoe popularly known as the Hush Puppy. The paragraph is a good example of how writers achieve coherence in their work. Notice the *repetition of key words* printed in red, the use of *pronouns* printed in blue, *synonyms referring to key words* printed in green, and *transitional expressions* highlighted in yellow.

> Sometimes even the most ordinary products can benefit from buzz. Remember Hush Puppies? When the company discovered that hip New York City kids were snapping up vintage pairs of its Hush Puppies at secondhand stores, it rushed into action. It began making its shoes in shades like Day-Glo orange, red, green and purple. Next, it sent free samples to celebrities, and not long after, David Bowie and Susan Sarandon were spotted wearing them. Then the company tightly controlled distribution, limiting the shoes to a handful of fashionable outlets. Soon high-end retailers like Saks, Bergdorf Goodman, and Barneys were begging for them. In just three years, from 1994 to 1996, Hush Puppies saw its annual sales of pups in North America skyrocket from fewer than 100,000 pairs to an estimated 1.5 million.

Repetition of Key Words

Notice that the key words *Hush Puppies* appear in the second sentence and again in the third sentence. In the last sentence, the words *Hush Puppies* occur for a third time and also a fourth time with a shortened, less formal name, *pups*.

Using Synonyms and Pronouns to Refer to Key Words

Writers often need to find other words or phrases to substitute for the key word so they will not have to repeat the key word over and over again. Notice in the paragraph how the author has twice used the common noun *shoes* to substitute for the proper noun *Hush Puppies.* Also, the words *samples* and *pairs* are used to refer to Hush Puppies.

Even more common is the use of pronouns to refer to key words. The pronoun *them* is used twice to refer to the Hush Puppies. In addition, notice the five pronouns (*its, it, it, it, its*) that refer to the shoe company.

Use of Transitional Expressions

Finally, coherence is achieved through the careful use of *transitions.* Transitions are words and expressions used in a piece of writing to show how the different ideas relate to each other. In the paragraph on Hush Puppies, several transitional expressions (marked in yellow highlighting) help the reader move through a sequence of events: *next, not long after, then, soon,* and *in just three years.* If you refer to Appendix E, you will find a list of many of these transitional words and expressions.

ACTIVITY 7 **Studying a Text for Coherence**

Read the following paragraph to discover the techniques used by the writer to achieve coherence. Find (1) four examples of the repetition of key words, (2) three examples of pronoun reference, (3) two examples of a word or phrase that takes the place of a key word, and (4) one example of a transitional word or expression. Label each of the examples that you find. (If necessary, refer to Appendix E for a list of transitional words and expressions.)

Nobody knows how many Web pages exist. Every day new pages are created. They are not numbered or put into any order. We might say they are dumped into the Internet. So then, how can we expect to find anything in this labyrinth of material? We need to use search engines, subject directories, and databases. These tools will lead us to the information we are seeking. Knowing how to use them will get us to the information we want within minutes. Although nearly everyone knows about the public search engines of Google and Yahoo, college students need to know much more about finding online sources using subject directories and databases. For instance, a database can tell you a number of things about a potential piece: how current the information is, the length of a piece, and the name of the periodical where the piece is found. This information helps a student evaluate whether or not the source is reliable and useful. Electronic sources of information have revolutionized research for students at every level.

WRITE FOR SUCCESS

What are some of the ways that successful students manage work, school, and personal life? Write a response that considers the following possibilities: (1) delegating more tasks to other family members, (2) postponing some personal matters until after graduation, (3) seeking out people who can help (4) trading with friends for babysitting and other needs, and (5) planning regular study times and finding quiet places to study.

Working Together

Matej Kastelic/Shutterstock.com

Knowing Your Audience

In planning a piece of writing, every writer must choose an approach to the subject, target the audience, and then keep that audience in mind as the work progresses. The following paragraph is from Patricia T. O'Conner's book on writing, *Words Fail Me*. In the passage, the author addresses the issue of a writer's audience and the importance of our awareness of audience in the writing process.

All writing has an intended audience, even the telephone book (it may be monotonous, short on verbs, and heavy on numbers and proper nouns, but it sure knows its readers!). Your audience probably won't be as wide as your area code, but it could be almost anyone—your landlord, a garden club, the parole board, Internet jocks, a college admissions director, fiction readers, the editorial page editor, the Supreme Court. Someone is always on the receiving end, but who? It's a big world out there, and before you write you have to narrow it down. Once you've identified your audience, everything you do—every decision you make about vocabulary, tone, sentence structure, imagery, humor, and the rest—should be done with this target, your reader, in mind.

After reviewing the text, divide into groups. Work together to fill in the following chart showing the relationship among audience, writer, topic, and voice. For example, who would write to a landlord; what might be the topic of such a letter; and would the writer use the first person (*I, we*), second person (*you*), or third person (*he, she, it, they*)?

Audience	Possible Writer	Possible Topic	Appropriate Choice of Voice
the Supreme Court	lawyer for store owners	interpretation of gun laws as it applies to store owners	formal (third person)
a microblog page			
a college admissions director			
dear diary			
a parole board			
the editor of a newspaper			
fiction readers			
a landlord			

If time permits, the class should come together to compare their charts. Choose one word that would describe the *tone* that should be set in each writing project.

PORTFOLIO SUGGESTION

When writers for advertising agencies work on ad campaigns, they must know their target audience. These writers choose every word for their ads with the greatest care. Because we live in such a visual culture, they also make sure that the photos and illustrations for their ads are compelling. Find and collect ads from magazines and newspapers that you find especially well designed and particularly effective. Take note of the modal or "hover" ads that pop up while you search the Internet. Study the words and pictures in these ads, noting the intended audience in each case. How does the ad target its audience? Preserve the ads and any notes for future writing projects that might interest you. You could choose from the following possible topics:

- audience in advertising
- the careful choice of vocabulary in advertisement
- the psychology of advertising

Creating Effective Sentences

Why Do College Students Need a Course in Writing?

You may think you will never need to know how to be a better writer. This is wishful thinking! As a student, you will need to express yourself in writing in nearly every course you take. In almost any professional job you may have in the future, it is likely that you will be required to send e-mails, write reports, and respond in writing for a variety of daily tasks. Even in your private life, there will be times when you will need to express yourself in writing. Perhaps no other course in college will prove to be more helpful than a writing course. The ability to write clear, effective prose is essential for every college-educated person.

- What are your plans for a future career?
- What part will writing play in that career choice?

Finding Subjects and Verbs in Simple Sentences

3

CHAPTER OBJECTIVES

In this foundational chapter, you will study what is essential to the basic sentence (also called the simple sentence). From here, you will be able to move to more complex sentence forms.

- finding the **subject** of a simple sentence, including sentences with prepositional phrases and appositive phrases

- finding the **verb** of a simple sentence

- identifying **six parts of speech** in a simple sentence

E+/Getty Images

Ideas may be communicated in more than one way. In informal situations, we might shake our head to mean yes or no, or we might use a single slang expression, such as "cool" to show our positive reaction to something. Such informal communication with friends is easy because we are with people who can see our gestures, can hear our tone of voice, and are familiar with our informal speech. When we write, however, we must express ourselves to an audience that does not see us or know us. In this case, our words must be chosen more carefully in order to be precise. One important way we, as writers, can be sure our ideas come across as clear and unmistakable is to use complete sentences.

What Is a Complete Sentence?

As writers, we need to express ourselves in complete sentences so that our ideas will be fully understood. This need for completeness means that every writing student must have a clear understanding of what makes up a sentence.

A **complete sentence** is a group of words that contains a subject and a verb and also expresses a complete thought.

How Do You Find the Subject of a Sentence?

The most basic sentence is called the *simple sentence. Simple* in this case does not mean *easy*, but it does mean that the sentence has only one subject-verb group. For most simple sentences, you can find the subject by keeping in mind five generalizations. Use generalizations 1 and 2 to complete the practice exercise that follows.

GENERALIZATION **1**   In a sentence, the subject usually answers the question "Who or what is the sentence about?"

GENERALIZATION **2**   The subject often occurs early in the sentence.

PRACTICE **1**   **In each of the following sentences, find the subject by asking yourself, "Who or what is the sentence about?"**

1. The gym seemed noisier than usual.

2. Our coach was shouting last-minute instructions.

3. He expected total concentration.

4. Three athletes were doing push-ups.

5. People were beginning to fill the bleachers.

GENERALIZATION **3**   The subject of a sentence is usually a noun or a pronoun.

Finding Nouns

A **noun** is a word that names a person, place, or thing. In the examples below, see how the noun *Avon* can function as a subject, an object, or a possessive.

Subject: *Avon* lifts weights.
Object: The coach trained *Avon.*
Possessive: *Avon's* coach always arrives early.

Two Categories of Nouns

1. **Common nouns or proper nouns.** Most nouns in English are *common nouns.* They are not capitalized. *Proper nouns* name particular persons, places, or things. They are always capitalized.

Common nouns	*Proper nouns*
aunt	Aunt Meriam
country	Brazil
watch	Rolex

2. **Concrete nouns or abstract nouns.** A second way to categorize nouns is to identify them as concrete nouns or abstract nouns. *Concrete nouns* name all the things we can see or touch, such as *desk, car,* or *friend. Abstract nouns* name the things we cannot see or touch, such as *justice, honesty,* or *friendship.*

Concrete nouns	*Abstract nouns*
face	loneliness
people	patriotism
jewelry	beauty

PRACTICE **2** **Underline every noun in each of the sentences below.**

1. The morning of June 27 was clear and sunny.

2. The flowers were blossoming profusely, and the grass was a rich green.

3. The people of the village began to gather in the square.

4. The lottery was conducted by Mr. Sommers.

5. The jovial man had time and energy to devote to civic activities.

Finding Pronouns

> A **pronoun** is a word that takes the place of a noun. Like a noun, a pronoun can be a subject or an object in a sentence. It can also be used to show possession.
>
> | | |
> |---|---|
> | *Subject:* | *He* lifts weights. |
> | *Object:* | The coach trained *him*. |
> | *Possessive:* | *His* coach always arrives early. |

There are four different categories of pronouns. (To see the complete list of these pronouns, consult Appendix B.) The chart on the next page lists only those pronouns that function as the subjects of sentences.

PRACTICE **3** **In each of the sentences below, replace the underlined word or words with a pronoun.**

1. The crowd arrived early. _____

2. The gym was noisy. _____

3. People waited eagerly. _____

4. Coach Ann Bradway had not lost a game yet this season. _____

5. Steven and I found the best seats in the front row. _____

6. Not one person could predict the outcome. _____

PRONOUNS THAT FUNCTION AS SUBJECTS

PERSONAL PRONOUNS THAT CAN BE SUBJECTS

	Singular	Plural
1st person:	I	we
2nd person:	you	you
3rd person:	he	they
	she	
	it	

RELATIVE PRONOUNS THAT CAN BE SUBJECTS

who   what

DEMONSTRATIVE PRONOUNS THAT CAN BE SUBJECTS

this   these

that   those

INDEFINITE PRONOUNS THAT CAN BE SUBJECTS

Singular

anyone	everyone	no one	someone
anybody	everybody	nobody	somebody
anything	everything	nothing	something
each	another	either (of)	neither (of)
one (of)	much	such (a)	

Plural

both	few	many	several

Singular or plural depending on meaning

all	more	none	some
any	most		

GENERALIZATION **4**   Noun or pronoun subjects in a sentence can be modified by adjectives.

An **adjective** is a word that modifies (describes or limits) a noun or a pronoun. Adjectives usually come directly in front of the nouns they modify, but they can also appear later in the sentence and refer back to the noun or pronoun.

young Avon   He is *young*.

PRACTICE **4**   **Underline the adjectives in each of the following sentences. Then draw an arrow to the noun each adjective modifies.**

1. The swimmer was confident.

2. Her long and strenuous workouts would soon pay off.

3. Several meters remained to reach the finish line.

4. Suddenly, she felt a terrible cramp in one leg.

5. A disappointing defeat would be the result.

GENERALIZATION 5   The subject of a sentence can be compound.

A **compound subject** is made up of two or more nouns or pronouns joined by one of the following: *and, or, either/or,* and *neither/nor.*
Avon and his *coach* lift weights.

PRACTICE 5   **Underline the compound subject in each of the following sentences.**

1. Exercise and thoughtful nutrition are the secrets to good health.

2. Mothers and fathers should help their children establish healthy lifestyles.

3. Unfortunately, biological factors and environmental factors can cause health problems.

PRACTICE 6   **The following sentences illustrate the different kinds of subjects you will encounter in this chapter. Examine each sentence and decide who or what the sentence is about. Underline the subject of each sentence. Then, on the line to the right, identify the subject with one or more of the following terms: common or proper noun; concrete or abstract noun; personal, relative or indefinite pronoun. Be as specific as possible.**

1. The young child played.   _____

2. Young Helen Keller played.   _____

3. She played.   _____

4. The park grew chilly.   _____

5. The leaves stirred.   _____

6. A thought suddenly struck her.   _____

7. Her parents and teacher would   _____
    be waiting   _____

8. Everyone would be worried.   _____

9. The time was getting late.   _____

10. Who would come and find her?   _____

NOTE: Not every noun or pronoun in a sentence is necessarily the subject of a verb. Remember that nouns and pronouns function as subjects, objects, and possessives. In the following sentence, which noun is the subject and which noun is the object?

Helen drank the water.

If you chose *Helen* as the subject and *water* as the object, you were correct.

In the exercises that follow, you will have the opportunity to practice finding subjects. Refer to the definitions, charts, and previous examples as often as needed.

EXERCISE **1**   **Finding the Subject of a Sentence**

Underline the subject in each of the following sentences. An example has been done for you.

The <u>loudspeaker</u> blared.

1. The train stopped.

2. Steven Laye had arrived.

3. She was passionate.

4. The decorations looked festive.

5. The fearful man held his bag tightly.

6. The pathway led to the stream.

7. Buses and cars choked the avenues.

8. People rushed everywhere.

9. The lights gave him a headache.

10. Enthusiasm filled his heart.

EXERCISE **2**   **Finding the Subject of a Sentence**

Underline the subject in each of the following sentences.

1. The road twisted and turned.

2. A young child hurried along briskly.

3. She carried an important message.

4. A white-tailed deer sprinted through the thicket.

5. Dark clouds and a sudden wind surprised her.

6. Her family would be elated to read the news.

7. Someone was shoveling the snow from the path.

8. Her aunt called out her name.

9. The old man tore open the envelope.

10. The message was brief.

EXERCISE ③   **Finding the Subject of a Sentence**

Underline the subject in each of the following sentences.

TIMOTHY A. CLARY/Getty Images

1. The Super Bowl has become very popular.

2. It has over 100 million viewers every year.

3. The commercials and halftime show attract even the non-football fans.

4. Halftime performers are not paid.

5. The media buzz is their reward.

6. Katy Perry and Beyonce are previous halftime performers.

7. A general Super Bowl ticket costs thousands.

8. Many hold private parties.

9. Wings, pizza, and beer are usually served.

10. The game has something for everyone.

EXERCISE ④   **Composing Your Own Sentences**

Create ten sentences using a variety of subjects. Use the following examples as suggestions.

Proper noun:	Amy Schumer
Common noun:	comedian
Abstract noun:	confidence
Compound subject:	actress and writer
Personal pronoun:	she

Exchange your sentences with those of a classmate. Then, for each sentence your classmate has written, underline and identify the subject to show that you understand the terms to describe various types of subjects.

Finding the Subject in Sentences with Prepositional Phrases

The sentences in Exercises 1 and 2 were short and basic. If we wrote only sentences of that type, our writing would sound choppy. Complex ideas would be difficult to express. One way to expand a simple sentence is to add one or more prepositional phrases.

He put his suitcase on the seat.

On is a preposition. *Seat* is a noun used as the object of the preposition. *On the seat* is a prepositional phrase.

A prepositional phrase is a group of words containing a preposition and an object of the preposition along with any modifiers. Prepositional phrases contain nouns or pronouns, but these nouns or pronouns are never the subject of the sentence.

> <u>on</u> the train
> <u>against</u> the wall
> <u>throughout</u> his life

In sentences with prepositional phrases, the subject may be difficult to spot. What is the subject of the following sentence?

> **In the young woman's apartment, books covered the walls.**

In the sentence above, what is the prepositional phrase? Who or what is the sentence about? To avoid making the mistake of thinking that a noun in the prepositional phrase could be the subject, a good practice is to cross out the prepositional phrase.

> ~~**In the young woman's apartment,**~~ **books covered the walls.**

With the entire prepositional phrase crossed out, it becomes clear that the subject of the sentence has to be the noun *books*.

GENERALIZATION **6**   The subject of a sentence is *never* found within the prepositional phrase.

If you memorize the prepositions in the following list, you will easily be able to spot prepositional phrases in sentences.

COMMON PREPOSITIONS

about	behind	except	onto	toward
above	below	for	out	under
across	beneath	from	outside	underneath
after	beside	in	over	unlike
against	between	inside	past	until
along	beyond	into	regarding	up
among	by	like	since	upon
around	concerning	near	through	with
as	despite	of	throughout	within
at	down	off	till	without
before	during	on	to	

In addition to these common one-word prepositions, many other prepositions are composed of two-word, three-word, and four-word combinations. The following list provides a sampling.

COMMON PREPOSITIONAL COMBINATIONS		
according to	for the sake of	in reference to
ahead of	in addition to	in regard to
at the time of	in between	in search of
because of	in care of	in spite of
by means of	in case of	instead of
except for	in common with	in the course of
for fear of	in contrast to	on account of
for the purpose of	in exchange for	similar to

EXERCISE ⑤ **Recognizing Prepositions**

In the following paragraph, find ten different prepositions and circle them.

We walked down the side streets under the trees toward the grocery store. There I poked among the fruit for a ripe melon. We walked home through solitary streets. Once we leaned over a fence to watch a woodchuck. We lingered at the sight until dark. The walk was enjoyable despite the rain.

EXERCISE ⑥ **Recognizing Prepositional Phrases**

In the following paragraph, find ten different prepositions. Circle each preposition and underline the entire prepositional phrase.

Michael Nava was raised in a neighborhood of Sacramento, California. The commercial district consisted mostly of shabby brick buildings. Beneath the railroad bridges, two rivers came together. The rivers passed between banks of thick undergrowth. A system of levees fed into the rivers. Uncultivated fields stretched behind ramshackle houses. The fields were littered with abandoned farming implements beside the foundations of long-gone houses. For a dreamy boy like Michael, this was a magical place to play.

EXERCISE **7**   **Finding Subjects in Sentences with Prepositional Phrases**

Remember that you will never find the subject of a sentence within a prepositional phrase. In each of the following sentences, cross out prepositional phrases. Then underline the subject of each sentence. An example follows:

~~In the late 1700s~~, an influential <u>author</u> named Jane Austen began writing stories ~~in the United Kingdom~~.

1. Jane would grow up in high-waisted floor-length dresses, with fans, bonnets, and parasols.

2. In that era, she wrote many humorous stories about social issues before her death in 1817.

3. In spite of the popularity of her stories, this author remained anonymous and relatively unknown at death.

4. Over 200 years later, artists remember Jane's appeal through movies and books.

5. In 1995, the instant movie classic *Clueless* came out in theaters.

6. Beneath the modern glamor of cell phones, malls, and short skirts, this movie portrayed Austen's character from 1815: the naïve matchmaker, *Emma*.

7. Throughout America and England, audiences enjoyed *Bridget Jones's Diary*, as a book in 1996 and then a movie in 2001.

8. Without Jane's *Pride and Prejudice* in 1813, Bridget Jones's complicated relationship with Mr. Darcy would not have existed.

9. On February 5, 2016, the movie *Pride and Prejudice and Zombies* was released as another contemporary twist on Jane's timeless work.

10. From beyond the grave, the Regency era author Jane Austen influences pop culture in the modern world.

Finding the Subject in Sentences with Appositive Phrases

An **appositive phrase** is a group of words within a sentence that gives us extra information about a noun or pronoun in that sentence. It is set off by commas.

Example:

Carmen Ruiz, *the new executive manager*, sat at her desk.

In this sentence, the words *the new executive manager* make up the appositive phrase. These words give extra information about Carmen Ruiz and are separated by commas from the rest of the sentence. If you were to leave out the appositive phrase, notice that what would remain would still be a complete sentence with the main idea undisturbed:

Example:

Carmen Ruiz sat at her desk.

Now the subject is clear: *Carmen Ruiz*

GENERALIZATION **7**   The subject of a sentence is never found within the appositive phrase.

PRACTICE **7**   **In each of the following sentences, cross out the appositive phrase and then underline the subject.**

1. Alex Harkavy, a high school senior, has an auditory-processing disorder.

2. Marcia Rubinstein, an educational consultant, can help him find the right college.

3. For instance, Landmark, a college in Putney, Vermont, specializes in programs for students with learning disabilities.

4. A federal law, the Americans with Disabilities Act, was enacted in 1990.

5. Now many colleges, both public and private, offer support for learning-disabled students.

6. One particular guidebook, Peterson's Colleges with Programs for Students with Learning Disabilities or Attention Deficit Disorder, is especially helpful.

Other Problems in Finding Subjects

Sentences with a Change in the Normal Subject Position

Some sentences begin with words that indicate a question is being asked. Such words as *why, where, how,* and *when* are adverbs, and they signal to the reader that a question will follow. These opening words are not the subjects. The subjects occur later in these sentences. The following sentences begin with words that signal a question:

Why is *he* going away?

How did *he* find his sister in the city?

Where is her *office*?

Notice that in each case the subject is not in the opening part of the sentence. However, if you answer the question or change the question into a statement, the subject becomes easier to identify.

***He* is going away because . . .**

***He* found his sister by . . .**

Her *office* is . . .

Sentences Starting with **There** *or* **Here**

Such words as *there* or *here* are adverbs. They cannot be the subjects of sentences.

There is a new teacher in the department.

Here comes the woman now.

Who or what is this first sentence about? This sentence is about a teacher. *Teacher* is the subject of the sentence. Who or what is the second sentence about? This sentence is about a woman. *Woman* is the subject of the second sentence.

Commands

Sometimes a sentence contains a verb that gives an order:

> **Go to Chicago.**
>
> **Help your sister.**

In sentences that give orders, *you* is not written down, but *you* is understood to be the subject. This is the only case where the subject of a sentence may be left out.

PRACTICE 8   **Underline the subject in each of the sentences below.**

1. Here in America the sale of human organs for transplant is against the law.

2. Unfortunately, there is a disturbing illegal market in the sale of these organs.

3. Where do some people desperately look for kidneys?

4. Why are so many donors exploited and unprotected?

5. Get involved. (you)

6. Work toward a solution to this tragic social problem. (you)

EXERCISE 8   ## Finding Subjects in Simple Sentences

In each of the following sentences, cross out prepositional phrases and appositive phrases. Then underline the subject. An example follows:

> ~~In the bustling airport of a busy city~~, <u>passengers</u> head ~~to their destinations~~.

1. Among the people in the airport's waiting areas are several college students on winter break.

2. Here on the black cushioned seating, a college freshman falls asleep.

3. There is plenty of noise around her.

4. The young woman's iPad, a gift from her mother, slips from her lap into the side pocket of her tote.

5. Outside the window on the tarmac, the connecting flight can be seen taxiing.

6. Some passengers are anxious near the time for boarding call.

7. Why are people afraid of flying?

8. Sometimes flyers take medication for their nerves.

9. Will the sleeping college freshman, a future English major, wake from her nap in time?

10. Before the boarding announcement, a fellow classmate wakes the exhausted freshman for her first return home from college.

EXERCISE ⑨ **Finding Subjects in Simple Sentences**

In each of the following sentences, cross out prepositional phrases and appositive phrases. Then underline the subject. An example follows:

Where ~~in the United States~~ can <u>we</u> find Lake Okeechobee?

1. Where can you find the only subtropical preserve in North America?

2. Look on a map at the southern tip of Florida. (You)

3. Here stretches the Everglades National Park, a natural treasure.

4. At one time, this Florida peninsula was not habitable.

5. Now, five million people live there.

6. The Everglades, a national park since 1947, has been in constant danger of destruction.

7. Marjory Stoneman Douglas, author of the book The Everglades: River of Grass, became a national crusader for the Everglades.

8. With the expansion of new development, these marshes are shrinking fast.

9. Do we have a responsibility to nature?

10. In 2000, Congress approved a bill for the restoration of the marshland.

EXERCISE ⑩ **Finding Subjects in Simple Sentences**

In each of the following sentences, cross out prepositional phrases and appositive phrases. Then underline the subject. An example follows:

~~According to various sources~~, many technology-related <u>careers</u> provide lucrative salaries ~~in different parts of the country~~.

1. Construction managers, the overall planners and supervisors of construction sites, will always be needed for building projects.

2. In the medical and health services field, leaders are needed as managers in the offices.

3. Here are some of the promising careers for number lovers: bookkeeping, accounting, and auditing clerks.

4. Also, many are needed as elementary school teachers for guiding our youth.

5. Which career category do you find the most interesting?

6. Think of what you enjoy.

7. Your career, a lifelong adventure, should reflect a basic interest inside of you.

8. Among the promising vocations, a physical therapist position could be great for those interested in the human body or sports.

9. For the visually creative and computer-minded, Web developers pave the way in organized Web content.

10. With a little research, you can make a well-informed career choice.

How Do You Find the Verb in a Sentence?

Verbs tell time. If a word functions as a verb in a sentence, you should be able to change it from one verb tense to another. The sentence should still make sense.

Because a verb tells time (past, present, or future), you can test which word in a sentence functions as the verb of that sentence by changing the time using the words *today, yesterday, or tomorrow*. Use the following sentences as models.

Present tense: Today, the woman *dances*.

HINTS   Change the time to the *past* by beginning the sentence with *yesterday*.

Past tense: Yesterday, the woman *danced*.

HINTS   Change the time to the *future* by beginning the sentence with *tomorrow*.

Future tense: Tomorrow, the woman *will dance*.

PRACTICE **9**   **Test the sentences below to determine which word functions as the verb in the sentence. Try three versions of each sentence: one beginning with *today*, one beginning with *yesterday*, and another beginning with *tomorrow*. Which is the word that changes? Circle that word. This is the word that functions as the verb in the sentence.**

1. The reason for his popularity is his foreign policy.

2. She has little control over the decision.

3. The test comes at a bad time.

A **verb** shows action, state of being, or occurrence. Verbs can change form to show the time (past, present, or future) of an action or state of being. Verbs fall into three classes: action verbs, linking verbs, and helping verbs.

Action Verbs

An **action verb** tells us what the subject is doing and when the action occurs.

For example:

The woman *studied* ballet.

What did the woman do? She *studied*. What is the time of the action? The action took place in the *past* (*-ed* is the regular past-tense ending).

Most verbs are *action verbs*. Here are a few examples.

EXAMPLES OF ACTION VERBS			
arrive	learn	open	watch
leave	forget	write	fly
enjoy	help	speak	catch
despise	make	teach	wait

EXERCISE **11** **Finding Action Verbs**

Each of the following sentences contains an action verb. Cross out prepositional phrases and appositive phrases. Next, underline the subject. Finally, circle the action verb. Is the action in the present, past, or future? An example follows:

   Many people (choose) unusual careers ~~in life~~.

1. Some professionals in China hug pandas for a living.

2. Golf ball divers dive to retrieve balls from ponds on golf courses.

3. In fancy restaurants, food stylists are paid to design food presentations.

4. For her wedding, the bride could hire an undercover bridesmaid as an assistant.

5. Some, with a pilot's license, legally steal planes back from wealthy persons in repossession.

6. One employee from a popular hotel warmed the bed for incoming guests.

7. A professional waterslide tester enjoys the slides and adventure in amusement parks and deluxe pools.

8. After a crime, crime scene cleaners are needed at the location.

9. Pet food tasters check pet food for flavor and quality.

10. With all the diverse careers out there, one will interest us.

EXERCISE **12**   **Finding Action Verbs**

Each of the following sentences contains an action verb. Cross out prepositional phrases and appositive phrases. Next, underline the subject. Finally, circle the action verb. Note that each verb you circle shows time (past, present, or future tense). An example follows:

~~With the rise of literacy,~~ the <u>demand</u> ~~for reading glasses~~ (increased).

1. Nero, an emperor of ancient Rome, gazed at gladiators in combat through a large emerald.

2. The Chinese manufactured sunglasses seven hundred years ago.

3. From quartz, monks carved the first magnifying glasses for reading.

4. In the fourteenth century, with the rise of the Venetian glass industry, glass lenses replaced quartz lenses.

5. In London in 1728, a man invented a pair of glasses with metal pieces and hinges.

6. George Washington bought a pair of these new glasses.

7. By 1939, movie producers in Hollywood devised colored contact lenses for special effects in horror movies.

8. In 1948, an American technician developed the first pair of modern contact lenses.

9. Now laser surgery repairs many eyesight problems.

10. Perhaps in the future nobody will need glasses or contact lenses.

Linking Verbs

A **linking verb** is a verb that links the subject of a sentence to one or more words that describe or identify the subject.

The <u>child</u> (is) a constant dreamer.   <u>She</u> (seems) distracted.

<u>We</u> (feel) sympathetic.

In each of these examples, the verb links the subject to a word that identifies or describes the subject. In the first example, the verb *is* links *child* with *dreamer.* In the second example, the verb *seems* links the pronoun *she* with *distracted.* Finally, in the third example, the verb *feel* links the pronoun *we* with *sympathetic.*

COMMON LINKING VERBS			
act	become	look	sound
appear	feel	remain	taste
be (am, is, are, was, were,	get	seem	turn
has been, or have been)	grow	smell	

EXERCISE **13**   **Finding Linking Verbs**

Each of the following sentences contains a linking verb. Cross out prepositional phrases and appositive phrases. Underline the subject of the sentence. Then draw an arrow to the word or words that identify or describe the subject. Finally, circle the linking verb. An example follows:

Dreams are very important in many cultures.

1. My dream last night was wonderful.

2. I had been transformed.

3. I looked young again.

4. The house was empty and quiet.

5. In a sunlit kitchen with a book in hand, I appeared relaxed and happy.

6. In the morning light, the kitchen felt cozy.

7. It seemed safe.

8. The brewing coffee smelled delicious.

9. The bacon, my usual Sunday morning treat, never tasted better.

10. In this dream, life felt satisfying.

EXERCISE **14**   **Finding Linking Verbs**

Each of the following sentences contains a linking verb. Cross out all prepositional phrases. Underline the subject of the sentence. Then draw an arrow to the word or words that identify or describe the subject. Finally, circle the linking verb. An example follows:

Many ~~of our elderly citizens~~ (are) vulnerable.

1. Sometimes a seemingly kind deed turns sour.

2. In one case, an elderly woman was the target of a scam.

3. A telephone caller seemed believable with a story about her grandson.

4. The caller sounded desperate for money for the grandson's release from jail.

5. The explanation appeared legitimate.

6. The elderly woman felt sympathetic and wired $5,000 through Western Union.

7. She later became suspicious.

8. Unfortunately, her discovery of the fraud was too late.

9. Elderly people often become easy prey for clever scam artists.

10. These scams are growing more numerous every year.

Helping Verbs (Also Called Auxiliary Verbs)

A **helping verb** is a verb that combines with a main verb to form a verb phrase. It always comes before the main verb and expresses a special meaning or a particular time.

In each of the following examples, a helping verb indicates what time the action of the verb *sleep* takes place.

Helping verbs	*Time expressed by helping verbs*
He *is* sleeping.	right now
He *might* sleep.	maybe now or in the future
He *should* sleep.	ought to, now or in the future
He *could have been* sleeping.	maybe in the past

COMMON HELPING VERBS

Major helping verbs		Forms of *be*		Forms of *have*	Forms of *do*
can	shall	being	are	has	does
could	should	been	was	have	do
may	will	am	were	had	did
might	would	is			
must					

Keep in mind that *be, do,* and *have* can also be used as the main verbs of sentences. In such cases, *be* is a linking verb and *do* and *have* are action verbs. The other helping verbs function only as helping verbs.

be, do, *and* **have** *used as helping verbs*	**be, do,** *and* **have** *used as main verbs*
I *am teaching* this class.	I *am* the teacher.
He *does work* hard.	He *does* the homework.
I *have borrowed* the money.	I *have* the money.

When we studied how to find the subject of a sentence, we learned that *nouns* and *pronouns* could be subjects and that *adjectives* could modify these nouns and pronouns. When we study how to find the verb of a sentence, we learn that the *adverb* is the part of speech that modifies a verb.

Adverbs are words that modify verbs, adjectives, or other adverbs.

An adverb modifying a verb:

Dreams **often** frighten young children.

An adverb modifying an adverb:

Dreams **very** often frighten young children.

An adverb modifying an adjective:

Dreams often frighten **very** young children.

Watch out for an adverb that comes between the helping verb and the main verb. In the following sentence, the word *often* is an adverb between the helping verb *can* and the main verb *frighten*.

Dreams can often frighten young children.

For more on adverbs, see Chapter 10. For a list of common adverbs, see Appendix B.

EXERCISE 15   **Finding Helping Verbs**

Circle the complete verb in each sentence below. An example follows:

Lifelong learning (is becoming) essential for all adults.

1. Graduation from high school does not signal the end of one's learning.

2. In today's world, workers must adjust to many changes in the workplace.

3. They will need to understand new technologies.

4. Can they recognize the difference between facts and opinions in news articles?

5. All citizens would benefit from annual refresher courses in their fields.

6. Everyone should read a daily newspaper.

7. Senior citizens might take courses at local community colleges.

8. Also, they could keep their minds active with crossword puzzles and other games.

9. Have people learned to try new recipes from television cooking programs?

10. Do we take responsibility for keeping our minds curious and engaged?

EXERCISE 16   **Finding Helping Verbs**

Each of the following sentences contains a helping verb in addition to the main verb. In each sentence, cross out prepositional phrases and underline the subject. Then circle the complete verb. An example follows:

~~In this country~~, daycare (has become) an important issue.

1. How does a person start a daycare center?

2. First, notices can be put in local churches and supermarkets.

3. Then that person should also use word of mouth among friends.

4. Many parents will need infant care during the day, after-school care, or evening and weekend care.

5. With luck, a nearby doctor may be helpful with the local health laws and legal requirements.

6. Of course, the licensing laws of the state must be thoroughly researched.

7. Unfortunately, the director of a daycare center could have trouble finding an affordable place.

8. Any child daycare center will depend on its ever widening good reputation.

9. In good daycare centers, parents should always be invited to attend meetings and planning sessions.

10. Finally, the center must be more interested in the character of its teachers than in the teachers' degrees.

How Do You Identify the Parts of Speech?

In this chapter, you have learned how most of the words in the English language function. These words can be placed into categories called *parts of speech*. You have learned to recognize and understand six of these categories: nouns, pronouns, adjectives, verbs, adverbs, and prepositions. (In later chapters, you will study the conjunction.) You can review your understanding of these parts of speech as you practice identifying them in the exercises provided here. You may also refer to Appendix B for a quick summary whenever you want to refresh your memory.

EXERCISE 17   **Identifying Parts of Speech**

In the sentences below, identify the part of speech for each underlined word. Choose from the following list:

a. noun	c. adjective	e. adverb
b. pronoun	d. verb	f. preposition

1. Some foods leave <u>you</u> more hungry than full.

2. An egg for breakfast with only 70 calories gives us more than 6 grams of <u>protein</u>.

3. Nutritionists also recommend oatmeal with fruit for <u>breakfast</u>.

4. Foods <u>with</u> a lot of water, like soup, are good choices at the beginning of a dinner.

5. By the end of your second course, you will <u>feel</u> full.

6. Nuts have the <u>perfect</u> combination of fiber, protein, and fats.

7. Do not eat more than one ounce of nuts <u>at</u> a time.

8. <u>Surprisingly</u>, an apple can be as filling as a meal with 4 grams of fiber and a high water content.

9. A six-ounce container of low-fat Greek yogurt with 17 grams of protein <u>prevents</u> hunger pangs.

10. The key to weight control is to eat protein, <u>healthy</u> fats, and fiber.

EXERCISE **18**   **Identifying Parts of Speech**

In the sentences below, identify the part of speech for each underlined word. Choose from the following list:

a. noun   c. adjective   e. adverb
b. pronoun   d. verb   f. preposition

1. The *Grand Ole Opry* is a <u>famous</u> radio program.

2. It began more than seventy <u>years</u> ago in Nashville, Tennessee.

3. By the 1930s, the <u>program</u> was the best source of country music on the radio.

4. In 1943, the program <u>could</u> be heard in every home in the nation.

5. <u>Many</u> people traveled to Nashville.

6. In Nashville, <u>they</u> could hear the performers for themselves.

7. The existing old concert hall, <u>poorly</u> constructed in the nineteenth century, was not an ideal place for modern audiences.

8. Television came in <u>during</u> the 1950s, and with it the demand for a new hall.

9. Now the Nashville hall is <u>modern</u> and air-conditioned.

10. More than six million people <u>visit</u> Nashville every year.

EXERCISE 19   **Identifying Parts of Speech**

In the sentences below, identify the part of speech for each underlined word. Choose from the following list:

a. noun   c. adjective   e. adverb
b. pronoun   d. verb   f. preposition

1. We all know some words from <u>catchy</u> songs by Taylor Swift, an American singer-songwriter.

2. At age five, the talented youth <u>began</u> forming her own songs.

3. A driven artist, <u>she</u> pursued a career in country music, becoming the youngest success story in writing and singing her own songs.

4. The performer was even able to <u>successfully</u> cross over into pop music, and has become one of the world's best-selling artists.

5. Her <u>influence</u> transcends entertainment.

6. To support music and literacy, this young professional donates hundreds of thousands of dollars <u>to</u> schools in need.

7. She has worked hard in aiding disaster relief <u>efforts</u> for Australia, Haiti, and America.

8. With children's hospital visits, and affiliation with around 60 charities and causes, she is hardly <u>idle</u>.

9. Winning awards and recognition from influential people such as Michelle Obama and Kerry Kennedy, <u>her</u> humanitarian work does not go unnoticed.

10. Swift has <u>proven</u> herself as not only an entertainer, but a young woman of hope, inspiration, and action.

Mastery and Editing Tests

TEST **1** **Finding Subjects and Verbs in Simple Sentences**

In each of the following sentences, cross out prepositional phrases and appositive phrases. Then underline the subject and circle the complete verb. An example follows:

(Have) <u>you</u> (thought) about the benefits of a two-year college degree?

1. With a struggling economy, community colleges have become more appealing than ever.

2. These schools offer a less expensive way to obtain a college education.

3. By living at home, college students avoid the costs of room and board.

4. Also, some young people are not very mature and benefit from family involvement in their lives.

5. Parents may have greater oversight of a young person in a community college.

6. The common problem of excessive drinking and casual sex at four-year schools worries many parents.

7. Is college academic work, in this case, the center of their lives?

8. Special job-related or certificate programs can make the local community college a desirable choice.

9. After two years of successful work at a community college, students may transfer to a four-year college.

10. Imagine a college degree without major debt!

TEST **2** **Finding Subjects and Verbs in Simple Sentences**

In each of the sentences in the following paragraph, cross out prepositional phrases and appositive phrases. Then underline the subject and circle the complete verb. An example follows:

(Has) anything strange ever (happened) ~~in your life?~~

In 1999, a young boy was playing baseball. Suddenly he was hit by a baseball bat. He could not breathe. In fact, his heart had stopped. Who would help? There was a nurse at the game. She acted quickly and performed CPR on the boy. The boy lived. Seven years later, this same nurse was eating dinner in a Buffalo restaurant. Unfortunately, a piece of food stuck in her throat. A worker at the restaurant did not hesitate. He had learned the Heimlich maneuver and successfully used the technique. Can you guess the young man's identity? The restaurant worker was the young baseball player from seven years earlier. Imagine everyone's amazement! What are the chances of such a coincidence?

TEST **3** **Student Writing: Finding Subjects and Verbs in Simple Sentences**

In each of the sentences in the following paragraph, cross out prepositional phrases and appositive phrases. Then underline the subject and circle the complete verb.

~~In an unmarked grave at the edge of the woods~~ (lies) Marley.

iStockphoto.com/kmoffitt

Here is a true story about a very bad dog. In rural Pennsylvania, John Grogan, a columnist for the Philadelphia Inquirer, lived with his wife Jenny. Soon they would be ready for children. In preparation, this young couple bought a Labrador retriever puppy. Into their home came the wildly energetic, highly dysfunctional Marley. Marley could chew door frames to the studs and separate steel bars on his crate. Drool covered the legs of all visitors to the Grogan home. He was expelled from obedience school. Marley's owner wrote a memoir about his dog titled *Marley and Me*. Its great success has led to several children's books and even a movie. Why has this book become such a big success? Apparently, everyone loves a book about a bad but lovable dog.

WRITE FOR SUCCESS

What are the factors that determine a student's success in college? Write a response that considers what part the following play: (1) ability, (2) attitude, (3) persistence, and (4) motivation.

Working Together

Crossword Puzzle: Reviewing the Terms for Sentence Parts

Review the names for sentence parts by doing this crossword puzzle. Feel free to work in pairs. If necessary, look back in the chapter for the answers.

Across

1. Verbs like *hop, sing,* and *play* are called ___ verbs.
4. Which of the following is a helping verb? *hear, when, will, only*
6. Every sentence has a(n) ___ and a verb.
8. A helping verb
9. Which of the following is a preposition? *must, upon, they, open*
12. A preposition
14. *Word, witch, wall,* and *willow* are examples of the part of speech called a(n) ___.
15. Most nouns are ___ nouns. They are not capitalized.
18. In the following sentence, which word is used as an adjective? *She has pet pigs for sale.*
21. Which of the following is a preposition? *he, be, by, if*
22. In the following sentence, which word is an abstract noun? *The era was not economically successful.*
23. A preposition
24. A word that can take the place of a noun

Down

1. *Joy, confidence,* and *peace* are examples of this kind of noun (the opposite of a concrete noun).
2. Which word is the subject in the following sentence? *Here is the tube of glue for Toby.*
3. An indefinite pronoun
4. A plural pronoun
5. *Look, appear, feel,* and *seem* are examples of ___ verbs.
7. Which word is the object of the preposition in the following sentence? *The car must weigh over a ton.*
10. The opposite of a common noun is a(n) ___ noun.
11. A personal pronoun
13. A preposition
16. In the following sentence, which word is a helping verb? *She may pay the fee for her son.*
17. Which of the following is a proper noun? *king, Nero, hero, teen*
19. In the following sentence, which word is an adjective? *Nan quickly ran toward the tan man.*
20. Which word is the verb in the following sentence? *Run down to the car for our bag.*
21. A common linking verb

Making Subjects and Verbs Agree

4

CHAPTER OBJECTIVES

In this chapter, you will practice making verbs agree with their subjects, especially in cases where subject-verb agreement is not immediately obvious.

You will learn about agreement when:

- the subject is a **personal pronoun**
- the verb is a form of *do or be*
- the subject is **hard to find**
- the subject is a **collective noun**
- the subject is an **indefinite pronoun**
- the subject is a **compound subject**
- the subject has an **unusual singular or plural form**

What Is Subject-Verb Agreement?

Subject-verb agreement means that a verb must agree with its subject in *number* (singular or plural).

RULE **1** | When the subject is a singular noun, the verb ends in *-s* (or *-es*) in the present tense.

> **The baby** *sleeps*.
>
> **The baby** *cries*.

RULE **2** | When the subject is a plural noun, the verb does not end in *-s* (or *-es*) in the present tense.

> **The babies** *sleep*.
>
> **The babies** *cry*.

Because a noun forms its **plural** by adding *-s* or *-es*, in contrast to a verb, which only adds an *-s* in the third person **singular** of the present tense, the student writer must pay attention to these endings. This rule causes a lot of confusion for student writers, especially those whose first language is not English. It may also be confusing to students who already speak and write English but whose local manner of speaking does not follow this rule. Although no one way of speaking is correct or incorrect, society does recognize a standard form that is acceptable in the worlds of school and business. Because we all must master this standard form, the material contained in this chapter is of the greatest importance to your success in college and beyond.

Subject-Verb Agreement with Personal Pronouns

The following chart shows personal pronouns used with the verb *sleep*.

PERSONAL PRONOUNS		
	Singular	Plural
First person:	I *sleep*	we *sleep*
Second person:	you *sleep*	you *sleep*
Third person:	he ⎫ she ⎬ *sleeps* it ⎭	they *sleep*

PRACTICE 1   **Circle the correct verb in each of the following sentences.**

1. The dog (bark, barks).

2. It (wake, wakes) up the neighborhood.

3. The neighbors (become, becomes) annoyed.

4. They (deserve, deserves) a quiet Sunday morning.

5. I (throws, throw) an old slipper at the dog.

Subject-Verb Agreement with the Verbs *do* and *be*

Although you might have heard someone say, "It don't matter" or "We was working," these expressions are not considered standard English because the subjects do not agree with the verbs. Study the two charts that follow to learn which forms of *do* and *be* are singular and which forms are plural.

THE VERB DO	
Singular	Plural
I *do*	we *do*
you *do*	you *do*
he ⎫ she ⎬ *does* it ⎭	they *do*
(Never use *he don't, she don't,* or *it don't.*)	

THE VERB *BE*

	PRESENT TENSE		PAST TENSE	
Singular	**Plural**		**Singular**	**Plural**
I *am*	we *are*		I *was*	we *were*
you *are*	you *are*		you *were*	you *were*
he	they *are*		he	they *were*
she } *is*			she } *was*	
it			it	

(Never use *we was, you was,* or *they was.*)

PRACTICE ② **Circle the verb that agrees with the subject.**

1. She (doesn't, don't) study in the library anymore.

2. We (was, were) hoping to find them there.

3. The library (doesn't, don't) close until eleven o'clock.

4. (Was, Were) you late tonight?

5. Irina (doesn't, don't) care if you stay until closing time.

EXERCISE ① **Making the Subject and Verb Agree**

In the blanks next to each sentence, write the subject of the sentence and the correct form of the verb.

	Subject	Verb
1. Mystery writers from around America (presents, present) an award called the Edgar, named after Edgar Allan Poe.	_____	_____
2. They (nominates, nominate) several writers each year for the award.	_____	_____
3. A successful mystery writer (lives, live) in our town.	_____	_____
4. She (doesn't, don't) live too far from me.	_____	_____
5. Sometimes we (sees, see) her out walking.	_____	_____
6. She always (wears, wear) an old wide-brimmed hat.	_____	_____
7. Her books usually (centers, center) around a sports theme.	_____	_____
8. Her latest book (is, are) about a murder at the U.S. Open Tennis Tournament.	_____	_____
9. She (was, were) nominated for the Edgar Award for best paperback of the year.	_____	_____
10. We (doesn't, don't) know yet if she will win the award.	_____	_____

EXERCISE ② **Making the Subject and Verb Agree**

In the blanks next to each sentence, write the subject of the sentence and the correct form of the verb.

	Subject	Verb
1. Many transportation companies today (tests, test) their workers for drugs.	_____	_____
2. To many people, it (seems, seem) an invasion of privacy.	_____	_____
3. Employers (worries, worry) about bus and train drivers' use of drugs on the job.	_____	_____
4. They (doesn't, don't) want the lives of their passengers at risk.	_____	_____
5. Even operators of rides in amusement parks (undergoes, undergo) tests.	_____	_____
6. Professional athletes on a team (has, have) special problems because of unwelcome publicity.	_____	_____
7. Some factories (installs, install) hidden video cameras for surveillance.	_____	_____
8. The General Motors Company (hires, hire) undercover agents as workers.	_____	_____
9. In Kansas City, drug-sniffing dogs (was, were) used in a newspaper office.	_____	_____
10. (Has, Have) you ever taken a drug test?	_____	_____

EXERCISE ③ **Making the Subject and Verb Agree**

In the blanks next to each sentence, write the subject of the sentence and the correct form of the verb.

	Subject	Verb
1. Many therapies (is, are) available today for people in need.	_____	_____
2. Talk therapy (encourages, encourage) troubled people to talk about problems with a trained therapist.	_____	_____
3. More recently, other treatments (has, have) become popular.	_____	_____
4. These (includes, include) music therapy, dance therapy, art therapy, and poetry therapy.	_____	_____
5. For example, professional writers (believes, believe) poetry has beneficial effects.	_____	_____

6. They (doesn't, don't) believe in repressing fear or anger.   _____   _____

7. Patients (creates, create) poetry as a form of self-healing.   _____   _____

8. A poem (gets, get) to the heart of a problem.   _____   _____

9. No invasive medical procedure (is, are) called for.   _____   _____

10. Poetry (allows, allow) these patients to explore emotions and organize thoughts.   _____   _____

Subject-Verb Agreement with Hard-to-Find Subjects

As you learned in Chapter 3, a verb does not always immediately follow the subject. Other words or groups of words called *phrases* (e.g., prepositional phrases or appositive phrases) can come between the subject and the verb. Furthermore, subjects and verbs can be inverted when they are used in questions or in sentences beginning with *there* or *here*.

When looking for subject-verb agreement in sentences where the subjects are difficult to find, keep two points in mind:

- Subjects are *not* found in prepositional phrases or appositive phrases.
- Subjects can be found after the verb in sentences that are questions and in sentences that begin with the word *there* or the word *here*.

EXERCISE 4 **Agreement with Hidden Subjects**

In each sentence below, cross out prepositional phrases, appositive phrases, and the word *there* or the word *here*. Then underline the subject. Finally, circle the correct verb.

1. There are many interesting words, current and past, hidden in the English language.

2. During the sixteenth century, an individual with an attractive face was called a *snoutfair*.

3. *Wonder-wench*, an affectionate term for a sweetheart of a woman, could flatter or offend women in today's world.

4. In the summer during the extreme heat, you can never forget to put deodorant on your *oxters*.

5. At dinner, by the dining table, the family's golden retriever might be guilty of *groaking*.

6. In order to groak, longingly stare at someone eating. (you)

7. After lack of sleep or too much drink, a person could become *mawmsey*.

8. How would you like your work to be described as *monsterful*?

9. Despite its sound, the definition means "wonderful and extraordinary."

10. Should English speakers resurrect interesting words long forgotten?

EXERCISE **5** **Agreement with Hidden Subjects**

In each sentence, cross out prepositional phrases, appositive phrases, and the word *there* or the word *here*. Then underline the subject. Finally, circle the correct verb.

1. Here (is, are) some basic medical supplies needed in every home.

2. A thermometer in the medicine chest (is, are) crucial.

3. There (is, are) a box of bandages on hand for minor injuries.

4. A vaporizer in the bedroom at night (relieves, relieve) bronchial congestion.

5. Pads of sterile gauze often (helps, help) dress wounds.

6. A small bottle of Coca Cola syrup (proves, prove) helpful for treating stomach upsets.

7. A useful tool, a pair of tweezers, (removes, remove) splinters.

8. In a home ready for emergencies, a list of important phone numbers (sits, sit) next to the telephone.

9. Why (has, have) cold compresses been useful in treating sprains?

10. Every person with a sense of responsibility (needs, need) a resource book on first aid.

Subject-Verb Agreement with Collective Nouns

Collective nouns name a group of people or things.

FREQUENTLY USED COLLECTIVE NOUNS

assembly	committee	faculty	jury	senate
audience	council	family	orchestra	team
board	couple	group	panel	tribe
class	crowd	herd	public	troop
club				

> A **collective noun** (also called a *group noun*) is considered singular unless the meaning is clearly plural.

Usually, a collective noun takes a singular verb or requires a singular pronoun to refer to that noun. The reasoning is that the group acts as a single unit.

The class *was waiting* for *its* turn to use the gym.

The Cub Scout troop *is holding its* jamboree in July.

The orchestra *performs* in Cincinnati next week.

Sometimes a collective noun takes a plural verb or requires a plural pronoun to refer to that noun because the members of the group are clearly acting as individuals, with separate actions as a result. One clue that a group noun will be considered plural is if the verb shows a difference of opinion: *disagree, argue, debate,* or *differ.*

The class *were putting* on their coats.

(Clearly, each member has his or her own coat.)

The Cub Scout troop *were having* difficulty with *their* tents.

(Here, the meaning is that each person is individually having trouble with his tent.)

The orchestra *are debating* whether or not to go on tour.

(Some individuals think they should go on tour; some think they should not.)

NOTE: The word *number* is a collective noun that is governed by the following rule:

If the definite article (*the*) is used with *number*, the meaning is singular.

The number of reality shows on television *has* increased.

If the indefinite article (*a, an*) is used with *number*, the meaning is plural.

A number of reality shows on television *have* been canceled.

EXERCISE 6   ## Agreement with Collective Nouns

Collective nouns can sometimes be singular or plural depending on the writer's intention. After each sentence of the following exercise, the words in parentheses indicate the writer's intended meaning. Underline the subject and circle the correct verb in each sentence.

1. The construction crew (is, are) being blamed for the accident. *(acting as a unit)*

2. In this case, the union (accuses, accuse) the crew. *(acting as a unit)*

3. A few days after the accident, the same group (files, file) charges. *(acting as a unit)*

4. The crew's legal team (is, are) uncertain about their strategy. *(acting as individuals)*

5. The public (voices, voice) their concerns to the media. *(acting as individuals)*

6. The crowd (grows, grow) more and more impatient. *(acting as a unit)*

7. The audience (interrupts, interrupt) the proceedings. *(acting as individuals)*

8. The jury (hears, hear) the evidence. *(acting as a unit)*

9. The group (has, have) very different opinions. *(acting as individuals)*

10. The crowd (sits, sit) on the edge of their seats to hear the verdict. *(acting as individuals)*

EXERCISE **7** **Agreement with Collective Nouns**

Use the following general rule for collective nouns: a collective noun is considered singular unless the members of the group are acting as individuals with different ideas or separate actions. In the following exercise, underline the subject and circle the correct verb in each sentence.

1. The couple (is, are) on a date.

2. The couple (pays, pay) separately for dinner.

3. The assembly (listens, listen) to the information from the speaker.

4. A family (argues, argue) over chores.

5. The faculty (supports, support) one another.

6. The public (knows, know) the details about the high profile case in the news.

7. The public (disagrees, disagree) on the outcome.

8. The sophomore class (is, are) deciding on their majors.

9. A club (was, were) formed by fans of science fiction.

10. The class (has, have) a good dynamic.

Subject-Verb Agreement with Indefinite Pronouns

Care should be taken to learn which indefinite pronouns are singular and which are plural.

INDEFINITE PRONOUNS

INDEFINITE PRONOUNS TAKING A SINGULAR VERB

everyone	one (of)	another	anything	nobody
everybody	someone	much	either (of)	nothing
everything	somebody	anyone	such (a)	neither (of)
each	something	anybody	no one	

Everyone *is* expecting a miracle.

(continued on next page)

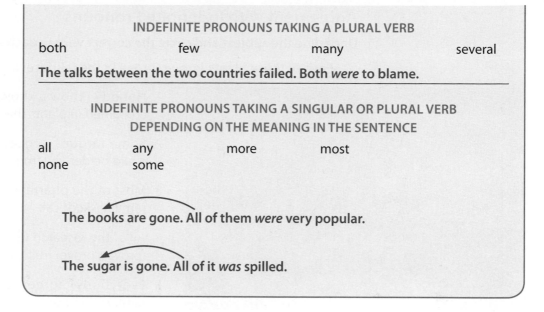

INDEFINITE PRONOUNS TAKING A PLURAL VERB

| both | few | many | several |

The talks between the two countries failed. Both *were* to blame.

INDEFINITE PRONOUNS TAKING A SINGULAR OR PLURAL VERB
DEPENDING ON THE MEANING IN THE SENTENCE

| all | any | more | most |
| none | some | | |

The books are gone. All of them *were* very popular.

The sugar is gone. All of it *was* spilled.

EXERCISE ⑧ **Agreement with Indefinite Pronouns**

Underline the subject and circle the correct verb in each sentence.

HINT   When a prepositional phrase follows an indefinite pronoun that is the subject, be sure the verb agrees with the indefinite pronoun subject.

1. Many of the paintings sold by Walter Keane (was, were) extremely popular in the 1960s.

2. They (features, feature) a variety of children and animals with hauntingly huge eyes.

3. Each of these pictures (was, were) actually painted by Walter's wife, Margaret Keane.

4. All of the credit for her work (was, were) taken by her husband.

5. Most of their contemporaries (was, were) shocked when she sued him years after their divorce.

6. Few (denies, deny) her claim after a 1986 court case.

7. Each of them (was, were) asked to paint a big-eyed painting in front of the judge.

8. One of these kinds of paintings (was, were) produced by Margaret in 53 minutes.

9. Nothing from Walter (was, were) produced.

10. Much of these events (is, are) shown in the movie *Big Eyes,* directed by Tim Burton in 2014.

EXERCISE **9** **Agreement with Indefinite Pronouns**

Underline the subject and circle the correct verb in each sentence.

<u>Each</u> of these plants (grows) grow) in the rainforest.

mathess/Getty Images

1. Nobody (knows, know) how many drugs are contained in plants that grow in the rainforest.

2. Some (argues, argue) that wonderful drugs could be derived from many plants.

3. Most of the pharmaceutical experts (remains, remain) skeptical.

4. All of the research (is, are) expensive and often (proves, prove) fruitless.

5. Everybody (agrees, agree) that the tropical rainforest is a source of medicine.

6. One of the dangers (is, are) the disappearance of the tropical rainforest.

7. One of the two U.S. companies in Costa Rica (is, are) Merck and Company.

8. Each of the companies (has been, have been) paying the country for the right to search the rainforest.

9. Among scientists, some (recommends, recommend) government-subsidized drug research.

10. Vincristine and vinblastine are two medicines found in the rainforest; both (is, are) used for cancer treatment.

Subject-Verb Agreement with Compound Subjects

RULE **3** | If the parts of a compound subject are connected by the word *and*, the verb is usually plural.

Alberto *and* Ramon *are* the winners.

The exception to this rule occurs when the two subjects are thought of as a single unit.

RULE **4** | If the parts of a compound subject connected by *and* are thought of as a single unit, the verb is singular.

Falafel *and* hummus *is* my favorite sandwich.

The rule becomes more complicated when the parts of the compound subject are connected by *or, nor, either, either/or, neither, neither/nor,* or *not only/but also.*

When the parts of a compound subject are connected with *or, nor, either, either/ or, neither, neither/nor,* or *not only/but also,* use the following rules:

1. If both subjects are singular, the verb is singular.

    Either Alberto *or* Ramon *is* at the concert.

2. If both subjects are plural, the verb is plural.

    Either my friends *or* my two brothers *are* at the concert.

3. If one subject is singular and one subject is plural, the verb agrees with the subject closer to the verb.

    Either my friends *or* my brother *is* at the concert.
    Either my brother *or* my friends *are* at the concert.

EXERCISE 10   **Subject-Verb Agreement with Compound Subjects**

Underline the compound subject and circle the correct verb in each sentence.

1. Macaroni and cheese (is, are) my son's favorite supper.

2. This meal and others like it (has, have) too much fat.

3. My mother and father, on the other hand, often (enjoys, enjoy) a spinach salad for their main meal.

4. For many of us, our shopping habits or cooking routine (needs, need) to be changed.

5. Either a salad or a cooked vegetable with a sprinkling of cheese (is, are) a better choice than macaroni and cheese.

6. Adults and children (does, do) need to watch their diets.

7. Too many pizzas and sodas (is, are) a disaster for people's health.

8. Either the lack of exercise or the eating of fatty foods (causes, cause) more problems than just weight gain.

9. Neither potato chips nor buttered popcorn (is, are) a good snack choice.

10. An apple or carrot sticks (makes, make) a better choice.

EXERCISE 11   **Subject-Verb Agreement with Compound Subjects**

In each sentence, underline the compound subject and circle the correct verb.

1. The hotel guests and the desk clerk (discusses, discuss) the problem with the hotel rooms.

2. Either the manager or someone in authority (needs, need) to be reached.

3. Frustration and outrage (shows, show) on the guests' faces.

4. The man with his daughter or the woman on the stairs (was, were) the first to complain.

5. According to the woman, the faucet and the showerhead in the bathroom (is, are) broken.

6. The swimming pool or the game rooms in the basement never (seems, seem) open.

7. Furthermore, both the man and the woman in this already upsetting situation (suspects, suspect) there are bedbugs.

8. Neither the people in the lobby nor the man behind the desk (is, are) happy about this situation.

9. Both the man with his daughter and the woman, along with her companion, (want, wants) their money back.

10. Unsanitary conditions and broken equipment (is, are) never appreciated by paying customers.

Subject-Verb Agreement with Unusual Nouns

Do not assume that every noun ending in -s is plural or that all nouns that do not end in -s are singular. There are some exceptions. Here are a few of the most common exceptions.

1. Some nouns are always singular in meaning but end in -s:

mathematics	diabetes	United States
economics	measles	Kansas

   Mathematics *is* my major.

2. Some nouns are always plural in meaning.

clothes	tweezers	pants
scissors	fireworks	pliers

   My blue pants *are* ripped.

3. Some nouns change internally or add endings other than -s:

Singular	_Plural_
foot	feet
tooth	teeth
child	children
man	men
woman	women
mouse	mice
ox	oxen
goose	geese

4. Some nouns remain the same whether singular or plural:

Singular	**_Plural_**
deer	deer
elk	elk
fish	fish
moose	moose

5. When some foreign words are used in English, they continue to form the plural by following the rules of their original languages. For example, here are four Latin words that follow the Latin rule (-*um* changes to -*a* to form the plural):

Singular	**_Plural_**
bacterium	bacteria
datum	data
medium	media
stratum	strata

Mastery and Editing Tests

TEST **1** **Making the Subject and Verb Agree**

In the blanks next to each sentence, write the subject of the sentence and the correct form of the verb. An example follows:

	Subject	Verb
Everybody (has, have) heard of injuries suffered by young athletes.	*Everybody*	*has*
1. Many of these injuries (happens, happen) to football quarterbacks.	_____	_____
2. One of the most serious sports injuries (is, are) a concussion.	_____	_____
3. Many young people (thinks, think) nothing of a minor blow to the head.	_____	_____
4. Now scientists (understands, understand) these injuries much better than before.	_____	_____
5. On impact, the arteries of the brain (is, are) constricted.	_____	_____
6. Some athletes unfortunately (suffers, suffer) a second concussion before healing from the first one.	_____	_____
7. Several minor concussions often (leads, lead) to permanent brain damage or even death.	_____	_____
8. Medical doctors all over the country (wants, want) stricter guidelines for athletes with concussions.	_____	_____

9. An athlete with one or more concussions (requires, require) a sufficient amount of rest. _____ _____

10. Today, nobody in contact sports (takes, take) a head injury lightly. _____ _____

TEST **2**   **Making the Subject and Verb Agree**

Using your own words and ideas, complete each of the following sentences. Be sure the subject and verb agree. An example follows:

The best <u>place</u> for wedding receptions (is) a restaurant with a view.

1. Our team _____

2. The box of chocolates _____

3. Both of my sisters _____

4. The effects of a pay cut on a family _____

_____

5. Where are _____

6. Not only the teacher but also the students _____

_____

7. The jury _____

8. Each of the contestants _____

9. There is _____

10. The table of contents in that book _____

TEST **3**   **Editing Student Writing: Making the Subject and Verb Agree**

The following paragraph contains seven errors in subject-verb agreement. For each sentence, cross out prepositional phrases and appositive phrases, underline the subject, and circle the verb. Place a check mark over errors in agreement. On the lines following, list the subject and the correct form of the verb for each sentence.

Smartphones: A Blessing and a Curse

¹Faces staring into smartphones throughout the world are commonly seen today. ²Gradually more and more people, including the older generation, has an addiction to their phone. ³How does these addictions get started? ⁴Access to social media on

the phone is one of the causes. ⁵True, social media is an effective way to connect individuals from all around the Earth. ⁶Furthermore, friends from the past is now able to keep up with one another. ⁷Once connected with many different people, the stream of pictures, posts and links on timelines keep you peering into each other's lives. ⁸Even the temporary gossip about various celebrities make us click and gawk at our mobile devices. ⁹Meanwhile, at a party or a dinner table, hardly anyone is listening to the lives right around him or her. ¹⁰Either a selfie opportunity or an incident to film make people aware of their surroundings for a bit (through their phones). ¹¹In fact, according to recent studies, we spend a few hours every day on social media on our phones. ¹²The instant access to information offers the new generations more potential than ever. ¹³However, each of us need to decide how much life will be spent looking at a phone.

Subject	Correct form of verb
1. _____	_____
2. _____	_____
3. _____	_____
4. _____	_____
5. _____	_____
6. _____	_____
7. _____	_____
8. _____	_____
9. _____	_____
10. _____	_____
11. _____	_____
12. _____	_____
13. _____	_____

TEST ❹   **Editing Student Writing Using Editing Symbols**

Instructors often use commonly accepted symbols to mark corrections in student writing. The editing symbol for subject-verb agreement is agr. (See the inside back cover for a list of common editing symbols.) The following paragraph contains five subject-verb agreement errors. Write agr above each error you find, and then write the subject and the correct verb form on the lines provided. (In sentence 9, consider *audience* as a collective noun that acts as a unit.).

¹Why don't everybody like a hair-raising horror movie? ²I don't see many of my college classmates at all the latest shows. ³My girlfriend doesn't like these kinds of movies, and neither do any of her friends. ⁴In fact, the theaters are filled almost exclusively with teenagers. ⁵My friends and I pays our thirteen bucks and anticipate a nightmare. ⁶Each of us hope for a thrill. ⁷Emotions like love, friendship, or kindness go by the wayside. ⁸The audience wants blood and guts! ⁹It don't matter if the plot is ridiculous and the acting is terrible. ¹⁰The typical horror movie with all its violent scenes appeal to our worst nature. ¹¹One of my favorite horror movies is *The Hills Have Eyes*. ¹²Fortunately for my friends and me, a popular horror movie these days usually has a sequel. ¹³We look forward to the next adrenaline rush.

Five subject-verb agreement corrections

	Subject	Correct form of verb
1.	_____	_____
2.	_____	_____
3.	_____	_____
4.	_____	_____
5.	_____	_____

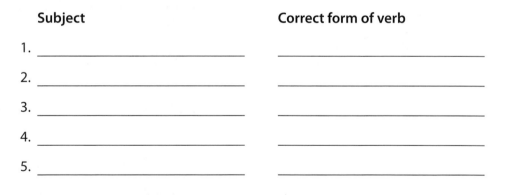

WRITE FOR SUCCESS

Many factors contribute to a student's success in college. Write a response that considers the importance of the following: grade point average in high school, number of credit hours taken each semester, choice of courses and instructors, attendance, knowledge of campus resources.

Digital Vision/Getty Images

Focused Freewriting: Preserving Family History

> Though it is more difficult to write about my father than about my mother, since I spent less time with him and knew him less well, it is equally as liberating. Partly this is because writing about people helps us to understand them, and understanding them helps us to accept them as part of ourselves. Since I share so many of my father's characteristics, physical and otherwise, coming to terms with what he has meant to my life is crucial to a full acceptance and love of myself.

Alice Walker, the well-known novelist and essay writer, expressed these thoughts in a journal that she kept for a time. She discovered that by writing down her thoughts and feelings about her father she felt liberated. We can all be liberated by a better understanding of the people who have shaped our lives. Obviously, we cannot know everything about another person, even a person with whom we have lived, but we can put together stories we have heard from relatives, along with memories that we have ourselves. When we write about family members, it is always good to remember that each person's perspective is colored by his or her own personality and by a memory that may not be entirely accurate. In this regard, you might want to create a portrait of a family member through the eyes of a person other than yourself, always keeping in mind that people's recollections can be distorted.

Questions for Class Discussion

1. On the basis of the Alice Walker quote above, can you explain why Alice Walker found writing about her father to be liberating?

2. To what extent should we feel that our family members are "part of ourselves"? What if we do not like or accept everything about a family member? In that case, what should we do about including that person in a memoir?

3. What types of information might you be tempted to write in a journal entry about a family member? Are there any people who could provide you with stories that you would like to include in your entry?

4. What would you like your grandchildren to know about you?

5. What characteristics, both physical traits and personality traits, do you believe you have inherited? Do you like what you have inherited? What traits do you wish were different?

6. Think about a person who has been adopted. How is preserving family history made more complicated for such a person? What advice could you offer?

7. What are the most common obstacles people face that prevent them from accepting themselves?

Freewriting

Freewrite for fifteen minutes. Share a story, a memory of some kind, or a description of a family member. You might tell a story about yourself, one that you would like your family to remember. Think of your piece of writing as the beginning of a memoir that future members of your family would like to have.

PORTFOLIO SUGGESTION

Save the freewriting you have done on your family's history. This is a topic that you may want to return to again and again. Children will appreciate all the stories and memories you can gather about your relatives. This may be one of the greatest gifts you can give your family.

Understanding
Fragments and Phrases 5

CHAPTER OBJECTIVES

Not all groups of words that go together are sentences. In this chapter, you will learn to recognize phrases so you can tell the difference between a phrase and a sentence.

- Distinguish a **fragment** from a sentence when one of the following elements is missing:

    a subject

    a verb

    a complete thought

- Identify the **six kinds of phrases** in English:

    noun phrases (including appositive phrases)

    prepositional phrases

    verb phrases

    infinitive phrases

    participial phrases

    gerund phrases

- Understand the three different functions of the **present participle**:

    as part of a verb phrase

    as an adjective

    as a noun

The fragment is a major problem for many student writers. A thought may be clear in a writer's mind, but on paper the expression of this idea may be incomplete because it does not include a subject, a verb, or a complete thought. In this section, you will improve your ability to spot fragments (incomplete sentences), and you will learn how to correct them. This practice will help you avoid fragments in your own writing.

Here, for example, is a typical conversation between two people in a laboratory. It is composed entirely of fragments, but the two people who are speaking have no trouble understanding each other.

Doug:	Had any test results yet?
Nelida:	Nothing statistically significant.
Doug:	Not good.
Nelida:	Back to step one.

Rewritten in complete sentences, this brief conversation might go as follows:

Doug:	Have you had any test results yet?
Nelida:	The results were not statistically significant.
Doug:	That is not good.
Nelida:	We will have to go back to step one.

In the first conversation, misunderstanding is unlikely since the two speakers stand face to face. Seeing the other's gestures and hearing the intonations in the other's voice help each one grasp the other's meaning. These short phrases are enough for communication because the speakers are using more than just words to convey their thoughts. They understand each other because each one has no difficulty completing the thoughts in the other's mind.

In writing, however, readers cannot be present to observe tone of voice, gestures, or other signals for themselves. They cannot be expected to read the writer's mind. For a reader, only words grouped into sentences and sentences grouped into paragraphs can provide clues to the meaning. Because writing often involves thoughts that are abstract and even complex, fragments cause great difficulty and sometimes result in total confusion for the reader.

EXERCISE ①   ## Putting a Conversation into Complete Sentences

The following conversation could have taken place between a couple preparing for a snowstorm. Rewrite the conversation in complete thoughts (or standard sentences). Remember the definition of a complete sentence:

> A **complete sentence** has a subject and a verb and expresses a complete thought.

Kyle:	What else?
Natalie:	Nothing except more wine.
Kyle:	One hour before the storm hits.
Natalie:	Going to be bad.
Kyle:	Hope no blackouts this time.
Natalie:	What about candles?
Kyle:	None.
Natalie:	The store on the corner.
Kyle:	Ready?
Natalie:	My coat.

Conversation rewritten in standard sentences

Kyle: _____

Natalie: _____

Kyle: _____

Natalie: _____

Kyle: _____

Natalie: _____

Kyle: _____

Natalie: _____

Kyle: _____

Natalie: _____

Remember that when you write in complete sentences, the results may differ from the way you would express the same ideas in everyday conversation with a friend.

Although you will occasionally spot incomplete sentences in professional writing, you may be sure the writer is using these fragments intentionally. In such cases, the fragment may be appropriate because it captures the way a person thinks or speaks or because it creates a special effect. A student developing his or her writing skills should be careful to use only standard-sentence form so that every thought will be communicated effectively. Nearly all the writing you will do in your life—business correspondence, papers in school, or reports in your job—will demand standard-sentence form. Fragments may be acceptable for an e-mail or text to a friend but they are not, as a rule, acceptable for more formal writing.

What Is a Fragment?

A **fragment** is a piece of a sentence.

A group of words may appear to be a sentence, but if one of the following elements is missing, the result is a fragment.

a. The subject is missing:

is shuffling the cards

b. The verb is missing:

the illusionist on the stage

c. Both the subject and the verb are missing:

on the stage

d. The subject and verb are present, but the group of words does not express a complete thought:

The illusionist shuffled

How Do You Correct a Fragment?

1. **Add the missing part or parts.**

   Fragment: across the lake

   To be added: subject and verb

   Complete sentence: I swam across the lake.

   The prepositional phrase *across the lake* is a fragment because a prepositional phrase cannot function as the subject or the verb in a sentence. Furthermore, the words *across the lake* do not express a complete thought.

2. **Join the fragment to the sentence where it belongs.**

   If you look at the context in which a fragment occurs, you will often find that the complete thought is already present. The writer did not recognize that the fragment belonged to the sentence that came just before or to the sentence that immediately followed. Therefore, another way to correct a fragment is to join the fragment to the sentence that precedes it or to the sentence that immediately follows it. Which sentence you choose depends on where the information in the fragment belongs. Study the example below.

   Incorrect: I swam. Across the lake in the middle of the night. The water was cool and inviting.

   Correct: I swam across the lake in the middle of the night. The water was cool and inviting.

Fragments can exist in a writer's work for a number of reasons. A writer may become careless for a moment or may not fully understand how all the parts of a sentence work. If the writer does not have a clear idea of what he or she is trying to say, fragments and other errors are more likely to occur. Sometimes another try at expressing the same idea may produce a better result.

EXERCISE **2** **Correcting Fragments by Adding the Missing Parts**

Make each of the following fragments into a complete sentence by adding the missing part or parts.

1. returned to the sea (add a subject)

   _____

2. a bird on the oak branch (add a verb)

   _____

3. between the island and the mainland (add a subject and a verb)

   _____

4. the hawk in a soaring motion (add a verb)

   _____

5. the fishing boats in the harbor (add a verb)

   _____

6. dropped like a stone into the water (add a subject)

   _____

7. the crescent moon (add a verb)

   _____

8. carried the fish to the tree (add a subject)

   _____

9. the fisherman put (complete the thought)

   _____

10. into the net (add a subject and a verb)

   _____

EXERCISE **3** **Correcting Fragments That Belong to Other Sentences**

Each of the following passages contains two or more fragments. First, read each passage carefully. Then place a check mark in front of each fragment you find. Finally, draw an arrow to indicate the sentence to which the fragment belongs. An example follows:

Adele assisted the dancers. She stood backstage during the performance. ✔ Between numbers. She helped the ballerinas change costumes.

1. Fishing is one of the oldest sports in the world. And can be one of the most relaxing. A person with a simple wooden pole and line can have as much fun as a sportsman. With expensive equipment. For busy executives, overworked teachers, and even presidents of nations. Fishing can be a good way to escape from the stress of demanding jobs.

2. The first electric car was built in 1887. Its popularity did not last long. The new gasoline engine became more widely used. However, with today's growing concern over carbon emissions and rising oil prices. Electric cars are becoming desirable once again. In fact, governments are now pushing to promote more electric cars. On the mass market. As of September 2015, about one million electric car models were sold in the United States, China, Japan. And parts of Western Europe. The return of the electric car could help us heal the planet.

3. Maya dropped out of college two years ago. She had found it hard to read the textbooks. And other assignments. Her mind wandered. She had never read for personal enjoyment. Except maybe a magazine now and then. Books had always seemed boring. She preferred to talk with her friends. She got a job instead working in a restaurant. For two years. Now Maya is back in school. With enough money saved to return to the local community college. She is ready. To put her mind on her coursework. She has decided to major in hospitality. To get a degree, she will need to learn much better study habits.

What Is a Phrase and How Many Kinds of Phrases Are There?

A **phrase** is a group of words belonging together but lacking one or more of the three elements necessary for a sentence.

Fragments are usually made up of phrases. These phrases are often mistaken for sentences because they are words that go together as a group. However, they do not fit the definition of a sentence. *Do not confuse a phrase with a sentence.*

The English language has six kinds of phrases, and you should learn to recognize each one. You have already studied three of these kinds of phrases in Chapter 3. Like the verb phrase, the infinitive phrase, the participial phrase, and the gerund phrase are all formed from verbs. However, these phrases do not function as verbs in sentences.

THE SIX TYPES OF PHRASES IN ENGLISH

1. **Noun phrase** — a noun with its modifiers:

   several graceful figure skaters

2. **Prepositional phrase** — a preposition with its object and modifiers:

   among the several graceful figure skaters

3. **Verb phrase** — a main verb with its helping verbs and modifiers:

   were carefully preparing

   have patiently rehearsed

4. **Infinitive phrase** — the word *to* with the base form of the verb and any other words that complete the phrase:

   to move gracefully

5. *Participial phrase* — a present or past participle and the other words that complete the phrase:

   moving gracefully

   greatly encouraged

   the participial phrase functions as an **adjective**:

   Moving gracefully, the skater looked like a ballet dancer.

   Greatly encouraged, the coach entered her into competition.

6. **Gerund phrase** — a present participle and the other words that complete the phrase:

   moving gracefully

   the gerund phrase functions as a **noun**:

   Moving gracefully is an important part of figure skating.

Infinitive Phrase

An infinitive phrase usually functions as a noun.

Infinitive phrase as subject

To continue this argument **would be useless.**

Infinitive phrase as object

She began *to move gracefully.*

NOTE: The word *to* can also be used as a preposition, as in *I wrote to my son.*

PRACTICE **1** **See whether you can distinguish between the infinitive phrases and the prepositional phrases. In each of the following sentences, label the italicized phrase as an infinitive phrase (INF) or prepositional phrase (PP).**

_____ 1. I stopped by his office *to say goodbye.*

_____ 2. The trail of evidence led directly *to him.*

_____ 3. We were lucky *to have discovered* his fraudulent activities.

_____ 4. The manager had forced him *to tell the truth.*

_____ 5. His leaving will be a relief *to the staff.*

Participial Phrase

How Is the Participle Formed?

The present and past participles are formed from the base verb:

Present participle:	base verb + *ing* **running, looking, trying**
Past participle:	base verb + the regular past tense ending -*ed* or -*d* **disappoint<u>ed</u>, turn<u>ed</u>, rais<u>ed</u>**

or

base verb + irregular past tense form
told, gone, given

The same particles are presented again, this time with words that might complete their phrases.

Examples of **present participial phrases**:

running home, looking very unhappy, trying hard

Examples of **past participial phrases**:

greatly disappointed, turned slightly, raised successfully

told tearfully, gone quickly, given gratefully

How Does a Participial Phrase Function?

A participial phrase functions as an **adjective** in a sentence. By studying the following sentences, you can observe how these phrases are used in complete sentences. These phrases function as adjectives for the noun or pronoun that follows them.

Running home, the worker lost her wallet.

Looking very unhappy, she retraced her steps.

Greatly disappointed, she could not find it.

Told tearfully, the story saddened her friends.

Gerund Phrase

The gerund is formed from the present participle. Along with any words that go with it, the gerund phrase functions as a **noun.** As such, it can be the subject or the object of a sentence.

    Gerund phrase as subject: *Long-distance running is strenuous exercise.*

    Gerund phrase as object: I like *long-distance running.*

PRACTICE 2 See whether you can distinguish between participial phrases and gerund phrases. In each of the following sentences, label the italicized phrase as a participial phrase (P) or a gerund phrase (G). Remember, the participial phrase functions as an adjective. The gerund phrase functions as a *noun.*

_____ 1. *Standing totally still,* the child hoped the bee would fly away.

_____ 2. *Playing the violin* requires a good ear for pitch.

_____ 3. The athlete will try *deep-sea diving.*

_____ 4. *Waiting patiently,* we ordered something to drink

_____ 5. *Weathered by many winters,* the barn badly needed paint.

EXERCISE 4 **Identifying Phrases**

Identify each of the underlined phrases.

Imagine paying $150 <u>for a concert ticket</u>, just

like everyone else, and then electing <u>to sit</u> in the

nosebleed section as high up and far away from the

action as you <u>could get</u>. Sitting in the back means

you are more likely to let <u>your mind</u> wander and less

likely to hear clearly. <u>Sitting in the front</u> means you'll

keep yourself accountable by being in full view of

the instructor and the rest of the class. Studies show

that there is <u>a definite connection</u> between students'

academic performance and their seat location.

What's the best spot for great concentration?

1. _____

2. _____

3. _____

4. _____

5. _____

6. _____

Front and center, literally—the "T zone." <u>In one study</u>   7. _____

students who sat at the back of a large auditorium

were six times more likely <u>to fail the course</u>, even   8. _____

though the instructor <u>had assigned</u> seats randomly!   9. _____

Not only will sitting in the T zone keep you alert

<u>throughout the class</u> but instructors tend to have   10. _____

higher opinions of the students who sit there.

EXERCISE **5**   **Identifying Phrases**

The following sentences make up a paragraph in *The Fault in Our Stars* by John Green. Identify each of the underlined phrases.

1. Augustus Waters drove horrifically. Whether <u>stopping or starting,</u>   _____

2. everything happened <u>with a tremendous JOLT</u>.   _____

3. I flew <u>against the seat belt</u> of his Toyota SUV each time he braked, and my neck snapped backward each time he hit the gas.   _____

4. I <u>might have been</u> nervous—   _____

5. what with sitting <u>in the car</u> <u>of a strange boy</u> <u>on the way</u> <u>to his house</u>,   _____
   _____

6. keenly aware that <u>my crap lungs</u> complicate efforts   _____

7. <u>to fend off</u> unwanted advances—   _____

8. but <u>his driving</u> was so astonishingly poor   _____

9. that I <u>could think</u> of nothing else.   _____

10. We'd gone perhaps a mile <u>in jagged silence</u> before Augustus said, "I failed the driving test three times."   _____

EXERCISE **6**   **Identifying Phrases**

Identify each of the underlined phrases.

1. <u>For years</u> scientists debated the existence of global warming.   _____

2. In the last five years, <u>the serious debate</u> has ended.   _____

3. <u>Pouring more and more greenhouse gases into the atmosphere,</u> humans are causing the earth to grow warmer.   _____

4. Massive sections of ice <u>are melting</u> in the Arctic and Antarctic.   _____

5. Sea levels are projected <u>to rise gradually</u>.   _____

6. <u>Warming a full degree Fahrenheit since 1970</u>, the oceans are fueling more intense typhoons and hurricanes.   _____

7. <u>By the year 2050</u>, more than a million animal species worldwide may be extinct.   _____

8. We <u>could be approaching</u> the point of no return.   _____

9. <u>Curbing greenhouse gases</u> is now a worldwide emergency.   _____

10. Congress needs <u>to regulate</u> greenhouse gases.   _____

The Three Functions of the Present Participle

The present participle causes problems for students working with sentence fragments. Because the participle is used sometimes as a verb (in a verb phrase), sometimes as an adjective (in a participial phrase), and sometimes as a noun (in a gerund phrase), it causes a good deal of confusion for students

The **present participle** can function in three different ways:

1. The participle functions as a *verb* in a **verb phrase.**

   The student *was taking* an exam.

2. The participle functions as an *adjective* in a **participial phrase.**

   ***Taking an exam,* the student felt stressed.**

3. The participle functions as a *noun* in a **gerund phrase.**

   ***Taking an exam* can be stressful.**

In each of these cases, the present participle is part of a phrase. Remember, a phrase is not a sentence.

EXERCISE 7 **Using the Present Participle in a Verb Phrase**

Below are five present participles. Add a helping verb to each one and use this verb phrase to write a complete sentence of your own. An example follows:

Present participle:	sitting
Verb phrase:	is sitting
Sentence:	The couple is sitting on the balcony.

1. building _____

2. crying _____

3. traveling _____

4. writing _____

5. thinking _____

EXERCISE **8**   **Using the Present Participle in a Participial Phrase**

Each of the following phrases contains a present participle. Use each participial phrase to compose a sentence in which the phrase functions as an adjective. An example follows:

Present participle:	sitting
Participial phrase:	sitting on the balcony
Participial phrase used as an adjective in a sentence:	Sitting on the balcony, the couple enjoyed the moonlight

1. <u>building</u> a house

   _____

   _____

2. <u>crying</u> over the broken vase

   _____

   _____

3. <u>traveling</u> in Mexico

   _____

   _____

4. hastily <u>writing</u> the text message

   _____

   _____

5. <u>thinking</u> about the problem

   _____

   _____

EXERCISE **9**   **Using the Present Participle in a Gerund Phrase**

Each of the following phrases contains a present participle. Use each gerund phrase to compose a sentence in which the phrase functions as a noun. An example follows:

Present participle:	sitting
Gerund phrase:	sitting on the balcony
Gerund phrase used as a noun in a sentence:	Sitting on the balcony is relaxing.

1. <u>building</u> a house

   _____

   _____

2. <u>crying</u> over the broken vase

   _____

   _____

3. <u>traveling</u> in Mexico

   _____

   _____

4. hastily <u>writing</u> the text message

   _____

   _____

5. <u>thinking</u> about the problem

   _____

   _____

How Do You Make a Complete Sentence from a Fragment That Contains a Participle?

When a participle is used incorrectly, the result is often a fragment. Here are three ways to turn a fragment containing a participle into a sentence.

> **Fragment: She *talking* in her sleep.**

1. Use the participle to form the **main verb** of the sentence.
   a. Add a helping verb (such as *is* or *was*) to the participle to form a verb phrase:

      > She *was talking* in her sleep.

   b. Change the participle to a different form of the verb (such as the past tense).

      > *She talked in her sleep.*

2. Use the participle to function as an **adjective** in a participial phrase, being sure to provide a subject and verb for the sentence.

   > *Talking in her sleep,* she muttered something about her basketball practice.

3. Use the participle to function as a **noun** in a gerund phrase.

   > *Talking in her sleep* revealed her innermost thoughts.

EXERCISE ⑩   **Correcting a Fragment That Contains a Participle**

Make four complete sentences from each of the following fragments. Use the following model as your guide.

Fragment: using the back stairway

a. She <u>is using</u> the back stairway. *(verb phrase)*

b. She <u>uses</u> the back stairway. *(simple present tense)*

c. <u>Using the back stairway</u>, she got away without being seen. *(participial phrase used as an adjective)*

d. <u>Using the back stairway</u> is not a good idea. *(gerund phrase used as a noun)*

1. moving out of the house

    a. _____

    b. _____

    c. _____

    d. _____

2. talking on the telephone

    a. _____

    b. _____

    c. _____

    d. _____

3. driving the car down Highway 60

    a. _____

    b. _____

    c. _____

    d. _____

EXERCISE ⑪   **Correcting a Fragment That Contains a Participle**

The following passage is made up of fragments containing participles. Rewrite the passage, creating complete sentences. Use any of the correction methods discussed previously in this chapter.

The zombie staggering forward in the cramped country cemetery. Tripping over disturbed tombstones. Graves not visited in years. A gravedigger working the night shift. Aware of unnatural moans growing louder in the distance. Looking out at the cemetery with his mouth open in disbelief.

_____

_____

_____

_____

EXERCISE ⑫   **Correcting a Fragment That Contains a Participle**

The following passage has four fragments containing participles. Place a check mark in front of each fragment. Then rewrite the passage using complete sentences. Use any of the four correction methods discussed previously in this chapter.

Finally at age 42 taking my driving test. I felt very nervous. My son was sitting in the backseat. All my papers sitting on the front seat. The inspector got into the car and sat on my insurance form. He looked rather sour and barely spoke to me. Trying not to hit the curb. I parallel parked surprisingly well. I managed to get through all the maneuvers. Now tensely waiting for the results.

_____

_____

_____

_____

EXERCISE ⑬   **Correcting Fragments**

Rewrite each fragment so that it is a complete sentence.

1. early morning a time of peace in my neighborhood

   _____

2. the gray mist covering up all but the faint outlines of nearby houses

   _____

3. the shapes of cars in the streets and driveways

   _____

4. to sit and look out the window

   _____

5. holding a steaming cup of coffee

_____

6. the only sound the rumbling of a truck

_____

7. passing by on the highway a quarter mile away

_____

8. children all in their beds

_____

9. no barking dogs

_____

10. in this soft, silent dream world

_____

EXERCISE **14**   **Correcting Fragments**

Each of the following groups of words is a phrase. First, name each phrase. Then make each phrase into a complete sentence.

1. two champion boxers

Name of phrase: _____

Sentence: _____

_____

2. to watch the fight

Name of phrase: _____

Sentence: _____

_____

3. in the ring

Name of phrase: _____

Sentence: _____

_____

4. are punching each other

Name of phrase: _____

Sentence: _____

_____

5. at the sound of the bell

   Name of phrases: _____

   Sentence: _____

   _____

6. gratefully supported

   Name of phrase: _____

   Sentence: _____

   _____

7. to referee the fight

   Name of phrase: _____

   Sentence: _____

   _____

8. the screaming fans

   Name of phrase: _____

   Sentence: _____

   _____

9. by the second round

   Name of phrase: _____

   Sentence: _____

   _____

10. knocked unconscious

    Name of phrase: _____

    Sentence: _____

    _____

Mastery and Editing Tests

TEST **1**   **Recognizing and Correcting Fragments**

The following is a summary description of one of *The Great Gatsby*'s famous parties at the mansion in New York. The description is made up entirely of fragments. Rewrite the description, making each fragment into a sentence.

Wild parties every weekend at the Long Island mansion. Packed with excited guests. Never-ending supply of free liquor. Partygoers mingling. Rumors about their unseen host. Fancy sights all around. Swimming pool. Beach. In the gardens, buffet tents bursting with all kinds of food. Live music from the orchestra. Feeling elegant and privileged for being invited. Scene crazier with guests getting drunk. Host Jay Gatsby nowhere to be found.

_____

_____

_____

_____

_____

_____

_____

_____

_____

_____

TEST ② **Recognizing and Correcting Fragments**

The following paragraph contains seven fragments. Read the paragraph and place a check mark in front of each fragment. Then rewrite the paragraph, being careful to use only complete sentences.

On that morning, the backyard was filled with neighborhood children. Running in and out of the sprinkler. Happy to feel the sudden cold drops of water on their skin. The day already a boiler. Maybe as much as 100 degrees. Some of the small children pranced around. In only their underwear. Others in and out of the water with all their clothes on. I loved the sound of their happy voices. The carefree sounds of the young.

_____

_____

_____

_____

_____

_____

_____

_____

_____

_____

TEST ③   **Editing Student Writing: Recognizing and Correcting Fragments**

The following paragraph contains six fragments. Read the paragraph and place a check mark in front of each fragment. Then rewrite the paragraph, being careful to use only complete sentences.

This was our home. It had only two rooms. On the second floor of a two-family house. Up a steep flight of stairs. Not so easy with several bags of groceries. A window in the living room overlooked the street. We liked to eat our dinners there. Looking out onto a busy scene. This was our entertainment. At night our mother pulled out two cots. For my sister and me. We often whispered late into the night. Always wishing for a real bedroom.

_____

_____

_____

_____

_____

_____

_____

_____

_____

TEST **4** **Editing Student Writing Using Editing Symbols**

As you learned in Test 4 of Chapter 4, instructors often use editing symbols to mark errors in student writing. The editing symbol for a fragment is frag. In the paragraph below, find five fragments (frag) and five errors in subject-verb agreement (agr). Mark each error with the commonly used editing symbol, and then correct the errors on the lines provided following the paragraph.

¹My older sister is delighted with her new job at the local pancake house. ²The most popular restaurant in town. ³Her boyfriend and a classmate also works there. ⁴Her required attire, a red shirt with embroidered large brown pancakes, are provided for free. ⁵One of the owners show her the routine. ⁶Everyone are expected to learn all the different tasks. ⁷Making the customers feel welcome. ⁸Keeping all the tables spotless. ⁹Either the manager or an experienced worker tell her how to operate the register. ¹⁰Everyone must work on weekends. ¹¹Also at least two nights a week. ¹²Saturdays are the best. ¹³The most tips!

Five suggestions for correcting the fragments.

1. _____

   _____

2. _____

3. _____

4. _____

5. _____

Five subject-verb agreement corrections

Subject	**Correct form of the verb**
6. _____	_____
7. _____	_____
8. _____	_____
9. _____	_____
10. _____	_____

WRITE FOR SUCCESS

What are some ways you could make use of the resources at your college? Are there writing labs, gym facilities, an office for students with disabilities, academic advisers, other student services? (Consult your college catalog for resource information.) Write a response describing at least three resources that you would like to use.

Working Together

Take home a Macintosh.
No purchase necessary.

All along, we've been telling you Macintosh™ is the easiest-to-use computer very little money can buy.

Now we're going to prove it.

By putting our Macintosh where our mouth is.

Right now, anyone who qualifies can walk into a participating authorized Apple dealer, and walk out with a Macintosh Personal Computer.

Absolutely free.

It's our way of letting you test drive a Macintosh for 24 hours in the comfort of your own office, home, RV, hotel room, dorm room or whatever.

And really experience, first-hand, how much your finger already knows about computers.

In less time than it takes you to get frustrated on an ordinary computer, you'll be doing real work on Macintosh.

Everything from writing memos to working with spreadsheets to creating charts to managing projects.

Because the hard part of test driving a Macintosh isn't learning how to use it.

The hard part is bringing it back.

Test drive a Macintosh.

984 Apple Computer Inc. Apple and the Apple logo are registered trademarks of Apple Computer Inc. Macintosh is a trademark licensed to Apple Computer Inc. For an authorized Apple dealer nest you call **(800) 538-9696.** In Canada, call **(800) 268-7796** or **(800) 268-7637.**

Image Courtesy of The Advertising Archives

Examining an Advertisement for Fragments

1. Advertising companies devote a great deal of their time and attention to market research. This research helps the company target its message to the most likely audience for its product or service. Who is the advertiser in this newspaper ad? Who is the intended audience? What is the product or service being advertised?

2. Like many advertisements we see in magazines, newspapers, and Web sites, this Macintosh advertisement is made up of short, snappy constructions that are not always complete sentences. Advertisers write in this way because they want to attract our attention. When we write for school or for work, however, our compositions must be made up of only complete sentences. Review the accompanying advertisement. Many of the paragraphs contain some fragments. Underline each fragment you find. With your classmates, rewrite the ad and correct all the fragments. Consider all the different answers and judge them for correctness. If needed, review the two ways to correct a fragment.

PORTFOLIO SUGGESTION

Choose a product or a service that particularly appeals to you. Clip or print newspaper or magazine ads, or both, that deal with this product or service. Take notes on television ads, Web site ads, or billboard ads. Review them at a later time for possible use in comparison and contrast essays.

Combining Sentences Using Coordination

6

CHAPTER OBJECTIVES

In this chapter, you will learn the three ways to use coordination to form compound sentences.

- using a comma plus a coordinating conjunction
- using a semicolon, an adverbial conjunction, and a comma
- using only a semicolon (no conjunction)

What Is Coordination?

So far you have worked with the simple sentence. If you review some of these sentences (such as the practice sentences in Chapter 3), you will see that writing only simple sentences results in a choppy style and also makes it difficult to express complicated ideas. You will need to learn how to combine simple sentences correctly by using coordination. To understand coordination, be sure you know the meaning of the following three terms.

A **clause** is a group of words that has a subject and a verb:

she spoke

when she spoke

NOTE: Of the two clauses above, only *she spoke* could be a sentence. The clause *when she spoke* could not stand alone as a sentence because it does not express a complete thought. (Chapter 7 will cover this second type of clause.)

An **independent clause** is a clause that can stand alone as a simple sentence:

She spoke.

A **compound sentence** is a sentence that is created when two or more independent clauses are correctly joined, using the rules of coordination:

She spoke, and we listened.

NOTE: Beginning here and continuing in the following chapters, whenever punctuation is the focus of a lesson, the punctuation marks will be enlarged to make them easier to see.

The three preceding terms are all part of the definition of coordination.

Coordination is the combining of two or more related independent clauses (you may think of them as simple sentences) that contain ideas of equal importance. The result is a **compound sentence**.

Two independent clauses:	She spoke. We listened.
Compound sentence:	She spoke**,** and we listened.

First Option for Coordination: Using a Comma plus a Coordinating Conjunction

The most common way to form a compound sentence is to combine independent clauses using a comma plus a coordinating conjunction.

FIRST OPTION FOR COORDINATION

Independent clause	Comma and coordinating conjunction	Independent clause
I had worked hard	**,** so	I expected results.

You will need to memorize the seven coordinating conjunctions given below. By doing this now, you will avoid confusion later when an additional set of conjunctions will be introduced to combine clauses.

CONNECTORS: COORDINATING CONJUNCTIONS

and	but	for (meaning *because*)	so
nor	yet	or	

PRACTICE **1**   **In each of the following compound sentences, draw a single line under the subject and draw two lines under the verb for each independent clause. Then add a comma and circle both the coordinating conjunction and the comma. An example follows:**

The <u>speaker</u> <u><u>rose</u></u> to her feet**,** and the <u>crowd</u> <u><u>became</u></u> quiet.

1. The audience listened   for this was a woman with an international reputation.

2. She could have told about all her successes   but instead she spoke about her disappointments.

3. Her words were electric   so the crowd was attentive.

4. I should have brought a recorder   or at least I should have taken notes.

Did you find a subject and verb for both independent clauses in each sentence? Now that you understand the structure of a compound sentence, be sure you understand the meanings of the different coordinating conjunctions. Keep in mind that these conjunctions are used to show the relationship between two ideas that have equal importance.

COORDINATING CONJUNCTIONS AND THEIR MEANINGS

CONJUNCTION	MEANING	EXAMPLE
and	to add an idea	He will call today, and he will call tomorrow.
nor	to add an idea when both clauses are in the negative	He will not call today, nor will he call tomorrow.
but	to contrast two opposing ideas	He will call today, but he might not call tomorrow.
yet	to emphasize the contrast between two opposing ideas (meaning: and despite this fact)	He promised to call today, yet he did not.
for	to introduce a reason	He will call today, for he wants a loan.
or	to show a choice	He will call today, or he will call tomorrow.
so	to introduce a result	He will call today, so I will wait for his call.

EXERCISE ① **Combining Sentences Using Coordinating Conjunctions**

For each of the following compound sentences, choose the coordinating conjunction that best supports the meaning of the sentence. Circle the letter corresponding to your choice.

1. The two detectives carefully checked the scene for fingerprints, _____ they could not find one clear print. (contrast)

   a. so   b. but   c. nor   d. or

2. The safe was open, _____ a single bag of coins remained. (add)

   a. but   b. and   c. or   d. for

3. There was no sign of forced entry, _____ they believed it was probably an inside job. (result)

   a. so   b. nor   c. but   d. or

4. The restaurant owner could not be found, _____ could the two waiters be located. (add, both clauses are in the negative)

   a. and   b. for   c. so   d. nor

5. Suddenly they became interested in one of the tables, _____ the surface seemed splattered with blood. (reason)

   a. and   b. for   c. yet   d. so

6. The missing tablecloth could also be significant, _____ they took photographs of the other tablecloths. (result)

   a. nor   b. so   c. but   d. or

7. One detective looked in the closets, _____ they contained nothing significant. (contrast)

   a. or   b. so   c. but   d. nor

8. Either they find another clue, _____ the blood stains might be their only evidence. (choice)

   a. or   b. yet   c. nor   d. but

9. There were no witnesses, _____ maybe DNA would tell a story. (contrast)

   a. for   b. nor   c. or   d. but

10. Either they get a break in the case, _____ the mystery may never be solved. (choice)

   a. and   b. nor   c. so   d. or

EXERCISE ❷   **Combining Sentences Using Coordinating Conjunctions**

Below are ten sentences. Some of them are compound sentences needing a comma and a coordinating conjunction. Some of them are simple sentences (with only compound subjects or compound verbs). These do not require a comma. Fill in each blank with a comma (if required) and a coordinating conjunction that best supports the meaning of the sentence.

1. The San Francisco Earthquake of 1906 may have shaken down hundreds of buildings _____ the fire that followed destroyed nearly everything left standing.

2. One hour after the earthquake, smoke could be seen from one hundred miles away _____ for three days and nights the sky was filled with smoke.

3. Outside the city the air was still _____ within the city the heated air of the fire produced an enormous gale.

4. This gale-force wind fed the flames _____ quickly spread the fire.

5. Firefighters tried valiantly to save buildings _____ before long the flames would reappear on all sides and destroy the structures.

6. The stories of many heroic deeds will never be told _____ will the number of dead ever be known.

7. The flames could not be stopped _____ people had no choice but to flee.

8. People pulling heavy trunks up and down the steep hills of the city eventually had to abandon them _____ survival depended on moving more quickly.

9. Tens of thousands of refugees camped around the city _____ fled to surrounding cities.

10. Nothing much remained of San Francisco following the fire except for memories _____ a few homes on the outskirts of the city.

EXERCISE ③ **Combining Sentences Using Coordinating Conjunctions**

The simple sentences in each of the following pairs could be combined with a coordinating conjunction. Decide what relationship the second sentence has to the first, and then choose the conjunction that makes the most sense. Write your compound sentence on the line provided. Use the following model as your guide.

Two simple sentences: She broke her arm.

She couldn't play in the finals.

Relationship of second sentence to first: result

Conjunction that introduces this meaning: so

Compound sentence: She broke her arm, **SO** she couldn't play in the finals.

1. Mr. Watson is kind and patient.

His brother is sharp and nagging.

Relationship of second sentence to first: _____

Conjunction that introduces this meaning: _____

_____

_____

2. The two adults are having great difficulty.

They are trying to raise a teenager.

Relationship of second sentence to first: _____

Conjunction that introduces this meaning: _____

_____

3. Young Michael has no family of his own.

He feels angry and alone.

Relationship of second sentence to first: _____

Conjunction that introduces this meaning: _____

_____

4. Michael hasn't been doing well in school.

   He isn't involved in any activities outside school.

   Relationship of second sentence to first: _____

   _____

   Conjunction that introduces this meaning: _____

   _____

   _____

5. Mr. Watson encouraged Michael to do volunteer work at the hospital.

   This might give Michael the satisfaction of helping other people.

   Relationship of second sentence to first: _____

   Conjunction that introduces this meaning: _____

   _____

   _____

6. Mr. Watson's brother wanted Michael to spend more time on his homework.

   He also wanted him to get a job after school to help with expenses.

   Relationship of second sentence to first: _____

   Conjunction that introduces this meaning: _____

   _____

   _____

7. Michael liked going to the hospital.

   He was doing something important.

   Relationship of second sentence to first: _____

   Conjunction that introduces this meaning: _____

   _____

   _____

8. He didn't earn any money.

   He liked helping people.

   Relationship of second sentence to first: _____

   _____

   Conjunction that introduces this meaning: _____

   _____

   _____

9. Michael has decided to have a career working in a hospital.

   He now has a reason to work harder in school.

   Relationship of second sentence to first: _____

   Conjunction that introduces this meaning: _____

   _____

   _____

10. Mr. Watson thinks the hospital volunteer work was a good idea.

    His brother has to agree.

    Relationship of second sentence to first: _____

    Conjunction that introduces this meaning: _____

    _____

    _____

Second Option for Coordination: Using a Semicolon, an Adverbial Conjunction, and a Comma

The second way to form a compound sentence is to combine independent clauses by using a semicolon, an adverbial conjunction, and a comma.

SECOND OPTION FOR COORDINATION		
Independent clause	Semicolon, adverbial conjunction, and comma	Independent clause
I had worked hard	**;** therefore**,**	I expected results.

The conjunctions used for this option are called adverbial conjunctions. These conjunctions are similar in meaning to the common coordinating conjunctions, but they sound more formal than the shorter conjunctions such as *and* or *but*. Using these adverbial conjunctions gives more emphasis to the clause than using coordinating conjunctions.

Less emphasis: He was late, and he had the wrong documents.

More emphasis: He was late; furthermore, he had the wrong documents.

Just as you memorized the list of coordinating conjunctions in the First Option for Coordination section, you should memorize the following list of adverbial conjunctions.

CONNECTORS: FREQUENTLY USED ADVERBIAL CONJUNCTIONS

Addition *(and)*	Contrast *(but)*	Alternative *(or)*	Result *(so)*	Likeness	Emphasis	To Show Time
also	however	instead	accordingly	likewise	indeed	meanwhile
besides	nevertheless	on the other hand	consequently	similarly	in fact	
furthermore	nonetheless	otherwise	hence			
in addition			therefore			
moreover			thus			

PRACTICE **2**   **In each of the following compound sentences, draw a single line under the subject and draw two lines under the verb for both independent clauses. Then circle the semicolon, adverbial conjunction, and comma. An example follows:**

> The jet was the fastest way to get there; moreover, it was the most comfortable.

1. The restaurant is always too crowded on Saturdays ; nevertheless, it serves the best food in town.

2. The land was not for sale ; however, the house could be rented.

3. The lawsuit cost the company several million dollars ; consequently, the company went out of business a short time later.

4. The doctor told him to lose weight ; furthermore, she instructed him to stop smoking.

EXERCISE **4**   ## Combining Sentences Using Adverbial Conjunctions

The simple sentences in each of the following pairs could be combined by using an adverbial conjunction. Decide on the relationship between the two sentences, and circle the letter of the adverbial conjunction that makes the most sense.

1. We are living in the age of the individual.

   More than 50 percent of adults are single.

   a. thus   b. otherwise

   c. hence   d. in fact

2. This means many households have only one occupant.

   In cities like Denver and Atlanta, more than 40 percent of households are occupied by only one person.

   a. besides   b. for example

   c. nevertheless   d. meanwhile

3. People today are less likely to stay in unhappy marriages and in other negative situations.

   Most of these people will continue to seek other meaningful relationships.

   a. nonetheless   b. in addition

   c. moreover   d. furthermore

4. Single people tend to join more organizations and visit friends.

   They have the time to contribute more to the vibrant life of their communities.

   a. however   b. nonetheless

   c. instead   d. also

5. Living alone means freedom to come and go as one pleases.

   A single person does not have to answer to anyone else.

   a. instead   b. nevertheless

   c. indeed   d. meanwhile

6. A single person working at home might stay in his or her pajamas all day.

   Those with families would be unlikely to have that choice.

   a. besides   b. hence

   c. however   d. likewise

7. Just a few decades ago, many people worked for large companies all their lives.

   These same people usually belonged to unions.

   a. on the other hand   b. however

   c. thus   d. in addition

8. Now most people do not work for large companies.

   They may work at home or work for short periods of time with small companies.

   a. also   b. furthermore

   c. instead   d. otherwise

9. In this new world, confident single people will have the flexibility to develop their individual talents.

   People without social skills may end up lonely or without any needed support system.

   a. besides   b. on the other hand

   c. consequently   d. for instance

10. The affluent single person may have increased opportunities.

    Children in poor one-parent households will have a harder time achieving rich and satisfying lives.

    a. meanwhile   b. otherwise

    c. similarly   d. therefore

Combining Sentences Using Adverbial Conjunctions

The simple sentences in each of the following pairs could be combined by using an adverbial conjunction. Decide what relationship the second sentence has to the first, and then choose the adverbial conjunction that makes the most sense. Be careful to punctuate correctly. An example follows:

Students must focus on their academic assignments **;** nonetheless**,** they often find themselves distracted.

1. Researchers cite many reasons for distraction _____ they offer us sound advice for more careful structuring of our time.

2. A bored person often loses concentration _____ a person with a very challenging task can lose concentration.

3. People feel a need to escape _____ they will often shop on the Web or read and answer e-mails.

4. The brain lends itself to distraction _____ even a moderately upsetting emotion such as frustration can disrupt your attention.

5. Many consider multitasking a positive activity _____ according to researchers, multitasking reduces our capacity to sustain attention.

6. Students need to take more control of their study time _____ their work will suffer.

7. The brain benefits from breaks _____ you might come back after a break feeling much more creative and focused.

8. Hunger, fatigue, or restlessness will not help a person to focus _____ a person should take a break at such times and eat, go to the gym, sleep, or take a walk.

9. A student might also stop and listen to music for a few minutes _____ he or she might take some deep breaths and do some stretching exercises.

10. Don't let your distractions control your life _____ find the healthiest ways to balance work and play.

Combining Sentences Using Adverbial Conjunctions

Add an adverbial conjunction and an independent clause to each of the following sentences to form a compound sentence that makes sense. Choose from the following adverbial conjunctions: *consequently, furthermore, however, in fact, instead, meanwhile, moreover, nevertheless, otherwise, therefore*. Remember to punctuate correctly. An example follows:

Members of the congressional committee met every day.

Members of the congressional committee met every day**;** nonetheless**,** they could not agree on the proposal.

1. The winter was unusually warm.

   _____

2. The governor was happy to see the unemployment rate fall.

   _____

3. The town installed video cameras in the park.

   _____

4. Our ambassador to Brazil speaks several languages.

   _____

5. Students should be careful about taking out large private loans for college.

   _____

6. The soccer player lifts weights three times a week.

   _____

7. The enthusiastic junior registered for creative writing.

   _____

8. Doctors advise elderly patients to get flu shots.

   _____

9. The candidates debated the issue of health care.

   _____

10. Most young athletes do not understand the consequences of using steroids.

    _____

Third Option for Coordination: Using a Semicolon

A third and less commonly used way to form a compound sentence is to combine two independent clauses by using only a semicolon.

THIRD OPTION FOR COORDINATION		
Independent clause	Semicolon	Independent clause
I had worked hard	;	I expected results.

You might choose the semicolon if the grammatical structure of each independent clause is similar or if the ideas in each independent clause are very closely related.

In the following sentence, the grammatical structure of each independent clause is similar:

The women pitched the tents; the men cooked the dinner.

In the following sentence, the two independent clauses contain closely related ideas:

The women pitched the tents; they were proud of their work.

EXERCISE **7**   **Combining Sentences Using a Semicolon**

Read each of the following sentences. If the sentence is a compound sentence that requires a semicolon, insert the semicolon where needed. If the sentence is a simple sentence, do not use punctuation.

1. Some people are afraid of public speaking   some fear it more than death.

2. It was dark   she couldn't find the light switch.

3. The resort had restaurants and a gym   the beach was lined with palm trees and blue lounge chairs.

4. The trains were running late   subway riders had to push their way into the train car.

5. Lisbeth worked hard for two years in her entry-level position before receiving a big promotion.

6. He decided to simplify his lifestyle in the city   his family was impressed.

7. She always spoke to everyone with respect   they all admired her.

8. The story touched my heart   I read it twice.

9. Many young adults today expect a lot in exchange for very little time and effort.

10. The instructor introduced new approaches in the course   sincere students were open to trying them.

EXERCISE **8**   **Combining Sentences Using a Semicolon**

Create a compound sentence by adding a semicolon and another independent clause to each of the following sentences. Both clauses in each compound sentence must have similar grammatical structures or have closely related ideas. Use the following example as your model.

Simple sentence:	Weight loss programs encourage proper nutrition.
Compound sentence:	Weight loss programs encourage proper nutrition; these programs also encourage consistent exercise.

1. Some people live to eat.

   _____

   _____

2. Children drink too much soda.

   _____

   _____

3. White bread is not a healthy food choice.

   _____

   _____

4. One very healthy exercise is jumping rope.

   _____

   _____

5. All children need healthy school lunch programs.

   _____

   _____

Before taking the mastery tests at the end of this chapter, review the information presented in the chapter by studying the following chart. (The same information is located on the inside front cover of this textbook.)

THREE OPTIONS FOR COORDINATION

OPTION 1

Independent clause + Comma and coordinating conjunction (*and, nor, but, yet, for, or, so*) + Independent clause

I had worked hard, so I expected results.

OPTION 2

Independent clause + Semicolon, adverbial conjunction, and comma + Independent clause

(*accordingly, also, besides, consequently, furthermore, hence, however, in addition, indeed, in fact, instead, likewise, meanwhile, moreover, nevertheless, nonetheless, on the other hand, otherwise, similarly, therefore, thus*)

I had worked hard; therefore, I expected results.

OPTION 3

Independent clause + Semicolon + Independent clause

I had worked hard; I expected results.

" Your vital signs are all healthy..."

Mastery and Editing Tests

TEST **1** **Combining Sentences Using Coordination**

In the blank to the left of each group of four sentences, write the letter of the sentence that is a correct example of coordination.

_____ 1. a. Childhood obesity is a serious problem in fact 12 million children in this country are overweight.

b. Childhood obesity is a serious problem, in fact 12 million children in this country are overweight.

c. Childhood obesity is a serious problem; in fact 12 million children in this country are overweight.

d. Childhood obesity is a serious problem; in fact, 12 million children in this country are overweight.

_____ 2. a. Childhood obesity leads to other health problems such as type 2 diabetes and hypertension so we must find ways to get this epidemic under control.

b. Childhood obesity leads to other health problems, such as type 2 diabetes and hypertension; so we must find ways to get this epidemic under control.

c. Childhood obesity leads to other health problems such as type 2 diabetes and hypertension, so we must find ways to get this epidemic under control.

d. Childhood obesity leads to other health problems such as type 2 diabetes and hypertension; so, we must find ways to get this epidemic under control.

_____ 3. a. Children should walk to school whenever possible they should walk the dog, do yard work, and play outside.

b. Children should walk to school whenever possible, they should walk the dog, do yard work, and play outside.

c. Children should walk to school whenever possible; they should walk the dog, do yard work, and play outside.

d. Children should walk to school whenever possible; they, should walk the dog, do yard work, and play outside.

_____ 4. a. Sodas and other sugary beverages should be avoided instead pure water and milk should be encouraged.

b. Sodas and other sugary beverages should be avoided, instead pure water and milk should be encouraged.

c. Sodas and other sugary beverages should be avoided; instead pure water and milk should be encouraged.

d. Sodas and other sugary beverages should be avoided; instead, pure water and milk should be encouraged.

_____ 5. a. It is important not to skip meals furthermore these meals should be eaten at regular times each day in order for the body to maintain energy.

b. It is important not to skip meals, furthermore these meals should be eaten at regular times each day in order for the body to maintain energy.

c. It is important not to skip meals, furthermore; these meals should be eaten at regular times each day in order for the body to maintain energy.

d. It is important not to skip meals; furthermore, these meals should be eaten at regular times each day in order for the body to maintain energy.

TEST ② Combining Sentences Using Coordination

In the blank to the left of each group of four sentences, write the letter of the sentence that is a correct example of coordination.

_____ 1. a. The theater was crowded, consequently, not everyone could get a good seat.

b. The theater was crowded; consequently not everyone could get a good seat.

c. The theater was crowded, so not everyone could get a good seat.

d. The theater was crowded; so not everyone could get a good seat.

_____ 2. a. The first apartment had no bedroom but it had a large beautiful living room.

b. The first apartment had no bedroom, however, it had a large, beautiful living room.

c. The first apartment had no bedroom; nevertheless, it had a large, beautiful living room.

d. The first apartment had no bedroom; yet it had a large, beautiful living room.

_____ 3. a. January had been bitterly cold; therefore, few people had attended the festival.

b. January had been bitterly cold, however, few people had attended the festival.

c. January had been bitterly cold also few people had attended the festival.

d. January had been bitterly cold; in addition few people had attended the festival.

_____ 4. a. The community waited for the news, nonetheless the crew kept digging.

b. The community waited for the news; and the crew kept digging.

c. The community waited for the news; meanwhile, the crew kept digging.

d. The community waited for the news, yet, the crew kept digging.

_____ 5. a. The village should balance its budget, likewise the taxes will have to be raised.

b. The village should balance its budget; otherwise, the taxes will have to be raised.

c. The village should balance its budget, besides the taxes will have to be raised.

d. The village should balance its budget; or the taxes will have to be raised.

TEST ③   **Editing Student Writing: Combining Sentences Using Coordination**

In the following paragraph, several simple sentences could be combined to form compound sentences by using coordination. Find three places in the paragraph where you can create compound sentences. Use each of the three options learned in this chapter. Write your new sentences on the lines provided after the paragraph.

¹My children were still in college. ²My old job with an accounting firm had ended. ³I needed to earn some money. ⁴The thought of a new job made me

nervous. ⁵What would it be like? ⁶Then I saw an ad for openings with Old Navy. ⁷I decided to apply. ⁸They offered a salary plus a good discount for employees. ⁹At the interview, I was the only person over twenty-five. ¹⁰They must have liked me. ¹¹They hired me the next day! ¹²I was sent to their largest downtown location. ¹³The first day on the job was scary. ¹⁴I was assigned to a "buddy." ¹⁵The young woman could have been one of my daughters. ¹⁶She explained how to be in control of the stockroom. ¹⁷She showed me how to use a scanner to find out the current price of an item. ¹⁸She advised me on how to keep items on hold for customers. ¹⁹She gave me a feeling of confidence. ²⁰I never thought I would feel that way. ²¹My spirit was willing. ²²I learned a lot. ²³My feet hurt by the end of the first day. ²⁴I spent half of my first month's salary on Old Navy clothes. ²⁵I had wanted new clothes for a long time. ²⁶Some of the clothes were for myself. ²⁷Some of the clothes were for my daughters.

Option 1: _____

_____

_____

Option 2: _____

_____

_____

Option 3: _____

_____

_____

TEST 4 **Editing Student Writing Using Editing Symbols**

The editing symbol for an error in coordination is coord. In the following paragraph, find five errors in coordination (coord), two fragments (frag), and three subject-verb agreement errors (agr). Mark the errors with these commonly used editing symbols, and then correct these errors on the lines provided after the paragraph.

¹Sometimes hardships make a person stronger ²Even in childhood. ³My mother has always been sickly so I have learned to be independent. ⁴It has happened gradually. ⁵The phone would ring I would answer it. ⁶Here is some of my weekly duties. ⁷I help my brothers with their homework and go to their baseball games. ⁸I cook nightly dinners once a week I do the grocery shopping. ⁹Friends of our family feels sorry for us but we are not unhappy. ¹⁰Especially sitting around the fire at night in the family room. ¹¹During the last few years, my father and I have

become very close. ¹²I have learned from adversity in fact I have found strength for the future. ¹³The knowledge of my father's love, kindness, and generosity remain my inspiration.

Five coordination corrections

1. _____

_____

2. _____

3. _____

_____

4. _____

_____

5. _____

_____

Two corrected fragments

6. _____

7. _____

_____

Three subject-verb agreement corrections

Subject	Correct form of the verb
8. _____	_____
9. _____	_____
10. _____	_____

WRITE FOR SUCCESS

What are some of the common mistakes that college students make? When you respond, consider the following: (1) skipping too many classes, (2) procrastinating with assignments, (3) failing to make use of advisement services, and (4) being afraid to ask questions.

Working Together

Beau Lark/Fancy/Corbis

Causes and Effects: College Dropout Rates

Many educational professionals are alarmed by the growing inability of Americans to compete with workers from many other countries. They point to the troubling dropout rate in our high schools and colleges. Leaders in industry claim there are jobs in skilled areas, but they cannot find people to fill these jobs. In recent years, the U.S. dropout rate has decreased slightly, but *PBS NewsHour* reported in February 2015 that the country still lags behind much of the world:

> While the increase is a step toward a White House–backed goal of having a 90 percent national on-time graduation rate by 2020, the U.S. ranked at the bottom of the Organisation for Economic Co-operation and Development's countries for graduation rates last year. Only Austria, Greece, Luxemburg, Mexico and Sweden had lower high school completion rates.

The class should divide into two groups. Working together, group 1 should develop a list of the causes of student dropout rates. Consider (1) the quality of prior education, (2) personal life experience, and (3) poor work habits. Group 2 should develop a list of the effects of students dropping out college. Consider what effects this might have on (1) the individual, (2) the U.S. economy, and (3) the country's future. The class should come together to present the lists. All students should keep their own separate copies of the ideas developed in the groups. A logical continuation of the discussion about these causes and effects might be the question of what could be done about this serious social problem.

PORTFOLIO SUGGESTION

You have just made lists on the topic of college dropouts. These lists include reasons for dropping out of college and the effects of dropping out of college. Save these notes in case you want to use the material in a future essay on this or on a related topic. For more information, consult the report on *PBS NewsHour's* Web page at http://www.pbs.org/newshour/rundown/high-school-graduation-rates-tick-u-s-still-lags-developed-countries/.

Combining Sentences Using Subordination

7

CHAPTER OBJECTIVES

In this chapter, you will learn how **subordination** is used to form **complex sentences**.

- Recognize the difference between an **independent clause** and a **dependent clause**.

- Understand the two options for combining an independent clause with a dependent clause that begins with a **subordinating conjunction**.

- Understand how to combine an independent clause with a dependent clause that begins with a **relative pronoun**.

What Is Subordination?

In the chapter about *coordination*, you learned that both clauses in a *compound sentence* are independent clauses. In *subordination*, only one clause can be an independent clause. Any other clause must be a dependent clause. A dependent clause is dependent on (that is, subordinate to) the independent clause, and together these clauses make up a *complex sentence*.

> **Subordination** is the method of combining two clauses that contain ideas not equally important. The more important idea is in the **independent clause,** and the less important idea is in the **dependent clause.** The result is a **complex sentence.**

Independent clause:	We listened.
Dependent clause:	when she spoke
Complex sentences:	We listened when she spoke.
	When she spoke, we listened.

The Difference between an Independent Clause and a Dependent Clause

An *independent clause* stands alone as a complete thought; it could be a simple sentence.

Independent clause: I drank the water.

A *dependent clause* begins with a connecting word, and even though the clause contains a subject and a verb, it does not stand alone as a complete thought. The idea is not complete.

Dependent clause: When I drank the water, . . .

Before you write your own complex sentences, practice the following exercises to be sure you recognize the difference between an independent clause and a dependent clause.

EXERCISE **1**   **Identifying Dependent and Independent Clauses**

In the blank to the left of each group of words, write *IC* if the group of words is an independent clause (a complete thought) or *DC* if the group of words is a dependent clause (not a complete thought, even though it contains a subject and a verb).

_____   1. Americans adore pets

_____   2. although high-end pet food is very expensive

_____   3. when Monty needs the right cut

_____   4. some pet stylists can earn one hundred dollars an hour

_____   5. wealthy pet owners may take their pets to daycare

_____   6. because pet play groups encourage socialization

_____   7. since veterinarians now treat animal obesity

_____   8. animals can also be treated for skin disorders by an animal dermatologist

_____   9. pets have been shown to lower their owner's blood pressure

_____10. even if some pets have been known to bite

EXERCISE **2**   **Identifying Dependent and Independent Clauses**

In the blank to the left of each group of words, write *IC* if the group of words is an independent clause (a complete thought) or *DC* if the group of words is a dependent clause (not a complete thought, even though it contains a subject and a verb).

_____   1. William Faulkner was a regional writer

_____   2. he was born near Oxford, Mississippi

_____   3. where he lived and died

_____   4. even though he used the dialect of the area

_____ 5. some of his books share the same characters and themes

_____ 6. because Faulkner devoted many pages to greed, violence, and meanness

_____ 7. until the year he died

_____ 8. he won the Nobel Prize in 1950

_____ 9. when he was recognized as one of America's greatest writers

_____10. although Faulkner departed from the traditional style of prose

EXERCISE 3   Identifying Dependent and Independent Clauses

In the blank to the left of each group of words, write _IC_ if the group of words is an independent clause (a complete thought) or _DC_ if the group of words is a dependent clause (not a complete thought, even though it contains a subject and a verb).

_____ 1. J. K. Rowling wrote her first book in a café

_____ 2. while her infant daughter slept

_____ 3. in one day, her first book sold 7 million copies

_____ 4. although the book was hundreds of pages long

_____ 5. the success of the Harry Potter series has been astonishing

_____ 6. Harry Potter mania swept the country

_____ 7. since the publication of the fourth book, _Harry Potter and the Goblet of Fire_

_____ 8. bookstores held midnight extravaganzas to release each new book in the series

_____ 9. J. K. Rowling kept writing for seventeen years

_____10. until she finished the last book in the series, _Harry Potter and the Deathly Hallows_

Warner Bros/Everett Collection

Using Subordinating Conjunctions

In _coordination,_ you combined ideas by using connecting words called _coordinating conjunctions_ and _adverbial conjunctions._ In _subordination,_ you combine ideas by using two different sets of connecting words called _subordinating conjunctions_ and _relative pronouns._ Begin this section by memorizing the list of subordinating conjunctions given in the chart below.

CONNECTORS: FREQUENTLY USED SUBORDINATING CONJUNCTIONS

after	in order that	unless
although	once	until
as, as if	provided that	when, whenever
as long as, as though	rather than	where, wherever
because	since	whereas
before	so that	whether
even though	though	while
if, even if		

We all went out for pizza *after the game was over*.

In the preceding sentence, the dependent clause *after the game was over* contains a subject (*game*) and a verb (*was*). The word *after* functions as a subordinating conjunction that joins the two clauses. The result is a *complex sentence* because the sentence contains an independent clause and a dependent clause.

However, we should remember that many of the words in the chart may also function as prepositions.

We all went out for pizza *after the game*.

In the preceding sentence, *after* functions as a preposition that introduces the prepositional phrase *after the game.* The sentence is a *simple sentence* because it contains only one independent clause.

In the next practice, see if you can recognize the difference between a word used as a preposition in a prepositional phrase and a word used as a subordinating conjunction at the beginning of a dependent clause.

PRACTICE 1 **Identify each of the following groups of words as a prepositional phrase (PP) or a dependent clause (DC).**

_____ 1. before the dance began

_____ 2. before the dance contest

_____ 3. since the first of the month

_____ 4. since I started this journal

_____ 5. after the Civil War

_____ 6. after my dad visited

The following chart contains a list of the subordinating conjunctions grouped according to their meanings. When you use one of these conjunctions, you must be sure that the connection made between the independent clause and the dependent clause conveys the meaning you intend.

THE FUNCTIONS OF SUBORDINATING CONJUNCTIONS

To introduce a condition: *if, even if, as long as, provided that, unless* (usually after a negative independent clause)

I will go *as long as* you go with me. I won't go *unless* you go with me.

To introduce a contrast: *although, even though, though, whereas, while*

I will go *even though* you won't go with me.

To introduce a cause: *as, because, since*

I will go *because* the meeting is very important.

To show time: *after, before, since, when, whenever, while, until*

I will go *when* it is time.

I have voted every year *since* I was eighteen.

I won't go *until* it is time.

Note: *Until* usually follows a negative independent clause.

To show place: *where, wherever*

I will go *wherever* you send me.

To show purpose: *in order that, so that*

I will go *so that* I can hear the candidate for myself.

When you write a complex sentence, you can choose the order of the clauses. You can begin with the *independent clause*, or you can begin with the *dependent clause*.

TWO OPTIONS FOR SUBORDINATION USING SUBORDINATING CONJUNCTIONS

OPTION 1

Begin with the independent clause. Do not use a comma.

We can finish our homework if Tamika leaves.

OPTION 2

Begin with the dependent clause followed by a comma.

If Tamika leaves, we can finish our homework.

Notice that you use a comma only when you choose option 2, beginning your sentence with the dependent clause. Your ear will remind you to use the correct punctuation. Read aloud the sample sentence given for option 2. Listen to the natural pause at the end of the dependent clause before continuing with the rest of the sentence. The place where you pause is the place where you put a comma.

If Tamika leaves, we can finish our homework.

PRACTICE ❷ **Use a subordinating conjunction to combine each of the following pairs of sentences.**

1. Use the subordinating conjunction *after*:

   Soraya went out to celebrate.

   She won the floor routine competition.

   a. Begin with an independent clause:

   _____

   b. Begin with a dependent clause:

   _____

2. Use the subordinating conjunction *when*:

   Carla returned from Venezuela this spring.

   The family was excited.

   a. Begin with an independent clause:

   _____

   b. Begin with a dependent clause:

   _____

EXERCISE ❹ **Combining Sentences Using Subordination**

Use subordination to combine each of the following pairs of sentences. Refer to the list of subordinating conjunctions if necessary.

1. She was eating breakfast.

   The results of the election came over the radio.

   _____

   _____

2. This year the town council voted in favor of the plan.

   Last year they voted against the identical plan.

   _____

   _____

3. I will see Shonda Rhimes tonight.

   She is speaking at the university.

   _____

   _____

4. The worker hoped for a promotion.

   Not one person in the department had received a promotion last year.

   _____

   _____

5. The worker hoped for a promotion.

   All his work was done accurately and on time.

   _____

   _____

EXERCISE  **Combining Sentences Using Subordination**

Use each of the following subordinating conjunctions to compose a complex sentence. An example has been done for you.

Subordinating conjunction: after

Complex sentence: After the game was over, we all went out for pizza.

1. as if

   _____

   _____

2. before

   _____

   _____

3. until

   _____

   _____

4. although

   _____

   _____

5. unless

   _____

   _____

EXERCISE  **Combining Sentences Using Subordination**

All the sentences in the following paragraph are simple sentences. Find three places in the paragraph where you could effectively combine two of the sentences to create a complex sentence (a sentence with one independent clause and at least one dependent clause). On the lines that follow the paragraph, write the three complex sentences you have created.

¹Many years ago, a woman was walking past an antique shop in New York City. ²She noticed a large beautiful bedspread in the window. ³She was an authority on antiques. ⁴She recognized it at once. ⁵The bedspread had belonged to Queen Marie Antoinette of France. ⁶The bedspread was embroidered with gold thread. ⁷It was worth a fortune. ⁸She bought the bedspread for fifty thousand dollars. ⁹It was worth more than one million dollars. ¹⁰This story is everyone's dream. ¹¹We would all like to discover a treasure in our attic, at a flea market, or at a garage sale. ¹²Recently, one man paid $1.00 for a strange hand-carved vase. ¹³Most people would have passed it up. ¹⁴He took it to the Antiques Roadshow. ¹⁵An expert evaluated the vase. ¹⁶She made an astonishing announcement. ¹⁷The vase was made from a rhinoceros horn. ¹⁸It was evaluated at $100,000.00. ¹⁹An object may appear worthless at first. ²⁰It may have real value in the marketplace.

1. _____

   _____

   _____

2. _____

   _____

   _____

3. _____

   _____

   _____

Using Relative Pronouns

Begin this section by studying the relative pronouns in the following box.

RELATIVE PRONOUNS			
who, whoever whom, whomever whose	refers to persons	where	refers to place
		when	refers to time
what, whatever which, whichever	refers to things		
that	usually refers to things sometimes refers to people		

Sentences can often be combined with a relative pronoun. These two simple sentences sound short and choppy:

The researcher had a breakthrough.

She was studying diabetes.

To avoid this choppiness, a writer might want to join the two related ideas by using a relative pronoun.

> A **relative clause** is a dependent clause that begins with a relative pronoun.
>
> *whom* the journalist interviewed
>
> *which* she incorporated into his article
>
> *that* we read in the magazine

If the relative clause is put in the wrong place, the result will confuse the reader.

Incorrectly combined: The researcher had a breakthrough *who* was studying diabetes.

The relative pronoun *who* refers to *researcher*, so the relative clause *who was studying diabetes* must be placed immediately after *researcher*.

Correctly combined: The researcher *who* was studying diabetes had a breakthrough.

RULE ❶   The relative pronoun and its clause must immediately follow the word to which it is related.

A sentence may have more than one relative clause. Study the following sentence, which contains two relative clauses. Notice that each relative pronoun immediately follows the word to which it is related.

The researcher *who* was studying diabetes had a breakthrough, *which* she reported to the press.

PRACTICE ❸   **Combine each pair of sentences into one complex sentence by using a relative pronoun. Do not use commas. An example follows:**

Simple sentence: The florist created the flower arrangement.

Simple sentence: He called us last weekend.

Complex sentence: The florist *who* called us last weekend created the flower arrangement.

1. The chemistry lab is two hours long. I attend that chemistry lab.

   Combined: _____

   _____

2. The student assistant is very knowledgeable. The student assistant is standing by the door.

   Combined: _____

   _____

3. The equipment was purchased last year.

   The equipment will make possible some important new research.

   Combined: _____

   _____

Punctuating Relative Clauses

In order to use correct punctuation in a sentence that contains a relative clause, the writer must understand the difference between two types of relative clauses.

1. A **restrictive clause** is a relative clause that is essential to the intended main idea of the sentence. Restrictive clauses often begin with the relative pronoun *that*. These clauses do not use any commas.

   You should never eat fruit that you haven't washed first.

   If we were to leave out the relative clause (*that you haven't washed first*), the idea that would remain is *You should never eat fruit*. Without the relative clause, the meaning of the main idea would have changed. Therefore, the dependent clause is essential.

2. A **nonrestrictive clause** is a relative clause that is not essential to the intended meaning of the main idea. Nonrestrictive clauses often begin with the pronoun *which*. They require commas to set off the relative clause.

   Mother's fruit salad, *which* she prepares every Sunday, is delicious.

   If we were to leave out the relative clause (*which she prepares every Sunday*), what would remain is *Mother's fruit salad is delicious*. The main idea is clear without the relative clause. Because the relative clause is not essential to this main idea, it is set off by commas.

SUBORDINATION: DISTINGUISHING BETWEEN TWO TYPES OF RELATIVE PRONOUN CLAUSES

RESTRICTIVE CLAUSE

The relative clause is essential to the meaning of the sentence. No commas are used.

You should never eat fruit *that you haven't washed first.*

NONRESTRICTIVE CLAUSE

The relative clause is not essential to the meaning of the sentence. Commas must be used.

Mother's fruit salad, *which she prepares every Sunday,* is delicious.

PRACTICE **4**   **Punctuating Relative Clauses**

In the sentences that follow, insert commas wherever they are needed. Be sure to study the following examples before you begin.

> **The man *who is wearing the Hawaiian shirt* is the bridegroom.**

In the sentence above, the bridegroom can be identified only by his Hawaiian shirt. Therefore, the relative clause *who is wearing the Hawaiian shirt* is essential to the meaning. No commas are needed.

> **Al, *who was wearing a blue polo shirt,* arrived late to the wedding.**

In the preceding sentence, the main idea is that Al was late. What he was wearing is not essential to that main idea. Therefore, commas are needed to set off this nonessential information.

1. The poem that my classmate read in class was very powerful.

2. The teacher who guided our class today is my favorite college professor.

3. Her biology course which met four times a week for two hours each session was extremely demanding.

4. You seldom learn much in courses that are not demanding.

5. My own poetry which has improved over the semester has brought me much satisfaction.

Now you are ready to practice combining your own sentences by using relative pronouns. The following exercises ask you to insert a variety of relative clauses into simple sentences. Pay careful attention to the punctuation.

EXERCISE **7**   **Writing Sentences Using Relative Pronouns**

Insert a relative clause into each of the following ten sentences. Use each of the possibilities (*who, whose, whom, which, that*) at least once. Be sure to punctuate correctly. An example has been done for you.

Simple sentence: The board recommends stricter regulations.

Complex sentence: The board, which is composed of five members, recommends stricter regulations.

1. The president _____
   asked her advisers for help.

2. Her advisers _____
   met with her in her office.

3. The situation _____
   was at a critical point.

4. Even her vice president _____
   appeared visibly alarmed.

5. Stacked on the table, the plans _____
   looked impressive.

6. The meeting _____
   began at two o'clock.

7. Every idea _____
   was examined in great detail.

8. Several maps _____
   showed the area in question.

9. One adviser _____
   was vehemently opposed to the plan.

10. Finally, the group agreed on a plan of action _____

EXERCISE ⑧   **Combining Sentences Using Relative Pronouns**

Combine each of the following pairs of sentences by using a relative pronoun.

1. Stress can do a great deal of harm.

   We experience stress every day.

   _____

2. People often use food to help them cope.

   Some people's jobs are demanding.

   _____

3. The practice of eating to cope with stress is often automatic.

   The practice of eating to cope usually goes back to childhood.

   _____

   _____

4. Some foods can actually increase tension.

   People turn to foods in times of stress.

   _____

5. Sweet foods are actually not energy boosters.

   Sweet foods are popular with people who need a lift.

   _____

   _____

6. Another substance is caffeine.

   People use other substances to get an energy boost.

   _____

7. One of the biggest mistakes is using alcohol to feel calm and relaxed.
   Alcohol is really a depressant.

   _____

   _____

8. People should eat three light meals a day and two small snacks.
   People want to feel a sense of calm.

   _____

   _____

9. Sufficient protein is needed throughout the day.
   Protein maintains an adequate energy level.

   _____

   _____

10. A person should eat regularly to avoid binges.
    Binges put on pounds and drain one's energy.

    _____

    _____

EXERCISE ⑨ **Combining Sentences Using Relative Pronouns**

Combine each of the following pairs of sentences by using a relative pronoun.

Blend Images - KidStock/Getty Images

1. a. Dr. Jose Abreo had an idea for social reform.
   b. He is a successful economist.

   _____

   _____

2. a. He believed classical music could save thousands of children.
   b. These children lived in crime-ridden neighborhoods throughout Venezuela.

   _____

   _____

   _____

3. a. In 1975 Dr. Abreo started a youth orchestra.

   b. This first orchestra had only eleven children.

   _____

   _____

4. a. Gradually, after-school centers were begun in many poor neighborhoods.

   b. In these neighborhoods, children were being lost to drugs and gang violence.

   _____

   _____

5. a. These centers offered free music lessons.

   b. These centers gave musical instruments to children as young as four.

   _____

   _____

6. a. The children seemed to love hard work.

   b. Children practiced six days a week.

   _____

7. a. Learning classical music instilled confidence and self-esteem.

   b. Classical music transported them to another world.

   _____

   _____

8. a. In thirty years, 800,000 children have passed through the system.

   b. The system has now grown to 220 youth orchestras.

   _____

   _____

9. a. Gustavo Dudamel is the first Venezuelan classical superstar.

   b. He conducts The Simon Bolivar National Youth Orchestra.

   _____

   _____

10. a. Classical music has a spiritual richness.

    b. Classical music can lift children's spirits from their physical poverty.

    _____

    _____

> **SUBORDINATION**
>
> **I: USE A SUBORDINATING CONJUNCTION**
>
> **a. Begin with the independent clause. Do not use a comma.**
>
>   We can finish our homework *if* Tamika leaves.
>
> **b. Begin with the dependent clause followed by a comma.**
>
>   *If* Tamika leaves, we can finish our homework.
>
> **II: USE A RELATIVE PRONOUN**
>
> **a. If the relative clause is essential information, the clause is restrictive. Do not use commas.**
>
>   You should never eat fruit *that you haven't washed first.*
>
> **b. If the relative clause is not essential information, the clause is nonrestrictive. Use commas.**
>
>   Mother's fruit salad, *which she prepares every Sunday,* is delicious.

Mastery and Editing Tests

TEST **1**   **Combining Sentences with a Subordinating Conjunction or a Relative Pronoun**

Combine each of the following pairs of sentences by using either a subordinating conjunction or a relative pronoun. Try to use a variety of subordinating conjunctions.

1. The *Titanic* sank on its maiden voyage in 1912.

   The captain ignored an iceberg warning.

   _____

   _____

2. The movie won several Academy Awards.

   It was three hours long.

   _____

   _____

3. Junior had a superhero costume.

   He was not a superhero.

   _____

   _____

4. The meme was insulting.

   Diamond decided not to share it.

   _____

   _____

5. The medical assistant always wore scrubs.

They were required for job.

_____

_____

6. The student saw the workload for the course.

She created a daily schedule.

_____

_____

7. I will pay attention to my written communication skills.

Prospective employers will think of me as the complete package.

_____

_____

8. The years passed.

The child grew.

_____

_____

9. The young professional committed herself to improvement.

She was satisfied with her progress.

_____

_____

10. The man was out shopping for ties.

A riot started on the street.

_____

_____

TEST ❷ **Finding Subordinating Conjunctions and Using Correct Punctuation**

Circle all the subordinating conjunctions in the following paragraph. Add commas wherever needed.

Although life in Russia today may differ widely from life in the United States Russian television has several shows that have similarities to American shows. *Let's Get Married* reminds us of *The Bachelor* because the single man has his choice of several eligible young women. Before he goes on a date with one of them he and the girls must answer questions from a panel of older women. While the American show has a budget to take the bachelor and his date to an exotic place the Russian show does not enjoy a budget that would allow for extravagant travel. Additionally, the contestants on the Russian show often wear outrageous costumes to amuse the viewers. The bachelor may be dressed as Aladdin and the young women as harem dancers as if they were characters in the *Tales from the Arabian Nights*. Another show, the popular *Fashion Verdict*, accuses some women of vulgar excess in the way they dress. The show takes place in a mock courtroom where a socialite woman, not unlike Paris Hilton, is prosecuted for her bad taste. Perhaps this show enjoys such great popularity because the real Russian legal system has such a bad reputation among the Russian population. Though many topics may still be taboo in Russian society, another Russian program, *Let Them Talk*, combines a Jerry Springer and Oprah Winfrey atmosphere. Unlike any previous Russian show this most popular show discusses taboo social topics and gives suggestions for self-help. For instance, until this program began airing the deplorable situation of severely handicapped persons often placed in institutions was not openly discussed. Finally, the Russians have their own version of the *Judge Judy* show. It differs from the American show probably because the Russian people yearn for real justice. Whereas *Judge Judy* is largely entertaining the Russian Judges on these television programs consider such cases as cheating landlords and lying ex-boyfriends much more seriously.

TEST ③ **Combining Sentences Using Coordination and Subordination**

The following paragraph is composed of mostly simple sentences. The result is very choppy. Read the entire paragraph, and then choose three places where sentences could be combined to create compound or complex sentences that will improve the style. Do not be afraid to change the wording to accommodate the changes you want to make. You can combine clauses using coordination or subordination. Write your new compound or complex sentences on the lines provided after the paragraph.

Our history is filled with stories of curious coincidences. One such example involves the two families of Lincoln and Booth. We all know the tragic story of the assassination of Abraham Lincoln in 1865. The president was murdered by a member of America's most famous theatrical family, the Booth family. The murderer's name was John Wilkes Booth. He was a handsome actor. He was greatly admired in many popular roles. About a year before this terrible event, another member of Lincoln's family was in great danger. This was Robert Todd Lincoln. He was the president's son. The young man was waiting for a train in the Jersey City train station. It was late at night. Passengers were crowding against the passenger car. They pressed against Robert. Then the train began to move. Robert lost his footing. He fell into the open space between the train and the platform. Suddenly, someone seized his coat collar and pulled him up and onto the platform. The man saved the boy's life. He was none other than Edwin Booth, the most famous actor in America. He was the brother of John Wilkes Booth!

1. _____
   _____
   _____

2. _____
   _____
   _____

3. _____
   _____
   _____

TEST ④ **Editing Student Writing Using Editing Symbols**

In the following paragraph, editing symbols mark the sentences that need revision or correction. Make your corrections on the lines provided after the paragraph. The editing symbol for a subordination error is *subord*.

[1]Fashion is always looking for a fresh idea. [2]Are you tired yet of the low-rise pants with the cropped shirts that reveals the bellybutton? [3]Have you seen too many young men, who walk along holding up their pants? [4]Are you glad to see lime green become last season's popular color? [5]And the wedding scene! [6]Every young female guest wears a black dress every bride wears a strapless gown. [7]One fact is for certain. [8]Another fad will replace a fading one. [9]Take, for example, shoe fashions. [10]After a generation of women enjoyed wearing comfortable shoes to work now young women are once again wearing pointed toes and spiked heels. [11]This new generation of women will ruin their feet, if they wear such shoes for very long. [12]While older people look for safety and comfort it seems younger people prefer

being provocative and even dangerously shocking. ¹³Another purpose of fads, of course, are to keep up our spirits. ¹⁴After the tragedy of 9/11, several fashion ads were recalled, because they were in bad taste. ¹⁵The patriotic look was in with a lot of red, white, and blue. ¹⁶The fashion industry is likely to be responsive to our nation's sobering circumstances however it is unlikely to come up with anything bordering on dowdy. ¹⁷Too many teens want to express themselves by the clothes they wear.

Corrections

1. agreement (sentence 2): _____

2. subordination (sentence 3): _____

   _____

   _____

3. fragment (sentence 5): _____

4. coordination (sentence 6): _____

   _____

5. subordination (sentence 10): _____

   _____

   _____

   _____

6. subordination (sentence 11): _____

   _____

   _____

7. subordination (sentence 12): _____

   _____

   _____

   _____

8. agreement (sentence 13): _____

9. subordination (sentence 14): _____

   _____

   _____

10. coordination (sentence 16): _____

_____

_____

_____

WRITE FOR SUCCESS

Many people are not realistic about their academic strengths and weaknesses. What do you believe are your academic strengths and weaknesses? For each strength you present, suggest how you might take advantage of this strength. For each weakness, suggest how you might minimize its negative impact.

MY FIRST JOB

BY MICHAEL POWELL

What Painting Rocks Has to Do with Army Precision

My first job was serving as an Army officer where I learned about painting rocks. If you step on a military base on the eve of an inspection you will discover soldiers painting things: rocks, curbs, tree-trunks, you name it. Seems like a mindless waste of time—classic busy work, or "spit and polish" taken to the extreme.

However, there are two important lessons I learned from years of watching folks in green brushing stones in bright white, yellow, and sometimes red. The first is that looking good, presenting well, and shining bright makes a powerful impression. Countless generals have strolled onto bases, smelling that new Sherman Williams in the air, and been immediately impressed. They form a quick impression that this is a squared-way unit.

It is easy to chuckle about it—how can good-looking rocks and curbs tell you anything about the fighting prowess of this unit? But truth be told, appearance and a strong initial impression cause an audience to form lasting impressions about the quality of what they see and the caliber of the person they are observing. A good speaker knows that the audience will form an impression in the first minute you step on stage, based on your appearance and tone of voice, that will dominate what they believe about the speech, no matter what its content.

As a solider I remember the obsession with highly shined boots, freshly pressed uniforms, and sharp haircuts. Sure, this was the act of "looking the part," but it was much more. The obsession with focus on detail, no matter how small, is frequently misunderstood as the military's adherence to conformity. That is wrong. The lesson really is twofold. First, it is about the power of forming habits. Experts say you must get in a pattern of consistent commitment if you want to form a lasting habit.

William Harris/Getty Images

Practicing the discipline of doing something important over and over again the exact same way forms habits that become instinctual. This is pretty critical for a solider in battle who may have not time to think, or is confused by the fog of war. He will instinctively know to flip his weapon off safe and fire in the right direction, because we ingrained in him a habit. This lesson easily can translate to any organization or in one's own personal growth.

Also, I learned the art of being intensely observant. To notice when something has changed, no matter how small or seemingly minor, is a powerful skill. I learned to be a ruthless observer—looking for patterns that are out of place. There is real power in, as Neo might put it, looking for a warp in the matrix. I learned to practice every day noticing the littlest things—I notice the first leaf to drop in fall, when someone changes a hairstyle, or a wall is painted, or a light left on, or someone's mood shifts. Observation obsession lets you see things others miss and gives you insight that can inspire creativity.

It also empowers you in another important way. It lets you look for what the painted rocks are hiding.

Narrowing the Topic Through Group Discussion: A Person's First Job

When you get your first job, you are not only earning your first paychecks but also learning your first lessons about the world of work. In this article, Michael Powell writes about the lessons he learned from his first job as an officer in the Army. After you have read the article, discuss the questions that follow. As you exchange ideas suggested by the article, you will find yourself concentrating on those aspects of the subject that interest you the most. These particular areas of interest would make good topics for your own writing.

Questions for Group Discussion

1. Michael Powell states that at first painting rocks and trees and curbs may seem "like a mindless waste of time," but actually serves to teach some important lessons. Have any students had a job where they had to perform tasks that they first thought were meaningless but later found to be important or meaningful?

2. One lesson the writer learned was that making a positive first impression is important to long-term success. This can be especially important during a job interview. How do students usually dress for a job interview? Do they dress up by wearing their nicest clothes, or do they simply dress as they do every day? What effect do they think this has on the boss or manager?

3. Soldiers obviously need to wear a uniform. Have any students had a job that required them to wear a uniform? Did it have any effect on job performance? Did it make the student take more pride in his or her work, or was it a nuisance?

4. Michael Powell's first job obviously had a lasting effect on his life. Did any students' first job teach them anything important? Did it teach them anything that they still find relevant to their lives today?

5. The writer says that his job as a soldier taught him to be observant of not just things but also people. For many of us, our first job is the first time we are really forced to interact with people of different age groups and walks of life outside of school and family settings. Did their first job teach any students about other people, how to deal with them when they are upset, how to negotiate with them, or how to work with them?

PORTFOLIO SUGGESTION

Save your notes from this discussion of a person's first job. From this general topic, narrow down the issues to three or four specific aspects that would be of interest to you for future writing projects.

Correcting Fragments and Run-Ons

8

This chapter builds on your previous work with phrases and clauses. Here you will study how to correct more complicated fragments and several types of run-on sentences.

- Identify **three types of fragments:**

  one or more phrases

  one or more dependent clauses

  a combination of phrases and dependent clauses

- Identify **three types of run-on sentences:**

  the *and* run-on

  the fused run-on

  the comma splice

What Is a Fragment?

A **fragment** is a piece of a sentence.

How Many Kinds of Fragments Are There?

1. A fragment could be a phrase:

   I picked up the newspaper. I recognized the face. *On the front page.*

NOTE: The prepositional phrase *on the front page* is a fragment, not a sentence.

2. A fragment could be a dependent clause:

   ***When I picked up the newspaper.* I recognized the face on the front page.**

NOTE: The dependent clause *when I picked up the newspaper* is a fragment, not a sentence.

3. A fragment could be a combination of phrases and dependent clauses:

   When I picked up the newspaper from the stand that is on the corner of the street.

NOTE: *When I picked up the newspaper* is a dependent clause; *from the stand* is a prepositional phrase; *that is* is a dependent clause; *on the corner* and *of the street* are prepositional phrases. A combination of phrases and dependent clauses is not a sentence.

How Do You Make a Complete Sentence from a Fragment?

1. **If the fragment is a phrase:**	I recognized the face. *On the front page*
Revision Option a:	The phrase might belong to the sentence that comes before it or after it. I recognized the face *on the front page.*
Revision Option b:	You might need to compose an independent clause to which the phrase will be added. I recognized the face. It was right there *on the front page.*
2. **If the fragment is a dependent clause:**	*When I picked up the newspaper*
Revision Option a:	The dependent clause might belong to the sentence that comes before it or after it. *When I picked up the newspaper,* I recognized the face on the front page.
Revision Option b:	You might need to compose an independent clause to add to the dependent clause. *When I picked up the newspaper,* I halted in my tracks. I recognized the face on the front page.
Revision Option c:	You might omit the subordinate conjunction, thereby leaving an independent clause. I picked up the newspaper. I recognized the face on the front page.
3. **If the fragment is a combination of phrases and dependent clauses:**	*When I picked up the newspaper from the stand that is on the corner of the street*
Revision Option a:	You need an independent clause. You might change a dependent clause to an independent clause by dropping the subordinate conjunction. *I picked up the newspaper* from the stand that is on the corner of the street.
Revision Option b:	You need an independent clause. You might add an independent clause. *When I picked up the newspaper from the stand that is on the corner of the street,* I recognized the face on the front page.

EXERCISE **1** **Recognizing Fragments**

Identify each of the examples below as one of the following:

a. sentence

b. fragment—phrase

c. fragment—dependent clause

d. fragment—combination of phrases and dependent clauses

_____ 1. At the bus stop.

_____ 2. While I was not looking.

_____ 3. Someone took my backpack.

_____ 4. Because so many people were watching.

_____ 5. Although someone must have seen the theft when they were waiting for the bus around three o'clock.

_____ 6. Even though I asked everyone.

_____ 7. Nobody seemed to have noticed.

_____ 8. After I reported the theft to the police because I knew I should since it is always important to document these kinds of incidents.

_____ 9. In the event of other similar thefts.

_____ 10. When I got home and called my husband who was very upset about the situation.

EXERCISE **2** **Recognizing and Correcting Fragments**

Revise the ten examples from Exercise 1. Put your revised sentences into paragraph form, correcting all fragments.

_____

_____

_____

_____

_____

_____

_____

EXERCISE ③   **Student Writing: Recognizing and Correcting Fragments**

Carefully read the following paragraph. Find five fragments and underline them. Then fix each fragment (using the options for correcting fragments, found in the How Do You Make a Complete Sentence from a Fragment section), and write the new sentences on the lines below.

Howard Crane the shortest kid in my entire seventh grade. He was always getting into fights, and he used terrible language. If you've ever known a bully. Howard was a prime example. One Friday afternoon as we sat in the school bus on our way home. Howard began taunting my younger brother. Because our parents had told us to ignore Howard. My brother just looked straight ahead. Saying nothing. I was growing angrier and angrier. I had to do something.

1. _____

   _____

2. _____

   _____

3. _____

   _____

4. _____

   _____

5. _____

   _____

What Is a Run-On?

In conversation, when we retell events that have occurred, we often link our thoughts together in one long narrative. Here is a young woman telling a friend about her scary dream:

I had this dream the other night and I was at some pool with my sister and the pool had seats all around it like a stadium but I can't remember if people were watching us or not but my sister suddenly fell into the pool so I had to jump in to save her and I swam to the bottom and these weird arms had appeared and they were keeping her down there but I got her free and we went to swim to the surface but someone above was putting boards over the top of the pool so we couldn't get out and that was when my dream ended.

The girl relating the dream sequence ran all the parts of this entire event together without any separations. As a result, the account appears as a **run-on**. In formal writing, a run-on is considered a serious error.

Run-ons are independent clauses that have been combined incorrectly.

How Many Kinds of Run-Ons Are There?

Run-ons may occur when the writer is unable to recognize where one complete thought ends and another thought begins. Run-ons also may occur if the writer is not sure of the standard ways of connecting ideas. Certain marks of punctuation are needed to show where two clauses join. Other punctuation signifies the end of a thought. Study the following three types of run-ons.

1. **The *and* run-on:** two or more relatively long independent clauses connected with a coordinating conjunction without any punctuation

   Incorrect: I met Charlyce in a yoga class at the YWCA and we soon became friends.

2. **The fused run-on:** two or more independent clauses run together without any punctuation

   Incorrect: I met Charlyce in a yoga class at the YWCA we soon became friends.

3. **The comma splice:** two or more independent clauses run together with only a comma

   Incorrect: I met Charlyce in a yoga class at the YWCA, we soon became friends.

How Do You Correct a Run-On Sentence?

There are three basic ways to correct a run-on sentence.

1. Make two sentences with end punctuation.

   Correct: I met Charlyce in a yoga class at the YWCA. We soon became friends.

2. Make a compound sentence using one of the three methods of coordination.

   Correct: I met Charlyce in a yoga class at the YWCA, and we soon became friends.

   I met Charlyce in a yoga class at the YWCA; indeed, we soon became friends.

   I met Charlyce in a yoga class at the YWCA; we soon became friends.

3. Make a complex sentence using subordination.

   Correct: Soon after I met Charlyce in a yoga class at the YWCA, we became friends.

   Charlyce and I became friends soon after we met in a yoga class at the YWCA.

NOTE: See the inside front cover for a quick review of coordination and subordination.

PRACTICE ①   **Below are several run-on sentences. Correct them by using any of the three strategies given above for correcting run-ons. If a sentence is correct as is, mark it with a "C."**

1. Chronic procrastinators are those people who put things off at school or at work they may also avoid obligations to their family members at home.

2. Most people would agree that nothing is so exhausting as thinking about an uncompleted task.

3. Sometimes a person feels inadequate or overwhelmed by a task and the result is he or she keeps putting off what has to be done.

4. Believe it or not, the average worker, according to recent research, wastes two hours a day on nonwork activities, this adds to the cost of doing business.

5. One way to deal with the tendency to procrastinate is to break up a complicated task into its smaller parts, another way is to reward oneself for accomplishing a task that seems too difficult or unpleasant.

EXERCISE ④   ## Recognizing and Correcting Run-Ons

Here is the same run-on sentence that you read earlier in this chapter. Rewrite the dream sequence correctly. Put a period at the end of each complete thought. You may have to omit some of the words that loosely connect the ideas, or you may want to use coordination and subordination. Remember to make each new sentence begin with a capital letter.

I had this dream the other night and I was at some pool with my sister and the pool had seats all around it like a stadium but I can't remember if people were watching us or not but my sister suddenly fell into the pool so I had to jump in to save her and I swam to the bottom and these weird arms had appeared and they were keeping her down there but I got her free and we went to swim to the surface but someone above was putting boards over the top of the pool so we couldn't get out and that was when my dream ended.

_____

_____

_____

_____

_____

_____

EXERCISE ⑤   ## Recognizing and Correcting Run-Ons

The following story is written as one sentence. Rewrite the story correctly. Put a period at the end of each complete thought. You may have to omit some of the words that loosely connect the ideas, or you may want to use coordination and subordination. Remember to make each new sentence begin with a capital letter.

My best friend is accident-prone if you knew her you'd know that she's always limping, having to write with her other hand or wearing a bandage on her head or ankle, like last week for example she was walking down the street minding her own business when a shingle from someone's roof hit her on the head and she had to go to the emergency room for stitches, then this week one of her fingers is purple because someone slammed the car door on her hand sometimes I think it might be better if I didn't spend too much time with her you know her bad luck might be catching!

_____

_____

_____

_____

_____

_____

_____

_____

EXERCISE ⑥   ## Student Writing: Recognizing and Correcting Run-Ons

The following story is written as one sentence. Rewrite the story correctly. Put a period at the end of each complete thought. You may have to omit some of the words that loosely connect the ideas, or you may want to use coordination and subordination. Remember to make each new sentence begin with a capital letter.

One morning, not too early, I will rise and slip downstairs to brew the coffee and no baby will wake me up and no alarm clock will rattle my nerves and the weather will be so warm that I will not have to put on my coat and hat to go out for the paper there will be no rush I will go to the refrigerator and take out eggs and sausage the bathroom will be free so I will be able to take a shower with no one knocking on the door and I will not have to run up and down the stairs looking first for someone's shoes and then for someone's car keys I will leisurely fix my hair and pick out a new outfit to wear the phone might ring and it will be a friend who would like to have lunch and share the afternoon with me money will be no problem maybe we'll see a movie or drive to the nearby city to visit a museum and the countryside will be beautiful and unspoiled my life will seem fresh and promising.

_____

_____

_____

_____

_____

_____

_____

_____

_____

_____

_____

Mastery and Editing Tests

TEST ① **Editing for Fragments and Run-Ons**

On the lines provided below the paragraph, identify each numbered group of words as a sentence (S), fragment (F), or run-on (R). Then rewrite the paragraph, correcting any fragments and run-ons.

[1]In laboratory experiments, scientists have discovered a diet. [2]That extends the life of their animals up to 50 percent or more. [3]This diet prevents heart disease, diabetes, and kidney failure and it greatly retards all types of cancer. [4]Even slowing down the aging process of cataracts, gray hair, and feebleness. [5]Staying on this diet keeps the mind flexible and the body active to an almost biblical old age. [6]These rats, fish, and worms stay very slim, they are fed a diet of necessary vitamins and nutrients but only 65 percent of the calories of the animal's normal diet. [7]Every creature fed this restricted diet has had a greatly extended life span. [8]The results of caloric restriction are spectacular. [9]Says Richard Weindruch, a gerontologist at the National Institute on Aging in Bethesda, Maryland. [10]Gerontologists have tried many things to extend life but this is the only experiment that works every time in the lab. [11]Animals that received enough protein, vitamins, and minerals to prevent malnutrition. [12]They survived to a grand old age and it does not seem to matter whether they ate a diet composed largely of fats or carbohydrates. [13]Researchers

warn people against undertaking this diet too hastily, it is very easy to become malnourished. ¹⁴Dr. Roy Walford is a pioneer in the field from the University of California he believes humans could live to an extraordinarily advanced age. ¹⁵If they were to limit their caloric intake.

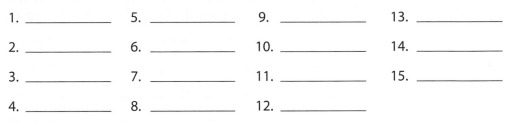

1. _____   5. _____   9. _____   13. _____

2. _____   6. _____   10. _____   14. _____

3. _____   7. _____   11. _____   15. _____

4. _____   8. _____   12. _____

Your version:

_____

_____

_____

_____

_____

_____

_____

_____

_____

_____

_____

_____

_____

_____

_____

_____

_____

TEST ❷ **Editing for Fragments and Run-Ons**

On the lines provided below, identify each numbered group of words as a sentence (S), fragment (F), or run-on (R). Then rewrite the paragraph, correcting any fragments and run-ons.

¹Every year more than 150 million people visit zoos and aquariums. ²All over the United States. ³It is not hard to imagine why zoos are so popular. ⁴First of all, a very pleasant place to spend an afternoon. ⁵Zoos are relatively quiet and peaceful. ⁶A welcome change from crowded and noisy amusement parks and other entertainment choices. ⁷Second, we are all attracted to the innocence of the animal

world. ⁸Often a person is drawn to an animal that is among the endangered species or he or she enjoys seeing an exotic animal that can be seen nowhere else. ⁹Families visit the zoo because it provides an activity that each family member can enjoy it also may strengthen family values and inspire concern for the welfare of animals. ¹⁰Zoo visitors focus on the lives of animals therefore they often rid their minds of stressful thoughts. ¹¹A Japanese study found zoo visitors leave with lower blood pressure. ¹²Feeling less stressed. ¹³The debate continues between two attitudes toward zoos. ¹⁴One side claims they are sanctuaries for animals, in addition they are places where children as well as adults can be educated about the animal world. ¹⁵The other side claims they are only cruel jails that are filled with unhappy animals for the sole purpose of entertaining humans.

1. _____   5. _____   9. _____   13. _____

2. _____   6. _____   10. _____   14. _____

3. _____   7. _____   11. _____   15. _____

4. _____   8. _____   12. _____

Your version:

_____

_____

_____

_____

_____

_____

_____

_____

_____

_____

_____

_____

_____

_____

_____

_____

TEST ③ **Editing Student Writing: Correcting Fragments and Run-Ons**

On the lines provided below, identify each numbered group of words as a sentence (S), fragment (F), or run-on (R). Then rewrite the paragraph, correcting any fragments and run-ons.

¹Many parents worry that their children are not reading enough others worry about what the children are reading. ²In fact, most children are not reading anything at all, houses are filled with the sounds from computer speakers, television shows, and video games. ³If children never see their parents reading or going to the library. ⁴They will most likely not develop good reading habits. ⁵Children who see their parents reading magazines, books, and newspapers. ⁶These children will grow up thinking that reading is a natural part of daily life. ⁷Parents can do many things to encourage reading. ⁸Like accompanying them to the library and helping them pick out books. ⁹Parents can encourage children to memorize poetry and they can show them how to read maps when they travel. ¹⁰Since most young people like children's magazines with pictures and short texts on current topics. ¹¹Parents could subscribe to these magazines for their children. ¹²Reading stories out loud as a family, with everybody participating. ¹³That is the best idea of all.

1. _____   5. _____   8. _____   11. _____

2. _____   6. _____   9. _____   12. _____

3. _____   7. _____   10. _____   13. _____

4. _____

Your version:

_____

_____

_____

_____

_____

_____

_____

_____

_____

_____

_____

_____

_____

TEST ④ **Editing Student Writing Using Editing Symbols**

The editing symbol for a run-on error is *ro*. In the paragraph below, ten errors are marked with editing symbols. Correct each error on the lines provided after the paragraph.

Sergio Pitamitz/Getty Images

¹If human development is to continue we will eventually have to develop forms of renewable energy. ²In the 1980s and 1990s, the United States lagged behind Europe and Asia in the development of wind power in fact, many of our machines were inefficient, of poor design, and expensive to maintain. ³Mostly only people living along coastal areas having high winds were attracted to investing in wind power. ⁴Because the major technology to enable the commercial use of wind power improved dramatically starting in 1999 wind farms have begun springing up in much broader geographical areas. ⁵ Not only along the coastal areas. ⁶ Undoubtedly, many refinements and improvements in the years to come. ⁷Wind power is extremely attractive, once the equipment is set up, nobody has to buy the wind that blows across the land. ⁸Portland, Oregon, is planning a wind farm that will supply all of that city's energy needs. ⁹And this would be the equivalent of taking 12,000 cars off the road every year. ¹⁰One farmer in the Portland area has several wind turbines, he tells everyone that he cultivates three crops: wheat, cattle, and wind. ¹¹He has power for his own use and he sells the extra power to the region's power grid. ¹²Each of his wind turbines bring in $3,000 to $4,000 a year in income.

Correction

1. subordination (sentence 1): _____

    _____

    _____

2. run-on (sentence 2): _____

    _____

    _____

    _____

    _____

3. subordination (sentence 4): _____

_____

_____

_____

_____

4. fragment (sentence 5): _____

_____

5. fragment (sentence 6): _____

_____

6. run-on (sentence 7): _____

_____

_____

7. fragment (sentence 9): _____

_____

8. run-on (sentence 10): _____

_____

_____

9. run-on (sentence 11): _____

_____

10. agreement (sentence 12): _____

_____

WRITE FOR SUCCESS

Everyone needs a financial plan in order to use one's resources wisely. Understanding the implications of the cost of education is no exception. What exactly are the costs of your education? To what degree will you depend on grants and loans? To what extent will your family be able to help? Will you work while you are going to school? What can you do now that will help you avoid excessive and burdensome loans after you graduate? Write a response that explains your personal plan for paying for your educational costs.

Working Together

Agencia Estado/AP Images

Discussion and Summary: Hazing on College Campuses

Often one of the most meaningful parts of college life is to belong to a campus organization. If a particular organization demands hazing as a condition for membership, being a victim of this hazing can be damaging and even life-threatening. Why would anybody be willing to submit to these abusive practices?

For many college students, joining a fraternity or sorority is an exciting part of the college experience. Joining one of these organizations gives a person a sense of belonging and an instant source of friends. However, think twice if one of these organizations requires hazing. We now know that there is a sad history of harmful and life-threatening behaviors. When hazing takes place among men, it is often said to be a test of strength. For example, it often includes tests of physical endurance, forced drinking of alcohol, paddling, and other forms of physical assault. Some studies on fraternities found that the emphasis of hazing is on toughness, enduring pain and humiliation, and the use of force to obtain obedience. Those who endorse hazing say that such traditions are needed to eliminate people unworthy of membership in the organizations. These ideas are entrenched in our assumptions about what we think of as masculinity.

As a class, discuss the following questions. All students should take notes. Then summarize the class responses to the questions.

1. Are you aware of any hazing on your college campus? If so, does the hazing include any women's groups?
2. Have you ever heard of any specific accounts (either on your campus or in the media) of hazing gone wrong?
3. What is the purpose of hazing?
4. Why do people agree to it?
5. What can be done to put an end to hazing that is dangerous?

PORTFOLIO SUGGESTION

Keep the notes and summary you have written on this topic in your portfolio. Your instructor may want you to return to this topic to develop your summary into a complete college essay. Research additional related information using the following search phrases: *hazing stories*, *hazing deaths*, *hazing statistics*, *hazing laws*, and *hazing prevention*.

Choosing Correct Pronouns

9

CHAPTER OBJECTIVES

This chapter will show you how to choose correct pronoun forms in constructions that are often confusing.

- Use the correct pronoun **case**

    with **comparisons**

    with **compound constructions**

    with *who/whom* **constructions**

- Understand the relationship between a pronoun and its **antecedent** in order to

    choose a pronoun that agrees **in number** with its antecedent

    choose a pronoun that agrees **in person** with its antecedent

    verify that the antecedent of a pronoun is not **missing, ambiguous,** or **repetitious**

Pronouns and Case

Most of us generally use the correct pronoun forms when we speak and write. However, the fact that pronouns have **case** (that is, they can change forms depending on their function in a particular sentence) causes confusion in three particular constructions: comparisons, compound constructions, and *who/whom* constructions.

Case refers to the form a noun or pronoun takes, depending on how it is used in a sentence. Notice in the following examples how the pronoun *I* changes its form when it changes its function:

Subject:	*I* needed a car.
Object:	Dad bought a used Honda for *me.*
Possessive:	*My* commute to work will now be easier.
	The title to the car is *mine.*
Reflexive:	I've assumed all responsibility for the car *myself.*

The following chart provides a helpful listing of the different pronoun forms.

PRONOUN CASE

	PRONOUNS USED AS SUBJECTS	PRONOUNS USED AS OBJECTS	PRONOUNS USED AS POSSESSIVES	PRONOUNS USED AS REFLEXIVES
Singular	I	me	my, mine	myself
	you	you	you, yours	yourself
	he	him	his	himself
	she	her	hers	herself
	it	it	its	itself
Plural	we	us	our, ours	ourselves
	you	you	your, yours	yourselves
	they	them	their, theirs	themselves
Singular or plural	who	whom	whose	

- As you study the chart, notice there are no such forms as *hisself, themself,* or *theirselves.*
- Be careful not to confuse *whose* with *who's* (who is, who has) or *its* with *it's* (it is).

Pronoun Case with Comparisons

Choosing the correct pronoun for a comparison is easier if you complete the comparison in your own mind. For example, choose the correct pronoun in the following sentence:

His competitor is much stronger than (he, him, his).

You might be tempted to choose the pronoun *him.* However, if you complete the comparison in your own mind, you will choose the correct pronoun:

His competitor is much stronger than (*he*, him, his) *is.*

The second sentence shows that *he* is the correct answer because the pronoun *he* is used as the subject in the clause *he is.* Now you can clearly see that "His competitor is much stronger than him is" would be the wrong choice.

PRACTICE **1** **First complete the comparison in your mind. Then circle the correct pronoun in each of the following sentences.**

1. My cousin did not enjoy the vacation as much as (I, me, mine).

HINT Before you choose, try adding *did* to complete the comparison:

My cousin did not enjoy the vacation as much as (I, me, mine) did.

2. The altitude in Quito affected my cousin more than (I, me).

HINT | Before you choose, try adding *it affected* to complete the comparison:

The altitude in Quito affected my cousin more than it affected (I, me).

3. The tour guide directed his speech to the travel agents rather than to my brother and (I, me).

HINT | Before you choose, try adding *to* after *and*.

The tour guide directed his speech to the travel agents rather than to my cousin and to (I, me).

EXERCISE ❶ **Choosing the Correct Pronoun with Comparisons**

Circle the correct pronoun in each of the sentences below. Remember to complete the comparison in your own mind.

1. I am as deeply involved in this proposal as (they, them).

2. We have done more research than (they, them).

3. She studied the final proposal more than (I, me).

4. The attractiveness of the competing proposal troubled my coworkers more than (I, me).

5. Their company had acquired fewer clients than (we, us, ourselves).

6. Our policies are much better than (them, theirs).

7. The contract was awarded to us rather than (they, them, themselves).

8. The results will matter more to the client than (she, her).

9. I will celebrate much longer tonight than (she, her).

10. An immediate vacation is more important for me than (he, him).

Pronoun Case in Compound Constructions

In a sentence that has a compound subject or a compound object, choosing the correct pronoun will be easier if you read the sentence and leave out one part of the compound construction.

Today, Diane and (I, me) should buy the tickets.

You might be tempted to choose the pronoun *me*. However, if you try reading this same sentence leaving out the first part of the compound subject (Diane), you will choose the correct pronoun.

Today, (*I*, me) should buy the tickets.

The second sentence shows that *I* is the correct answer because the pronoun *I* is used as the subject for the verb *should buy.* Now you can clearly see that "Today, me should buy the tickets" is the wrong choice.

PRACTICE **2**   **Circle the correct pronoun in each of the sentences below. Remember to leave out one part of the compound construction to test your answer.**

1. Developers and (he, him) hope to renovate that building.

HINT   Try the sentence without the words *developers and:*

   (He, Him) hopes to renovate that building.

2. They spoke to the construction company and (I, me).

HINT   Try the sentence without the words *the construction company and:*

   They spoke to (I, me).

EXERCISE **2**   **Choosing the Correct Pronoun in Compound Constructions**

In each of the following sentences, circle the correct pronoun. Remember to leave out one part of the compound construction to test your answer.

1. The head nurse called from the hospital to speak to my husband or (I, me).

2. The other nurses and (she, her) had been very supportive throughout Sasha's illness.

3. We were relieved to get the test results from the lab and (she, her).

4. Both my husband and (I, me) were encouraged by the news.

5. Unlike my husband Tyrone and (I, me), Sasha was very calm.

6. Tyrone and (I, me) were thrilled that Sasha was in remission.

7. Because our children and (we, us) were so exhausted, we decided to take a weekend vacation.

8. Tyrone, Sasha, and (I, me) got out the map.

9. (He, Him) and Sasha decided to drive to the harbor in Baltimore.

10. The vacation would give Sasha and (we, us) a chance to unwind.

Pronoun Case in *Who/Whom* Constructions

At times, most of us are confused about when we should use *who* or *whom*, partly because *whom* has become increasingly uncommon in spoken English. In written English, however, it is still important to understand the difference in how these two words function in a sentence.

Who is always used in the subject position in a sentence.

Who is going with you to the performance?

Who is the subject of the verb phrase *is going.*

Who did you say is going with you to the performance?

Who is the subject of the verb phrase *is going* (even though a second clause, *did you say,* interrupts the first clause).

He is the person *who* is going with me.

Who is the subject of the verb phrase *is going* in the second clause, *who is going with me.*

Whom is always used in the object position in a sentence.

Whom did the director choose for the part?

Whom is the direct object of the verb phrase *did choose.*

To *whom* did the director give the part?

Whom is the object of the preposition *to.*

When a sentence has more than one clause, it is helpful to cross out all the words except the relative clause beginning with the *who/whom* pronoun. Then you will better understand how *who/whom* functions within its own clause.

~~The scholarship will be given to~~ (whoever, whomever) wins the poetry contest.

In the clause (*whoever, whomever*) *wins the poetry contest,* the pronoun *whoever* is the correct choice. *Whoever* is the subject of the verb *wins.* (The entire clause is considered the object of the preposition *to.*)

PRACTICE **3**   In each of the sentences below, cross out all the words except the clause containing the *who/whom* pronoun. Then decide whether the *who/whom* functions as a subject or as an object within that clause and circle the correct choice.

   1. She is the friend (who, whom) I treasured.

      Look at: **(who, whom) I treasured**

   2. She is the friend (who, whom) I knew could be trusted.

      Look at: **(who, whom) could be trusted**

3. They will award the prize to (whoever , whomever) is the best.

Look at: (whoever, whomever) **is the best**

4. I don't know (who, whom) should do the work.

5. That is the girl (who , whom) I hope will win.

EXERCISE **3** **Choosing the Correct Pronoun Using** *Who/Whom*

Circle the correct pronoun in each of the sentences below. Remember, to avoid confusion, cross out other clauses in the sentence so you can focus on the clause in question.

~~I don't know~~ (who, whom) ~~you think~~ is good at money management.
~~This is the woman~~ (who, whom) ~~I was told~~ would give us good advice.

Jose Luis Pelaez/Blend Images/Getty Images

1. In relationships, the issue (who, whom) is best suited to run the family's finances is always critical.

2. Everyone knows couples for (who, whom) money is the source of endless squabbles.

3. Most couples quickly decide (who, whom) is the right person to balance the bank account.

4. (Who, Whom) should the couple trust for financial advice?

5. Another question is (who's, whose) responsible for the final decisions about making large purchases?

6. To (who, whom) do most people listen about long-range financial planning?

7. Researchers (who, whom) have studied this area of human behavior have reached some surprising conclusions.

8. Couples (who's, whose) weddings were costly like to remember those expenses.

9. However, these same couples (who, whom) have children to educate seldom want to talk about college costs.

10. Two people for (who, whom) future goals are very different need to listen to expert advice.

EXERCISE **4** **Choosing the Correct Pronoun Using** *Who/Whom*

Circle the correct pronoun in each of the sentences below.

1. To (who, whom) did you give the textbook?

2. (Who, Whom) will Tania ask for help?

3. The couple will sublet their apartment to (whoever, whomever) they like.

4. (Whose, Who's) shoe is this?

5. Desiree cannot remember (who, whom) told her that.

6. The CEO wants to figure out (who's, whose) to blame for this.

7. Give these old coats to (whoever, whomever) needs them the most.

8. (Who, Whom) shall I say is calling?

9. Derek is the one (whom, who) the casting director has chosen.

10. The man seemed to argue with (whomever, whoever) he didn't like.

EXERCISE **5** **Choosing Correct Pronoun Forms**

Practice pronoun case with all three constructions (comparisons, compound constructions, and *who/whom* constructions). Circle the correct pronoun in each of the sentences below.

1. Jamel and (she, her) presented the project today.

2. Between you and (I, me), I think it was outstanding.

3. Their visual materials will help (whoever, whomever) will study the project later

4. He is usually a better speaker than (she, her).

5. Everyone (who, whom) heard them was impressed.

6. (Who, Whom) do you think made the best points?

7. I am not as deeply involved in my project as (they, them).

8. To (who, whom) should I turn for guidance?

9. The professor gave both Carolyn and (he, him) A's.

10. My partner and (I, me) will have to work harder to reach the professor's standard.

EXERCISE **6** **Student Writing: Choosing Correct Pronoun Forms**

Practice pronoun case with all three constructions. In the following paragraph, circle the correct pronoun wherever you have a choice.

When my mother and (I, me) decided to care for my very ill father at home, some of our friends objected. My sister and (they, them) said we would be exhausted and unable to handle the stress. The people (who, whom) we met at the hospital had the same opinion. To (who, whom) could we go for help in the middle of the night? My father, (who, whom) we believed would be happier at home, had been our first consideration. Of course, we would have benefited if either my mother or (I, me) had been a nurse. However, we did have a visiting nurse available at times. We were more confident than (they, them) that we could handle the situation. We were the only ones for (who, whom) this work would be a labor of love.

Pronoun-Antecedent Agreement

When you use a pronoun in your writing, that pronoun must refer to a word used previously in the text. This previously used word is called the *antecedent*.

> An **antecedent** is a word (or words) that is replaced by a pronoun later in a piece of writing.
>
> The *pool* was crowded. *It* was a popular place on a hot summer day.
>
> In this example, the pronoun *it* replaces the word *pool*. *Pool*, in this case, is referred to as the *antecedent* of the pronoun *it*.

The next three rules concerning pronouns are often troublesome to writers. Study each rule carefully, and complete the exercises that follow.

RULE **1**   A pronoun must agree in *number* (singular or plural) with any other word to which it refers.

The following sentences illustrate a lack of pronoun-antecedent agreement in **number**.

> **Lacks agreement:**   The *pool* was crowded. *They* were popular places on a hot summer day.

In this example, *pool* is the antecedent of the pronoun *they*. However, *pool* is singular and *they* is plural. The pronoun *it* must be used to agree in number with the antecedent *pool*.

Pronoun-antecedent agreement can be particularly complicated if the pronoun is an indefinite pronoun. Words like *everyone* or *nobody* are singular. They require a singular pronoun.

> **Lacks agreement:**   *Everyone* worked on *their* final draft.

Even though you may hear people use the plural pronoun *their* to refer to a singular subject, this usage is not correct in formal writing. Here are two other approaches writers often take:

Sexist construction:	*Everyone* worked on *his* final draft.
Awkward construction:	*Everyone* worked on *his or her* final draft.

This last form is technically correct, but the continual use of the construction *his or her* will soon begin to sound awkward and repetitious. Often, the best solution to the problem is to revise the construction so that both the pronoun and the antecedent are plural:

Pronouns agree:	*All* the students worked on *their* final drafts.

Another way around the problem is to avoid the pronoun altogether or use the article:

Avoids the pronoun:	Everyone worked on final drafts.
	Everyone worked on the final drafts.

Another problem with pronoun-antecedent agreement in *number* occurs when a demonstrative pronoun (*this, that, these, those*) is used with a noun. In such a case, the pronoun must agree with the noun it modifies:

Singular:	this kind, that kind; this type, that type
Incorrect:	*These kind* of shoes hurt my feet.
Correct:	*This kind* of shoe hurts my feet.
Plural:	these kinds, those kinds, these types, those types
Incorrect:	*Those type* of cars always need oil.
Correct:	*Those types* of cars always need oil.
One solution:	rewrite to avoid the pronoun altogether.

PRACTICE 4 **Rewrite each of the following sentences so that the pronoun agrees with its antecedent in *number*. It may be helpful to draw an arrow from the pronoun to its antecedent.**

1. Everyone should bring their suggestions to the meeting.

   _____

2. This sorts of clothes are popular now.

   _____

3. No one knew what they were eating.

   _____

4. If the bird watchers hope to see anything, one must get up early.

   _____

5. These type of book appeals to me.

One solution: rewrite to put the antecedent into the plural.

RULE **2**   A pronoun must agree with its antecedent in *person*.

The following sentence illustrates a lack of pronoun-antecedent agreement in **person**.

Lacks agreement: When mountain climbing, *one* must maintain *your* concentration at all times.

When you construct a piece of writing, you choose a "person" as the voice in that piece of writing. Your instructor may advise you which personal pronoun to use for a particular writing assignment. Whatever guidelines you are given, the important point is to be consistent and use the same **person**. Below are some examples in which the pronouns agree:

When mountain climbing, *you* must maintain *your* concentration at all times.

When mountain climbing, *I* must maintain *my* concentration at all times.

When mountain climbing, *we* must maintain *our* concentration at all times.

PRACTICE **5**   **Correct each of the following sentences so that the pronoun agrees with its antecedent in *person*.**

1. I enjoy math exams because you can demonstrate what you know.

2. When I took geometry, we discovered that frequent review of past assignments helped make the course seem easy.

3. People always need to practice your skills.

4. Math games can be fun for a student if you have a spirit of curiosity.

5. When studying math, you must remember that we have to "use it or lose it."

RULE **3**   The antecedent of a pronoun should not be *missing*, nor should the pronoun be *ambiguous* or *repetitious*.

● **Missing antecedent:**

In Florida, *they* have beautifully developed retirement areas.

In this sentence, we do not know to whom *they* refers. If the text has not told us that *they* refers to the Florida government, real estate developers, or some other group, then we must say that the antecedent is *missing*. The sentence should be rewritten to avoid *they*.

Acceptable revision: Many Florida communities have beautifully developed retirement areas.

- **Ambiguous pronoun:**

    Margaret told Lin that *she* needed to earn $1,000 during the summer.

In this sentence, *she* could refer to either Margaret or Lin. The sentence should be revised in a way that will avoid this confusion.

Acceptable revision: Margaret told Lin that Lin needed to earn $1,000 during the summer.

Acceptable revision: Margaret said that Lin needed to earn $1,000 during the summer.

- **Repetitious pronoun and antecedent:**

    The book, *it* describes the Great Depression.

The subject in this sentence should be either the noun *book* or, if there is already an antecedent, the pronoun *it.* Using both the noun and the pronoun as subjects for the verb results in needless repetition.

Acceptable revision: The book describes the Great Depression.

PRACTICE **6**   **Rewrite the following sentences so that the antecedents are not *missing* and the pronouns are not *ambiguous* or *repetitious*.**

1. The biologist asked the director to bring back his microscope.

    _____

    _____

2. The report, it says that both the atmosphere and oceans have gotten warmer since the 1950s.

    _____

    _____

    _____

3. At the laboratory, they said the research had run into serious difficulties.

    _____

    _____

4. The testing equipment was accidentally dropped into the aquarium, and it was badly damaged.

    _____

    _____

    _____

5. I don't watch the 10 o'clock news anymore because they have become too slick

_____

_____

_____

EXERCISE **7**   **Making Pronouns and Antecedents Agree**

The following sentences contain errors with the use of pronouns. In each sentence, circle the pronoun that is problematic. Next, identify the problem: (1) the pronoun does not agree in person or number with the antecedent, (2) the antecedent is missing, (3) the pronoun is ambiguous, (4) the pronoun is sexist, or (5) the pronoun is repetitious. Then rewrite the sentence correcting the problem.

1. Vanessa asked her friend to take her video off the site.

_____

_____

2. Before you decide on a treatment, a person must think about the side effects involved.

_____

_____

3. When the student received the award, their name was misspelled on it.

_____

_____

4. They used to think that drilling holes in one's head would help with seizures and migraines.

_____

_____

5. Everybody was looking forward to their winter break.

_____

6. Each of the contestants chose songs from his childhood.

_____

_____

7. You need to wear gloves because they said the temperature will drop tonight.

_____

_____

8. These kind of videos are disturbing.

_____

9. The lady, she said we had to leave the movie theater.

_____

10. Those type of people need to think before posting things.

_____

EXERCISE ⑧   ## Making Pronouns and Antecedents Agree

The following sentences contain errors with the use of pronouns. In each sentence, circle the pronoun that is problematic. Next, identify the problem: (1) the pronoun does not agree in person or number with the antecedent, (2) the antecedent is missing, (3) the pronoun is ambiguous, (4) the pronoun is sexist, or (5) the pronoun is repetitious. Then rewrite the sentence correcting the problem. If a sentence is correct, mark a **C** on the line provided.

1. The teacher told the parent he needed the test results.

_____

2. The county submitted their proposal for the bridge repairs.

_____

3. Retail stores must be profitable, but if you overprice your products, you will lose business.

_____

_____

4. Anyone who fails the final will be unlikely to get his or her diploma.

_____

_____

5. A young person seldom receives enough advice on how he should choose his career.

_____

_____

6. These type of watch are very popular.

_____

7. People were rescued from our homes.

_____

8. No one brought their books today.

_____

9. The college, it is holding homecoming weekend on October 5.

_____

10. They call Indiana the Hoosier state.

_____

EXERCISE **Making Pronouns and Antecedents Agree**

Each of the following sentences contains an error with the use of the pronoun. Edit each sentence so that antecedents are not missing, pronouns agree with their antecedents, and pronouns are not ambiguous, repetitious, or sexist.

1. Everyone should go to a live concert once in their life.

2. Last month, Cynthia invited Vermell to a Mary J. Blige concert because she loves her music.

3. They said the tickets would be sold out quickly.

4. If you get up early enough, a person has a good chance to buy decent seats.

5. These type of events are very expensive.

6. The night of the concert, the arena it was jammed with young people.

7. The security guards told the fans that they must be more patient.

8. People have been trampled in these sort of crowds.

9. Finally, you could hear the music begin; our long wait for tickets had been worth the trouble.

10. Her songs have positive lyrics; that's why I like it so much.

Mastery and Editing Tests

TEST ① **Using Pronouns Correctly**

Each of the following sentences contains at least one pronoun. Edit each sentence to correct errors in any of the following: pronoun case; pronouns that do not agree with their antecedents; and missing, ambiguous, or repetitious antecedents. If the sentence does not contain an error, mark it with a C.

1. Whom do you think will be our next Supreme Court justice?

2. Frank sent his cousin his favorite playlist.

3. One must understand anatomy if you want to go into a medical field.

4. Doctor Mustafa does these math calculations much faster than I.

5. In the newspaper, it said that Bruno would be going on tour soon.

6. My professor and me have a plan to work together on the research this summer.

7. They ought to give more grants for scientific research.

8. The tailor and he agreed on the fitting.

9. He decided to complete the group project by hisself.

10. These type of projects demand serious commitment.

TEST **2**   **Using Pronouns Correctly**

Each of the following sentences contains at least one pronoun. Edit each sentence to correct errors in any of the following: pronoun case; pronouns that do not agree with their antecedents; and missing, ambiguous, or repetitious antecedents. If the sentence does not contain an error, mark it with a C.

1. In the ad it said you should send a résumé.

2. To who do you think we should send these bulletins?

3. A pharmacist must triple-check every order he fills.

4. Just between you and I, the firm is in financial trouble.

5. Those lessons helped Karen more than him.

6. We always buy these type of coats.

7. The bank warns people that you should always balance your checking account.

8. Janelle's sister brought her plan to the council.

9. The assignments they are going to require library research.

10. Everyone did his part.

TEST ③   **Editing Student Writing: Using Pronouns Correctly**

The following paragraph contains ten errors in pronoun usage. Edit the paragraph to correct all errors with pronouns.

¹Nobody wants to give up their dreams. ²Last Friday, my husband went to see a friend about his choice of career. ³The friend he shared details of his own career path. ⁴As a child, he had dreamed of becoming a Supreme Court justice whom would make important decisions such as the case of *Roe v. Wade*. ⁵This had been his childhood fantasy. ⁶As he grew older, him and his sister enjoyed watching *Law and Order*. ⁷He was more interested in the legal court scenes than her. ⁸His dream slowly changed to having a career as a criminal lawyer. ⁹His dream it was to defend innocent people. ¹⁰Four years later, as he was finishing college, they advised him to take the LSAT, the test that qualifies a student for law school. ¹¹Although he took the test several times, he was unable to achieve a qualifying score. ¹²This friend, whom eventually concluded that he must be realistic, then studied to become a paralegal. ¹³Now with a satisfying and challenging job, he had advice for my husband. ¹⁴Dreams are important, but everyone must also be realistic about what they are able to achieve.

TEST ④   **Editing Student Writing Using Editing Symbols**

In the following paragraph, editing symbols mark the sentences that need revision or correction. These editing symbols include the following: agr (agreement), frag (fragment), ro (run-on), subord (subordination), pron ca (pronoun case), and pron ref (pronoun reference). Make your corrections on the lines provided after the paragraph.

     pron ca
¹John Dickens, whom was the father of the great novelist Charles Dickens, was
         pron ref
never able to handle their money successfully. ²The family had to move to smaller and smaller houses as the finances of the family became worse. ³Eventually, they found
    pron ca
themself living in a small part of a house. ⁴Young Charles was sent to a pawnbroker's
      frag
shop. ⁵To sell the family's books, silver teapots and spoons, and other family possessions.

⁶Little by little, even the family furniture had to be sold, and he was placed in

debtor's prison. [7]In those days, this is what they *(pron ref)* did to the head of the family if he or she could not pay debts. [8]When Charles was twelve he *(subord)* suffered another traumatic event because of his family's situation. [9]He was taken out of school *(ro)* and his parents put him to work pasting labels on bottles of shoe polish. [10]He never recovered from the psychological shock. [11]His formal education, it was over. *(pron ref)* [12]As a result of these childhood traumas, Charles Dickens's numerous novels, which are filled with many a colorful character, portrays children trapped by circumstances they cannot control. *(agr)*

Corrections

1. pronoun case (sentence 1): _____

2. pronoun reference (sentence 1): _____

3. pronoun case (sentence 3): _____

4. fragment (sentence 5): _____

5. pronoun reference (sentence 6): _____

6. pronoun reference (sentence 7): _____

7. subordination (sentence 8): _____

8. run-on sentence (sentence 9): _____

9. pronoun reference (sentence 11): _____

10. agreement (sentence 12): _____

WRITE FOR SUCCESS

No one can always feel happy and upbeat. How can you recognize when someone is more than temporarily discouraged and may be clinically depressed? Consider the following signs in your response: suicidal thoughts, sleep disorders, trouble concentrating, feelings of emptiness or worthlessness, weight change.

Working Together

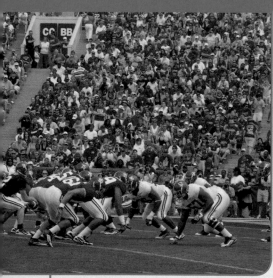

The Library of Congress

Discussion and Summary: the Big Business of College Sports

The following passage indicates the value that some colleges now place on sports. As you read the passage, think about the amount of money it takes to run a sports program and where that money should originate. Consider the advantages the student athletes and the student body derive from college sports. If colleges devote so many resources and attention to sports, what are the consequences on academic programs?

A river of cash is flowing into college sports, financing a spending spree among elite universities that has sent coaches' salaries soaring and spurred new discussions about whether athletes should be paid. But most of that revenue is going to a handful of elite sports programs, leaving some colleges to rely heavily on students to finance their athletic ambitions.

In the past five years, public universities pumped more than $10.3 billion in mandatory student fees and other subsidies into their sports programs.

Many universities are demanding that their students pay more to support sports at the same time they are raising tuition, forcing many students to take out bigger loans to pay the bill.

Questions for Group Discussion

1. Should colleges offer coaches multi-million dollar contracts? Do you think all coaches of all sports receive equal wages? What might account for the salaries that different coaches receive?

2. Explain why it is or is not fair that students, through tuition and fees, subsidize a sports program.

3. In recent years a public debate has raged about paying student athletes. What additional facts need to be collected to help resolve this debate? What are some of the factors that should be considered in offering student athletes a salary?

4. What part does sports play on your college campuses? In your opinion, is the current emphasis on college sports acceptable?

5. What are some of the consequences for institutions of higher learning if their attention to sports is greater than their attention to academics? What are the implications for society at large?

Writing a Summary

Considering the facts from the text and the in-class discussion of the issues, write a response that summarizes the main controversies with the big business of sports on college campuses.

PORTFOLIO SUGGESTION

Do some research at your school. What part do sports play in campus life? Is the football stadium at the center of your school's college culture? If this topic interests you, read the essay "Sports at Any Cost" (*Huffington Post*, November 15, 2015, projects.huffingtonpost.com/ncaa/sports-at-any-cost). These issues could be the basis for a very timely and fascinating research paper.

Working with Adjectives, Adverbs, and Parallel Structure

10

CHAPTER OBJECTIVES

Adjectives and **adverbs** describe, limit, or qualify other words. In the first part of the chapter, you will study common problems using adjectives and adverbs correctly.

Adjectives and Adverbs

- **adjectives and adverbs used in comparisons,** especially irregular forms
- the most commonly **confused adjectives and adverbs,** including *good* and *well*
- **misplaced modifiers and dangling modifiers**
- the adverb *not* and the avoidance of **double negatives**

In the second part of this chapter, you will learn to recognize when parallel structure is required.

Parallel Structure

Items listed in a series need to have similar grammatical elements.

- making **words in a series** the same parts of speech
- making **phrases in a series** the same kinds of phrases
- making certain that **clauses in a series** are not mixed with phrases or words

What Is the Difference between an Adjective and an Adverb?

Adjectives modify nouns and pronouns.

Charlene is a *studious* person.

She is *studious*.

Adverbs modify verbs, adjectives, and other adverbs. They often end in *-ly*. They usually answer one of the following questions: *How? When? Where? Why?* or *To what extent?*

The adverb *happily* modifies the verb *dreams*:

Charlene *happily* dreams about her vacation.

The adverb *too* modifies the adjective *careful*:

You cannot be *too* careful.

The adverb *very* modifies another adverb, *quickly*:

Charlene worked *very* quickly.

Because not all adverbs end in *-ly*, you should learn to recognize some of the other common adverbs.

LIST OF COMMON ADVERBS

always	later	not	seldom	very
even	more	now	sometimes	yesterday
ever	much	often	tomorrow	
just	never	quite	too	

PRACTICE 1 **In each of the following sentences, an adjective or an adverb has been underlined. Draw an arrow from the underlined word to the word that it modifies. Then identify the underlined word as an adjective (adj) or an adverb (adv). An example has been done for you.**

adj   The sunlight felt warm.

_____ 1. Seasonal Affective Disorder (SAD) is a unique type of depression sometimes called the "winter blues."

_____ 2. An estimated 25 percent of the population suffers from a mild form of SAD.

_____ 3. About 5 percent suffers from a more severe form of the disorder.

_____ 4. Young people and women are at a very high risk for the disorder.

iStockphoto.com/Lise Gagne

_____ 5. The symptoms occur <u>regularly</u> during the fall or winter months.

_____ 6. People with SAD may feel <u>anxious</u>.

_____ 7. They may crave sugary or <u>starchy</u> foods.

_____ 8. A brisk walk in the morning sunlight can be <u>helpful.</u>

Adjectives and Adverbs Used in Comparisons

For most adjectives and adverbs of one *syllable*, add *-er* to create the comparative form and *-est* to create the superlative form.

The following chart lists some one-syllable adjectives (adj) and adverbs (adv) along with their comparative and superlative forms.

COMPARATIVE FORMS OF ONE-SYLLABLE ADJECTIVES AND ADVERBS

ADJECTIVE OR ADVERB	COMPARATIVE FORM (COMPARES TWO THINGS OR GROUPS)	SUPERLATIVE FORM (COMPARES THREE OR MORE THINGS OR GROUPS)
light (adj)	lighter	lightest
short (adj)	shorter	shortest
fast (adv)	faster	fastest
hard (adj or adv)	harder	hardest

Some adjectives and adverbs of *two syllables* take *-er* and *-est*, while others use *more* (or *less*) and *most* (or *least*). When in doubt, consult a dictionary.

The following chart lists some two-syllable adjectives and adverbs along with their comparative and superlative forms.

COMPARATIVE FORMS OF TWO-SYLLABLE ADJECTIVES AND ADVERBS

ADJECTIVE OR ADVERB	COMPARATIVE FORM (COMPARES TWO THINGS OR GROUPS)	SUPERLATIVE FORM (COMPARES THREE OR MORE THINGS OR GROUPS)
easy (adj)	easier	easiest
funny (adj)	funnier	funniest
happy (adj)	happier	happiest
lovely (adj)	lovelier	loveliest
helpful (adj)	more helpful	most helpful
famous (adj)	more famous	most famous
quickly (adv)	more quickly	most quickly
slowly (adv)	more slowly	most slowly

For adjectives and adverbs of *three or more syllables*, use *more* or *less* to create the comparative form and *most* or *least* to create the superlative form.

The following chart lists some three-syllable adjectives and adverbs along with their comparative and superlative forms.

COMPARATIVE FORMS OF THREE-SYLLABLE ADJECTIVES AND ADVERBS

ADJECTIVE OR ADVERB	COMPARATIVE FORM (COMPARES TWO THINGS OR GROUPS)	SUPERLATIVE FORM (COMPARES THREE OR MORE THINGS OR GROUPS)
successful (adj)	more successful	most successful
delicious (adj)	more delicious	most delicious
easily (adv)	more easily	most easily
carefully (adv)	more carefully	most carefully

Some commonly used adjectives and adverbs have irregular forms. Study the following chart of commonly used adjectives and adverbs that have irregular comparative and superlative forms.

IRREGULAR COMPARATIVE FORMS

ADJECTIVE OR ADVERB	COMPARATIVE FORM (COMPARES TWO THINGS OR GROUPS)	SUPERLATIVE FORM (COMPARES THREE OR MORE THINGS OR GROUPS)
bad (adj)	worse	worst
badly (adv)	worse	worst
good (adj)	better	best
well (adj or adv)	better	best
many (adj)	more	most
much (adj or adv)	more	most
more (adj or adv)	more	most
far (adj or adv)	farther or further	farthest or furthest
little (adj or adv)	less	least

farther/further   Use *farther* or *farthest* to indicate physical distance.

She could not walk any *farther*.

Use *further* or *furthest* to indicate mental distance.

The lawyer made a *further* argument.

little/few   Do not confuse *little* with *few*. Use *little* when you cannot easily count the item modified.

They had *little grain* for the cattle.

Use *fewer* when you can count the item modified.

They had *fewer cattle* this year than last year.

EXERCISE 1   ## Adjectives and Adverbs Used in Comparisons

In each of the following sentences, fill in the blank with the correct form of the adjective or adverb given in parentheses.

1. This chapter is _____ than the last one.
   (easy)

2. She is the _____ woman in the police department.
   (tall)

3. That machine is _____ operated than the one in the other room.   (easily)

4. He feels _____ today than he did yesterday.
(good)

5. That woman is the _____ chef in San Francisco.
(famous)

6. This paralegal is the _____ person in the office.
(helpful)

7. Would you please drive _____ than your father?
(slowly)

8. Unfortunately, this was my _____ business trip.
(bad)

9. His illness became _____ .
(bad)

10. This lasagna is the _____ lasagna I have ever tasted.
(delicious)

EXERCISE  **Adjectives and Adverbs Used in Comparisons**

In each of the following sentences, fill in the blank with the correct form of the adjective or adverb given in parentheses.

1. The Gonzalez home was the _____ building from the school.
(far)

2. Out of all the students, she had the _____ approach to learning.
(good)

3. The meatloaf was the _____ Alberto had ever tasted.
(bad)

4. Not trying at all is _____ than trying and failing.
(bad)

5. Dwelling on positive thoughts is _____ for your body than dwelling on negative thoughts.   (healthy)

6. *Star Wars: The Force Awakens* has made many original fans _____ than the earlier prequels.   (happy)

7. They looked at the evidence in the case _____ than the initial investigators did.   (carefully)

8. Some people think that golf is the _____ sport to watch.
   (boring)

9. Naomi finished the assignment _____ when she cut out all
   distractions.   (fast)

10. The _____ street in the neighborhood was the one in front of
    (busy)   the corner store.

The Most Commonly Confused Adjectives and Adverbs

To strengthen your understanding of modifiers, study not only the list of adjectives and adverbs given below but also the sample sentences that show how each modifier is used.

awful/awfully | **awful (adj):** | Those peaches look *awful*. (*Awful* is a predicate adjective after the linking verb *looks.*)

| **awfully (adv):** | Those peaches look *awfully* fuzzy. (*Awfully* is an adverb modifying the adjective *fuzzy.*)

bad/badly | **bad (adj):** | The play was *bad*. (meaning *not good*)

| | He feels *bad*, even though the fever is down. (meaning *sick*)

| | He feels *bad* about losing the money. (meaning *sorry* or *upset*)

| **badly (adv):** | The crew painted *badly*. (meaning *not well*)

| | The garage *badly* needs a coat of paint. (meaning *very much*, with verbs such as *want* or *need*)

good/well | **good (adj):** | Alice Walker is a *good* writer.

| | The food tastes *good*.

| | He feels *good* about his work. (Remember that *good* is always an adjective.)

| **well (adv):** | She dances *well*. (meaning *skillfully*)

| | The children behaved *well*. (meaning *in a proper manner*)

| | The praise for her book was *well* deserved. (meaning *fully*)

| | He gets along *well* with people. (meaning *successfully*)

| **well (adj):** | He feels *well*. (*Well* is an adjective only when referring to *health.*)

poor/poorly	poor (adj):	The *poor* man was now homeless. (meaning *pitiful* or *penniless*)
	poorly (adv):	He scored *poorly* on the exam.
quick/quickly	quick (adj):	She is *quick* at word games.
	quickly (adv):	She works *quickly*.
quiet/quietly	quiet (adj):	After ten at night, the dorm has *quiet* hours.
	quietly (adv):	Talk *quietly* after ten o'clock.
real/really	real (adj):	The medics responded to a *real* emergency. (meaning *genuine, not imaginary*)
	really (adv):	The student is *really* determined to do well. (meaning *genuinely, truly*)
sure/surely	sure (adj):	I am *sure* she was the person driving the car. (meaning *certain, confident, firm*)
	surely (adv):	He *surely* was speeding.
		(meaning *certainly, truly*)

NOTE: *Real* and *sure* are often used informally in everyday conversation as adverbs to mean *very* or *certainly*, as in "I'm real sorry about your illness," or "I'm sure sorry about your illness." However, this usage is not acceptable in formal writing.

PRACTICE ②   **Choose the correct adjective or adverb in each of the following sentences. You may find it helpful to draw an arrow to the word that the adjective or adverb is modifying.**

1. Do not compose your résumé too (quick, quickly)

2. A résumé must be (real, really) accurate without any typos or misspellings.

3. Many résumés look (awful, awfully) because they lack parallel structure.

4. You should feel (good, well) about the finished product.

5. If a résumé has been written (good, well), the individual may get an interview.

Misplaced and Dangling Modifiers

Study the following five sentences. Notice how the meaning of each sentence is changed depending on where in the sentence the modifier *only* is placed.

Only Charlene telephoned my brother yesterday. (Nobody else telephoned.)

Charlene *only* telephoned my brother yesterday. (She did not e-mail or visit.)

Charlene telephoned *only* my brother yesterday. (She called no one else.)

Charlene telephoned my *only* brother yesterday. (The writer has only one brother.)

Charlene telephoned my brother *only* yesterday. (She didn't telephone until yesterday.)

A **modifier** is a word, phrase, or clause that functions as an adjective or an adverb.

my only brother

Only modifies the noun *brother*; therefore, *only* functions as an adjective.

the marine *who is my brother*

Who is my brother is a clause that modifies the noun *marine*; therefore, *who is my brother* functions as an adjective clause.

just yesterday

Just modifies the adverb *yesterday*; therefore, *just* functions as an adverb.

Misplaced Modifiers

A **misplaced modifier** is a modifier whose placement in a sentence makes the meaning of that sentence confusing, awkward, or ambiguous.

Below is a list of modifiers that are often misplaced. When you use one of these words, be sure it immediately precedes, or comes before, the word or word group it modifies.

MODIFIERS OFTEN MISPLACED

almost	exactly	just	nearly	scarcely
even	hardly	merely	only	simply

Big Cheese Photo/Thinkstock

1. The modifier is in a **confusing** position because it does not immediately precede the word it modifies.

   Confusing placement of a word modifier:

   > *Nearly* the salesperson sold the used car to the customer.

   Nearly, an adverb, cannot modify the noun *salesperson*.

   Revised: The salesperson *nearly* sold the used car to the customer.

   ***Nearly* correctly modifies the verb *sold*.**

   Confusing placement of a *phrase* modifier:

   > *With all the rusty spots,* the salesperson could not sell the car.

   Is it the salesperson who has rusty spots or the car?

   Revised: The salesperson could not sell the car *with all the rusty spots.*

   Confusing placement of a *clause* modifier:

   > The salesperson could not sell the used car to the customer *that needed extensive body work.*

   Is it the customer or the car that needed extensive body work?

   Revised: The salesperson could not sell the used car *that needed extensive body work* to the customer.

2. The modifier is in an **awkward** position, interrupting the flow of the sentence.

   Awkward placement:

   > We want *to* before the summer ends buy a used car.

   In this case, the infinitive *to buy* has been split or interrupted by the modifying phrase. The result is awkward sounding.

   Revised: Before summer ends, we want to *buy a used car.*

3. The modifier is in an **ambiguous** position (sometimes called a "squinting modifier").

   Ambiguous placement:

   > The used car salesperson when questioned *seriously* doubted he could sell the rusty car.

   Was the salesperson seriously questioned or did he seriously doubt? From the placement of *seriously*, it is impossible to know.

   Revised: When *seriously questioned,* the used car salesperson doubted he could sell the rusty car.

   or, depending on the intended meaning:

   When questioned, the used car salesperson *seriously doubted* he could sell the rusty car.

EXERCISE **3**   **Revising Misplaced Modifiers**

Revise each of the following sentences to avoid misplaced modifiers.

1. I gave the puppy to my sister with the white paws.

   _____

2. I am looking for the keys to the filing cabinets that are missing.

   _____

3. We decided to before the camping trip buy better sleeping bags.

   _____

4. As a pilot, passenger safety had always come first.

   _____

5. They need to immediately after the party go home.

   _____

6. The dance contestants waited eagerly watching the faces of the judges.

   _____

7. The jeweler wanted to for his new customer design a special charm bracelet.

   _____

8. I took my daughter to my office who loved a day off from school.

   _____

9. The accountant forgot almost to tell his client about the change in the law.

   _____

10. Take one tablet every day only.

    _____

Dangling Modifiers

A **dangling modifier** is a modifier without a logical or identifiable word, phrase, or clause to modify in the sentence.

Sentence with a dangling modifier: Working on the car's engine, the dog barked all afternoon.

Who was working on the engine? According to the sentence, it is the dog who was working on the engine. *Working on the car's engine* is a participial phrase that modifies the subject *dog*. As it stands, the sentence makes no sense.

> ## TWO OPTIONS FOR REVISING A DANGLING MODFIER
>
> ### Option 1: Create a new subject for the independent clause.
>
> Working on the car's engine, *I* heard the dog barking all afternoon.
>
> Now the modifying phrase *working on the car's engine* modifies the subject pronoun *I*.
>
> ### Option 2: Create a dependent clause (a dependent clause begins with a subordinating conjunction or relative pronoun and has a subject and a verb).
>
> *While I was working on the car's engine,* the dog barked all afternoon.
>
> Now the modifying phrase *working on the car's engine* has been changed into a dependent clause.

EXERCISE ④   **Revising Dangling Modifiers**

Revise each of the following sentences to avoid misplaced or dangling modifiers.

1. Victor fed the pit bull wearing his tuxedo.

   _____

2. Scrolling through Instagram, the photo caught her eye.

   _____

3. Hoping to see the news, the television set was turned on at seven o'clock.

   _____

4. Running up the stairs, the train had already left for Philadelphia.

   _____

5. After dancing around the room, the temperature felt much warmer.

   _____

6. Dressed in a Dracula costume, I thought my son looked perfect for Halloween.

   _____

7. Hanging from the ceiling in her bedroom, she saw three spiders.

   _____

8. After wiping down the window, the hummingbird flew away.

   _____

9. Howling without a stop, we listened to the neighbor's dog all evening.

   _____

10. After painting my room all afternoon, my cat demanded her dinner.

   _____

EXERCISE ⑤   **Revising Misplaced or Dangling Modifiers**

Revise each of the following sentences to avoid misplaced or dangling modifiers.

1. Blinking on and off with a green glow, we captured a lot of fireflies.

   _____

2. At the age of ten, my family took a trip to Washington, D.C.

   _____

3. Taking good notes, grades were improved.

   _____

4. I bought a dress for my mother that was made of lace.

   _____

5. Working extra hours last week, his salary dramatically increased.

   _____

6. We watched a movie in the theater that had won an Academy Award for best picture.

   _____

   _____

7. The breakup depressed her, which had happened years ago.

   _____

8. Last week while shopping, my friend's purse was stolen.

   _____

9. While eating lunch outdoors, the picnic table collapsed.

   _____

10. She drew unicorns on her notebook prancing.

   _____

Avoiding the Double Negative with the Adverb Not and Other Negative Words

The adverb *not* is one of several words that carry a negative meaning. In Standard English, having two negative words in the same sentence is not acceptable.

WORDS THAT CARRY A NEGATIVE MEANING

no	no one	neither	barely
not	none	never	hardly
nobody	nothing	nowhere	scarcely

You can correct a sentence that contains a double negative by removing either one of the two negative words.

Incorrect:	I *don't* have *no* food in my house.
Possible corrections:	I *don't* have any food in my house.
	I have *no* food in my house.

PRACTICE ③ **Revise each of the following sentences to correct the double negative.**

1. A person shouldn't never go out with something cooking on the stove.

2. You haven't neither a bike nor a car.

3. I don't want nothing.

4. I won't never-break my promise.

5. I can't hardly wait until summer.

Parallel Structure: Making a Series of Words, Phrases, or Clauses Balanced within the Sentence

Which one of the following sentences has the more balanced structure?

> Her favorite hobbies are playing the trumpet, listening to jazz, and to go to concerts.

> Her favorite hobbies are playing the trumpet, listening to jazz, and going to concerts.

If you selected the second sentence, you made the better choice. The second sentence uses parallel structure to balance the three phrases in the series (*playing the trumpet, listening to jazz, going to concerts*). Matching each of the items in the series with the same *-ing* structure makes the sentence easier to understand and more pleasant to read. Words, phrases, and even sentences in a series should be made parallel.

RULE ① For parallel structure, **words** in a series should have the same parts of speech.

Not parallel: The town was small, friendly, and the atmosphere was peaceful.

The series is composed of two adjectives and one clause.

Parallel: The town was small, friendly, and peaceful.

The series is composed of three adjectives: *small, friendly,* and *peaceful.*

RULE ② For parallel structure, **phrases** in a series should be the same kinds of phrases *(infinitive phrase, prepositional phrase, verb phrase, noun phrase, or participial phrase).*

Not parallel: Her lost assignment is in her closet, on the floor, and a pile of clothes is hiding it.

The series is composed of two prepositional phrases and one clause.

Parallel: Her lost assignment is in her closet, on the floor, and under a pile of clothes.

The series is composed of three prepositional phrases beginning with *in, on,* and *under.*

RULE ③ For parallel structure, **clauses** in a series should not be combined with phrases or words.

Not parallel: The street was narrow, the shops were charming, and crowds in the café.

The series is composed of two clauses and one phrase.

Parallel: The street was narrow, the shops were charming, and the café was crowded.

Now the series is composed of three clauses.

PRACTICE ④ **Each of the following sentences lacks parallel structure. In each sentence, revise the underlined section to make the series parallel.**

1. My favorite armchair is lumpy, worn, and <u>has dirt spots everywhere.</u>

2. She enjoys reading novels, studying the flute, and <u>sews her own clothes.</u>

3. He admires teachers who make the classroom an exciting place and

   <u>willingly explaining the lesson more than once.</u>

EXERCISE 6   **Revising Sentences for Parallel Structure**

Each of the following sentences lacks parallel structure. Underline the word, phrase, or clause that is not parallel, and revise it so that its structure balances with the other items in the pair or series. An example has been done for you.

> Not parallel: The best leather comes from Italy, from Spain, and <u>is imported from Brazil</u>.
>
> Parallel: The best leather comes from Italy, Spain, and Brazil.

1. Winter in Chicago is very windy, extremely snowy, and has many bitterly cold days.

2. I would prefer to download music rather than watching television.

3. Mr. Lee is a helpful neighbor, a loyal friend, and dedicated to his children.

4. The apartment is crowded and without light.

5. The dancer is slender, tall, and moves gracefully.

6. The nursery was cheerful, large, and had a lot of sun.

7. My friend loves to play chess, to read science fiction, and working out at the gym

8. For homework today I must read a chapter from my medical terminology book, do five exercises for my English class, and filling out my calendar.

9. The essay showcased the student's powerful research skills and his strong writing voice was showcased.

10. Her eyes darted around the room, down at the floor, and then she finally looked at him.

EXERCISE 7   **Revising Sentences for Parallel Structure**

Each of the following sentences lacks parallel structure. Underline the word, phrase, or clause that is not parallel, and revise it so that its structure balances with the other items in the pair or series.

1. The driver had to choose between driving into the railing or he would hit the deer.

2. She disliked going to the beach, hiking in the woods, and she didn't care for picnics, either.

3. The singers have been on several road tours, have recorded for two record companies, and they would like to make a movie someday.

4. In their free time, the young couple enjoys house renovations, taking long hikes in the mountains, and volunteering at the local animal shelter.

5. They would rather order a pizza than eating their sister's cooking.

6. I explained to the teacher that my car had broken down, my books had been stolen, and no assignment pad.

7. That night the prisoner was sick, discouraged, and she was filled with loneliness.

8. As the truck rumbled down the street, it suddenly lurched out of control, smashed into a parked car, and then the truck hit the storefront of my uncle's hardware store.

9. The teacher is patient, intelligent, and demands a lot.

10. He wanted more than just to pass his college course, but also being able to apply the information.

EXERCISE ⑧   ## Revising Sentences for Parallel Structure

Each of the following sentences lacks parallel structure. Underline the word, phrase, or clause that is not parallel, and revise it so that its structure balances with the other items in the pair or series.

1. The first-grade teacher told us that our child was unruly, mischievous, and made too much noise.

2. The dog's size, its coloring, and whenever it barked reminded me of a wolf.

3. The puppy was energetic, hungry, and it loved everyone.

4. Zelda came up to me coughing violently, sweating profusely, and she kept scratching her skin.

5. Jordan would rather travel and see the world than staying home and reading about other places.

6. For weeks he tried to decide whether he should major in chemistry, continue with accounting, or to take a year off.

7. Her depression was a result of the loss of her job, the breakdown of her marriage, and a teenage daughter who was a problem.

8. She must either cut back on her expenses or selling her car.

9. The burglar ran out of the house, over the porch, and he flew through the front driveway.

10. He went through four years of college, one year of graduate school, and doing one year teaching seventh-grade science.

Mastery and Editing Tests

TEST ① **Revising Sentences to Correct Modifiers and Create Parallel Structure**

Each sentence has an error in the use of a modifier or in parallel structure. Rewrite each sentence to correct the error you find.

1. The puppy devoured the bone, tore up his new bed, and jumping up on the new sofa.

   _____

   _____

2. The student almost received enough money from his aunt to pay for his semester's tuition.

   _____

   _____

3. She returned from vacation rested, with a great deal of energy, and happy.

   _____

4. Joseph managed to find time to coach the team with two other day jobs.

_____

_____

5. I am the most happiest man alive.

_____

6. Discovered by accident, the football fan took the diamond ring to the lost and found.

_____

_____

7. Books were piled on the reading tables, magazines were tossed on chairs, and scraps of paper everywhere.

_____

_____

8. Being hard of hearing, the whistle of the train did not warn him of the danger.

_____

_____

9. The audience was restless because the speaker talked slow.

_____

10. The bus, judging the fog was too thick, stopped by the side of the road.

_____

_____

TEST **2** **Revising Sentences to Correct Modifiers and Create Parallel Structure**

Each sentence has an error in the use of a modifier or in parallel structure. Rewrite each sentence to correct the error you find.

1. The job demands computer skills, math ability, and with accounting background.

_____

2. My sister is not only a talented musician, but she is also teaching with great success.

_____

3. Raking the leaves this morning, more than a hundred geese flew overhead.

_____

_____

4. Follow the directions for writing the essay carefully.

_____

5. The astronomer completed the calculation at the observatory that he had been working on for nearly a decade.

_____

_____

6. The politician is the baddest speaker I have ever heard.

_____

7. My older brother is guilty of lecturing me instead of a good example.

_____

8. The new highway follows the river, bypasses the small towns, and you can save a lot of time.

_____

_____

9. The committee chairperson works good with others.

_____

10. I don't want nothing to eat.

_____

 TEST **3**   ## Revising Sentences to Correct Modifiers and Create Parallel Structure

Each sentence has an error in the use of a modifier or parallel structure. Rewrite each sentence to correct the error you find.

1. The car stopped quick to avoid the child.

_____

2. My friend is generous, hardworking, and a talker.

_____

3. The members of Congress would rather stonewall the proposal than to pass the new law.

_____

_____

4. When covered with thin ice, you should not skate on the lake.

_____

5. Last year, the citizen just paid half of his taxes.

_____

6. From the airport, I will either take the bus or the shuttle to the hotel.

_____

7. For the holidays, we plan to do some cooking, see a few good movies, and listening to jazz.

_____

_____

8. Working late into the night, the page numbering on my report kept printing out incorrectly.

_____

_____

9. I haven't seen nobody today.

_____

10. The child behaved real good during the performance.

_____

TEST ④ **Editing Student Writing Using Editing Symbols**

The commonly used editing symbols for errors in modifiers are *adj* (adjective), *adv* (adverb), and *dm* (dangling modifier). The editing symbol for an error in parallel structure is //. In the paragraph below, ten errors are marked with editing symbols. Correct each error on the lines provided after the paragraph.

¹The criminal justice system in the United States has changed dramatically in recent years. ²We have come a long way since the nineteenth century, when the use of fingerprint evidence was all that an investigator had to help them. *pron ref* ³The use of DNA has led to this *adv* real important change. ⁴DNA testing is a scientific method of determining whether two samples of organic material *agr* comes from the same source. ⁵Testing *dm* for DNA, an individual may be placed at a particular crime scene. ⁶These scientific tests may contradict criminal convictions from the past. ⁷In such cases, this evidence becomes more *adj* strong than any jury finding. ⁸Just a few years ago, the discoveries made through the use of DNA testing in Illinois were so dramatic that the governor ordered all executions in that state canceled. ⁹In other states, people have also been wrongfully convicted and jailed for many kinds of

offenses, including first-degree murder, sexual assault, and people *who* were dealing //
drugs. ¹⁰People who have been in prison for years, in New York, in Ohio, and the
state of California, have been found innocent and have been released. ¹¹One of the //
few problems with DNA evidence are the expense of running the tests. ¹²However, *agr*
the most best news for the future is that problems of wrongful convictions by juries *adj*
will occur a lot less often. ¹³Because DNA evidence will be presented whenever *frag*
possible as part of courtroom evidence.

Corrections

1. pronoun reference (sentence 2): _____

    _____

2. adverb (sentence 3): _____

    _____

3. agreement (sentence 4): _____

    _____

4. dangling modifier (sentence 5): _____

    _____

5. adjective (sentence 7): _____

6. parallel structure (sentence 9): _____

    _____

7. parallel structure (sentence 10): _____

    _____

8. agreement (sentence 11): _____

9. adjective (sentence 12): _____

10. fragment (sentence 13): _____

_____

_____

_____

_____

WRITE FOR SUCCESS

What qualities do you have that will make you a desirable student to your instructors in class or to your future employers? Consider your abilities, your personality, and any other factors that could be important.

Preparing and Editing a Résumé

Below is a draft of a résumé written by a college student who is looking for a summer job. This draft already has many of the elements needed for an effective résumé, but it also contains at least twenty errors (such as misspelling, typographical errors, faulty punctuation, or inconsistent design). Before it can be submitted to a potential employer, it will need to be edited and revised. Study each item listed on the résumé, and then answer the questions that follow.

Gary Sommers
645 Franklin AVe
Norman, OK 73071
(405)-662-1919 gsommers@oku.edu

<u>Present Job Objective:</u>	A summer position as an assistant in teh mayors office where I hope to experience how city government offices work
<u>Education:</u>	High School Diploma, Kennedy High School, Norman, Oklahoma
	B.A., Business Administration, University of Oklahoma
	Expected date of graduation: june 2016
	Courses in Business and Computers: Principles of Accounting, Microeconomic Theory, Problem solving and Structured Programming, Computer Systems and Assembly

WORK EXPERIENCE:

9/14–2016	Tutor, Math Lab, University of Oklahoma
2013–2014	Summer Volunteer at Camp Sunshine, a day camp for disabled children
2012–present	Volunteer at community gardens
<u>Special Skills:</u>	fluent in spanish
<u>Computer Skills:</u>	familiar with Microsoft Office, Excel, Lotus, Photoshop
<u>Interests:</u>	Soccer, guitar
<u>References:</u>	Available on request

Questions for Résumé Editing

1. Can you find typos, or errors in spelling, capitalization, or punctuation?
2. Can you find several inconsistencies in the design or layout? (Look for places where parallel structures are needed.)
3. Is there any missing information in this résumé?
4. Why has Mr. Sommers not included facts such as date of birth and marital status?
5. When a person looks for a job, how many references should be listed? How does the person obtain these references?
6. How could Mr. Sommers highlight his interest in the particular job for which he is applying?

PORTFOLIO SUGGESTION

Using the same headings found in this sample résumé, draft a résumé of your own. Copy it onto a flash drive that you will keep. Remember to update the résumé regularly. You may want to highlight a particular skill or emphasize different parts of your background by creating two or more versions of your résumé.

Mastering Irregular Verb Forms

11

CHAPTER OBJECTIVES

In this chapter, you will learn the principal parts of **fifty irregular verbs**. These verbs are divided into four groups.

- eight verbs that do not change their forms
- two verbs with the same simple and past participle forms
- twenty verbs with the same past tense and past participle forms
- twenty verbs that differ in all three forms

What Are the Principal Parts of Irregular Verbs?

The English language has more than 100 verbs that do not form the past tense or past participle with the usual -*ed* ending. Their forms are irregular. When you listen to children age four or five, you often hear them use -*ed* to form the past tense of every verb, as in "Yesterday, I *goed* to my aunt's house." Later on, they will learn that the verb *to go* is unusual, and they will change to the irregular form: "Yesterday, I *went* . . ." The best way to learn these verbs is to listen to how they sound. In Appendix C of this book, you will find an extensive list of the three principal parts of these verbs: the **simple form** (also called *dictionary form, infinitive form,* or *basic form*), the **past tense**, and the **past participle** (used with perfect tenses, after *has, have, had,* or *will have,* or with the passive voice, after the verb *to be*).

Practicing Fifty Irregular Verbs

Learn the three principal parts of all fifty irregular verbs given in this chapter. Pronounce them out loud until you have learned them. If you don't know the meaning of a particular verb or you cannot pronounce a verb and its forms, ask your instructor for help. Most irregular verbs are very common words that you will be using often in your writing and speaking. You will want to know them well.

EIGHT VERBS THAT DO NOT CHANGE THEIR FORMS

(Notice that all the verb forms end in *t* or *d*.)

SIMPLE FORM	PAST TENSE	PAST PARTICIPLE	SIMPLE FORM	PAST TENSE	PAST PARTICIPLE
bet	bet	bet	hurt	hurt	hurt
cost	cost	cost	put	put	put
cut	cut	cut	quit	quit	quit
hit	hit	hit	spread	spread	spread

TWO VERBS WITH THE SAME SIMPLE AND PAST PARTICIPLE FORMS

SIMPLE FORM	PAST TENSE	PAST PARTICIPLE
come	came	come
become	became	become

PRACTICE **1**   In each of the following sentences, fill in the correct form of the verb given in parentheses.

1. Last year, the financing of a college education _____ a more difficult task. (become)

2. For example, the tuition for the typical education _____ 7 percent more this past year than it did two years ago. (cost)

3. Unfortunately, many families trying to help have also been _____ with decreased income. (hit)

4. The message has _____ that college costs will continue to spiral. (spread)

5. I have _____ trying to guess my expenses for next year. (quit)

TWENTY VERBS WITH THE SAME PAST TENSE AND PAST PARTICIPLE FORMS

SIMPLE FORM	PAST TENSE	PAST PARTICIPLE	SIMPLE FORM	PAST TENSE	PAST PARTICIPLE
bend	bent	bent	creep	crept	crept
lend	lent	lent	keep	kept	kept
send	sent	sent	sleep	slept	slept
spend	spent	spent	sweep	swept	swept
catch	caught	caught	weep	wept	wept
teach	taught	taught	bring	brought	brought
bleed	bled	bled	buy	bought	bought
feed	fed	fed	fight	fought	fought
lead	led	led	seek	sought	sought
speed	sped	sped	think	thought	thought

PRACTICE **2**   In each of the following sentences, fill in the correct form of the verb given in parentheses.

1. Last semester, the school district _____ new chemistry texts. (buy)

2. Some citizens felt the district had _____ too much money on these new books. (spend)

3. They claimed the taxpayers were being _____ dry.
   (bleed)

4. These citizens argued that the school should have _____ the old books.
   (keep)

5. The teachers _____ the old books were worn out.
   (think)

6. Parents, on the other hand, _____ to hire two new teachers.
   (seek)

7. They _____ for a smaller class size.
   (fight)

8. Most teachers _____ classes that were too large.
   (teach)

9. One father _____ a campaign to educate the community.
   (lead)

10. He _____ every citizen a letter to explain the problem.
    (send)

PRACTICE ③ **In each of the following sentences, fill in the correct form of the verb given in parentheses.**

1. In 2007, the British singer and songwriter Adele Laurie Blue Adkins _____ her journey to becoming one of the world's best-selling artists. (begin)

2. The year before in 2006, this sultry-voiced performer _____ to the spotlight because of social media. (rise)

3. A friend of hers posted a demo that Adele had _____ for a school project. (sing)

4. Britain immediately recognized the exceptional quality of her voice, and her audiences _____.
   (grow)

5. Adele's success in America was sealed when she was _____ over here to appear on *Saturday Night Live*. (fly)

6. America has _____ great voices before, but many quickly fell in love
   (know)
   with Adele's rich vocals.

7. Her second album _____ the number one position in America longer
   (ride)
   than any other album since 1985.

8. Many opportunities have _____ up for her since then.
   (spring)

9. She has _____ a popular song for the James Bond movie, *Skyfall*, in 2012. (write)

10. So far, this artist has _____ that her talent and appeal are not at all small. (show)

TWENTY VERBS THAT DIFFER IN ALL THREE FORMS

SIMPLE FORM	PAST TENSE	PAST PARTICIPLE	SIMPLE FORM	PAST TENSE	PAST PARTICIPLE
blow	blew	blown	begin	began	begun
fly	flew	flown	drink	drank	drunk
grow	grew	grown	ring	rang	rung
know	knew	known	shrink	shrank	shrunk
throw	threw	thrown	sing	sang	sung
bite	bit	bitten (or bit)	sink	sank	sunk
drive	drove	driven	spring	sprang	sprung
hide	hid	hidden (or hid)	swim	swam	swum
ride	rode	ridden			
rise	rose	risen			
stride	strode	stridden			
write	wrote	written			

EXERCISE 1   Practicing Irregular Verb Forms

For each verb given in parentheses, supply the past tense or the past participle.

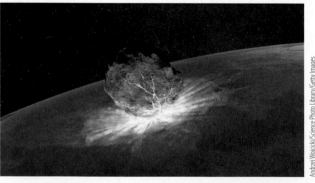

Andrzej Wojcicki/Science Photo Library/Getty Images

Ever since scientists _____ studying the
                 (begin)

dinosaur, they have _____ about what may have
               (write)

caused its extinction. In past attempts to find an answer,

many theories were suggested, but no one _____
                      (know)

for sure. Now most scientists have _____ on one
                   (bet)

strong possibility. That theory suggests that 65 million years

ago, a six-mile-wide chunk of rock _____ the earth and _____ up
                 (hit)   (throw)

a thick cloud of dust. The dust _____ the sunlight from the earth, causing
               (keep)

certain life forms to disappear. Some scientists have _____ to the conclusion
               (come)

that this could have _____ the earth's animal population by as much as
          (shrink)

70 percent. Other scientists are still not convinced. They believe time has

_____ the true reason for the disappearance of the dinosaurs.
   (hide)

EXERCISE **2**   **Practicing Irregular Verb Forms**

For each verb given in parentheses, supply the past tense or the past participle.

Nearly everyone has _____ a cold at some time or another. Medical
                                      (catch)

researchers have long _____ a cure for the common cold, but so far they
                               (seek)

have had no success. The cold virus has _____ throughout the world,
                                                  (spread)

and the number of its victims has _____ every year. Experience has
                                            (rise)

_____ us that people who have _____ plenty of liquids and
      (taught)   (drink)

taken aspirin have gotten over colds more quickly than those who have not, but

this is not a good enough remedy. People once believed that you _____
                                                                          (feed)

a fever and starved a cold, but recent research has _____ to a disclaimer
                                                              (lead)

of this belief. Other research, including the search for a vaccine, has _____
                                                                                  (cost)

a lot of time and effort. So far, the new knowledge has not _____ a cure.
                                                                     (hring)

EXERCISE **3**   **Practicing Irregular Verb Forms**

The following paragraph is written in the present tense. Rewrite the paragraph using the past tense.

The jockey drives his pickup truck to the racetrack. He strides into the stalls

where the horses are kept. His head swims with thoughts of the coming race. He

springs into the saddle and rides to the starting gate. The bell rings, and the horses

fly out of the gate. They speed around the first turn. The crowd grows tense, and

excitement spreads as the horses sweep across the finish line.

_____

_____

_____

_____

_____

More Irregular Verbs

Appendix C gives an alphabetical listing of nearly every irregular verb. Use that list to supply the correct form for each verb in the following exercises.

EXERCISE ④   **Practicing More Irregular Verb Forms**

For each verb given in parentheses, supply the past tense or the past participle.

1. The paparazzi had _____ her for a celebrity.
   (mistake)
2. I was very mad when I realized he had _____ my favorite tool.
   (break)
3. The comedian had _____ the joke too far.
   (take)
4. The incident had _____ the young mother.
   (shake)
5. Yesterday, she _____ several possible outfits for the garden party.
   (see)
6. After getting caught in the rain, the executive _____ out her shirt.
   (wring)
7. We had _____ shopping for appetizers for the event.
   (go)
8. Last night, the child _____ into tears when he was scolded.
   (burst)
9. The family had _____ the prisoner years ago.
   (forgive)
10. Have you already _____?
    (eat)

EXERCISE ⑤   **Practicing More Irregular Verb Forms**

Read the following paragraph. Find and circle the ten irregular verbs that are written incorrectly. In the spaces provided, write the correct forms of the ten irregular verbs.

Mr. Weeks, an alumnus of our university, had gave a large sum of money to the school just before he died. A committee was choosen to study how the money should be used. Each member thunk about the possibilities for several weeks before the meeting. Finally, the meeting begun in late November. Each member brung his or her ideas. One gentleman fealt the school should improve the graduate program by hiring two new teachers. Another committee member layed out a proposal for remodeling the oldest dormitory on campus. Janice Spaulding had writen a plan for increasing scholarships for deserving students. A citizen unexpectedly swang open the door and strode into the room. She pleaded with the school to provide more programs for the community. After everyone had spoke , the committee was asked to make a more thorough study of each project.

1. _____   6. _____
2. _____   7. _____
3. _____   8. _____
4. _____   9. _____
5. _____   10. _____

EXERCISE 6   **Practicing More Irregular Verb Forms**

For each verb given in parentheses, supply the past tense or the past participle.

1. He _____ his book bag across his chest.
   (sling)
2. The earth _____ as the truck roared down the road.
   (shake)
3. She _____ their clothes out on the bed.
   (lay)
4. No one has _____ what happened the last time he was over.
   (forget)
5. The cook _____ the pancake into the air.
   (fling)
6. The reporter _____ for more details in the case.
   (dig)
7. The camper _____ on the grass, exhausted from the hike.
   (lie)
8. The director had _____ to her about her lateness on the set.
   (speak)
9. The pool _____ running in the area.
   (forbid)
10. The small animal was _____ in fear.
    (freeze)

Mastery and Editing Tests

TEST 1   **Using Correct Irregular Verb Forms**

In each of the following sentences, underline the irregular verb. If the verb form is wrong, correct it. If the form is correct, mark it with a C.

1. He lended his son the money.

2. The fan blowed the smoke across the room.

3. The stuffing was shook out of the teddy bear.

4. She has rode on many spirited horses.

5. The members of the team had swum in the pool for two hours.

6. The children had fed the cat.

7. The famous soprano sung for the president when he was inaugurated.

8. The soldiers creeped up on the enemy position.

9. The novel was written in just two years.

10. The galleon sunk shortly after it had left Puerto Rico for Spain.

TEST **2**   **Using Correct Irregular Verb Forms**

For each irregular verb given in parentheses, supply the past tense or past participle.

1. Mike Wallace was _____ for his "ambush" interviews.
   (know)

2. He often _____ his subjects unaware.
   (catch)

3. He never _____ from asking a tough question.
   (shrink)

4. He _____ very high ratings to the television program *60 Minutes*.
   (bring)

5. He _____ all over the world interviewing people like Iran's President
   (fly)
   Mahmoud Ahmadinejad.

6. Facing a lawsuit from General Westmoreland, Mike Wallace _____
   (grow)
   depressed.

7. He _____ badly and couldn't eat.
   (sleep)

8. Finally, he suffered a nervous breakdown and _____ in a hospital bed
   (lie)
   for a week before returning home.

9. The producers of *60 Minutes* _____ their documentary practices and
   (rethink)
   decided to be less confrontational.

10. Mike Wallace _____ working well into his eighties and lived to the age
    (keep)
    of 93, dying on April 7, 2012.

TEST **3**   **Using Correct Irregular Verb Forms**

In each of the following sentences, underline the irregular verb. If the verb form is wrong, correct it. If the form is correct, mark it with a C.

1. The sales associate seen a lot of personalities in that store.

2. Maria's story had took an unexpected turn.

3. Too many things were shook up by that statement.

4. The teenager was hurt by the unkind comments.

5. Dancing had began to take her mind off of things.

6. Before it could escalate, the official sweeped it under the rug.

7. Jada brung everything with her.

8. Silas had threw the game on purpose.

9. The kids had drunk all the soda.

10. Daisy sprung from her seat.

TEST ④ **Editing Student Writing Using Editing Symbols**

The correction symbol for an error in verb form is *vb*. In the paragraph below, ten errors are marked with editing symbols. Correct each error on the lines provided after the paragraph.

¹In 1903, Horatio Nelson Jackson made a bet of $50.00 that he could drive across the country in less than three months. ²No one at that time had ever *vb* drove an automobile from California to New York. ³When he *vb* begun his trip, he had no worries about traffic problems. ⁴*frag* Because there were hardly any cars. ⁵However, there were other concerns. ⁶One major problem a hundred years ago *agr* were the absence of service stations along the way. ⁷When his car broke down, Horatio *vb* slept in whistle-stop towns, waiting for parts to be delivered by train. ⁸The roads were trails of mud or dust. ⁹*frag* If they existed at all. ¹⁰Furthermore, the cars at that time had no shock absorbers, power steering, air conditioning, seatbelts, and *//* they had no radios either. ¹¹Despite these difficulties, Horatio won his bet. ¹²He rumbled down Fifth Avenue in New York with his mechanic and his bulldog named Bud. ¹³He *vb* become the first person to drive an automobile across the country. ¹⁴Recently, an Indiana dentist and his wife reenacted that trip of a century ago in a 1904 Winton, a car that is no longer produced. ¹⁵The century-old car *vb* speeded along at twenty-five or thirty miles an hour. ¹⁶The couple faced problems when a wheel fell off, the brakes *vb* catched fire, and a tire went flat. ¹⁷After the trip, the dentist commented, "By comparison, driving in a modern car is like riding on a magic carpet."

Corrections

1. verb form (sentence 2): _____

2. verb form (sentence 3): _____

3. fragment (sentence 4): _____

   _____

   _____

4. agreement (sentence 6): _____

5. verb form (sentence 7): _____

6. fragment (sentence 9): _____

   _____

7. parallel structure (sentence 10): _____

   _____

   _____

8. verb form (sentence 13): _____

9. verb form (sentence 15) _____

10. verb form (sentence 16): _____

WRITE FOR SUCCESS

Everyone has his or her own learning style. Some people enjoy listening to lectures and taking notes. These same people often can read for long periods of time and study textbook chapters. Others need to be more active and do better in lab classes, field trips, and projects that take them outside the classroom. In other words, they prefer to do something physically while learning the material. Still others work best when they team with a partner or a person who can advise and offer special help. Write a response that details how you learn best.

Working Together

Blend Images - Jose Luis Pelaez Inc/Getty Images

Preparing for a Job Interview

Among the most important moments in our working lives are those times when we are searching for a first job or when we find ourselves moving from one job to another. Because a critical part of any job search is a successful interview, it is essential to be prepared to answer direct questions from the person who may hire you. Personnel officers of companies, along with counselors who help people get jobs in those companies, all agree that a job applicant should expect certain questions in an interview.

Here are five questions considered to be the most important:

1. What is your idea of the ideal job?
2. What image do you have in mind of the supervisor or manager you would like to work for?
3. What qualifications separate you from any other candidate for this job?
4. What is the most balanced portrait you can give of yourself?
5. What are your greatest strengths? What weaknesses about yourself have you recognized?

Experts say that the last two questions are especially tricky because they call for very personal answers. Also, when people respond to these questions, they tend either to talk too much about themselves or to give answers that are too brief.

The president of one counseling service suggests that an effective way to answer the question about a self-portrait is to ask another question, such as "Can you tell me about some problems you have had in your company, so I can focus my response?" In this way, you will have some good examples to use as part of your answer. Another counselor says that, when you are interviewed, you should "be honest, be yourself, and do your homework."

Working in Groups

Divide into five groups. Each group should take one of the five questions from the preceding list. Each student should devote ten minutes of freewriting to respond to his or her group's question. Following the freewriting, the group should then spend another ten minutes discussing the responses generated by its members. Sometimes groups like to exchange their freewriting so others can read their responses aloud or silently. One member of the group will then present a summary of the group's response to the rest of the class.

PORTFOLIO SUGGESTION

Use this opportunity to work on your own answers to these job interview questions. Write out your answers and save them for future reference. You may find them useful when you are preparing for an actual job interview.

Using Verb Tenses Correctly

12

CHAPTER OBJECTIVES

Using verb tenses correctly is at the heart of understanding a language. In this chapter, you will focus on six issues.

- using the **present perfect** and **past perfect tenses** correctly
- understanding the **sequence of tenses**
- avoiding unnecessary **shifts in verb tense**
- understanding when to choose the **active voice** and when to choose the **passive voice**
- recognizing constructions that require the **subjunctive mood**
- knowing how to use *should/would, can/could, will/would,* and *used to/supposed to,*

How Many Verb Tenses Are There in English?

Not all languages express time by using exactly the same verb tenses. Students for whom English is a second language know that one of their major tasks in learning English is to understand how to use each of the tenses. Because the next sections of this chapter concern common problems with tense, a chart of the English verb tenses is provided. You may want to refer to this list from time to time. Notice that the chart gives example sentences for each tense and continuous form.

THE SIX ENGLISH VERB TENSES AND THEIR CONTINUOUS FORMS

THREE SIMPLE TENSES	SIMPLE CONTINUOUS FORMS	THREE PERFECT TENSES	PERFECT CONTINUOUS FORMS
1. Present	**Present continuous**	**4. Present perfect**	**Present perfect continuous**
you walk	you are walking	you have walked	you have been walking
I run	I am running	I have run	I have been running
2. Past	**Past continuous**	**5. Past perfect**	**Past perfect continuous**
you walked	you were walking	you had walked	you had been walking
I ran	I was running	I had run	I had been running
3. Future	**Future continuous**	**6. Future perfect**	**Future perfect continuous**
you will walk	you will be walking	you will have walked	you will have been walking
I will run	I will be running	I will have run	I will have been running

How Do You Use the Present Perfect and the Past Perfect Tenses?

The perfect tenses need special attention because they are generally not well understood nor consistently used in the accepted way.

How Do You Form the Perfect Tenses?

The **present perfect tense** consists of *has* or *have* plus the past participle of the main verb:

has worked

have worked

The **past perfect tense** consists of *had* plus the past participle of the main verb:

had worked

What Do These Tenses Mean?

> The **present perfect tense** can be used to describe an action that started in the past and continues to the present time.

Jennifer *has worked* at the hospital for ten years.

This sentence indicates that Jennifer began to work at the hospital ten years ago and is still working there now. The following timeline shows that the action began ten years ago and continues up to the present time.

Study these other examples of sentences using the present perfect tense: in each case, the action started in the past and continues up to the present time.

She *has studied* violin since 1990.

I *have* always *appreciated* his generosity.

> The **present perfect tense** can also be used to describe an action that has just taken place or an action that took place at an indefinite time in the past.

An action that has just taken place:

***Has* Jennifer *found* a job yet?**

Jennifer *has* (just) *found* a new job in Kansas City.

An action that took place at an indefinite time:

***Have* you ever *been* to San Diego?**

Yes, I *have been* there three times.

NOTE: If the time were definite, you would use the simple past:

Jennifer *found* a new job yesterday.

Yes, I *was* in San Diego last week.

PRACTICE ❶   **Complete the following sentences by filling in the blanks with either the simple past tense or the present perfect tense.**

1. I _____ to Mexico in 2002.
      (go)

2. I _____ deep-sea diving a few times.
      (go)

3. The drummer in the band _____ percussion since he was five.
                             (study)

4. It _____ the jury two hours to reach their verdict yesterday.
      (take)

5. Washington, D.C., _____ the capital of our country for many years.
                  (be)

> The **past perfect tense** describes an action completed in the past before another past action or a specific time.

Jennifer *had worked* at the hospital for ten years before she *moved* away.

In this sentence, there are two past actions: Jennifer *worked* and Jennifer *moved*. The action that took place first is in the past perfect (*had worked*). The action that took place later, but was also completed in the past, is in the simple past (*moved*). The following timeline shows that one past action (*had worked*) was completed before another past action (*moved*).

	moment of speaking		
first action in the past	second action in the past		
x	x		
PAST		**PRESENT**	**FUTURE**
had worked	moved		

Study these other examples of sentences using the past perfect tense:

I *had* just *finished* when the bell *rang*.

He *said* that Randall *had told* the class about the experiment.

We *had provided* the information long before last week's meeting.

He *had left* for work by 8 a.m.

NOTE: In informal speech and writing, the simple past tense is often used to express the past perfect tense.

Informal writing or speech: **The child *witnessed* the accident before he ran away.**

Formal writing: **The child *had witnessed* the accident before he ran away.**

PRACTICE **2** Complete the following sentences by filling in the blanks with either the present perfect tense or the past perfect tense of the given verb.

1. Mexico City _____ visitors for many years.
   (fascinate)

2. This city _____ the third-largest city in the world, and people
   (become)

   _____ it grow larger every year.
   (watch)

3. The suburbs of the city _____ old villages that _____
   (replace)   (exist)

   peacefully since the days of the Aztecs.

4. Yolanda told us that she _____ in Fort Worth before she moved to
   (live)

   Mexico City.

5. Today, Mexico City _____ a computer-controlled subway system to
   (build)

   deal with its huge transportation problem.

What Is the Sequence of Tenses?

The term *sequence of tenses* refers to the logical relationship of verb tenses in sentences that have more than one clause.

If the tense of the independent clause is in the **present** (he *knows*), here are the possibilities for the dependent clause:

Independent clause (IC)	Dependent clause (DC)	Time of the DC in relation to the IC
	that she studies.	same time
He knows	that she studied.	earlier
	that she *will* study.	later

If the tense of the independent clause is in the **past** (he *knew*), here are the possibilities for the dependent clause:

Independent clause (IC)	Dependent clause (DC)	Time of the DC in relation to the IC
	that she studied.	same time
He knew	that she *had* studied.	earlier
	that she *would* study.	later

If the independent clause is in the **future** (he *will know*), here are the possibilities for the dependent clause:

Independent clause (IC)	Dependent clause (DC)	Time of the DC in relation to the IC
	if she studies.	same time
He will know	if she *has* studied.	earlier
	if she *will* study.	later

EXERCISE **1**   **Practicing with Sequence of Tenses**

In each of the following sentences, the verb in the independent clause has been underlined. Choose the correct verb tense for the verb in the dependent clause. Use the preceding examples if you need help.

1. The program <u>will continue</u> only after the coughing and fidgeting _____.
   (stop)

2. Because he was poor and unappreciated by the music world when he died in 1791,

   Mozart <u>did not realize</u> the importance that his music _____ in the future.
   (have)

3. Dad <u>will tell</u> us tonight if he _____ a new car next month.
   (buy)

4. Albert Einstein <u>failed</u> the entrance exam at the Swiss Federal Institute of

   Technology because he _____ a very disciplined student.
   (be + never)

5. Einstein <u>studied</u> only subjects that he _____ .
   (like)

6. Cancer researchers <u>think</u> it's likely that a cure for most cancers _____
   (be + soon)

   found.

7. We <u>know</u> that scientists _____ now close to finding a cure for leukemia.
   (be)

8. The interviewer felt that the young woman _____ more than she <u>was</u>
   (know)

   <u>telling</u> him.

9. The doctor went into the operating room. She <u>hoped</u> that the operation

   _____ as planned.
   (go)

10. The doctor came out of the operating room. She <u>said</u> that the operation was

    over and _____ well.
    (go)

Library of Congress Prints and Photographs Division, LC-USZ62-27663

EXERCISE **2**   **Practicing with Sequences of Tenses**

Complete each of the following sentences by choosing the verb tense that makes the meaning clear. Circle the letter of the correct answer.

1. In 1896, the Olympic Games consisted of forty-one events with thirteen nations competing; since then, the number of events and the number of nations participating _____.

   a. is increasing   c. has increased

   b. increased   d. had increased

2. In 1936, the Olympic Games _____ place in Berlin, Germany.

   a. take   c. took

   b. had taken   d. has taken

3. Adolf Hitler, the Nazi dictator, _____ only blond, blue-eyed athletes to win all the gold medals in track.

   a. is expecting   c. has been expecting

   b. was expecting   d. will expect

4. One year earlier, Jesse Owens, a student at Ohio State University, _____ three world records in track.

   a. breaks   c. had been breaking

   b. was breaking   d. had broken

5. As a result, young Owens _____ in Berlin in 1936 to represent the United States in track.

   a. is arriving   c. arrived

   b. will arrive   d. has arrived

6. To Hitler's dismay, Jesse Owens stunned the crowds when he _____ the world records in the 100-meter, the 200-meter, and the broad jump events.

   a. set   c. was setting

   b. had set   d. has set

7. After he _____ these events, he then helped his team win the 400-meter relay race as well.

   a. wins   c. had won

   b. has won   d. had been winning

8. At the time, Adolph Hitler was furious at the victories a black athlete _____; he refused to acknowledge him.

   a. has achieved   c. achieves

   b. had achieved   d. will achieve

9. Today, everyone _____ that Jesse Owens was the outstanding athlete at the Olympic Games that year.

    a. will realize   c. realized

    b. realizes   d. had realized

10. His achievements _____ young athletes of color ever since that historic day.

    a. have been inspiring   c. inspire

    b. had been inspiring   d. will inspire

Avoiding Unnecessary Shifts in Verb Tense

Unless there is some reason to change tenses, inconsistent shifting from one tense to another should be avoided. Study the following examples:

Shifted tenses: **The customer demanded** (past tense) **to see the manager. He** *was* (past tense) **angry because every jacket he** *tries* **on (Why present tense?)** *has* **(Why present tense?) something wrong with it. A button** *was* (past tense) **missing on the first, the lining** *did* **not** *hang* (past tense) **properly on the second, and the collar** *had* (past tense) **a stain on the third.**

Revised: **The customer demanded** (past tense) **to see the manager. He** *was* (past tense) **angry because every jacket he** *tried* **on (past tense)** *had* (past tense) **something wrong with it. A button** *was* (past tense) **missing on the first, the lining** *did* **not** *hang* (past tense) **properly on the second, and the collar** *had* (past tense) **a stain on the third.**

NOTE: When the subject is a created work such as a book, play, poem, or piece of music, be especially careful about the verb tense. Although the work was created in the past, it is still enjoyed in the present. In such a case, the present tense is used.

    Shakespeare's *Hamlet* <u>is</u> **a great play. It** <u>was</u> **written four centuries ago.**

EXERCISE **3**   **Correcting Unnecessary Shifts in Verb Tense**

Each sentence has an unnecessary shift in verb tense. Revise each sentence so that the tenses remain consistent.

1. After I complete that writing course, I took the required history course.

2. In the beginning of the movie, the action was slow; by the end, I am sitting on the edge of my seat.

3. The textbook gives the rules for writing a bibliography, but it didn't explain how to do footnotes.

4. While working on her report in the library, my best friend lost her note cards and comes to me for help.

5. The encyclopedia gives several pages of information about astronomy, but it didn't give any information about black holes.

6. "Salvation" was written by Langston Hughes; it continued to be widely read today.

7. This is a TV series, but it had too many characters.

8. The senator was leading in the polls until along comes a younger and more energetic rival.

9. At the end of *Gulliver's Travels,* the main character rejects the company of people; he preferred the company of horses.

10. My friend arrives late, as usual, and then complained when the movie was sold out.

EXERCISE **4**   **Correcting Unnecessary Shifts in Verb Tense**

The following paragraph contains unnecessary shifts in verb tense. Correct all verb tenses that are inconsistent.

Anyone who starts the novel *Black Boy* by Richard Wright will have a hard time putting it down. Wright calls it a "fictionalized autobiography" that tells the truth. In the three months following its publication, it sells 400,000 copies. Richard Wright knew about the universal problems that can destroy a man. He was born in Natchez, Mississippi, in 1908. His father, a poor farmer, abandons the family when Wright is only six. Living with an aunt, he experiences racial hatred when his uncle is lynched. He decided by nineteen that he wanted to be a writer and moves to Chicago where he has access to public libraries. He was an avid reader. His first novel, *Native Son,* is an immediate success. The story was a brutally honest picture of black, urban, ghetto life. Wright wanted his main character to symbolize all the poorly treated people around the world, but critics were more interested in Wright's powerful depiction of white racism in America. When Wright was invited to France after the publication of *Black Boy* in 1948, he finds it exhilarating to be treated as an equal. Eventually Wright moved permanently to Paris, France, with his wife and daughter. Although he continued to write, he seems to lose touch with the American reality. None of the novels written in France succeed, and he dies in 1960.

EXERCISE 5   **Editing Student Writing: Correcting Unnecessary Shifts in Verb Tense**

The following paragraph was part of an essay written by a first-year college student. It contains unnecessary shifts in verb tense. Correct all verb tenses that are inconsistent.

I remember last year when I was trying to choose the right school and worrying about it a lot. One day, a friend says that, instead of talking about it all the time, I should visit a few places and actually see them. One afternoon, I decide to do just that. I take the bus, get off in the center of town, and from there walked to the campus. It's very clean, with no graffiti on any of the walls. Behind the visitor's desk stood two students passing out brochures on programs and majors. The student union looks inviting, so I went in to get a soda and check it out. I sit down and started listening to the students at the other tables. I was curious to hear bits of their conversations. Students seemed to be treating each other with respect. I did not hear one sarcastic remark, and no one is rude to anyone else. I went to the library and had the same experience. Everyone seems so helpful and friendly. I knew this was the kind of atmosphere I would like. On my way out, I pick up an application from the visitors' desk. Both of the students behind the desk are smiling at me as I leave.

What Is the Difference between the Passive Voice and the Active Voice?

In the **active voice**, the subject of the verb does the acting:

Chinua Achebe wrote *Things Fall Apart*.

In general, you should choose the active voice to achieve direct, economical, and forceful writing. Most writing should be in the active voice.

In the passive voice, the subject of the verb receives the action.

***Things Fall Apart* was written by Chinua Achebe.**

> The passive voice is used to deemphasize the actor in cases where the actor is not important or perhaps not known.

Study the three sentences that follow. All three deal with President Kennedy's assassination. The first is in the active voice, and the other two are in the passive voice. Discuss with your classmates and instructor what would cause a writer to choose each of the following sentences to express the same basic fact.

Active Voice

Lee Harvey Oswald shot John F. Kennedy in 1963.

Passive Voice

President John F. Kennedy was shot by Lee Harvey Oswald in 1963.

President John F. Kennedy was shot.

How Do You Form the Passive Voice?

A sentence in the passive voice consists of the subject acted upon, followed by a form of the verb *to be* and the past participle. The actor may appear at the end in a phrase beginning with *by*.

FORMING THE PASSIVE VOICE

SUBJECT ACTED UPON +	VERB TO *BE* +	PAST PARTICIPLE +	*BY* PHRASE (OPTIONAL)
The race	was	won	(by the runner)
The meals	have been	cooked	(by the chef)
The books	are	illustrated	(by the artists)

EXERCISE 6   **Forming Active Voice and Passive Voice**

Complete each of the following examples by supplying either the active or the passive voice. Then discuss with the rest of the class the reasons a writer would choose either the active or the passive voice to express each idea.

Active Voice

1. _____
   _____

2. _____
   _____

Passive Voice

1. The wrong number was dialed (by the child).

2. The sweater was crocheted very carefully (by my grandmother).

3. The tornado struck Cherry Creek last spring.

3. _____

_____

4. The wind blew the leaves across the yard.

4. _____

_____

5. _____

_____

_____

5. In the seventies, platform shoes were worn (by many fashionable young men and women).

EXERCISE ⑦ **Forming Active Voice and Passive Voice**

Complete each of the following examples by supplying either the active or the passive voice. Then discuss with the rest of the class the reasons a writer would choose either the active or the passive voice to express each idea.

Active Voice

1. The Internet provider increased its prices.

2. _____

_____

3. The hotel will be installing security cameras near the exercise room.

4. _____

_____

5. The new intern broke the printer.

Passive Voice

1. _____

_____

2. A boycott was proposed (by Hollywood's leading actresses).

3. _____

_____

4. Comic Con is loved by many gamers.

5. _____

_____

What Is the Subjunctive Mood?

Verbs in the English language have three possible moods.

1. The **indicative mood** expresses statements of fact:

   He *drives* home every Sunday.

   Most sentences call for the indicative mood.

2. The **imperative mood** expresses commands:

   ***Drive* home on Sunday!**

3. The **subjunctive mood** expresses conditions contrary to fact:

If I were you, I would drive home on Sunday.

or follows certain verbs of demand or urgency:

I insist that he drive home on Sunday.

Of the three moods possible for verbs in English, the subjunctive mood has the most limited use.

> The **subjunctive mood**, the most limited of the three moods for English verbs, uses special verb forms to express statements contrary to fact or to express demand or urgency after certain verbs.

Three instances follow that call for the subjunctive. In each of these three instances, notice that the *-s* is *not* added in the third person singular present tense.

1. For unreal conditions introduced with *if* or *wish*, use *were* if the verb is *be*.

   If he were my teacher, I would be pleased.

   I wish he were my teacher.

2. For clauses starting with *that* after verbs such as *ask, request, demand, suggest, order, insist,* or *command*, use the infinitive form of the verb.

   I demand that she be on time.

   Sullivan insisted that Jones report on Tuesday.

3. For clauses starting with *that* after adjectives expressing urgency, as in *it is necessary, it is imperative, it is urgent, it is important,* and *it is essential,* use the infinitive form of the verb.

   It is necessary that she wear a net covering her hair.

   She insisted that Robert be ready by 5 a.m.

PRACTICE 3   **In the following sentences, underline the word or phrase that determines the subjunctive, and circle the subjunctive. An example has been done for you.**

Truman <u>suggested that</u> the country adopt the Marshall Plan in 1947.

1. When President Roosevelt died in 1945, the law required that Vice President Truman take over immediately.

2. It was essential that President Truman act quickly and decisively.

3. Truman must have wished that he were able to avoid using the atomic bomb to bring an end to World War II.

4. He felt it was necessary that the United States help Europe recover from the destruction of World War II.

5. President Truman always insisted that other countries be economically strong.

Knowing How to Use *Should/Would, Can/Could, Will/Would,* and *Used To/ Supposed To*

should/would

Do not use more than one modal auxiliary (*can, may, might, must, should, ought*) with the main verb.

Incorrect:	Joel *shouldn't ought* to sell his car.
Correct:	Joel *ought not* to sell his car.

or

Joel *shouldn't* sell his car.

Do not use *should of, would of,* or *could of* to mean *should have, would have,* or *could have.*

Incorrect:	Elana *would of* helped you if she *could of.*
Correct:	Elana *would have* helped you if she *could have.*

can/could; will/would

Use *could* as the past tense of *can.*

I *see* that he *can do* the job.

I *saw* that he *could do* the job.

Use *would* as the past tense of *will.*

I *see* that they *will do* a good job.

I *saw* that they *would do* a good job.

used to/supposed to

Do not omit the final *-d* in the phrases *used to* and *supposed to.*

Incorrect:	I am *use to* walking to school.
Correct:	I am *used to* walking to school.
Incorrect:	We are *suppose to* meet him for dinner.
Correct:	We are *supposed to* meet him for dinner.

Mastery and Editing Tests

TEST **Using Correct Verb Forms**

Revise each of the following sentences to avoid problems with verbs.

1. A specific seat was not requested by you. *(Use active voice.)*

   _____

2. It is imperative that Mr. Garcia returns to the office after his appointment.

   _____

3. The project should of been finished by Thursday.

   _____

4. The girl from Iowa was not use to the sight of the vast blue ocean.

   _____

5. The best-selling novel was reviewed by the book club before they saw the movie adaptation. *(Use active voice.)*

   _____

   _____

6. Today, all athletes stretched to avoid injuries and improve performance.

   _____

7. A great white shark was turned upside down; the creature goes into a trance.

   _____

8. If it was up to me, we would all have Mondays off.

   _____

9. The ambassador arrived at the garden gala and realized she choose the wrong shoes for the event.

   _____

   _____

10. The agent would of blown her cover if not for her partner's quick thinking.

    _____

TEST **Editing Student Writing: Using Correct Verb Forms**

In the following paragraph, change nine incorrect verb forms to their correct forms and change one passive sentence into an active sentence.

¹When the day arrived, my mother was jubilant. ²We drive to the synagogue. ³My aunt Sophie and her daughters come with us. ⁴Once in the temple, the women

were separated from the men. ⁵They sat upstairs in their assigned places. ⁶I was ask to keep my hat on and was given a shawl to wear that I seen before. ⁷I was suppose to wait for the rabbi to call me. ⁸My turn finally comes. ⁹I walked up to a table in the front. ¹⁰There I read from the sacred scriptures in Hebrew. ¹¹My mother had told me that if I was to read the scriptures fluently, she would be very proud. ¹²I knew. I could of read more loudly, but I was nervous. ¹³Afterward, I was taken by my family to a fine kosher restaurant for a celebration. *(Change to the active voice.)* ¹⁴There I receive a beautiful gold charm bracelet.

TEST ③ Editing Student Writing: Using Correct Verb Forms

In the following paragraph, change the ten incorrect verb forms to their correct forms.

¹My semester of chemistry seemed ill-fated from the very start. ²When I lost my textbook the first week of classes, I should of known I was in for trouble. ³The second week, I had the flu and miss two classes. ⁴On the following Monday, when I finally start off for class again, the bus was so delayed that I walked into the classroom half an hour late. ⁵The teacher scowls at me and ask to speak to me after class. ⁶I always use to sit in the front row so I could see the board and hear the lectures. ⁷Because I am late, I will have to take a seat in the last row. ⁸I wish I was able to start this class over again the right way. ⁹No one had ought to have such an unlucky start in any class.

TEST ④ Editing Student Writing: Using Correction Symbols

In the paragraph below, ten errors are marked with editing symbols. Correct each error on the lines provided after the paragraph.

¹Our college professor was amazed last year when a man comes to our English [*vb*] class to deliver a pizza to a student. ²The student later explained that he missed [*vb*] lunch. ³The professor was surprised that the student seen no problem with this [*vb*] incident. ⁴The pizza was confiscated. ⁵Across America today, cell phones and other electronic gadgets in the classrooms are a cause for concern among teachers, administrators, and sometimes even students are getting upset. [*//*] ⁶Going off in class, [*dm*] the lessons are disturbed by cell phones. ⁷Some students leave classes, they go out [*ro*] into the hallways to make calls. ⁸Others play video games or watch movies, that they [*subord*]

have downloaded onto their laptops. ⁹Cheating with handheld organizers and cell

phone messaging *agr* are also problematic for teachers. ¹⁰At the college I attend, many

professors have made policies regarding electronic devices in their classrooms.

¹¹Banning these devices is *vb* suppose to result in a more controlled classroom.

¹²I am not convinced this is a good idea. ¹³*frag* Because a student may urgently need to

communicate with someone.

Corrections

1. verb form (sentence 1):   _____

2. verb form (sentence 2):   _____

        _____

3. verb form (sentence 3):   _____

4. parallel structure (sentence 5):   _____

        _____

        _____

        _____

        _____

        _____

5. dangling modifier (sentence 6):   _____

6. run-on (sentence 7):   _____

        _____

7. subordination (sentence 8):   _____

        _____

        _____

8. Agreement (sentence 9):   _____

9. verb (sentence 11):   _____

10. fragment (sentence 13):   _____

        _____

        _____

WRITE FOR SUCCESS

How can one be sure to get the most out of a class? What constitutes good working habits in class? Write a response that considers the following: preparation, having the proper materials, ability to take notes, readiness to ask questions, and readiness to focus mentally.

Working Together

Problem Solving: Integrity in the Workplace

Recently, a young office worker went to his superior and reported that a fellow worker was incorrectly reporting the company's profits. It was clear that the intention was to give the impression the company was doing better than it really was. His superior told the young worker not to worry about the situation, and that he himself would take care of it. Before long, this same worker was let go. He believed he was fired because of his honesty, and he began to suspect a conspiracy of dishonesty among the others in his company. The worker may have paid a high price for being a whistleblower: he lost his job.

The lack of integrity in today's workplace has reached the level of a national disgrace. Consider the following list of scandals that reached the public's awareness in recent years.

- Predatory lenders misled customers into risky mortgage loans that resulted in huge numbers of foreclosures by 2008.
- For over a decade, Penn State administrators looked the other way when witnesses continued to report sexual abuse of children by the assistant football coach.
- The lobbyist Jack Abramoff defrauded Indian tribes by promising them favors he could not or would not act upon.
- Red Cross workers stole money donated for the victims of Hurricane Katrina.
- Government officials attempted to silence a NASA scientist when he tried to publish his findings on global warming.
- Bernard Madoff, a Wall Street money manager, defrauded investors (including many charities) of $50 billion.

Working in Groups

Divide into groups. In addition to the examples given above, each group should add other examples of dishonesty in the workplace. Examples might include actual situations that members of the group have personally observed, or these examples may be scandals that are currently in the news. Then each group should discuss how each of these betrayals of trust might have been avoided. Develop a list of procedures that institutions should take to protect the public. Each group should present these examples and suggestions to the other groups.

Each member of the class should take notes during the presentations and jot down questions, along with any points of disagreement. After the presentations, discuss whether the suggestions for dealing with the examples of dishonesty would be effective. Are there additional problems to be addressed?

PORTFOLIO SUGGESTION

All groups (charitable organizations, educational institutions, political institutions, and social institutions) are affected by dishonesty. Depending on your interests and job goals, you might want to study how a scandal or case of corruption has affected one of these institutions. A fascinating research paper could develop from the notes you save from the class presentations.

iStockphoto.com/ArtisticCaptures

Learning the Rules for Capitalization and Punctuation

13

CHAPTER OBJECTIVES

In this chapter, you will learn the basic rules of capitalization and punctuation that govern English. Many of these rules you undoubtedly already know, but several of them are likely to be new for you.

- ten basic rules for **capitalization**
- ten basic uses of the **comma**
- three uses for the **apostrophe**
- four uses for **quotation marks**
- three uses for the **semicolon**
- four uses for the **colon**
- use of the **dash** and **parentheses**

In college and at work, you will have to be in control of capitalization and punctuation. When is a word important enough to need a capital letter? Where are commas needed in a sentence? These and other questions will be answered when you know the fundamental rules and how to apply them. Carefully study the examples that are given under each rule. Notice that you will often learn how to capitalize and punctuate by learning what *not* to do.

Ten Basic Rules of Capitalization

RULE **1**   Capitalize the first word of every sentence.

> **Every building was old. Our house was the oldest.**

RULE **2**   Capitalize the names of specific things and places.

Specific buildings:

> **I went to the Jamestown Post Office.**
>
> > but
>
> **I went to the post office.**

Specific streets, cities, states, and countries:

> **The mayor lives on Elam Avenue.**
>
> > but
>
> **The mayor lives on the same street as my mom and dad.**

Specific organizations:

> **Our neighbor collected money for the March of Dimes.**
>
> but
>
> **Our neighbor collected money for his favorite charity.**

Specific institutions:

> **The loan is from the First National Bank.**
>
> but
>
> **The loan is from one of the banks in town.**

Specific bodies of water:

> **My uncle fishes every summer on Lake Michigan.**
>
> but
>
> **My uncle spends every summer at the lake.**

RULE **3**   Capitalize days of the week, months of the year, and holidays. Do not capitalize the names of seasons.

> **The fourth Thursday in November is Thanksgiving Day.**
>
> but
>
> **I cannot wait until spring.**

RULE **4**   Capitalize the names of all languages, nationalities, races, religions, deities, and sacred terms.

> **My friend who is Ethiopian speaks very little English.**
>
> **The Koran is the sacred book of Islam.**

RULE **5**   Capitalize the first word and generally every important word in a title. Do not capitalize articles, prepositions, coordinating conjunctions, nor the *to* in infinitives unless they are the first or last word in the title.

> *For Whom the Bell Tolls* **is a famous novel by Ernest Hemingway.**
>
> **Her favorite short story is "A Rose for Emily."**

RULE **6**   Capitalize the first word of a direct quotation.

> **The teacher said, "You have been chosen for the part."**
>
> but
>
> **"You have been chosen," she said, "for the part."**

NOTE: In the second sentence, *for* is not capitalized because it is a continuation of the sentence in quotation marks.

RULE **7**   Capitalize historical events, periods, and documents.

> **the American Revolution**
>
> **the Colonial Period**
>
> **the Bill of Rights**

RULE **8**   Capitalize the words *north, south, east,* and *west* when they are used as places rather than as geographical directions.

> **He comes from the Midwest.**
>
> but
>
> **The farm is about twenty miles west of Omaha.**

RULE **9**   Capitalize people's names.

Proper names:

> **Charles Wong**

Professional titles when they are used with the person's proper name:

> **Justice Sotomayor**   but   **the justice**
>
> **Professor Shapiro**   but   **the professor**

Terms for relatives (mother, sister, nephew, uncle) when they are used in the place of proper names:

> **I told Grandfather I would meet him later.**
>
> but
>
> **I told my grandfather I would meet him later.**

NOTE: Terms for relatives are not capitalized if a pronoun, article, or adjective is used with the name.

RULE **10**   Capitalize brand names.

> **Lipton's Noodle Soup**   but   **noodle soup**
>
> **Velveeta Cheese**   but   **cheese**

EXERCISE **1**   Capitalization

In each of the following sentences, correct any word that requires capitalization.

1. The artist replied, "we are hoping for space in the newly renovated commercial center."

2. All of the villagers celebrated the winter solstice with a festival in the town square.

3. The head of general motors came to Washington, D.C., looking for a loan.

4. The movie was based on a story from the old testament.

5. In 1803, American ambassadors negotiated the louisiana purchase with france.

6. Many senior citizens go to the southwest in the winter.

7. The members of the automobile workers union appealed to president Obama.

8. Many dominican students are in one of the health-related programs in this university.

9. My sister's favorite television programs are *game of Thrones* and *the voice*.

10. The law professor wrote a letter to judge Johnson.

EXERCISE **2**   Capitalization

In each of the following sentences, correct any word that requires capitalization.

1. Every tuesday the general visits the hospital.

2. On one level, the book *the lord of the rings* can be read as a fairy tale; on another level, the book can be read as a christian allegory.

3. The golden gate bridge in san franscisco may be the most beautiful bridge in the world.

4. She is the sister of my french teacher.

5. I've always wanted to take a trip to the far east in spring.

6. The kremlin, located in moscow, once housed the soviet government.

7. I needed to see dr. Ghavami, but the nurse told me the doctor would not be in until next week.

8. He shouted angrily, "why don't you ever arrive at your history class on time?"

9. The college level examination program will start on january 18.

10. While yet a teenager growing up in harlem, james Baldwin became a baptist preacher.

EXERCISE  3 **Capitalization**

In each of the following sentences, correct any word that requires capitalization.

1. The lawyer's office is located on north pleasant street.

2. My uncle lives farther west than grandmother.

3. I'd like to move to the south by next summer.

4. The well-known anthropologist Margaret Mead was for many years director of the museum of natural history in new york city.

5. The constitution of the united states was signed in constitution hall on september 17, 1787.

6. Sculptor John Wilson was commissioned to create a bust of rev. Martin Luther King, jr.

7. The project will be funded partly with money from the national endowment for the arts.

8. I read the magazine article in *sports illustrated* while I was waiting in the dentist's office yesterday.

9. The tour took the retired teachers above the arctic circle.

10. Many gerber baby foods no longer have sugar and salt.

Ten Basic Uses of the Comma

You may feel uncertain about when to use commas. One of the best ways to become more confident with using commas is to concentrate on a few basic rules. These rules will cover most of your needs.

The tendency now in English is to use fewer commas than in the past. There is no one complete set of rules on which everyone agrees. However, if you learn these ten basic uses, your common sense will help you figure out what to do in other cases. Remember that a comma usually signifies a pause in a sentence. As you read a sentence out loud, listen to where you pause within the sentence. This pause is often a clue that a comma is needed. Notice that in each of the examples for the following ten uses, you can pause where the comma should be placed.

RULE 1   Use a comma to separate three or more items in a series. These items can be composed of words, phrases, or clauses.

Three words (in this case, adjectives) in a series:

He was *silent, lonely,* and *afraid.*

Three phrases (in this case, verb phrases) in a series:

He *ran in the race, finished among the top ten,* and *collapsed happily on the ground.*

Three clauses in a series:

Dee Gordon, *who won the batting title for the Miami Marlins, who also won a Gold Glove at Shortstop,* and *who is widely viewed as one of the future stars of Major League Baseball,* tested positive for performance-enhancing drugs in 2016.

NOTE: Although some grammar authorities omit the comma between the last item of a series and the coordinating conjunction, check with your instructor to determine the preferred style. Be mindful that omitting the final comma may change the meaning, as in the following examples.

The cell phones come in red, green, pink, and black.

The cell phones come in red, green, pink and black.

NOTE: No comma is used for only two items:

He was *silent and lonely.*

RULE ② | Use a comma to set off parts of dates, addresses, and geographical names.

I was born on August 29, 1996, in the middle of a hurricane.

I lived at 428 Wilderness Road, Silver Lake, North Carolina, for many years.

I dreamed of spending a semester in Quito, Ecuador, to study art.

RULE ③ | Use a comma to set off a number of adjectives that modify a noun.

I carried my *favorite, old, green* coat.

Sometimes two adjectives in front of a noun go together to give a distinct meaning. In this case, they would not be separated by commas:

I carried my *favorite, dark green* coat.

The words *dark* and *green* belong together to give the meaning of a single color: *dark* modifies the color *green,* and the two words together describe the color of the coat.

PRACTICE ① | **In each of the following sentences, insert a comma wherever needed.**

1. On October 8 2015 the city of Flint Michigan announced that its water source would switch back to Detroit's water system.

2. Problems with the water supply of the United States Europe Canada and other parts of the world are growing.

3. Water is colorless tasteless odorless and free of calories.

4. You will use—on an average day—twenty-four gallons of water for flushing thirty-two gallons for bathing and washing clothes and twenty-five gallons for other uses.

5. It took 120 gallons of water to create the eggs you ate for breakfast 3,500 gallons for the steak you might eat for dinner and more than 60,000 gallons to produce the steel used to make your car.

RULE **4**   Use a comma along with a coordinating conjunction to combine two simple sentences (also called independent clauses) into a single compound sentence. (See Chapter 6 on coordination.)

The hour was late, but I was determined to finish the assignment.

Be careful to use the comma with the conjunction only when you are combining sentences. When you are combining words or phrases, no comma is used.

My sister was safe but not happy.

My mother and father were searching for her.

She was neither in class nor at work.

PRACTICE **2**   **In each of the following sentences, insert commas wherever they are needed.**

1. The most overused bodies of water are our rivers but they continue to serve us daily.

2. American cities often developed next to rivers and industries followed soon after in the same locations.

3. The people of the Industrial Age can try to clean the water they have used or they can watch pollution take over.

4. The Great Lakes are showing signs of renewal yet the struggle against pollution there must continue.

5. Many people have not yet been educated about the dangers to our water supply nor are all our legislators fully aware of the problem.

RULE **5**   Use a comma to follow introductory words, phrases, or dependent clauses.

- introductory words (such as *yes, no, oh, well*) or transitional expressions (*such as therefore, finally, however*):

Oh, **I never thought he would do it.**

Therefore, **we were very surprised.**

- introductory phrases:

Long prepositional phrase:	*In the beginning of the course,* I thought I would never be able to do the work.
Participial phrase:	*Walking on tiptoe,* the young mother quietly peeked into the nursery.
Infinitive phrase:	*To be quite honest,* I don't believe he's feeling well.

- introductory dependent clauses beginning with a subordinating conjunction:

When the food arrived, we all grabbed for it.

(For more examples, see Chapter 7 on subordination.)

PRACTICE ❸   **In each of the following sentences, insert commas wherever they are needed.**

1. To many people from the East the plans to supply more water to the western states seem unnecessary.

2. However people in the West know that they have no future without a good water supply.

3. When they entered Salt Lake Valley in 1847 the Mormons found dry soil that needed water before crops could be grown.

4. Confidently the new settlers dug ditches that brought the needed water.

5. Learning from the past modern farmers are trying to cooperate with nature.

RULE ❻   Use commas to set off a word, phrase, or clause when the word, phrase, or clause interrupts the main idea.

- interrupting word:

We will, *however*, take an X-ray.

- interrupting phrase:

Prepositional phrase:	I wanted, *of course*, to stay.
Appositive phrase:	Mariella, *the girl with the braids*, has a wicked sense of humor.

- interrupting clause:

He won't, *I think*, try that again.

Mariella, *who wears braids*, has a wicked sense of humor.

NOTE: Keep in mind that the same word, phrase, or clause may function in more than one way. The way the word functions determines the rule for punctuation. Consider again the word *however*. Although we have seen that commas set off the word when it interrupts in the middle of a clause, we use a semicolon and a comma if the word connects two independent clauses:

We will, *however*, take an X-ray.

We will take an X-ray; *however*, the doctor cannot read it today.

Another example of how function determines punctuation is in the case of a relative clause. Commas *are used* if the relative clause interrupts and is not essential to the main idea:

> **My sister, *who wears braids*, has a wicked sense of humor.**

Commas are *not* used if the clause is part of the identity, necessary to the main idea:

> **The girl *who wears braids* is my sister.**

The clause *who wears braids* is necessary for identifying which girl is the sister.

(For more examples of the use of the comma with relative clauses, see Chapter 7.)

PRACTICE **4**   **In each of the following sentences, insert commas wherever they are needed.**

1. Some parts of our country I believe do not have ample supplies of water.

2. The rocky soil of Virginia for example cannot absorb much rainwater.

3. Johnstown Pennsylvania a town of 21,000 is situated in one of the most flood-prone valleys of America.

4. It is not therefore a very safe place to live.

5. The Colorado which is one of our longest rivers gives up most of its water to farmers and cities before it reaches the sea.

RULE **7**   Use commas around nouns in direct address. (A noun in *direct address* is the name or title used in speaking to someone.)

> **I thought, *Rosa*, that I saw your picture in the paper.**

PRACTICE **5**   **In each of the following sentences, insert commas wherever they are needed.**

1. Dear your tea is ready now.

2. I wonder Jason if the game has been canceled.

3. Dad could I borrow five dollars?

4. I insist sir on speaking with the manager.

5. Kim is that you?

RULE **8**   Use commas in numbers of 1,000 or larger.

> **1,999**
>
> **1,999,999,999**

PRACTICE **6**   **In each of the following numbers, insert commas wherever they are needed.**

1. 4 876 454

2. 87 602

3. 156 439 600

4. 187 000

5. 10 000 000 000 000

RULE **9**   Use a comma to set off exact words spoken in dialogue.

"Let them," she said, "eat cake."

NOTE: Commas (as well as periods) are placed inside the quotation marks. *(This rule, which is standard American practice, will be unfamiliar to students who have been educated in the British system.)*

PRACTICE **7**   **In each of the following sentences, insert commas wherever they are needed.**

1. "I won't " he insisted "be a part of your scheme."

2. He mumbled "I plead the Fifth Amendment."

3. "I was told " the defendant explained "to answer every question."

4. "This court case " the judge announced "will be televised."

5. "The jury " said Al Tarvin of the press "was handpicked."

RULE **10**   Use a comma wherever it is necessary to prevent a misunderstanding.

Before eating, the cat prowled through the barn.

PRACTICE **8**   **In each of the following sentences, insert commas wherever they are needed.**

1. Kicking the child was carried off to bed.

2. To John Russell Baker is the best columnist.

3. When you can come and visit us.

4. We surveyed the students in the class; out of the twenty seven were married.

5. Some types of skin cancers can kill doctors say.

EXERCISE **4**   **Using the Comma Correctly**

In each of the following sentences, insert commas wherever they are needed.

1. In Miami Florida, a valedictorian gets ready to give a speech in front of a full auditorium of about 4 000 friends and family.

2. Even though she is nervous she has properly prepared.

3. The determined youth did research in fact on how to manage her anxiety.

4. Her findings which were taken from a study on communication apprehension explained that heart rates during public speaking reveal four different styles of nervousness.

5. The styles were identified as the Average the Insensitive the Confrontational and the Inflexible.

6. The people with the average heart rate reaction have the expected amount of adrenaline pumping and they feel generally positive about public speaking.

7. Those identified as having an insensitive nervousness style are much less apprehensive about speaking in public have a much lower heart rate and usually have a lot of experience in front of an audience.

8. The people with a confrontational reaction to public speaking have a very high heart rate in the moments right before they speak but after they start the rate relaxes to average.

9. The inflexible have the highest heart rate of all and this incredible anxiety can be used to enhance their performance or diminish it.

10. The valedictorian in Florida steps to the podium takes a deep breath and says "Congratulations graduates."

EXERCISE **5**   **Using the Comma Correctly**

In each of the following sentences, insert commas wherever they are needed.

1. Abraham Lincoln was born on February 12 1809 in Kentucky.

2. In 1816 after selling most of their possessions the Lincoln family moved to Indiana.

3. During their first weeks in Indiana the family hunted for food drank melted snow and huddled together for warmth.

4. After a little formal education Lincoln worked on a ferryboat on the Ohio River.

5. The first large city that Lincoln visited was New Orleans an important center of trade in 1828.

6. Among the 40,000 people living in New Orleans at the time of Lincoln's visit there were people from every state and several foreign countries.

7. New Orleans also showed Lincoln such city luxuries as fancy clothes gleaming silverware expensive furniture and imported china and glassware.

8. As a result of this visit Lincoln must have compared the log cabin of his childhood with the wealthy houses of the big city.

9. A few years later Lincoln became a merchant but his failure in business left him in debt for more than ten years.

10. How fortunate that Lincoln who started off with a career in business turned his attention to politics.

EXERCISE **6** **Using the Comma Correctly**

In each of the following examples, insert commas wherever they are needed.

1. First appearing in the 1870s psychology is considered a relatively new discipline.

2. Psychologists study behavior and its relationship with the brain and the environment.

3. A psychologist for example might concentrate on behaviors that affect the mental health of an individual.

4. Alas opportunities in psychology are much greater for those who have masters and doctoral degrees.

5. An undergraduate degree however is excellent preparation for continuing on to other graduate degrees in a variety of fields.

6. This is because psychology majors learn how to collect analyze and interpret data.

7. In order to develop these skills psychology majors take courses that involve statistics and experimental design.

8. People with bachelor's degrees often possess good research and writing skills are good problem solvers and have higher-level thinking abilities.

9. With a bachelor's degree in psychology you may find a job as an interviewer a personnel analyst a probation officer an employment counselor a correction counselor or a guidance counselor in an educational setting.

10. Most people working in the area of psychology love their work and they cannot imagine ever dropping out of their field.

Three Uses for the Apostrophe

RULE ❶   Use an apostrophe to form the possessive.

- For most singular nouns, add **'s**:

    the pen of the teacher = **the teacher's pen**

    the strategy of the boss = **the boss's strategy**

    the wheel of the car   = **the car's wheel**

Be careful to choose the right noun when you form the possessive. Always ask yourself *who* or *what* possesses something. In the previous examples, the teacher possesses the pen, the boss possesses the strategy, and the wheel belongs to the car. Note the following unusual possessives:

Hyphenated words:	**mother-in-law's advice**
Joint possession:	**Lucy and Desi's children**
Individual possession:	**John's and Steve's ideas**

- For most indefinite pronouns, add **'s**:

    everyone's responsibility

    somebody's wallet

    another's problem

NOTE: A possessive pronoun (*his, hers, its, ours, yours, theirs, whose*) never takes an apostrophe.

    Whose **key is this?**

    The key is *his.*

    The car is *theirs.*

- For nouns that form their plurals in a regular way (by adding **-s** or **-es**), add only an apostrophe:

    the coats of the ladies   = **the ladies' coats**

    the store of the brothers = **the brothers' store**

- For nouns that form their plural in an irregular way (they do not end in **-s**), add **'s**:

    the hats of the children = **the children's hats**

    the harness of the oxen = **the oxen's harness**

NOTE: A few singular nouns ending in the **s** or **z** sound are awkward to pronounce if another **s** sound is added. In those cases, the final **-s** is optional. Let your ear help you make the decision.

    Jesus's robe or Jesus' robe

    Moses's law or Moses' law

RULE **2**

> Use **'s** to form certain plurals to prevent confusion.

- letters of the alphabet:

  When he writes, all his *a*'s look like *o*'s.

- abbreviations with periods:

  My sisters both have Ph.D.'s from the University of Buffalo.

- words referred to in a text:

  He uses too many *you know*'s when he speaks.

NOTE: Never use an apostrophe to form any other plurals.

RULE **3**

> Use an apostrophe to show where one or more letters have been omitted in a contraction.

cannot	**= can't**
should not	**= shouldn't**
will not	**= won't** (This is the only commonly used contraction that changes its spelling.)
I am	**= I'm**
she will	**= she'll**

EXERCISE **7**   **Using the Apostrophe**

Fill in each of the blanks below with the correct form of the word; follow the rules for using the apostrophe.

1. rays of the sun   the _____ rays

2. the reputation of the press   the _____ reputation.

3. length of the room   the _____ length

4. the house of Anthony and Maria   _____ house
   (*joint possession*)

5. the idea of nobody   _____ idea

6. The book belongs to him.   The book is _____.

7. in the reign of Queen Elizabeth   in _____

8. That is her opinion. (*form a contraction*)   _____ her opinion.

9. shirts for boys   _____ shirts

10. the cover of the book   the _____ cover

EXERCISE **8** **Using the Apostrophe**

Fill in each of the blanks below with the correct form of the word; follow the rules for using the apostrophe.

1. the value of the property   the _____ value

2. the plans of the developers   the _____ plans

3. the guess of anybody   _____ *guess*

4. Visitors cannot park on this block.   Visitors _____ park
   (*form a contraction*)   on this block.

5. the rights of the owners   the _____ rights

6. the claims of the father-in-law   the _____ claims

7. the inventions of Westinghouse   _____
   and Edison (*individual possession*)   inventions

8. The money belongs to him.   The money is _____.

9. the windshield of the bus   the _____ windshield

10. the enamel of the teeth   the _____ enamel

EXERCISE **9** **Using the Apostrophe**

Fill in each of the blanks below with the correct form of the word; follow the rules for using the apostrophe.

1. the engine of the train   the _____ engine

2. the spirit of the class   the _____ spirit

3. the center for women   the _____ center

4. the wish of everybody   _____ wish

5. The toys belong to them.   The toys are _____.

6. The child mixes up *b* and *d*.   The child mixes up _____
   (*use the plural*)

7. I will not leave this house.   I _____ leave this house.
   (*form a contraction*)

8. the grain of the wood   the _____ grain

9. the verdict of the jurors   the _____ verdict

10. the policies of Ridge School   _____
    and Orchard School   policies
    (*individual possession*)

Four Uses for Quotation Marks

RULE   Use quotation marks for a direct quotation (a speaker's or writer's exact words).

> **"Please," I begged, "go away."**

Do not use quotation marks for an indirect quotation (reporting a speaker's or writer's words).

> **I begged her to go away.**

RULE   Use quotation marks for material copied word for word from a source.

The *New York Times* reported, "The average adult body contains 40 to 50 quarts of water. Blood is 83 percent water; muscles are 75 percent water; the brain is 74 percent water; and even bone is 22 percent water."

RULE ③   Use quotation marks for titles of shorter works such as short stories, poems, articles in magazines and newspapers, songs, essays, and chapters of books.

> **"A Modest Proposal," an essay by Jonathan Swift, is a masterpiece of satire.**

> **"The Lottery," a short story by Shirley Jackson, created a sensation when it first appeared in *The New Yorker*.**

NOTE: The title of a full-length work (such as a book, a play, a magazine, or a newspaper) is italicized in print and underlined when handwritten.

> **In print:**   **Many famous short stories have first appeared in *The New Yorker*.**

> **Handwritten form:**   **Many famous short stories have first appeared in <u>The New Yorker</u>.**

RULE ④   Use quotation marks for terms referred to in a special way.

> **"Duckie" is a term of affection used by the British, in the same way we would use the word "honey."**

PRACTICE   **In each of the following sentences, insert quotation marks wherever they are needed.**

1. The Gift of the Magi is one of the short stories in O. Henry's book *The Four Million*.

2. Franklin Delano Roosevelt said, We have nothing to fear but fear itself.

3. The president told his cabinet that they would have to settle the problem in the next few days.

4. The term reggae refers to a popular musical style originating in Jamaica.

5. She read the article Can Empathy Be Taught? in a recent issue of *Academe.*

If these five sentences had been handwritten, which words would have been underlined?

Three Uses for the Semicolon

RULE **1** Use a semicolon to join two independent clauses whose ideas or sentence structures are related.

He decided to consult the map; she decided to use their GPS.

RULE **2** Use a semicolon in front of an adverbial conjunction used to combine two sentences.

He decided to consult the map; however, she decided to use their GPS.

RULE **3** Use a semicolon to separate items in a series when the items themselves contain commas.

I had lunch with Linda, my best friend; Mrs. Armstrong, my English teacher; and Jan, my sister-in-law.

NOTE: If the writer had used only commas to separate the items in this example, the reader might think five or six people had gone to lunch together.

PRACTICE **10** **In each of the following sentences, insert a semicolon wherever needed.**

1. One of the best ways to remember a vacation is to take numerous photos one of the best ways to recall the contents of a book is to take notes.

2. The problem of street crime must be solved otherwise, the number of vigilantes will increase.

3. The committee was made up of Kevin Corey, a writer Anita Poindexter, a professor and Jorge Rodriguez, a politician.

4. The bank president was very cordial however, he would not approve the loan.

5. The retailer wants higher profits the customer wants lower prices.

Four Uses for the Colon

RULE **1**   Use a colon after an independent clause when the material that follows is a series of items, an illustration, or an explanation.

- a series of items:

  Please order the following items: five dozen pencils, twenty rulers, and five rolls of tape.

Notice that in the sentence below, no colon is used because there is not a complete sentence (or independent clause) before the list.

  The courses I am taking this semester are Introduction to College Writing, Introduction to Psychology, Art Appreciation, and Biology 101.

Do not use a colon directly after a verb; after the prepositions *except* or *regarding*; or after expressions *such as, for example, especially,* or *including.*

  The merchant ordered the following items: belts, handbags, and shoes.

  The merchant *ordered* belts, handbags, and shoes.

  The merchant ordered everything in the catalog: belts, handbags, and shoes.

  The merchant ordered everything in the catalog *except* belts, handbags, and shoes.

  The merchant ordered many items: belts, handbags, and shoes.

  The merchant ordered many items *including* belts, handbags, and shoes.

- an illustration or explanation:

  She was an exceptional child: at seven she was performing on the concert stage.

RULE **2**   Use a colon after the salutation of a formal or business letter.

  Dear Sales Office Manager:

  Dear President Gonzalas:

RULE **3**   Use a colon when using numerals to indicate time.

  We will eat at 5:15.

RULE **4**   Use a colon between the title and the subtitle of a book.

  Plain English Please: A Rhetoric

PRACTICE **11**   **In each of the following sentences, insert colons wherever they are needed.**

1. Three vocalists performed in Los Angeles recently   Ariana Grande, Adele, and Sam Smith.

2. The official has one major flaw in his personality   greed.

3. The restaurant has lovely homemade desserts such as German chocolate layer cake and baked Alaska.

4. The college offers four courses in English literature   Romantic Poetry, Shakespeare's Plays, The British Short Story, and The Modern Novel.

5. Visiting me at the weight loss retreat center, Marlene brought me a sausage and cheese pizza, soda, and a gallon of ice cream.

Use of Dashes and Parentheses

Commas, dashes, and parentheses can all be used to show an interruption of the main idea. The particular form of punctuation you choose depends on the degree of interruption.

RULE **1**   Use dashes for a less formal and more emphatic interruption of the main idea. Dashes are seldom used in formal writing.

He came—I thought—by car.

She arrived—and I know this for a fact—in a pink Cadillac.

RULE **2**   Use parentheses to insert extra information that some of your readers might want to know but that is not at all essential for the main idea. Such information is not emphasized.

Johann Sebastian Bach (1685–1750) composed the six Brandenburg Concertos.

Plea bargaining (see Section 4.3) was developed to speed court verdicts.

PRACTICE **12**   **Insert dashes or parentheses wherever needed.**

1. Herbert Simon is and I don't think this is an exaggeration a genius.

2. George Eliot her real name was Mary Ann Evans wrote *Silas Marner*.

3. You should in fact, I insist see a doctor.

4. Unemployment brings with it a number of other problems see the study by Brody, 2010.

5. Mass media television, radio, movies, magazines, and newspapers are able to transmit information over a wide range and to a large number of people.

EXERCISE **10**   **Other Marks of Punctuation**

In each of the following sentences, insert marks of punctuation wherever they are needed. Choose from quotation marks, semicolon, colon, dashes, and parentheses.

1. To measure crime, sociologists have used three different techniques official statistics, victimization surveys, and self-report studies.

2. The Bells is one of the best-loved poems of Edgar Allan Poe.

3. The lake has one major disadvantage to swimmers this summer weeds.

4. E. B. White wrote numerous essays for adults however, he also wrote some very popular books for children.

5. Tuberculosis also known as consumption has once again become a serious health issue.

6. The Victorian Period 1837–1901 saw a rapid expansion of industry.

7. He promised me I know he promised that he would come to my graduation.

8. Do you know what the French expression déjà vu means?

9. She wanted to go to the movies he wanted to watch a movie at home.

10. She has the qualifications needed for the job a teaching degree, a pleasant personality, two years' experience, and a love of children.

EXERCISE **11**   **Other Marks of Punctuation**

In each of the following sentences, insert marks of punctuation wherever they are needed. Choose from quotation marks, semicolon, colon, dashes, and parentheses.

1. Many young people have two feelings about science and technology awe and fear.

2. The three people who helped work out the real estate transaction were Mr. Doyle, the realtor Mrs. White, the bank officer and Scott Castle, the lawyer.

3. The book was titled *American Literature The Twentieth Century*.

4. I decided to walk to school, she said, because the bus fare has been raised again.

5. She brought the following items to the beach towel, sunglasses, sunscreen, a beach chair, and several books.

6. The conference I believe it is scheduled for sometime in January will focus on the development of a new curriculum.

7. The song Memories comes from the Broadway show *Cats*.

8. The complex lab experiment has these two major problems too many difficult calculations and too many variables.

9. The mutt that is to say, my dog is smarter than he looks.

10. Violent crime cannot be reduced unless the society supports efforts such as strengthening the family structure, educating the young, and recruiting top-notch police.

EXERCISE **12**   **Other Marks of Punctuation**

In each of the following sentences, insert marks of punctuation wherever they are needed. Choose from quotation marks, semicolon, colon, dashes, and parentheses.

1. Boomerang child was a new term in the dictionary of 2011 and means a young adult who returns to live at his or her family home, especially for financial reasons.

2. My father enjoyed spending money my mother was frugal.

3. The student's short story Ten Steps to Nowhere appeared in a collection titled *The Best of Student Writing*.

4. The report stated specifically that the company must if it wants to grow sell off at least 10 percent of its property.

5. The foreign countries she visited were Mexico, Israel, and Morocco.

6. Remember, the doctor told the patient, the next time I see you, I want to see an improvement in your condition.

7. These students made the high school honor roll Luis Sanchez, Julie Carlson, and Tenesha Moore.

8. The chemist showed the students a container of NaCl salt and asked them to identify the granules.

9. He said that he would give us an extension on our term papers.

10. The work was tedious nevertheless, the goal of finding the solution kept him motivated.

Mastery and Editing Tests

TEST **Editing for Correct Capitalization and Punctuation**

In each of the following sentences, insert correct capitalization and marks of punctuation wherever they are needed.

1. Many people no matter their background feel that the job search process can be intimidating.

2. Unless they come from career-focused schools many graduates arent trained for this.

3. Of the five phases in the job search process the first two can set the tone for the rest of the search.

4. The first phase is knowing what you can offer but you must also learn what your target career expects of you.

5. One job searcher spent an entire week in june simply looking up job postings in her field reading the descriptions and taking notes.

6. Even though she lived in richmond virginia job posts from New York city still informed her about workplace expectancy.

7. After she made lists of her qualifications and matched them to the expectancies of the workforce she was ready to begin phase two writing her master resume and master cover letter.

8. Her resume s profile was influenced by the language she had seen on the various job postings.

9. She had learned that overused phrases like team player could be replaced by more descriptive phrases like experience with collaborating and performing cross-functionally.

10. This job searcher s process a job in and of itself was approached in a positive orderly and humble manner.

TEST **2** **Editing for Correct Capitalization and Punctuation**

Read the following paragraph and insert the correct capitalization and marks of punctuation wherever they are needed.

[1]The expression your name is mud has its origin in a person from history. [2]Samuel Mudd was a doctor in Maryland during the civil war. [3]About 4 a.m. on april 15 1856 at his home in charles county Maryland dr. Mudd was awakened by men who needed medical attention. [4]One was john wilkes booth who had just shot

president Abraham Lincoln at ford's theatre in Washington d.c. ⁵Mudd set and bandaged booth s broken leg before the assassin went on his way. ⁶A few days later the doctor was arrested and charged with being part of the conspiracy to kill the president. ⁷He was convicted by a military court and sentenced to life in prison but in 1869 president Andrew Johnson commuted his sentence. ⁸Since that time dr. Mudd s descendants have tried without success to overturn that original conviction. ⁹One politician united states representative Steny Hoyer introduced a bill (the Samuel Mudd relief act) that would have cleared the doctor's name but it failed to pass. ¹⁰after yet another setback Richard Mudd the grandson of Samuel Mudd made a statement to reporters. ¹¹As long as the United States lasts the tragic story of my 31-year-old grandfather given a life sentence for setting a broken leg is never going to end. ¹² Sadly Dr. Richard Mudd died in 2002 after 70 years of trying to clear his grandfather s name.

TEST ③ Editing for Correct Capitalization and Punctuation

Read the following paragraph and insert the correct capitalization and marks of punctuation wherever they are needed.

Victorian Traditions/Shutterstock.com

¹Valentine s day is celebrated on february 14 as a romantic festival. ²People send their sweethearts greeting cards that say won t you be my valentine? ³echildren like to make their own cards from paper doilies red construction paper bright foils and samples of wallpaper. ⁴All of these customs probably have their origin in the ancient roman festival of lupercalia which took place every winter. ⁵The festival honored juno the goddess of women and marriage and pan the god of nature. ⁶According to the book *popular antiquities* which was written in 1877 England began observing this holiday as early as 1446. ⁷In the united states the holiday became popular after the civil war. ⁸Admirers today continue to send their sweethearts cards chocolates and flowers.

TEST ④   Editing Student Writing Using Editing Symbols

In the following paragraph, ten errors are marked with editing symbols. Correct each error on the lines provided after the paragraph. The symbol for a capitalization error is *cap*, and the symbol for a punctuation error is *punc*.

¹When I was growing up in Honduras, my G̲rͨaͣnpdmother made me a delicious cup of hot chocolate every morning. ²I've only recently learned about its interesting history. ³Chocolate is made from the seeds of the fruit of the cacao tree w̲hͦich is an unusual plant that produces flowers and fruits on its trunk, not on its branches. ⁴The story of chocolate goes back to its origins in c̲eͨnͣtpral America more than 1,500 years ago. ⁵Recently, t̲hͦeͦy ͦffound a piece of chocolate in a tomb that dates back to 600 BC. ⁶The ancient m̲aͨyͣap made the cacao into a d̲rͦiͦnͦkͦ but it was the foam, not the liquid, that they most enjoyed. ⁷Scientists had a̲lͮwbays believe that the common people had not been allowed access to cacao plants, but this idea was proved wrong. ⁸Cacao plants were found in the ashes of the ancient Salvadoran village of Ceren. ⁹A v̲iͦlͦlͦagge that had been buried by a volcano in 590. ¹⁰The people of Ceren made beautiful ceramics into which they mixed cacao p̲aͦsͦtͦeͦ vanilla chilies and other spices to concoct a delicious drink. ¹¹In some marketplaces in southern Mexico, it is still possible to buy a similar drink, referred to by the locals as p̲oͦpͦo. ¹²You are lucky if you have the opportunity to sample a cup.

Corrections

1. capitalization (sentence 1): _____

2. punctuation (sentence 3) subordination: _____

_____

_____

_____

3. capitalization (sentence 4): _____

4. pronoun reference (sentence 5): no antecedent _____

5. capitalization (sentence 6): _____

6. punctuation (sentence 6): coordination _____

_____

7. verb form (sentence 7): _____

8. fragment (sentence 9) : _____

_____

_____

_____

_____

9. punctuation (sentence 10): items in a series _____

_____

_____

_____

_____

10. punctuation (sentence 11) special term: _____

WRITE FOR SUCCESS

Part of success in college, in a career, or in running a household depends on a person's ability to organize all of his or her responsibilities. Write a response that explains your plan to organize this current week or month of your life. How will you organize your days to ensure that you have the necessary time put aside to complete your college assignments?

Working Together

Writing a Review: Eating Out

Newspapers and magazines hire writers to review movies and plays, restaurants, concerts, art gallery openings, and other events. You might think that being paid to eat out would be the perfect way to earn a living!

Read the following newspaper review of a typical neighborhood restaurant. The review contains important information that a customer would need to know, such as location, days and hours of operation, menu, atmosphere, price, and other special features.

Eating Out

If you appreciate authentic Chinese food, you should go for lunch or dinner to the Golden Fortune Restaurant, located at 99 Elm Avenue in Ellington. It is just above the South Side Plaza, walking distance from the center of town. The Golden Fortune Restaurant is the kind of restaurant you will want to visit more than once. The food is expertly prepared, the prices are moderate, and the service is always friendly. We particularly liked the warm and relaxed atmosphere, partly the result of soft classical music playing in the background.

Many of the lunch and dinner selections at the Golden Fortune are traditional, with a few surprises. All of the vegetables used are fresh, and a special section of the menu is devoted to dieters. The appetizers are large enough to serve two people. On our first visit, we were delighted with the combination platter. It is the most popular appetizer on the menu because it allows diners to sample a half dozen of the house specialties.

One unique touch at this restaurant is the choice of twenty-four different teas. Instead of having an ordinary pot of green tea placed in front of you, as in most Chinese restaurants, at the Golden Fortune you can choose from a wide variety. These include green tea with passion fruit, peach tea, and even milk tea with oatmeal. Customers enjoy trying new combinations each time they visit. Our favorite is the black tea with plum. If you like, you may bring your own wine or beer, and the waiters will be happy to serve it.

Some of the most popular main courses are beef with garlic sauce, crispy honey chicken on a bed of rice and vegetables, and a variety of delicious stir-fry dishes. If you choose a stir-fry at the Golden Fortune, you may select a favorite sauce and type of noodle along with a meat or fish, and the kitchen will make up the dish you want.

The Golden Fortune is open for lunch from noon to 4 p.m. and for dinner from 5 p.m. until 11 p.m. every day of the week. No reservations are needed. For takeout orders, call 548-4407 after 11 a.m.

Divide into groups of five. Each group should decide on a restaurant or event to review and list the basic subjects that will be covered in that review. Each person in the group should then select one subject and write a paragraph of at least five sentences about it. Return to the group to listen to each other's paragraphs as they are read. Decide on the best order for the paragraphs, and together compose an introduction and conclusion for the piece. Then put these paragraphs together to construct a complete review.

PORTFOLIO SUGGESTION

Keep this review in your portfolio. Whenever you go to a restaurant, musical event, or movie, keep in mind that these are all places where reviewers go and write down their reactions. You can, too!

PART 3

National Archives

Understanding the Power of Words

Find Your Voice

Many people are content to keep their thoughts to themselves. They are often reluctant to make their voices heard. Now that you are in college, however, you will be encouraged to express your ideas, both vocally and in writing. College is the time to evaluate your beliefs, find your voice, and speak up. Your voice is vital, whether as a student, an employee in the workplace, or a citizen who is part of a community. Our families, schools, workplaces, and institutions need your voice.

Choosing Words That Work

- What are those ideas that you are passionate about?
- What values do you believe are worth fighting for?

Choosing Words That Work

14

CHAPTER OBJECTIVES

The right choice of words is always critical for a writer's finished product. In this chapter, you will explore ways to improve your word choices.

- use words rich in meaning
- understand the denotations and connotations of words
- avoid wordiness:
  - redundant expressions
  - wordy phrases
  - overuse of the verb *to be*
  - unnecessary repetition of the same word
  - unnecessary use of *there is* or *there are*
  - flowery or pretentious language
  - apologetic, tentative expressions
- avoid language inappropriate for formal writing:
  - slang
  - clipped language
  - sexist language
  - trite expressions (clichés)

Using Words Rich in Meaning

Writing involves a constant search to find the right words to express thoughts and feelings as accurately as possible. When a writer wants to be precise or wants to give a certain flavor to a piece of writing, the creative possibilities for word choice and sentence construction are almost endless. The creative writer looks for words that have rich and appropriate meanings and associations.

For instance, if you were describing a person under five years of age, you might choose one of these words:

imp	brat	preschooler	child
toddler	tot	youngster	infant

Some words have no associations beyond their strict dictionary meaning; these words are said to be neutral. Which words in the above list do you consider neutral, communicating no negative or positive emotional associations?* Some of these words suggest a child's age or stage of development. A person writing a brochure for a nursery school would probably choose the word *preschooler* because it typically

*Your answer should be *child*.

identifies a child as between the ages of three and five. A person talking about a child who has just learned to walk might use the word *toddler* because it carries the association of a small child who is toddling along a bit unsteadily. What informal and unkind word might an angry older sibling shout when a younger brother or sister has just colored all over a favorite book?† When you write, choosing the word with the appropriate connotations will give your writing richness and depth.

EXERCISE **1**   **Using Words Rich in Meaning**

The five words in Column A all have the basic meaning of *confident*. However, an additional meaning makes each word richer and more specific. Match each word in Column A with the letter of the definition from Column B that best fits the word.

Column A	Column B
_____ 1. bold	a. characterized by a sense of superiority, self-importance, or entitlement
_____ 2. courageous	b. arrogant; pertly self-assertive; conceited
_____ 3. cocky	c. not influenced or controlled by others in matters of opinion, conduct, etc.; thinking or acting for oneself
_____ 4. arrogant	d. not deterred by danger or pain; brave
_____ 5. independent	e. not hesitating or fearful in the face of actual or possible danger or rebuff; courageous

Most languages are rich with words that describe eating. Column A contains several words that mean *to eat*. Match each word in Column A with the letter of the definition from Column B that best fits the word.

Column A	Column B
_____ 1. taste	a. to eat with small quick bites
_____ 2. devour	b. to bite or chew on something persistently
_____ 3. nibble	c. to eat between meals
_____ 4. gorge	d. to test the flavor of a food
_____ 5. gnaw	e. to stuff oneself with food
_____ 6. snack	f. to eat up greedily

EXERCISE **2**   **Using Words Rich in Meaning**

The words *eat, drink, song, and walk* are neutral words (having no positive or negative associations). Each neutral term is followed by four words, each one with its own precise meaning. In each case, give a definition for the word. Use your dictionary.

Example: crunch: <u>to eat with a noisy, crackling sound</u>

†Your answer should be *brat*.

to eat

1. gobble: _____

2. savor: _____

3. munch: _____

4. devour: _____

to drink

1. sip: _____

2. gulp: _____

3. slurp: _____

4. lap: _____

a song

1. aria: _____

2. lullaby: _____

3. ballad: _____

4. hymn: _____

to walk

1. lumber: _____

2. amble: _____

3. stride: _____

4. roam: _____

Understanding Loaded Words: Denotation/Connotation

The careful writer considers more than the dictionary meaning of a word. Some words have different meanings for different people.

> The **denotation** of a word is its strict dictionary meaning. The **connotation** of a word is the meaning (apart from the dictionary meaning) that a person attaches to a word because of that individual's personal experience with the word.
>
> | | |
> |---|---|
> | **Word:** | hacker (noun) |
> | **Denotation (computers):** | a person who uses computers to gain unauthorized access to data |
> | **Possible connotations:** | thief, pirate, data liberator, rebel, one who enjoys the intellectual challenge of creatively overcoming or circumventing limitations |

Computer users, the FBI, and journalists all understand word connotations differently. Consider the term *hacker*. It is easy to see a range of biases and associations appear when people discuss hackers. Some may think of a thief. Others might fear a dangerous outlaw. Somebody else might picture a gamer trying to solve a complex riddle. Still others imagine a computer programmer working on the side of justice. The dictionary meaning of *hacker* is "a person who uses computers to gain unauthorized access to data." This definition does not address the ethics or legality of hacking. Your personal experience with the word may be influenced by news reports, movies, the Internet, or even having been hacked yourself.

Choosing words that are not neutral but that have more exact or appropriate meanings is a powerful skill for a writer, one that will help your reader better understand the ideas you want to communicate. As your vocabulary grows, your writing will become richer and deeper. Your work will reflect your understanding of the many shades of meaning that words can have.

EXERCISE 3   **Denotation/Connotation**

In this exercise, you have the opportunity to think of words that are richer in associations than the neutral words underlined in the sentences below. Write your own word choice in the space to the right of each sentence. Discuss with others in your class the associations you make with the words you have chosen.

1. I live in a <u>house</u> not far from downtown.   _____

2. I <u>walk</u> home from work every night.   _____

3. Usually the same <u>person</u> is always walking behind me.   _____

4. He is always carrying a lot of <u>stuff</u>.   _____

5. He looks as if he is <u>old</u>.   _____

6. He has <u>marks</u> all over his face.   _____

7. Sometimes I try to <u>talk</u> with him.   _____

8. He has such <u>damaged</u> clothing.   _____

9. Sometimes I can hear him <u>talking</u> to himself.   _____

10. At night when I am <u>sitting</u> in my favorite armchair, I often think of him and wish he could tell me the story of his life.   _____

EXERCISE 4   **Denotation/Connotation**

Each of the following sentences contains a word or phrase that has positive or negative associations for some people. Read each sentence and study the underlined word or phrase. Below each sentence, write the emotional meaning the underlined word or phrase has for you. Discuss your answers with your classmates. An example follows.

Sentence: Her <u>brother</u> went with her so that she would not have to drive alone.

Explanation: The word *brother* usually has a positive connotation. We expect a brother to be someone who is helpful and protective.

1. The <u>dog</u> stood at the door; it practically took up the whole doorway.

   _____

   _____

2. The <u>foreigner</u> had been working at the ranch for months.

   _____

   _____

3. His <u>pickup truck</u> was parked in front of the garage.

   _____

   _____

4. A woman and child were peering through the chain-link <u>fence</u>.

   _____

   _____

5. The <u>farmhand</u> carried a long object of some kind.

   _____

   _____

EXERCISE **5**   **Denotation/Connotation**

When you write, you create a tone by the words you choose. Review the sentences you worked with in Exercise 4. For each sentence, create a more positive tone, either by changing the underlined word or phrase to a different word or phrase or by adding adjectives to modify the underlined word or phrase.

1. _____

   _____

2. _____

   _____

3. _____

   _____

4. _____

_____

5. _____

_____

Wordiness: In Writing, Less Can Be More!

In his book *The Elements of Style,* the famous writer E. B. White quotes his old teacher William Strunk Jr., who said that a sentence "should contain no unnecessary words" and a paragraph "no unnecessary sentences." Strunk's philosophy of writing also includes the commandment he gave many times in his classes at Cornell University: "Omit needless words!" It was a lesson that E. B. White took to heart, with the wonderful results that we see in his own writing.

Following is a summary of some important ways you can cut the number of your words to strengthen the power of your ideas. Read each example of wordiness, and notice how the revision makes the idea more concise.

1. Redundant expressions   **Revisions**

circle around   circle

blue in color   blue

past history   history

connect together   connect

true fact   fact

surrounded on all sides   surrounded

very unique   unique

2. Wordy phrases   **Revisions**

in the event that   if

due to the fact that   because

for the stated reason that   because

in this day and age   today

at this point in time   now

in the neighborhood of   about

3. Overuse of the verb *to be*   **Revisions**

The man is in need of help.   The man needs help.

They are of the opinion that a lawyer should be They believe a lawyer should
called.   be called.

4. Unnecessary repetition of the same word   **Revision**

The book is on the table. The book is my favorite.   The book on the table is my
I have read the book five times.   favorite. I have read it five
                                                     times.

5. **Unnecessary use of *there is* or *there are***	**Revisions**
There are two major disadvantages to the new proposal.	The new proposal has two major disadvantages.
There is no doubt but that the sun will rise tomorrow.	No doubt the sun will rise tomorrow.
6. **Flowery or pretentious language**	**Revision**
It is delightful to contemplate the culinary experience we will enjoy after the termination of this cinematic event.	I can't wait until we have pizza after the movie.
7. **Apologetic, tentative expressions**	**Revisions**
In my opinion, the grading policy for this course should be changed.	The grading policy for this course should be changed.
Right now, it seems to me that finding a job in my field is very difficult.	Right now, finding a job in my field is very difficult.
In this paper, I will try to explain my views on censorship of the campus newspaper.	Censoring the campus newspaper is a mistake.

EXERCISE ⑥ **Revising Wordy Sentences**

In each of the following sentences, underline the wordy phrase. Then revise each sentence to avoid wordiness.

1. The date for the final completion of your project is a week from this Friday.

   _____

   _____

2. The thought of the exam is causing her to be in a constant state of tension.

   _____

3. There is no better place to study than in our library.

   _____

4. Some people have the belief that astrology is a science.

   _____

5. We are all in need of better organizational skills.

   _____

6. As far as mechanical ability is concerned, Mike is very handy.

   _____

7. She is in the process of wrapping a present.

   _____

8. Due to the fact of the rain, the concert might be canceled.

   _____

9. In my opinion, it would seem to me that the causes for unemployment are complex.

   _____

10. The box had an oblong shape.

    _____

EXERCISE ⑦   **Revising Wordy Sentences**

In each of the following sentences, underline the wordy phrase. Then revise each sentence to avoid wordiness.

1. The academic advisor is of a kindly nature.

   _____

2. I was told he is a male actor.

   _____

3. The price was in the neighborhood of fifty dollars.

   _____

4. In regard to the package, it was sent to the wrong address.

   _____

5. It is everyone's duty to be in attendance at the meeting today. (Avoid the verb *to be*.)

   _____

6. My best friend is above me in height.

   _____

7. I tiptoed down the stairs on my toes in order to surprise everyone.

   _____

8. They made the discovery that I was not upstairs.

   _____

9. A member of the teaching staff at this institution of higher learning failed to submit in a timely fashion the fruits of my endeavors for the course during this entire period from September to December.

   _____

10. Even though I am not an expert, I think that more neighborhood health clinics are needed.

    _____

Recognizing Language Appropriate for Formal Writing

When we have conversations with family and friends, or when we write to them, we use informal language. This relaxed use of language may include slang and other informal words and phrases familiar to our particular group or region. When we write or speak in public, however, we need to use more formal language. In this case, slang is not appropriate, nor is it appropriate to use any words that could be considered sexist or disrespectful of any individual or group.

> **Slang** is a term that refers to special words or expressions used by a particular group of people, often with the intention of keeping that meaning private. One characteristic of a slang word or expression is that it is often used only for a limited time and then forgotten. For example:
>
> The party was *swell*. (1940s)
>
> The party was *groovy*. (1960s)
>
> The party was *awesome*. (1980s)
>
> The party was *phat*. (1990s)
>
> The party was *hot*. (2000s)
>
> The party was on *fleek*. (2010s)

Slang or informal words	Acceptable words
bucks / dough	dollars
kids	children
a bummer / drag	a bad experience
off the wall / cray	crazy
yummy	delicious
chow / grub	food

> **Clipped language** refers to the use of shortened words to make communication more relaxed and informal. Clipped language is not appropriate in more formal writing, which requires standard English.

Clipped language	Acceptable words
doc	doctor
pro	professional
info	information
rep	reputation
stats	statistics

Sexist language refers to the use of single-gender nouns or pronouns to apply to both men and women. This was standard usage in the past, but writers and publishers today avoid such language.

Sexist language: Everyone must bring *his* project on Tuesday.

Options for revising sexist language:

1. Use plural pronouns and plural antecedents.

   **All** students must bring _**their**_ projects on Tuesday.

2. Change the pronoun to an article.

   **Everyone** must bring _**a**_ project on Tuesday.

3. Replace a single-gender term with an inclusive term.

   **Everyone** must bring _**his or her**_ project on Tuesday.

4. Use the passive voice, thus avoiding the need for a pronoun.

   Projects must be brought to class on Tuesday.

5. Use a gender-neutral term.

   Sexist language: **The teacher is an important _man_. _He_ can influence the lives of many children in a community.**

   Nonsexist language: **The teacher is an important _person_ who can influence the lives of many children in the community.**

The following partial list of sexist terms is accompanied by present-day acceptable forms.

Sexist terms	*Acceptable terms*
businessman	business executive, businessperson
chairman	chairperson
common man	average person
congressman	member of congress, legislator
fireman	firefighter
forefathers	ancestors
mailman	mail carrier, postal worker
mankind	humanity, people
salesman	sales associate, salesperson, sales representative
stewardess	flight attendant

> **Trite expressions** (or **clichés**) are expressions that may have been fresh at one time but now have become stale from overuse.

Trite expressions	*Acceptable expressions*
cool as a cucumber	calm
mad as a hornet	angry
a golden opportunity	an exceptional opportunity
light as a feather	light
busy as a bee	busy
dead as a doornail	dead
slowly but surely	gradually
without rhyme or reason	senseless

EXERCISE ⑧ ## Recognizing Language Inappropriate for Formal Writing

The following sentences contain words that are informal, slang, sexist, or trite. Circle the word or phrase in each sentence that is inappropriate for formal writing, and on the line to the right of each sentence, provide a more formal word or expression to replace the inappropriate one.

1. My ex couldn't tell a story without beating around the bush. _____

2. Friday evening is a good time to chill out. _____

3. She told the dude to get out of her sight. _____

4. The businessmen in the community support the science project. _____

5. It is time to come clean with the director. _____

6. The first experiment turned out to be a downer. _____

7. The scientist has guts to continue the research. _____

8. The entire lab is a dump. _____

9. The guys often spend the night there. _____

10. They work until two or three in the morning and then crash. _____

EXERCISE ⑨   **Recognizing Language Inappropriate for Formal Writing**

The following sentences contain words that are informal, slang, sexist, or trite. Circle the word or phrase in each sentence that is inappropriate for formal writing, and on the line to the right of each sentence, provide a more formal word or expression to replace the inappropriate one.

1. Don't bug me about studying.   _____

2. I aced the last French test.   _____

3. Bring me some grub, I've got the munchies.   _____

4. He's my buddy .   _____

5. How crummy is the weather outside?   _____

6. The bodybuilder is as strong as an ox .   _____

7. He was well-known on the block.   _____

8. The medical doctor is a well-respected person in most communities; he is considered a role model for our children.   _____

9. I think it's gonna be nice tomorrow.   _____

10. I ain't seen the new neighbors yet.   _____

Studying a Student Essay for Word Choices

ACTIVITY ①   **Making Better Word Choices**

When Sandra Russell wrote an essay on the experience of living through a tornado, she composed more than one draft. Below are six sentences that she could have written when she worked on the first draft of her essay. Rewrite each sentence, focusing particularly on revising the underlined words. Your revisions could include different word choices or additional words, phrases, and clauses that make the sentences more descriptive and interesting.

1. All afternoon, <u>clouds were forming</u>. (*Add more descriptive detail.*)

   _____

   _____

2. I could <u>hear the wind blow and expected thunder and lightning</u>. (*Add more descriptive detail.*)

   _____

   _____

3. She <u>took</u> my hand and <u>took</u> me to the storm cellar. (*Choose more descriptive verbs.*)

_____

_____

4. We <u>sat</u> in the <u>cellar</u>. *(Choose more descriptive words.)*

_____

_____

5. <u>Stuff</u> lay around our yard. *(Be more specific.)*

_____

_____

6. <u>The storm</u> came through my neighborhood, <u>destroying lots of property</u>. *(Be more specific.)*

_____

_____

ACTIVITY ➋   Sharing Sentence Revisions

Share your revised sentences with other members of your class. For each of the six sentences, choose three revised examples for the class to review.

ACTIVITY ➌   Working with a Student Essay

Read the complete student essay out loud. Following the reading, search the essay to discover how Sandra Russell expressed the six ideas you revised in Activity 1. Underline the six sentences as you find them. Discuss with class members how these ideas were successfully expressed by the student writer.

Perspectives - Jeff Smith/Shutterstock.com

BAD WEATHER

I was born in Booneville, Arkansas, and grew up on a small farm about five miles south of Paris. Naturally, I grew up in an area where tornados are feared each spring. I didn't really understand this until one humid, still night in April of 1985.

All afternoon, dark threatening clouds had been building up in the west, blocking out the sun. I could see the lightning dance about the sky as the thunder responded by shaking the ground beneath my feet. The wind softly stirred the tree tops but then quickly died as it got darker and darker.

I walked outside and listened to the silence ringing in my ears. In the distance, I could hear a rumble, soft at first but slowly and steadily intensifying. My mom came outside and stood at my side and listened to the rumbling noise. Everything

(continued on next page)

was still; nothing dared to move. Even my dog Moose lay quietly, as if punished, in his doghouse. It was almost as if he knew what was about to happen.

"Mama, what's that noise?" I asked her, but she didn't answer. She grabbed my hand and dragged me to the storm cellar. I didn't have time to argue with her before I heard the rumble nearly upon us. We huddled in the musty-smelling cellar. The roar was so loud it hurt my ears. I could hear the whistling of the wind above us. I cried and screamed for the awful noise of the whistle to stop, but no one could hear me above the ferocious noise. The rumble barreled on us, and it seemed as if it would never end. The air was still in the dark cellar, but I could hear it as it moved violently above our heads. I didn't think the thundering noise would ever end.

I hadn't realized that I had quit breathing until it finally stopped. I drew a quick breath and thanked God it was over and my mother and I were safe. We crawled out of the cellar and took the first real look at our home. Trees were uprooted. Glass and boards and even a stop sign lay scattered around our yard. The roof on our house was damaged and a few windows were broken out, but that was all. Even most of our animals had survived that day, including Moose.

That night is one that I'll never forget. A moderately sized tornado (about an F3 on the Fujita scale) ripped through my neighborhood, destroying ten houses and damaging fifty others. No tornado warnings had been issued for that area until ten minutes after it was already over. Luckily, no one was seriously injured. The local television station didn't even bother to comment on its mistake. Until that night I had never realized how an event could change the way you feel about something for the rest of your life. Now I look at the television and see tornado, hurricane, and even flood victims with new eyes. They are real, just like me.

by Sandra Russell

Mastery and Editing Tests

TEST **1** **Student Writing: Editing for Inappropriate Language**

Each sentence in the following paragraph contains at least one example of inappropriate language. Underline the inappropriate words, and then rewrite the paragraph, revising any language that is not appropriate in formal writing.

When my sis was hired by a major electronics company last summer, we were a little worried about her. She had flunked math in school, so we wondered if she had chosen the right kind of company. The person who had the job before her was let go because he had an attitude. Imagine our surprise when she soon announced that she had been selected chairman of an important committee at work. She said that she really didn't want to be in a leadership position, but we all knew she was nuts about it.

_____

_____

_____

_____

_____

_____

_____

TEST ❷ **Student Writing: Editing for Wordiness**

Below are a student's beginning thoughts about teenagers hanging out at the mall. On the lines that follow, revise the paragraph to eliminate wordiness.

In this day and age, the mall is the most popular place for a large number of American teenagers to gather. I am of the opinion that the suburban mall encourages young people to want and desire things and stuff they cannot afford and probably don't need. This results and ends in a constant feeling of dissatisfaction. People from other countries look at these young people and conclude that American culture is much too materialistic. Why don't parents insist that teenagers and adolescents involve themselves in clubs, organized sports, volunteer organizations, musical groups, and other more productive and satisfying activities? I would like to say that the mall is good in one sense: it is a relatively safe place for kids to hang out and congregate. However, owing to the more negative effects of hanging out at malls, I have arrived at the conclusion that parents should encourage other activities for their teenagers.

TEST 3 **Editing for Wordiness and Inappropriate Language**

The following paragraph contains examples of wordiness as well as inappropriate language (slang, clipped words, and sexist terms). Underline each problem as you find it, and then revise the paragraph. (*Hint*: Fifteen words or phrases need revision. Find and revise at least ten.)

One of the most outstanding scientists in the U.S. came from China in 1936. She is Chien-Hsiung Wu, and her story is the story of how she greatly influenced the development of physics. When Miss Wu came to America in 1936, she intended to do grad work and hightail it back to China. However, World War II broke out, and she remained to teach at Smith College, where she enjoyed working with the Smithies. Very soon after that, she was employed by Princeton U. At that time, she was the only girl physicist hired by a top research university. Later, she became an important workman on Columbia University's Manhattan Project, the project that developed the A bomb. She hunkered down at Columbia for more than thirty years, her many scientific discoveries bringing her world recognition. In 1990, Chien-Hsiung Wu became the first living scientist to have an asteroid named in her honor. This celestial object whirling in the darkest corners of outer space is now carrying her name.

_____

_____

_____

_____

_____

_____

_____

_____

_____

_____

_____

_____

WRITE FOR SUCCESS

What do you consider to be your core values? Perhaps they include spirituality, family life, career success, or independence. Write a response that explains the values that matter to you most.

Working Together

Alina Vincent Photography, LLC/Getty Images

Being Tactful in the Workplace

Words are charged with meanings that can be either encouraging and supportive or hurtful and wounding. Although workers in government offices and other public places are there to help the public, they often are so overworked that they do not always respond in positive ways. Below are several comments or questions that might be heard in an office where a person has gone to get help. In each case, revise the language so that the comment or question is more encouraging.

1. I don't have any idea what you're talking about.

   _____

   _____

2. Why don't you learn to write so people can read it?

   _____

   _____

3. We don't accept sloppy applications.

   _____

   _____

4. How old are you anyway?

   _____

   _____

5. Can't you read directions?

   _____

   _____

6. What's the matter with you? Why can't you understand this simple procedure?

   _____

   _____

7. I don't have time today for people like you!

   _____

   _____

Share your revisions with each other. Then, as a class, discuss some individual experiences in which the use of language made you or someone you know feel hurt or upset. These experiences may have occurred at a campus office, a local bank, or a local shop. How could a change of language have improved each situation?

279

PORTFOLIO SUGGESTION

Using the "Working Together" Activity and class discussion, write about one of the following:

- Discuss the importance of using polite language in the workplace. (You can use the examples given during the classroom discussion.)

- Give advice to employers on how to train employees to speak in an encouraging and supportive way while on the job.

- Describe the difficulty workers have when customers or clients are rude. (If you have had a job, you may have experienced such a situation. How did you deal with it?)

- Over the course of the semester, keep a record of actual incidents that happen to you in which the language used was less than respectful. In the future, you could write an essay analyzing each situation and suggesting how the experiences could have been more positive.

Paying Attention to Look-Alikes and Sound-Alikes

15

CHAPTER OBJECTIVES

In this chapter, you will focus on forty-eight sets of words that are frequently confused.

- Group I: ten sets of words that sound alike

- Group II: ten additional sets of words that sound alike

- Group III: five sets of words including contractions that sound like other words

- Group IV: ten sets of words that sound or look almost alike

- Group V: ten additional sets of words that sound or look almost alike

- Group VI: three sets of verbs that are often confused: *lay/lie, raise/rise,* and *set/sit*

Many words in English are confusing because they either look alike or sound alike but are spelled differently and have completely different meanings. Every student needs to watch out for these troublesome words, often called "look-alikes" and "sound-alikes." Students whose first language is not English will find this chapter especially helpful.

In this chapter, words that are often confused have been grouped into six manageable sections so that you can study each section in one sitting. Within each set of confused words, each word is defined and used in a sentence. After you have studied the spellings and definitions, fill in the blanks with the correct words. Master each group before you proceed to the next.

Group I: Words That Sound Alike

aural/oral

aural (adj):   related to hearing
oral (adj):   related to the mouth

The ear specialist gave the child an *aural* exam.

The dentist urged him to improve his *oral* hygiene.

The student dreaded giving _____ reports in class because a high fever

had caused _____ nerve damage and affected his hearing.

capital/capitol

capital (adj):   ¹adding financial value; ²fatal
capital (noun):   ¹leading city; ²money
capitol (noun):   a legislative building

The new addition is a *capital* improvement on their home.

The governor opposes *capital* punishment.

The *capital* [leading city] of Wyoming is Cheyenne.

The retailer has *capital* to invest in remodeling.

The dome of the state *capitol* [legislative building] is gold.

She needed _____ to rebuild her home, but she first went to the _____ [legislative building] to obtain needed permits.

close/clothes

close (verb):   to shut
close (noun):   end or conclusion
clothes (noun):   garments

Please *close* the door.

Finally, the war came to a *close*.

The *clothes* were from the local women's store.

NOTE: Cloth is a piece of fabric, not to be confused with the word *clothes*, which as a noun is always plural.

The *cloth* for the table was my mother's.

Because she wanted to buy new _____, she was glad she didn't _____ her checking account.

coarse/course

coarse (adj):   [1]rough, not fine in texture; [2] lacking in refinement, vulgar
course (noun):   [1]direction; [2]part of a meal; [3]unit of study

The coat was made from a *coarse* tweed.

He told a *coarse* joke.

What is the *course* of the plane?

The main *course* of the meal was served.

English is a required *course* at my school.

A few students in that _____ complained about the teaching assistant's _____ comments.

complement/ compliment

complement (noun):   [1]what is required to make a thing complete; [2]something that completes
complement (verb):   to complete
compliment (noun):   an expression of praise
compliment (verb):   to praise

The kitchen has a full *complement* of pots and pans.

Her shoes *complement* the outfit.

The chef received a *compliment* on his dessert.

The food critic *complimented* the chef.

Because the library had such a full _____ of books in my field, I felt I had

to _____ the librarian.

forward/foreword		
forward (verb):	to send a letter or a package to another address	
forward (adj):	[1]bold or pushy; [2]going toward the front or the future	
forward (adv):	toward the front or the future	
foreword (noun):	introduction to a book, usually written by someone other than the author of the book	

Please *forward* my mail.

She was so *forward*, she pushed her way in.

He took one step *forward*.

Read the *foreword* first.

Even though the book was written by his colleague, the new professor was so

_____ as to severely criticize its _____.

passed/past		
passed (verb):	(past tense of *to pass*) to move ahead or to move by	
past (noun):	the time before the present	
past (prep):	beyond	
past (adj):	no longer current	

She *passed* the library.

Don't live in the *past*.

He walked *past* the house.

Her *past* failures have been forgotten.

Walking _____ the professor's message board, he found out he had

_____ both tests that he had taken during the _____ week.

peace/piece		
peace (noun):	the absence of war; inner contentment	
piece (noun):	a part or portion of a larger thing	
piece (verb):	to mend or join by adding to something	

The diplomat is negotiating a *peace* settlement.

I ordered a *piece* of peach pie.

We hope to *piece* together what happened in Syria.

She had the _____ of mind of offering the last _____ of pizza to

the hungrier student.

plain/plane		
plain (adj):	[1]ordinary; [2]clear	
plain (noun):	flat land without trees	
plane (noun):	[1]aircraft; [2]carpenter's tool for shaving wood; [3]level of development	

We ate a *plain* meal of soup and bread.

The directions were given in *plain* English.

Many pioneers crossed the *plain* by covered wagon.

The passengers were seated on the *plane*.

A carpenter's *plane* and drill are needed for the job.

Astrophysicists think on a different *plane* from most people.

He wanted _____ advice on how to find the cheapest _____ tickets.

presence/presents   **presence (noun):**   [1]the state of being present; [2]a person's manner
                     presents (noun):   gifts
                     presents (verb):   (third person singular of *to present*) to introduce or offer

Your *presence* is needed in the dean's office.

Daniel Radcliffe has a wonderful stage *presence*.

The child received many birthday *presents*.

Every spring the dean *presents* the English prize.

The singer showed great _____ as she accepted _____ from her fans.

EXERCISE ①   **Group I Words**

Circle the words that correctly complete each of the following sentences.

1. When I telephoned the doctor, he warned me that the (aural, oral) medicine was to be used only in my child's ear; this pill was not an (aural, oral) medicine.

2. I read a (peace, piece) in today's news about the (peace, piece) accords.

3. The senators met in Athens, the (capital, capitol) of Greece, to discuss the question of (capital, capitol) punishment.

4. I hurried to take several yards of wool (close, clothes, cloth) to the tailor, who had agreed to make some new winter (close, clothes, cloth) for my family; I knew he would (close, clothes, cloth) at five o'clock.

5. Every (coarse, course) of the meal was delicious, but the bread was rather (coarse, course).

6. She always chooses colors that (complement, compliment) each other, but she never expects a (complement, compliment).

7. I so much looked (forward, foreword) to reading the new book that I read the (forward, foreword) the very first day.

8. I have spent the (passed, past) few days wondering if I (passed, past) the exam.

9. The storm had been raging over the (plain, plane) for hours before the passengers on the (plain, plane) suddenly went down.

10. Each year, the mayor (presence, presents) a number of awards as well as several lovely (presence, presents) to outstanding members of the community.

EXERCISE ② **Group I Words**

In the following paragraph, find ten often confused words that you have just studied in Group I. Circle each of the words. Then, on the lines below the paragraph, correct those words that are incorrect. If a word has been used correctly, write C for *correct*.

Wolfgang Mozart was a child star of the eighteenth century. At three years old, he could pick out chords and tunes on the piano. At the age of four, he composed his first piano peace. As a musical genius, Mozart had an extremely well-developed oral sense. When Mozart was only six, he and his sister played before the emperor in Vienna, the capitol of Austria. The emperor paid Mozart a complement by having his portrait painted. Among other presence was an embroidered suit of cloths. In the course of his life, Mozart wrote church music, sonatas, operas, and chamber music. Like many great artists of the passed, he was ahead of his time and created on such a different plain from other composers of his day that his own era never fully appreciated him. Today, Mozart is recognized as one of music's greatest composers. You might be interested in reading a book of Mozart's letters. Be sure to read the forward.

_____   _____

_____   _____

_____   _____

_____   _____

_____   _____

Group II: More Words That Sound Alike

principal/principle

principal (adj):	[1]most important; [2]main
principal (noun):	[1]head of a school; [2]sum of money invested or borrowed
principle (noun):	rule or standard

The *principal* dancer was superb.

What is the *principal* reason for your decision?

The *principal* of the school arrived late.

The *principal* and interest on the loan were due.

He is a man of *principle.*

The _____ reason the _____ resigned was a matter of _____.

rain/reign/rein

rain (noun):	water falling to earth in drops
reign (noun):	period of a king or queen's rule
rein (noun):	strap attached to a bridle, used to control a horse

I'm singing in the *rain.*

When was the *reign* of Henry VIII?

I grabbed the pony's frayed *rein.*

The queen's _____ began on a day of heavy _____.

sight/site/cite

sight (noun):	[1]ability to see; [2]something seen
site (noun):	[1]plot of land where something is, was, or will be located; [2]place for an event
cite (verb):	to quote as an authority or example

His *sight* was limited.

The Grand Canyon is an awesome *sight.*

Here is the *site* for the new courthouse.

Please *cite* the correct law.

The ancient burial _____ was a very impressive _____. Many famous archaeologists still _____ the old inscriptions when they publish their findings.

stationary/stationery

stationary (adj):	standing still, not moving
stationery (noun):	writing paper, usually with matching envelopes

She hit a *stationary* object.

He wrote the letter on his *stationery.*

She remained _____ as she read the letter written on the hotel _____.

to/too/two   **to (prep):**   in a direction toward
                    too (adv):   [1]also; [2]excessively
                    two (noun, adj):   the number 2

        We walked *to* the movies.

        We walked home *too*.

        The tickets were *too* expensive.

        She has *two* children.

Billy and Maria are _____ film buffs who go _____ a movie every

week; sometimes their daughter goes _____.

vain/vane/vein   **vain (adj):**   [1]conceited; [2]unsuccessful
                      vane (noun):   ornament, often in the shape of a rooster, that turns in the wind (seen on the tops of buildings, particularly barns)
                      vein (noun):   [1]blood vessel; [2]branching framework of a leaf; [3]area in the earth where minerals such as gold or silver are found; [4]passing attitude

        He was handsome but *vain*.

        We made a *vain* attempt to contact his brother.

        The weather *vane* pointed southwest.

        The *veins* carry blood to the heart.

        The *veins* on the maple leaf are red.

        The miner found a *vein* of silver.

        She spoke in a humorous *vein*.

The artist was incredibly _____ about the realism of the _____

he sculpted into the statue's neck.

waist/waste   **waist (noun):**   middle portion of the body
                   waste (verb):   to use carelessly
                   waste (noun):   discarded objects

        His *waist* is thirty-six inches around.

        He *wasted* too much time watching television.

        The *waste* was put into the garbage pail.

Jewel's pants have elastic fabric around the _____ so that she doesn't

have to _____ any time taking them on and off.

weather/whether   **weather (noun):**   atmospheric conditions
                      whether (conj):   if it is the case that

        The *weather* in Hawaii is gorgeous.

        I'll go *whether* I'm ready or not.

I will go to the islands on vacation, _____ the _____ is good or not.

whole/hole   **whole (adj):**   complete
              hole (noun):   opening

> He ate the *whole* pie.

> I found a *hole* in the sock.

Just to win a dare, he ate the _____ package of donut _____.

write/right/rite   **write (verb):**   ¹to form letters and words; ²to compose
                    right (adj):   ¹correct; ²conforming to justice, law, or morality
                    right (noun):   ¹power or privilege to which one is entitled; ²direction opposite to the left
                    rite (noun):   traditional, often religious, ceremony

> I will *write* a poem for your birthday.

> What is the *right* answer?

> Trial by jury is a *right* under the law.

> The senator's position is to the *right* of center.

> A bridal shower is a *rite* of passage.

Many music historians still _____ about whether the crowds were

_____ to riot at the debut of *The* _____ *of Spring*, Stravinsky's

ballet of 1913.

EXERCISE ③ **Group II Words**

Circle the words that correctly complete each of the following sentences.

1. The (principal, principle) was respected because he would not compromise his one fundamental (principal, principle).

2. The museum had on display a horse's (rain, reign, rein) that dated from the (rain, reign, rein) of Queen Isabella.

3. You do not have to (sight, site, cite) statistics to convince me of the risk of losing my (sight, site, cite).

4. He bought the (stationary, stationery) from a clerk who said nothing and remained (stationary, stationery) behind the counter the entire time.

5. The (to, too, two) of us should go (to, too, two) the new noodle restaurant, and I hope Riley will come (to, too, two).

6. I could tell the actor was (vain, vane, vein) when a (vain, vane, vein) popped out of his head when she mentioned his age.

7. It is a (waist, waste) of time to ask him to measure the size of his (waist, waste).

8. We always listen to the (weather, whether) report to decide (weather, whether) we should bring a sweater or not.

9. Nobody knows the (whole, hole) story about the (Whole, Hole) in the Wall Gang.

10. Every American has the (write, right, rite) to participate in any religious (write, right, rite) of his or her choosing.

EXERCISE ④ **Group II Words**

In the following paragraph, find ten often confused words that you have just studied in Group II. Circle each of the words. Then, on the lines below the paragraph, correct those words that are incorrect. If a word has been used correctly, write C for _correct_.

The company officials searched for years until they found the proper sight for their gem mine. First, they investigated legal records to make sure they had the rite to drill in the area. After drilling several wholes to see if any vanes were worth exploring, they were surprised to learn the area had been a principal mining area for Spanish colonizers in the sixteenth century. No exploration had been done there since the rein of King Philip IV. Company officials even found stationary containing written orders from the king. These modern explorers eventually determined they were to late to find any more emeralds, but they did have a good chance of discovering semiprecious stones. Since they did not want to waist any more time, work began immediately. In all kinds of whether, the work progressed. The results were worth their efforts.

_____   _____

_____   _____

_____   _____

_____   _____

_____   _____

Group III: Contractions That Sound Like Other Words

it's/its   **it's:**   contraction of *it is*
            its: possessive pronoun of *it*

    It's **early.**

    Its **tail is short.**

_____ too late now to put the space vehicle into _____ orbit.

they're/their/there   **they're:**   contraction of *they are*
                       their: possessive pronoun of *they*
                       there: at that place

    They're **happy.**

    Their **children are healthy.**

    Look over *there.*

_____ excited about the new apartment; _____ is more light, and _____ son will have his own room.

we're/were/where   **we're:**   contraction of *we are*
                    were: past tense of *are*
                    where: at or in what place

    We're **happy.**

    The days *were* **too short.**

    Where **are we?**

We need to know _____ you were last night. _____ you safe? After all, _____ your parents.

who's/whose   **who's:**   contraction of *who is*
               whose: possessive pronoun

    Who's **the author of this book?**

    Whose **clothes are these?**

_____ pancakes are these, and _____ to blame for the mess in the kitchen?

you're/your   **you're:**   contraction of *you are*
               your: possessive pronoun of *you*

    You're **the boss.**

    Your **team has won.**

When _____ diploma is in hand, _____ a happy graduate.

EXERCISE **5** **Group III Words**

Circle the words that correctly complete each of the following sentences.

1. (It's, Its) obvious that the car has lost (it's, its) muffler.

2. The pie has lost (it's, its) freshness, and (it's, its) time to throw it out.

3. When (they're, their, there) in school, (they're, their, there) parents work in the restaurant on the corner over (they're, their, there).

4. Now that (they're, their, there) living in the country, (they're, their, there) expenses are not so great, so they might stay (they're, their, there).

5. (We're, Were, Where) hoping our friends (we're, were, where) not hurt at the place (we're, were, where) the accident occurred.

6. (We're, Were, Where) did the coupons go that (we're, were, where) saving?

7. (Who's, Whose) car is double-parked outside, and (who's, whose) going to move it?

8. (Who's, Whose) the pitcher in the game today, and (who's, whose) idea was it to buy tickets?

9. When (you're, your) a parent, (you're, your) free time is never guaranteed.

10. Please give me (you're, your) paper when (you're, your) finished writing.

EXERCISE **6** **Group III Words**

In the following paragraph, find ten often confused words that you have just studied in Group III. Circle each of the words. Then, on the lines below the paragraph, correct those words that are incorrect. If a word has been used correctly, write C for *correct*.

Psychologists tell us that laughter is found only among human beings. Of all creatures, where the only ones who laugh. Psychologists are interested in what makes people laugh, but so far there best explanations are only theories. From a physical point of view, your healthier if you laugh often. Laughter is good for you're lungs, and it's an outlet for extra energy. Another effect of laughter is it's beneficial release of anxiety and anger. The comedian, who's job depends on figuring out what makes people laugh, often pokes fun at the behavior of other people. However, a joke about a local town might not be funny in front of an audience of people who like living their. Were all familiar with jokes that are in bad taste. Its a good idea to recognize who your audience is.

_____   _____

_____   _____

_____   _____

_____   _____

_____   _____

Group IV: Words That Sound or Look Almost Alike

accept/except   **accept (verb):**   [1]to receive with consent; [2]to admit; [3]to regard as true or right
except (prep):   other than, but

> I *accept* the invitation with pleasure.
>
> I *accept* responsibility.
>
> I *accept* your explanation.
>
> Everyone *except* me was ready.

I will _____ all the applications _____ the late ones.

advice/advise   **advice (noun):**   opinion as to what should be done
advise (verb):   [1]to suggest; [2]to counsel

> I need good *advice.*
>
> He *advised* me to take a different course.

I _____ you to get the best _____ possible.

affect/effect   **affect (verb):**   [1]to influence; [2]to change
effect (noun):   result
effect (verb):   to bring about

> Smoking will *affect* your health.
>
> The *effects* of the hurricane were evident.
>
> The hurricane *effected* devastating changes in the county.

His low grades will _____ his chances of getting into law school; this

could have a serious _____ on his future plans.

breath/breathe   **breath (noun):**   [1]air that is inhaled or exhaled; [2]the act of inhaling or exhaling
breathe (verb):   to inhale or exhale

> You seem out of *breath.*
>
> Don't *breathe* in these fumes.

When they went mountain climbing, every _____ was difficult. By the

time they reached the summit, they could hardly _____.

choose/chose   **choose (verb):**   to select

               chose (verb):   past tense of *choose*

               I *choose* a bagel for breakfast every day.

               Yesterday I *chose* to sleep late.

This year I will _____ my clothes more carefully because last year

I _____ several items that I never wore.

conscience/   **conscience (noun):**   a person's recognition of right and wrong
conscious/   **conscious (adj):**   ¹awake; ²aware of one's own existence
conscientious   **conscientious (adj):**   ¹careful; ²thorough

               His *conscience* bothered him.

               The patient was *conscious* and able to talk.

               The student was *conscientious* about doing her homework.

In the story of Pinocchio, Jiminy Cricket acts as the puppet's _____

because Pinocchio is not _____ of right and wrong. The cricket does a

very _____ job.

costume/custom   **costume (noun):**   special style of dress for a particular occasion
               custom (noun):   common tradition

               The child wore a clown *costume* for Halloween.

               One *custom* at Thanksgiving is to serve turkey.

My cousin in New Orleans enjoys the _____ of wearing a special

_____ for Mardi Gras.

council/   **council (noun):**   group that governs
counsel/   **counsel (verb):**   to give advice
consul   **counsel (noun):**   ¹advice; ²a lawyer
               consul (noun):   government official in the foreign service

               The student *council* meets every Tuesday.

               Please *counsel* the elderly couple.

               The candidate appreciated his campaign adviser's *counsel*.

               The defendant has requested *counsel*.

               He was appointed a *consul* by the president.

When I appeared before the _____, they gave me good _____,

advising me to meet with El Salvador's _____.

desert/dessert   **desert (verb):**   to abandon
desert (noun):   barren land
dessert (noun):   last part of a meal, often sweet

> **Don't *desert* me now.**
>
> **The cactus flowers in the *desert* are beautiful.**
>
> **We had apple pie for *dessert*.**

When the caravan became lost in the _____, they did not think about a

full meal with _____. All they wanted was some water.

diner/dinner   **diner (noun):**   [1]person eating a meal; [2]restaurant with a long counter and booths
dinner (noun):   main meal of the day

> **The *diner* waited for her check.**
>
> **I prefer a booth at the *diner*.**
>
> **What is for *dinner*?**

That _____ is a good place for _____. You can tell by the number

of satisfied _____ there.

EXERCISE ⑦   **Group IV Words**

Circle the words that correctly complete each of the following sentences.

1. The judge refused to (accept, except) most of the evidence (accept, except) for the testimony of one expert witness.

2. I need some good (advice, advise); is there anyone here who could (advice, advise) me?

3. How does the asthma medicine (affect, effect) you? Some medicine may have more than one adverse side (affect, effect).

4. The injured mountain climber was advised to (breath, breathe) deeply and exhale slowly; the park ranger could see her (breath, breathe) in the chilly air.

5. Now we (choose, chose) cars based on fuel efficiency; in the past we usually (choose, chose) based on power.

6. When the thief became (conscience, conscientious, conscious), he gave himself up to the police because his (conscience, conscientious, conscious) was bothering him.

7. Before you visit China, you should read about its (costumes, customs), including its New Year celebration at which colorful (costumes, customs) are worn.

8. The town (council, counsel, consul) needs its own legal (council, counsel, consul) to help interpret the laws.

9. In some (desert, dessert) environments, the only thing that is served for (desert, dessert) is hot tea.

10. All I want for (diner, dinner) is a salad; do you think I can get a good one at this corner (diner, dinner)?

EXERCISE 8   **Group IV Words**

In the following paragraph, find ten often confused words that you have just studied in Group IV. Circle each of the words. Then, on the lines below the paragraph, correct those words that are incorrect. If a word has been used correctly, write C for *correct*.

For thousands of years, it has been a costume to enjoy wine. Today, some people chose to drink wine with diner, while others wait until desert. There are wine clubs where people look for advise as to what they should drink; these people are very conscience about making the correct choice. Others look for council in magazines that tell them how to chose the correct wine for a food. They except the words of the experts on some wines whose prices would take your breath away.

_____   _____
_____   _____
_____   _____
_____   _____
_____   _____

Group V: More Words That Sound or Look Almost Alike

emigrate/	**emigrate (verb):**	to leave a country or region
immigrate/	**immigrate (verb):**	to come into a country or region
emigrant/	**emigrant (noun):**	person who leaves one country to settle in another country
immigrant	**immigrant (noun):**	person who comes into a country to settle there

They *emigrated* from Europe.

Many people have *immigrated* to the United States.

Each *emigrant* left home with childhood memories.

Nearly every *immigrant* landed first at Ellis Island.

People who _____ from Eastern Europe often _____ to the United States. In their native countries, the _____ are missed by their relatives; in the adopted country, they become valued _____.

farther/further

farther (adj, adv):	a greater distance (physically)
further (adj, adv):	a greater distance (mentally); additional
further (verb):	to help advance (a person or a cause)

They had to walk *farther* down the road.

The speaker made a *further* point.

Working with the tutor will *further* my chances for a good grade on the exam.

The council made a _____ decision that the new town hall should be built _____ from the creek.

loose/lose

loose (adj):	not tightly fitted
lose (verb):	[1]to be unable to keep or find; [2]to fail to win

The dog's collar is *loose*.

Don't *lose* your keys.

Don't *lose* the game.

The child has a couple of _____ teeth, and he might _____ one of them.

personal/personnel

personal (adj):	[1]relating to an individual; [2]private
personnel (noun):	people employed by an organization

Is this your *personal* account or your corporate account?

He asked for his *personal* mail.

All *personnel* in the company were interviewed.

The manager took a _____ interest in the _____ in his department.

quiet/quit/quite

quiet (adj):	[1]free from noise; [2]calm
quit (verb):	[1]to give up; [2]to stop
quite (adv):	[1]completely; [2]rather

They loved the *quiet* village.

He *quit* smoking.

She is not *quite* alone.

She is coming *quite* soon.

Christina was _____ determined to find a _____ spot to study before she _____ for the day.

receipt/recipe   **receipt (noun):**   paper showing that a bill has been paid
                  recipe (noun):   formula for preparing a mixture, especially in cooking

No exchanges can be made without a *receipt*.

I found my *recipe* for caramel flan.

Here is your sales _____ for the cookbook; I hope you enjoy each

_____.

special/especially   **special (adj):**   not ordinary
                    especially (adv):   particularly

We're planning a *special* weekend.

She is *especially* talented in art.

A sixteenth birthday party is a _____ event for a girl, _____ when all of her friends can attend.

than/then   **than (conj or prep):**   used to make a comparison
                then (adv):   [1]at that time; [2]next

This cake is sweeter *than* that one.

I was at work *then*.

First he blamed his parents; *then* he blamed me.

Michael and Janice cook at home rather _____ eating out; _____ they usually go to a movie.

thorough/though/   **thorough (adj):**   accurate and complete
thought/through/   **though (adv or conj):**   despite the fact that
threw   **thought (verb):**   past tense of *think*
                through (prep):   from one end to the other (*Note:* thru is not standard spelling.)

                threw (verb):   past tense of *throw*

She always does a *thorough* job.

I worked even *though* I was exhausted.

I *thought* about my goals.

We drove *through* the tunnel.

He *threw* the ball to me.

We _____ they did a _____ job of cleaning the apartment,

even _____ they _____ out some papers that they should have

looked _____ more carefully.

use/used to **use (verb):** to employ for a purpose (past tense is *used*)

used to: [1]an expression indicating that an activity is no longer done in the present; [2]accustomed to or familiar with

Yesterday, I *used* my father's car.

I *used to* take the bus to school, but now I ride my bike.

I am *used to* walking to school.

I _____ repair my car myself, but then I _____ my local garage

for a difficult repair; now I _____ that garage all the time.

EXERCISE 9 **Group V Words**

Circle the word that correctly completes each of the following sentences.

1. The band's guitarist (emigrated, immigrated) from Sierra Leone.

2. Let's not travel any (farther, further) tonight.

3. (Loose, Lose) lips sink ships.

4. Most of the (personal, personnel) at this company are well trained.

5. Please be (quiet, quit, quite) while she is performing.

6. Keep this (receipt, recipe) for tax purposes.

7. He made a (special, especially) trip to visit his daughter.

8. I would rather read a good book (than, then) watch the inflight movie.

9. When she walked (thorough, though, thought, through, threw) the door, he didn't recognize her even (thorough, though, thought, through, threw) he had known her all his life.

10. I am not (use, used) to staying up so late.

EXERCISE 10   **Group V Words**

In the following paragraph, find ten often confused words that you have just studied in Group V. Circle each of the words. Then, on the lines below the paragraph, correct those words that are incorrect. If a word has been used correctly, write C for *correct*.

Advertising is very old: some advertisements on paper go back further then three thousand years. In ancient Greece, it was quiet common to see signs advertising different kinds of services, but it was not until printing was invented that modern advertising was born. In Europe in the seventeenth century, people use to place ads in newspapers; some of these ads were personnel messages, but most were for business. When emigrants came to the United States, they used advertisements to find jobs; we can imagine them going thorough each newspaper very carefully. Today, advertising is all around us, special on television. If we are not careful, we can loose our focus when we watch a program. When a commercial interrupts a chef who is giving us a receipt for a complicated new dish, perhaps we should mute the sound until the commercial ends.

_____   _____

_____   _____

_____   _____

_____   _____

Group VI: *Lay/Lie, Raise/Rise, and Set/Sit*

These six verbs (*lay/lie, raise/rise,* and *set/sit*) are perhaps the most troublesome verbs in the English language. Not only are their principal parts nearly all irregular and easily confused with each other, but in addition, one set must always take a direct object while the other set is intransitive and never takes an object. First learn the principal parts of the set that always takes a direct object.

Verbs Always Taking a Direct Object: *lay, raise,* and *set*

The three verbs *lay, raise,* and *set* always require a direct object.

I *lay* the book down.

I *raise* a flag.

I *set* the table.

PRINCIPAL PARTS OF VERBS LAY, RAISE, AND SET

VERB MEANING	PRESENT	PRESENT PARTICIPLE	PAST	PAST PARTICIPLE
lay: to put something down	lay	laying	laid	has laid or have laid
raise: to move something up	raise	raising	raised	has raised or have raised
set: to place something	set	setting	set	has set or have set

Here are some additional examples of these verbs in the past tense. Notice that each verb takes a direct object.

> **The child *laid the ball* on the rug.**

> **The sunshine *raised our spirits*.**

> **The woman *set her hat* on the sofa.**

PRACTICE ❶ **Fill in the first blank in each of the following sentences with the correct form of the verb. Then choose a direct object for each verb and write it in the second blank.**

1. The postal worker said he had _____ the _____ on the back porch.
(lay)

2. The father _____ his _____ to be a caring person. (*Use past tense.*) (raise)

3. We always _____ the _____ on the counter.
(set)

4. They are _____ down the new _____ today.
(lay)

5. Every night, I _____ out my _____ for the following day.
(lay)

6. The citizen _____ many _____ whenever the board meets.
(raise)

7. She has _____ the _____ to record tonight's program.
(set)

8. The principal has _____ down the law for the new dress code.
(lay)

9. We were _____ the _____ for dinner.
(set)

10. He has _____ a substantial amount of _____ for the charity.
(raise)

Verbs Never Taking a Direct Object: *lie, rise,* and *sit*

The intransitive verbs *lie, rise,* and *sit* are used when the subject is doing the action without any help. No other person or object is needed to accomplish the action.

The verbs *lie, rise,* and *sit* do not require an object.

I *lie* down.

I *rise* up.

I *sit* down.

PRINCIPAL PARTS OF *LIE, RISE, AND SIT*

VERB MEANING	PRESENT	PRESENT PARTICIPLE	PAST	PAST PARTICIPLE
lie: to recline	lie	lying	lay	has lain *or* have lain
rise: to stand up or move upward	rise	rising	rose	has risen *or* have risen
sit: to take a sitting position	sit	sitting	sat	has sat *or* have sat

Here are some additional sentences with intransitive verbs in the past tense:

The *cat lay* on the rug.

The *sun rose* in the east.

The *woman sat* on the sofa.

PRACTICE ② **Fill in the blank in each of the following sentences with the correct form of the intransitive verb.**

1. As I write this postcard, the sun is _____ .
   (rise)

2. The new paint brushes _____ on the workbench. (*Use present tense.*)
   (lie)

3. He was _____ at the breakfast table when his sister called.
   (sit)

4. Last night, we _____ on the couch watching a television show.
   (lie)

5. Yesterday morning, the couple _____ at five o'clock to see the sunrise.
   (rise)

6. The cat is always _____ on my favorite chair.
   (lie)

7. It was very late when they _____ down to dinner.
   (sit)

8. The price of college has _____ dramatically.
   (rise)

9. The newspapers have _____ in the driveway for days.
   (lie)

10. The child has _____ a long time in front of the camera.
    (sit)

EXERCISE 11 **Group VI Words**

Fill in the blank in each of the following sentences with the correct form of the correct verb.

1. I have _____ the suitcases in your room.
   (lie, lay)

2. I am _____ near the bonfire.
   (sit, set)

3. She likes me to _____ by her bed and read to her in the evening.
   (sit, set)

4. Last spring, the manufacturers _____ the prices.
   (rise, raise)

5. Yesterday, the price of gasoline _____ by twenty cents.
   (rise, raise)

6. When I entered the room, the woman _____ to greet me.
   (rise, raise)

7. The woman _____ her head when I entered the room.
   (rise, raise)

8. I usually _____ down in the afternoon.
   (lie, lay)

9. The auto mechanic is _____ under the car.
   (lie, lay)

10. I can't remember where I _____ my keys.
    (lie, lay)

EXERCISE 12 **Group VI Words**

Fill in the blank in each of the following sentences with the correct form of the correct verb.

1. The cat has _____ in the sun all afternoon.
   (lie, lay)

2. If you feel sick, _____ down on that bed.
   (lie, lay)

3. The elevator always _____ quickly to the tenth floor.
   (rise, raise)

4. The boss _____ her salary twice this year.
   (rise, raise)

5. His parents _____ down the law when he came home late.
   (lie, lay)

6. The carpenters _____ the roof when they remodeled the house.
   (rise, raise)

7. The dog _____ up every evening and begs for food.
   (sit, set)

8. Last week, Neda _____ at the computer every night.
   (sit, set)

9. I always watch the waiter _____ on a stool after his shift is done.
   (sit, set)

10. We have _____ out cookies and milk for Santa Claus every year since
    (sit, set)
    the children were born.

Mastery and Editing Tests

TEST 1 **Choosing Correct Words**

Circle the words that correctly complete the sentences.

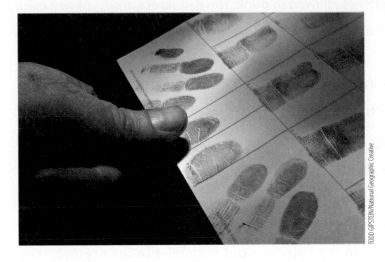

TODD GIPSTEIN/National Geographic Creative

In the (past, passed), the major way to identify people was (thorough, though, thought, through, threw) the use of fingerprints. That technique was developed during the (rain, reign, rein) of Queen Victoria in England. Now a new technology called iris recognition has been developed. This method of identification uses the information stored in the iris, the colored section of the eye that surrounds the pupil. The iris contains more information (than, then) any other part of the body. Every one of (it's, its) 266 features can be measured fully. In contrast, fingerprints contain only thirty features. Iris recognition was developed in 1994 by a computer scientist at Cambridge University in England, and now (it's, its) used to identify people at airport security checkpoints and in some banks. To scan a person's iris, a machine directs a beam of infrared light on the person from 14 inches away. The (whole, hole) procedure takes about one minute. This is (quiet, quite) an advantage over fingerprinting, which is very time-consuming. Unfortunately, however, a bank's customers would have to use only (they're, their, there) own bank's ATMs. The other problem with this new technology concerns the cost, but (who's, whose) to say what safeguarding an individual's privacy is worth?

TEST 2 **Choosing Correct Words**

Circle the words that correctly complete the sentences.

Coffee has a long history and an interesting one. Long before it was brewed, coffee was enjoyed (plain, plane) or mixed with vegetables and eaten as food. The (sight, site, cite) of the first cultivated coffee was most likely Kaffa, a part of Ethiopia not far from the (capital, capitol) of that country. That is (we're, were, where) coffee most likely got (it's, its) name. (Than, Then) in the fourteenth century, merchants came across the (desert, dessert) from Arabia to Kaffa, obtained coffee seeds, and began to grow coffee in their own countries. The people of Arabia were (quiet, quite, quit) happy to enjoy coffee, (special, especially) because it took the place of alcohol, which they were not allowed to drink. The first (loose, lose) coffee beans came to Europe in 1615, and the drink has remained popular ever since.

TEST ③ **Choosing Correct Words**

Circle the words that correctly complete the sentences.

People have pierced their ears (thorough, though, thought, through, threw) every period of recorded history. Ancient Egyptians, Persians, Hebrews, and others would (sit, set) jewels, pearls, and other precious stones into gold and silver to make earrings. They even (use, used) to hang earrings from the statues of their gods and goddesses. When the Egyptians put mummies in their tombs, they would (lie, lay) earrings in the coffins as decorations for the people to wear in the afterlife. Centuries ago, both men and women wore earrings, but one Roman emperor thought his people were becoming (to, too, two) (vain, vane, vein). After speaking out against the use of earrings, he went (farther, further) and ruled that men could no longer wear them. Today, hardly anyone would (accept, except) such a regulation. People would rebel because they believe wearing (they're, their, there) jewelry is a personal (right, write, rite).

WRITE FOR SUCCESS

What motivates a person to do well in college? Some motivators may be said to be extrinsic (the motivation comes from without), such as (1) getting good grades, (2) getting college credits, and (3) hoping for higher pay in a future job. Other motivators are intrinsic (the motivation comes from within), such as (1) having curiosity about learning something new, (2) being fascinated with a topic, and (3) taking satisfaction in meeting a challenge. Write a response that considers both extrinsic and intrinsic motivators that influence your work in school.

Working Together

kaczor58 /Shutterstock.com

Examining the Issue of Plagiarism

Plagiarism is the unlawful use of another writer's words or ideas as if they were your own. When you use material from the work of another writer, you must give credit to that author, or you will be guilty of plagiarism. All writers are expected to acknowledge the sources they use for their own work, and college students should be especially careful in this regard. Students are often under pressure to submit assignments on time; they may be tempted to use already published work and copy too much from that work. If a student writer is found to have turned in plagiarized material, the consequences can be serious indeed.

A professional writer who should have been fully aware of plagiarism and its implications is Alexander Theroux. Theroux, who has taught at Harvard and Yale, published a collection of essays under the title *The Primary Colors*. A reader happened to be examining Theroux's book, and was reminded of passages in another work, a volume titled *Song of the Sky*, by an aviator named Guy Murchie. Murchie's book had been published in 1954 and was not well known. In fact, it had been out of print for some time.

The reader noticed remarkable similarities between some passages from the two books. Compare the following passages from the Theroux book and *Song of the Sky*.

Song of the Sky, page 29	*The Primary Colors,* page 16
"Blue water is salty, warm, and deep and speaks of the tropics where evaporation is great and dilution small—the Sulu Sea, the Indian Ocean, the Gulf Stream. Green water is cool, pale with particles, thin with river and rain, often shallow."	"Incidentally, blue water is invariably salty, warm, and deep and speaks of the tropics, where evaporation is great and dilution minimal—the Sulu Sea, the Indian Ocean, the Gulf Stream. Green water, on the other hand, is cool, pale with particles, thin with river and rain, often shallow."

Questions for Small-Group Discussion

1. Discuss the extent to which the two passages differ.
2. When asked about the striking similarities between his book and *Song of the Sky*, Alexander Theroux stated, "I just thought it was my own work. I can't always remember the source of where I found something." Discuss the writer's explanation. Is it satisfactory? Do you think there is a more likely explanation?
3. When this example of plagiarism was discovered, the publisher of the Theroux book announced that future editions would either leave out the plagiarized passages or give direct credit to *Song of the Sky*. Was this a good solution? In your opinion, is there anything else the publisher should do in such a case?

4. If a college student is found guilty of plagiarism, what should the penalty be?
5. It has been said that when students plagiarize material in school, those students really cheat themselves because any benefit from learning is lost. Discuss.
6. What is the policy on plagiarism given in the catalog of the educational institution you attend?

PORTFOLIO SUGGESTION

A democracy depends on the integrity of its institutions and its individual citizens to function. Based on your observations, make a list of the ways college students reveal a lack of integrity. Have you observed cheating on tests, buying papers on the Internet, or copying of other students' assignments? You may want to write an essay in which you predict the effects this behavior will have when these same students graduate and assume leadership positions in their communities.

PART 4

Pete Saloutos/Shutterstock.com

Creating Effective Paragraphs

Practice, Practice, Practice

Even people who seem to have natural talent—award-winning athletes, performers, and writers—must practice and work hard to become the best in their fields. The good news for writers is that writing is like other skills—it can be developed. No matter what your current level of ability, you can always get better. The secret is really about focus and perseverance. For every skill, practice will always be the major way to improve.

- What natural skills do you have?
- How have you worked to improve them?
- Can you use these same techniques for improving your writing?

Working with Paragraphs: Topic Sentences and Controlling Ideas

16

The well-developed paragraph almost always has a topic sentence. In this chapter, you will learn how to recognize and generate your own strong topic sentences.

- identifying the characteristics of an acceptable paragraph

- finding the topic sentence of a paragraph

- distinguishing between a topic sentence and a title

- finding the topic in a topic sentence

- finding the controlling idea of a topic sentence

- writing topic sentences

- choosing controlling ideas

What Is a Paragraph?

> A **paragraph** is a group of sentences constructed to develop one main idea. A paragraph may stand by itself as a complete piece of writing, or it may be a section of a longer piece of writing, such as an essay.

No single rule can prescribe how long a paragraph should be, but a paragraph that is too short can make a reader think that some basic information is missing. On the other hand, a paragraph that is too long will likely make a reader lose interest. An effective paragraph must be long enough to develop the main idea the writer is expressing, usually six or seven sentences in length, but no more than ten or twelve sentences. While it is true that newspapers and magazines take liberties with the paragraph form and often have paragraphs as short as a single sentence, a well-developed piece of writing will seldom present a single sentence as a paragraph (unless the sentence is a piece of dialogue).

Before you begin writing and printing out your own paragraphs, your instructor may want you to demonstrate your ability to work with the computer. You may need to show your ability to set margins, to double-space the text, and to paginate. Your instructor will also explain other specific information (such as your name, the class, and the date of submission) needed for turning in written assignments. This information may be placed on a separate title page. Standard paragraph form will require consistent margins, an indented first sentence, a capitalized word at the beginning of each sentence, and correct punctuation to end each complete sentence. These are the basic requirements that all students must be able to meet in order to do college-level work.

While you are studying in college, you will need to become comfortable using a computer, so take this opportunity to learn new word-processing skills. For example, if you have never paginated a paper before or you have never used the spell-check option, explore these features. Find something new to learn. Because jobs for your generation will demand computer literacy, you will need to have an enthusiastic attitude about learning new skills on the computer.

EXERCISE ① **Standard Paragraph Form**

Type the following sentences into a standard paragraph. Follow your instructor's requirements for margins and spacing. Then print out your work, being sure to check the page for typos and other errors.

1. The local library became a haven for disaster victims.

2. In the large basement, thirty families huddled in groups of four or five.

3. Volunteer workers were busy carrying boxes of clothing and blankets.

4. Two Red Cross workers stood at a long table sorting through boxes to find sweaters and blankets for the shivering flood victims.

5. One dedicated woman in a red woolen hunting jacket stirred a huge pot of soup.

6. Men and women with tired faces sipped steaming coffee and wondered if they would ever see their homes again.

7. Outside, the downpour continued.

Michael Rieger/FEMA

What Is a Topic Sentence?

A **topic sentence** states the main idea of a paragraph. It is the most general sentence of the paragraph. All the other sentences serve to explain, describe, extend, or support this main-idea sentence.

Most paragraphs you read will begin with the topic sentence. However, some topic sentences come in the middle of the paragraph; others come at the end. Some paragraphs have no stated topic sentence at all; in those cases, the main idea is implied. Students are usually advised to use topic sentences in all their work. This will ensure that the writing will have a focus and will develop only one idea at a time. Whether the task is an essay exam in a history course, a research paper for a sociology course, or an essay in a composition course, thoughtful use of topic sentences will create better results. Good topic sentences help both the writer and the reader think clearly about the main points.

Below are two paragraphs. Each paragraph makes a separate point, which is stated in its topic sentence. In both of these paragraphs, the topic sentence happens to be first. Read the paragraphs and notice how the topic sentence is the most general sentence; in each case, it states the main idea of the paragraph. The other sentences explain, describe, extend, or support the topic sentence.

I went through a difficult period after my father died. I was moody and sullen at home. I spent most of the time in my bedroom listening to music on the radio, which made me feel even worse. I stopped playing soccer after school with my friends. My grades in school went down. I lost my appetite and seemed to get into arguments with everybody. My mom began to look worried, but I couldn't bring myself to participate in an activity with any spirit. It seemed life had lost its joy for me.

Fortunately, something happened that spring that brought me out of my depression. My uncle, who had been disabled while serving in the army, came to live with us. I learned many years later that my mother had asked him to come and live with us in the hope that he could bring me out of myself. I, on the other hand, was told that it was my responsibility to help my uncle feel at home. My mother's plan worked. My uncle and I were both lonely people. A friendship began that was to change both our lives for the better.

EXERCISE ② **Finding the Topic Sentence of a Paragraph**

Each of the following five paragraphs contains a topic sentence that states the main idea of the paragraph. Find the sentence that best states the main idea and underline it. Keep in mind that the topic sentence will not always be the first sentence of the paragraph.

1.　　This situation was one of the worst I had ever been in. There was a tube in my nose that went all the way to the pit of my stomach. I was being fed intravenously, and there was a drain in my side. Everybody came to visit me, mainly out of curiosity. The girls were all anxious to know where I had gotten shot. They had heard all kinds of tales about where the bullet struck. The bolder ones wouldn't even bother to ask: they just snatched the cover off me and looked for themselves. In a few days, word got around that I was in one piece.

2.   Anyone who has been in the hospital with a serious illness can tell you that the sight of a good nurse is the most beautiful view in the world. Today, the hospital nurse has one of the hardest jobs of all. Although a doctor may direct the care and treatment of a patient, it is the nurse who must see to it that the care and treatment are carried out. A nurse must pay attention to everything, from the condition of the hospital bed to the scheduling of medication throughout the day and night. In addition to following a doctor's orders for the day, the nurse must respond to whatever the patient might need at any given moment. A sudden emergency requires the nurse to make an immediate judgment: can the situation be handled without the doctor being called in? More recently, nurses have become increasingly burdened by paperwork and other administrative duties. Many people worry that the increasing demands on nurses will take them away from what they do best—namely, caring for people on a one-to-one basis.

3.   A person's life at any given time incorporates both external and internal aspects. The external system is composed of our memberships in the culture: our job, social class, family and social roles, how we present ourselves to and participate in the world. The internal realm concerns the meanings this participation has for each of us. In what ways are our values, goals, and aspirations being invigorated or violated by our present life system? How many parts of our personality can we live out and what parts are we suppressing? How do we *feel* about our way of living in the world at any given time?

4.   Mountains of disposable diapers are thrown into garbage cans every day. Tons of yogurt containers, soda cans, and a variety of plastic items are discarded without so much as a stomp to flatten them out. If the old Chevy is not worth fixing, tow it off to sit with thousands of others on acres of fenced-in junkyards. Radios, televisions, and toasters get the same treatment because it is easier and often less expensive to buy a new product than to fix the old one. Who wants a comfortable old sweater if a new one can be bought on sale? No thought is given to the fact that the new one will look like the old one after two or three washings. We are the great "Let's junk it" society!

5.   Many people go to the grocery store without much thought. Once there, they become victims to clever product placement. In order to shop wisely, several basic rules should be kept in mind. First, the wise shopper should make a list. This will keep a focus on the person's needs, not wants. Grocery stores purposely place tempting items such as candy and magazines near the checkout counters; these are things that are not basic needs on anyone's list. A person who sticks to the list will save a substantial amount of money within a few months. Second, the shopper should avoid delis and convenience stores where the markups tend to be higher than in the large grocery chains. Next, buying store brands can result in big savings. In many cases, these store brands are of the same quality as the higher priced brands. Of course, we all know we should clip coupons, but be careful not to buy items that are not really necessary. Sometimes a store brand is still cheaper than the more expensive item even after the coupon amount has been deducted. Some people claim they can save by buying in bulk. They might buy a bushel of apples or 40 pounds of potatoes. However, if the food spoils before you can eat it, this may be a big mistake. It is true that a bargain is not always a bargain.

EXERCISE ③ **Finding the Topic Sentence of a Paragraph**

Each of the following five paragraphs contains a topic sentence that states the main idea of the paragraph. Find the sentence that best states the main idea and underline it. Keep in mind that the topic sentence will not always be the first sentence of the paragraph.

1.   Last evening at a party, a complete stranger asked me, "Are you a Libra?" Astrology is enjoying increasing popularity all across the United States. My colleague reads the horoscope every morning before coming to work. At the local stores, cards, books, T-shirts, and other useless astrological products bring fat profits to those who have manufactured them. Even some public officials, like the British royal family, are known to consider the "science" of astrology before scheduling an important event.

2.   Participating in fund-raising walks and runs can raise needed research money for good causes, such as cures for multiple sclerosis or breast cancer. Donating used clothing to organizations like the Salvation Army is better than having closets full of clothes you never wear. It only takes an hour to donate blood, and this one hour of your time may save someone's life. Volunteers are badly needed at animal shelters and food pantries. What about volunteering to tutor a child or

take an elderly person to medical appointments? Anyone with a caring heart can find some time in the week to make a difference in another person's life.

3.   When we remember something, our brain uses more than one method to store the information. Short-term memory helps recall recent events; long-term memory brings back items that are further in the past; and deep retrieval gives access to long-buried information that is sometimes difficult to recall. Whether these processes are chemical or electrical, we do not yet know, and much research remains to be done before we can say with any certainty. The brain is one of the most remarkable organs, a part of the body that we have only begun to investigate. It will be years before we even begin to understand all its complex processes.

4.   Most of the homes were wooden cottages painted a deep red. This is the color farmers have been using for hundreds of years. We were curious to see what the insides would look like. The rooms were light and airy, with the walls painted white or light shades of grey, cream, or yellow. Where the ceilings met the walls, white or pastel moldings with carved details were attached. We noticed that much of the furniture was painted. Sometimes beautiful old tiled stoves stood in the living rooms. Visiting these cottages was a look at the Swedish traditional use of colors. Although the overall feeling inside was white on white, one should mention that bright splashes of color were added for pillows and other accessories.

5.   Advertisements that claim you can lose five pounds overnight are not to be trusted. Nor are claims that your luck will change if you send money to a certain post office box in a distant state. You should avoid chain letters you receive in the mail that promise large amounts of money if you cooperate and keep the chain going. Many people are suspicious of the well-publicized million-dollar giveaway promotions that offer enormous cash prizes, even if you do not try the company's product. We should be skeptical of offers that promise something for little or no effort or money.

EXERCISE ④ **Finding the Topic Sentence of a Paragraph**

The topic sentence is missing in each of the following four paragraphs. Read each paragraph carefully and circle the letter of the best topic sentence for that paragraph.

1.   I would probably have lived my entire existence within a one-mile radius of where I was born. I would undoubtedly have married a woman of my identical

religious, socioeconomic, and cultural background. I would almost certainly have become a medical doctor, an engineer, or a software programmer. I would have socialized within my ethnic community and had cordial relations, but few friends, outside that group. I would have a whole set of opinions that could be predicted in advance; indeed, they would not be very different from what my father believed, or his father before him.

a.   If I had remained in India, my destiny would to a large degree have been predictable.

b.   If I had remained in India, I would have been very happy living in the neighborhood where I grew up.

c.   If I had remained in India, I would have married someone very like my own mother.

d.   If I had remained in India, I would have had an excellent education.

2.   It is not that poor people in the Third World don't work hard. On the contrary, they labor incessantly and endure hardships that are almost unimaginable to people in the West. In the villages of Asia and Africa, for example, a common sight is a farmer beating a pickax into the ground, women wobbling under heavy loads, children carrying stones. These people are performing very hard labor, but they are getting nowhere. The best they can hope for is to survive for another day. Their clothes are tattered, their teeth are rotted, and disease and death constantly loom over their horizon.

a.   Poor people from the Third World live in small villages in Asia and Africa.

b.   The lives of many poor people in the Third World are defined by an ongoing struggle to exist.

c.   Disease is a constant threat to poor people in the Third World.

d.   Poor people in the Third World work constantly.

3.   The roads are not properly paved. The water is not safe to drink. Pollution in the cities has reached hazardous levels. Public transportation is overcrowded and unreliable. There is a two-year waiting period to get a telephone. Government officials, who are very poorly paid, are inevitably corrupt, which means that you must pay bribes on a regular basis to get things done. Most important, there are limited prospects for the children's future.

a.   It is difficult to live in a Third World country where corruption is so widespread.

b.   Everyday life in the Third World is filled with hardships for everyone.

c.   Only the very poor in the Third World suffer; the upper and middle classes live an easy life.

d.   Governments in the Third World do not care about the common people.

4.   Let me illustrate with the example of my sister, who got married several years ago. My parents began the process by conducting a comprehensive survey of all the eligible families in our neighborhood. First they examined primary criteria such as religion, socioeconomic position, and educational background. Then my parents investigated subtler issues: the social reputation of the family, reports of an eccentric uncle, the character of the son, and so on. Finally, my parents were down to a dozen or so eligible families, and they were invited to our house for dinner with suspicious regularity. My sister was "free to choose." My sister knew about, and accepted, the arrangement; she is now happily married with two children. I am not quarreling with the outcome.

a.   Children in India are free to choose the person they want to marry.

b.   In India, the reputation of the family into which you are married is very important.

c.   A person's future in India is largely determined by the parents.

d.   In all cultures, parents want their children to marry for love.

Distinguishing a Topic Sentence from a Title

The topic sentence works like a title by announcing the subject of the paragraph. However, keep in mind that the title of an essay or book is usually a single word or short phrase, whereas the topic sentence of a paragraph must *always* be a complete sentence.

Title:	**Backpacking in the mountains**
Topic sentence:	**Backpacking in the mountains last year was an exhausting experience.**
Title:	**The stress of college registration**
Topic sentence:	**College registration can be stressful.**

EXERCISE 5   **Distinguishing a Topic Sentence from a Title**

Indicate whether each of the following examples is a title (T) or a topic sentence (TS) by writing *T* or *TS* in the space provided.

_____ 1.   The benefits of a college education

_____ 2.   The outstanding achievements of aviator Amelia Earhart

_____ 3.   The president's cabinet proposed two possible solutions

_____ 4.   The basis of the Arab-Israeli conflict

_____ 5.   The Mediterranean diet is perhaps the healthiest diet in the world

_____ 6.   The astounding beauty of the Rocky Mountains at dusk

_____ 7. The fastest sports car on the market

_____ 8. Fast-food restaurants are popular with families who have fussy eaters

_____ 9. The expense of maintaining a car

_____10. Maintaining an old house is expensive

EXERCISE ⑥   **Distinguishing a Topic Sentence from a Title**

Indicate whether each of the following examples is a title (T) or a topic sentence (TS) by writing _T_ or _TS_ in the space provided.

_____ 1. Dreams can be frightening

_____ 2. The advantages of term limits for people in public offices

_____ 3. _The Imitation Game_ tells the tragic story of a famous mathematician

_____ 4. The job of my dreams

_____ 5. Taking a walk can be calming

_____ 6. Cooking requires great patience as well as skill

_____ 7. Selecting the right camera for an amateur

_____ 8. A regular routine is healthy for children

_____ 9. The worst bargain of my life

_____10. My last used car was a bargain

EXERCISE ⑦   **Distinguishing a Topic Sentence from a Title**

Indicate whether each of the following examples is a title (T) or a topic sentence (TS) by writing _T_ or _TS_ in the space provided.

_____ 1. How to make friends at college and still have time to study

_____ 2. With the widespread use of computers, word-processing skills are needed for many jobs

_____ 3. The disadvantages of living alone

_____ 4. The fight to keep our neighborhood park clean

_____ 5. The peacefulness of a solitary weekend in nature

_____ 6. Our investigation into the mysterious death of Walter D.

_____ 7. The flea market looked promising

_____ 8. The two main reasons divorce rates are rising

_____ 9. The single life did not turn out to be as glamorous as I had hoped

_____10. The continued popularity of board games

Finding the Topic in a Topic Sentence

To find the topic in a topic sentence, ask yourself what subject the writer is going to discuss. In the first sentence that follows, the topic is underlined. Underline the topic in the second example.

Backpacking in the mountains last year **was an exhausting experience.**

College registration **can be stressful.**

Note that a topic sentence may have a two-part topic:

The differences between **softball and baseball** **may not be readily apparent to the person who is unfamiliar with the games.**

EXERCISE **8** **Finding the Topic in a Topic Sentence**

Find the topic in each of the following topic sentences. For each sentence, ask yourself this question: What topic is the writer going to discuss? Then underline the topic.

1. Remodeling an old house can be frustrating.

2. College work demands more independence than high school work.

3. A well-made suit has three easily identified characteristics.

4. Growing up near a museum had a profound influence on my life.

5. My favorite room in the house would seem ugly to most people.

6. The huge trade imbalance of the United States has several sobering consequences.

7. One of the drawbacks of skiing is the expense.

8. Spanking is not a successful way to discipline a child.

9. An attractive wardrobe does not have to be expensive.

10. Of all the years in college, the first year is usually the most demanding.

EXERCISE **9** **Finding the Topic in a Topic Sentence**

Find the topic in each of the following topic sentences. For each sentence, ask yourself this question: What topic is the writer going to discuss? Then underline the topic.

1. Taking care of a house can easily be a full-time job.

2. Many television news programs are more interested in entertaining than providing newsworthy information.

3. One of the undisputed goals in teaching is to be able to offer individualized instruction.

4. Whether it's a car, a house, or a college, bigger isn't always better.

5. Many child psychologists find the amount of violence on television disturbing.

6. In today's economy, carrying at least one credit card is probably advisable.

7. Much highway advertising is not only ugly but also distracting for the driver.

8. Figuring out a semester course schedule can be a complicated process.

9. In recent years, we have seen a dramatic revival of interest in quilting.

10. Working for a small company can be more rewarding than working for a large corporation.

EXERCISE **10**   **Finding the Topic in a Topic Sentence**

Find the topic in each of the following topic sentences. For each sentence, ask yourself this question: What topic is the writer going to discuss? Then underline the topic.

1. To my surprise, the basement had been converted into a small studio apartment.

2. Of all the presidents, Abraham Lincoln probably enjoys the greatest popularity.

3. Nature versus nurture is a controversial issue in child psychology.

4. Many people find dependence on public transportation frustrating.

5. When we met for dinner that night, I was shocked at the change that had come over my friend.

6. According to the report, current tax laws greatly benefit those who own real estate.

7. Sam Cooke, the famous singer, began his career in a gospel choir.

8. As we rode into town, the streets seemed unusually empty.

9. Excellent long-term benefits are rare these days.

10. Many people claim that finding coupons online can save them as much as 30 percent on their food bills.

What Is a Controlling Idea?

A topic sentence should contain not only the topic but also a controlling idea.

> The **controlling idea** is the part of a topic sentence that expresses the point the writer wants to make about the topic.
>
> **Backpacking trips are *exhausting*.**

A particular topic could have any number of possible controlling ideas, depending on the writer's focus. On the topic *backpacking,* three writers might want to make different points:

A family backpacking trip can be much more *satisfying* than a trip to an amusement park.

or

Our recent backpacking trip was a *disaster*.

or

A backpacking trip *should be a part of every teenager's experience.*

Finding the Controlling Idea of a Topic Sentence

When you look for the controlling idea of a topic sentence, ask yourself this question: What is the point the writer is making about the topic?

In each of the following examples, underline the topic and circle the controlling idea.

Sealfon's Department Store is the most popular store in town.

The writer of this topic sentence announces that the focus will be on what makes the store a favorite.

Sealfon's Department Store is too expensive for a student's budget.

The writer of this topic sentence announces that the focus will be on the store's high prices.

EXERCISE 11 **Finding the Controlling Idea**

Below are ten topic sentences. For each sentence, underline the topic and circle the controlling idea.

1. Vigorous exercise is a good way to reduce the effects of stress on the body.

2. Buffalo and Toronto differ in four major ways.

3. Television violence causes aggressive behavior in children.

4. Athletic scholarships available to women are increasing.

5. Caffeine has several adverse effects on the body.

6. Serena Williams and her sister Venus have dominated the world of women's tennis.

7. Training a cat to do tricks takes great patience.

8. Babysitting for a family with four preschool children was the most exhausting job I've ever had.

9. The hours between five and seven in the morning are my most productive.

10. The foggy night was spooky.

EXERCISE **12**   **Finding the Controlling Idea**

Below are ten topic sentences. For each sentence, underline the topic and circle the controlling idea.

1. Piano lessons turned out to be an unexpected delight.

2. The training of Japanese police officers is quite different from that of American police officers.

3. An Olympic athlete has five distinctive characteristics.

4. The candidate's unethical financial dealings will have a negative impact on this campaign.

5. A bicycle ride along the coast is a breathtaking trip.

6. The grocery store is another place where people waste a significant amount of money every week.

7. Being an only child is not as bad as people think.

8. Rewarding children with candy or desserts is an unfortunate habit of many parents.

9. A childhood hobby often develops into a promising career.

10. The writing of a dictionary is an incredibly detailed process.

EXERCISE **13**   **Finding the Controlling Idea**

Below are ten topic sentences. For each sentence, underline the topic and circle the controlling idea.

1. Learning to type takes more practice than talent.

2. Shakespeare's vocabulary is challenging for some of today's students.

3. Atlanta, Georgia, is one of the cities in the Sunbelt that is experiencing significant population growth.

4. Half a dozen new health magazines are enjoying popularity.

5. The importance of good preschool programs for children has been sadly underestimated.

6. The disposal of toxic wastes has caused problems for many manufacturers.

7. Censorship of school textbooks is a controversial issue in some school districts.

8. Finding an inexpensive method to make saltwater drinkable has been unsuccessful so far.

9. Developing color film is more complicated than developing black and white.

10. The cloudberry is one of the rare berries of the world.

Choosing Controlling Ideas

Teachers often assign one general topic on which all students must write. Likewise, when writing contests are announced, the topic is often the same for all contestants. Because very few people have exactly the same view or attitude toward a topic, it is likely that no two papers will have the same controlling idea. In fact, there could be any number of controlling ideas. The secret to writing a successful topic sentence is to find the controlling idea that is right for you.

EXERCISE **14**   ### Choosing Controlling Ideas for Topic Sentences

Below are two topics. For each topic, think of three possible controlling ideas, and then write a topic sentence for each of these controlling ideas. An example has been done for you.

Topic: My mother

Three possible controlling ideas:

1. **Unusual childhood**

2. **Silent woman**

3. **Definite ideas about alcohol**

Three different topic sentences:

1. **My mother had a most unusual childhood.**

2. **My mother is a silent woman.**

3. **My mother has definite ideas about alcohol.**

1. **Topic: My neighborhood**

First controlling idea: _____

First topic sentence: _____

_____

Second controlling idea: _____

Second topic sentence: _____

_____

Third controlling idea: _____

Third topic sentence: _____

_____

2. **Topic: Cell phones**

First controlling idea: _____

First topic sentence: _____

_____

Second controlling idea: _____

Second topic sentence: _____

_____

Third controlling idea: _____

Third topic sentence: _____

_____

EXERCISE **15** **Choosing Controlling Ideas for Topic Sentences**

Below are two topics. For each topic, think of three possible controlling ideas, and then write a topic sentence for each of these controlling ideas. An example has been done for you.

Topic: The movie *Mad Max: Fury Road*

Three possible controlling ideas:

1. **Explores the effects of environmental damage on a future society**
2. **Shows George Miller's directing and visual storytelling talents**
3. **Reveals how working together can overthrow a corrupt regime**

Three different topic sentences:

1. *Mad Max: Fury Road* **explores the effects of environmental damage on a future society.**
2. *Mad Max* **shows George Miller's great talents for both directing and visual storytelling.**
3. *Fury Road* **is a movie whose main characters, played by Charlize Theron and Tom Hardy, work together to overthrow a corrupt regime.**

1. **Topic: Late-night talk shows**

First controlling idea: _____

First topic sentence: _____

_____

Second controlling idea: _____

Second topic sentence: _____

_____

Third controlling idea: _____

Third topic sentence: _____

_____

2. **Topic: Working in a nursing home**

First controlling idea: _____

First topic sentence: _____

_____

Second controlling idea: _____

Second topic sentence: _____

_____

Third controlling idea: _____

Third topic sentence: _____

_____

EXERCISE 16 **Choosing Controlling Ideas for Topic Sentences**

Below are two topics. For each topic, think of three possible controlling ideas, and then write a topic sentence for each of these controlling ideas. An example has been done for you.

Topic: Physical fitness

Three possible controlling ideas:

1. **The growth of new lines of products**
2. **Increased popularity of health clubs**
3. **Use of exercise videos and equipment at home**

Three different topic sentences:

1. **Recent years have seen the creation of entire lines of products devoted to fitness and health.**
2. **The high level of interest in physical fitness has resulted in a widespread growth of health clubs across the country.**
3. **A person can improve his or her physical fitness by exercising at home with a professional video or working out on one of the many pieces of equipment available for private use.**

1. **Topic: Music** (You can choose any music genre if you prefer.)

First controlling idea: _____

First topic sentence: _____

_____

Second controlling idea: _____

Second topic sentence: _____

_____

Third controlling idea: _____

Third topic sentence: _____

_____

2. **Topic: Junk food**

First controlling idea: _____

First topic sentence: _____

_____

Second controlling idea: _____

Second topic sentence: _____

_____

Third controlling idea: _____

Third topic sentence: _____

_____

Mastery and Editing Tests

TEST ① **Further Practice Writing Topic Sentences**

Develop each of the following topics into a topic sentence. In each case, the controlling idea is missing. Decide on the point you wish to make about the topic. Then include this controlling idea as part of your topic sentence. When you have finished, underline the topic and circle your controlling idea. Be sure your topic sentence is a complete sentence and not a fragment. An example has been done for you.

Topic:	**My brother's car accident**
Controlling idea:	**Tragic results**
Topic sentence:	**My brother's car accident had (tragic results) for the entire family.**

1. **Topic: Cyberbullying**

Controlling idea: _____

Topic sentence: _____

_____

2. **Topic: Two years in the military**

Controlling idea: _____

Topic sentence: _____

_____

3. **Topic: Living with in-laws**

Controlling idea: _____

Topic sentence: _____

_____

4. **Topic: Moving to a new location**

   Controlling idea: _____

   Topic sentence: _____

   _____

5. **Topic: Cheating**

   Controlling idea: _____

   Topic sentence: _____

   _____

TEST **2**   **Further Practice Writing Topic Sentences**

Develop each of the following topics into a topic sentence. In each case, the controlling idea is missing. Decide on the point you wish to make about the topic. Then include this controlling idea as part of your topic sentence. When you have finished, underline the topic and circle your controlling idea. Be sure your topic sentence is a complete sentence and not a fragment.

1. **Topic: College dormitories**

   Controlling idea: _____

   Topic sentence: _____

   _____

2. **Topic: College meal plans**

   Controlling idea: _____

   Topic sentence: _____

   _____

3. **Topic: Student fees**

   Controlling idea: _____

   Topic sentence: _____

   _____

4. **Topic: College parking**

   Controlling idea: _____

   Topic sentence: _____

   _____

5. **Topic: College clubs**

   Controlling idea: _____

   Topic sentence: _____

   _____

TEST ③ **Further Practice Writing Topic Sentences**

Develop each of the following topics into a topic sentence. In each case, the controlling idea is missing. Decide on the point you wish to make about the topic. Then include this controlling idea as part of your topic sentence. When you have finished, underline the topic and circle your controlling idea. Be sure your topic sentence is a complete sentence and not a fragment.

1. **Topic: Computer programming**

   Controlling idea: _____

   Topic sentence: _____

   _____

2. **Topic: Body piercing**

   Controlling idea: _____

   Topic sentence: _____

   _____

3. **Topic: Allergies**

   Controlling idea:_____

   Topic sentence: _____

   _____

4. **Topic: Airport security**

   Controlling idea: _____

   Topic sentence: _____

   _____

5. **Topic: Text messaging**

   Controlling idea: _____

   Topic sentence: _____

   _____

WRITE FOR SUCCESS

Research shows that a person's brain functions better when there is regular physical activity. How do you keep yourself physically energized? Do you incorporate some form of exercise into your daily routine? Write a response that describes your routine for physical activity or describes what could be a realistic plan for a routine. Consider your particular set of circumstances and interests.

Working Together

Tony Latham/Corbis

Exploring Controlling Ideas: A Person's Lifestyle

In developing a topic into a paragraph, a writer can choose from an endless number of controlling ideas. Student writers are often surprised by another writer's approach to a given topic. We will explore some of these approaches as we brainstorm for different controlling ideas on the following topic: a person's lifestyle. The controlling idea in the following topic sentence uses *comparison or contrast* as a method of development. It contrasts a person's lifestyle with his or her parents' lifestyle.

My parents' lifestyle is *a completely different arrangement* from my own.

Divide into groups. Each group should prepare a list of possible controlling ideas for a paragraph or essay on the topic of *a person's lifestyle.* Each person in the group should contribute two controlling ideas. Then come together as a class and share the controlling ideas with each other. (If possible, write them on a board for all to see.) When all the groups have shared their lists, the following questions should be answered:

1. How many different controlling ideas have emerged from the work of all the groups?
2. How many methods of development (*description, example, narration, process, classification, cause and effect, definition, comparison and contrast, or argument*) are represented in the several controlling ideas generated by the groups in the class?

PORTFOLIO SUGGESTION

Each student in the class should copy a complete list of controlling ideas that has been developed by the class. Organize the ideas into groups according to the most obvious method of development. Save this list in your portfolio as a reminder of the ways you could develop your own thinking on a given topic. Put a check mark beside the controlling ideas that you would consider for your own writing. Your instructor may ask you to write a paragraph or essay using the controlling idea that is most interesting to you.

Another interesting topic to write about might be the lifestyle of a particular group. Consider looking for material on the lifestyles of the rich and famous, the lifestyles of people in religious ministries, the lifestyles of people with a particular disability, the lifestyles of "successful" people, or the lifestyles of "happy" people.

Working with Paragraphs: Supporting Details

CHAPTER OBJECTIVES To develop a paragraph successfully, you must use appropriate details to support the main idea of that paragraph. In this chapter, you will learn several skills that will help you use supporting details in your own writing. These skills are as follows:

- identifying supporting details

- choosing supporting details based on the method of paragraph development

- avoiding restatement of the topic sentence

- making supporting details specific

What Is a Supporting Detail?

Once you have constructed a topic sentence made up of the topic and its controlling idea, you are ready to support your statement with details. The quality and number of these details will largely determine the effectiveness of the writing. You can hold your readers' attention with your choice of details, or you can lose your readers' interest because your details are not compelling.

A **supporting detail** is a piece of evidence used by a writer to make the controlling idea of the topic sentence convincing and interesting to the reader. A piece of evidence might be a descriptive image, an example taken from history or personal experience, a reason, a fact (such as a statistic), a quotation from an expert, or an anecdote used to illustrate a point.

Poor supporting detail: **Many people died of the flu in the 1960s.**

Effective supporting detail: **In 1968, seventy thousand people died of the Hong Kong flu in the United States.**

How Do You Choose Supporting Details?

For a paragraph to be well developed, the main idea must be supported by the use of several appropriate details. As you work through the chapters in this section, you will have opportunities to use many types of supporting details. The following chart lists the various methods of paragraph development. A writer chooses supporting details according to what best fits the method of development. For instance, if the writer is describing someone's appearance, the details are made up of sensory images (e.g., *a raspy voice, olive skin,* and *the scent of Old Spice cologne*).

METHODS OF PARAGRAPH DEVELOPMENT

Narration:	telling a story using a sequence of events
Description:	using sensory images to create a picture with words
Process:	using steps explaining how to do something or explaining how something works
Illustration or example:	giving instances of the main idea
Comparison/contrast:	showing similarities or differences
Cause and effect:	examining reasons or outcomes
Extended definition:	analyzing at some length the meaning of a word or concept
Classification:	dividing a subject into groups or parts

As you choose your supporting details, keep in mind that your readers do not necessarily have to agree with your point of view. However, your supporting details must be good enough to make your readers at least appreciate your details. Your goal should be to educate your readers. Try to give them some understanding of your subject. Don't assume they know about your topic or are interested in it. If you provide enough specific details, your readers will feel they have learned something new about the subject, and this alone is a satisfying experience for most people. Effective supporting details will encourage readers to keep on reading. Such details will make your points more memorable, and they will give pleasure to those who are learning new material or picturing the images you have created.

Read the following paragraph and observe how it provides effective details that support the controlling idea of the topic sentence.

Most people are surprised to learn that there are more than 200 distinct cold viruses. Twenty-five million people in the United States have a cold every year. Certainly we all need to know how to care for a cold most effectively. Everyone has heard of the two common recommendations: get lots of rest and drink plenty of fluids. Actually, this advice is good. Getting enough rest puts less stress on the body, which results in a quicker recovery. Studies have found that less than seven hours of sleep a night makes a person three times more likely to catch a cold in the first place. Drinking fluids, particularly warm fluids and hot soups, is also good. Warm fluids raise your body temperature. Viruses do not replicate as well at higher temperatures. While most people know about rest and drinking fluids, many people do not know about the negative effects of taking antibiotics, aspirin, or Tylenol when fighting a cold. Antibiotics are effective only if you have a bacterial infection. Aspirin and Tylenol are actually dangerous because they will suppress your body's natural production of antibodies. These antibodies normally will fight a cold virus. While many people believe large doses of

(continued on next page)

vitamin C or echinacea will shorten the effects of a cold, recent studies have not been able to confirm this. On the other hand, one positive finding from recent studies confirms that supplements with the mineral zinc will help reduce the duration and severity of the common cold in healthy people.

PRACTICE 1   **Using the lines provided, copy the topic sentence from the previous paragraph. Then answer the questions about the details that support the topic sentence.**

Topic sentence: _____

_____

What are two examples of how to care for a cold that most people already know?

_____

_____

What are the examples of information people may not know?

_____

What studies have had mixed results?

_____

Tetra Images/Alamy

_____

What mineral supplement has been proven effective?

_____

_____

EXERCISE 1   **Finding the Topic Sentence and Supporting Details**

Read each paragraph below. On the lines that follow, write the topic sentence and identify the supporting details.

1.   Diabetes, a disease of the pancreas, falls into two types. Type 1 diabetes is sometimes called juvenile diabetes because most people are diagnosed before the age of 40. People with this type of diabetes must inject or pump insulin two or three times a day because the pancreas produces very little insulin or none at all. Only 5 to 10 percent of all the people with diabetes have type 1. Type 2 diabetes usually develops in adults over 35 years old and seems to be connected to obesity, poor diet, lack of exercise, and sometimes ethnicity. In this case, the pancreas may produce some insulin but not enough, or it has trouble using the insulin. Sadly, type 2 diabetes has recently begun to appear in overweight children and teenagers.

Topic sentence: _____

What is the first type of diabetes: _____

What is the age factor?: _____

What is the second type of diabetes? _____

What is the age factor? _____

_____

2.   As time passed, the Gonzalez family became a melting-pot success story by anyone's measure. One by one, each of us completed high school and joined the first college-educated generation in the family's history. My uncle Sergio and aunt Catin produced a college instructor in Greek and Latin, another son who rose to be an official in the Nixon and Reagan administrations, and a South Bronx social worker. I went to Ivy League Columbia University and eventually on to a career in journalism; my sister became a public school teacher and later a college instructor. One cousin became a doctor, another a psychiatric social worker, and another a police detective.

FROM JUAN GONZALEZ
A Harvest of Empire

Topic sentence: _____

_____

First example: _____

_____

Second example: _____

_____

Third example: _____

Fourth example: _____

Fifth example: _____

_____

Sixth example: _____

Seventh example: _____

Eighth example: _____

EXERCISE **2** **Finding the Topic Sentence and Supporting Details**

Read each paragraph below. On the lines that follow, write the topic sentence and identify the supporting details.

1.   Hilda takes an enormous amount of space, though so little time, in my adolescence. Even today, her memory stirs me; I long to see her again. She was three years older than I, and for a short while all I wanted was to look like, sound like, and dress like her. She was the only girl I knew who told me I wrote excellent letters. She made a plaster cast of my face. She had opinions on everything. She took a picture of me, at sixteen, which I have still. She and I were nearly killed, falling off a hillside road in her small car. Hilda was so full of life, I cannot believe her dead.

FROM HAN SUYIN,
A Mortal Flower

Topic sentence: _____

_____

First detail: _____

_____

Second detail: _____

Third detail: _____

Fourth detail: _____

Fifth detail: _____

Sixth detail: _____

2.   A steadily accumulating body of evidence supports the view that cancers are caused by things that we eat, drink, breathe, or are otherwise exposed to. That evidence is of three kinds. First, the incidence of many types of cancers differs greatly from one geographic region of the world to another. Second, when groups of people permanently move from one country to another, the incidence of some types of cancer changes in their offspring. For example, when Japanese move to this country, the relatively high rate of occurrence of stomach cancer they experience in Japan falls so that their children experience such cancer only a fifth as frequently, the same incidence as other Americans. Asians have low incidence of breast cancer, but when they come to the United States, it increases sixfold. Third, we are becoming aware of an increasing number of chemical pollutants in air and water and food that have proven to be cancer-producing.

FROM MAHLON B. HOAGLAND,
The Roots of Life

Topic sentence: _____

_____

First piece of evidence: _____

_____

Second piece of evidence (and example): _____

_____

_____

_____

Third piece of evidence: _____

_____

EXERCISE ③ **Finding the Topic Sentence and Supporting Details**

Read each paragraph below. On the lines that follow, write the topic sentence and identify the supporting details.

1.   Transportation was simple then. Two good horses and a sturdy wagon met most needs of a villager. Only five or six individuals possessed an automobile in the Pueblo of 300. A flatbed truck fixed with wooden rails and a canvas top made a regular Saturday trip to Santa Fe. It was always loaded beyond capacity with Cochitis taking their wares to town for a few staples. With an escort of a dozen barking dogs, the straining truck made a noisy exit, northbound from the village.

FROM JOSEPH H. SUINA,
And Then I Went to School

Topic sentence: _____

First example: _____

Second example: _____

_____

Third example: _____

_____

_____

2.   Fairness is the ability to see more than one side in a situation, and sometimes it even means having the ability to decide against your own interests. For example, in San Antonio, Texas, a woman was involved in a complicated custody dispute that involved her thirteen-year-old son. The mother loved her son and wanted custody of him, even though she had a major health problem. She listened patiently while her ex-husband argued for full custody of the child. The woman felt that she had presented a good case before the judge, but when the boy was asked for his feelings in the matter, the mother found herself faced with a difficult situation: her son wanted to live with his father.

Topic sentence: _____

_____

Anecdote: _____

_____

_____

_____

_____

_____

_____

Avoiding Restatement of the Topic Sentence

Writers need to recognize the difference between a genuine supporting detail and a simple restatement of the topic sentence. The following is a poor paragraph because all its sentences merely restate the topic sentence.

iStockphoto.com/fornmt

> The wedding day was the highest point in a girl's life—a day to which she looked forward all her unmarried days and to which she looked back for the rest of her life. All the events of the day were unlike those of any other day in her life before or after. Everyone would remember this day. Each event was unforgettable. The memories would last a lifetime. A wedding was the beginning of living "happily ever after."

By contrast, this paragraph, from Margaret Mead's "From Popping the Question to Popping the Pill," has excellent supporting details:

> The wedding day was the highest point in a girl's life—a day to which she looked forward all her unmarried days and to which she looked back for the rest of her life. The splendor of her wedding, the elegance of dress and veil, the cutting of the cake, the departure amid a shower of

(continued on next page)

rice and confetti, gave her an accolade of which no subsequent event could completely rob her. Today people over fifty years of age still treat their daughter's wedding this way, prominently displaying the photographs of the occasion. Until very recently, all brides' books prescribed exactly the same ritual they had prescribed fifty years before. The etiquette governing wedding presents—gifts that were or were not appropriate, the bride's maiden initials on her linen—was also specified. For the bridegroom the wedding represented the end of his free, bachelor days, and the bachelor dinner the night before the wedding symbolized this loss of freedom. A woman who did not marry—even if she had the alibi of a fiancé who had been killed in war or had abilities and charm and money of her own—was always at a social disadvantage, while an eligible bachelor was sought after by hostess after hostess.

EXERCISE ④ **Distinguishing a Supporting Detail from a Restatement of the Main Idea**

Each topic sentence below is followed by four additional sentences. Three of these additional sentences contain acceptable supporting details, but one of the sentences is simply a restatement of the topic sentence. In the spaces provided, identify each sentence as *SD*, for supporting detail, or *R*, for restatement.

1. I used to be so organized before I went to college.

  _____ a. In my closet, I had my clothes arranged in matching outfits with shoes, hats, and even jewelry to go with them.

  _____ b. In the past, I always kept my things in order.

  _____ c. If I opened my desk drawer, compartments of paper clips, erasers, staples, pens, pencils, stamps, and rulers greeted me, without a penny or safety pin out of place.

  _____ d. On top of my chest of drawers sat a comb and brush and two oval frames with pictures of my best friends; that was all.

2. Iceland has a very barren landscape.

  _____ a. One-tenth of the island is covered by ice.

  _____ b. There is not a single forest on the entire island.

  _____ c. Nearly everywhere you look in Iceland, you see vast desolate areas.

  _____ d. Three-fourths of the island is uninhabitable.

3. Until recently, books have been the most important method of preserving knowledge.

  _____ a. Without books, much of the knowledge of past centuries would have been lost.

_____ b. Leonardo da Vinci kept notebooks of his amazing inventions and discoveries.

_____ c. During the Middle Ages, monks spent their entire lives copying books by hand.

_____ d. The Library of Congress in Washington, D.C., is given a copy of every book published in the United States.

4. Most adults no longer wonder whether cigarette smoking is bad for their health.

_____ a. Based on the evidence from more than 30,000 studies, a federal law requires that cigarette manufacturers place a health warning on their packages.

_____ b. Studies have shown that smoking causes nearly 80 percent of lung cancer deaths in this country.

_____ c. Few people today have any doubts about the connection between cigarette smoking and poor health.

_____ d. We know that 30 percent of the deaths from coronary heart disease can be attributed to smoking.

5. When an earthquake struck Mexico in 1985, scientists and city planners learned a great deal about the kinds of buildings that can survive an earthquake.

_____ a. Buildings that had foundations resting on giant rollers suffered very little damage.

_____ b. Buildings that were made only of adobe material simply fell apart when the earthquake struck.

_____ c. Many modern buildings were designed to vibrate in an earthquake, and these received the least amount of shock.

_____ d. After the 1985 earthquake in Mexico, officials realized why some buildings were destroyed and others suffered hardly any damage at all.

EXERCISE 5 **Distinguishing a Supporting Detail from a Restatement of the Main Idea**

Each topic sentence below is followed by four additional sentences. Three of these additional sentences contain acceptable supporting details, but one of the sentences is simply a restatement of the topic sentence. In the spaces provided, identify each sentence as *SD*, for supporting detail, or *R*, for restatement.

1. In the last thirty years, the number of people living alone in the United States has increased by 400 percent.

_____ a. People are living alone because the number of divorces has dramatically increased.

_____ b. Many young people are putting off marriage until they are financially more secure or emotionally ready.

_____ c. More and more Americans are finding themselves living alone.

_____ d. An increasing percentage of our population is in the age group over sixty-five, and many of them are widows and widowers.

2. Today, people are realizing the disadvantages of using credit cards too often.

_____ a. People should think twice before borrowing money on credit.

_____ b. Interest rates on credit cards can reach alarming rates.

_____ c. Credit cards encourage buying on impulse, rather than planning a budget carefully.

_____ d. Many credit card companies charge an annual fee for the privilege of using their cards.

3. In medicine, prevention is just as important as treatment.

_____ a. A good way for a person to keep in touch with his or her health is to have an annual physical.

_____ b. To stay healthy, people should watch their weight.

_____ c. Some researchers claim that taking an aspirin every day thins the blood, which prevents clotting.

_____ d. Where health is concerned, warding off a disease is as critical as curing it.

4. Since World War II, the status of women in Japan has changed.

_____ a. In 1947, women won the right to vote.

_____ b. Women's position in Japanese society has altered over the past seventy years.

_____ c. Many Japanese women now get a higher education.

_____ d. A woman can now own property in her own name and seek divorce.

5. Certain factors that cannot be changed have been shown to contribute to heart attacks and stroke.

_____ a. Three out of four heart attacks and six out of seven strokes occur after the age of sixty-five, so age is definitely a factor.

_____ b. Heart attacks and strokes have many causes, some of which we can do nothing about.

_____ c. African-Americans have nearly a 45 percent greater risk of having high blood pressure, a major cause of heart attacks and strokes.

_____ d. Men are at greater risk than women in their chance of suffering from cardiovascular disease.

How Do You Make Supporting Details Specific?

Students often write paragraphs that are made up of too many general statements. With such paragraphs, the writer's knowledge is in doubt, and the reader may suspect that the point being made has no basis in fact. Here is one such paragraph that never rises beyond generalities.

> Doctors are terrible. They cause more problems than they solve. I don't believe most of their treatments are necessary. History is full of the mistakes doctors have made. We don't need all those operations. We should never ingest all those drugs doctors prescribe. We shouldn't allow them to give us all those unnecessary tests. I've heard plenty of stories that prove my point. Doctors' ideas can kill you.

Here is another paragraph on the same topic. It is much more interesting and convincing because the writer has used supporting details rather than relying on general statements.

> Evidence shows that "medical progress" has been the cause of tragic consequences and even death for thousands of people. X-ray therapy was thought to help patients with tonsillitis. Now many of these people are found to have developed cancer from these X-rays. Not so long ago, women were kept in bed for several weeks following childbirth. Unfortunately, this cost many women their lives because they developed fatal blood clots from being kept in bed day after day. One recent poll estimates that 30,000 people die each year from the side effects of drugs that were prescribed by doctors. Recently, the Centers for Disease Control and Prevention reported that 25 percent of the tests done by clinical laboratories were done poorly. All this is not to belittle the good done by the medical profession, but to impress on readers that it would be foolish to rely totally on the medical profession to solve all our health problems.

This paragraph is much more likely to be of real interest. Even if the reader wanted to disprove the author's point, it would be very hard to dismiss these supporting details, which are based on facts and information that can be verified. Because the writer sounds reasonable, the reader has respect for the presentation of specific facts, even if he or she has a different position on the topic.

In writing effectively, the ability to go beyond the general statement and get to the accurate pieces of information is what counts. A good writer tries to make his or her reader an expert on the subject. Readers should go away excited to share the surprising information they have just learned. A writer who has a statistic, a quotation, an anecdote, a historical example, or a descriptive detail has the advantage over all other writers, no matter how impressive these writers' styles may be.

Good writing, therefore, is filled with supporting details that are specific, accurate, and appropriate for the subject. Poor writing is filled with generalizations, stereotypes, vagueness, untruths, and sometimes even sarcasm and insults.

EXERCISE 6 **Creating Supporting Details**

Below are five topic sentences. Supply three supporting details for each one (inventing, when necessary). Be sure each detail is specific, not general or vague, and use complete sentences for your answers.

1. Several learning disabilities today can be treated.

   a. _____

   b. _____

   c. _____

2. At certain times, a student should ask for help.

   a. _____

   b. _____

   c. _____

3. More than one strategy can help students remember information.

   a. _____

   b. _____

   c. _____

4. Many issues affect reading comprehension.

   a. _____

   b. _____

   c. _____

5. At least three ways of learning have been described by educators.

   a. _____

   b. _____

   c. _____

EXERCISE **7** **Creating Supporting Details**

Below are five topic sentences. Supply three supporting details for each one (inventing, when necessary). Be sure each detail is specific, not general or vague, and use complete sentences for your answers.

1. The recent financial crisis has had far-reaching consequences for many American families.

    a. _____

    b. _____

    c. _____

2. On a college campus today, current trends in fashion are noticeable.

    a. _____

    b. _____

    c. _____

3. Each sport has its own particular injuries.

    a. _____

    b. _____

    c. _____

4. My manager at work often exhibits very odd behavior.

    a. _____

    b. _____

    c. _____

5. There are several reasons why people today do not get enough exercise.

    a. _____

    b. _____

    c. _____

EXERCISE **8** **Creating Supporting Details**

Below are five topic sentences. Supply three supporting details for each one (inventing, when necessary). Be sure each detail is specific, not general or vague, and use complete sentences for your answers.

1. A democracy depends on an educated populace.

    a. _____

    b. _____

    c. _____

2. An only child is not necessarily a lonely child.

   a. _____

   b. _____

   c. _____

3. Lending money to a friend is not recommended.

   a. _____

   b. _____

   c. _____

4. Everyone should get up and walk or stretch after 50 minutes of inactivity.

   a. _____

   b. _____

   c. _____

5. Video games can stimulate the mind.

   a. _____

   b. _____

   c. _____

WRITE FOR SUCCESS

How does a person set goals for himself or herself? Consider the importance of having both short- and long-term goals. Experts would say such goals need to be realistic and useful. These goals also need to be concrete and specific. Finally, they should fit into your value system. Write a response that explores your personal goals, both short-term and long-term. Be sure these goals are realistic, useful, and specific. Explain how they reflect what you value most in life.

Working Together

Stuart Monk/Dreamstime.com

Peer Editing: Recording Family, Community, or National Traditions

Rituals and celebrations are important milestones for individuals, groups, and even entire nations. These milestones affirm people's lives and help them feel connected. They also support a nation's need to preserve its history.

Our country observes two major holidays to honor our soldiers. The first of these is Memorial Day, a holiday that honors all those who have died in the service of our nation. It was originally called Decoration Day and was officially proclaimed in 1868. Memorial Day is observed on the last Monday in May; on that day in many areas of the country, war veterans collect donations and give people red paper poppies in return. This is also a time to fly the flag at half staff to commemorate the war dead. The graves of fallen soldiers are decorated with American flags, and some communities hold parades in honor of the day. Veterans Day, on the other hand, is a day intended to honor *all* American veterans, living and dead. Originally known as Armistice Day, Veterans Day marked the end of World War I on November 11, 1918. With all the war veterans returning from Iraq and Afghanistan, many Americans today are concerned that these war veterans be better supported in their efforts to adjust to civilian life.

The class should divide into an even number of groups, each group choosing a different topic, either from the list below or from topics given by the instructor. Each person within a group will then write two sentences that demonstrate supporting details for the topic.

Possible Topics: Description of a Memorial Day Parade

Description of a soldier's grave

Ways individuals can be supportive of living veterans

What the government or private industry should do for jobless or homeless veterans

What should be done for veterans who return home with psychological problems

What financial support is available to veterans for higher education and/or job training

After students have written their sentences, each group should pass these sentences to another group. This group will read all the sentences and evaluate them in three ways:

a.   Using the editing symbols from the inside back cover, mark any errors.

b.   Give each sentence a rating from 1 (the lowest) to 4 (the highest), judging the sentences for the specificity of the supporting details.

Use the following sentences as your guide:

Rating #1: The sentence is too general, containing no specific details.

Americans fly the flag on important days.

Rating #2: The sentence is more specific but still too general.

Americans fly the flag on national holidays.

Rating #3: The sentence has some specific detail.

It is customary to fly the American flag on national holidays such as the Fourth of July.

Rating #4: The sentence has very specific details.

It is customary to fly the American flag on our national holidays: Memorial Day, Veterans Day, Flag Day, and the Fourth of July.

c.   Rewrite at least two of the sentences, making the details more specific.

When your sentences are returned to you, be sure to note how each sentence was evaluated. Has your ability to recognize the difference between a specific detail and a general statement improved?

PORTFOLIO SUGGESTION

Information discussed while working together may lead you to further exploration of these topics. An interesting research topic would be a discussion of some specific ways Americans around the country are helping returning veterans. You might contact a veterans' organization in your community and ask what programs are available for local veterans. You also might talk to local veterans to ask them what they would like to see made available.

Developing Paragraphs: Illustration 18

CHAPTER OBJECTIVES

To give clarity to a general idea or an abstract notion, a writer may choose **illustration**, or **example**, to develop a paragraph.

- learning about three ways to illustrate a point
- recognizing four sources of examples
- using transitions to introduce examples
- analyzing paragraphs with examples
- taking a step-by-step approach to create paragraphs that use illustration
- studying models to create paragraphs that use illustration

What Is Illustration?

A main idea must be supported by details. Using an illustration is one of the best ways to do this.

> *Illustration* (often called **example** or **exemplification**) is a method of developing an idea by providing one or more instances of that idea. Illustrations, or examples, serve to clarify the idea, make the idea more convincing, or make an abstract idea more concrete.
>
> One example of American craftsmanship is the Tiffany lamp.

Writers use illustration in three basic ways.

1. To provide a list of brief examples, given without any particular grouping:

Topic sentence

> <u>As a child, I had pen pals from all over the world.</u> These included my cousin Britt-Marie from Sweden, Ying from Hong Kong, Simone from France, Etsuko from Japan, and several children from Kenya.

2. To provide a list of brief examples arranged into groups:

Topic sentence

> <u>As a child, I had pen pals from all over the world</u>. From Europe were my Swedish cousin Britt-Marie and a pretty French girl named Simone. From the Pacific came the beautiful monthly letters of Etsuko and an occasional postcard from Ying in Hong Kong. Finally, from Africa came a number of charming letters from several schoolchildren in Kenya.

3. To select one item from a possible list and develop it more fully into a longer and more developed example, called an **extended example** (possibly consisting of an **anecdote** based on the principles of narration):

Topic sentence

> <u>As a child, I had pen pals from all over the world</u>. It all started when my cousin Britt-Marie in Sweden sent me a funny little letter in half English, half Swedish. Sitting on our front porch swatting flies one morning in August, I was considering walking the two miles uptown to the library when the mail carrier handed me an envelope with colorful stamps on it. It was probably the first piece of mail I had ever received. I barely knew I had a cousin Britt-Marie. But there she was—a young girl writing just to me from across the Atlantic Ocean. I was hooked from that very day. Although I eventually had pen pals from many other countries, Britt-Marie remained my favorite. In fact, we still communicate, now by e-mail, at least once every few weeks.

Always remember that the anecdote must support the larger point contained in the topic sentence—namely, the writer had pen pals from all over the world.

Where Does the Writer Find Examples?

Writers draw on four main sources for examples.

1. **Personal experience and knowledge of the world.** Writers find supporting examples for their work everywhere, beginning with their own experience. What you have observed and what has happened to you are two excellent sources of examples for your writing. You have gained a great deal of knowledge either formally or informally, and you can call upon that knowledge when you look for examples to illustrate your points.

2. **Imagination.** When writers need examples to clarify their ideas, they often find it useful to draw upon their imagination for their examples, or they visualize hypothetical situations that suggest specific details. Humorous writers do this all the time when they tell jokes. You, too, can use your imagination to generate examples when your writing does not require strictly factual information. A hypothetical example is particularly useful to illustrate a point, and it often begins with a phrase such as "Imagine the following situation" or "Consider this hypothetical case" or "Ask yourself what would happen if. . . ."

3. **Interviews and surveys.** Obtaining examples through interviews and informal surveys can enrich your writing by allowing you to present very specific information and facts about your main idea. We see and hear interviews on television and radio every day, as people from all walks of life tell their stories on every topic imaginable. We are accustomed to seeing professional interviewers ask questions, but you can also gain examples in this way by talking to your friends and classmates and learning from them.

4. **Outside research.** Printed or electronic material from outside sources can provide specific examples for your work. This research may involve the resources of a library, with its online databases as well as other online resources. This kind of research is necessary for term papers and many other kinds of college work, and it always requires a careful listing of the sources used.

EXERCISE ①   **The Sources for Illustrations**

Each of the following four paragraphs develops an idea by using illustration. Read each paragraph and decide what source the writer used to obtain the illustration. Choose from the following list:

- example from personal experience or knowledge
- imaginary or hypothetical example
- information from an interview or survey conducted by the writer
- outside research (material found in books, in articles, or on the Internet)

Topic sentence   1.   <u>For those who want to land a full-time job after college, an internship is often a very good idea.</u> Our college career services office asked twelve students who had been chosen for internships the summer after their junior year to answer some questions about their experiences. Of the twelve individuals, six had enjoyed internships that paid a stipend, while the other six had received no money at all. Eight of the interns (both paid and unpaid) reported that being an intern had been a positive experience with opportunities to learn skills that would be needed in their future careers; the four other interns did not feel they had learned anything new, but they were nevertheless hopeful that the experience would look good on their résumés and thus, in the end, have been worthwhile. The college career services office was eager to pursue those sources of internships in which students would be exposed to real job experiences in their field of study.

Type of illustration: _____

Topic sentence   2.   <u>For those who want to land a full-time job after college, an internship is often a very good idea.</u> In the current job market, many are finding it difficult to get a job in their field. If you are one of these people, consider what an internship could do for you. A person might, for example, get an internship in the entertainment industry. While you may find yourself getting people coffee or answering telephones, you would at least get to see how that particular company operates from the inside. You also might make several valuable contacts that could later turn out to be instrumental in your finding a permanent position. People who create most internships like this one would make an effort to give you some experience in your field. This might help you assess whether this is truly the career for you. Even if there would not be any pay for the internship, you might decide that the time spent is an investment in your future.

Type of illustration: _____

Topic sentence 3. <u>For those who want to land a full-time job after college, an internship is often a very good idea.</u> The summer after my junior year at Arizona State, I applied for a number of internships, without much success. I approached some broadcasting companies, but when I found out they would pay nothing at all, I realized that I could not afford to have no income during the summer. On one occasion, I contacted a financial company, only to be told that they did not have any internships. The manager was amused when I asked him if I could be the first! I sent him a follow-up e-mail, and two weeks later I was taken by surprise when he wrote back and told me that indeed I would be their first intern if I still wanted it. Did I! They offered me enough of a stipend that I could take the internship without going into debt.

Type of illustration: _____

Topic sentence 4. <u>For those who want to land a full-time job after college, an internship is often a very good idea</u>. Companies are offering more internships now than ever before. According to Edwin W. Koc, research director at the National Association of Colleges and Employers, people who serve as interns eventually receive more job offers than those who do not, and those who do obtain jobs after completing internships command higher salaries when they begin than those who have not had internships. Of course, competition for these internships is intense. A student should visit the college career services center and see what might be available in his or her major. A student can also go online to Internships.com, which posts openings. They claim that 34 percent of internships are paid positions with the amount of pay varying depending on the industry. Jobs in such areas as fashion and entertainment tend not to pay or to pay very little, while positions in areas such as engineering, technology, and finance are likely to offer modest payment. Lauren Berger, chief executive of Internqueen.com, suggests you also make a list of ten companies you would like to work for and contact them for information about any possible internships. Sometimes colleges will even give stipends to students who have received unpaid internships. This growing trend of summer internships is an opportunity a student should not pass up.

Type of illustration: _____

 EXERCISE 2 | The Sources for Illustrations

Below is a topic sentence. Write a paragraph in which you support the idea of the topic sentence by using an example from your personal experience or knowledge. Topic sentence: *Many advertising claims are deceptive.*

Your paragraph:

_____

_____

_____

_____

_____

_____

_____

EXERCISE 3 | The Sources for Illustrations

Below is a topic sentence. Write a paragraph in which you support the idea by using information from a survey of several of your classmates.

Topic sentence: *Taste in music is very personal.*

Your paragraph:

_____

_____

_____

_____

_____

_____

_____

Achieving Coherence

Choosing an Order Depending on the Type of Illustration Used

1. If the illustration is a *story* or an *anecdote,* the writer usually uses *time order.*
2. If the illustration is made up of *several descriptive examples,* the writer might use *spatial order* (top to bottom, right to left, etc.).
3. If the illustration calls for a *logical order,* this logic will determine the sequence.
4. If no special order seems necessary, the writer often places the *strongest or most important example last* because this is what the reader is likely to remember best.

Using Transitions

Writers often signal the beginning of an illustration by using a key phrase. Following is a list of phrases commonly used to signal the beginning of an illustration.

Transitions Commonly Used in Illustration

For example, . . .	Consider the case of . . .
Another example is . . .	A case in point . . .
To illustrate, . . .	For instance, . . .
An illustration of this is . . .	An anecdote illustrating this is . . .
One such case is . . .	To be specific, . . .

EXERCISE **4**   **Analyzing Paragraphs That Use Examples**

Read the following paragraph by Suzanne Britt, and then answer the questions about it.

Topic sentence   Being a connoisseur of junk has wonderfully mucked up my entire life. You know the song about favorite things like raindrops on roses and whiskers on kittens? Well, I've got my own list of favorite things: I like the insides of filthy bus stations, unsavory characters, a Dr Pepper can floating on the sun-flecked water, Jujubes, the greasy tug and tang of beef jerky wrapped in cellophane, the kitchen drawer beside the phone, the Sunday clutter around the house, the noble whiff of manure, the sweaty odor of a person I love, the smoke-filled room in which I get to inhale the equivalent of eleven cigarettes without breaking my promise to quit, the pigeon droppings in the square, the grease under the fingernails of a gas station attendant (if I can still find one), the rusty Brillo on the sink, the bathroom glass placidly growing bacteria for the whole family, *People* magazine, a dog-eared paperback, a cold pork chop eaten at the refrigerator door.

1. State the topic sentence in your own words. _____

   _____

2. How many examples are given in the paragraph? _____

3. Underline the examples in the paragraph.

4. Does the author use any words or phrases to signal any of the examples? If so, circle each one. _____

5. If there is more than one example, can you suggest any order for them?

   _____

EXERCISE **5**   **Analyzing Paragraphs That Use Examples**

Read the following paragraph and then answer the questions about it.

Topic sentence   Cheating no longer seems to be considered as shameful as it once was. Some say the increased competition to get into colleges and graduate schools may account for why more students are willing to cheat. Whatever the reasons, the Educational Testing Service has provided us with some very sobering facts about academic cheating in American schools. In a poll of students selected for *Who's Who Among American High School Students*, more than half of the students surveyed thought cheating was no big deal. In fact, what might stun most people, is that 80% of these students said they had cheated in order to get to the top of their class. In another survey, this one conducted by the Josephson Institute of Ethics, the results showed that 70% of the 20,000 students surveyed from middle school and high school admitted to cheating. What should really worry our society is the knowledge that this cheating is not likely to stop at graduation. Do we want to live in a society of people who believe that the ends justify the means?

1. State the topic sentence in your own words. _____

   _____

2. How many surveys were cited in the paragraph? _____

3. Who are the experts named? _____

   _____

4. What are the statistics given? _____

   _____

5. What alarming conclusion does the author make? _____

   _____

   _____

EXERCISE **6**   **Analyzing Paragraphs That Use Examples**

Read the following paragraph and then answer the questions about it.

Topic sentence    One of the most wonderful aspects of Sabatini's teaching was his desire to give encouragement. Even if the student did not have a great voice or did not show true promise, Sabatini would find something to praise, some little ray of hope that might help the student continue in the right direction. Let me relate an anecdote that will demonstrate this instructor's positive approach. One day, I was called in to Sabatini's studio to play the piano for a new pupil. This young student had come many miles to study with Sabatini, and I could see at once that she was very nervous. That she knew just a few words of Italian only made her more apprehensive. I started to play the music for the test aria. As usual, Sabatini sat in his chair with his eyes closed, listening. The young voice floated through the room, small and shaky at first, but growing a little more confident as she went on. Finally, after it was over, we all waited for the great man's judgment. Sabatini looked up and spoke through me. "I cannot do much for this young student," he said slowly, "because God has already done so much for her." When I translated this for the student, her face gained a new color and she smiled for the first time. That day started her period of study with Sabatini, and three years later she made her first appearance in the opera house. I have always known that her great career really began with those first words of encouragement from her teacher.

1. State the topic sentence in your own words. _____

   _____

2. How many examples are given in the paragraph? _____

3. Mark the example (or examples) in the paragraph.

4. Does the author use any words or phrases to signal the use of an illustration?

   If so, circle each one. _____

Writing a Paragraph Using a Step-by-Step Approach to Illustration

Mastering any skill, including writing, requires a disciplined attitude. One way to master the skill of creating a piece of writing is to take a step-by-step approach, focusing on one issue at a time. This approach results in a minimum of stress. Another advantage is that the writer does not miss important points or misunderstand any part of the process. Of course, there are other ways to build effective paragraphs through illustration, but here is one logical method you can use that will always achieve good results.

STEP-BY-STEP APPROACH TO WRITING A PARAGRAPH USING ILLUSTRATION

1. Compose your topic sentence, being sure to consider carefully your choice of controlling idea.

2. When using examples, consider the options: personal experience, hypothetical examples, interviews or surveys, and research. What type of example will fit your idea best? At this stage, brainstorming with a group of classmates is usually helpful.

3. Decide how many examples you will provide to develop your paragraph. Will there be one extended example with several sentences or several brief examples of one sentence each?

4. If you have more than one example, decide on the order in which to present them. Many writers start with the least important example and end with the most important.

5. Use complete sentences when you write down your examples. Each example must support the main idea, or the paragraph will lack unity.

6. Write a final sentence that concludes what you want to say about this idea.

7. Copy your sentences into standard paragraph form. Indent five spaces to begin the paragraph and be sure to double-space.

8. Always make a final check for spelling errors and other mistakes such as omitted words.

NOTE: When you use a computer spell-check feature, keep in mind that this feature will alert you only to spellings that do not match words in its dictionary. If you type *there* when you mean *their*, the spell-checker will see an acceptable word. When it comes to a final editing, there is no substitute for your own careful reading.

EXERCISE 7 **Writing a Paragraph Using a Step-by-Step Approach to Illustration**

This exercise will guide you through the construction of a paragraph using illustration. Start with the topic suggested below. Use the eight steps to help you work through the stages of the writing process.

Ben Molyneux / Alamy

Topic: Animals that make good pets

People have many reasons for keeping pets, ranging from the desire for simple companionship to a need for protection. In recent years, the list of animals has expanded beyond the traditional animals we all know— dogs, cats, fish, and birds—as people have chosen some very exotic animals. People have been known to keep deadly snakes in their homes, and in New York City a resident was discovered to have a dangerous Bengal tiger in his small apartment. Keeping in mind the subject of traditional and nontraditional pets, choose a controlling idea about keeping a pet, an idea that will give you the opportunity to use several specific examples of pets people like to have. Do you know if there are any specific laws that your community has enacted to outlaw certain pets as inappropriate or too dangerous? If you could choose two or three pets for yourself, describe which ones you would choose and why.

1. Topic sentence:

   _____

   _____

2. Which type of example (or types of examples) will you use?

   _____

   _____

3. How many examples will you give? _____

   _____

4. List your examples in an order that makes sense to you. (One good example may be enough. Probably no more than three or four brief examples would fit in one paragraph.)

   a. _____

   b. _____

   c. _____

   d. _____

5. Working from your list in number 4, construct at least one sentence for each of your examples.

_____

_____

_____

_____

_____

_____

_____

_____

_____

_____

6. Write the sentence that will conclude your paragraph.

_____

_____

7. On a separate sheet of paper or on a computer, copy your sentences into standard paragraph form.

8. Do a final reading to check for errors and omissions.

EXERCISE 8 **Writing a Paragraph Using a Step-by-Step Approach to Illustration**

This exercise will guide you through the construction of a paragraph using illustration. Start with the topic suggested below. Use the eight steps to help you work through the stages of the writing process.

Topic: Examples of art in our daily lives

We often think of _art_ as something far removed from our lives, intended only for galleries and museums. However, if we think about the items we use every day (our dishes, our clothes, the colors we choose to paint our walls), we realize that our choices of these items represent our individual attempts to make our lives more beautiful and more satisfying. What examples can you give that show your own artistic taste or style? In what ways have you tried to make your own world include things of beauty or artistic value?

1. Topic sentence:

_____

_____

2. Which type of example (or types of examples) will you use?

   _____

   _____

3. How many examples will you give? _____

4. List your examples in an order that makes sense to you. (One good example may be enough. Probably no more than three or four brief examples would fit in one paragraph.)

   a. _____

   b. _____

   c. _____

   d. _____

5. Working from your list in number 4, construct at least one sentence for each of your examples.

   _____

   _____

   _____

   _____

   _____

   _____

   _____

   _____

   _____

6. Write the sentence that will conclude your paragraph.

   _____

   _____

7. On a separate sheet of paper or on a computer, copy your sentences into standard paragraph form.

8. Do a final reading to check for errors and omissions.

Studying Model Paragraphs to Create Paragraphs Using Illustration

Assignment 1: A Person's Passion

Many people are passionate about something in their lives. Perhaps it is a sport or perhaps it is an interest in music or collecting. Study the paragraph below. Use it as a model to write your own paragraph giving examples that show how a person's passion occupies an important place in his or her life. The following paragraph is taken from "The Joy of Reading and Writing: Superman and Me," by Sherman Alexie.

MODEL PARAGRAPH: A PASSION FOR READING

Topic sentence

My father, who is one of the few Indians who went to Catholic school on purpose, was an avid reader of westerns, spy thrillers, murder mysteries, gangster epics, basketball player biographies, and anything else he could find. He bought his books by the pound at Dutch's Pawn Shop, Goodwill, Salvation Army, and Value Village. When he had extra money, he bought new novels at supermarkets, convenience stores, and hospital gift shops. Our house was filled with books. They were stacked in crazy piles in the bathroom, bedrooms, and living room. In a fit of unemployment-inspired creative energy, my father built a set of bookshelves and soon filled them with a random assortment of books about the Kennedy assassination, Watergate, the Vietnam War, and the entire 23-book series of the Apache westerns. <u>My father loved books.</u> Since I loved my father with an aching devotion, I decided to love books as well.

Ten suggested topics   **Activities many people are passionate about:**

1. Playing video games
2. Following the news
3. Watching movies
4. Listening to music
5. Cooking
6. Learning a new technology
7. Caring for a pet
8. Playing a sport
9. Keeping up with fashion
10. Volunteering

Assignment 2: Shopping

Most people have very strong feelings about shopping. Write a paragraph that gives one or more examples of your best or worst shopping experiences. The following paragraph is taken from Phyllis Rose's essay "Shopping and Other Spiritual Adventures in America Today."

Topic sentence

MODEL PARAGRAPH: SHOPPING FOR BLUE JEANS

<u>Try to think of a kind of shopping in which the object is all important and the pleasure of shopping is at a minimum.</u> For example, consider the purchase of blue jeans. I buy new blue jeans as seldom as possible because the experience is so humiliating. For every pair that looks good on me, fifteen look grotesque. But even shopping for blue jeans at Main Surplus on First Street—no frills, bare-bones shopping—is an event in the life of the spirit. Once again I have to come to terms with the fact that I will never look good in Levi's. Much as I want to be mainstream, I never will be.

Ten suggested topics **Shopping:**

1. For weekly groceries
2. For a bathing suit
3. For an outfit to wear to a party
4. For a gift for a very fussy relative
5. On the Internet
6. At thrift stores or garage sales
7. For a used car
8. For bargains
9. For a gift for a child
10. Using coupons

Assignment 3: Our Expectations of Others

We enter into relationships believing that people will behave in an expected way. Often we are sadly disappointed. Write a paragraph in which you give one or more examples of how you expect people to act when they are in certain relationships. The following paragraph could be from a newspaper columnist giving advice to parents.

MODEL PARAGRAPH: ADVICE TO PARENTS

Topic sentence

Children should have to help out with the daily chores. All children of school age should understand that it is only fair that everyone should take part. Even the youngest can put away their toys at the end of the day and help set the table. Older children should help with the cooking, make their own beds, put away their clothes, and take out the garbage. Teenagers should be expected to help with shopping and housecleaning. They should help with childcare when necessary. By the way, teenagers who do such tasks for a family should not feel entitled to be paid for their efforts; there are very few families in our society that can afford hired help. Moreover, if you think all of the above applies to girls only, think again! Boys, now more than ever, must learn to be responsible for any and all of the family household tasks. Children who grow up sharing in the household work will be more self-sufficient than the princess or prince who will certainly grow up to be a very disappointing spouse.

Ten suggested topics

Expectations of:

1. Domestic partners
2. Grandparents
3. Teachers
4. Students
5. Waiters
6. Roommates
7. Patients
8. Employers
9. Coworkers
10. Friends

Assignment 4: Remedies to Cure What Ails Us

Health food stores are enjoying great popularity, partly because so many people believe that natural products can alleviate a wide range of complaints. Write a paragraph in which you give examples of popular trends for solving an everyday problem. The following paragraph offers several examples of remedies that are currently used in place of traditional medicine.

MODEL PARAGRAPH: THE POPULARITY OF NATURAL REMEDIES

Topic sentence

   Many stores today are selling newly accepted natural remedies for all types of human ailments. For instance, people with AIDS use the herb astragalus as a natural way to boost their immune systems. Other people concerned about their immune systems but only worried about colds or flu use echinacea, a plant extract, to help them resist sickness. People who want to lose weight are also seeking help from natural remedies. One of the most popular examples of remedies for overweight people is the Chinese herb *ma huang*. This is a powerful substance and can be dangerous for some because it can cause heart attacks or strokes, especially if it is used with caffeine. One of the cures most sought after is the cure for cancer, and again natural substances hold out some promise of relief. For example, shark cartilage is believed by many to stop the growth of cancerous tumors or even eliminate them altogether. Many users of herbs and other natural healing substances take these supplements to improve their general health. For instance, ginseng is used throughout the world as a revitalizing tonic, and garlic has been said to combat infections, prevent blood clots, and lower blood pressure. Although many claims are made for natural remedies, we often do not have proof that they work as well as a few people say they do.

Ten suggested topics **Remedies for:**

1. Stress
2. The common cold
3. The "blues"
4. The hiccups
5. A sore back
6. Smoking
7. Shyness
8. Writer's block
9. Insomnia
10. Procrastination

WRITE FOR SUCCESS

Some people arrive at college with attitudes or habits that may have seemed all right in high school or in their lives preceding college. Have you observed students who exhibit signs of immaturity, arrogance, a chip on their shoulder, unwillingness to respect those in authority, or an easygoing lack of responsibility? Write a response that explores this question: Do some people need to make an attitude adjustment when they get to college? Look at your own life as well. What attitude adjustments will ensure a more successful college experience?

Working Together

Tetra Images/Getty Images

Researching Examples: Phobias

Angela Gomez has a problem. She just received a promotion at work, and her new position will require her to speak in front of large groups of people. However, Angela has an abnormal fear of public speaking. She now feels that she may have to give up her new position if she cannot overcome this fear.

A phobia is deep fear of an object or situation. All of us fear one thing or another, but when a fear is abnormally deep and does not have any logical basis, we call it a phobia. People who suffer from phobias often realize that their emotional reactions are unreasonable, but they cannot control them. They also suffer from real physical reactions, including a pounding of the heart, a sinking feeling in the stomach, trembling, and a feeling of faintness. Very often, phobias are the result of traumatic experiences in childhood.

Working in Groups

Working in groups of three or so, locate information on at least three phobias. Common ones include *claustrophobia, agoraphobia, acrophobia,* and *xenophobia.* Find enough information about these phobias so that you can write a well-developed paragraph on each one. This could be the basis for an essay on the topic. You will want to define each phobia, and you will also want to explain how the phobia complicates the life of the person who has to deal with it.

PORTFOLIO SUGGESTION

When your group finds an article or some other source of information on one of the selected phobias, print out or make copies of the material. Each group member will then have the information. Add your paragraphs on phobias to your portfolio. You are building material for possible essays and research papers.

Developing Paragraphs: Narration 19

CHAPTER OBJECTIVES

Some people are good storytellers, and we all enjoy a good story told to us. This chapter on narration will help you improve your writing skills as you focus on these narrative elements.

- **making a point**
- ordering details according to **time sequence**
- using **transitions** to show a shift in time
- taking a step-by-step approach to create narrative paragraphs
- studying model paragraphs to create narrative paragraphs

What Is Narration?

Narration is the oldest and best-known form of verbal communication. It is, quite simply, the telling of a story.

Every culture in the world, past and present, has used narration to teach its children, entertain its people, and inform the citizenry of important matters. Because everyone likes a good story, the many forms of narration, such as stories told around a fire, or written short stories and novels, or visual soap operas and movies, will always have an audience.

The following narrative paragraph, taken from Helen Keller's autobiography, tells the story of her realization that every object has a name. The paragraph shows the enormous difficulties faced by a seven-year-old girl who was unable to see, hear, or speak.

The morning after my teacher came, she led me into her room and gave me a doll. The little blind children at the Perkins Institution had sent it and Laura Bridgman had dressed it; but I did not know this until afterward. When I had played with it a little while, Miss Sullivan slowly spelled into my hand the word "d-o-l-l." I was at once interested in this finger play and tried to imitate it. When I finally succeeded in making the letters correctly, I was flushed with childish pleasure and pride. Running downstairs to my mother I held up my hand and made the letters for *doll*. I did not know that I was spelling a word or even that words existed; I was simply making my fingers

(continued on next page)

Topic sentence

go in monkey-like imitation. In the days that followed I learned to spell in this uncomprehending way a great many words, among them *pin, hat, cup,* and a few verbs like *sit, stand,* and *walk.* <u>But my teacher had been with me several weeks before I understood that everything has a name.</u>

Using Narration to Make a Point

At one time or another, you have probably met a person who loves to talk on and on without making any real point. This person is likely to tell you everything that happened during the day, including every sight and every sound. Your reaction to the unnecessary and seemingly endless supply of details is probably one of fatigue and hope for a quick getaway. This is not narration at its best! A good story is almost always told to make a point: it can make us laugh, it can make us understand, or it can change our attitudes.

When Helen Keller tells the story of her early experiences with her teacher, she is careful to use only those details that are relevant to her story. For example, the doll her teacher gave her is an important part of the story. This doll reveals not only something about Helen Keller's teacher but also the astounding fact that Helen did not know that objects have names. With this story, we see the beginning of Helen's long struggle to communicate with other people.

EXERCISE ❶   **Using Narration to Make a Point**

Below are the brief summaries of two stories that were made into movies. One is fiction, the other one true. For each one, write your ideas of what point the author may have intended. Use complete sentences.

1. A young man goes with his girlfriend to meet her parents for the first time. She is apologetic and embarrassed by the chaos of her large and extended family. The young man, who has no close family members other than his mother, finds these eccentric people lovable and charming.

    _____

    _____

2. George VI, an introverted man with a severe stutter, is suddenly thrust upon the throne of England when his older brother, Edward VII, who was in line for the throne, chooses to marry a commoner and abdicate the throne. The story tells of the struggles of this younger brother who tries valiantly to overcome his stutter so he can address his nation in a time of war when people need the leadership of their king.

    _____

    _____

    _____

EXERCISE **2**   **Using Narration to Make a Point**

Below are the brief summaries of two famous short stories. For each one, write your idea of what point the author may have intended. Use complete sentences.

1. A young boy becomes infatuated by a girl in his neighborhood, a girl he has never spoken to but admires from a distance. One day, the girl does speak to the boy, asking him if he plans to go to a special fair, Araby, being held in the city. The boy says he will go and bring back a present for her. From then on, all he can think about is getting to Araby. When he finally catches a train to the bazaar, he finds that it is nearly over. His growing sense of frustration is only made worse when the lights are turned off. At the end, gazing into the darkness, he feels nothing but anguish and anger.

    _____

    _____

2. A woman, unhappy in her marriage, is given the news that the train her husband was on has crashed and he is believed to have died. She is secretly relieved to think that at last she will be free. However, when he returns alive and well, she dies of a heart attack, ironically leaving everyone to believe she died of happiness.

    _____

    _____

EXERCISE **3**   **Using Narration to Make a Point**

Below are the brief summaries of two famous short stories, one fiction and one autobiographical. For each one, write your idea of what point the author may have intended. Use complete sentences.

1. At the beginning of the twentieth century, two artists are living in New York's Greenwich Village. One is dying and being cared for by the other. A tree outside the window announces that autumn has arrived. The dying artist promises that she will live as long as one leaf remains on the tree. Wanting to extend the dying artist's life, the friend skillfully paints a leaf on the garden wall that will remain there after all the other leaves have fallen.

    _____

    _____

2. A twelve-year-old girl, along with the entire black community, has anticipated with excitement the graduation day for the children of Stamps, Arkansas. It is 1940, and the schools in the town are segregated. The girl is in a mood of exhilaration until a white official arrives to give the commencement speech and quickly rushes off. His speech has the cruel effect of reminding everyone of their limited opportunities in a society of racial inequality. It takes the high school valedictorian to turn the dispirited group around. He leads the students

in what is known as the *African-American National Anthem* with the stirring words by the black poet James Weldon Johnson. The mood of pride and self-worth returns. The day is saved.

_____

_____

Achieving Coherence

Placing Details in Order of Time Sequence

When you write a narrative paragraph, the details given are usually ordered according to time sequence. That is, you tell what happened first, then what happened next, and next, until finally you get to the end of the story. In your narrative, you could be describing events that took place in a matter of minutes or over a period of many years.

In the following paragraph, the story takes place in a single day. The six events that made the day a disaster are given in the order in which they occurred. Although some stories flash back to the past or forward to the future, most use the chronological order of the events.

Topic sentence

My day was a disaster. First, it had snowed during the night, which meant I had to shovel before I could leave for work. I was mad that I hadn't gotten up earlier. Then I had trouble starting my car, and to make matters worse, my daughter wasn't feeling well and said she didn't think she should go to school. When I eventually did arrive at work, I was twenty minutes late. Soon I found out my assistant had forgotten to make copies of a report I needed at nine o'clock. I quickly had to make another plan. By five o'clock, I was looking forward to getting my paycheck. Foolish woman! When I went to pick it up, the office assistant told me that something had gone wrong with the computers. I would not be able to get my check until Tuesday. Disappointed, I walked down the hill to the parking lot. There I met my final defeat. In my hurry to park the car in the morning, I had left my parking lights on. Now my battery was dead. Even an optimist like me had the right to be discouraged!

EXERCISE **4** **Placing Details in Order of Time Sequence**

The topic given is followed by supporting details. These supporting details are not in any particular order. Put the events in order according to time sequence by writing the appropriate number in the space provided.

An emergency in an apartment building

_____ He ran to the corner and pulled the fire alarm.

_____ The fire began around six o'clock.

_____ When the firefighters came, they found flames leaping out of the third-floor windows.

_____ A man walking his dog spotted smoke coming from the building.

_____ Official orders were given to evacuate the building.

EXERCISE 5 **Placing Details in Order of Time Sequence**

The topic below is followed by supporting details. These supporting details are not in any particular order. Put the events in order according to time sequence by writing the appropriate number in the space provided.

The story of Flight 1549

_____ Another possibility was to try to get to an airport in New Jersey, but again there was not enough power.

_____ A flock of birds had hit the engines without warning.

_____ Amazingly, everybody survived this crash, which has become known as "Miracle on the Hudson."

_____ The flight began at La Guardia Airport without incident.

_____ The pilot, Captain Chesley B. Sullenberger, spoke to the air traffic controllers and discussed the options.

_____ One possibility was to return to the original airport, but the airplane did not have enough power.

_____ Everyone was shocked when the pilot announced he would have to ditch the plane in the frigid Hudson River.

_____ Suddenly, the pilot and copilot experienced a loss of power in both engines.

EXERCISE 6 **Placing Details in Order of Time Sequence**

The topic given is followed by supporting details. These supporting details are not in any particular order. Put the events in order according to time sequence by writing the appropriate number in the space provided.

From the life of Sojourner Truth, crusader, preacher, and the first African American woman to speak out against slavery

_____ She was received by Abraham Lincoln in the White House the year before his assassination in 1865.

_____ She was forty-six when she took the name Sojourner Truth.

_____ Sojourner Truth began life as a slave when she was born in 1797, but she was set free in 1827.

_____ She spent her final years giving lectures throughout the North.

_____ At the age of 52, she traveled to the West, where her speeches against slavery and for women's rights drew large crowds.

_____ In 1860, at the beginning of the Civil War, she was active in gathering supplies for the black regiments that were fighting in the war.

_____ Not long after her first trip west, she settled in Battle Creek, Michigan.

Using Transitions That Show a Shift in Time

> *Transitions* are words and phrases that help a reader not only move smoothly from one idea to another but also make the proper connection between those ideas.

Although transitions must not be overused, they are important tools for every writer. Here is the Helen Keller paragraph you studied previously, this time with each of the transitional words and phrases printed in boldface.

> **The morning after** my teacher came, she led me into her room and gave me a doll. The little blind children at the Perkins Institution had sent it and Laura Bridgman had dressed it; but I did not know this **until afterward**. When I had played with it **a little while**, Miss Sullivan slowly spelled into my hand the word "d-o-l-l." I was **at once** interested in this finger play and tried to imitate it. When I **finally** succeeded in making the letters correctly, I was flushed with childish pleasure and pride. Running downstairs to my mother I held up my hand and made the letters for *doll*. I did not know that I was spelling a word or even that words existed; I was simply making my fingers go in monkey-like imitation. **In the days that followed** I learned to spell in this uncomprehending way a great many words, among them *pin, hat, cup*, and a few verbs like *sit, stand*, and *walk*. But my teacher had been with me **several weeks** before I understood that everything has a name.

Notice how the time transitions used in this paragraph make the order of events clear. *"The morning after* my teacher came" gives the reader the sense that the action of the story is being told day by day. In the second sentence, Helen Keller gives information she learned *afterward.* The writer then tells us that when she had played with the doll *a little while,* she *at once* became interested in the connection between an object and the word for that object. This realization was one of the central lessons in young Helen Keller's education, and it became the starting point for all of her later learning. She uses two more transitional phrases to tell us about the beginning of this education: *In the days that followed,* we learn, she mastered a great many words, although it took her *several weeks* before she learned the even more important concept that everything has a name. In addition to the fact that these transitions make the sequence of events clear, they further emphasize the intended meaning of the paragraph, that it was the gradual dawning on Helen

Keller's part that led to her realization that every object has a name. We need transitions in narration to establish the passage of time.

As you write your own narrative paragraphs, you will find yourself using your own transitional words and expressions. However, as a reminder and a guide, the following chart will serve as a helpful reference.

TRANSITIONS COMMONLY USED IN NARRATION TO SHOW A SHIFT IN TIME

Expresses the past	Expresses the present	Expresses time close to the present	Expresses a long passage of time
recently	now; by now	within a few minutes	several weeks later
previously	at once	soon; soon afterward	the following month
earlier	suddenly	later; later on	finally
in the past	immediately	after a little while	eventually
a few days ago	meanwhile	then	in the end
a hundred years ago	at the same time	next; the next day	

EXERCISE 7 **Working with Transitions**

Below is a paragraph taken from an essay by John McMurtry on the topic of the violent nature of football. Fill in each of the blanks with a transition of time that might have been the author's choice.

^{1}_____ my neck got a hard crick in it. I couldn't turn my head; to look left or right I'd have to turn my whole body. ^{2}But I'd had cricks in my neck since I started playing grade-school football and hockey, so I just ignored it. ^{3}_____ I began to notice that when I reached for any sort of large book (which I do pretty often as a philosophy teacher at the University of Guelph) I had trouble lifting it with one hand. ^{4}I was losing the strength in my left arm, and I had such a steady pain in my back I often had to stretch out on the floor of the room I was in to relieve the pressure. ^{5}_____ I mentioned to my brother, an orthopedic surgeon, that I'd lost the power in my arm since my neck began to hurt. ^{6}_____ I was in a Toronto hospital not sure whether I might end up with a wasted upper limb. ^{7}Apparently the steady pounding I had received playing college and professional football in the late 1950s and early 1960s had driven my head into my backbone so that the discs had crumpled together at the neck—"acute herniation"—and had cut the nerves to my left arm like a pinched telephone wire (without nerve stimulation, of course, the muscles atrophy, leaving the arm crippled). [8]So I spent my Christmas holidays in the hospital in heavy traction and for much of _____ my neck was in a brace. [9]_____ most of the pain has gone, and I've recovered most of the strength in my arm. [10]But _____ I still have to don the brace, and surgery remains a possibility.

EXERCISE **8** ## Working with Transitions

Below is a narrative paragraph by the American essayist E. B. White. On the lines provided, list all the transitions of time that give order to the paragraph.

One summer, along about 1904, my father rented a camp on a lake in Maine and took us all there for the month of August. We all got ringworm from some kittens and had to rub Pond's Extract on our arms and legs night and morning, and my father rolled over in a canoe with all his clothes on, but outside of that the vacation was a success and from then on none of us ever thought there was any place in the world like that lake in Maine. We returned summer after summer—always on August 1 for one month. I have since become a salt-water man, but sometimes in summer there are days when the restlessness of the tides and the fearful cold of the sea water and the incessant wind that blows across the afternoon and into the evening make me wish for the placidity of a lake in the woods. A few weeks ago this feeling got so strong I bought myself a couple of bass hooks and a spinner and returned to the lake where we used to go, for a week's fishing and to revisit old haunts.

_____   _____

_____   _____

_____   _____

EXERCISE **9** ## Working with Transitions

Below is a narrative paragraph taken from a story by the Russian writer Ivan Turgenev. On the lines provided, list all the transitions of time that give order to the paragraph.

I went to the right through the bushes. Meantime the night had crept close and grown up like a storm cloud; it seemed as though, with the mists of evening, darkness was rising up on all sides and flowing down from overhead. I had come upon some sort of little, untrodden, overgrown path; I walked along it, gazing intently before me. Soon all was blackness and silence around—only the quail's cry was heard from time to time. Some small nightbird, flitting noiselessly near the ground on its soft wings, almost flapped against me and scurried away in alarm. I came out on the farther side of the bushes, and made my way along a field by the hedge. By now I could hardly make out distant objects; the field showed dimly white around; beyond it rose up a sullen darkness, which seemed to be moving up closer in huge masses every instant. My steps gave a muffled sound in the air that grew colder and colder. The pale sky began again to grow blue—but it was the blue of night. The tiny stars glimmered and twinkled in it.

_____   _____

_____   _____

_____   _____

Writing a Narrative Paragraph Using a Step-by-Step Approach

Mastering any skill, including writing, requires a disciplined attitude. One way to master the skill of creating a piece of writing is to take a step-by-step approach, focusing on one issue at a time. This approach results in a minimum of stress. Another advantage is that the writer does not miss important points or misunderstand any part of the process. Of course, there are other ways to build effective narrative paragraphs, but here is one logical method you can use that will always achieve good results.

STEP-BY-STEP APPROACH TO WRITING A NARRATIVE PARAGRAPH

1. Study the given topic, and then plan your topic sentence with its controlling idea.

2. List all the events that come to your mind when you think about the story you have chosen.

3. Choose the important events, dropping any that do not directly relate to your controlling idea.

4. Put your list in the correct time sequence.

5. Write one complete sentence for each of the events you have chosen from your list, adding any significant details.

6. Write a concluding statement that gives some point to the events of the story.

7. Copy your sentences into standard paragraph form.

8. Always make a final check for spelling errors and other mistakes, such as omitted words.

NOTE: When you use a computer spell-check feature, keep in mind that this feature will alert you only to spellings that do not match words in its dictionary. If you type _there_ when you mean _their_, the spell-checker will see an acceptable word. When it comes to a final editing, there is no substitute for your own careful reading.

EXERCISE **10** **Writing a Narrative Paragraph Using a Step-by-Step Approach**

Cpl. Timothy Childers

This exercise will guide you through the construction of a complete narrative paragraph. Start with the suggested topic. Use the eight steps to help you work through the stages of the writing process.

Topic: Nearly every family has a favorite story they like to tell about one of their members, often a humorous incident that happened to one of them. There are also crises and tragic moments in the life of every family. Choose a story, funny or tragic, from the life of a family member you have known.

1. Topic sentence: _____

   _____

   _____

2. Make a list of the events that took place.

   a. _____

   b. _____

   c. _____

   d. _____

   e. _____

   f. _____

   g. _____

   h. _____

   i. _____

   j. _____

3. Circle the five or six events you believe are the most important for the point of the story.

4. Put your final choices in order by numbering each of them.

5. Using your final list, write at least one sentence for each event you have chosen.

   a. _____

   _____

   b. _____

   _____

c. _____

_____

d. _____

_____

e. _____

_____

f. _____

_____

6. Write a concluding statement. _____

_____

_____

7. On a separate sheet of paper or on a computer, copy your sentences into standard paragraph form.

8. Do a final reading to check for errors and omissions.

EXERCISE **11** **Writing a Narrative Paragraph Using a Step-by-Step Approach**

This exercise will guide you through the construction of a complete narrative paragraph. Start with the suggested topic. Use the eight steps to help you work through the stages of the writing process.

Topic: Tell the story of an incident you witnessed that revealed an unfortunate lack of sensitivity (or even cruelty) on someone's part. What did you observe the person doing? How did other people react? What did you do or what do you wish you had done in response to this incident?

1. Topic sentence: _____

_____

2. Make a list of the events that took place.

a. _____

b. _____

c. _____

d. _____

e. _____

f. _____

g. _____

h. _____

i. _____

j. _____

3. Circle the five or six events you believe are the most important for the point of the story.

4. Put your final choices in order by numbering each of them.

5. Using your final list, write at least one sentence for each event you have chosen.

a. _____

_____

b. _____

_____

c. _____

_____

d. _____

_____

e. _____

_____

f. _____

_____

6. Write a concluding statement. _____

_____

_____

7. On a separate sheet of paper or on a computer, copy your sentences into standard paragraph form.

8. Do a final reading to check for errors and omissions.

Studying Model Paragraphs to Create Paragraphs Using Narration

Assignment 1: The Story of How You Faced a New Challenge

Write a paragraph telling the story of a day when you faced an important challenge of some kind. It could have been a challenge in school, at home, or on the job. The following paragraph is adapted from a story by the journalist Betty Rollin.

Topic sentence

MODEL PARAGRAPH: DEADLINE

    <u>When I awoke that morning I hit the floor running.</u> I washed my face, brushed my teeth, got a pot of coffee going, tightened the sash on my bathrobe, took my laptop out of its case, placed it on the kitchen table, retrieved my notes from the floor where they were stacked in manila folders, unwrapped a pack of legal notepads, opened the word processor software, looked at the blank screen, put my head on the keys, wrapped my arms around the machine and cried.

Ten suggested topics

1. The day I started a new job
2. My first day in a difficult course
3. The day I began my first research paper
4. The day I finally organized my room
5. The day I conducted an important job interview
6. The day I found out I was deeply in debt
7. The day I had to end a relationship
8. The day I lied, but for a good reason
9. The day I learned of a death in the family
10. The day I finally fulfilled an obligation

Assignment 2: The Story of a Fight or Argument

Write a paragraph in which you tell the story of a fight or confrontation you were involved in or witnessed. Include the important details that will hold your reader's attention. The following paragraph, from Albert Halper's short story "Prelude," tells the story of a street fight.

MODEL PARAGRAPH: THE FIGHT

Topic sentence

But the people just stood there afraid to do a thing. Then while a few guys held me, Gooley and about four others went for the stand, turning it over and mussing and stamping on all the newspapers they could find. Syl started to scratch them, so they hit her. Then I broke away to help her, and then they started socking me too. My father tried to reach me, but three guys kept him away. Four guys got me down and started kicking me and all the time my father was begging them to let me up and Syl was screaming at the people to help. And while I was down, my face was squeezed against some papers on the sidewalk with stories about Austria and I guess I went nuts while they kept hitting me, and I kept seeing the headlines against my nose.

Ten suggested topics

A confrontation between:

1. Two friends
2. Two neighbors
3. An angry customer and a store employee
4. A frustrated parent and a child
5. A manager and an unhappy employee
6. Two people trying to solve a problem in different ways
7. A local citizen and a careless tourist
8. A politician and an angry citizen
9. Two siblings
10. Two roommates

Assignment 3: The Moment a Relationship Changed

Write a paragraph that tells the story of how your relationship with another person changed. You might select one particular moment when the relationship changed from casual friendliness to something deeper and more lasting or a moment that led to a separation of some kind. The following paragraph, taken from Morley Callaghan's short story "One Spring Night," tells of a young man who is falling in love.

MODEL PARAGRAPH: FALLING IN LOVE

Topic sentence

Bob had taken her out a few times when he had felt like having some girl to talk to who knew him and liked him. And tonight he was leaning back good-humoredly, telling her one thing and then another with the wise self-assurance he usually had when with her; but gradually, as he watched her, he found himself talking more slowly, his voice grew serious and much softer, and then finally he leaned across the table toward her as though he had just discovered that her neck was full and soft with her spring coat thrown open, and that her face under her little black straw hat tilted back on her head had a new, eager beauty. Her warm, smiling softness was so close to him that he smiled a bit shyly.

Ten suggested topics

1. A moment when my relationship with a parent changed
2. The moment my relationship with a friend changed
3. A moment when I understood my child in a new way
4. The day I learned something new about a neighbor
5. The day I shared an experience with a fellow worker
6. The day I made friends with someone older or younger than myself
7. The moment my relationship with a classmate changed
8. The moment when I understood something new about a teacher
9. The time when a stranger became a friend
10. The time when a close relationship deepened

Assignment 4: You Won't Believe What Happened to Me Today!

Tell the story of a day you found yourself facing a difficult or frustrating situation. The following paragraph, from Berton Roueché's short story "Phone Call," describes a day in the life of a young man, a day when nothing seemed to go right.

MODEL PARAGRAPH: THE TRUCK BREAKS DOWN

I got out of the truck and got down on my knees and twisted my neck and looked underneath. Everything looked O.K. There wasn't anything hanging down or anything. I got up and opened the hood and looked at the engine. I don't know too much about engines—only what I picked up working around Lindy's Service Station the summer before last. But the engine looked O.K., too. I slammed down the hood and lighted a cigarette. It really had me beat. A school bus from that convent over in Sag Harbor came piling around the bend, and all the girls leaned out the windows and yelled. I just waved. They didn't mean anything by it—just a bunch of kids going home. The bus went on up the road and into the woods and out of sight. I got back in the truck and started it up again. It sounded fine. I put it in gear and let out the clutch and gave it the gas, and nothing happened. The bastard just sat there. So it was probably the transmission. I shut it off and got out. There was nothing to do but call the store. I still had three or four deliveries that had to be made and it was getting kind of late. I knew what Mr. Lester would say, but this was *Topic sentence* one time when he couldn't blame me. <u>It wasn't my fault.</u> It was him himself that told me to take this truck.

Ten suggested topics
1. The day I discovered I had been deceived
2. The day I was falsely accused
3. The day I lost an important game
4. The day I lost my temper
5. The day I was shocked by . . .
6. The day nothing went right
7. The day I failed to . . .
8. The day I lost my keys (or some other important item)
9. The day I could have used some help
10. The day I lost my job

WRITE FOR SUCCESS

What story could you tell about a member of your family that demonstrates some important strength? It could be a character trait, a special talent, or an ability to persevere in the face of adversity. Recount this story so that readers will understand why this person is worthy of admiration.

Working Together

Telling Stories That Make a Point

It is believed that Aesop was a Greek slave who lived about 2,500 years ago. He is credited with over 200 fables, short tales that point to an instructive moral at the end. Aesop's fables have become part of our international literary heritage. The following fable is a classic example of a tale from Aesop, one with a timeless moral at the end.

iStockphoto.com/Kevin Miller

> A farmer realized he was dying. He did not want to leave this world without being sure that all of his sons knew how to be good farmers. He called them to his bedside and said, "My sons, I am about to depart from this world. After I go, however, I want you to search for what I have hidden in the vineyard. When you find it, you will possess all that I am able to leave you."
>
> The young men were convinced their father had buried some great treasure on the property. After he died, they all took their shovels and dug up every part of the vineyard. They found no treasure at all, but their digging helped the grapevines so much that the next year's harvest saw the best crop of grapes in many years.
>
> **Moral:** Our greatest treasure is what comes from our own hard work.

Group Discussion

Nearly all of us would like to get something for nothing. Have you ever heard of someone who reminds you of the farmer's sons in the fable? Do you know people who gamble? Have you heard of people who expect their family to support them instead of taking responsibility for themselves? Have you read about people who have inherited money or have won a lottery but who did not know how to handle the money? Share these stories with your classmates.

On the other hand, what is a story you could share about someone who has worked very hard? To what extent is Aesop's moral true, that our greatest treasure is what we achieve by our own hard work?

PORTFOLIO SUGGESTION

Write one of the following narratives to keep in your portfolio:

1. A fable with a one-sentence moral at the end.

2. A narrative paragraph that tells the story of someone you know who either tried to get something for nothing or worked very hard to achieve a goal. Be sure your story has a point at the end.

3. An essay titled "Important Lessons to Learn in Life." Locate a book containing Aesop's fables and review them. Choose three of the fables that you believe contain the most important lessons to learn in life and write an essay that uses these three morals as examples in your essay.

379

Developing Paragraphs: Description

20

CHAPTER OBJECTIVES

This chapter focuses on several skills important to descriptive writing, chief among them the use of the five senses.

- creating a topic sentence containing a **dominant impression**

- avoiding vague dominant impressions

- supporting the topic sentence with details that evoke **sensory images**

- putting the details in a logical order, usually a **spatial order** of some kind

- taking a step-by-step approach to create descriptive paragraphs

- studying model paragraphs to create descriptive paragraphs

What Is Description?

One method of developing a paragraph is to use descriptive details. For example, when you read the opening chapter of almost any novel, you notice that the author has begun the story with one or more paragraphs of description that set the stage for that story.

> **Description** uses sensory images to create a picture with words.

The following example comes from a personal essay written by Native American writer and language advocate Joseph H. Suina. In this paragraph, he describes his childhood home. As you study this description, look for the details that make this paragraph effective.

Topic sentence

    During those years, Grandmother and I lived beside the plaza in a humble one-room house. It consisted of a traditional fireplace, a makeshift cabinet for our few tin cups and dishes, and a wooden crate that held our two buckets of all-purpose water. At the far end of the room were two rolls of bedding we used as comfortable sitting "couches." Consisting of thick quilts, sheepskin, and assorted blankets, these bed rolls were undone each night. A wooden pole the length of one side of the room was suspended about 10 inches from the ceiling beams. A modest collection of colorful shawls, blankets, and sashes draped over the pole making this part of the room most interesting. In one corner was a bulky metal trunk for our

(continued on next page)

ceremonial wear and few valuables. A dresser, which was traded for some of my grandmother's well-known pottery, held the few articles of clothing we owned and the "goody bag." Grandmother always had a flour sack filled with candy, store bought cookies, and Fig Newtons. These were saturated with a sharp odor of mothballs. Nevertheless, they made a fine snack with coffee before we turned in for the night. Tucked securely in my blankets, I listened to one of her stories or accounts of how it was when she was a little girl. These accounts seemed so old fashioned compared to the way we lived. Sometimes she softly sang a song from a ceremony. In this way, I fell asleep each night.

When you use effective sensory images in your writing, the descriptive details that result will be memorable and convincing to your reader. Such details will make a tremendous difference in how well your reader is able to imagine what you are describing. You can demonstrate this to yourself by answering the following questions about the descriptive paragraph above.

1. What can you see? _____

_____

_____

2. What can you hear? _____

3. What suggests how something would feel to the touch? _____

_____

4. What can you smell? _____

5. What can you taste? _____

Working with Description

Selecting the Dominant Impression

It is not enough to give random pieces of information about the particular person, object, or place you are describing. The overall effect of a paragraph of descriptive writing should be the sense of a *dominant impression*. Each individual sentence that you write should be part of a picture that becomes clear when the reader finishes the paragraph.

The **dominant impression** is the overall impression created by a descriptive piece of writing. This impression is often summed up by one word or phrase in the topic sentence.

Topic sentence: My childhood home was *humble*.

When you write a descriptive paragraph, you should know what impression you are trying to achieve with your supporting details. For example, when you describe a place, the dominant impression you want to create could be one of *comfort* or it could be one of *elegance*. When you write a description of a person, you might want to present the impression of an *outgoing, gregarious* person or perhaps the very opposite, that of a *shy, withdrawn* sort of person. Often it is useful to incorporate the dominant impression into the topic sentence. This will help you focus as you write and will leave no doubt in the reader's mind as to the direction of your thinking. All the other sentences should support this impression you are working to create.

The following charts contain two short lists of possible dominant impressions. Use them as a guide while you work through this chapter.

DOMINANT IMPRESSIONS FOR DESCRIPTIONS OF PLACES

crowded	cozy	inviting	cheerful	dazzling
romantic	restful	dreary	drab	uncomfortable
cluttered	ugly	tasteless	unfriendly	gaudy
stuffy	eerie	depressing	spacious	sunny

DOMINANT IMPRESSIONS FOR DESCRIPTIONS OF PEOPLE

creative	angry	independent	proud	dependable
tense	shy	aggressive	generous	sullen
silent	witty	pessimistic	responsible	efficient
snobbish	placid	bumbling	bitter	easygoing

EXERCISE **1** ## Selecting the Dominant Impression

Each one of the following places could be the topic for a descriptive paragraph. For each topic, provide an appropriate dominant impression. Use the list in the box if you need help. Remember that there is no single right answer; the word you choose should represent the impression you want to create.

Topic	Dominant impression
A hotel lobby	spacious
1. A college bookstore	_____
2. An auto repair shop	_____
3. A park pavilion	_____
4. A bus stop	_____
5. A gambling casino	_____
6. An older relative's house	_____
7. A bridge underpass	_____

8. An elevator   _____

9. A company's corporate headquarters   _____

10. A train station   _____

EXERCISE ② **Selecting the Dominant Impression**

Each one of the following people could be the topic for a descriptive paragraph. For each topic, provide an appropriate dominant impression. Use the list in the box if you need help. Remember that there is no single right answer; the word you choose should represent the impression you want to create.

Topic   **Dominant impression**

1. A comedian being interviewed on television   _____

2. A resident at a nursing home   _____

3. A computer tech   _____

4. A bank teller on a busy day   _____

5. A farmer   _____

6. A politician running for office   _____

7. A cab driver   _____

8. A volunteer at a pet rescue   _____

9. A bride   _____

10. A family welcoming a soldier home   _____

Revising Vague Dominant Impressions

Certain words have become so overused that they no longer have any specific meaning for a reader. Careful writers avoid these words because they are almost useless in descriptive writing. Here is a list of the most commonly overused words:

VAGUE AND OVERUSED WORDS		
good	fine	typical
bad	okay	interesting
nice	normal	beautiful

The following paragraph is an example of the kind of writing that suffers from the continued use of vague words:

> I had a typical day. The weather was nice and my job was interesting. The food for lunch was okay; supper was good. After supper I saw my fiancée, who is beautiful. That's when my day really became fun.

Notice that all the details in the paragraph are vague. The writer has told us what happened, but we cannot visualize any of the details that are mentioned. The writer has made the mistake of using words that have lost much of their meaning.

The next group of exercises will give you practice in recognizing and eliminating overused words.

EXERCISE 3   **Revising Vague Dominant Impressions**

In each of the spaces provided, write a word or phrase that creates a more specific dominant impression than the underlined word. An example has been done for you. You might want to work in groups to think of words and phrases that are more specific.

> **Vague: The tablecloth was <u>beautiful</u>.**
>
> **Revised: The tablecloth was <u>of white linen with delicate blue embroidery</u>.**

1. The sky was <u>beautiful</u>. _____

2. The water felt <u>nice</u>. _____

3. Walking along the beach was <u>fun</u>. _____

4. The storm was <u>bad</u>. _____

5. The diner was <u>typical</u>. _____

6. The main street is <u>interesting</u>. _____

7. The dessert tasted <u>good</u>. _____

8. My brother seems <u>normal</u>. _____

9. Our house is <u>fine</u>. _____

10. My job is <u>okay</u>. _____

EXERCISE 4   **Revising Vague Dominant Impressions**

In each of the spaces provided, write a word or phrase that creates a more specific dominant impression than the underlined word. Working in groups may be helpful.

1. The reunion turned out to be a <u>nice</u> event. _____

2. The window display was <u>beautiful</u>. _____

3. The boat ride was <u>fine</u>. _____

4. The circus was <u>fun</u>. _____

5. The milk tasted <u>awful</u>. _____

6. The play was <u>bad</u>. _____

7. His new suit looked <u>okay</u>. _____

8. The dance class was <u>fine</u>. _____

9. Her new watch was <u>nice</u>. _____

10. It was a <u>good</u> lecture. _____

EXERCISE **5** **Revising Vague Words**

Below is a previously used paragraph that is filled with vague words. Rewrite the paragraph, replacing the vague words with more specific details.

I had a typical day. The weather was nice and my job was interesting. The food for lunch was okay; supper was good. After supper I saw my fiancée, who is beautiful. That's when my day really became fun.

_____

_____

_____

_____

_____

_____

_____

Recognizing and Creating Sensory Images

One of the basic ways all good writers communicate experiences to their readers is by using sensory images. We respond to writing that makes us _see_ an object, _hear_ a sound, _touch_ a surface, _smell_ an odor, or _taste_ a flavor. When a writer uses one or more sensory images in a piece of writing, we tend to pay more attention to what the writer is saying, and we tend to remember the details of what we have read.

For example, if you came across the word _door_ in a sentence, you might or might not pay attention to it. However, if the writer told you it was a _heavy wooden door, rough to the touch and creaking loudly when it opened,_ you would not be as likely to forget it. The door would stay in your mind because the writer used sensory images.

Sensory images are those details that relate to our senses: sight, sound, touch, smell, and taste.

Effective description:

The floors were of black and white tile, the walls cream-colored with huge casement windows that opened onto a long veranda where the strains of violin music, soft voices, and the clink of glasses could be heard.

Less effective description:

The room had tiled floors, painted walls, and big windows. We could hear music and voices coming from outside.

PRACTICE ❶ **The following sentences describe a delicatessen. Each sentence contains at least one sensory image. For each of the sentences, identify which of the physical senses (sight, sound, touch, smell, taste) the writer has appealed to.**

1. A large refrigerator case against one wall was always humming loudly from the effort of keeping milk, cream, and several cases of soda and beer cool at all times.

   Physical senses: _____

   _____

2. Stacked on top of the counter were baskets of fresh rolls and breads that gave off an aroma containing a mixture of onion, caraway seed, and pumpernickel.

   Physical senses: _____

3. Mr. Rubino was always ready with a sample piece of cheese or smoked meat as a friendly gesture.

   Physical senses: _____

When you use sensory images, you will stimulate readers' interest, and these images will stay in their minds.

EXERCISE ❻ **Recognizing Sensory Images**

The following paragraph contains examples of sensory images. Find the images and list them in the spaces provided.

It was only when he had reached the door that he realized what it actually was that had drawn him over to it; it was the smell of something to eat. By the door there was a dish filled with sweetened milk with little pieces of white bread floating in it. He was so pleased he almost laughed, as he was even hungrier than he had been that morning, and immediately dipped his head into the milk, nearly covering his eyes with it. But he soon drew his head back again in disappointment; not only did the pain in his tender left side make it difficult to eat the food—he was only able to eat if his whole body worked together as a snuffling whole—but the milk did not taste at all nice. Milk like this was normally his favorite drink, and his sister had certainly left it there for him because of that, but he turned, almost against his own will, away from the dish and crawled back into the center of the room.

FROM FRANZ KAFKA,
The Metamorphosis

Sensory images

Touch and bodily feelings: _____

_____

_____

Taste: _____

Smell: _____

EXERCISE **7** ## Recognizing Sensory Images

The following paragraph contains examples of sensory images. Find the images and list them in the spaces provided.

The lake ice split with a sound like the crack of a rifle. Thick slabs of ice broke apart, moving ponderously, edge grinding against edge, up-thrusting in jagged peaks, the green-gray water swirling over half-submerged floes. In an agony of rebirth, the splitting and booming of the ice reverberated across the thawing land. Streams raced toward the lake, their swift currents carrying fallen branches and undermining overhanging banks of earth and softened snow. Roads became mires of muck and slush, and the meadows of dried, matted grass oozed mud.

FROM NAN SALERNO,
Shaman's Daughter

Sensory images

Sight: _____

_____

Sound: _____

_____

Touch: _____

EXERCISE **8** ## Recognizing Sensory Images

The following paragraph contains examples of sensory images. Find the images and list them in the spaces provided.

Topic sentence   In the waiting room there were several kerosene stoves, placed about to warm the shivering crowd. The stoves were small black chimneys with nickel handles. We stood around them rubbing hands and watching our clothes steam. An American lady, in a slicker, like the men, and rubber boots up to her knees, kept bringing bowls of soup and shiny tin cups with hot coffee. Whatever she said to us and whatever we said to her neither understood, but she was talking the language of hot soup and coffee and kindness and there was perfect communication.

FROM ERNESTO GALARZA,
Barrio Boy

Sensory images

Sight: _____

_____

Sound: _____

Touch: _____

Taste: _____

Smell: _____

EXERCISE **9**   ## Creating Sensory Images

Each of the following topic sentences contains an underlined word that identifies a physical sense. For each topic sentence, write three sentences that give examples of sensory images. For example, in a sentence describing *sounds* near a hospital, a writer could use ambulance sirens, loudspeakers calling doctors, and the voices of patients and staff members.

1. As the baseball fans entered the stadium, they recognized the usual <u>sounds</u>.

    Write three sentences with sensory images:

    a. _____

    _____

    b. _____

    _____

    c. _____

    _____

2. I can't help stopping in the bakery every Sunday morning because the <u>smells</u> are so tempting.

    Write three sentences with sensory images:

    a. _____

    _____

    b. _____

    _____

    c. _____

    _____

3. The diplomat wasn't prepared for the <u>sight</u> that greeted her when she walked off the plane.

    Write three sentences with sensory images:

    a. _____

    _____

    b. _____

    _____

    c. _____

    _____

EXERCISE 10   **Creating Sensory Images**

Each of the following topic sentences contains an underlined word that identifies a physical sense. For each topic sentence, write three sentences that give examples of sensory images.

1. In the dark hallway, the dog walker <u>felt</u> in his pocket for the keys.

   Write three sentences with sensory images:

   a. _____

   _____

   b. _____

   _____

   c. _____

   _____

2. They knew the garbage strike had gone on for a long time when they had to <u>hold their noses</u> as they walked down the street.

   Write three sentences with sensory images:

   a. _____

   _____

   b. _____

   _____

   c. _____

   _____

3. Sitting on the cabin porch early in the morning, the hunters could hear the <u>sounds</u> of a world waking up.

   Write three sentences with sensory images:

   a. _____

   _____

   b. _____

   _____

   c. _____

   _____

EXERCISE 11   **Creating Sensory Images**

Each of the following topic sentences contains an underlined word that identifies a physical sense. For each topic sentence, write three sentences that give examples of that underlined sensory image.

1. Going to a dance club can be an overwhelming experience because of the many different <u>sounds</u> you hear there.

   Write three sentences with sensory images:

   a. _____

   _____

   b. _____

   _____

   c. _____

   _____

2. My friend says he loves the <u>taste and texture</u> of the chocolate, the nuts, and the coconut when he eats that candy bar.

   Write three sentences with sensory images:

   a. _____

   _____

   b. _____

   _____

   c. _____

   _____

3. The tour guide could <u>see</u> that the group standing on the corner was confused.

   Write three sentences with sensory images:

   a. _____

   _____

   b. _____

   _____

   c. _____

   _____

Achieving Coherence: Putting Details in Spatial Order

In descriptive writing, supporting details are usually arranged according to **spatial order.** The writer describes items in much the same way as a camera might move across a scene. Items could be ordered from top to bottom, from left to right, from outside to inside, from nearby to farther away, or even around in a circle. Sometimes the most important image is saved for last in order to give the greatest impact to that image.

Here is a description of a hotel room in Bogota, Colombia.

> The room was about the size of New York's Grand Central Station. It had been painted a fiendish dark green. A single light bulb hung from the thirteen-foot-high ceiling. The bed was oversized. The desk was gigantic, and the leather-covered chairs engulfed us. Although hot water ran from the cold faucet and cold from the hot, we were delighted.
>
> FROM VIRGINIA PAXTON
> *Penthouse in Bogota*

Notice how the writer begins with a general description of the room, including its size and color, the height of the ceiling, and the source of light. Then the writer moves on to give details about the furniture. The final detail is one that is meant to be humorous (the mix-up with the hot and cold water); the writer wants to amuse us and convince us that she enjoyed the adventure of staying in an unusual hotel room. You might also conclude that the order of details here goes from the outer edges of the room to the center. When writing a descriptive paragraph, no matter which method of spatial order you choose, the details should be in a sequence that will allow your reader to visualize the scene in a logical order. Can you explain why the dominant impression is the last word of the paragraph?

EXERCISE 12 **Using Spatial Order**

Each of the following topic sentences is followed by four or more descriptive sentences that are not in any particular order. Put these descriptive sentences in order by placing the appropriate number in the space provided.

1. The Statue of Liberty, now completely restored, is a marvel to visitors from all over the world.

   (Order the details from bottom to top.)

   _____ With current restoration finished, the crown continues to be used as a place where visitors can get a good view of New York Harbor.

   _____ The granite for the base of the statue was quarried and cut many miles from New York City and then taken by boat to Bedloe's Island, where the statue was built.

   _____ The torch has been repaired and will now be illuminated by outside lights, not lights from inside the torch itself.

   _____ The seven spikes that rise above the crown represent the seven seas of the world.

   _____ The body was covered with copper that was originally mined on an island off the coast of Norway.

2. The runway models in the designer's winter fashion show presented a classic look.

   (Order the details from top to bottom.)

   _____ The skirts were beautifully designed and made of quality fabrics.

   _____ The shoes were all high-heeled, basic, black pumps.

   _____ Exquisite silk scarves flowed as the models walked past the audience.

   _____ Meticulous attention was paid to hairstyles and makeup.

   _____ The sweaters were all made of cashmere in vibrant colors.

3. My aunt and uncle's kitchen is an orderly place.

   (Order the details from near to far.)

   _____ As usual, in the center of the table sits a vase with fresh yellow daffodils.

   _____ Nearby on the refrigerator, a magnet holds the week's menu.

   _____ Sitting at the kitchen table, I am struck by the freshly pressed linen tablecloth.

   _____ Looking across the room through the stained glass doors of her kitchen cupboards, I can see neat rows of dishes, cups, and saucers, exactly eight each, matching the colors of the tablecloth and wallpaper.

EXERCISE **13** **Using Spatial Order**

Each of the following topic sentences could be expanded into a fully developed paragraph. In the spaces provided, give four appropriate sensory images for the topic sentence. Be sure to give your images in a particular order. That is, the images should go from top to bottom, from outside to inside, from close to far, or around the area you are describing.

1. The airport terminal was as busy inside as it was outside.

   a. _____

   _____

   b. _____

   _____

   c. _____

   _____

   d. _____

   _____

2. The student lounge is a quiet and relaxing place in our school.

a. _____

_____

b. _____

_____

c. _____

_____

d. _____

_____

3. The motel lobby had once been elegant, but now it was beginning to look shabby.

a. _____

_____

b. _____

_____

c. _____

_____

d. _____

_____

EXERCISE **14** **Using Spatial Order**

Each of the following topic sentences could be expanded into a fully developed paragraph. In the spaces provided, give four appropriate sensory images for the topic sentence. Be sure to give your images in a particular order. That is, the images should go from top to bottom, from outside to inside, from close to far, or around the area you are describing.

1. The shopping mall was supposed to be enjoyable, but the experience gave me a headache.

a. _____

_____

b. _____

_____

c. _____

_____

d. _____

_____

2. The pizza shop is so tiny that people are not likely to stay and eat.

a. _____

_____

b. _____

_____

c. _____

_____

d. _____

_____

3. The bus was filled with a strange assortment of people.

a. _____

_____

b. _____

_____

c. _____

_____

d. _____

_____

Writing a Descriptive Paragraph Using a Step-by-Step Approach

Mastering any skill, including writing, requires a disciplined attitude. One way to master the skill of creating a piece of writing is to take a step-by-step approach, focusing on one issue at a time. This approach results in a minimum of stress. Another advantage is that the writer does not miss important points or misunderstand any part of the process. Of course, there are other ways to build effective descriptive paragraphs, but here is one logical method you can use that will always achieve good results.

STEP-BY-STEP APPROACH TO WRITING A DESCRIPTIVE PARAGRAPH

1. Study the given topic, and then plan your topic sentence, especially the dominant impression.

2. List at least ten sensory images that come to your mind when you think about the topic you have chosen.

3. Choose the five or six most important images from your list. Be sure these details support the dominant impression.

4. Put your list in a spatial order.

5. Write at least one complete sentence for each of the images you have chosen from your list.

6. Write a concluding statement that offers some reason for describing this topic.

7. Copy your sentences into standard paragraph form.

8. Always make a final check for spelling errors and other mistakes, such as omitted words.

NOTE: When you use a computer spell-check feature, keep in mind that this feature will only alert you to spellings that do not match words in its dictionary. If you type *there* when you mean *their,* the spell-checker will see an acceptable word. When it comes to a final editing, there is no substitute for your own careful reading.

EXERCISE 15   **Writing a Descriptive Paragraph Using a Step-by-Step Approach**

The following exercise will guide you through the construction of a descriptive paragraph. Start with the suggested topic. Use the eight steps to help you work through the stages of the writing process.

Topic: **A place you have visited**

1. Topic sentence (including a dominant impression): _____

_____

2. Make a list of possible sensory images.

a. _____

b. _____

c. _____

d. _____

e. _____

f. _____

g. _____

h. _____

i. _____

j. _____

3. Check the five or six images you believe are the most important for the description.

4. Put your selected details in a spatial order by numbering them.

5. Using your final list, write at least one sentence for each image you have chosen.

a. _____
_____

b. _____
_____

c. _____
_____

d. _____
_____

Courtesy of John Scarry

e. _____
_____

f. _____
_____

6. Write a concluding statement. _____
_____

7. On a separate sheet of paper or on a computer, copy your sentences into standard paragraph form.

8. Do a final reading to check for errors and omissions.

EXERCISE **16** **Writing a Descriptive Paragraph Using a Step-by-Step Approach**

The following exercise will guide you through the construction of a descriptive paragraph. Start with the suggested topic. Use the eight steps to help you work through the stages of the writing process.

Topic: **The memory box in your bedroom**

1. Topic sentence (including a dominant impression): _____
_____
_____

2. Make a list of possible sensory images.

   a. _____

   b. _____

   c. _____

   d. _____

   e. _____

   f. _____

   g. _____

   h. _____

   i. _____

   j. _____

3. Check the five or six images you believe are the most important for the description.

4. Put your selected details in order by numbering them.

5. Using your final list, write at least one sentence for each image you have chosen.

   a. _____

   _____

   b. _____

   _____

   c. _____

   _____

   d. _____

   _____

   e. _____

   _____

   f. _____

   _____

6. Write a concluding statement. _____

   _____

7. On a separate sheet of paper or on a computer, copy your sentences into standard paragraph form.

8. Do a final reading to check for errors and omissions.

Studying Model Paragraphs to Create Descriptive Paragraphs

Assignment 1: A Description of a Home

Write a paragraph in which you describe a house or room that you remember clearly. Choose your dominant impression carefully, and then select your sensory images to support that impression. In your description you may want to include the person who lives in the house or room. The following is a model paragraph from Charles Chaplin's *My Autobiography*.

MODEL PARAGRAPH: THE BUNGALOW

Topic sentence

It was dark when we entered his bungalow, and when we switched on the light I was shocked. The place was empty and drab. In his room was an old iron bed with a light bulb hanging over the head of it. A rickety old table and one chair were the other furnishings. Near the bed was a wooden box upon which was a brass ashtray filled with cigarette butts. The room allotted to me was almost the same, only it was minus a grocery box. Nothing worked. The bathroom was unspeakable. One had to take a jug and fill it from the bath tap and empty it down the flush to make the toilet work. This was the home of G. M. Anderson, the multimillionaire cowboy.

Ten suggested topics

1. A student's apartment
2. A vacation home
3. A dormitory
4. The house of your dreams
5. Your bedroom
6. The garage
7. The messiest room you have ever seen
8. The front yard
9. A tool shed
10. The backyard

Assignment 2: A Description of a Person

Write a paragraph in which you describe a person whose appearance made a deep impression on you. You might recall someone you have personally known, or you might choose a familiar public figure. Brainstorm by making a list of the images you remember when you think of this person, images that will create a vivid picture for your readers. What dominant impression do you want to leave with the reader? Is there one single word that would convey this impression? Remember that your supporting details should all support your choice of dominant impression. In the model paragraph that follows, Colin Powell, the first African-American chair of the Joint Chiefs of Staff, gives us a picture in words of the most memorable person he recalls from his youth. Notice how each part of the description reveals a personality trait.

> ### MODEL PARAGRAPH: THE DOMINANT FIGURE OF MY YOUTH
>
> *Topic sentence*
>
> <u>The dominant figure of my youth was a small man, five feet two inches tall.</u> In my mind's eye, I am leaning out the window of our apartment, and I spot him coming down the street from the subway station. He wears a coat and tie, and a small fedora is perched on his head. He has a newspaper tucked under his arm. His overcoat is unbuttoned, and it flaps at his sides as he approaches with a brisk, toes-out stride. He is whistling and stops to greet the druggist, the baker, our building super, almost everybody he passes. To some kids on the block, he is a faintly comical figure. Not to me. This jaunty, confident little man is Luther Powell, my father.

Ten suggested topics

1. An elderly relative
2. Your favorite television character
3. An outstanding athlete
4. A loyal friend
5. An overworked employee
6. A cab driver
7. A fashion model
8. A gossipy neighbor
9. A street vendor
10. A pushy salesperson

Assignment 3: A Description of a Time of Day

Write a paragraph in which you describe the sights, sounds, and events of a time of day in a place that you know well. For instance, it could be a Sunday morning at your house or Friday night at the movies. In the model paragraph that follows, Neil deGrasse Tyson, astrophysicist and director of the Hayden Planetarium in New York City, describes a life-changing night when he was nine years old.

MODEL PARAGRAPH: A DARK AND STARRY NIGHT

Topic sentence

It was a dark and starry night. I felt as though I could see forever. Too numerous to count, the stars of the autumn sky, and the constellations they trace, were rising slowly in the east while the waxing crescent moon was descending into the western horizon. Aloft in the northern sky were the Big and Little Dippers just where they were described to appear. The planets Jupiter and Saturn were high in the sky. One of the stars seemed to fall toward the horizon. It was a meteor streaking through the atmosphere. I was told there would be no clouds that night, but I saw one. It was long and skinny and stretched across the sky from horizon to horizon. No, I was mistaken. It wasn't a cloud. It was the Milky Way. I had never seen the sky of the Milky Way with such clarity and majesty as that night. Forty-five minutes swiftly passed when the house lights came back on in the planetarium sky theater. That was the night—the night the universe poured down from the sky and flowed into my body. I had been called. The study of the universe would be my career, and no force on Earth would stop me.

Ten suggested topics

1. A Saturday afternoon filled with errands
2. The dinner hour at my house
3. Lunchtime in a cafeteria
4. A midnight raid on the refrigerator
5. Breakfast at a restaurant
6. Monday morning
7. Getting ready to go out on a Friday night
8. My Sunday morning routine
9. Coming home from school or work
10. Watching late-night movies

Assignment 4: A Description of a Time of Year

Write a paragraph in which you describe a particular time of year. Make sure that all of the details you choose relate specifically to that time of year. In the model paragraph that follows, from "Boyhood in Jamaica" by Claude McKay, the writer remembers springtime on his native island.

MODEL PARAGRAPH: SEASONS IN JAMAICA

Topic sentence

Most of the time there was hardly any way of telling the seasons. To us in Jamaica, as elsewhere in the tropics, there were only two seasons—the rainy season and the dry season. We had no idea of spring, summer, autumn, and winter like the peoples of northern lands. Springtime, however, we did know by the new and lush burgeoning of grasses and the blossoming of trees, although we had blooms all the year round. The mango tree was especially significant of spring because it was one of the few trees that used to shed its leaves. Then, in springtime, the new leaves sprouted—very tender, a kind of sulfur brown, as if they had been singed by fire. Soon afterwards the white blossoms came out and we knew that we would be eating juicy mangoes by August.

Ten suggested topics

1. A winter storm
2. New Year's Eve
3. Summer in the country
4. A winter walk
5. Jogging in the spring rain
6. Sunbathing on a beach
7. Thanksgiving dinner
8. The leaves in autumn
9. Christmas morning
10. Halloween night

WRITE FOR SUCCESS

Finding a good place to study is not always easy. What determines a good place? Is it soft music or available food and beverage? Is it absolute silence and absence of distractions? Describe the place on campus that you find the most conducive to studying. Be sure to use as many of the senses as possible in your description.

Working Together

James Woodson/Getty Images

Writing a Character Sketch

The following personal ad appeared on the bulletin board of a college campus center:

> College girl seeks neat, responsible roommate to share off-campus apartment for next academic year. Person must be a nonsmoker and respect a vegetarian who cooks at home. Furniture not needed, but microwave and printer would be awesome!

Different personal habits often have a way of causing friction between two people who share the same living space. This is the reason it can be very difficult to find the right roommate in a college dormitory, the right person to share an apartment, or the right long-term companion to share a lifestyle.

Divide into groups. The members of each group should develop a list of habits that can become problems when people share a living space. Then, working together, group the items on your list into categories with general headings. For example, one general heading might be *food issues*. You might find it useful to group items in order of increasing importance.

Finally, each student should choose from one of the topics below and write a serious or amusing character description.

1. Write a paragraph or two in which you provide a character description of yourself for an agency that will match you with a roommate. As you write, be sure to include information about your interests, habits, attitudes, and other personal characteristics that could make a difference in the kind of person the agency will select for you.

2. Write a paragraph or two in which you provide a character sketch of the roommate you would like the agency to find for you.

3. Write a description of what you imagine would be the "roommate from hell."

PORTFOLIO SUGGESTION

Keep your character sketch in your portfolio. You may want to collect other examples of paragraphs of description that you find effective. These models may suggest ways that you can revise your own character sketch, or they may inspire you to write other character sketches of people you observe or know well.

Developing Paragraphs: Process Analysis

21

CHAPTER OBJECTIVES

Giving instructions or explaining how something is done involves careful reconstruction of a sequence of steps. If any part of the instructions is missing, an entire process can be misunderstood. In this chapter, you will learn the elements of writing good process paragraphs.

- distinguishing between **directional** and **informational** process writing

- understanding the importance of **completeness**

- achieving coherence through **logical sequence** and the use of **transitions**

- taking a step-by-step approach to create process paragraphs

- studying model paragraphs to create process paragraphs

What Is Process Analysis?

Process analysis is a method of development that provides a step-by-step explanation of how something is done (directional) or how something works (informational).

If parents were to find a tick in their child's hair, they would need to know what to do. They might go online for help. Read the following advice, which is an example of process analysis that is directional.

Tick Bites

Example of process writing that is directional

Remove the tick with a pair of tweezers. Never try to remove a tick by burning it or applying kerosene or other substances. Gently grasp the tick with the tweezers as close to the skin as possible. Slowly pull the insect straight out. Do not twist as you pull, or the tick's body will separate from its head, leaving the head buried under your skin. As you pull, do not squeeze the body of the tick. Squeezing can inject infectious fluids from the tick into you. After removing the tick, thoroughly clean the bite area and your hands, preferably with an antiseptic such as rubbing alcohol. If the tick came from an area with a high incidence of Lyme disease, save the tick and consult a

Topic sentence

doctor. Otherwise, monitor the bite area. If small raised bumps appear at the bite site or if you develop a rash around the bite or flu-like symptoms, see your doctor. <u>In the case of a tick bite, time is critical because the longer the tick is attached to a person's body, the greater the risk of contracting Lyme disease.</u>

You can find examples of directional process writing everywhere you look—in newspapers, magazines, and books, as well as on the containers and packages of products you use every day. Your daily life is filled with activities that involve the need for directional process. Instructions on a test, directions on how to get to a wedding reception, and your favorite spaghetti recipe are a few examples of the kinds of process writing you see and use regularly.

The other type of process writing is **informational**. In this case, you explain how something works or how something worked in the past. There is no expectation or even possibility that the reader will or could act upon it. The purpose of describing the process is purely to provide information. History books are filled with such writing. For instance, if you described how a Civil War general planned his battle strategy, this would be informational process writing. The following example tells how the writer and social activist Malcolm X accomplished his self-education. In the paragraph, the transitional words that signal the steps or stages of the process have been italicized.

The Education of Malcolm X

Topic sentence

Example of process writing that is informational

When Malcolm X was in prison, he became very frustrated because he could not express his thoughts in letters written to his family and friends. Nor could he read well enough to get the meaning from a book. He decided to change this situation. *First*, he got hold of a dictionary along with some paper and pencils. He was astounded at how many words there were. Not knowing what else to do, he turned to the first page and *began* by copying words from the page. It took him the entire day. *Next*, he read what he had written aloud, over and over again. He was excited to be learning words he never knew existed. *The next morning*, he reviewed what he had forgotten and then copied the next page. He found he was learning about people, places, and events from history. This process *continued until* he had filled a tablet with all the A's and *then* all the B's. *Eventually*, Malcolm X copied the entire dictionary!

Making Sure All the Steps Are Included

All of us have been given directions that seemed very clear at first but that did not produce the result we expected. Perhaps we misunderstood one of the steps in the process, or perhaps the writer left out a step. Maybe the person giving the information assumed that we already knew certain parts of the process or didn't think through the process carefully enough to identify all the steps. Directions must always be accurate and complete, even down to any special equipment needed to carry out the process.

The writer who presents a process is almost always more of an authority on the subject than the reader. In providing information or giving directions on how to do something, it is easy to leave out steps because they may seem too obvious to be worth mentioning. A writer should never assume that the reader will be able to fill in any missing steps. An important part of process writing is always being aware of the audience.

EXERCISE **1** **Is the Process Complete?**

Read the steps in the following recipe. Imagine yourself baking the cake using only the information provided. Has any information been left out, or have any needed steps been omitted? (Although recipes are generally not presented in paragraph or essay form, they are good examples of process writing in which the order and completeness of the step-by-step procedure are of critical importance.)

How to make a Swedish spice cake

1. Butter an 8-inch tube pan and sprinkle with 2 tbsp. of fine dry bread crumbs.

2. Cream ½ cup of butter; add 1 cup firmly packed brown sugar and cream until light and fluffy.

3. In a small bowl, beat 2 egg yolks until light and add to the creamed mixture.

4. Sift together 1½ cups all-purpose flour, 1 tsp. baking powder, 2 tsp. ground cardamom, and 2 tsp. ground cinnamon.

5. Add the dry ingredients to the creamed ingredients, mixing alternately with ½ cup light cream.

6. Beat egg whites until stiff and fold into the batter.

7. Turn into a prepared pan, bake, and serve unfrosted.

Missing step or steps: _____

_____

_____

EXERCISE **2** **Is the Process Complete?**

Imagine that, at long last, a family is ready to remodel a bathroom or a kitchen. Read the following steps, which should be followed for successful completion of the job. Can you think of any steps that might be missing?

Steps to remodeling a room in your home

1. Have a good idea of what you want before contacting a carpenter or contractor.

2. Be realistic about what you can afford to spend.

3. Get at least two estimates for the job.

4. Plan to be present when the work is being done.

5. Do not pay the final payment until everything is finished and you are satisfied with the job.

Missing step or steps: _____

_____

_____

_____

_____

EXERCISE ③   **Is the Process Complete?**

In the following process, determine whether any important steps have been omitted. Imagine yourself going through the process using only the information provided.

How to prepare for an oral presentation

1. Research your topic thoroughly, taking notes and recording the sources for your information.

2. Prepare your speech on special large note cards, with each point on a different card.

3. Decide on a transitional word to use before each new point. Do not hesitate to use typical transitions such as *my first point*, *second*, or *in conclusion*.

4. Rehearse your speech more than once.

5. Just before you begin, remind yourself that you will speak slowly and clearly.

Missing step or steps: _____

_____

_____

_____

Achieving Coherence

Ordering in Logical Sequence

When you are working with a process, it is important not only to make sure that the steps in the process are complete but also to present the steps in the right sequence. For example, if you are describing the process of cleaning an electric mixer, it is important to point out that you must first unplug the appliance before you remove the blades. A person could lose a finger if this part of the process were missing. Improperly written instructions have caused serious injuries and even death.

EXERCISE 4   **Ordering in Logical Sequence**

The following steps describe the process of refinishing hardwood floors. Put the steps into their proper sequence.

_____   Sanding with coarse sandpaper continues until the hardwood is exposed.

_____   A coat of polyurethane finish is applied.

_____   When the sanding is finished, the floor is thoroughly cleaned with a vacuum sweeper to remove all the sawdust.

_____   The finish must then dry for three days before waxing and buffing.

_____   All furnishings are removed from the room.

_____   The initial sanding is done with coarse sandpaper on the sanding machine.

_____   The edger and hand sander are used after the machine sanding to get to hard-to-reach places.

_____   A second coat of polyurethane finish is applied on the following day, using a brush or a roller.

_____   The coarse sandpaper on the machine is changed to fine sandpaper for the final sanding.

_____   Nails sticking out from the floor should be either pulled out or set below the surface of the boards before starting the sanding.

EXERCISE 5   **Ordering in Logical Sequence**

The following steps describe the process of devising a filing system. Put the steps into their proper sequence.

_____   Filing of additional items should stop when mental fatigue sets in.

_____   Now the file folder is labeled, and the sheet of paper is slipped in.

_____   All the pages to be filed should be gathered in one area, perhaps in the room where the filing cabinet is located.

_____   The file folders are alphabetized and put away in the file drawer. Your session for that time is finished.

_____   In addition, a wastebasket, file folders, labels, and a pen will be needed.

_____   The same procedure should be repeated with the next sheet of paper, keeping in mind that this sheet of paper might have a place in an existing file rather than a new one.

_____   Any page can be picked up at random to be studied. Does the item need to be saved? If the item has no value, it should be recycled. If the item has value, then the process moves to the next step.

_____   Once the filing system has been established, it is easy to maintain if, every time a particular file is consulted, the complete file is scanned quickly to identify any items that are no longer useful and need to be discarded.

_____   When the item seems worth saving, the question should be asked: What is this item about? That subject will be the title for the label on the file folder.

Using Transitions

Like writers of narration, writers who analyze a process usually order their material by time sequence. Although it would be tiresome to use the words *and then* for each new step, some transitions are necessary for the process to read smoothly and coherently. Here is a list of transitions frequently used in a process paragraph.

TRANSITIONS COMMONLY USED IN PROCESS ANALYSIS

the first step	the second step	the last step
in the beginning	as you are…	the final step
to start with	next	finally
to begin with	now	at last
first of all	once you have	eventually
	then	
	after you have…	

EXERCISE ⑥   **Using Transitions to Go from a List to a Paragraph**

Select one of the three processes presented in exercise 2. Use the list of steps, including missing steps that you supplied, to write a process paragraph. Be sure to include transitions to make the paragraph read smoothly and coherently.

_____

_____

_____

_____

_____

_____

_____

_____

_____

_____

_____

_____

_____

_____

_____

_____

Writing a Process Paragraph Using a Step-by-Step Approach

Mastering any skill, including writing, requires a disciplined attitude. One way to master the skill of creating a piece of writing is to take a step-by-step approach, focusing on one issue at a time. This approach results in a minimum of stress. Another advantage is that the writer does not miss important points or misunderstand any part of the process. Of course, there are other ways to build effective process paragraphs, but here is one logical method you can use that will always achieve good results.

STEP-BY-STEP APPROACH TO WRITING A PROCESS PARAGRAPH

1. After you have chosen your topic and controlling idea, plan your topic sentence.

2. List as many steps or stages in the process as you can.

3. Eliminate irrelevant steps, add any equipment or materials needed, and explain any special circumstances of the process.

4. Put the steps in order.

5. Write at least one complete sentence for each of the steps you have chosen from your list.

6. Write a concluding statement that says something about the results of completing the process.

7. Copy your sentences into standard paragraph form.

8. Make a final check for spelling errors and other mistakes, such as omitted words.

NOTE: When you use a computer spell-check feature, keep in mind that this feature will alert you only to spellings that do not match words in its dictionary. If you type *there* when you mean *their*, the spell-checker will see an acceptable word. When it comes to a final editing, there is no substitute for your own careful reading.

EXERCISE 7   **Writing a Process Paragraph Using a Step-by-Step Approach**

This exercise will guide you through the construction of a complete process paragraph. Start with the topic suggested below. Use the eight steps to take you through each stage of the writing process.

   Topic: How to lose weight

Perhaps no topic has filled more book and magazine pages than the "lose five pounds in one week" promise. The wide variety of diet plans boggles the mind. Here is your chance to add your own version.

Terry Vine/Getty Images

1. Topic sentence: _____

    _____

    _____

    _____

    _____

2. Make a list of all necessary steps.

    a. _____

    b. _____

    c. _____

    d. _____

    e. _____

    f. _____

    g. _____

    h. _____

    i. _____

    j. _____

3. Eliminate irrelevant steps, add any equipment or materials needed, and explain any special circumstances.

4. Put your steps in order by numbering them.

5. Using your final list, write at least one sentence for each step you have chosen.

    a. _____

    _____

    b. _____

    _____

    c. _____

    _____

    d. _____

    _____

    e. _____

    _____

    f. _____

    _____

    g. _____

    _____

6. Write a concluding statement. _____

_____

_____

7. On a separate sheet of paper or on a computer, copy your sentences into standard paragraph form.

8. Do a final reading to check for errors and omissions.

EXERCISE 8   **Writing a Process Paragraph Using a Step-by-Step Approach**

This exercise will guide you through the construction of a complete process paragraph. Start with the topic suggested below. Use the eight steps to take you through each stage of the writing process.

   Topic: How to set up a budget

Imagine you are the expert who has been hired by a couple to help them sort out their money problems. Together they bring in a reasonable salary, but they always spend more than they earn.

1. Topic sentence: _____

_____

_____

_____

_____

_____

_____

2. Make a list of all necessary steps.

   a. _____

   b. _____

   c. _____

   d. _____

   e. _____

   f. _____

   g. _____

   h. _____

   i. _____

   j. _____

3. Eliminate irrelevant steps, add any equipment or materials needed, and explain any special circumstances.

4. Put your steps in order by numbering them.

5. Using your final list, write at least one sentence for each step you have chosen.

   a. _____

   _____

   b. _____

   _____

   c. _____

   _____

   d. _____

   _____

   e. _____

   _____

   f. _____

   _____

   g. _____

   _____

6. Write a concluding statement. _____

   _____

   _____

7. On a separate sheet of paper or on a computer, copy your sentences into standard paragraph form.

8. Do a final reading to check for errors and omissions.

Studying Model Paragraphs to Create Process Paragraphs

Assignment 1 (Directional): How to Accomplish a Familiar Task

Write a paragraph in which you describe the process of carrying out a task. The following paragraph describes a process for organizing a pickup game.

> ### MODEL PARAGRAPH: HOW TO ORGANIZE A PICKUP GAME
>
> *Topic sentence*
>
> <u>Though it sounds like the easiest thing in the world, organizing a pickup game of basketball, soccer, or ultimate Frisbee can be frustrating.</u> First, you have to have the right number of players. Even when the correct number of people say they will play, you cannot guarantee that they will all be there, let alone show up on time. Then, you have to confirm that the field, court, or park is not already occupied. Don't assume that somebody else will automatically bring the necessary equipment; if you cannot bring it yourself, you must communicate to another player to bring the ball, goals, Frisbee, or whatever gear is needed. Organizing the players and the location is just the beginning. Let the players know that they should bring two colors of shirts, one white and one dark. That way you can split into two clear teams. Never show up with a grey shirt—it's so confusing! Are you light or dark? Once everyone is present with the proper clothing and has had a chance to warm up, divide into two even sides. Teams should have equal numbers, but they should also have an equal distribution of talent. This can be challenging. Avoid having all the skilled or most experienced players come together on a single team. When play starts, be patient with the beginners, be sure to communicate, and of course practice good sportsmanship. During pickup games, try not to lose your temper, curse your teammates, or be selfish. Do, however, take the opportunity to practice new moves, make friends, and get some great exercise.

Ten suggested topics

1. How to plan a move from one home to another
2. How to transfer contacts to a new cell phone
3. How to save money at the grocery store
4. How to change the oil in your car
5. How to make the best … (choose your favorite dish)
6. How to mail a fragile object
7. How to pack a suitcase
8. How to furnish an apartment inexpensively
9. How to organize a small room or apartment
10. How to plan a barbecue

Assignment 2 (Directional): How to Care for Your Health

Awareness of the importance of health and physical fitness has increased, bringing in big profits to health-related magazines, health clubs, health food producers, and sports equipment manufacturers. Write a paragraph in which you show steps you can take for your mental or physical health. The following paragraph tells how to get a good night's sleep.

> ### MODEL PARAGRAPH: HOW TO GET A GOOD NIGHT'S SLEEP
>
> *Topic sentence*
>
> <u>Getting a good night's sleep depends on following several important steps.</u> First, the conditions in the bedroom must be correct. The temperature should be around sixty-five degrees, and the room should be as quiet as possible. Next, an important consideration is the bed itself. A good-quality mattress goes a long way toward preventing aches, which often wake people up when they turn over during the night. Using natural fabrics such as cotton and wool is a much better choice than using sheets and blankets made of synthetic materials that do not allow air to circulate. In addition, pillows that are either too soft or too hard can cause stiffness of the neck and lead to a poor night's sleep. Once the room is prepared, sleep is still not ensured. The next requirement is that the person going to bed feels relaxed and tired enough to sleep. This will not happen if the person has been lying around all day napping and leading an inactive life. People who have trouble sleeping should try to keep an active schedule. Then, as bedtime nears, activities should become less stimulating and more relaxing. Finally, people often forget the importance of what they eat in the hours preceding bedtime. People should not go to bed hungry, nor should they overeat. Foods such as candy bars or cookies are full of sugar and act as stimulants. Such foods, along with all caffeinated beverages, should be avoided. When these steps are followed, nearly everyone can look forward to a good night's sleep.

Ten suggested topics

1. How to plan a wholesome diet
2. How to care for someone who is ill
3. How to plan a daily exercise program
4. How to choose a sport that is suitable for you
5. How to organize preventative care
6. How to pick a doctor
7. How to deal with anger
8. How to limit junk food
9. How to recognize and treat depression
10. How to find a spiritual side to life

Assignment 3 (Informational): How Teamwork Accomplishes a Task

Write a paragraph in which you describe the process used by an agency or group of people to achieve some important goal. The following paragraph, describing how wildfires are fought, is an example of informational process writing.

MODEL PARAGRAPH: FIGHTING WILDFIRES

Topic sentence

   When a wildfire starts, a process to protect lives and property is set in motion. At first, the fire is watched. Many fires do not go beyond the initial burn. If the fire appears to be spreading, the next step is to call on weather forecasters to study the weather patterns to predict where the fire will spread next. Firefighters called "hot shots" may hike into the area to begin their work of scraping, cutting, and clearing the brush that gives fuel to the fire. The first goal of the hot shots is to cut a containment perimeter around the fire rather than put it out. If it is too far to hike into an area, parachutists called "smoke jumpers" will go in to do the work. If the fire is moving too fast or is burning in extremely rugged terrain, helicopter pilots drop chemicals or water on the fire to retard it. Although some fires are set by Mother Nature during lightning storms, the sad fact is that most fires are set by humans who carelessly toss away cigarette butts that have not been completely extinguished.

Ten suggested topics

1. How a charity accomplishes its goal
2. How lab experiments use teamwork
3. How a band requires cooperation
4. How a family requires communication
5. How a neighborhood crime-watch group functions
6. How an ambulance crew works together
7. How a local government operates
8. How an office should be run
9. How a study group requires flexibility and patience
10. How a sports team requires sportsmanship and positive communication

WRITE FOR SUCCESS

Some students arrive at college knowing exactly what they want to major in and what their career goals are. The majority of students, however, are less than sure what they should major in and may feel pressured to figure out what major they should pursue.

Use this writing response to explore one possible major that interests you. What do you already know about the major? If you can, find a senior classmate who can give you information about pursuing this major. Consider the following questions:

(a) Are there any courses you must complete before you can start the major?

(b) Which of the courses offered in the major are required?

(c) Which of the courses offered in the major most interest you? Why?

(d) What do you believe will be the most challenging courses for you? Why?

(e) What are the job prospects for students who graduate with this major?

(f) Is this a major for which you would have a wholehearted interest? Explain.

Working Together

vgajic/Getty Images

Building a Team

Either in school or in business, being able to work well with a group is of vital importance. If a team member does not understand or respect how groups should function, the experience may be frustrating at best and a failure at worst. Below are several questions for a discussion on teamwork. Select one student in the class to direct the discussion while another student writes the main points of the discussion on the board.

Class Discussion

1. When a group meets to work, what procedure should be followed?

2. How important is it that everybody first understand the task?

3. How can a group avoid the situation in which only one person seems to be doing all the work?

4. What should be done about a person who tends to dominate all the discussions?

5. What can be done for a person who is very shy?

6. What can be done about a person who has an "attitude"?

7. How can the team be sure that the meeting does not end up with people chatting instead of focusing on the task?

8. How can personality conflicts be avoided?

9. How should disagreements be handled?

Use the material from the classroom discussion to write a process essay. In your essay, describe the procedure that should be followed when a group of people meets to work on a project. It might be helpful to use as an example a group of workers doing a particular job: teachers getting together to design a series of courses, magazine editors meeting to decide on a theme for their next issue, or a school's coaches planning their strategies for the upcoming season.

PORTFOLIO SUGGESTION

Record some of the comments that you heard during the group discussion, making special note of two or three points you found especially interesting. Write at least one or two sentences for each of these special points, concentrating on some aspect about which you feel strongly. Place these completed sentences in your portfolio for possible use in future writing assignments. As you record the general comments and generate your own sentences, keep in mind that your notes may apply directly to your work in other college courses. The idea of building team spirit or learning to work with others has many direct applications, including in the fields of sports, science, psychology, and sociology.

Developing Paragraphs: Comparison/Contrast

22

CHAPTER OBJECTIVES

Writing a paragraph using comparison or contrast requires the development of two topics at the same time. In this chapter, you will concentrate on the special needs of this challenging rhetorical form.

- choosing a **two-part topic**

- ordering material using the **point-by-point method** or the **block method**

- improving coherence by using **transitional phrases** common to comparison/contrast writing

- taking a step-by-step approach to create comparison/contrast paragraphs

- studying model paragraphs to create comparison/contrast paragraphs

What Is Comparison/Contrast?

We use comparison and contrast every day. In the grocery store, we judge similar products before we decide to buy one of them; we listen to two politicians on television and think about the differences between their positions before we vote for one of them; and we read college catalogs and talk to our friends before we make a final choice about which school we should attend.

When we compare or contrast two items, we need to consider exactly which points should be compared. We usually have a purpose or a need for making our decision about which item is better or worse. For instance, when making an expensive purchase, a person who has not analyzed the situation might be tempted to rely on a clever salesperson who may want to make an easy sale. A person might also be swayed by the price alone or make the decision based on impulse. We have all experienced the sad consequences of making such a decision without thinking it through. Comparison or contrast uses a logical process that will help us think through critical similarities or differences.

Consider the common experience of finding the best apartment to rent. The search for an appropriate place to live directly affects one's budget and has many implications for a person's daily life. Does the monthly rent include utilities, and if not, how high could those costs go? Can you rent month-to-month, or are you obliged to sign a lease? How much of a security deposit will you have to put down? Are pets allowed? Is the apartment available now? Is it furnished or unfurnished? What condition is it in?

Aside from the apartment itself, some basic questions about the building and the neighborhood come to mind. What floor is the apartment on, and if it is on one of the upper floors, is there an elevator? Is the building well maintained? Does it have good security? Is the building close to public transportation? Is there shopping nearby?

If your piece of writing were concerned with this subject of choosing the right apartment, the points listed above would make your writing fall into the category of *comparison/contrast*. In this case, because the search for the right apartment is such an important one, you can see that comparison or contrast is not only a useful tool—it is an absolutely essential one.

> **Comparison/contrast,** as a method of development, examines similarities or differences between people, objects, or ideas in order to arrive at a judgment or conclusion.

NOTE: Although the term *comparison* is sometimes used in a general sense to include both comparisons and contrasts, here we use the term *comparison* when we focus on similarities, and we use the term *contrast* when we focus on differences.

Choosing a Two-Part Topic

Much of the difficulty in writing a paragraph of comparison or contrast is caused by having a two-part topic. Therefore, careful thought must be given to creating the topic sentence for that paragraph. You must choose a two-part topic that has a sufficient number of points to compare or contrast, but you must avoid selecting two-part topics that would have so many points to compare or contrast that you would not be able to discuss all the material in one paragraph. For example, a student trying to compare the Spanish word *río* with the English word *river* might be able to come up with only two sentences of material. With only a dictionary to consult, it is unlikely that the student would find enough material for several points of comparison. On the other hand, contrasting the United States with Europe would present such an endless supply of points that the tendency would be to give only general facts that the reader would already know. When the subject is too broad, the writing is often too general. A better two-part topic might be to compare traveling by train in Europe with traveling by train in the United States.

Once you have chosen a two-part topic that you feel is not too limiting and not too broad, you must remember that a good comparison/contrast paragraph devotes an equal or nearly equal amount of space to each of the two parts. If the writer is interested in only one of the topics, the danger is that the paragraph will be one-sided.

Here is a sentence with a one-sided contrast:

> **American trains go to only a few towns, are infrequent, and are often shabby and uncomfortable. In contrast, European trains are much nicer.**

The following sentences show a better-written contrast, giving attention to both topics:

> **American trains go to only a few large cities, run infrequently, and are often shabby and uncomfortable. In contrast, European trains go to nearly every small town, are always dependable, and are clean and attractive.**

EXERCISE **1**   **Evaluating the Two-Part Topic**

Study the following topics. Decide whether each topic is *too broad* or could be *suitable* for a paragraph of comparison or contrast. Mark your choice in the appropriate space to the right of each topic given. Be prepared to explain your choices.

Topic	Too broad	Suitable
1. Plants and animals	_____	_____
2. Print books and e-books	_____	_____
3. Leasing a car and buying a car	_____	_____
4. Alligators and crocodiles	_____	_____
5. Colombia and Peru	_____	_____
6. Off-campus housing and on-campus housing	_____	_____
7. Parents and grandparents	_____	_____
8. A registered nurse and a licensed practical nurse	_____	_____
9. Careers in medicine and careers in finance	_____	_____
10. Baseball and soccer	_____	_____

EXERCISE 2   **Working with Comparison/Contrast**

For each comparison or contrast, supply your own two parts of the topic. Each two-part topic should be one that you could develop as an example of comparison or contrast.

1. Compare/contrast two personality types:

   The _____ person with the _____ person

2. Compare/contrast two kinds of pants:

   _____ with _____

3. Compare/contrast two kinds of gambling:

   _____ with _____

4. Compare/contrast two kinds of exercise equipment:

   _____ with _____

5. Compare/contrast two types of TV shows:

   The _____ show with the _____ show

6. Compare/contrast two types of architecture:

   _____ with _____

7. Compare/contrast two places where you can relax:

   Relaxing in the _____ with relaxing in the _____

8. Compare/contrast two ways to invest money:

_____ and _____

9. Compare/contrast two sports stadiums:

_____ with _____

10. Compare/contrast two political parties:

_____ with _____

EXERCISE **3** **Working with Comparison/Contrast**

For each comparison or contrast, supply your own two parts of the topic. Each two-part topic should be one that you could develop as an example of comparison or contrast.

1. Compare/contrast two kinds of popular video games:

Playing _____ with playing _____

2. Compare/contrast two ways of watching movies:

Watching movies _____ with watching movies _____

3. Compare/contrast two careers:

A career in _____ with a career as a(n) _____

4. Compare/contrast two ways of paying for a purchase:

Using _____ to buy something with using _____ to buy something

5. Compare/contrast two different lifestyles:

The life of _____ with the life of _____

6. Compare/contrast two places to go swimming:

Swimming in a(n) _____ with swimming in a(n) _____

7. Compare/contrast two types of phone:

_____ with _____

8. Compare/contrast two popular Web sites:

_____ with _____

9. Compare/contrast two leisure activities:

_____ with _____

10. Compare/contrast two different teaching styles or classroom types:

_____ with _____

Achieving Coherence: Two Approaches to Ordering Material

Point-by-Point Method

One method for ordering material in a paragraph of comparison or contrast is known as the **point-by-point method**. When you use this method, you compare/contrast point 1 of topic 1 and then point 1 of topic 2. Then you continue with your second points for each of the two topics. You continue until you have covered all the points. For example, here is a paragraph from Julius Lester's *All Is Well.* In the paragraph, the writer uses the point-by-point method to compare the difficulties of being a boy in our society more than a generation ago with the difficulties of being a girl at that same time.

Topic sentence

<u>Now, of course, I know that it was as difficult being a girl as it was a boy, if not more so.</u> While I stood paralyzed at one end of a dance floor trying to find the courage to ask a girl for a dance, most of the girls waited in terror at the other, afraid that no one, not even I, would ask them. And while I resented having to ask a girl for a date, wasn't it also horrible to be the one who waited for the phone to ring? And how many of those girls who laughed at me making a fool of myself on the baseball diamond would have gladly given up their places on the sidelines for mine on the field?

Notice how, after the opening topic sentence, the writer uses half of each sentence to describe a boy's situation growing up and the other half to describe a girl's experience. This technique is often used in longer pieces of writing in which many points of comparison are made. This method helps the reader keep the comparison or contrast carefully in mind at each point.

If the paragraph is broken down into its parts, this is how the **point-by-point method** might look in chart form:

Topic Sentence: Now, of course, I know that it was as difficult being a girl as it was a boy, if not more so.

Point-by-Point Method			
Points to Compare or Contrast	**First Topic: Boys**		**Second Topic: Girls**
Point 1 ⟶	While I stood paralyzed at one end of a dance floor trying to find the courage to ask a girl for a dance, ...	⟶	... most of the girls waited in terror at the other, afraid that no one, not even I, would ask them.
Point 2 ⟶	And while I resented having to ask a girl for a date, ...	⟶	... wasn't it also horrible to be the one who waited for the phone to ring?
Point 3 ⟶	And how many of those girls who laughed at me making a fool of myself on the baseball diamond ...	⟶	... would have gladly given up their places on the sidelines for mine on the field?

Block Method

The other method for ordering material in a paragraph of comparison or contrast is known as the **block method**. When you use this approach, you present all of the facts and supporting details about one part of your topic, and then you give all of the facts and supporting details about the other part. Here, for example, is another version of the paragraph by Julius Lester, this time written according to the block method:

Topic sentence

Now, of course, I know that it was as difficult being a girl as it was a boy, if not more so. I stood paralyzed at one end of the dance floor trying to find the courage to ask a girl for a dance. I also resented having to ask a girl for a date. Furthermore, I often felt foolish on the baseball diamond. On the other hand, most of the girls waited in terror at the other end of the dance floor, afraid that no one, not even I, would ask them to dance. In addition, it was a horrible situation for the girls who had to wait for the phone to ring, hoping for a date. And how many of those girls who stood on the sidelines would have gladly traded places with me on the baseball diamond?

Notice how the first half of this version presents all of the details about the boy, and the second part of the paragraph presents all of the information about girls. This method is often used in shorter pieces because the reader will easily remember three or four short points and thus not need each comparison/contrast side by side.

If the paragraph is broken down into its parts, this is how the **block method** might look in chart form:

Topic Sentence: Now, of course, I know that it was as difficult being a girl as it was a boy, if not more so.

Block Method					
Topics	Point 1		Point 2		Point 3
First topic →	I stood paralyzed at one end of the dance floor trying to find the courage to ask a girl for a dance.	→	I also resented having to ask a girl for a date, …	→	Furthermore, I often felt foolish on the baseball diamond.
Second topic →	On the other hand, most of the girls waited in terror at the other end of the dance floor, afraid that no one, not even I, would ask them to dance.	→	In addition, it was a horrible situation for the girls who had to wait for the phone to ring, hoping for a date.	→	And how many of those girls who stood on the sidelines would have gladly traded places with me on the baseball diamond?

You will want to choose one of these methods before you write a comparison or contrast assignment. Keep in mind that, although the block method is most often used in shorter writing assignments, such as a paragraph, you can often effectively employ the point-by-point method as well.

EXERCISE **4**   **Recognizing the Two Approaches to Ordering Material**

Each of the following passages is an example of comparison or contrast. Read each paragraph carefully, and decide whether the writer has used the point-by-point method or the block method. Also decide whether the piece emphasizes similarities or differences. Indicate your choices in the spaces provided after each passage.

Topic sentence   1.   <u>Female infants speak sooner, have larger vocabularies, and rarely demonstrate speech defects.</u> (Stuttering, for instance, occurs almost exclusively among boys.) Girls exceed boys in language abilities, and this early linguistic bias often prevails throughout life. Girls read sooner, learn foreign languages more easily, and, as a result, are more likely to enter occupations involving language mastery. Boys, in contrast, show an early visual superiority. They are also clumsier, performing poorly at something like arranging a row of beads, but excel at other activities calling on total body coordination. Their attentional mechanisms are also different. A boy will react to an inanimate object as quickly as he will to a person. A male baby will often ignore the mother and babble to a blinking light, fixate on a geometric figure, and at a later point, manipulate it and attempt to take it apart.

_____ Point-by-point   _____ Block

_____ Similarities   _____ Differences

Topic sentence   2.   <u>Often a writer is inspired by a piece of literature from the past.</u> The obvious parallels between Shakespeare's *Romeo and Juliet* and the musical *West Side Story* have been frequently noted. *Romeo and Juliet* opens with a fight between two feuding families, the Montagues and the Capulets. Romeo meets Juliet at a masked ball, and it is love at first sight. They meet secretly. Unfortunately, through a series of events, Romeo commits suicide thinking Juliet has died. In *West Side Story*, the musical also opens with a fight, in this case between two feuding gangs, the Jets and the Sharks. When Tony, a former Jet, meets Maria, the sister of a Shark, at a gymnasium dance, like Romeo and Juliet, they immediately fall in love. They too must meet secretly. However, misfortune occurs, and Tony believes Maria to be dead. The musical ends tragically for the young lovers.

_____ Point-by-point   _____ Block

_____ Similarities   _____ Differences

Topic sentence   3.   <u>I first realized that the act of writing was about to enter a new era five years ago when I went to see an editor at *The New York Times*.</u> As I was ushered through the vast city room I felt that I had strayed into the wrong office. The place was clean and carpeted and quiet. As I passed long rows of desks, I saw that almost every desk had its own computer terminal and its own solemn occupant—a man or a woman typing at the computer keyboard or reading what was on the terminal screen. I saw no typewriters, no paper, no mess. It was a cool and sterile environment; the drones at their machines could have been processing insurance claims or tracking a spacecraft in orbit. What they didn't look like were newspaper people, and what the place didn't look like was a newspaper office. I knew how a newspaper office should look and sound and smell—I worked in one for thirteen years. The paper was the *New York Herald Tribune,* and its city room, wide as a city block, was dirty and disheveled. Reporters wrote on ancient typewriters that filled the air with clatter; copy editors labored on coffee-stained desks over what the reporters had written. Crumpled balls of paper littered the floor and filled the wastebaskets—failed efforts to write a good lead or a decent sentence. The walls were grimy—every few years they were painted over in a less restful shade of eye-rest green—and the atmosphere was hazy with the smoke of cigarettes and cigars. At the very center, the city editor, a giant named L. L. Engelking, bellowed his displeasure with the day's work, his voice a rumbling volcano in our lives. I thought it was the most beautiful place in the world.

_____ Point-by-point   _____ Block

_____ Similarities   _____ Differences

4.   We went fishing the first morning. I felt the same damp moss covering the worms in the bait can, and saw the dragonfly alight on the tip of my rod as it hovered a few inches from the surface of the water. <u>It was the arrival of this fly that convinced me beyond any doubt that everything was as it always had been, that the years were a mirage and there had been no years.</u> The small waves were the same, chucking the rowboat under the chin as we fished at anchor, and the boat was the same boat, the same color green and the ribs broken in the same places, and under the floorboards the same freshwater leavings and debris—the dead hellgrammite°, the wisps of moss, the rusty discarded fishhook, the dried blood from yesterday's catch. We stared silently at the tips of our rods, at the dragonflies that came and went. I lowered the tip of mine into the water, tentatively, pensively dislodging the fly, which darted two feet away, poised, darted two feet back, and came to rest again a little farther up the rod. There had been no years between the ducking of this dragonfly and the other one—the one that was part of memory. I looked at the boy, who was silently watching his fly, and it was my hands that held his rod, my eyes watching. I felt dizzy and didn't know which rod I was at the end of.

Topic sentence

hellgrammite°

the larva of the dobsonfly, often used as bait for fishing

_____ Point-by-point   _____ Block

_____ Similarities   _____ Differences

EXERCISE ⑤ **Using the Point-by-Point Method for Contrast**

Passage 3 in exercise 4 uses the block method to make its points of contrast. Rewrite the passage using the point-by-point approach.

_____

_____

_____

_____

_____

_____

_____

_____

EXERCISE **6** **Using the Point-by-Point and Block Methods for Comparison or Contrast**

Below is how one student prepared for the writing of a paragraph comparing life in the city with life in the suburbs. Review the student's chart, and add your own ideas and omit any you do not wish to include. Then, selecting either the block method or the point-by-point method, write a comparison or contrast paragraph of your own on this topic. (Feel free to change the topic sentence to reflect your own point of view.)

Topic Sentence: If I could move back to the city from the suburbs, I know I would be happy.

Life in the City/Life in the Suburbs				
Points to Compare or Contrast	**Topic 1: Living in the City**		**Topic 2: Living in the Suburbs**	
Point 1 ⟶	A quick ride on the bus or subway gets you to work.	⟶	Commuting to work from the suburbs to the city is often time-consuming, exhausting, and expensive.	
Point 2 ⟶	Men are as visible as women in the neighborhood.	⟶	Because most men in the suburbs work in the city, few of them are active in the suburban community.	
Point 3 ⟶	The architecture and diversity of people are stimulating.	⟶	The sameness of streets and people is monotonous.	
Point 4 ⟶	Shopping for nearly everything can be done on foot.	⟶	Most shopping requires a car.	
Point 5 ⟶	People walk in their neighborhoods.	⟶	People go everywhere by car.	

Notice that the writer who created this list emphasized the disadvantages of the suburbs, in contrast to the advantages of the city. No mention was made, for example, of overcrowding or high crime rates in the city. Another list could be created from the point of view of a person who prefers the suburbs.

Achieving Coherence: Using Transitions

In addition to ordering your material using either the block method or the point-by-point method, the careful use of transitions will also help to achieve coherence. The transitions in the following chart are useful to keep in mind when writing a comparison or contrast paragraph. Some of them are used in phrases, some in clauses. For example, notice the difference between *like* and *as*. *Like* is used as a preposition in a prepositional phrase:

My sister is just <u>*like*</u> me.

As is used as a subordinating conjunction to begin a clause:

Every evening my sister reads in bed, <u>*as* does her older daughter</u>.

TRANSITIONS COMMONLY USED IN COMPARISON/CONTRAST

again	like	although	instead
also	likewise	and yet	nevertheless
as well as	moreover	but	on the contrary
both	the same as	despite	on the other hand
equally	similar to	different from	otherwise
furthermore	similarly	even though	still
just as	so	except for	though
just like	too	however	unlike
		in contrast with	whereas

EXERCISE **7**

Using Transitions in Comparisons and Contrasts

Read each of the following pairs of sentences and decide whether the idea being expressed is a comparison or a contrast. Next, combine the two sentences by using a transition you have chosen from the list above. Then write your new sentence on the lines provided. If needed, you may reword your new sentence to make it grammatically correct. An example has been done for you.

> **Mr. Costello is a teacher.**
>
> **His wife is a teacher.**

First you decide that the two sentences show a comparison. Then you combine the two by using an appropriate transition:

> **Both Mr. Costello and his wife are teachers.**

Use a variety of transitions.

1. Dr. Rappole has an excellent bedside manner.

    Dr. Connolly is very withdrawn.

Your combined sentence: _____

_____

2. The first apartment had almost no furniture, was badly in need of painting, and felt dark and cheerless.

    The second apartment was bare, felt totally neglected, and looked out onto a brick wall.

Your combined sentence: _____

_____

_____

3. In the United States, interest in soccer has become apparent only in recent years.

   Soccer has always been immensely popular in Brazil.

   Your combined sentence: _____

   _____

   _____

4. The French Revolution relied heavily on the common people.

   The Russian Revolution was dominated by an elite group of thinkers.

   Your combined sentence: _____

   _____

   _____

5. Sandro is carefree and fun loving, with more interest in theater than math.

   Noreen, Sandro's sister, takes math more seriously and wants to become an engineer.

   Your combined sentence: _____

   _____

   _____

EXERCISE 8 **Using Transitions in Comparisons and Contrasts**

First, identify each of the following pairs of sentences as a comparison or a contrast. Then combine the two sentences by using a transition from the list included in the Achieving Coherence section. Do not use the same transition more than once. Finally, write your new sentence on the lines provided.

1. *The View* is a daytime talk show that often deals with serious current issues that are of interest to viewers.

   Stephen Colbert's talk show provides light entertainment in the late evening.

   Your combined sentence: _____

   _____

   _____

2. Shakespeare's *Romeo and Juliet* is a famous love story that takes place in Italy.

   West Side Story is a more contemporary version of Shakespeare's love story that takes place in New York City.

   Your combined sentence: _____

   _____

   _____

3. The movie *Wild* deals with the theme of a woman against nature.

   The movie *127 Hours* deals with the theme of man against nature.

   Your combined sentence: _____

   _____

4. Some scientists believe that dinosaurs became extinct because they ran out of food.

   Some scientists think that dinosaurs were victims of a climate change induced by dust clouds thrown up by a meteor hitting earth.

   Your combined sentence: _____

   _____

   _____

5. The Museum of Modern Art in New York City is limited to art from the twentieth and twenty-first centuries.

   The Metropolitan Museum of Art in New York City contains art that dates back thousands of years.

   Your combined sentence: _____

   _____

   _____

Writing a Comparison/Contrast Paragraph Using a Step-by-Step Approach

Mastering any skill, including writing, requires a disciplined attitude. One way to master the skill of creating a piece of writing is to take a step-by-step approach, focusing on one issue at a time. This approach results in a minimum of stress. Another advantage is that the writer does not miss important points or misunderstand any part of the process. Of course, there are other ways to build effective comparison or contrast paragraphs, but here is one logical method you can use that will always achieve good results.

STEP-BY-STEP APPROACH TO WRITING A COMPARISON/CONTRAST PARAGRAPH

1. After you have chosen your two-part topic, plan your topic sentence.

2. List each point that could be compared or contrasted.

3. Choose the three or four most important points from your list.

4. Decide whether you want to use the point-by-point method or the block method for organizing your paragraph.

5. Write at least one complete sentence for each of the points you have chosen from your list.

6. Write a concluding statement that summarizes the main points, makes a judgment, or emphasizes what you believe is the most important point.

7. Copy your sentences into standard paragraph form.

8. Always make a final check for spelling errors and other mistakes, such as omitted words.

NOTE: When you use a computer spell-check feature, keep in mind that this feature will alert you only to spellings that do not match words in its dictionary. If you type *there* when you mean *their*, the spell-checker will see an acceptable word. When it comes to a final editing, there is no substitute for your own careful reading.

EXERCISE 9 **Writing a Comparison or Contrast Paragraph Using a Step-by-Step Approach**

This exercise will guide you through the construction of a comparison or contrast paragraph. Start with the suggested topic. Use the eight steps as a guide.

Hero Images/Getty Images

Topic: **Compare or contrast how you spend your leisure time with how your parents (or friends) spend their leisure time.**

1. Topic sentence: _____

_____

_____

_____

2. Make a list of possible comparisons or contrasts.

a. _____

b. _____

c. _____

d. _____

e. _____

f. _____

g. _____

h. _____

i. _____

j. _____

3. Circle the three or four comparisons or contrasts that you believe are most important, and put them in order.

4. Choose either the point-by-point method or the block method.

5. Using your final list, write at least one sentence for each comparison or contrast you have chosen.

a. _____

_____

b. _____

_____

c. _____

_____

d. _____

_____

6. Write a concluding statement. _____

_____

_____

7. On a separate sheet of paper or on a computer, copy your sentences into standard paragraph form.

8. Do a final reading to check for errors and omissions.

EXERCISE **10**   **Writing a Comparison or Contrast Paragraph Using a Step-by-Step Approach**

This exercise will guide you through the construction of a comparison or contrast paragraph. Start with the suggested topic. Use the eight steps as a guide.

Topic: **Compare or contrast the styles of two television personalities (or two other public figures often in the news).**

1. Topic sentence: _____

   _____

   _____

2. Make a list of possible comparisons or contrasts.

   a. _____

   b. _____

   c. _____

   d. _____

   e. _____

   f. _____

   g. _____

   h. _____

   i. _____

   j. _____

3. Circle the three or four comparisons or contrasts that you believe are most important, and put them in order.

4. Choose either the point-by-point method or the block method.

5. Using your final list, write at least one sentence for each comparison or contrast you have chosen.

   a. _____

   _____

   b. _____

   _____

   c. _____

   _____

   d. _____

   _____

6. Write a concluding statement. _____

   _____

   _____

7. On a separate sheet of paper or on a computer, copy your sentences into standard paragraph form.

8. Do a final reading to check for errors and omissions.

Studying Model Paragraphs to Create Comparison or Contrast Paragraphs

Assignment 1: Contrasting a Place Then and Now

Write a paragraph in which you compare or contrast the appearance of a place when you were growing up with the appearance of that same place now. The following paragraph contrasts the way a small city appeared some years ago with how it appeared to the writer on a recent visit.

> ### MODEL PARAGRAPH: THIRTY YEARS LATER
>
> As I drove up Swede Hill, I realized that the picture I had in my mind all these years was largely a romantic one. It was here that my father had boarded, as a young man of eighteen, with a widow who rented rooms in her house. Now the large old wooden frame houses were mostly two-family homes; no single family could afford to heat them in the winter. The porches, which had once been beautiful and where people had passed their summer evenings, had peeling paint and were in need of repair. No one now stopped to talk; the only sounds to be heard were those of cars whizzing past. The immigrants who had come to this country and worked hard to put their children through school were now elderly and mostly alone. Their more educated children had long ago left the small upstate city for better opportunities elsewhere. From the top of the hill, I looked down fondly on the town built on the hills and noticed that a new and wider highway now went through the town. My father would have liked that; he would not have had to complain about Sunday drivers on Foote Avenue. In the distance I could see the large shopping mall, which had attracted most of the area shoppers. Local in-town businesses had gradually been forced to close. The center of town no longer hummed with
>
> *Topic sentence*   activity, as it once had. The years had not been kind. <u>My town was not the same place I had known as a child.</u>

Ten suggested topics   Contrast the way a place appears now with how it appeared some years ago:

1. A city, town, or village

2. Your childhood home

3. A barber shop or beauty salon

4. A friend's home

5. A local corner store (or some other local establishment)

6. Your elementary school

7. A downtown shopping area

8. A restaurant or diner

9. An undeveloped place such as an open field or wooded area

10. A library

Assignment 2: Comparing Two Individuals Who Share Similar Qualities

Write a paragraph in which you compare two individuals you know or you have observed. The following paragraph is a classic comparison by the historian Bruce Catton. Using the point-by-point method, he compares two legendary generals from the U.S. Civil War, Ulysses S. Grant, head of the Union Army, and Robert E. Lee, leader of the Confederate forces of the South.

MODEL PARAGRAPH: GRANT AND LEE

Topic sentence

<u>Different as they were—in background, in personality, in underlying aspiration—these two great soldiers had much in common.</u> Each man had, to begin with, the great virtue of utter tenacity and fidelity. Grant fought his way down the Mississippi Valley despite acute personal discouragement and profound military handicaps. Lee hung on in the trenches at Petersburg after hope itself had died. In each man there was an indomitable quality . . . the born fighter's refusal to give up as long as he can still remain on his feet and lift his two fists. Daring and resourcefulness they had, too; the ability to think faster and move faster than the enemy. These were the qualities that gave Lee the dazzling campaigns of Second Manassas and Chancellorsville and won Vicksburg for Grant.

Ten suggested topics   Compare:

1. Two friends who have similar qualities
2. Two singers who have similar musical styles
3. Two politicians who both demonstrate leadership qualities
4. Two social reformers who have similar goals or who perform similar duties
5. Two talk show hosts
6. A plumber and a doctor
7. Two brothers or two sisters who share certain personality traits
8. A baby and an elderly person
9. Two athletes who demonstrate similar talents
10. A ballet dancer and a football player

Assignment 3: Contrasting Two Approaches to a Subject

Write a paragraph in which you contrast two ways of considering a particular topic. The following paragraph contrasts two approaches to the art of healing—the traditional medical approach and the approach that involves less dependence on chemicals and more reliance on the body's natural defense system.

Topic sentence

MODEL PARAGRAPH: THE MEDICAL PROFESSION AND NATURAL HEALING

Natural healing is basically a much more conservative approach to health care than traditional medical practice. Traditional medical practice aims for the quick cure by means of introducing substances or instruments into the body that are highly antagonistic to whatever is causing the disease. A doctor wants to see results, and he or she wants you to appreciate that traditional medicine is what is delivering those results to you. Because of this desire for swift, decisive victories over disease, traditional medicine tends to be dramatic, risky, and expensive. Natural healing takes a slower, more organic approach to the problem of disease. It first recognizes that the human body is superbly equipped to resist disease and heal injuries. But when disease takes hold or an injury occurs, the first instinct in natural healing is to see what might be done to strengthen that natural resistance and those natural healing agents so that they can act against the disease more effectively. Results are not expected to occur overnight, but neither are they expected to occur at the expense of the body, which may experience side effects or dangerous complications.

Ten suggested topics   Contrast:

1. Two attitudes toward required courses in college
2. Two attitudes toward writing research papers
3. Keeping an elderly person with health problems at home in contrast to moving her or him to a nursing home
4. Being your own boss or working for someone else
5. Two views about online dating
6. Two attitudes toward divorce
7. Two radically different political viewpoints
8. Your lifestyle today and five years ago
9. Two views on prison sentences for drug possession
10. Two attitudes on the right-to-die issue

Assignment 4: Contrasting Cultural Approaches

Write a paragraph in which you compare or contrast two cultures or an aspect of culture that may be observed in two societies. The following paragraph was written by Brenda David, a U.S. teacher who worked with schoolchildren in Milan, Italy, for several years.

MODEL PARAGRAPH: CHILDREN OF TWO NATIONS

Topic sentence

   All young children, whatever their culture, are alike in their charm and innocence—in being a clean slate on which the wonders and ways of the world are yet to be written. <u>But during the three years I worked in a school in Milan, I learned that American and Italian children are different in several ways.</u> First, young American children tend to be active, enthusiastic, and inquisitive. Italian children, on the other hand, tend to be passive, quiet, and not particularly inquisitive. Second, American children show their independence while their Italian counterparts are still looking to their parents and grandparents to tell them what to do or not do. Third, and most important to those who question the influence of environment on a child, the American children generally surpass their Italian schoolmates in math, mechanical, and scientific abilities. But American children are overshadowed by their Italian counterparts in their language, literature, art, and music courses. Perhaps the differences, which those of us at the school confirmed in an informal study, were to be expected. After all, what priority do Americans give to the technological skills? And what value do Italians—with the literature of poets and authors like Boccaccio, the works of Michelangelo, and the music of the world-famous La Scala opera at Milan—place on the cultural arts?

Ten suggested topics   Contrast:

1. Two different cuisines

2. Courtship in two cultures

3. Attitudes toward women's roles in two societies

4. Two musical traditions, generations, or genres

5. Raising children in two different cultures

6. Urban people with small-town people

7. Care for the elderly in two cultures

8. The culture of your neighborhood with the general culture of your society

9. The culture you live in now with the culture in which your parents were raised

10. Medical care in our society with the medical care of another society

WRITE FOR SUCCESS

The academic demands of college can be quite a change from the academic demands of high school. In addition, many other aspects of college life make college a different experience from high school. Write a response that compares your experience in high school with your experience in college. Be sure to include academic issues among the points you make.

Working Together

WR Publishing / Alamy Stock Photo

A Before-and-After Story

Below is an account of a radical change in one person's life. When you have read this before-and-after report (which uses the block method), share with your classmates some stories of changes in the lives of people you have known. Then write a before-and-after story of your own. Use the following chart to help you plan your approach to the two-part topic.

Before

Since I was fifteen, I've saved all kinds of stuff: bureau handles, small bottles, marbles, mirrors, nuts, screws, wire, cord, bathtub stoppers, mothballs, empty cigarette packs, frying pans, pencils that say different things on them, trusses, parking tickets. In 1997, my brother Harry, with whom I lived, slipped on some of my papers and got brought to a nursing home. The social worker wouldn't let him come back unless I got rid of my collections. So I bought a bus pass and visited him once a week. He died last year at eighty-five. If he'd had a hobby like me, he might have lived longer. I liked living in my junk, and I always knew where everything was. In the living room, the junk came up to about my chest. In the bedroom, it wasn't too bad; it just came up to my knees. I made paths to get around. It made me feel important. But I guess I overdid it. The landlord wanted me to get rid of my junk. A third of my neighbors wouldn't talk to me. I suspected I might get evicted. So this summer I had to let my junk go.

After

My nephew cleaned it out with some friends of his. It took ten days. I wasn't there. When I came back, I was disappointed. I thought more stuff would be saved. I had an empty feeling, like I was robbed. I lost memories of my four brothers and my mother. But things happen—what can you do? I'm too old to worry anymore. All that's left is my necktie collection and my cat, Wagging. The emptiness is a little hard to get used to. For one thing, the traffic noise is very loud now. And I feel hollow. My junk was sort of a freedom. I put so much work into saving—years and years—and it's suddenly gone. It's like somebody had died, a fire or an earthquake. It's like the change from hot to cold water. I may start saving certain things, like books, but I don't go out as much as I used to, so I can't collect as much. From now on, I'll have fewer hobbies.

Preparing to write a comparison or contrast paragraph involves noting points o comparison or contrast. Use the chart provided below.

Points to Compare or Contrast	Before	After
Point 1		
Point 2		
Point 3		
Point 4		
Point 5		

PORTFOLIO SUGGESTION

You might find it interesting to do some research on a personality type known as the pack rat: a person who fills an apartment or house with useless stuff that is never thrown away. Television programs about hoarders have presented the personal stories of some of these people. Go online and find information on two other hoarders, the Collyer brothers, who died in New York City shortly after World War II. Use the information you find on Homer and Langley Collyer to write an essay about people who cannot bring themselves to throw anything away.

Developing Paragraphs: Cause and Effect 23

CHAPTER OBJECTIVES

In our daily lives, we often look for connections between two actions or events. We wonder if these events are accidental, coincidental, or connected in some more causal way. When writers examine causal relationships, they are using a cause-and-effect method of development.

- recognizing **terms** that signal causal relationships

- avoiding errors in **logic**

- identifying **immediate causes, underlying causes, immediate effects,** and **long-term effects**

- improving coherence by using **transitional phrases** common to cause and effect

- taking a step-by-step approach to create cause-and-effect paragraphs

- studying model paragraphs to create cause-and-effect paragraphs

What Is Cause and Effect?

Cause and effect, as a method of development, is the search for the relationship between two actions or two events, one of which we conclude is the reason for the other action or event.

People have always looked at the world and asked, "Why did this happen?" or "What will be the result?" Ancient societies created beautiful myths and legends to explain the mysteries of the universe. Modern civilization has emphasized the use of scientific methods of observation to find answers to mysteries such as the cause of autism or the reason why the planet Mars appears to be covered by canals. When we examine the spiritual or physical mysteries of our world, we are trying to discover the connections or links between events. In this chapter, we will refer to such connections between events as **causal relationships**.

Not everything that happens to us is due to luck or chance. For instance, a magic trick may appear to have no logical explanation to the child who watches, but the person performing that trick knows the secret of the connection between the rabbit and the hat. The search for causes or effects is a bit like detective work. A person looks for clues that will explain what might at first seem unexplainable. Learning to recognize causal relationships can help us better understand some of the events that happen to us over the course of our lives. This search for connections can be complex. Often the logical analysis of a problem reveals more than one possible explanation. Sometimes the best one can do is find **possible causes** or **probable effects**.

Recognizing Terms that Signal Cause and Effect

Writers who examine the causal relationship between two events are likely to use one or more of the terms in the following chart. Study the chart to become familiar with these terms associated most often with cause and effect.

TERMS THAT SIGNAL CAUSAL RELATIONSHIPS

Causes: explaining **why**

giving **reasons**

understanding **problems**

determining **immediate causes** and **underlying causes**

presenting **contributing factors**

Effects: predicting **results**

understanding **consequences**

providing **solutions**

determining **immediate effects** and **long-term effects**

Following are some examples of how a writer could signal causal relationships. Notice the two sentences in the second example. The cause does not always have to be mentioned first. Sometimes, the effect will be mentioned before the cause depending on how the sentence is worded.

1. *If . . . , then . . . .*

   If the school budget is defeated, **then** several teachers will have to be dismissed.

2. *The cause/reason/result/consequence/effect . . . was that . . . .*

   The **reason** several teachers were dismissed **was that** the school budget was defeated.

   The **result** of the school budget defeat **was that** several teachers were dismissed.

3. *The problem . . . could be solved . . . .*

   The problem of funding the school's wrestling team **could be solved** if enough people in the community would get together to raise the needed money.

PRACTICE ① **Use the preceding patterns to create sentences of your own on the following topic: The challenge of writing a research paper.**

1. If _____

   then _____ .

2. A contributing factor is _____.

3. The cause for _____

is that _____.

4. The consequence of _____

is that _____.

5. The problem of _____

could be solved _____

EXERCISE 1 **Finding Causes and Effects in Paragraphs**

The following two paragraphs have the same topic: headaches. However, their controlling ideas differ. One paragraph examines the causes of headaches, while the other describes the effects of recurring headaches.

Cause: explaining why, giving reasons, understanding problems

Topic sentence

Headaches can have several causes. Many people think that the major cause of a headache is nervous tension, but strong evidence suggests diet and environment as possible factors. Some people get headaches because they are dependent on caffeine. Other people may be allergic to salt, or they may have low blood sugar. Still other people are allergic to household chemicals, including polishes, waxes, bug killers, and paint. If they can manage to avoid these substances, their headaches tend to go away. When a person has recurring headaches, it is important to look for the underlying cause, especially if the result of that search is freedom from pain.

According to the above paragraph, what causes a headache?

1. _____

2. _____

a. _____

b. _____

c. _____

3. _____

    a. _____

    b. _____

    c. _____

    d. _____

Effect: predicting results, understanding consequences, suggesting solutions

Topic sentence

> <u>Recurring headaches can have several disruptive effects on a person's life.</u> Severe headaches are more than temporary inconveniences. In many cases, these headaches make a person nauseated to the point that he or she must go to bed. Sleep is often interrupted because of the pain. This worsens the physical and emotional state of the sufferer. Those who try to maintain a normal lifestyle often rely on drugs to get through the day. Such drugs, of course, can have negative side effects. Productivity on a job can certainly be reduced, even to the point of regular absences. Finally, perhaps the most distressing aspect of all this is the seemingly unpredictable occurrence of these headaches. The interruption to a person's family life is enormous: plans canceled at the last minute and relationships with friends and family strained. It is no wonder that many of these people feel discouraged and even depressed.

According to the preceding paragraph, what are some of the effects of recurring headaches?

1. _____

2. _____

3. _____

4. _____

5. _____

EXERCISE **2**   **Separating the Cause from the Effect**

In each sentence, separate the *cause* (reasons or problems) from the *effect* (results, consequences, or solutions). Remember that the cause is not necessarily given first.

1. In this country, more than half of the mothers with children under one year of age work outside the home; this has resulted in the unprecedented need for daycare.

   Cause: _____

   _____

   Effect: _____

2. Today, more than two-thirds of all preschool children and four out of five school-age children have working mothers; this has led to increased strains on the daycare system.

   Cause: _____

   _____

   Effect: _____

3. In one national survey, more than half the working mothers reported that they had either changed jobs or cut back on their hours to be more available for their children.

   Cause: _____

   Effect: _____

4. Because they feel their children need the supervision of a parent, many mothers who work do so only when their children are in school, and other mothers work only occasionally during the school year.

   Cause: _____

   Effect: _____

   _____

5. Many mothers experience deep emotional crises as a result of the conflict between the financial obligations of their home and their own emotional needs as parents.

   Cause: _____

   _____

   Effect: _____

Avoiding Errors in Logic

Here is an example of a possible error in logic:

> **Every time I try to write an essay in the evening, I have trouble getting to sleep. Therefore, writing must prevent me from sleeping.**

In this case, the act of writing may indeed stimulate the person and prevent that person from getting to sleep. However, if the person is serious about finding the cause of the insomnia, he or she must find out whether other *factors* are to blame. For instance, if the person is drinking several cups of coffee while writing each evening, this caffeine intake could cause the person's sleep problems.

AVOID THESE COMMON ERRORS IN LOGIC

1. Do not confuse coincidence or chronological sequence with evidence of a causal relationship.

2. Look for underlying causes beneath the obvious ones and for far-reaching effects beyond the ones that first come to mind. Often what appears to be a single cause or a single effect is part of a much more complex relationship.

Here is an example of a coincidental relationship: **Whenever I leave for work late, I get stopped at all the red lights.**

Why is this a coincidental relationship? It is purely coincidental that someone would get all of the red lights just because of leaving late for work.

Here is an example of a causal relationship: **When I realized that the discussion between my husband and me was becoming an argument, I calmed down and spoke in a gentle tone; as a result, our attitudes toward each other changed for the better.**

Why is this a causal relationship? People will calm down during arguments if one remains calm and uses a pleasant tone.

EXERCISE ③   ### Looking for the Causal Relationship

Study each of the following situations. If the sequence of events is merely coincidental or the conclusion is unfounded, write *U* (unfounded) in the space provided. If the relationship is most likely causal, write *C*. Be prepared to explain your answers in class.

_____ 1. Every time I carry my umbrella, it doesn't rain. I am carrying my umbrella today; therefore, it won't rain.

_____ 2. We put fertilizer on the grass. A week later, the grass had grown two inches and turned a deeper green.

_____ 3. On Tuesday morning, I walked under a ladder. On Wednesday morning, I walked into my office and was told I had lost my job.

_____ 4. The child grew up helping her mother cook. In adulthood, she became a famous chef.

_____ 5. Tar and nicotine from cigarettes damage the lungs. People who smoke cigarettes increase their chances of dying from lung cancer.

_____ 6. A political scandal was exposed in the city on Friday. On Saturday night, only twenty-four hours later, a power blackout occurred in the city.

_____ 7. Increasing numbers of tourists came to the island last year. The economy of the island reached new heights.

_____ 8. Many natural disasters have occurred this year. The world must be coming to an end.

_____ 9. The biggest factory in a nearby town decided to relocate to another country. The town officials invited different industries to consider moving to the town.

_____10. That woman sings beautifully. She must have an equally beautiful personality.

EXERCISE ④ **Immediate or Underlying Causes**

Five topics follow. For each topic, give a possible immediate or direct cause and then give a possible underlying cause. Discuss your answers in class. An example has been done for you.

Causes of a particular disease, such as tuberculosis

Immediate cause: contact with a carrier of the disease

Underlying cause: immune system weakened by poor nutrition

1. Causes for a tuition increase at a college

    Immediate cause: _____

    Underlying cause: _____

2. Causes for cutting a particular sports program from a school or college

    Immediate cause: _____

    Underlying cause: _____

3. Causes for new development in a city

    Immediate cause: _____

    Underlying cause: _____

4. Causes of closing a restaurant

    Immediate cause: _____

    Underlying cause: _____

5. Causes of debt

Immediate cause: _____

Underlying cause: _____

EXERCISE ⑤   **Immediate or Long-Term Effects**

Below are five topics. For each topic, give an immediate effect and then give a possible long-term effect. Discuss your answers in class. An example has been done for you.

Effects of using credit cards

Immediate effect: money available on the spot for purchases

Long-term effect: greater cost because of interest payments

1. Effects of horror movies on young children

Immediate effect: _____

Long-term effect: _____

2. Effects of students taking out loans to complete college

Immediate effect: _____

Long-term effect: _____

3. Effects on family life when both parents work outside the home

Immediate effect: _____

Long-term effect: _____

4. Effects of major industry leaving town

Immediate effect: _____

Long-term effect: _____

5. Effects of having a family member with special needs

Immediate effect: _____

Long-term effect: _____

Achieving Coherence: Using Transitions

Several transitional words and expressions are particularly useful in writing about causes or effects. You will need to feel comfortable using these words and expressions, and you will need to know what punctuation is required.

TRANSITIONS COMMONLY USED IN CAUSE-AND-EFFECT WRITING

COMMON TRANSITIONS FOR CAUSE

because	He missed the opportunity because he was ill.
caused by	The missed opportunity was caused by illness.
the reason . . . is that	The reason he missed the opportunity is that he became ill.
resulted from	The missed opportunity resulted from his illness.

COMMON TRANSITIONS FOR EFFECT

accordingly	He was ill; accordingly, he missed the opportunity.
as a result	He was ill; as a result, he missed the opportunity.
consequently	He was ill; consequently, he missed the opportunity.
for this reason	He was ill. For this reason, he missed the opportunity.
resulted in	His illness resulted in his missing the opportunity.
so	He was ill, so he missed the opportunity.
therefore	He was ill; therefore, he missed the opportunity.
thus	He was ill; thus, he missed the opportunity.

EXERCISE **6**   **Using Transitional Words and Expressions to Signal Cause**

Use each of the following words or phrases in a complete sentence that demonstrates you understand how to use the given term to express a causal relationship.

1. caused by

   _____

   _____

2. because

   _____

   _____

3. resulted from

   _____

   _____

4. the reason for . . . is that

   _____

   _____

EXERCISE **7**   **Using Transitional Words and Expressions to Signal Effect**

Use each of the following words or phrases in a complete sentence that demonstrates you understand how to use the given term to point to an effect.

1. accordingly

_____

_____

2. as a result

_____

_____

3. resulted in

_____

_____

4. consequently

_____

_____

5. for this reason

_____

_____

6. so

_____

_____

7. therefore

_____

_____

8. thus

_____

_____

Writing a Cause-and-Effect Paragraph Using a Step-by-Step Approach

Mastering any skill, including writing, requires a disciplined attitude. One way to master the skill of creating a piece of writing is to take a step-by-step approach, focusing on one issue at a time. This approach results in a minimum of stress. Another advantage is that the writer does not miss important points or misunderstand any part of the process. Of course, this is not the only way to build a paragraph using cause and effect, but it is one logical method that will achieve good results.

STEP-BY-STEP APPROACH TO WRITING A CAUSE-AND-EFFECT PARAGRAPH

1. After you have chosen your topic, plan your topic sentence.

2. Brainstorm by jotting down all possible causes or effects. Ask others for their thoughts. Do research if necessary. Consider long-range effects or underlying causes.

3. Choose the three or four best points from your list.

4. Decide on the best order for these points. (One way to organize them is from least important to most important.)

5. Write at least one complete sentence for each of the causes or effects you have chosen from your list.

6. Write a concluding statement.

7. On a separate sheet of paper or on a computer, copy your sentences into standard paragraph form.

8. Always make a final check for spelling errors and other mistakes, such as omitted words.

NOTE: When you use a computer spell-check feature, keep in mind that this feature will alert you only to spellings that do not match words in its dictionary. If you type *there* when you mean *their*, the spell-checker will see an acceptable word. When it comes to a final editing, there is no substitute for your own careful reading.

EXERCISE **8** **Writing a Causal Paragraph Using a Step-by-Step Approach**

This exercise will guide you through writing a paragraph using cause as the method of development. Start with the suggested topic. Use the eight steps to help you work through the stages of the writing process.

    Topic: Why do many Americans have pets?

1. Topic sentence: _____

    _____

    _____

2. Make a list of possible causes. *(Consider immediate and underlying causes.)*

    a. _____

    b. _____

c. _____

d. _____

e. _____

3. Cross out any points that may be illogical or merely coincidental.

4. Put your list in order.

5. Using your final list, write at least one sentence for each of the causes you have found.

a. _____
_____

b. _____
_____

c. _____
_____

d. _____
_____

e. _____
_____

6. Write a concluding statement. _____
_____
_____

7. On a separate sheet of paper or on a computer, copy your sentences into standard paragraph form.

8. Do a final reading to check for errors and omissions.

EXERCISE 9   **Writing an Effect Paragraph Using a Step-by-Step Approach**

This exercise will guide you through writing a paragraph using effect as the method of development. Start with the suggested topic. Use the eight steps to help you work through the stages of the writing process.

Topic: It is claimed that people today do not read as much as people of previous generations. Has the nature of reading changed? What are the effects (both immediate and long-term) for our society?

Library of Congress Prints and Photographs Division[LC-DIG-ds-05448]

1. Topic sentence: _____

_____

_____

2. Make a list of possible effects. *(Consider immediate and long-term effects.)*

   a. _____

   _____

   b. _____

   _____

   c. _____

   _____

   d. _____

   _____

   e. _____

   _____

3. Cross out any points that may be illogical or merely coincidental.

4. Put your list in order.

5. Using your final list, write at least one sentence for each of the effects you have found.

   a. _____

   _____

   b. _____

   _____

   c. _____

   _____

   d. _____

   _____

   e. _____

   _____

6. Write a concluding statement. _____

_____

_____

7. On a separate sheet of paper or on a computer, copy your sentences into standard paragraph form.

8. Do a final reading to check for errors and omissions.

Studying Model Paragraphs to Create Cause-and-Effect Paragraphs

Assignment 1: The Causes of a Social Problem

Write a paragraph about the causes of a social problem that is of concern to you. The following paragraph by Lillian Neilson looks at possible causes for placing an elderly relative in a nursing home.

MODEL PARAGRAPH: OLD AGE IN MODERN SOCIETY

Topic sentence

    <u>Industrialized societies have developed homes for the elderly who are unable to care for themselves.</u> Despite much criticism, these homes care for a growing percentage of our nation's elderly. Why do some people feel forced into placing parents in a nursing home? The most immediate cause is that, following serious illness, there is often no place for the elderly person to go where he or she can be cared for. In the family of today, it is often the case that both partners work outside the home, so no one is home during the day to care for the person. Hiring a full-time nurse is beyond the budget of nearly every family. Even when a family member can be home to care for the elderly person, the problems can be overwhelming. The older person can be too heavy for one or even two caretakers to manage. Giving a bath can be especially dangerous in these circumstances. In addition, many elderly people have to be watched very carefully because of their medical condition. Many families do not have the proper training to meet these needs. Finally, elderly people who are suffering from senility and are often unpredictable can make it impossible for a caregiver to leave the house or get a proper night's rest. Perhaps improving the system of home health care could help families keep their loved ones in their homes longer.

Ten suggested topics

1. The causes of homelessness

2. The causes of losing a job

3. The causes of a child running away from home

4. The causes of dropping out of high school or college

5. The causes of divorce

6. The causes of low voter turnout

7. The causes of obesity

8. The causes of high stress among college students

9. The causes of road rage

10. The causes of hate crimes

Assignment 2: The Causes That Led to a Particular Historical Event

Write a paragraph about the causes that led to a particular event in history. This assignment will require some research. The following model paragraph looks at the causes for the loss of life when a supposedly unsinkable ship sank on its maiden voyage more than one hundred years ago.

Topic sentence

MODEL PARAGRAPH: THE SINKING OF THE TITANIC

After the British ship *Titanic* sank in the Atlantic Ocean on April 15, 1912, with the loss of more than 1,500 lives, investigators began an exhaustive search for the causes of the tragedy. The immediate cause of this terrible loss of life was a large iceberg that tore a three-hundred-foot gash in the side of the ship, flooding five of its watertight compartments. Some believe that the tragedy took place because the crew members did not see the iceberg in time, but others see a chain of different events that contributed to the tragedy. First was the fact that the ship was not carrying enough lifeboats for all of its passengers: It had enough boats for only about half of the people onboard. Furthermore, the ship's crew showed a clear lack of caring about the third-class, or "steerage," passengers, who were left in their cramped quarters below decks with little or no help as the ship went down. It has often been said that this social attitude of helping the wealthy and neglecting the poor was one of the real causes of the loss of life that night. Indeed, some of the lifeboats were not filled to capacity when the rescue ships eventually found them. Finally, the tragedy of the *Titanic* was magnified by the fact that some ships nearby did not have a radio crew on duty and therefore missed the distress signals sent by the *Titanic*. Out of all this, the need to reform safety regulations on passenger ships became obvious.

Ten suggested topics

1. Causes of an economic recession or depression

2. Causes of the growth of the civil rights movement in the 1960s in the United States

3. Causes of the war in Iraq

4. Causes of the decreasing number of trees in our forests

5. Causes of the victory (or loss) of a particular political candidate in a recent election

6. Causes of the loss of life and property after Hurricane Katrina

7. Causes of the low home ownership rates

8. Causes of the American Revolution

9. Causes of the victory (or loss) of a sports team

10. Causes of the repeal of Prohibition in 1933

Assignment 3: The Effects of a Substance or an Activity on the Human Body

Write a paragraph about what happens to the human body when it uses a substance or engages in some activity. The following model paragraph is adapted from Norman Taylor's *Plant Drugs That Changed the World*.

MODEL PARAGRAPH: EFFECTS OF CAFFEINE

Topic sentence

How much caffeine is too much? The ordinary cup of coffee, of the usual breakfast strength, contains between 100 and 200 mg of caffeine. That "second cup of coffee," therefore, means twice that amount of caffeine at one sitting. Its effects upon the nervous system, the increased capacity for thinking, its stimulating effects on circulation and muscular activity, not to speak of its sparking greater fluency—these are attributes of the beverage that few will give up. If it has any dangers, most of us are inclined to ignore them. But there is no doubt that excessive intake of caffeine at one time, say up to five or six cups, has harmful effects such as restlessness, nervous irritability, insomnia, and muscular tremor. The lethal dose in humans is unknown, for there are no records of it. Experimental animals die in convulsions after overdoses, and from such studies, it is assumed that a fatal dose of caffeine in humans may be about one hundred cups of coffee!

Ten suggested topics

1. The effects of alcohol on the body

2. The effects of regular exercise

3. The effects of overeating

4. The effects of a strict diet

5. The effects of fasting

6. The effects of substance abuse

7. The effects of smoking

8. The effects of staring at the computer for long periods of time

9. The effects of a sedentary lifestyle

10. The effects of taking vitamin supplements

Assignment 4: The Effects of a Community Emergency or Disaster

Think of an emergency or disaster that took place in or around your community. This could be an event that you witnessed or that you heard about in the media. Describe the effects this disaster had on you or the people who were involved. The following model paragraph describes the effects that a large power outage had on the communities of the Northeast.

MODEL PARAGRAPH: THE BLACKOUT OF 2003

Topic sentence

On Thursday, August 14, 2003, a large area of the northeastern United States was plunged into darkness because of a power failure, resulting in what has become known as the Blackout of 2003. This unprecedented power failure, which affected several states and parts of Canada, struck in an instant and without warning. The result was a near paralysis of normal activity. Most seriously affected, of course, were those individuals, businesses, and institutions caught in a variety of dangerous situations. For example, many people were stuck in elevators; others were underground in dark, hot, crowded subways. In hospitals, patients requiring life support depended on emergency equipment to work properly. Apart from these dangerous aspects of the blackout, the financial loss to certain businesses was considerable. Restaurants and other food-related industries were forced to throw away much of their food. In such states as Michigan and Ohio, the National Guard had to distribute water. Sewage treatment plants that could not operate had to release raw sewage into waterways. Transportation became another major problem. People who needed gasoline for their cars found that most gasoline pumps depended on electricity. The absence of working traffic lights made for huge traffic nightmares, and many airline flights were canceled. Even farmers needed generators rushed to them so they could operate their milking machines. Sadly, one effect of the emergency was that a few greedy individuals took advantage of the situation and overcharged people for items or services they needed. Reports surfaced of people paying $40.00 for simple $9.00 flashlights. Luckily, the power returned for most people within twenty-four hours and ended their discomfort. A more lasting effect, however, was the emerging realization that our electrical infrastructure is much more vulnerable than the general public had ever realized. In fact, the first thought on everyone's mind when the blackout occurred was that terrorists might have caused it. Some experts fear that even if terrorists did not initiate the blackout, the event will become a model or case study for future terrorist plans and activities. As soon as the emergency had passed, blame was placed on power company officials for not paying attention to the long-standing needs of the electrical system. People now must face the truth that creating a better system is going to involve huge amounts of money.

Without any question, we can expect an increase in the cost of electricity. Surprisingly, not all of the long-term effects may be negative: officials may now be forced to plan and execute improvements that will lead to improved monitoring and maintenance of our power supply.

Ten suggested topics

1. The effects of a drought

2. The effects of an unexpected outbreak of a disease

3. The effects of a flood or other extensive water damage on a home or community

4. The effects of a prolonged heat wave

5. The effects of a strike on a community

6. The effects of a major fire in a commercial district

7. The effects of the loss of small businesses in a community

8. The effects of the loss of an important community leader

9. The effects of decreased services in communities

10. The effects of a home invasion in a city neighborhood

WRITE FOR SUCCESS

Many students fail to recognize the value of seeking advice from experts. Write a response that explores the effects of good advisement. Consider how an expert could have a positive effect on some of the following issues: how many college credits to take, how to plan the semester's schedule, how to find out more about particular courses and the faculty members teaching them, how to plan for your major, how to tackle an issue that may turn out to be big problem later on, how to decide whether to drop a course, how to make a financial decision, and how to manage a personal problem.

Looking at Immediate and Long-Term Effects: The Story of Rosa Parks

Rosa Parks (1913–2005), who refused to give up her seat on an Alabama bus, set off a spark that inflamed the civil rights movement of that era. Her action is the subject of the following article by Ruth Edmonds Hill. The instructor or a member of the class should read the excerpt aloud while the rest of the class listens, noting immediate or long-term effects and marking the text where each effect is given.

1   The incident that changed Parks's life occurred on Thursday, December 1, 1955, as she was riding home on the Cleveland Avenue bus from her job at Montgomery Fair, a downtown department store where she worked as an assistant tailor. The first ten seats on the city buses, which were always reserved for whites, soon filled up. She sat down next to a man in the front of the section designated for blacks, when a white male got on and looked for a seat. In such situations, the black section was made smaller. The driver, who was white, requested that the four blacks move. The others complied, but Parks refused to surrender her seat, so the driver called the police. Parks had been evicted from a bus twelve years earlier by the same driver, but this time it was different. In a *Black Women Oral History Project* interview, she said, "I didn't consider myself breaking any segregation laws . . . because he was extending what we considered our section of the bus." And in *Black Women* she explained, "I felt just resigned to give what I could to protest against the way I was being treated."

2   At this time there had been fruitless meetings with the bus company about the rudeness of the drivers and other issues— including trying to get the bus line extended farther into the black community, because three-quarters of the bus riders were from there. In the previous year, three black women, two of them teenagers, had been arrested for defying the seating laws on the Montgomery buses. The community had talked many times about a citywide demonstration, such as boycotting the bus line, but it never developed. The Women's Political Council already had a network of volunteers in place and had preprinted flyers; they needed only a time and place for a meeting.

3   About six o'clock that evening, Parks was arrested and sent to jail. She was later released on a one-hundred-dollar bond, and her trial was scheduled for December 5. Parks agreed to allow her case to become the focus for a struggle against the system of segregation. On December 2, the Women's Political Council distributed more than fifty-two thousand flyers throughout Montgomery calling for a one-day bus boycott on the day of Parks's trial. There was a mass meeting of more than seven thousand blacks at the Holt Street Baptist

Church. The black community formed the Montgomery Improvement Association and elected Martin Luther King Jr. president. The success of the bus boycott on December 5 led to its continuation. In the second month, it was almost 100 percent effective, involving thirty thousand black riders. When Parks was tried, she was found guilty and fined ten dollars plus court costs of four dollars. She refused to pay and appealed the case to the Montgomery Circuit Court.

4 Following her release from jail, Parks went back to work but later lost her job, as did her husband. At home, the couple had to deal with threatening telephone calls. Rosa Parks devoted her time to arranging rides in support of the boycott. Blacks were harassed and intimidated by the authorities in Montgomery, and there was an attempt to break up their carpools. Parks served for a time on the board of directors of the Montgomery Improvement Association and often was invited elsewhere to speak about the boycott.

5 On February 1, 1956, in an attempt to have the Alabama segregation laws declared unconstitutional, the Montgomery Improvement Association filed a suit in the U.S. District Court in the names of four women and on behalf of all who had suffered indignities on the buses. On June 2, the lower court declared segregated seating on the buses unconstitutional. The Supreme Court upheld the lower court order that Montgomery buses must be integrated, and on December 20, 1956, the order was served on Montgomery officials. After 381 days of boycotting, resulting in extreme financial loss to the bus company, segregation and other discriminatory practices were outlawed on the city buses. Parks's refusal to give up her seat on a bus was the beginning of the civil rights movement of the 1950s and 1960s. Her action marked the beginning of a time of struggle by black Americans and their supporters as they sought to become an integral part of America.

6 With the notoriety surrounding her name, Parks was unable to find employment in Montgomery. Her husband became ill and could not work, so Parks, her husband, and her mother moved to Detroit in 1957 to join Parks's brother. Although her husband did not have a Michigan barber's license, he found work in a training school for barbers. In 1958 Parks accepted a position at Hampton Institute in Virginia for one year, after which she returned to Detroit and worked as a seamstress. She continued her efforts to improve life for the black community, working with the Southern Christian Leadership Conference in Detroit. In 1965, Parks became a staff assistant in the Detroit office of United States Representative John Conyers; she retired in 1988.

Working in Groups

After the excerpt has been read, the class should divide into groups. Each group should create two lists: the immediate effects and the long-term effects of Rosa Parks's decision, as presented in the article. Come together again as a class and compare the lists. Has each group agreed on which effects were immediate and which effects were long-term?

Since the day in 1955 when Rosa Parks took her historic stand, many changes have taken place in civil rights in our society. Your instructor may want you to choose another area of civil rights (such as one of those listed below) to study the causes of that particular group's discontent or to study the effects of that group's struggle to obtain legal rights.

- rights of the dying
- rights of the unborn
- gay and transgendered rights
- rights of immigrants

PORTFOLIO SUGGESTION

Because civil rights are constantly evolving in our society, and because many different groups are continuing to press for their rights, we need to understand the underlying causes and the long-term effects of those struggles. Investigate newspapers, magazines, and the Internet for material on current civil rights struggles. You may have a particular struggle in which you are deeply interested. Keep the results in your portfolio. The material you collect could well be useful later when you might want to write about some aspect of this important topic.

Developing Paragraphs: Definition and Analysis

24

CHAPTER OBJECTIVES

Definition and analysis is another method used to develop ideas. To avoid misunderstandings and confusion, definitions are needed for any terms that may be unfamiliar to the reader or that are open to different interpretations. In fact, defining terms is a part of most nonfiction writing.

- placing the term into a larger **class**
- identifying the term's **characteristics**
- using **negation**
- providing **examples**
- using **extended definition** or **analysis**
- taking a step-by-step approach to create definition paragraphs
- studying model paragraphs to create definition paragraphs

What Is Definition?

Definition, as a method of development, explores the meaning or significance of a term.

Placing a Term in Its Larger Class

The starting point for any good definition is to place the word into a larger **category** or **class**. For example, a *trout* is a kind of fish; a *doll* is a kind of toy; a *shirt* is an article of clothing. Here are the first four meanings of a dictionary entry for the word *family*.

> **family (fam´e -le, fam´le)** *n., pl.* **-lies. Abbr. fam.** 1. The most instinctive fundamental social or mating group, traditionally consisting of two parents rearing their children. 2. One's spouse and children. 3. A group of persons sharing a common ancestry: relatives, kinfolk, clan. 4. All the members of a household; those who share one's domestic home.

According to this dictionary entry, the *family* is the most basic of social groups. Therefore, the larger category that the term *family* can be placed into is a *social group*.

EXERCISE **1**   **Defining by Class**

Define each of the following terms by placing it in a larger class. Keep in mind that when you define something by *class,* you are placing it in a larger category so that the reader can see where it belongs. Use the dictionary if you need help. An example has been done for you.

Chemistry is *one of the branches of science.*

1. Mythology is _____

2. Nylon is _____

3. An amoeba is _____

4. A tricycle is _____

5. Cabbage is _____

6. Democracy is _____

7. Asbestos is _____

8. A piccolo is _____

9. Poetry is _____

10. A university is _____

Giving a Term Its Identifying Characteristics

Once a term has been put into a larger class, the next step is to provide the **identifying characteristics** that make the term different from other members in that class. What makes a *trout* different from a *bass,* a *doll* different from a *puppet,* a *shirt* different from a *sweater*? Here a definition can give examples. Look back again at the dictionary definition of *family.* Notice that the first meaning gives an example of a family: "traditionally … two parents rearing their children." The three additional meanings provide suggestions for some other variations.

EXERCISE **2**   **Identifying Characteristics**

Using the same terms as in Exercise 1, give one or two identifying characteristics that differentiate your term from other terms in the same class. Use a dictionary. An example has been done for you.

Chemistry is *the study of the structure, properties, and reactions of matter.*

1. Mythology is _____

_____

2. Nylon _____

_____

3. An amoeba _____

_____

4. A tricycle _____

_____

5. Cabbage _____

_____

Melba Photo Agency/Alamy/Houghton Mifflin Harcourt

6. Democracy _____

_____

7. Asbestos _____

_____

8. A piccolo _____

_____

9. Poetry _____

_____

10. A university _____

_____

Defining by Negation

The writer could also have defined *family* by **negation.** That is, the writer could have described what a family is *not*:

A family is not a corporation.

A family is not a formal school.

A family is not a religion.

When a writer defines a concept using negation, the definition should be completed by stating what the subject actually *is*:

A family is not a corporation, but it is an economic unit of production and consumption.

A family is not a formal school, but it is a major center for learning.

A family is not a religion, but it is where children learn their moral values.

EXERCISE **3**   **Defining by Negation**

Define each of the following terms, using negation to construct your definition. Keep in mind that such a definition is not complete until you have also included a positive statement about the topic that you are defining. You may want to work in groups to arrive at your answers.

1. A disability does not mean _____

    but it may mean _____

2. The perfect car need not be _____

    but it should be _____

3. Drugs are not _____

    but they are _____

4. Freedom is not _____

    but it is _____

5. A good job does not have to _____

    but it should _____

6. Exercise should not be _____

    but it should _____

7. A university is not _____

    it is _____

8. A legislator should not _____

    but he or she should _____

9. The ideal pet is not _____

    it _____

10. A boring person is not _____

    but he or she is _____

Defining with Examples

Examples make a concept more concrete. For each of the following terms, provide one good example that would help make a stronger definition. You may need to consult an encyclopedia. An example has been done for you.

Term: Chemistry

Example: Chemistry teaches us that hydrogen has the simplest structure of all the elements, with only one electron and one proton. It is colorless, highly flammable, the lightest of all gases, and the most abundant element in the universe.

EXERCISE ④   **Providing Examples**

Provide an example of each of the following terms.

1. Cliché _____

_____

2. Fairy tale _____

_____

_____

_____

3. Fable _____

_____

4. Folktale _____

_____

_____

5. Myth _____

_____

6. Superstition _____

_____

_____

_____

_____

_____

7. Proverb _____

_____

_____

8. Metaphor _____

_____

9. Legend _____

_____

_____

10. Epic _____

_____

_____

Defining with Analysis or Extended Definition

When you write a paragraph or an essay that uses definition, the dictionary entry is only the beginning. It is not the function of a dictionary to go into great depth. A dictionary can provide only basic meanings and synonyms. To help a reader understand a difficult term or idea, a writer needs to expand this definition into what is called an **extended definition**. With an *extended definition*, a concept is analyzed so that the reader will have a more complete understanding of it. For instance, an extended definition might include a historical perspective. When or how did the concept begin? How did the term change or evolve over the years, or how do different cultures understand the term? Asking these questions involves you in the term's *connotations*. An extended definition, or *analysis* as it is also called, draws on more than one method to arrive at an understanding of a term.

> An **extended definition** is an expanded analysis of a concept or term, giving additional information that conveys a fuller meaning.

The following paragraph, taken from *Sociology: An Introduction* by John E. Conklin, is the beginning of a chapter on the family. The author's starting point is very similar to the dictionary entry given earlier.

> In every society, social norms define a variety of relationships among people, and some of these relationships are socially recognized as family or kinship ties. A *family* is a socially defined set of relationships between at least two people who are related by birth, marriage, or adoption. We can think of a family as including several possible relationships, the most common being between husband and wife, between parents and children, and between people who are related to each other by birth (siblings, for example) or by marriage (a woman and her mother-in-law, perhaps). Family relationships are often defined by custom, such as the relationship between an infant and godparents, or by law, such as the adoption of a child.

The author begins this definition by putting the term into a larger class. *Family* is one type of social relationship among people. The writer then identifies the people who are members of this group. Family relationships can be formed by marriage, birth, adoption, or custom. The author does not stop here. Following this paragraph, the writer explores the functions of the family, conflicts in the family, the structure of the family, and the special characteristics of the family.

TERMS COMMONLY USED FOR DEFINITION

characteristics	includes	signifies
connotes	indicates	suggests
consists of	is/is not	symptoms
constitutes	is more than	is thought to be
denotes	is not only	traits
defined as	means	is understood to be

TRANSITIONS COMMONLY USED FOR DEFINITION	
For multiple meanings:	first; second; third; in one case; in another case
For identifying characteristics:	one trait; another trait; a third quality
For examples:	for example; for instance; like; such as; to illustrate
To show change over time:	at one time; now
To specify:	in particular; specifically; in fact
To add:	also; in addition; furthermore

Writing a Definition Paragraph Using a Step-by-Step Approach

Mastering any skill, including writing, requires a disciplined attitude. One way to master the skill of creating a piece of writing is to take a step-by-step approach, focusing on one issue at a time. This approach results in a minimum of stress. Another advantage is that the writer does not miss important points or misunderstand any part of the process. Of course, there are other ways to build effective paragraphs using definition as the method of development, but here is one logical method you can use that will always achieve good results.

STEP-BY-STEP APPROACH TO WRITING A DEFINITION PARAGRAPH

1. After you have selected a term, put that term into its larger class.

2. Give the term its identifying characteristics.

3. Construct your topic sentence. You may want to provide a framework around the term you are defining by putting it into the context of a specific time and place.

4. If helpful, use *negation* to tell what your term does not mean.

5. Provide examples. Write at least one or two sentences for each example.

6. Provide any additional analysis necessary for an understanding of the term.

7. Write a concluding statement.

8. On a separate sheet of paper or on the computer, copy your sentences into standard paragraph form. Redraft as necessary.

9. Do a final reading to check for errors and omissions.

EXERCISE **5**   **Writing a Definition Paragraph Using a Step-by-Step Approach**

This exercise will guide you through the construction of a paragraph using definition as the method of development. Start with the suggested term. Use the nine steps shown above to help you work through the stages of the writing process.

Term: Cyberbullying

1. Put the term into a larger class. _____

2. What are the identifying characteristics of the term?

   _____

   _____

3. Construct the topic sentence.

   _____

4. Define the term using negation. (optional)

   _____

5. Give examples of the term. Write at least one or two complete sentences for each example.

   _____

   _____

   _____

   _____

   _____

   _____

6. Provide further analysis, historical or cultural, that would help the reader understand the term.

   _____

   _____

   _____

   _____

   _____

   _____

7. Write a concluding sentence.

8. Copy your sentences into standard paragraph form. Redraft as necessary.

9. Do a final reading to check for errors and omissions.

Studying Model Paragraphs to Create Definition Paragraphs

Assignment 1: Definition of a Medical Condition

Write a paragraph that defines a current medical concern, one that is gaining a good deal of national attention. The following paragraph attempts to define the phenomenon of *autism* and includes some of the symptoms that are used to help diagnose the condition.

MODEL PARAGRAPH: WHAT IS AUTISM?

Topic sentence

Autism is a developmental disability that, until the 1940s, was unrecognized. In 1988, the film *Rain Man* starring Dustin Hoffman brought the condition to greater public awareness. Now some researchers claim that one in every 91 American children has some form of autism. This is because the definition has broadened to include a wide range of identifying symptoms. The three most distinctive symptoms that lead to a diagnosis of autism are (1) a difficulty with social interaction, (2) a problem with verbal and nonverbal communication, and (3) repetitive actions or obsessive interests. For instance, a parent may slowly realize that a child is not making eye contact or smiling. Sometimes a child is developing normally and then suddenly loses language and social skill. Experts point out that autism is not to be confused with mental retardation. Autistic children are often gifted in one or more areas. While there is still much to learn about the syndrome, doctors all agree that the earlier parents start intervention therapies, the better the outcome.

Ten suggested topics

1. ADD (attention deficit disorder)

2. Childhood obesity

3. Alzheimer's disease

4. Asthma

5. Munchausen syndrome

6. Generalized Anxiety Disorder

7. Dyslexia

8. Anorexia nervosa

9. Postpartum depression

10. Type 1 diabetes

Assignment 2: Definition of a Controversial Term

Write a paragraph that defines a controversial term. The following extended definition is how Lawrence M. Friedman, professor of law at Stanford University, defines the term *crime*.

MODEL PARAGRAPH: WHAT IS CRIME?

Topic sentence

There is no real answer to the question, What is crime? There are popular ideas about crime: crime is bad behavior, antisocial behavior, blameworthy acts, and the like. <u>But in a very basic sense crime is a *legal* concept; what makes some conduct criminal, and other conduct not, is the fact that some, but not others, are "against the law."</u> Before some act can be isolated and labeled as a crime, there must be a special, solemn, social and political decision. In our society, Congress, a state legislature, or a city government has to pass a law or enact an ordinance adding the behavior to the list of crimes. Then this behavior, like a bottle of poison, carries the proper label and can be turned over to the heavy artillery of law for possible enforcement.

Ten suggested topics

1. Pornography
2. Child abuse
3. Torture
4. Freedom
5. Intelligence
6. Patriotism
7. Marriage
8. Masculinity
9. Justice
10. Violence

Assignment 3: Your Definition of a Type of Person

Write a paragraph that defines a type of person according to your own opinion. In the following paragraph, semantics expert S. I. Hayakawa defines his idea of the creative person.

MODEL PARAGRAPH: THE CREATIVE PERSON

Topic sentence

A creative person, first, is not limited in his thinking to "what everyone knows." "Everyone knows" that trees are green. The creative artist is able to see that in certain lights some trees look blue or purple or yellow. The creative person looks at the world with his or her own eyes, not with the eyes of others. The creative individual also knows his or her own feelings better than the average person. Most people don't know the answer to the question, "How are you? How do you feel?" The reason they don't know is that they are so busy feeling what they are supposed to feel, thinking what they are supposed to think, that they never get down to examining their own deepest feelings.

Ten suggested topics

1. The couch potato

2. The anxious type

3. The drama queen

4. The abusive person

5. The hypochondriac

6. The enabler

7. The taker (or the giver)

8. The artist

9. The narcissist

10. The dependent person

WRITE FOR SUCCESS

The nature of intelligence has been widely debated. Some believe intelligence is a matter of inherited abilities. Others believe it is largely learned. What abilities should be included in an assessment of intelligence? Is it mainly math and reading ability, which SAT college entrance tests seem to suggest? Write a response that looks more deeply into the question of intelligence. How would you judge your own intelligence? Is it fixed, or can it be improved?

Working Together

Who Is a Hero?

Some words or ideas are hard to define, either because they are complicated or because they are controversial. One such idea is the concept of *heroism*. The following paragraph examines the traits that might define a hero.

Ivy Close Images/Alamy

In ancient Greece, the hero was less than a god but more than the average man. He had to exhibit great bravery. Today, most people would agree that heroes have to be brave. Certainly, cowardice is not heroic. Is the quality of bravery enough to provide a definition of a hero? If a person is brave enough to participate in extreme sports, should that person be called a hero? Many of us would say no. The hero must be a person who seeks an admirable goal that is easily regarded as helpful to society. In addition to bravery and pursuing a noble goal, we might also add self-sacrifice. Few would disagree that a mother who rescues her child in a fire only to lose her own life in the process is a hero. On the other hand, if one is brave only for selfish reasons, few would call that person a hero. A final quality that some would say defines a hero is that the hero must be successful. This is controversial because if we call a person like Jonas Salk, who discovered a vaccine for polio, a hero, then are all those scientists who worked tirelessly to discover cures but failed not heroes? Agreeing on the qualities of a hero is not as simple as one first might think.

Working in Groups

Working together as a class, discuss the following Americans. Which ones would you consider heroes? Explain your reasoning.

- Pilot Chesley Sullenberger, who guided a disabled US Airways jetliner to land safely in the Hudson River in the winter of 2009
- Roberto Clemente, famous Puerto Rican baseball player, who was killed in an airplane crash trying to deliver relief supplies to earthquake victims in Nicaragua
- Hollywood celebrity Angelina Jolie, who has adopted several children from other lands and does humanitarian work around the world
- Bill Gates, a wealthy businessperson, who gives away millions of dollars
- A bone marrow donor
- A firefighter killed in the World Trade Center attacks
- The boxer Muhammad Ali, also known for his political courage in the civil rights era

- Sally Ride, the first American woman to go into space
- A citizen in the armed services who has been killed in battle
- Wesley Autrey, the 50-year-old man from Harlem who jumped into the path of a subway train to save the life of a stranger

Work together to create a definition of *heroism* in a single sentence. Then look up the dictionary definition. How close are the two definitions?

PORTFOLIO SUGGESTION

Using the list from the group exercise, research more about some of these outstanding individuals. Examine these people's lives, and then make judgments about them. Do you think these people have the qualities of true heroes? Keep a list of heroic individuals and their deeds for possible use in a future essay.

Developing Paragraphs: Classification

25

CHAPTER OBJECTIVES

When a topic involves a large body of information, classification can be a very useful method of development. This chapter will explain the thinking behind classification and give you more than one opportunity to practice this method of development.

- finding a **basis for classification**
- making **distinct categories**
- making the classification **complete**
- making sure the classification has a **useful purpose**
- using **transitions** to achieve coherence
- using a step-by-step approach to create classification paragraphs
- studying model paragraphs to create classification paragraphs

What Is Classification?

Every day we are helped by systems that take large amounts of information and organize that information into groups or categories so that we can better manage it. Libraries classify books and periodicals according to a specific system; in biology, plants and animals are classified into groups and subgroups (e.g., *kingdom, phylum, class, genus, species*). In our jobs, office documents must be organized into some logical filing system both in physical files and on computers or the Cloud. Classification is also a method for developing a piece of writing. This chapter will guide you through the thinking process needed to create paragraphs using classification.

Classification is a logical way of thinking that enables us to separate a large number of items into categories. The result is a more manageable way to understand or analyze the material.

- A marketing analyst might write a brochure to classify the types of products a company offers.
- A historian might classify a century of history into its time periods, decades, or eras.

Finding the Basis for Classification

Not all topics are suitable for classification. To break something down into its parts, you must find an important basis for those divisions. For instance, if you were a travel agent, a customer who wanted to go on a vacation might ask you to provide a list of vacation spots ranging from least expensive to most expensive. Another customer might ask for vacation possibilities that would be near a beach. Still another might want to know about vacations that involve renting a cabin in a fishing area. In other words, there could be many ways to approach the classification of vacations.

Topic: Vacation spots

Three possible bases for classifying vacations:

1. By price (first class, second class, economy)
2. By special attractions (the beach, the mountains, the desert)
3. By accommodations (motel, cabin, trailer)

EXERCISE ① **Finding the Basis for Classification**

For each of the following topics, pick three different ways the topic could be classified.

1. **Topic: Movies**

Ways to divide the topic: _____

_____

2. **Topic: Cars**

Ways to divide the topic: _____

_____

3. **Topic: Houses**

Ways to divide the topic: _____

_____

4. **Topic: Animals**

Ways to divide the topic: _____

_____

5. **Topic: Caffeinated drinks**

Ways to divide the topic: _____

_____

Making Distinct Categories

To classify items properly, we must find *distinct categories* into which these items will fit. Each item must belong to only one category. For example, classifying motorcycles into three categories—imported motorcycles, U.S.-made motorcycles, and used motorcycles—would not be an effective use of classification because an *imported* motorcycle or a U.S.-made motorcycle could also be a *used* motorcycle. Thus, these categories would not be distinct.

EXERCISE ❷ **Making Distinct Categories**

For each of the following topics, first choose a basis for classification. Then divide the topic into as many distinct categories as you think the classification requires. Write your answers on the lines provided.

Keep in mind that, when you divide your topic, each item must belong to only one category. For example, if you were to classify cars by type, you would not want to make sports cars and imported cars two of your categories because several kinds of sports cars are also imported cars.

1. **Dogs**

Basis of classification: _____

Distinct categories:

_____   _____   _____

_____   _____   _____

2. **Television commercials**

Basis of classification: _____

Distinct categories:

_____   _____   _____

_____   _____   _____

3. **College sports**

Basis of classification: _____

Distinct categories:

_____   _____   _____

_____   _____   _____

4. **Doctors**

Basis of classification: _____

Distinct categories:

_____   _____   _____

_____   _____   _____

5. **The courses offered in one of your college's departments**

Basis of classification: _____

Distinct categories:

_____   _____   _____

_____   _____   _____

Making the Classification Complete

A classification must also be *complete*. For example, if you classified motorcycles into the two categories of *new* and *used*, your classification would be complete because all motorcycles have to be either *new* or *used*. If this is your choice for classifying motorcycles, your classification is complete. There is no other possible category. Depending on your purpose, however, there could be other possible bases for classifications that would also have distinct and complete categories.

The following paragraph is one writer's classification of different types of people and their ways of dealing with money.

Topic sentence

 When it comes to handling money, we can observe four distinct types. The first type is the spendthrift. This is the person who gives little thought to the future, spending money recklessly and wastefully. Even if this person is lucky enough to inherit some money, within a very short time, every penny will be squandered on foolish purchases. The second type is the moderate spender. This person carefully pays his or her bills on time, and if some money is left over, he or she might save a certain amount but is likely to also spend a portion of the money on items that could be considered luxuries. Perhaps most of us fall into this group. The third type is the one who believes in frugality. This is the person who clips coupons, wears hand-me-downs if given the chance, and declines invitations to go out if the cost is not within a strict budget. Although being frugal used to be considered a virtue, in good economic times most people forget to be frugal. We ought to admire the frugal person because this person is looking ahead and understands that life can bring unexpected downturns in which a nest egg will save the day. The fourth type is the miser, sometimes called by other names: tightwad, skinflint, penny-pincher or scrooge. This poor soul is unable to enjoy any of his or her wealth. The total focus is on hoarding every penny, even doing without basic necessities. The character Ebenezer Scrooge in Charles Dickens's *A Christmas Carol* is an example of a miser. Of these four types, which one are you?

In the paragraph above, notice that the writer gives us not only the basis of the classification (the different approaches to handling money) but also gives a name to each of the four types of the classification. The categories are distinct and the classification feels complete.

Making Sure the Classification Has a Useful Purpose

Finally, a classification should serve some *useful purpose*. For a person thinking about buying a motorcycle, classifying motorcycles into the categories of *new* or *used* may be a helpful way to make a wise decision.

EXERCISE ③   **Making Sure the Classification Has a Useful Purpose**

For each example, suggest a reason why a writer might want to classify the following topics:

1. Housing _____

2. Musical instruments _____

3. Criminal charges _____

4. Snacks _____

5. Newspapers _____

Achieving Coherence

In a paragraph or essay that uses classification to develop the ideas, certain terms are almost always to be found. These terms are used to signal that the writer is transitioning from one category to the next. Often the number of categories will be indicated, such as *the first group, the second group,* and *the third group.*

TERMS THAT SIGNAL CLASSIFICATION		
areas	features	principles
aspects	forms	qualities
brands	groups	sorts
categories	kinds	systems
classes	levels	traits
components	parts	types

Writing a Classification Paragraph Using a Step-by-Step Approach

Mastering any skill, including writing, requires a disciplined attitude. One way to master the skill of creating a piece of writing is to take a step-by-step approach, focusing on one issue at a time. This approach results in a minimum of stress. Another advantage is that the writer does not miss important points or misunderstand any part of the process. Of course, there are other ways to build effective classification paragraphs, but here is one logical method you can use that will always achieve good results.

STEP-BY-STEP APPROACH TO WRITING A CLASSIFICATION PARAGRAPH

1. After you have selected a topic, decide on the basis for your classification.

2. Determine the categories for your classification. Give each category an identifying title or name. Be as creative as possible. You may want to take a humorous tone. Remember, no item should belong in more than one group, and your classification should be complete.

3. Write your topic sentence. Use one of the terms (such as *group* or *type*) that signals a classification.

4. Write at least one or two sentences for each group, remembering that each group should be given approximately equal space and importance.

5. Write a concluding statement. If you have not already indicated a useful purpose for the classification, do so in the conclusion.

6. On a separate sheet of paper or on a computer, copy your sentences into standard paragraph form. Before printing, read the paragraph again to check for any changes that may be needed.

7. Do a final reading once you have printed the paragraph to check for any errors or omissions.

EXERCISE 4   **Writing a Classification Paragraph Using a Step-by-Step Approach**

The following exercise will guide you through the construction of a classification paragraph. Start with the suggested topic. Use the seven steps to help you work through the stages of the writing process.

Topic: Games I have played

1. What is the basis for your classification? _____

    _____

2. What are the categories for your classification? Give each category a name.

    a. _____

    b. _____

    c. _____

    d. _____

3. Write your topic sentence. (Use one of the classification terms given in the Achieving Coherence section.)

_____

_____

4. Write at least one or two sentences about each category.

a. _____

_____

b. _____

_____

c. _____

_____

d. _____

_____

5. Write a concluding sentence. Suggest a useful purpose for the classification.

_____

_____

_____

6. On a separate sheet of paper or on a computer, copy your sentences into standard paragraph form.

7. Do a final reading to check for errors and omissions.

Studying Model Paragraphs to Create Classification Paragraphs

Assignment 1: Classifying Everyday Items

Write a paragraph that classifies items we use every day. The following paragraph classifies types of automobiles now being developed.

MODEL PARAGRAPH: THE FUTURE CAR

Everyone knows that this country must develop cars that are more efficient and less polluting. Today's internal combustion engine uses only 13 percent of its fuel to move the vehicle. The race is on to find the car of the future. *Topic sentence* At present, five basic types of cars are in different stages of development.

(Continued)

The first type is the *hypercar*. This automobile continues to use gasoline or alternative fuels like ethanol to power the car, but the car itself as well as the engine has dramatic new designs that improve its efficiency. The second type of car is the *electric car*. This car uses hybrid electric batteries to store energy, but its main disadvantage is its dependence on frequent recharging. The third type is the *hybrid car*. While this car continues to use gasoline, it also uses batteries that can improve its efficiency. The fourth type is a car run by *hydrogen fuel cells*. Its advantage is that the only emission it produces is water, but many other problems remain, like water supply. The fifth type is the *solar-powered car*. Unfortunately, whenever there is no sunlight for a number of days, there is no power. No single type of car has yet emerged as the perfect solution, although some, like the hybrid, are available for purchase now. We will have to wait and see if any alternative energy-saving car will be a clear winner in the race for a better and more environmentally friendly car.

Ten suggested topics   **Everyday items that could be classified:**

1. Work clothes

2. Cell phones

3. Hairstyles

4. Desserts

5. Shoes

6. Jewelry

7. Magazines

8. Tools

9. Makeup

10. Computers

Assignment 2: Classifying Places

Write a paragraph that classifies places with which you are familiar. The following paragraph is a famous example of classification, written in the late 1940s by the master American essayist E. B. White.

MODEL PARAGRAPH: THE THREE NEW YORKS

Topic sentence

There are roughly three New Yorks. There is, first, the New York of the man or woman who was born here, who takes the city for granted and accepts its size and its turbulence as natural and inevitable. Second, there is the New York of the commuter—the city that is devoured by locusts each day and spat out each night. Third, there is the New York of the person who was born somewhere else and came to New York in quest of something. Of these three trembling cities the greatest is the last—the city of final destination, the city that is a goal. It is this third city that accounts for New York's high strung disposition, its poetical deportment, its dedication to the arts, and its incomparable achievements. Commuters give the city its tidal restlessness; natives give it solidity and continuity; but the settlers give it passion. And whether it is a farmer arriving from Italy to set up a small grocery store, or a young girl arriving from a small town in Mississippi to escape the indignity of being observed by her neighbors, or a boy arriving from the Corn Belt with a manuscript in his suitcase and a pain in his heart, it makes no difference: each embraces New York with the intense excitement of first love, each absorbs New York with the fresh eyes of an adventurer, each generates heat and light to dwarf the Consolidated Edison Company.

Ten suggested topics   Places that could be classified:

1. Colleges

2. Parks

3. Clubs

4. Restaurants

5. Places to study

6. Party locations

7. Clothing stores

8. Neighborhoods

9. Places to play sports

10. Honeymoon locations

Assignment 3: Classifying Types of People

Write a paragraph that classifies a group of people. The following paragraph divides movie heroes into three distinct groups.

MODEL PARAGRAPH: MOVIE HEROES

Topic sentence

<u>Heroes in American movies usually fall into one of three types</u>. In adventure movies, the hero is usually one-dimensional. James Bond, Batman, and Wonder Woman are examples of heroes who will predictably battle evil against all odds and emerge victorious. In romantic comedies, the heroine is likely to be loveable but offbeat. These roles have been superbly played by actresses like Jennifer Lawrence or Emma Stone. The third type of hero is the silent loner type. Who could forget some of the characters portrayed by Clint Eastwood, Denzel Washington, or Matthew McConaughey?

Ten suggested topics   People to classify:

1. Politicians

2. Authority figures

3. Heroes

4. Celebrities

5. Supervisors

6. Babysitters

7. Pet owners

8. Coworkers

9. People in the neighborhood

10. Relatives

WRITE FOR SUCCESS

If you were to classify the types of health hazards that often affect college students, you might include (1) lack of sleep, (2) too much partying, (3) poor diet, (4) stress, and (5) unprotected sex. Pick two or three from those items listed, or other health concerns of your own choosing, and write a response that describes each of your categories.

Working Together

svetikd/iStock/Getty Images

Classification: Personalities in the Classroom

How could you categorize students in the classrooms you have known? Here are a few popular stereotypes that could be used when exploring this topic:

> The class clown
>
> The overachiever
>
> The teacher's pet
>
> The quiet student
>
> The easily distracted student

Brainstorming

Brainstorm with the class for the names of other student types found in the classroom. Put all the possibilities on the board. Then decide which combinations would work well together for a classification paragraph or essay, remembering that the categories should be distinct and complete. (Of course, there could be some flexibility with the completeness of the categories if your intention is humorous.) How many different groupings can the members of the class arrange?

Writing

Each student should then write a classification paragraph using one of the groupings from the class brainstorming session.

Peer Editing

After fifteen minutes or so, pass the paragraphs around so that all students can read each other's work. On a separate sheet of paper that accompanies each paragraph, each student should make one positive criticism and one constructive criticism. Return the paragraph with its separate page of comments to the owner.

PORTFOLIO SUGGESTION

The paragraph you have written in class would make a good introductory paragraph for a full-length essay in which you could devote an entire paragraph to each student type. Keep your paragraph as well as the brainstorming list developed in the class. You might find this material useful when writing an essay in your current class or in a future writing class.

PART 5

Structuring the College Essay

Welcome Help from Others

In our everyday lives, we often call on others for help. In college, you need to feel comfortable asking for help. You may need it from your teachers, librarians, deans, tutors, peers, and even family members. In a future job, you may have a mentor, a more experienced person, who will give you advice and help you advance. As you face the challenge of writing full-length college essays, be sure to ask for and value support from others.

- Who has been a mentor in your life?
- Who at your school could you ask to be a mentor?
- In what ways could a mentor help you?

Moving from the Paragraph to the Essay

26

CHAPTER OBJECTIVES

To prepare you for writing fully developed college essays, the work in this chapter will focus on the essential parts of the essay form.

- recognizing and writing a **thesis statement**
- writing an effective **introductory paragraph**
- using **transitions** to achieve coherence between body paragraphs
- writing an effective **concluding paragraph**
- composing **titles**

What Is a College Essay?

No matter what major a student declares in college, developing writing skills is a critical part of that student's growth and progress. Nearly every course requires at least some writing. This writing most often takes the form of the college essay (also called *composition, theme,* or simply *paper*).

When we constructed paragraphs in Part 4, with topic sentences and supporting details, we were aiming for an organized result with unity and coherence. The full-length essay must have this same objective. Making all the parts of an essay work together is a greater challenge than writing a paragraph because in an essay, a topic is developed at greater length and in greater depth.

A **college essay** is a piece of writing that develops a topic in five or more paragraphs, including an introductory paragraph that states the thesis, three or more supporting paragraphs that develop the topic, and a concluding paragraph.

Kinds of Paragraphs in the Complete College Essay

1. The **introductory paragraph** is the first paragraph of the essay. Its purpose is to lead the reader to the **thesis statement** in an inviting and interesting way that will encourage the reader to continue reading.

2. **Support paragraphs** (sometimes called **body paragraphs**) provide evidence that the thesis is valid. An acceptable college essay must have at least three well-developed support paragraphs. (You have studied these types of support paragraphs in Part 4 of this book.) Each support paragraph should flow logically to the next support paragraph. This is often accomplished by the careful use of **transitional expressions**.

3. The **concluding paragraph** is the final paragraph of the essay. Its purpose is to give the reader a sense that the essay has come to a satisfying conclusion. By this point, the reader should have the feeling that everything the essay needed to say has been said.

What Is a Thesis Statement?

A **thesis statement** gives the main idea of an essay.

The thesis statement of an essay tells what the writer intends to prove, defend, or explain about the topic. It may show the writer's viewpoint toward the topic or show how the writer intends to treat the topic. We say that the thesis has a *controlling idea*. This most important sentence is usually placed at the end of the introductory paragraph.

Sample thesis statement: **All-day kindergarten programs benefit children in several important ways.**

Do not confuse a thesis statement with a title or a simple fact. A **title** is usually a phrase, not a complete sentence.

Sample title: **The Advantages of an All-Day Kindergarten**

A **fact** is something known for certain. It can be verified. A fact does not suggest a personal viewpoint.

Sample fact: **Very few kindergartens in the United States offer a full day of instruction.**

PRACTICE 1   **Read each of the following statements. If the statement is a thesis, mark *TH* on the blank line. If the statement is a title, mark *T*. If the statement is a fact, mark *F*.**

_____ 1. In the United States, kindergarten is not compulsory.

_____ 2. Children should begin learning to read in kindergarten.

_____ 3. Putting a child into kindergarten before he or she is ready can have several unfortunate effects on that child.

_____ 4. Learning to read in kindergarten

_____ 5. In some European countries, children do not begin formal schooling until the age of seven.

EXERCISE 1   **Recognizing a Thesis Statement**

Identify each of the following as a *title* (T), a *thesis* (TH), or a *fact* (F).

_____ 1. It is estimated that two hundred grizzly bears live in Yellowstone National Park.

_____ 2. The survival of grizzly bears in our country should be a top priority.

_____ 3. When bears are young cubs, there are twice as many males as females.

_____ 4. Only about 60 percent of bear cubs survive the first few years of life.

_____ 5. Bears, a precious natural resource

_____ 6. The average life span of a bear today is only five or six years.

_____ 7. The plight of the American grizzly bear has drawn the attention of many writers and naturalists.

_____ 8. Five actions need to be taken to save the grizzly bear from extinction.

_____ 9. To save the grizzly bear, we need laws from Congress, the cooperation of hunters and campers, and an educated general public.

_____ 10. A decision to save the grizzly bear

EXERCISE 2 **Recognizing a Thesis Statement**

Identify each of the following as a _title_ (T), a _thesis_ (TH), or a _fact_ (F).

_____ 1. The merchandising madness of pharmaceutical companies

_____ 2. Americans are spending approximately $10.4 billion a year on the four leading antidepressants, namely, Zoloft, Paxil, Wellbutrin, and Celexa.

_____ 3. The American love affair with pills

_____ 4. Washing your blues away with Prozac

_____ 5. Consumers need to be better educated about the questionable promises made by the marketers of antidepressants.

_____ 6. After the attacks of September 11, national sales for the top-selling antidepressants rose 20 percent.

_____ 7. Advertisements for antidepressants after September 11 featured American flags, candles, and firefighters.

_____ 8. A culture seeking self-stimulation and self-sedation

_____ 9. In recent years, we have seen an unfortunate blurring between real and imagined medical need.

_____ 10. Americans should understand the difference between normal anxiety and pathological anxiety.

EXERCISE 3 **Recognizing a Thesis Statement**

Identify each of the following as a _title_ (T), a _thesis_ (TH), or a _fact_ (F).

_____ 1. The disparity between the salaries of average American workers and the highest earners should concern the citizens of our country.

_____ 2. Outrage over salaries of chief executive officers (CEOs)

_____ 3. The average American worker received an annual salary of $34,053 in 2011.

_____ 4. A healthy democracy should ideally include a large and prosperous middle class.

_____ 5. Increasing protests over large CEO salaries

_____ 6. On average, chief executive officers received $9.6 million in 2010 and $12.9 million in 2011.

_____ 7. Wages for the average worker rose only 2.8 percent in 2010 and even less in 2011.

_____ 8. Profound changes within the American middle class

_____ 9. The chief of Oracle, Larry Ellison, earned $77.6 million in 2011.

_____10. When the wealth of any nation is controlled by fewer and fewer people, we must examine the consequences.

Creating an Effective Thesis Statement

Narrowing the Scope of the Topic

Student writing suffers when the chosen topic is too general. A good writer must recognize when the topic needs to be narrowed or qualified so that the material will fit the length of an essay (which is often only a few paragraphs long) and also fit the writer's knowledge and experience. Consider the following example:

General topic: **Swimming**

A student decides to write on the general topic of *swimming*, but that topic seems too general for an effective essay. The writer, therefore, thinks about how to (1) limit or (2) qualify that topic.

1. To *limit the topic*, the writer might choose a different term that covers a smaller part of the topic and thus narrows the scope.

   Limited topic: **Floating**

2. To *qualify the topic*, the writer might add a descriptive word or phrase to the general topic. This change will also result in narrowing the scope of the topic.

   Qualified topic: **Swimming two hours a week**

EXERCISE **4** **Building the Thesis Statement: Limiting or Qualifying a Topic**

Below are four topics. For each one, show how a writer could narrow the scope by either limiting the topic or qualifying the topic. An example has been done for you.

General topic: **Dentistry**

Limited topic: **Orthodontics**
(changes the general term to a more narrowed focus)

Qualified topic: **Preventive dentistry**
(adds a descriptive word that narrows the focus)

1. **Language**

   limited topic: _____

   qualified topic: _____

2. **Illness**

   limited topic: _____

   qualified topic: _____

3. **Games**

   limited topic: _____

   qualified topic: _____

4. **Vacations**

   limited topic: _____

   qualified topic: _____

Choosing a Controlling Idea That Can Be Supported

The controlling idea is what you want to show or prove about your topic. It is your point of view. A controlling idea must be something you can defend. Often this controlling idea is expressed by an adjective such as *beneficial, difficult,* or *unfair.* The writer who narrowed the scope of the topic *swimming* to either *floating* or *swimming two hours a week* may have chosen the following italicized words as the **controlling ideas** for an essay.

Topic:	Swimming
Limited topic:	Floating
Possible thesis statement:	Learning to float at the age of twenty was a *terrifying* experience.
Qualified topic:	Swimming two hours a week
Possible thesis statement:	Swimming two hours a week can *dramatically change a person's health.*

EXERCISE **5**   **Building the Thesis Statement: Adding the Controlling Idea**

Each of the following topics has been limited or qualified. In each case, provide a possible controlling idea.

1. **Dancing**

   limited topic: **Tango** _____

   controlling idea: _____

2. **School**

   qualified topic: **After-school programs** _____

   controlling idea: _____

3. **Transportation**

limited topic: **Electric cars** _____

controlling idea: _____

4. **Personality**

qualified topic: **Common personality flaws** _____

controlling idea: _____

5. **Clubs**

qualified topic: **Our local clubs** _____

controlling idea: _____

Planning for the Strategy of Development

Sometimes the strategy of development is included in the thesis statement. The reader recognizes the strategy by the use of specific words that signal the strategy:

description (sight, sound, taste, smell, touch)	**advantages, disadvantages**
	causes, effects, reasons, why
example, anecdote	**definition (meaning, analysis)**
classification (groups, types, kinds)	**persuasion, argument**
comparison, contrast	**process (steps, stages, how to)**

Study the following thesis statement:

Studying in a group can sometimes be more helpful than studying alone.

Now look at the thesis statement again and analyze its parts.

General topic:	**Studying**
Qualified topic:	**Studying in a group (contrasted with studying alone)**
Controlling idea:	**More helpful**
Strategy of development:	**Contrast**

Here the writer has not used the word *contrast* in the thesis, but it is clear that a contrast will be made between *studying alone* and *studying in a group.* A writer should always have in mind what major strategy will be used to defend the viewpoint of the essay. While it is true that professional writers often use more than one strategy within an essay, student writers would do well to develop essays using one strategy at a time. By working in this way, a writer can concentrate on understanding and developing the skills needed for each specific strategy.

EXERCISE **6**   **The Thesis Statement: Adding the Strategy of Development**

In each of the following thesis statements, underline the topic, circle the controlling idea, and indicate on the line provided what you believe will be the strategy of development. (Refer to the previously noted list of strategies.)

1. The effects of gambling are disastrous.

    Strategy of development: _____

2. Learning how to do your own tax return can be frustrating.

    Strategy of development: _____

3. The sight of our neighborhood park is dismaying.

    Strategy of development: _____

4. The meaning of the term patriotism is often controversial.

    Strategy of development: _____

5. Student loans fall into several categories.

    Strategy of development: _____

EXERCISE **7**   **Composing the Thesis Statement**

Three general topics follow. For each one, develop a thesis statement by (a) limiting or qualifying the general topic, (b) choosing a controlling idea (what you want to explain or prove about the topic), and (c) selecting a strategy that you can use to develop that topic. An example has been done for you.

General topic:	Community services
Qualified topic:	Community services for senior citizens in Ann Arbor, Michigan
Controlling idea:	Explain the different types of services available.
Strategy of development:	Classification
Thesis statement:	The community services available to senior citizens in Ann Arbor, Michigan, can be classified into three major groups: services to deal with health, housing, and leisure.

1. **General topic: Female vocalist**

    a. Limited or qualified topic:

    _____

    b. Controlling idea:

    _____

    c. Strategy of development (see the list under Planning the Strategy of Development):

    _____

Thesis statement:

_____

_____

_____

2. **General topic: Credit cards**

    a. Limited or qualified topic:

    _____

    b. Controlling idea:

    _____

    c. Strategy of development (see the list under Planning the Strategy of Development):

    _____

Thesis statement:

_____

_____

_____

3. **General topic: Medical technology**

    a. Limited or qualified topic:

    _____

    b. Controlling idea:

    _____

    c. Strategy of development (see the list under Planning the Strategy of Development):

    _____

Thesis statement:

_____

_____

_____

EXERCISE **8**   **Creating Thesis Statements**

Three general topics follow. For each one, develop a thesis statement by (a) limiting or qualifying the general topic, (b) choosing a controlling idea (what you want to explain or prove about the topic), and (c) selecting a strategy that you can use to develop that topic. Review the example given in Exercise 7.

1. **General topic: Housing**

   a. Limited or qualified topic:

   _____

   b. Controlling idea:

   _____

   c. Strategy of development (see the list under Planning the Strategy of Development):

   _____

   Thesis statement:

   _____

   _____

   _____

2. **General topic: Politics**

   a. Limited or qualified topic:

   _____

   b. Controlling idea:

   _____

   c. Strategy of development (see the list under Planning the Strategy of Development):

   _____

   Thesis statement:

   _____

   _____

   _____

   3. **General topic: Snacks**

      a. Limited or qualified topic:

           _____

      b. Controlling idea:

           _____

      c. Strategy of development (see the list under Planning the Strategy of Development):

           _____

Thesis statement:

_____

_____

_____

Writing an Effective Introductory Paragraph

> An **introductory paragraph** is the first paragraph of an essay. It has one main purpose: to make its readers eager to read more. In most essays, this introductory paragraph contains a thesis statement.

Although there is no single way to write an introductory paragraph, many effective introductions follow predictable patterns. A list of the most commonly found patterns follows. When you are ready to create your own introductions, you can consider trying some of these patterns.

COMMON INTRODUCTORY PATTERNS

1. Begin with a general subject that can be narrowed down into the specific topic of your essay.

2. Begin with specifics (a brief anecdote, a specific example or fact) that will broaden into the more general topic of your essay.

3. Give a definition of the concept that will be discussed.

4. Make a startling statement.

5. Start with an idea or statement that is a widely held point of view, and then surprise the reader by stating that this idea is false or that you hold a different point of view.

6. Start with a familiar quotation from a famous book or a famous person.

7. Give a number of descriptive images that will lead to the thesis of your essay.

8. Ask a question that you intend to answer.

9. Use classification to indicate how your topic fits into the larger class to which it belongs or how your topic can be divided into categories that you are going to discuss.

EXERCISE ⑨ **Identifying Common Introductory Patterns**

Below are the introductions for three essays. Each one is an example of a common introductory pattern. Using the Common Introductory Patterns chart, identify each paragraph by its pattern.

1. Here is the introduction to the essay "Some American Drugs Familiar to Everybody," by Adam Smith:

> Our attitude toward the word "drug" depends on whether we are talking about penicillin or heroin or something in between. The unabridged three-volume Webster's says a drug is "a chemical substance administered to prevent or cure disease or enhance physical and mental welfare" or "a substance affecting the structure or function of the body." Webster's should have added "mind," but they probably thought that was part of the body. Some substances that aren't drugs, like placebos, affect "the structure or function of the body," but they work because we *think* they're drugs.

Introductory pattern: _____

2. Here is the opening of the essay "Obsessed with Sport: On the Interpretation of a Fan's Dreams" by Joseph Epstein:

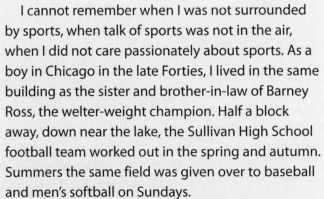

muzsy/Shutterstock.com

> I cannot remember when I was not surrounded by sports, when talk of sports was not in the air, when I did not care passionately about sports. As a boy in Chicago in the late Forties, I lived in the same building as the sister and brother-in-law of Barney Ross, the welter-weight champion. Half a block away, down near the lake, the Sullivan High School football team worked out in the spring and autumn. Summers the same field was given over to baseball and men's softball on Sundays.
>
> A few blocks to the north was the Touhy Avenue Field House, where basketball was played, and lifeguards trained, and behind which, in a softball field frozen over in winter, crack-the-whip, hockey, and speed skating took over. To the west, a block or so up Morse Avenue, was the Morse Avenue "L" Recreations, a combined pool hall and bowling alley. Life, in short, was games.

Introductory pattern: _____

3. Here is an introduction to an essay about a family making cider on their farm. It is titled "Falling for Apples," by Noel Perrin.

> The number of children who eagerly help around a farm is rather small. Willing helpers do exist, but many more of them are five years old rather than fifteen. In fact, there seems to be a general law that says as long as a kid is too little to help effectively, he or she is dying to. Then, just as they reach the age when they really could drive a fence post or empty a sap bucket without spilling half of it, they lose interest. Now it's cars they want to drive, or else they want to stay in the house and listen for four straight hours to The Who. There is one exception to this rule. Almost no kid that I have ever met outgrows an interest in cidering.

Introductory pattern: _____

_____

EXERCISE 10 Identifying Common Introductory Patterns

Below are the introductions for four essays. Each one is an example of a common introductory pattern. Using the Common Introductory Patterns chart, identify each paragraph by its pattern.

1. Below is the introduction to the essay "Getting Dizzy by the Numbers," by Frank Trippett.

°*Matthew 10:30: Chapter 10, verse 30 of the Book of Matthew found in the New Testament of the Bible*

> "The very hairs of your head," says **Matthew 10:30**,° "are all numbered." There is little reason to doubt it. Increasingly, everything tends to get numbered one way or another, everything that can be counted, measured, averaged, estimated or quantified. Intelligence is gauged by a quotient, the humidity by a ratio, pollen by its count, and the trends of birth, death, marriage, and divorce by rates. In this epoch of runaway demographics, society is as often described and analyzed with statistics as with words. Politics seems more and more a game played with percentages turned up by pollsters, and economics a learned babble of ciphers and indexes that few people can translate and apparently nobody can control. Modern civilization, in sum, has begun to resemble an interminable arithmetic class in which, as **Carl Sandburg**° put it, "numbers fly like pigeons in and out of your head."

°*Carl Sandburg: American poet (1878–1967)*

Introductory pattern: _____

2. This is how Stanley Milgram begins his essay "Confessions of a News Addict."

°*Walter Cronkite: news anchor for 19 years with CBS News (1916–2009)*

> Let me begin with a confession. I am a news addict. Upon awakening I flip on the *Today* show to learn what events transpired during the night. On the commuter train which takes me to work, I scour the *New York Times*, and find myself absorbed in tales of earthquakes, diplomacy and economics. I read the newspaper as religiously as my grandparents read their prayerbooks. The sacramental character of the news extends into the evening. The length of my workday is determined precisely by my need to get home in time for **Walter Cronkite**.° My children understand that my communion with Cronkite is something serious and cannot be interrupted for light and transient causes. What is news, and why does it occupy a place of special significance for so many people?

Introductory pattern: _____

_____

3. Here is how the American composer Aaron Copland began an essay on listening to music:

> We all listen to music according to our separate capacities. But, for the sake of analysis, the whole listening process may become clearer if we break it up into its component parts, so to speak. In a certain sense we all listen to music on three separate planes. For lack of a better terminology, one might name these: the sensuous plane, the expressive plane, the sheerly musical plane. The only advantage to be gained from mechanically splitting up the listening process into these hypothetical planes is the clearer view to be had of the way in which we listen.

Introductory pattern: _____

4. Marya Mannes wrote this introduction for her essay "How Do You Know It's Good?"

> Suppose there were no critics to tell us how to react to a picture, a play, or a new composition of music. Suppose we wandered innocent as the dawn into an art exhibition of unsigned paintings. By what standards, by what values would we decide whether they were good or bad, talented or untalented, successes or failures? How can we ever know that what we think is right?

Introductory pattern: _____

What *Not* to Say in Your Introduction

1. Avoid telling your reader that you are beginning your essay:

   In this essay I will discuss . . .

   I will talk about . . .

   I am going to prove . . .

2. Do not apologize:

   Although I am not an expert . . .

   In my humble opinion . . .

3. Do not refer to later parts of your essay:

   By the end of this essay, you will agree . . .

   In the next paragraph, you will see . . .

4. Do not use trite expressions. Because these expressions have been overused, they have lost all interest and effectiveness. Using such expressions shows that you have not taken the time to use your own words to express your ideas. The following are some examples of trite expressions:

   busy as a bee

   you can't judge a book by its cover

   haste makes waste

EXERCISE 11   **Composing an Introductory Paragraph**

Compose your own introductory paragraph using one of the nine patterns that you have just studied. You may want to use one of the topics that were provided in Exercises 7 and 8 and for which you have already written a thesis statement. On the line below, write the number from the list of given patterns you have chosen to use. When you have finished, underline your thesis statement.

Pattern number: _____

_____

_____

_____

_____

_____

_____

_____

_____

Achieving Coherence

A. Use Transitions

Successful essays use transitional expressions to help the reader understand the logic of the writer's thinking. Usually they occur when the writer is moving from one point to the next. They can also occur whenever an idea is complicated. The writer may need to summarize the points so far, emphasize a point already made, or repeat an important point. The transition may be a word, a phrase, a sentence, or even a paragraph.

Here are some transitional expressions that might be used to help the reader make the right connections.

1. To make your points stand out clearly:

the first reason	second, secondly	finally
first of all	another example	most important
in the first place	even more important	all in all
	also, next	in conclusion
	then	to summarize

2. To provide an example of what has just been said:

   for example

   for instance

3. To show the consequence of what has just been said:

   therefore

   as a result

   then

4. To make a contrasting point clear:

   on the other hand

   but

   contrary to current thinking

   however

5. To admit a point:

   of course

   granted

6. To resume your argument after admitting a point:

   nevertheless

   even though

   nonetheless

   still

7. To call the reader's attention to your organization:

> **Before attempting to answer these questions, let me . . .**
>
> **In our discussions so far, we have seen that . . .**
>
> **At this point, it is necessary to . . .**
>
> **It is beyond the scope of this paper (essay) to . . .**

B. Repeat a Word from a Preceding Sentence

A subtler way to link one idea to another in an essay is to repeat a word, phrase, or a variation of either from the preceding sentence.

> **I have many memories of my childhood in Cuba. These *memories* include the aunts, uncles, grandparents, and friends I had to leave behind.**

C. Use a Pronoun to Refer to a Word or Phrase from a Preceding Sentence

> **My family and I have had to build a new life from almost nothing. *It* was often difficult, but I believe the struggle made us strong.**

EXERCISE **12**   **Finding Transitional Expressions**

Following are four paragraphs from a selection titled "Politics and the World," by Kathryn and Ross Petras. Find the words that give this selection its coherence. Circle all the transitional expressions, underline pronouns that refer to antecedents, and box key terms that are repeated.

Some world problems have a way of lingering and festering. They appear, disappear, then reappear again in the daily newspapers of the world. Usually they're based on land: who controls it, who gets to live on it.

In the past the U.S. and the Soviet Union usually took opposing sides in these conflicts. Sometimes there were very real moral reasons for backing one side or another, but many times the reasons were said to be "geopolitical," which really meant if the Soviets were on one side, we decided to join the other—and vice versa.

All this could get pretty cynical. For one thing, almost every obscure corner of the world was declared "geopolitically strategic" at one point or another. For another, the morality could get very dicey. For example, during the 1970s we supported Ethiopia and the Soviets supported Somalia in their dispute over the Ogaden, a dry and remote desert region populated by Somali nomads but controlled by Ethiopia.

Naturally, we set up military posts in our ally Ethiopia and the Soviets put in military bases in their ally Somalia, and each superpower talked of its love of and historic ties to its ally. Then local Marxists seized control in Ethiopia—and after a short while the U.S. and the Soviets calmly switched client states. The U.S. moved into the former Soviet bases in Somalia, the Soviets moved into Ethiopia, and both sides started talking about their *real* ties to their new ally.

Of course, once the Cold War was over, no one cared about either nation anymore, and they both degenerated into anarchy, aided by mounds of heavy weapons and automatic rifles helpfully supplied by both sides. Finally we moved in to save Somalia from itself and our legacy of arms sales—and congratulated ourselves on our humanity.

Writing an Effective Concluding Paragraph

A concluding paragraph has one main purpose: to give the reader the sense of having reached a satisfying ending to the topic discussed. Students often feel they have nothing to say at the end. A look at how professional writers frequently end their essays may ease your anxiety about writing an effective conclusion. You have more than one possibility. Here are some of the most frequently used patterns for ending an essay:

1. **Come full circle—that is, return to the material in your introduction.** Finish what you started. Remind the reader of the thesis. Be sure to restate the main idea using different wording. Here is the conclusion to the essay "Confessions of a News Addict." (The introductory paragraph appears in Exercise 10.)

   > Living in the modern world, I cannot help but be shaped by it, suckered by the influence and impact of our great institutions. The *New York Times*, CBS, and *Newsweek* have made me into a news addict. In daily life I have come to accept the supposition that if the *New York Times* places a story on the front page, it deserves my attention. I feel obligated to know what is going on. But sometimes, in quieter moments, another voice asks: If the news went away, would the world be any worse for it?

2. **Summarize by repeating the main points.** This example is the concluding paragraph to an essay on African art.

   > In summary, African art explains the past, describes values and a way of life, helps man relate to supernatural forces, mediates his social relations, expresses emotions, and enhances man's present life as an embellishment denoting pride or status as well as providing entertainment such as with dance and music.

3. **Show the significance of your thesis by making predictions, giving a warning, giving advice, offering a solution, suggesting an alternative, or telling the results.** This example is the concluding paragraph to "Falling for Apples." (The introductory paragraph appears in Exercise 9.)

> This pleasure goes on and on. In an average year we start making cider the second week of September, and we continue until early November. We make all we can drink ourselves, and quite a lot to give away. We have supplied whole church suppers. One year the girls sold about ten gallons to the village store, which made them some pocket money they were prouder of than any they ever earned from babysitting. Best of all, there are two months each year when all of us are running the farm together, just like a pioneer family.

4. **End with an anecdote that illustrates your thesis.** This example is the concluding paragraph to the essay "Obsessed with Sport." (The introductory paragraph appears in Exercise 9.)

> When I was a boy I had a neighbor, a man who, after retirement, had a number of strokes. An old man and a young boy, we had in common a love of sports, which, when we met on the street, was our only topic of conversation. He once inspected a new glove of mine, and instructed me to rub it down with Neat's-foot-oil, place a ball firmly in the pocket, wrap string tightly around the glove, and leave it like that for the winter. I did, and it worked. After his last stroke but one, he seldom left his house. Afternoons he spent in a chair in his bedroom, a blanket over his lap, listening to Cub games over the radio. It was while listening to a ball game that he quietly died. I cannot imagine a better way.

What *Not* to Say in Your Conclusion

1. Do not introduce a new point.
2. Do not apologize.
3. Do not end vaguely, leaving the reader feeling unsatisfied. This sometimes happens if the very last sentence is not strong enough.

A Note about Titles

Be sure to follow the standard procedure for writing your title.

1. Capitalize the first and last words and all other principal words. This excludes articles (*the, a, an*), coordinating conjunctions (*and, but, or, nor, for, yet, so*), prepositions, and the *to* in infinitives.
2. Do not underline the title or put quotation marks around it.
3. Think of a short and catchy phrase (three to six words). Often writers wait until they have written a first draft before working on a title. A phrase taken from the essay might be perfect. If you still cannot think of a clever title after you have written a draft, choose some key words from your thesis statement.
4. Center the title at the top of the page, and remember to leave about an inch of space between the title and the beginning of the first paragraph.

WRITE FOR SUCCESS

Philosophers, spiritual leaders, and indeed most people at one time or another ponder the meaning of life. For most people, the meaning is derived from doing something that matters, something that serves humankind. Write a response that explains specifically how you believe success in college can lead you to a more meaningful life.

Working Together

Planning the Parts of an Essay

The cartoon above uses a multiple-choice quiz to suggest some of the problems facing education in America. As a class, discuss each of the four areas of concern raised by the cartoonist. What do you think is the thesis for this cartoon?

Break into groups of five or six and, using the organization and content suggested by Tom Toles, create a six-paragraph essay. Include ideas that were presented in the class discussion or in your group. Assign each person in your group to one of the following paragraphs:

Introductory paragraph

Four paragraphs of support:

1. **Learning versus sports**
2. **Reading versus television**
3. **A new idea versus a new car**
4. **Studying versus shopping**

Concluding paragraph

Before you write, review the basic content for each paragraph so that each group member understands what the supporting details should be.

PORTFOLIO SUGGESTION

Keep this group essay in your portfolio. How well did the members of your group succeed in helping each other build one unified essay? Because, throughout their careers, many people are expected to work with their colleagues to produce work such as annual reports, write-ups of experiments, or advertising brochures, you should seek to improve your ability to work with others both in school and at work.

Following the Progress of a Student Essay

27

CHAPTER OBJECTIVES

In this chapter, you will develop an essay of your own as you follow the progress of a student essay. It was written by Raluca, a woman who was raised in another culture and whose second language is English.

- using the **prewriting techniques** of freewriting, brainstorming (to create a list), and clustering

- finding a **controlling idea** for the thesis statement

- deciding on the **topic sentences** for three or more body paragraphs

- writing an **introductory paragraph**

- studying the student essay for the **development of the body paragraphs**

- arranging the paragraphs in essay form, adding a **concluding paragraph**

- **revising the draft** using peer evaluation

- **proofreading** the final essay for any errors or omissions

The Assignment: Description of a School Experience

In many college courses, you will have an opportunity to pick your own topic for a writing project. In other courses, topics will be assigned. For the greatest benefit in the work of this chapter, all students will be developing the same general assignment: the description of a school experience. Notice that *description* is the method of development.

> **Your Assignment:** Write an essay describing your experience in a school you once attended.

> **Raluca's narrowed topic:** The school I attended as a child in Romania

Notice that the topic has been narrowed from *a school* to the very specific school the writer attended. By narrowing the focus, the writer will be better able to avoid generalities and produce a unique and interesting piece of writing.

Used with permission from the author.

Now narrow your topic to a specific school experience. You are free to select any educational institution that you have attended. Your topic could be based on your experience in a grade school, middle school, high school, driving school, summer school, institute, or the college you are now attending.

Your narrowed topic: _____

_____

Step 1: Using Prewriting Techniques to Explore What You Know About the Topic

As you already know, writers may choose from a number of prewriting techniques to help gather their first thoughts on a topic. We will consider *freewriting, brainstorming* (to create a list), and *clustering.* You will have the chance to experiment with these three techniques and decide which of them works best for you.

Focused Freewriting: Letting Your Mind Make Free Associations

The purpose of freewriting is to put on paper whatever ideas come to mind when the topic is explored. Without any concerns about form or content, this freewriting can often create a flow of thoughts that surprises even the writer. New and different ideas, some of which the writer is not consciously aware of, may emerge.

Raluca chose freewriting as her prewriting technique. She expressed her first thoughts on the topic without any concern for grammar or organization. Below is her piece of freewriting.

RALUCA'S FREEWRITING

Its hard to explain what life in an communist country was like. Besides the fears, the unfulfilled needs and the constant untrust, life continued to be lived. School in Romania was mandatory and free. We had uniforms, this was a way of making all of us equal, we wore red scarfs, white socks and blue jumpers. The classrooms were very austere, with 15 double-desks, a blackboard and a map on the wall. The framed portrait of our president was present in the middle of the wall, above the blackboard, in every classroom. One teacher was teaching all subjects, and the day was divided in hours, with a 10 minutes break between hours. We didn't have to switch classrooms and we didn't spent a lot of time in school. Every day we had 4 or

(continued on next page)

5 hours, every hour with another subject. In literature, a lot of emphasis was placed on memorization, poems of the important Romanian authors, and during the vacations, mandatory lecture. We had to bring every day a soap and a towel, to wash our hands before eating. Food was brought from home and eaten in the classroom. The teachers were tough. Communist education was based on humiliation, it was a shame if you didn't give the right answer to a question or if you got bad grades. Sometimes the teachers enjoyed their power. It was like a sort of social stratification, based on how good your grades were. The results of the tests and the grades were communicated in front of the class. The grades were from 1–10. There were no multiple-choice tests. You had to memorize and give the answers, written, on the paper.

In this piece of freewriting, Raluca has recalled several memories from her school days. When she wrote this, she did not worry about mistakes or the order of her details. Because English is her second language, she has several phrases that are not idiomatic. She has some errors with spelling and punctuation. She also has a run-on sentence. However, these kinds of mistakes should not be her concerns at this stage in the process.

Freewriting is very different from a more finished piece of writing. Freewriting usually has no title, lacks an introduction and conclusion, and contains no carefully planned paragraphs that include topic sentences. A piece of freewriting may also be repetitious and hard to follow. For all of these reasons, freewriting should never be confused with a finished essay. Student writers must always be aware that freewriting is a first response to a topic, not a carefully constructed college-level essay.

ACTIVITY 1A   **Your Freewriting**

Keeping Raluca's freewriting in mind, write down your own thoughts about a school you have attended. Your freewriting may be shorter or longer than Raluca's, but at this point, length is not important. Do not allow the fear of making mistakes slow you down.

Name of your school: _____

_____

_____

_____

_____

_____

_____

_____

_____

_____

Making a Brainstorming List

Making a list of words or phrases that come to mind is another helpful method of gathering information on any topic. When asked to provide a brainstorming list, Raluca produced the following items (notice there is no particular order):

RALUCA'S BRAINSTORMING LIST

communism	testing and grading
president's portrait	humiliation and shame
uniforms: red scarves, blue jumpers	one teacher for all subjects
soap and towel	atmosphere of fear
bring your own lunch	teachers enjoyed power
blackboard	no place for joy
map	dreary room

ACTIVITY **1B** ## Constructing Your Brainstorming List

Make a list of words or phrases that come to mind when you think about a specific school you attended. Identify your topic by placing the name of your school at the top of your brainstorming list.

Name of your school: _____

_____	_____
_____	_____
_____	_____
_____	_____
_____	_____
_____	_____

Different prewriting techniques may bring different ideas to the surface. For instance, a brainstorming list might very well include different details from those produced in the freewriting. Is there any item included in your brainstorming list that was not part of your freewriting?

Clustering

A third prewriting technique that writers use to explore their ideas is called *clustering*. This technique demands more organizational skill than freewriting or listing because, when a writer uses clustering, words or phrases are put into groups that have specific headings. We can think of the cluster as an outline in visual form. Some writers find that the act of drawing a circle and inserting an idea, resulting in a kind of diagram, to be a helpful way to express their thinking on a topic.

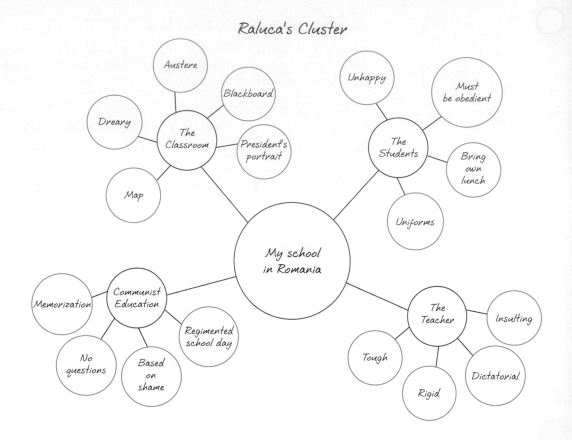

Raluca's Cluster

ACTIVITY **1C**   **Your Cluster**

Now explore how you could arrange your thoughts as a visual cluster, placing your topic in the middle of your cluster and grouping related ideas around that central topic.

Step 2: Finding the Controlling Idea for the Thesis Statement

Once a writer has explored the topic with the use of prewriting techniques and has generated ideas and details important for the essay, it is time to find the controlling idea for the thesis statement. The freewriting, listing, or clustering that a writer produces during the prewriting stage will not necessarily result in an obvious controlling idea. The writer must search for the word or phrase that best states the overriding attitude or viewpoint of the essay.

Raluca Works on Her Controlling Idea for the Thesis Statement

The material in Raluca's prewriting activities produced many ideas and details that Raluca will use in her essay. However, she must still compose her thesis statement. To do this, Raluca needs to decide on a controlling idea that will unify all the details about her childhood school. Here are some of the possible thesis statements that Raluca could have considered. In each example, the controlling idea has been circled.

1. Life for a schoolchild in Romania was (regimented).
2. The Romanian schoolroom was (austere).
3. Life under communism was (filled with fear).
4. The experience of schoolchildren in Romania in the 1970s was (harsh).
5. Most teachers in Romanian schools during the 1970s were (dictatorial).

PRACTICE **1** **Review Raluca's possible thesis statements and answer the following questions:**

1. Which thesis statement is too general and off the topic of the assignment?
   _____

2. Which thesis statements seem too narrow and might provide only enough material for one or two paragraphs? _____

The success of an entire essay often depends on taking the time to determine what word or phrase would best express your controlling idea. Without a clear controlling idea in mind, the essay is much less likely to develop into a unified piece.

In writing about the school you have attended, here are some possible controlling ideas you might consider for your thesis sentence.

Possible Controlling Ideas

supportive	unsupportive
well run	not well run
a happy place	an unhappy place
carefully maintained	run-down
safe	dangerous
challenging	unchallenging
technologically up-to-date	not well equipped
academically solid	academically weak
disciplined	undisciplined

Remember, it is your *controlling idea* that will unify the essay. All the body paragraphs will have to serve and support the controlling idea.

ACTIVITY **2** **Choosing Controlling Ideas for Possible Thesis Statements**

Keeping in mind your prewriting activities as well as the suggested list of controlling ideas given previously, think of three words or phrases that could be possible controlling ideas for your essay. Then compose a thesis statement for each one. Place a check mark beside the thesis statement you intend to use.

Controlling idea: _____

Thesis statement: _____

_____

Controlling idea: _____

Thesis statement: _____

_____

Controlling idea: _____

Thesis statement: _____

_____

Step 3: Deciding on the Topic Sentences For Three or More Body Paragraphs

Raluca Plans the Main Divisions of Her Essay and Writes a Topic Sentence for Each of These Divisions

When Raluca did her freewriting, she was not thinking about how to divide her material into body paragraphs. Now she must invest her time organizing that material. Thinking about all the details she has generated, she decides on possible major divisions. Each of these main divisions could become a developed paragraph, each one beginning with a topic sentence. Here is the list she initially considered:

What the classroom looked like

How teachers treated students

How students were dressed

What a day was like

What subjects were studied

The communist approach to education

How students felt about school

Notice how this list differs from her brainstorming list. Here, Raluca is working on the major divisions that will form the different sections of her essay. The details she uses will all fall within one of these divisions. Here are the four main divisions Raluca chose for her essay and the topic sentence she composed for each one.

Paragraph Divisions	Topic Sentences
1. How the classroom appeared:	**The classroom was *stark*.**
2. How the students were treated:	**Students were expected to be *obedient*.**
3. What a class day was like:	**The school day was very *rigid*.**
4. The communist approach to education:	**Communist education was based on *humiliation*.**

Notice that each topic sentence has the topic and a controlling idea (in italics). Now Raluca realizes exactly which details to place in each of these paragraphs. She will use only details that support the controlling idea of each topic sentence.

ACTIVITY ③ **Composing the Topic Sentences for Your Body Paragraphs**

Think about your material. What three or four main divisions could you make? Each one of these will be developed into a paragraph. Write a topic sentence for each one of these. Circle the controlling idea in each sentence.

1. _____

2. _____

3. _____

4. _____

Step 4: Writing the Introductory Paragraph

Raluca Composes the Introductory Paragraph, Ending with the Thesis Statement

Raluca's freewriting lacks an introductory paragraph with a thesis statement that will unify the entire piece of writing. She needs to compose her introduction, perhaps starting with the same general remarks she made in her freewriting. These general remarks can lead to the more narrowed focus of her thesis statement.

Below is the introductory paragraph that Raluca used in her final draft. The thesis statement is in bold. Compare this introduction with the first two sentences of Raluca's freewriting. How do they differ? Circle her controlling idea.

°*term to explain the Communist takeover of Eastern Europe after 1945*

> Forty years ago, life in a Communist country such as Romania was filled with fears, unfulfilled needs, and the constant distrust of others who might be spying on their neighbors. To a person born in the West, on this side of the **Iron Curtain**,° it is hard to imagine what schoolchildren faced. Nevertheless, life had to be lived, and children went off to school every day. Remembering my childhood school days does not bring back many happy memories. **The experience of a schoolchild in Romania in the 1970s was harsh.**

ACTIVITY ④ **Composing Your Introductory Paragraph**

Write an introductory paragraph for your own essay. You might do as Raluca did by starting with general remarks that will lead to your more specific thesis statement with its controlling idea. Aim for at least four or five sentences, ending with the thesis statement. Underline the thesis statement.

(For more ideas of common patterns used to write introductory paragraphs, review Common Introductory Patterns in Chapter 26.)

_____
_____
_____
_____
_____
_____
_____
_____
_____
_____
_____
_____
_____
_____

Step 5: Studying the Student Essay for Paragraph Development

Before you work on developing your body paragraphs, read Raluca's essay and discuss her body paragraphs. What are the strengths and weaknesses of each paragraph? Are there any additional details you would like to have known?

Raluca's Final Draft

TITLE	**Going to School Behind the Iron Curtain**
INTRODUCTION: BEGINS WITH A GENERAL SUBJECT LEADING TO THE SPECIFIC TOPIC	Life in a communist country such as Romania in the 1970s was filled with fears, unfulfilled needs, and the constant distrust of others who might be spying on their neighbors. To a person born in the West, on this side of the Iron Curtain, it is hard to imagine what schoolchildren faced. Nevertheless, life had to be lived, and children went off to school every day. Remembering my childhood school days does not bring back many happy memories. **The**
THESIS STATEMENT	**experience of a schoolchild in Romania in the 1970s was harsh.**
PARAGRAPH DEVELOPMENT TOPIC SENTENCE 1	**The classroom was stark.** The only pieces of furniture in the room were the fifteen double desks for students and the teacher's desk at the front. A blackboard was on the front wall. The room was often quite cold and only on very dark days were the old ceiling lights turned on. When you entered the room, the only object to look at was the framed portrait of the country's president dominating the front wall above the blackboard. His unsmiling face and somber eyes looked down on everything we did. All across the country his face was at the head of every classroom. We were never allowed to forget who controlled our lives.

(continued on next page)

PARAGRAPH
DEVELOPMENT
TOPIC SENTENCE 2

Students were expected to be obedient. We all wore uniforms: blue jumpers or blue pants, white blouses or shirts, red scarves or ties and white socks. This dress code kept us all looking the same. No one should look different or special in any way. I cannot remember that anyone complained. Each child brought his or her own lunch and soap. We ate our lunch in the classroom. We accepted our situation and did not expect anyone to provide us with any food or supplies. We understood our teachers would not have tolerated any complaints or unwillingness to follow orders.

PARAGRAPH
DEVELOPMENT
TOPIC SENTENCE 3

The school day was very rigid. One teacher taught us all the subjects. The school day was divided into four or five hour-long classes, each one with a different subject. There was a ten-minute break between hours. We did not have to change rooms, and we were finished by early afternoon, sent home with lessons to do. Subjects were taught largely by memorization of facts. The individual teacher had no say in what material to cover. The curriculum was set by the authorities and rigidly adhered to. For instance, in literature classes, most of the emphasis was placed on memorizing poems by important Romanian authors. Children were not encouraged to ask questions, and discussions were most uncommon. When it was test time, we were given blank sheets of paper. There was no such thing as multiple-choice tests. Answers were right or wrong. Grading was from one to ten, with ten being the best.

PARAGRAPH
DEVELOPMENT
TOPIC SENTENCE 4

Communist education was based on humiliation. It was shameful if we did not give the right answer to a question or if we received bad grades. Sometimes we could see that the teachers enjoyed their power. When test results were returned, our grades were shared in front of the entire class. Everyone knew that the only way to get ahead was to do well on the tests. There was no misbehaving. Bad behavior was not tolerated. Corporal punishment was allowed.

CONCLUSION
A RETURN TO
THE IDEAS IN THE
INTRODUCTION

My memory of school in Romania is of days of dutiful work. There was little room for the joy of learning or the freedom of expression. If I were to pick a color to describe my school time, it would be gray. Education was memorizing and repeating what we were told—that was all.

ACTIVITY **5**   ## Developing Your Body Paragraphs

On a computer or on the lines provided below, develop each of your body paragraphs. Use only details that support the controlling idea in each topic sentence you have created. Underline your topic sentences.

Body Paragraph 1

_____

_____

_____

_____

_____

_____

Body Paragraph 2

_____

_____

_____

_____

_____

_____

_____

Body Paragraph 3

_____

_____

_____

_____

_____

_____

_____

Step 6: Putting the Draft into Essay Form with a Concluding Paragraph

Here is Raluca's conclusion. Do any key words from her introduction appear again in the conclusion? Notice how Raluca has summed up the points of her essay in a creative way. Review Raluca's conclusion as a possible model for the ending of your own essay.

> My memory of school in Romania is of days of dutiful work. There was little room for the joy of learning or the freedom of expression. If I were to pick a color to describe my school time, it would be gray. Education was memorizing and repeating what we were told—that was all.

ACTIVITY ⑥   **Putting Your Paragraphs into Essay Form and Adding a Conclusion**

On a computer, follow your instructor's specifications for typing your introduction and body paragraphs. Add a concluding paragraph that will bring the essay to a satisfying end.

(For more ideas of common patterns used to write conclusions, review Writing an Effective Concluding Paragraph in Chapter 26.)

Step 7: Revising the Draft Using Peer Evaluation

In the revision process, you must think, rethink, and think again about all the parts that will make up the whole. One of the most helpful ways to begin thinking about your revision is to have others read your work and make suggestions. The peer evaluation form that follows will help others analyze your work.

ACTIVITY ⑦   **Using a Peer Evaluation Form**

Ask an individual or a group of individuals to use the following form to evaluate your work. With the feedback you receive, you will be ready to revise your draft.

PEER EVALUATION FORM

1. Introductory paragraph

    a. Is the introduction interesting? Could you make any suggestions for improvement?

    b. Underline the thesis. Circle the controlling idea.

2. Body paragraphs

    a. Has the writer used description as the method of development?

    b. Does each body paragraph have a topic sentence? Draw a wavy line under each topic sentence.

    c. Has each body paragraph been adequately developed with at least six to eight sentences?

    d. Do the topic sentences all support the controlling idea of the thesis?

    e. Does the material in each body paragraph relate to its topic sentence? Place a check mark next to any sentence that should be dropped.

3. Details

    a. What is the overall quality of the details? Are they specific enough? Does the writer give names, dates, titles, places, colors, shapes, etc.? In the margin, suggest better details wherever they occur to you.

(continued on next page)

   b. You might be able to count the number of details in each paragraph. Do you believe there are enough details? Indicate in the margin where you believe additional details would improve the essay.

4. Coherence

   a. Does the essay follow a logical progression? If not, place a question mark where you begin to feel confused.

   b. Has the writer used transitional words or phrases at any point to move from one idea to another? If so, put a box around these expressions. Can you suggest a spot where adding a transitional word or phrase would be an improvement?

   c. Has the writer used synonyms, substitutions, or pronouns to replace key words? If so, put a box around these words. If the writer repeats certain words too often, can you suggest in the margin any other synonyms, substitutions, or pronouns that would be an improvement?

5. What detail or idea did you like best about this essay?

6. Does the essay come to a satisfying conclusion?

Step 8: Proofreading the Final Essay for Errors and Omissions

Below are four sentences taken from Raluca's freewriting. Can you find any errors that need to be corrected?

1. Its hard to explain what life in an communist country was like.

2. Besides the fears, the unfulfilled needs and the constant untrust, life continued to be lived.

3. We didn't spent a lot of time in school.

4. Communist education is based on humiliation, it was a shame if you didn't give the right answer to a question or if you received bad grades.

ACTIVITY **8**   **Proofread Your Essay**

After your revisions are complete, you will need to proofread your essay. In a dictionary, look up any word that you suspect might have been misspelled. Run the spell-check program on your computer. Read each sentence aloud to check for omitted words, typos, or other corrections that might have to be made. Sometimes hearing a sentence read out loud helps a writer hear that place where a better word choice or a punctuation mark is needed. In fact, don't be embarrassed to ask someone else to proofread your essay.

WRITE FOR SUCCESS

An educator recently divided people into two categories: those who take responsibility for their actions and those who always blame others for what happens. It is not hard to imagine which mind-set is the healthier one. Write a response that looks at two or three situations and explains your own reactions. Are you a person who looks for someone to blame, or do you look within yourself to see if you bear some responsibility? You might consider an argument with a partner or other family member, an unhappy result with an academic issue, or a complaint about a person in authority.

Working Together

Image Source/Getty Images

Peer Editing: The Revision Stage

Below are four paragraphs taken from a student essay titled "How Students Are Managing the High Costs of a College Education."

Paragraph 1

[1]Going to college is now a big investment for many students and their families. [2]Total costs at private four-year colleges can be as much as $60,000 a year. [3]A state school can cost as much as half that amount. [4]To make matters worse, many states are cutting their budgets for colleges and universities, which will only result in higher tuition rates. [5]Unfortunately, many students and parents do not have a realistic understanding of how much debt they will have to take on.

Paragraph 2

[1]In fact, 74 percent of full-time students now must combine school with work. [2]This is much higher than in the past. [3]And nearly half of those students work more than twenty-five hours a week. [4]It is hard to believe. [5]Of those who work more than twenty-five hours a week, 20 percent work full-time and go to school full-time. [6]Students who work twenty-five hours or more a week are more likely to earn lower grades and often have to drop out of courses.

Paragraph 3

[1]Perhaps the best jobs are the ones that are right on campus. [2]Work-study programs are popular at most schools, and some jobs such as designing websites or maintaining websites can be well paid. [3]If a school offers a cooperative education program, it is usually a good thing. [4]Real-world work experience can give a student the experience they need to qualify for good paying jobs as soon as they graduate and they are also building up their résumés for future job hunting. Some professional services charge a lot of money to help students polish their résumés.

Paragraph 4

[1]There are some ways to afford an education even when your family cannot help you. [2]There are some young people who work for companies like UPS, who help their workers go to college by providing $2,000 to $3,000 for their school costs. [3]There are others who join the military so they can receive a free education. [4]Some people feel that a soldier's free education comes with another sort of high price. [5]More students are going to community colleges and living at home, cutting down on costs. [6]And you can always work during the summer saving money for the next semester's courses.

Working in Groups

Each of the paragraphs has at least one major need for revision.

> **Paragraph 1:** Read the entire essay, and then compose a thesis statement at the end of the first paragraph.
>
> **Paragraph 2:** Paragraph 2 lacks a topic sentence. Create a topic sentence for that paragraph.
>
> **Paragraph 3:** Revise any sentences that contain errors with pronouns. To maintain unity, find a sentence that does not belong. Correct the run-on sentence.
>
> **Paragraph 4:** Revise the first three sentences so that they avoid the repetitious and wordy "There are" expression. Is the meaning of sentence 4 clear? What is your understanding about beginning a sentence with *and*, as in sentence 6?

Each group should decide on what revisions are needed for the four paragraphs and be prepared to present these revisions to the class.

PORTFOLIO SUGGESTION

Remember that, when you are preparing a class writing assignment, you must frequently save your file, preferably giving each draft a different name. Keep your earlier drafts until you have made a final review of your last draft and you feel certain you will have no further need to consult your old drafts again. Be sure to keep a backup copy as well as a hard copy of papers submitted to your instructors. These safety measures help avoid lost or misplaced submissions.

Writing an Essay Using Examples, Illustrations, or Anecdotes

28

Exploring the Topic: Living with a Disability

Most of us have to cope with a variety of disadvantages in our lives. For some people, however, these disadvantages can be serious disabilities that threaten the quality of their lives. Society's view of people with disabilities has changed a great deal over the years. In the past, people with serious disabilities tended to avoid being in public and often did not try to join the rest of society in seeking an education or job advancement. Today, the situation is very different because laws have been passed to protect the rights of people who have limitations. Being disabled should no longer mean being deprived of a productive life.

andres balcazar/Getty Images

1. What, in your judgment, are the most serious disabilities some people have to endure? What disabilities are less obvious than others?

_____

_____

_____

_____

_____

2. Despite the more open and supportive atmosphere in our society today, many people are unsure how to interact with disabled people. What are some misconceptions people have about those with disabilities? What mistakes do people often make when they encounter a disabled person?

_____

_____

_____

_____

_____

3. An American man who had lost the use of both legs reached the top of Japan's Mount Fuji by riding a bicycle with a central hand crank. What other remarkable accomplishments have been made by people with serious disabilities?

_____

_____

_____

_____

_____

4. What are some special accommodations currently provided by schools and employers to help people with disabilities? In your opinion, what more could be done?

_____

_____

_____

_____

_____

Reading a Model Essay with Examples, Illustrations, or Anecdotes

Darkness at Noon
Harold Krents

In the following essay, which appeared in the *New York Times,* the lawyer Harold Krents gives us a frank picture of his daily life as a sightless person who is trying to retain his dignity in a world that is not always supportive.

°narcissistic
characterized by excessive admiration of oneself

°enunciating
clearly pronouncing

°conversely
in the opposite or reverse way

°graphically
in sharp and vivid detail

1   Blind from birth, I have never had the opportunity to see myself and have been completely dependent on the image I create in the eye of the observer. To date, it has not been narcissistic°.

2   There are those who assume that since I can't see, I obviously cannot hear. Very often people will converse with me at the top of their lungs, enunciating° each word very carefully. Conversely°, people will also often whisper, assuming that since my eyes don't work, my ears don't either.

3   For example, when I go to the airport and ask the ticket agent for assistance to the plane, he or she will invariably pick up the phone, call a ground hostess and whisper: "Hi, Jane, we've got a 76 here." I have concluded that the word "blind" is not used for one of two reasons: Either they fear that if the dread word is spoken, the ticket agent's retina will immediately detach, or they are reluctant to inform me of my condition of which I may not have been previously aware.

4   On the other hand, others know that of course I can hear, but believe that I can't talk. Often, therefore, when my wife and I go out to dinner, a waiter or waitress will ask Kit if *"he* would like a drink" to which I respond that "indeed *he* would."

5   This point was graphically° driven home to me while we were in England. I had been given a year's leave of absence from my Washington law firm to study for a diploma-in-law degree at Oxford University. During the year I became ill and was hospitalized. Immediately after admission, I was wheeled down to the X-ray room. Just at the door sat an elderly woman—elderly I would judge from the sound of her voice. "What is his name?" the woman asked the orderly who had been wheeling me.

6   "What's your name?" the orderly repeated to me.

7   "Harold Krents," I replied.

8   "Harold Krents," he repeated.

9   "When was he born?"

10   "When were you born?"

11   "November 5, 1944," I responded.

°**intoned**
said in a monotone

12   "November 5, 1944," the orderly intoned°.

13   This procedure continued for approximately five minutes, at which point even my saint-like disposition deserted me. "Look," I finally blurted out, "this is absolutely ridiculous. Okay, granted I can't see, but it's got to have become pretty clear to both of you that I don't need an interpreter."

14   "He says he doesn't need an interpreter," the orderly reported to the woman.

°**cum laude**
"with honors," a distinction bestowed at graduation from a college or university

15   The toughest misconception of all is the view that because I can't see, I can't work. I was turned down by over forty law firms because of my blindness, even though my qualifications included a cum laude° degree from Harvard College and a good ranking in my Harvard Law School class.

16   The attempt to find employment, the continuous frustration of being told that it was impossible for a blind person to practice law, the rejection letters, not based on my lack of ability but rather on my disability, will always remain one of the most disillusioning experiences of my life.

17   I therefore look forward to the day, with the expectation that it is certain to come, when employers will view their handicapped workers as a little child did me years ago when my family still lived in Scarsdale.

18   I was playing basketball with my father in our backyard according to procedures we had developed. My father would stand beneath the hoop, shout, and I would shoot over his head at the basket attached to our garage. Our next-door neighbor, aged five, wandered over into our yard with a playmate. "He's blind," our neighbor whispered to her friend in a voice that could be heard distinctly by Dad and me. Dad shot and missed; I did the same. Dad hit the rim; I missed entirely; Dad shot and missed the garage entirely. "Which one is blind?" whispered back the little friend.

19   I would hope that in the near future when a plant manager is touring the factory with the foreman and comes upon a handicapped and nonhandicapped person working together, his comment after watching them work will be, "Which one is disabled?"

Analyzing the Writer's Strategies

1.   In the opening paragraph, the writer establishes that his blindness has placed him in a peculiar situation: he must form an image of himself based on the observations of others who can see him. Explain what the writer means when he tells us that, up until now, his own image of himself "has not been narcissistic."

2.   Harold Krents points out three misconceptions people have about blind people. Find where in the essay the writer states each of these misconceptions, and mark them.

3. Each of the misconceptions is followed by one or two anecdotes that illustrate that misconception. Locate each anecdote and indicate whether it makes use of a quotation or a piece of dialogue. Why do you think Harold Krents has included these quotations or conversations?

4. Despite the essentially serious nature of the subject, Harold Krents is able to maintain his sense of humor. Where in the essay do you see him demonstrating this sense of humor?

Writing an Essay Using Examples, Illustrations, or Anecdotes

Of the many ways writers choose to support their ideas, none is more useful or appreciated than the example. All of us have ideas in our minds, but these ideas will not become real for our readers until we use examples to make our concepts clear, concrete, and convincing. Writers who use good examples will be able to hold the attention of their readers.

> **Illustration** or **example** is a method of developing ideas by providing one or more instances of the idea in order to make what is abstract more concrete, give more clarity to the idea, or make that idea more convincing.

Closely Related Terms Used in Example Essays

Example: a specific instance of something being discussed

Extended example: an example that is developed at some length, often taking up one or more complete paragraphs

Illustration: an example used to clarify or explain

Anecdote: a brief story used to illustrate a point

Choosing a Topic and Controlling Idea for the Thesis Statement

Here is a list of possible topics that could lead to an essay in which *example* is used as the main method of development. The rest of this chapter will help you work through the various stages of the writing process.

1. Three challenges I have overcome
2. The three greatest inventions of all time
3. The difficulties in completing a college education
4. Three things I cannot live without
5. Three ways to enjoy music
6. The world's worst habits
7. The three biggest needs in my community
8. Superstitions
9. Poor role models
10. Health problems I have had to overcome

Using this list or drawing upon ideas of your own, jot down two or three topics that you could develop by providing examples.

_____

_____

_____

From these topics, select the one that seems most promising. Which one is most likely to interest your readers? Which one appeals to you the most?

Selected topic: _____

Your next step is to decide what your controlling idea will be. What is the point you want to make about the topic you have chosen? For instance, if you chose to write about the world's worst habits, your controlling idea might be "unhealthy" or "dangerous."

Controlling idea: _____

Now put your topic and controlling idea together to form your thesis statement.

Thesis statement: _____

_____

Gathering Information Using Brainstorming Techniques

Take at least fifteen minutes to jot down every example you can think of that could be used in your essay. If the topic is not too personal, you might form a group to help each other think of examples, anecdotes, and illustrations. Later, if you feel your examples need to be improved, you may want to refer to material from magazines or newspapers. If you do use outside sources, be sure to take notes, checking the correct spelling of names and the accuracy of dates and facts.

_____

_____

_____

_____

_____

_____

_____

_____

_____

_____

_____

Selecting and Organizing the Material

Review your list of examples, crossing out any ideas that are not useful. Do you have enough material to develop three body paragraphs? This might mean using three extended examples, some anecdotes, or several smaller examples that could be organized into three different groups. Decide on the order in which you want to present your examples. Do you have any ideas about how you might want to write the introduction? On the lines that follow, show your plan for organizing your essay. You may want to make an outline that shows your major points, putting supporting details under each major point.

_____

_____

_____

_____

_____

_____

Writing the Rough Draft

Now you are ready to write your rough draft. Approach the writing with the attitude that you are going to write down all your thoughts on the subject without worrying about mistakes of any kind. It is important that your mind be relaxed enough to allow your thoughts to flow freely. You do not need to follow your plan exactly. Just get your thoughts on paper. You are free to add ideas, drop others, or rearrange the order of your details at any point. Sometimes a period of freewriting leads to new ideas that are better than the ones you had in your brainstorming session. Once a writer has something on paper, he or she usually feels a great sense of relief, even though it is obvious that revisions lie ahead.

Keep in mind that, in a paragraph with several examples, you will achieve coherence if these examples are ordered in a logical progression. You could start with the less serious and then move to the more serious, or you might start with the simpler one and move to the more complicated. If your examples consist of events, you might begin with examples from the more distant past and move forward to examples from the present day. Whatever logical progression you choose, you will find it helpful to signal your examples by using some of the transitional expressions that follow.

TRANSITIONS COMMONLY USED IN EXAMPLES

an example of this is	for example	a typical case	The following story illustrates the point.
to illustrate this	for instance	such as	To illustrate my point, let me tell you a story.
as an illustration	specifically	one such case	An anecdote will clarify the point.

Revising the Rough Draft

You may revise your rough draft alone, with a group, with a peer tutor, or directly with your instructor. Here are some of the basic questions you should consider at this most important stage of your work.

GUIDELINES FOR REVISING AN ESSAY DEVELOPED BY EXAMPLE

1. Does the rough draft satisfy the conditions for the essay form? Is there an introductory paragraph? Are there at least three well-developed paragraphs in the body of the essay? Does each of these paragraphs include at least one example? Is there a concluding paragraph? Remember, a single sentence is not considered an acceptable paragraph in standard essay writing unless it is a piece of dialogue with quotation marks.

2. Have you used *example* as your major method of development? Could you make your examples even better by being more specific or by looking up statistics or facts that would lend more authority to your point of view? Could you quote an expert on the subject?

3. What is the basis for the ordering of your examples? Whenever appropriate, did you use transitions to signal the beginning of an example?

4. Is any important part missing? Are there any parts that seem irrelevant or out of place?

5. Are there words or expressions that could have been better chosen? Are any sentences or paragraphs repetitious?

6. Find at least two verbs (usually some form of the verb *to be*) that could be replaced with more descriptive verbs. Add at least two adjectives that will provide better sensory images for the reader.

7. Find at least one place in your draft where an additional sentence or two would make an example better.

8. Can you think of a more effective or creative way to begin or end?

9. Show your draft to two other readers, and ask each one to give you at least one suggestion for improvement.

Preparing the Final Copy, Printing, and Proofreading

The typing of the final version should follow the traditional rules for an acceptable submission.

CHECKLIST FOR THE FINAL COPY

- Use only 8½-by-11-inch paper (never paper torn out of a spiral-bound notebook).
- Print on only one side of the paper.
- Double-space.
- Leave approximately a 1½-inch margin on each side of the paper.
- Put your name, the date, the title of your paper, and any other relevant information either on a separate title page or at the top of the first page. (Ask your instructor for specific advice on what information to include.)
- Center the title. Do not put quotation marks around the title, and do not underline it.
- Do not hyphenate a word at the end of a line unless you are willing to consult a dictionary to check on the acceptable division of the word into syllables.
- Indent each paragraph five spaces.
- If your paper is more than one page, number the pages and staple the pages together so they will not get lost.
- Do not forget to save a copy before you submit the paper.

NOTE: In most cases, college instructors will not accept handwritten work. If you are permitted to submit handwritten work, however, be sure your handwriting is legible. Certainly everyone today is expected to type and be familiar with current computer technology.

Once you have typed your final version and printed it, an important step still remains. Paying attention to this step can often improve your grade. You must *proofread* your paper. Even if you have used a spell-check feature available on your word-processing program, errors could remain in your paper. The spell-check feature finds only groupings of letters that are not words. For example, if you typed the word *form* when you meant to type *from*, the spell-checker would not catch this error. The secret of good proofreading is to look at each word and sentence construction by itself without thinking about the paper's content.

CHECKLIST FOR PROOFREADING

Study each sentence: One way to proofread is to read backward, starting with the last sentence and examining every sentence, one at a time. First, check that the sentence is really complete and is not a fragment or a run-on. Then check the punctuation. Go to the next sentence and do the same. In this way, you will develop a critical eye for spotting any problems with sentence-level errors.

Study each word: Read the paper again, this time studying each word in every sentence. Look at the letters of the word. Have you transposed any letters, or have you left off an ending such as *-ed* or *-s*? If there are any words you are not sure how to spell, check a dictionary for the correct spelling. Have you omitted any words?

WRITE FOR SUCCESS

What do you believe are the qualities of successful people? Write a response that looks at the lives of three people. They could be famous or not. What qualities have led to their success in life? And remember, *successful* does not always mean the same as *rich*!

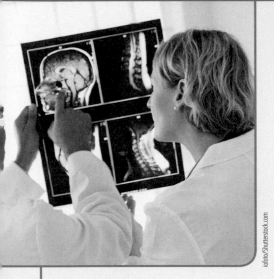

Brainstorming for Examples: Job Advancement

Many people think that, to keep a good job, they need to demonstrate that they are especially clever or smart, that they are a favorite of their employer, or that they are special in some other way. However, when employers have been surveyed, their responses show that the first item on their list of priorities is a surprisingly simple one: they just want their workers to show up!

Assume that a worker is dependable and does show up every day. How does that worker obtain good performance evaluations that will lead to a more permanent position, a salary increase, or a job promotion?

Working in Groups

Sometimes, without being aware of it, people act in ways at work that harm their chances for job advancement. Bad evaluations can even result in a person being fired. Develop a list of examples of actions or attitudes that keep workers from moving ahead in their careers. Then come together as a class and make a composite list of examples. Do any class members recall an actual incident they observed that would illustrate one of the examples?

PORTFOLIO SUGGESTION

Keep your list of examples in your portfolio for a possible essay on the topic of job advancement. Following are a few other work-related topics that you might want to consider for longer research papers:

- What is the place of labor unions in the workforce?
- Explain the problems with health insurance in this country.
- Argue for or against tenure for teachers.
- Compare working for a big company versus working for a small one.
- Tell the stories of some famous whistleblowers (John Dean, Erin Brockovich, Mary McCarthy, Harry Markopolos).
- What are some of the best-rated companies to work for and why? (Search on the Web "companies good to work for.")

Writing an Essay Using Narration

29

CHAPTER OBJECTIVES

This chapter will take you through the process of writing an essay using narration.

- exploring the topic: A Lasting Childhood Memory

- reading and analyzing a childhood memory: "Salvation," by Langston Hughes

- following the writing process to develop your own essay using narration

Exploring The Topic: A Lasting Childhood Memory

For most of us, childhood holds a mixture of happy and painful memories. Some memories are so lasting that they become part of our permanent consciousness. The recollection that the writer Langston Hughes shares with us in the following selection is one of these lasting memories, in which a child finds his perceptions to be in conflict with those of the adults around him. The essay you will write in this chapter will be a narrative based on a childhood experience that made a lasting impression on you. As you answer the following questions, think about what childhood experience you might want to recall.

1. What different roles should adults play in the various stages of a child's life?

   _____

   _____

   _____

   _____

   _____

2. What are some of the demands made by adults that children typically resist?

   _____

   _____

   _____

   _____

   _____

3. What are some of the experiences common to most childhoods?

   _____

   _____

   _____

   _____

   _____

4. What are some examples of painful experiences that occur in some childhoods?

   _____

   _____

   _____

   _____

   _____

Reading a Model Essay with Narrative Elements

Salvation

Langston Hughes

Langston Hughes (1902–1967) was one of the most important writers of the twentieth century, bringing to his poetry, fiction, and essays profound commentary on the black experience in the United States. He was a leader of the Harlem Renaissance, a movement that took place during the 1920s when African-American arts flourished in New York. Although Langston Hughes is perhaps best known for his poetry, the following selection, from his 1940 autobiography *The Big Sea,* has become famous. In it, he looks back on a central event of his youth, an event he realizes changed his vision of himself and his world.

°**revival**
meeting for the purpose of bringing people into the faith

1   I was saved from sin when I was going on thirteen. But not really saved. It happened like this. There was a big revival° at my Auntie Reed's church. Every night for weeks there had been much preaching, singing, praying, and shouting, and some very hardened sinners had been brought to Christ, and the membership of the church had grown by leaps and bounds. Then just before the revival ended, they held a special meeting for children, "to bring the young lambs to the fold." My aunt spoke of it for days ahead. That night I was escorted to the front row and placed on the mourners' bench° with all the other young sinners, who had not yet been brought to Jesus.

°**mourners' bench**
first pew in a church, where those who have not been saved await conversion

2   My aunt told me that when you were saved you saw a light, and something happened to you inside! And Jesus came into your life! And God was with you from then on! She said you could see and hear and feel Jesus in your soul. I believed her. I had heard a great many old people say the same thing and it seemed to me they ought to know. So I sat there calmly in the hot, crowded church, waiting for Jesus to come to me.

°**dire**
terrible

°**fold**
fenced enclosure for animals

3   The preacher preached a wonderful rhythmical sermon, all moans and shouts and lonely cries and dire° pictures of hell, and then he sang a song about the ninety and nine safe in the fold°, but one little lamb was left out in the cold. Then he said: "Won't you come? Won't you come to Jesus? Young lambs, won't you come?" And he held out his arms to all us young sinners there on the mourners' bench. And the little girls cried. And some of them jumped up and went to Jesus right away. But most of us just sat there.

°**work-gnarled**
misshapen from hard work

4   A great many old people came and knelt around us and prayed, old women with jet black faces and braided hair, old men with work-gnarled° hands. And the church sang a song about the lower lights are burning, some poor sinners to be saved. And the whole building rocked with prayer and song.

5   Still I kept waiting to see Jesus.

6   Finally all the young people had gone to the altar and were saved, but one boy and me. He was a rounder's° son named Westley. Westley and I were surrounded by sisters and deacons° praying. It was very hot in the church, and getting late now. Finally Westley said to me in a whisper: "God damn! I'm tired o' sitting here. Let's get up and be saved." So he got up and was saved.

7   Then I was left all alone on the mourners' bench. My aunt came and knelt at my knees and cried, while prayers and songs swirled all around me in the little church. The whole congregation prayed for me alone, in a mighty wail of moans and voices. And I kept waiting serenely° for Jesus, waiting, waiting—but he didn't come. I wanted to see him, but nothing happened to me. Nothing! I wanted something to happen to me but nothing happened.

8   I heard the songs and the minister saying: "Why don't you come? My dear child, why don't you come to Jesus? Jesus is waiting for you. He wants you. Why don't you come? Sister Reed, what is this child's name?"

9   "Langston," my aunt sobbed.

10   "Langston, why don't you come? Why don't you come and be saved? Oh, Lamb of God! Why don't you come?"

11   Now it was really getting late. I began to be ashamed of myself, holding everything up so long. I began to wonder what God thought about Westley, who certainly hadn't seen Jesus either, but who was now sitting proudly on the platform, swinging his knickerbockered° legs and grinning down at me, surrounded by deacons and old women on their knees praying. God had not struck Westley dead for taking his name in vain or for lying in the temple. So I decided that maybe to save further trouble, I'd better lie, too, and say that Jesus had come, and get up and be saved.

12   So I got up.

13   Suddenly the whole room broke into a sea of shouting, as they saw me rise. Waves of rejoicing swept the place. Women leaped in the air. My aunt threw her arms around me. The minister took me by the hand and led me to the platform.

14   When things quieted down, in a hushed silence, punctuated by a few ecstatic "Amens," all the new young lambs were blessed in the name of God. Then joyous singing filled the room.

15   That night, for the last time in my life but one—for I was a big boy of twelve years old—I cried. I cried, in bed alone, and couldn't stop. I buried my head under the quilts, but my aunt heard me. She woke up and told my uncle I was crying because the Holy Ghost had come into my life, and because I had seen Jesus. But I was really crying because I couldn't bear to tell her that I had lied, that I had deceived everybody in the church, that I hadn't seen Jesus, and that now I didn't believe there was a Jesus any more, since he didn't come to help me.

°**rounder**
someone who makes rounds, such as a security guard or a policeman

°**deacons**
members of the church chosen to help the minister

°**serenely**
calmly

°**knickerbockered**
dressed in short pants gathered below the knees

Analyzing the Writer's Strategies

1. A narration is a story, usually set in a particular time, place, and culture. Several details in "Salvation" refer to religious ideas and rituals that may be unfamiliar to some readers. Review the story and make a list of any religious references that are unfamiliar to you. Learn their meanings through the Internet, library resources, or discussion with your classmates.

2. A narration achieves coherence when details are placed in order of time sequence. Review the essay and underline the transitional words and expressions that indicate time, starting with "every night for weeks" in paragraph 1.

3. What do you believe is Hughes's purpose in telling this story? (See Chapter 2 for a review of the three purposes for writing.)

4. Many of the sentences in this story provide descriptive details that capture the sights or sounds of a particular moment. Choose the five sentences that you found to be the most effective. Mark them in the text so you can discuss them with your classmates.

5. Three individuals are heard speaking in the story, but the narrator himself is never heard directly. As we read the story, what effect is created by being able to hear other people, but not the storyteller himself?

6. In life and in literature, the gap between what we expect and what actually takes place is called *irony*. Study the ending of this story. Why is the ending *ironic*?

Writing an Essay Using Narration

Narration is the oldest and best-known form of verbal communication. It is, quite simply, the telling of a story.

Choosing a Story and the Point You Wish to Make with That Story

Here is a list of possible topics that could lead to an essay in which *narration* is the main method of development.

1. The experience (positive or negative) of moving to a new neighborhood
2. Experiencing a parent's separation or divorce
3. A lesson learned from the mistake (or success) of an older brother or sister (or other relative)
4. Gaining new perspective through a cultural or artistic work
5. When I stood alone against others
6. An experience that made me feel alone

7. An experience that made me more confident in myself
8. A memorable classroom experience
9. An accident that affected my childhood
10. A story of triumph or victory

Using this list of suggested topics to start you thinking, jot down two or three powerful memories you have from your own childhood. These will be possible topics for your writing.

_____

_____

_____

From these topics, select the one that seems the most promising. Which one do you feel strongest about? Which one is most likely to interest your readers? Which topic is most suitable for a college essay?

Selected topic: _____

Good narration makes a point. A writer may not always come right out and state the point, but the reader should understand the point by the time he or she reaches the end of the story. Think about your story. What is the point you would like to make?

Point of your story: _____

The introductory paragraph for a story usually sets the scene. What time (for example, the time of year or the time of day), place, and mood will you establish in your introductory paragraph?

Time: _____

Place: _____

Mood: _____

Gathering Information Using Brainstorming Techniques

Take at least fifteen minutes to jot down the sequence of events for your story as you remember it. Try to remember the way things looked at the time, how people reacted (what they did, what they said), and what you thought as the events were happening. If you can go to the actual spot where the events took place, you might go there and take notes on the details of the place. Later on, you can sort through the material and pick out what you want to use.

_____

_____

_____

_____

_____

Selecting and Organizing the Material

Review your brainstorming list, crossing out any details that are not appropriate. Prepare to build on the ideas that you like. Put these remaining ideas into an order, perhaps writing an outline. This will serve as your temporary guide.

_____

_____

_____

_____

_____

Writing the Rough Draft

Find a quiet place where you will not be interrupted for at least one hour. With the plan for your essay in front of you, sit down and write the story that is in your mind. Do not try to judge what you are putting down as right or wrong. What is important is that you let your mind relax and allow the words to flow freely. Do not worry if you find yourself not following your plan exactly. Keep in mind that you are free to add parts, drop sections of the story, or rearrange details at any point. Sometimes, if you allow your thoughts to take you wherever they lead, new ideas may emerge. You may like these inspirations better than your original plan. Writing a rough draft is a little like setting out on an expedition; there are limitless possibilities, so it is important to be flexible. Keep in mind that, in a narrative essay, you will achieve coherence when the details are ordered according to a time sequence. One way to make the time sequence clear is to use transitional words that signal a time change. Here are some examples of transitional words that will help the reader move smoothly from one part of a story to the next.

TRANSITIONS COMMONLY USED IN NARRATION

in December of 2013	suddenly	after a little while	several weeks passed
the following month	now; by now	then	later; later on
at first	immediately	meanwhile	at the same time
at once	in the next month	next; the next day	finally

Revising the Rough Draft

You may revise your rough draft alone, with a group, with a peer tutor, or directly with your instructor. If you are working on a computer, making changes is so easy that you will feel encouraged to explore alternatives. Unlike making changes using traditional pen and paper, inserting or deleting material on a computer is a simple matter. Here are some of the basic questions you should consider when the time comes to revise your narration.

GUIDELINES FOR REVISING AN ESSAY DEVELOPED BY NARRATION

1. Does the rough draft satisfy the conditions for the essay form? Is there an introductory paragraph? Are there at least three well-developed paragraphs in the body of the essay? Is there a concluding paragraph? Remember, a single sentence is not considered an acceptable paragraph in standard essay writing unless it is a piece of direct dialogue using quotation marks. (In the case of dialogue, a new paragraph is begun each time a different person speaks.)

2. Is your essay a narration? Does it tell the story of one particular incident that takes place at a specific time and location? A writer who talks about incidents in a general way in order to comment on the meaning of these incidents is not using narration. You must be a storyteller. Where does the action take place? Can the reader visualize it? What time of day, week, or year is it? What is the main character in the story doing?

3. Have you put the events of the story in a time order? Find the expressions you have used to show the time sequence.

4. Can you think of any part of the story that is missing and should be added? Is there any material that is irrelevant and should be omitted?

5. Are any sentences or paragraphs repetitious?

6. Find several places where you can substitute stronger verbs or nouns. Add adjectives to give the reader better sensory images.

7. Find at least three places in your draft where you could add details. Perhaps you might add an entire paragraph that will describe more fully the person or place that is central to your story.

8. Can you think of a more effective or creative way to begin or end?

9. Does your story have a point? If a person told you every little thing that happened in the day, this would not make an interesting story. A good story should have a point.

10. Show your rough draft to at least two other readers and ask for suggestions.

Preparing the Final Copy, Printing, and Proofreading

Follow the traditional rules for an acceptable submission when you type your final version.

CHECKLIST FOR THE FINAL COPY

- Use only 8½-by-11-inch paper (never paper torn out of a spiral-bound notebook).

- Print on only one side of the paper.

- Double-space.

(continued on next page)

- [ ] Leave approximately a 1½-inch margin on each side of the paper.

- [ ] Put your name, the date, the title of your paper, and any other relevant information either on a separate title page or at the top of the first page. (Ask your instructor for specific advice on what information to include.)

- [ ] Center the title. Do not put quotation marks around the title, and do not underline it.

- [ ] Do not hyphenate a word at the end of a line unless you are willing to consult a dictionary to check on the acceptable division of the word into syllables.

- [ ] Indent each paragraph five spaces.

- [ ] If your paper is more than one page, number the pages and staple the pages together so they will not get lost.

- [ ] Do not forget to save a copy before you submit the paper.

NOTE: In most cases, college instructors will not accept handwritten work. If you are permitted to submit handwritten work, however, be sure your handwriting is legible. Certainly everyone today is expected to type and be familiar with current computer technology.

Once you have typed your final version and printed it, an important step still remains. Paying attention to this step can often improve your grade. You must *proofread* your paper. Even if you have used a spell-check feature available on your word-processing program, errors could remain in your paper. The spell-check feature finds only groupings of letters that are not words. For example, if you typed the word *there* when you meant to type *their,* the spell-checker would not catch this error. The secret of good proofreading is to look at each word and sentence construction by itself without thinking about the paper's content.

CHECKLIST FOR PROOFREADING

Study each sentence: One way to proofread is to read backward, starting with the last sentence and examining every sentence, one at a time. First, check that the sentence is really complete and is not a fragment or a run-on. Then check the punctuation. Go to the next sentence and do the same. In this way, you will develop a critical eye for spotting any problems with sentence-level errors.

Study each word: Read the paper again, this time studying each word in every sentence. Look at the letters of the word. Have you transposed any letters, or have you left off an ending such as *-ed* or *-s*? If there are any words you are not sure how to spell, check a dictionary for the correct spelling. Have you omitted any words?

WRITE FOR SUCCESS

We all know that small children want instant gratification. Part of becoming an adult is learning the value of waiting and planning. A greater reward will likely come to those who can postpone gratification. Write a response that tells the story of someone who wisely deferred pleasures in order to achieve a greater long-term goal.

Hudiemm/iStock/Getty Images Plus/Getty Images

Sharing Our Narratives

Everyone loves a good story. We especially value those stories about ourselves and our family members that reveal some personal truth that we hold dear. In the 1950s, a series of radio broadcasts titled "This I Believe" became immensely popular. These brief essays, written by people from all walks of life, were reflections on a personal belief. A few years ago, National Public Radio reintroduced the idea. Below is a portion of one of these essays. Read Melissa Weiler Gerber's essay about why she believes it is important to pay attention to the little things in life.

1   I believe in details. I know this runs counter to well-meaning advice that seeks to liberate us from sweating the little stuff. I am painfully aware that my conviction places me at risk for lost sleep and moments of distraction. Dare I say it may even make this forty-one-year-old a bit old-fashioned. So be it.

2   It's in my blood. My grandmothers remembered everyone's birthday and acknowledged all sicknesses, deaths, weddings, and other major life events with handwritten notes. My father, a lawyer and one-time English teacher, edited my early writing diligently and, along with my ninth grade grammar teacher, instilled in me the importance of a comma, the difference one word choice can make. My mother wrote a special message on the paper napkin in my lunch box each birthday during every school year.

3   Details bring me joy—the feel of quality paper, the heft of a rocks glass, the foam on a well-made latte. These are little gifts that lift my spirit and elevate ordinary experiences. But I also recognize that my commitment to particulars has a dark side. I feel compelled to try on three pairs of the same size jeans before making my final choice. I have to read every greeting card in the store to find just the right one. And discovering I've committed a typo nearly kills me.

4   Yes, it's hard work to focus on details, but focus I must, for details are fleeting—the circumstances of a first kiss, a lost loved one's laugh, that shortcut we always used to take. Unless purposefully tended to, the components of even the most important of life's events are apt to fade and then disappear.

5   Okay, I'm a bit obsessed, but let's face it, it's the sum of all these details that add up to the whole person we are—the eyeglass frames we select, the unique flair of our signature, our choice of seat on a roller coaster—these things provide each of us with our own unique identity. They tell the world in a million tiny ways who we are, what we value.

6   This is why those things play such an important role in relationships. Taking the time to notice, acknowledge, and recall details makes those around us feel appreciated and understood. We draw on the best of our humanity when we slow down enough to listen—really listen—to a story being told. I certainly notice when someone does that for me.

7   And so, I pledge to try my best to remember whether you like the toilet paper to roll under or over, whether you are a cat or dog person, and the date of that big birthday you have coming up. I'll be grateful if you remember that my ears are not pierced, I like peppermint tea, and chocolate is always the right answer. Yes, I believe in details.

1. Melissa Weiler Gerber thinks that it's the details of our lives that help make us individuals. Do you agree that paying attention to these details is important? Discuss what details of your life or personality make you unique.

2. Melissa Weiler Gerber began her essay by stating, "I believe in details." Here are some first sentences from other contributing essays in the series:

I believe in the power of perfume.

I believe in the power to forget.

I learned everything I needed to know from my dog.

After dividing into groups, each group should develop a list of ten first lines that might begin an essay on "This I Believe." Be creative. Share these ideas with the entire class. Your instructor may then assign a writing project in which you are to select one sentence from these class lists and write an essay titled "This I Believe." Using Melissa Weiler Gerber's writing as a model, be sure to include examples that illustrate your belief.

PORTFOLIO SUGGESTION

- Go to the website *thisibelieve.org*. Read a number of these essays and print out several that you find powerful, creative, or memorable. Consider sending in your own essay on "This I Believe."

- Keep all the narratives you have worked on in this chapter in your portfolio. These narratives could be the beginning of a series of stories written to capture the memories of your own family members. These stories may become the basis for a wonderful gift to your own children someday.

Writing an Essay Using Process Analysis 30

Exploring the Topic: Preparing for a Job Interview

You are in the market for a job. You have searched the Internet, read the ads, asked your friends for suggestions, made phone calls to all your contacts, and sent out résumés. Now you have a very promising interview coming up next week. What should you do to prepare for this important interview? How can you be sure you will make a good impression?

1. If you have ever interviewed for a job, share your experience with the class. What was the best or worst aspect of the interview? What questions were you asked? Were you prepared? Did you get the job?

   _____

   _____

   _____

2. Imagine you are the person conducting a job interview. What would you be looking for in a prospective employee?

   _____

   _____

   _____

iStockphoto.com/sdominick

3. From what you have heard or read, what advice would you give to someone preparing for a job interview?

_____

_____

_____

4. What should a person *never* do in a job interview?

_____

_____

_____

Reading a Model Essay with Steps in a Process
How to Ace a Job Interview
Richard Koonce

In the following essay, Richard Koonce takes us through the stages of the interview process, giving valuable pointers to job seekers. Whether you are heading toward an interview yourself or advising a friend who is looking for a job, the following essay is filled with practical wisdom about what it takes to have a successful job interview.

1   Next to public speaking, most people think that enduring a job interview is one of the most stressful human experiences.

°quibble
disagree

2   I wouldn't quibble° with that. However, a lot of people not only manage to master the art of effective interviewing as they go about job searches, but actually grow to enjoy the interview experience.

3   Good thing! Job interviews are something we all have to deal with from time to time in our careers. So it pays to know how to handle yourself effectively when you're sitting across the desk from a prospective employer. Indeed,

°navigate the terrain
find the way

knowing how to navigate the terrain° of job interviews can pay off big time for your career, land you a better job than the one you initially interview for, and position you for the job success and satisfaction you deserve.

4   How do you ace a job interview? Here are some tips.

5   Recognize that when you interview for a job, employers are looking for evidence of four things: your ability to do the job, your motivation, your compatibility with the rest of the organization, and your self-confidence. If you understand how all those things play into an interviewer's questions (and an employer's hiring decisions), you'll have a better chance of getting hired.

6   Often the first thing an employer wants to know is, "Will you fit in?" Presuming a company has seen your résumé ahead of time and invited you for an interview, it may assume you have certain skills. Now the employer wants to know, "Will you be compatible with everyone else who works here?"

7   Fitting in is a real hot button for employers. That's because it's expensive to go through the rehiring process if someone doesn't work out.

8   Along with determining compatibility, employers want to know that you're motivated to do a job. And they want to know why you want to work for their organization. So be ready with career highlights that illustrate why hiring you would be a good decision for the organization. Showcase your talents as an instructional designer, for example, or tell the interviewer about the process improvement efforts you've put in place in your current job that ensure continuous refinement of training courses. Concise oral vignettes° like these can make a great impression on interviewers.

°vignettes
short descriptive accounts

9   Throughout the interview, breathe deeply, speak slowly, and focus on projecting yourself confidently. This is important. Employers want to see self-confidence in job seekers. A lot of job seekers are too modest. They downplay their accomplishments. Don't embellish or exaggerate, but don't be a shrinking violet either. Rehearse ahead of time the answers to key questions that you expect to be asked, especially that all-time favorite: "Tell me about yourself."

10   Some other points to keep in mind:

11   Before the interview, do some research on the company you're interviewing with. That will enable you to demonstrate knowledge of the company when you meet the interviewer. It may also prompt questions that you'll want to get answers to, even as questions are being asked of you.

12   There are lots of research options. You can tap into the Internet and pull down everything from company profiles to *Dun and Bradstreet* financial reports. You can talk to friends or coworkers who may know something about the organization. And don't forget to watch the paper for late-breaking developments about the company. (If you read in the paper the day of your interview that your prospective employer is about to file Chapter 11°, you may want to think twice about working there!)

°Chapter 11
one type of bankruptcy under federal bankruptcy laws

13   Arrive for the interview early enough to go to the restroom to check yourself out. The last thing you want is to arrive for your interview beaded with sweat, having just sprinted there from the subway stop two blocks away.

14   Once in the interview, concentrate on making a pleasant and strong first impression. Eighty percent of the first impression an interviewer gets of you is visual—and it's formed in the first two minutes of the meeting! So, men, wear a well-made suit, crisply starched white or blue shirt, and polished shoes. Women, you can get away with more color than men, but dress conservatively in dresses, or jacket and skirt combinations. Wearing a colorful scarf is a good way to weave in color, but keep jewelry to a minimum.

15   As you answer questions, be sure to emphasize as often as you can the reasons why your skills, background, and experience make you a good fit for the job that you're interviewing for.

16   After the interview, immediately send a thank-you note to the interviewer. This is a critical point of interview etiquette. Many job candidates eliminate themselves from competition for a job because they don't do this.

17   Finally, learn from every job interview you have. Don't be hard on yourself if things don't go your way. Even job interviews that don't go well can be great learning experiences. And in my own life, I can look back on interviews where I'm glad I didn't get the job!

Analyzing the Writer's Strategies

1. Had Richard Koonce followed a more traditional college essay structure, how many of his first paragraphs would have been combined to comprise the introductory paragraph?

2. What criticism would writing instructors have of paragraph 10?

3. According to the author, what are the four pieces of information employers want to know about a prospective employee?

4. According to Richard Koonce, the stages in the interview process consist of the following: (a) what you should know before the interview, (b) how you should prepare for the interview, (c) what you should do upon arrival at the interview, (d) how you should conduct yourself during the interview, and (e) what you should do after the interview. Mark each of these stages in your text. What is the author's advice at each of these stages?

5. This essay was written in 1997. Do you think the advice on how to dress for an interview (paragraph 14) would be any different today?

6. From your own experience, can you think of any other advice that should have been included?

7. How does the writer's last paragraph provide a useful conclusion to the essay?

Writing an Essay Using Process Analysis (How to...)

Process analysis, as a method of developing ideas, involves giving a step-by-step explanation of how to do something (called *directional process*) or how something works (called *informational process*).

The how-to section of a library or bookstore is usually a busy area. Although many of us can now find much of this information on the Web, most people also enjoy browsing through books on shelves. People find books that help them perform thousands of different tasks—from plumbing to flower arranging. If you want to learn how to cook Chinese meals, assemble a child's bicycle, start your own business, or remodel your bathroom, you can find a book that will tell you how to do it. Thousands of books and articles have been written that promise to help people accomplish their goals in life. What do you think are the best-selling how-to books in America? Perhaps you have guessed the answer: books on how to lose weight!

Choosing a Topic and Controlling Idea for the Thesis Statement

Here is a list of possible topics for an essay in which process analysis is the main method of development. Be sure to pick a process with which you are already familiar.

1. How to choose a major in college
2. How to prepare for a driver's test
3. How to plan a budget
4. How to buy a used car
5. How to study for a test
6. How to change a tire
7. How to redecorate a room
8. How to buy clothes on a limited budget
9. How to find the right place to live
10. How to make new friends

Using this list of topics or ideas of your own, jot down two or three processes with which you are familiar.

_____

_____

_____

_____

_____

From all these topics, which one will give you the best opportunity for writing? Which one is most likely to interest your readers? For which topic do you have the most firsthand experience?

   Selected topic: _____

Your next step is to decide on your purpose for writing. Which of the two types of process writing will you be doing? Do you want to give directions on how to carry out each step in a process so that your readers can do this process themselves? For instance, will you provide directions on how to change a tire, perhaps suggesting that your readers keep these directions in the glove compartments of their cars? Or do you want to provide information on how a process works because you think your readers might find it interesting? For instance, you might explain the process involved in getting an airplane off the ground. Not many of us understand how this works, and very few of us will ever pilot a plane. Perhaps you know a lot about an unusual process that might interest or amuse readers. Place a check mark next to the process type you will use.

Your choice of process: Directional _____ Informational _____

What will be your controlling idea? _____

Now put your topic and controlling idea together into a thesis statement.

Thesis statement: _____

_____

Gathering Information Using Brainstorming Techniques

Take at least fifteen minutes to list as many steps or stages in the process as you can. If the process is one that others in your class or at home already know, consult with them about additional steps that you may have overlooked. You may also need to think of the precise vocabulary words associated with the process (such as the names of tools used for building or repairing something). The more specific you are, the more helpful and interesting the process analysis will be for your readers. List below the steps or stages in the process you have chosen:

_____

_____

_____

_____

_____

Selecting and Organizing the Material

In a process essay, the most essential elements are the **completeness**, the **accuracy**, and the **order** of all the steps.

Completeness and Accuracy

Review your brainstorming list, asking yourself whether or not the list is complete. For someone who is unfamiliar with this process, is there any step he or she might need to know? (The step may seem obvious to you, but for someone else, it may be a necessary step to mention.) Is there any additional piece of information that, while not essential, would be helpful or encouraging? Perhaps you have a special warning about something that the reader should be careful *not* to do. Finally, you might consider telling your readers exactly where in the process most problems are likely to occur.

Order

Now make an outline dividing the process into its major steps or stages. Underneath each major stage, list all the details, including any vocabulary words that are particular to the process, and the name of any special tool or piece of equipment that is needed at any stage of the process. If your process involves a sequence that must be followed in a definite order, be careful that the order is correct.

_____

_____

_____

_____

_____

Writing the Rough Draft

Write your rough draft, keeping in mind that your outline is only a guide. As you write, you will find yourself reevaluating the logic of your ideas, a perfectly natural step that may involve making some changes to your outline. You may think of some special advice that would help the reader; if you do, feel free to add the details. Your main goal is to get the process on paper as completely and accurately as possible.

Unfortunately, process essays can sometimes turn into simple numbered lists of items. This is fine for an instruction booklet that goes with a company's product. In an essay, however, the steps are usually not numbered. Instead, the movement from one step to another is signaled by changing to a new paragraph and using a transitional expression. Like other methods for developing ideas, *process analysis* has its own special words and expressions that can be used to signal movement from one step to the next. Below are some of the most common transitions used in process writing.

TRANSITIONS COMMONLY USED IN PROCESS ANALYSIS

the first step	first of all	then	the last step
in the beginning	while you are	the second step	the final step
to start with	as you are	after you have	finally
to begin with	next	at last	eventually

Revising the Rough Draft

If you can set aside your rough draft and return to it later, you will be able to view your work with more objectivity and thus revise your writing more effectively.

You may revise alone, with a group, with a peer tutor, or directly with your instructor. The following guidelines contain basic questions you should consider when you approach this most important stage of your work.

GUIDELINES FOR REVISING AN ESSAY DEVELOPED BY PROCESS ANALYSIS

1. Does the rough draft satisfy all the conditions for the essay form? Is there an introductory paragraph? Are there at least three well-developed paragraphs in the body of the essay? Have you written a concluding paragraph? Remember, a single sentence is not considered an acceptable paragraph in standard essay writing unless it is a piece of direct dialogue using quotation marks.

2. Is the process essay directional or informational?

3. Are the steps of the process in the correct order? In a process essay, the sequence of the steps is crucial. Placing a step out of order could have disastrous results.

4. Are the directions accurate and complete? Check more than once that no important piece of information has been left out. Have you considered the points where some special advice might be helpful? Are there any special tools that would be useful?

5. Is any of the material irrelevant?

6. Are any sentences or words repetitious?

7. Find several places where more specific verbs, nouns, or adjectives can be substituted. Always try to use vocabulary that is appropriate for the process being described.

8. Can you think of a more effective way to begin or end?

9. Does the essay flow logically from one idea to the next? Could you improve this flow with better use of transitional expressions?

10. Show your draft to at least two other readers and ask for suggestions.

Preparing the Final Copy, Printing, and Proofreading

Follow the traditional rules for an acceptable submission when you type your final version.

CHECKLIST FOR THE FINAL COPY

- Use only 8½-by-11-inch paper (never paper torn out of a spiral-bound notebook).

- Print on only one side of the paper.

- Double-space.

- Leave approximately a 1½-inch margin on each side of the paper.

- Put your name, the date, the title of your paper, and any other relevant information either on a separate title page or at the top of the first page. (Ask your instructor for specific advice on what information to include.)

(continued on next page)

- Center the title. Do not put quotation marks around the title, and do not underline it.

- Do not hyphenate a word at the end of a line unless you are willing to consult a dictionary to check on the acceptable division of the word into syllables.

- Indent each paragraph five spaces.

- If your paper is more than one page, number the pages and staple the pages together so they will not get lost.

- Do not forget to save a copy before you submit the paper.

NOTE: In most cases, college instructors will not accept handwritten work. If you are permitted to submit handwritten work, however, be sure your handwriting is legible. Certainly everyone today is expected to type and be familiar with current computer technology.

Once you have typed your final version and printed it, an important step still remains. Paying attention to this step can often improve your grade. You must *proofread* your paper. Even if you have used a spell-check feature available on your word-processing program, errors could remain in your paper. The spell-check feature finds only groupings of letters that are not words. For example, if you typed the word *then* when you meant to type *than,* the spell-checker would not catch this error. The secret of good proofreading is to look at each word and sentence construction by itself without thinking about the paper's content.

CHECKLIST FOR PROOFREADING

Study each sentence: One way to proofread is to read backward, starting with the last sentence and examining every sentence, one at a time. First, check that the sentence is really complete and is not a fragment or a run-on. Then check the punctuation. Go to the next sentence and do the same. In this way, you will develop a critical eye for spotting any problems with sentence-level errors.

Study each word: Read the paper again, this time studying each word in every sentence. Look at the letters of the word. Have you transposed any letters, or have you left off an ending such as *-ed* or *-s*? If there are any words you are not sure how to spell, check a dictionary for the correct spelling. Have you omitted any words?

WRITE FOR SUCCESS

Do you know how a student transfers to another college? What is the process? What are the problems involved? Write a response that gives advice to a friend who is thinking of transferring. Provide a sequence of steps for the procedure. Feel free to consult any available information.

Working Together

MachineHeadz/Getty Images

Deciding on a Logical Order: Sexual Harassment in the Workplace

The following letter was sent to a well-known advice column:

DEAR ABBY: I am a young woman who has entered the workforce for the first time. I work at a large company that employs very few women. Abby, I am a very average girl who has never been the center of attention, but here at work it's a different story. Here, I get treated like a supermodel.

People fawn over me, ask me personal questions, ask me out and just want to be my friend. It's hard to get work done with so many men coming by every day, and it's embarrassing for me.

I have tried to be cold to some of them to get them to stop coming by, but it doesn't work. How can I discourage random people from coming by just to say "Hi" and have a conversation all the time? They don't start conversations with all the men who sit near me, so why should they start one with me? It's making me want to leave the company and never come back.

Plain Jane in Texas

Being harassed at work can create very complicated issues on the job. In many cases, the situation comes down to one person's word against that of another. Often, the person in the less powerful position is afraid to report a more powerful person to outside authorities. Fear of losing one's job is a strong incentive to remain silent. However, a person should not have to endure unacceptable behavior.

Consider the specific example described in the letter to Dear Abby. Divide into groups and discuss the following questions concerning the woman who wrote the letter. Decide on the most logical order for the steps this person should take.

1. Should she confront the men who are harassing her?
2. Should she go to her supervisor? Should she tell other coworkers about the problem?
3. Should she share her problem with her friends?
4. Should she avoid the problem by quitting her job?
5. How important is evidence for a person in this situation? How and when should she gather documentation for a possible formal action?
6. Does she need a lawyer? Does she need to consider the consequences of a formal action?

PORTFOLIO SUGGESTION

Write a process essay in which you outline the steps a person should take if he or she is being harassed on the job.

Discussion of this issue may remind you of other problems that arise in the workplace. If so, you may want to start gathering ideas on some of these other problems that are of interest to you. Your examination of these issues could relate directly to other subject areas you might study, such as psychology, sociology, business ethics, or business management.

Writing an Essay Using Comparison/Contrast 31

CHAPTER OBJECTIVES

This chapter will take you through the process of writing an essay using comparison/contrast.

- exploring the two-part topic: Men and Women Look at Beauty

- reading and analyzing a model essay: "The Ugly Truth about Beauty," by Dave Barry

- following the writing process to develop your own essay using comparison/contrast

Exploring the Topic: Men and Women Look at Beauty

Standards of beauty may change, but the search for beauty is a continual one in our lives. Whether we accept society's definition of beauty or have our own ideas on the subject, the question of how we see ourselves in the context of our culture is of genuine interest to most people.

1. When you look at another person, what is the first thing you notice about that person? Is this the feature or quality you always find most attractive about someone else?

   _____

   _____

   _____

   _____

   _____

2. To what extent do you judge someone by his or her appearance? Are you critical of people who do not pay a great deal of attention to how they look?

   _____

   _____

   _____

   _____

   _____

iStockphoto.com

3. All of us have met people who are very attractive, and our first tendency is to admire such people. Are there some possible disadvantages to being very handsome or very beautiful?

_____

_____

_____

_____

_____

4. What are some of the more extreme measures people take to make themselves more attractive? Do you think these attempts are the result of pressures from society, the media, and the fashion and makeup industries, or do they result from inborn desires that people have?

_____

_____

_____

_____

_____

5. What public figure (an entertainer, politician, or sports figure) do you consider to be especially handsome or beautiful? Why?

_____

_____

_____

_____

_____

6. Is there too much emphasis in the media today on impossible standards of beauty? At what point does this affect people's health?

_____

_____

_____

_____

_____

Reading a Model Essay That Uses Comparison/Contrast

Beauty and The Beast

by *Dave Barry*
from the Miami Herald, February 1, 1998

The writer Dave Barry has been called "the funniest man in America." His career has been largely devoted to pointing out the lighter side of life. After graduating from college, he worked as a newspaper reporter before discovering his true talent as a writer of humorous essays. The wry observations about modern life that filled his columns earned Barry a Pulitzer Prize in 1988. In the following essay, which first appeared in the *Philadelphia Inquirer* in 1998, the writer gives us an amusing look at how both sexes view beauty.

1   If you're a man, at some point a woman will ask you how she looks.

2   "How do I look?" she'll ask.

3   You must be careful how you answer this question. The best technique is to form an honest yet sensitive opinion, then collapse on the floor with some kind of fatal seizure. Trust me, this is the easiest way out. Because you will never come up with the right answer.

4   The problem is that women generally do not think of their looks in the same way that men do. Most men form an opinion of how they look in seventh grade, and they stick to it for the rest of their lives. Some men form the opinion that they are irresistible stud muffins, and they do not change this opinion even when their faces sag or their noses bloat to the size of eggplants and their eyebrows grow together to form what appears to be a giant forehead-dwelling tropical caterpillar.

5   Most men, I believe, think of themselves as average-looking. Men will think this even if their faces cause heart failure in cattle at a range of 300 yards. Being average does not bother them; average is fine, for men. This is why men never ask anybody how they look. Their primary form of beauty care is to shave themselves, which is essentially the same form of beauty care that they give to their lawns. If, at the end of his four-minute daily beauty regimen, a man has managed to wipe most of the shaving cream out of his hair and is not bleeding too badly, he feels that he has done all he can, so he stops thinking about his appearance and devotes his mind to more critical issues, such as the Super Bowl.

6   Women do not look at themselves this way. If I had to express, in three words, what I believe most women think about their appearance, those words would be: "not good enough." No matter how attractive a woman may appear

571

to be to others, when she looks at herself in the mirror, she thinks: woof. She thinks that at any moment a municipal animal-control officer is going to throw a net over her and haul her off to the shelter.

7   Why do women have such low self-esteem? There are many complex psychological and societal reasons, by which I mean Barbie. Girls grow up playing with a doll proportioned such that, if it were a human, it would be seven feet tall and weigh 81 pounds, of which 53 pounds would be bosoms. This is a difficult appearance standard to live up to, especially when you contrast it with the standard set for little boys by their dolls . . . excuse me, by their action figures. Most of the action figures that my son played with when he was little were hideous-looking. For example, he was very fond of an action figure (part of the He-Man series) called "Buzz-Off," who was part human, part flying insect. Buzz-Off was not a looker. But he was extremely self-confident. You could not imagine Buzz-Off saying to the other action figures: "Do you think these wings make my hips look big?"

8   But women grow up thinking they need to look like Barbie, which for most women is impossible, although there is a multibillion-dollar beauty industry devoted to convincing women that they must try. I once saw an Oprah show wherein supermodel Cindy Crawford dispensed makeup tips to the studio audience. Cindy had all these middle-aged women applying beauty products to their faces; she stressed how important it was to apply them in a certain way, using the tips of their fingers. All the women dutifully did this, even though it was obvious to any sane observer that, no matter how carefully they applied these products, they would never look remotely like Cindy Crawford, who is some kind of genetic mutation.

9   I'm not saying that men are superior. I'm just saying that you're not going to get a group of middle-aged men to sit in a room and apply cosmetics to themselves under the instruction of Brad Pitt, in hopes of looking more like him. Men would realize that this task was pointless and demeaning°. They would find some way to bolster° their self-esteem that did not require looking like Brad Pitt. They would say to Brad: "Oh YEAH? Well what do you know about LAWN CARE, pretty boy?"

°**demeaning**
degrading

°**bolster**
support or buoy up

10   Of course many women will argue that the reason they become obsessed with trying to look like Cindy Crawford is that men, being as shallow as a drop of spit, WANT women to look that way. To which I have two responses:

11   1. Hey, just because WE'RE idiots, that does not mean YOU have to be; and

12   2. Men don't even notice 97 percent of the beauty efforts you make anyway. Take fingernails. The average woman spends 5,000 hours per year worrying about her fingernails; I have never once, in more than 40 years of listening to men talk about women, heard a man say, "She has a nice set of fingernails!" Many men would not notice if a woman had upward of four hands.

13   Anyway, to get back to my original point: If you're a man, and a woman asks you how she looks, you're in big trouble. Obviously, you can't say she looks bad. But you also can't say that she looks great, because she'll think you're lying, because she has spent countless hours, with the help of the multibillion-dollar beauty industry, obsessing about the differences between herself and Cindy Crawford. Also, she suspects that you're not qualified to judge anybody's appearance. This is because you have shaving cream in your hair.

Analyzing the Writer's Strategies

1. Underline the thesis of Barry's essay.

2. Read the introduction (paragraphs 1–3) and the conclusion (paragraph 13) of the essay and explain how Barry's conclusion echoes what he wrote in the introduction.

3. Find three sentences in the essay that you find humorous, and explain what makes these sentences funny.

4. Dave Barry uses informal language. Find five examples of informal language or slang.

5. Find an example of Barry's use of simile (a comparison using *like* or *as*).

6. Summarize how Barry contrasts each of the following:
   a. A man's daily regimen and a woman's daily regimen
   b. A man's attitude about himself and a woman's attitude about herself
   c. A Barbie doll and an action figure called Buzz-Off
   d. A woman's attitude toward Cindy Crawford and a man's attitude toward Brad Pitt

Writing an Essay Using Comparison/ Contrast

Comparison/contrast, as a method for developing ideas, involves the careful examination of similarities and differences between people, objects, or ideas to arrive at a judgment or conclusion.

Choosing a Topic and Controlling Idea for the Thesis Statement

Here is a list of possible topics for an essay in which comparison/contrast is the main method of development.

1. High school classes and college classes
2. Studying with a friend and studying alone
3. Advertising targeting female audiences and male audiences
4. Your best friend in childhood and your best friend now
5. Using public transportation and driving your own car
6. Our current president and any previous chief executive
7. Government student loans compared with private student loans
8. Two places where you have lived
9. Cooking dinner at home and eating out
10. Live music compared with recorded music

Using this list of topics or ideas of your own, jot down a few two-part topics that appeal to you.

_____

_____

_____

_____

From your list of two-part topics, which one will give you the best opportunity for writing? Which one is most likely to interest your readers? For which topic do you have the most firsthand experience?

Selected topic: _____

Your next step is to decide what your controlling idea should be. What is your main purpose in comparing or contrasting these two topics? Do you want to show that, although people think the two topics are similar, they actually differ in important ways? Do you want to show that one topic is better in some ways than the other? Do you want to analyze how something has changed over the years (a "then and now" essay)?

Controlling idea: _____

At this point, combine your two-part topic and controlling idea into one thesis statement.

Thesis statement: _____

_____

Gathering Information Using Brainstorming Techniques

Take at least fifteen minutes to brainstorm (using listing or clustering) as many points of comparison or contrast as you can on your chosen topic. You will probably want to think of at least three or four points. Under each point, brainstorm as many details as come to mind. For instance, if you are comparing two friends and the first point concerns the interests they have in common, recall as much as you can about the activities they share together. If you are brainstorming on a topic that other classmates or family members might know something about, ask them to help you think of additional points to compare. If special vocabulary comes to mind, jot that down as well. The more specific you are, the more helpful and interesting your comparison or contrast will be for your readers.

POINTS TO COMPARE OR CONTRAST

	Topic One _____	Topic Two _____
Point 1		
Point 2		
Point 3		
Point 4		
Point 5		

Selecting and Organizing the Material

Comparison/contrast always involves a two-part topic. For instance, you might compare the school you attend now with a school you attended in the past. We often need to make choices or judgments, and we can make better decisions if we compare or contrast the two items in front of us. Because of the two-part topic, you have a choice in organizing the essay:

1. **The block method.** With this method, write everything you have to say about one topic or idea, and then in a later paragraph or paragraphs, write entirely about the other topic. If you choose this method, when you discuss the second topic, be sure to bring up the same points and keep the same order as when you discussed the first topic.

2. **The point-by-point method.** With this method, discuss one point and show in one paragraph how both topics relate to this point. Then, in a new paragraph, discuss the second point and relate it to both topics, and so forth.

Which method will be better for the topic you have selected—the block method or the point-by-point method?

At this stage, review your brainstorming list, asking yourself if you have a complete list. Have you left out any point that might need to be considered? Do you have at least three points, and do you have enough material to develop both parts of the topic? You do not want the comparison or contrast to end up one-sided, with most of the content focused on only one part of the topic.

Depending on your choice of block method or point-by-point method, outline your topic based on one of the two formats below. The example contrasts high school classes with college classes.

Outline for Block Method

I.	**Topic 1**	**High school classes**
	A. First point (how often classes meet)	meet five days a week
	B. Second point (homework)	daily homework
	C. Third point (research papers)	seldom require research papers
	D. Fourth point (discipline)	discipline problems
II.	**Topic 2**	**College classes**
	A. First point (how often classes meet)	meet only two or three days a week
	B. Second point (homework)	long-term assignments
	C. Third point (research papers)	often require research papers
	D. Fourth point (discipline)	few discipline problems

Outline for Point-by-Point Method

I. First point	How often classes meet	
Topic 1	high school classes:	meet five days a week
Topic 2	college classes:	meet only two or three days a week

II. Second point	Homework	
Topic 1	high school classes:	have daily homework
Topic 2	college classes:	have long-term assignments

III. Third point	Research papers	
Topic 1	high school classes:	seldom require research papers
Topic 2	college classes:	often require research papers

IV. Fourth point	Discipline	
Topic 1	high school classes:	often have discipline problems
Topic 2	college classes:	seldom have discipline problems

Your Outline

_____

_____

_____

_____

_____

_____

_____

_____

_____

_____

_____

_____

_____

Writing the Rough Draft

Write your rough draft. Remember that your outline is a guide. Most writers find that additional details occur to them as they write. If you have new thoughts, you should feel free to explore them. Of course, you must then reevaluate the logic of your ideas.

As is true with other methods of developing ideas, comparison/contrast has its particular words and expressions to indicate movement from one point to the next.

TRANSITIONS COMMONLY USED IN COMPARISON/CONTRAST

TRANSITIONS FOR COMPARISON		TRANSITIONS FOR CONTRAST	
again	like	although	instead
also	likewise	and yet	nevertheless
as well as	moreover	but	on the contrary
both	the same as	despite	on the other hand
equally	similar to	different from	otherwise
furthermore	similarly	even though	still
just as	so	except for	though
just like	too	however	unlike
		in contrast with	whereas
		in spite of	while

Revising the Rough Draft

If you are able to leave your rough draft and return to it later for revision, you will view your work with greater objectivity. In the best circumstances, you might be able to set your first draft aside for a day or two before you revise.

When you revise, you may work alone, with a group, with a peer tutor, or directly with your instructor. Here are some of the basic questions you should consider during this most important stage of your work.

GUIDELINES FOR REVISING AN ESSAY DEVELOPED BY COMPARISON/CONTRAST

1. Does the rough draft satisfy the conditions for the essay form? Is there an introductory paragraph? Are there at least three well-developed paragraphs in the body of the essay? Have you written a concluding paragraph? Remember, a single sentence is not considered an acceptable paragraph in standard essay writing unless it is a piece of direct dialogue using quotation marks.

2. Does the essay compare or contrast a two-part topic and come to some conclusion about the comparison or contrast?

3. Has the essay been organized by the point-by-point method or the block method?

4. Have important points been omitted? Is any of the material irrelevant?

5. Are there repetitious sentences or paragraphs?

(continued on next page)

6. Find several places where more specific verbs, nouns, or adjectives can be substituted. Use vocabulary that is appropriate for the topic being discussed.

7. Can you think of a more effective or creative way to begin or end?

8. Does the essay flow logically from one idea to the next? Could you improve this flow with better use of transitional expressions?

9. Show your draft to at least two other readers and ask for suggestions.

Preparing the Final Copy, Printing, and Proofreading

Follow the traditional rules for an acceptable submission when you type your final version.

CHECKLIST FOR THE FINAL COPY

- Use only 8½-by-11-inch paper (never paper torn out of a spiral-bound notebook).
- Print on only one side of the paper.
- Double-space.
- Leave approximately a 1½-inch margin on each side of the paper.
- Put your name, the date, the title of your paper, and any other relevant information either on a separate title page or at the top of the first page. (Ask your instructor for specific advice on what information to include.)
- Center the title. Do not put quotation marks around the title, and do not underline it.
- Do not hyphenate a word at the end of a line unless you are willing to consult a dictionary to check on the acceptable division of the word into syllables.
- Indent each paragraph five spaces.
- If your paper is more than one page, number the pages and staple the pages together so they will not get lost.
- Do not forget to save a copy before you submit the paper.

NOTE: In most cases, college instructors will not accept handwritten work. If you are permitted to submit handwritten work, be sure your handwriting is legible. Certainly everyone today is expected to type and be familiar with current computer technology.

Once you have typed your final version and printed it, an important step still remains. Paying attention to this step can often improve your grade. You must *proofread* your paper. Even if you have used a spell-check feature available on your word-processing program, errors could remain in your paper. The spell-check feature finds only groupings of letters that are not words. For example, if you typed the word *van* when you meant to type *ban*, the spell-checker would not catch this error. The secret of good proofreading is to look at each word and sentence construction by itself without thinking about the paper's content.

TIPS FOR PROOFREADING

Study each sentence: One way to proofread is to read backward, starting with the last sentence and examining every sentence, one at a time. First, check that the sentence is really complete and is not a fragment or a run-on. Then check the punctuation. Go to the next sentence and do the same. In this way, you will develop a critical eye for spotting any problems with sentence-level errors.

Study each word: Read the paper again, this time studying each word in every sentence. Look at the letters of the word. Have you transposed any letters, or have you left off an ending such as *-ed* or *-s*? If there are any words you are not sure how to spell, check a dictionary for the correct spelling. Have you omitted any words?

WRITE FOR SUCCESS

Review your time in college so far. What were your expectations when you came to college? Compare these expectations with what you have actually experienced. Were some aspects of college life better than you expected? Have some aspects not met your expectations? Include three different areas of college life in your response.

iStockphoto.com

Contrasting Men and Women

The essay included earlier in this chapter is a humorous look by Dave Barry as he examines one of the major differences between men and women. Below is a more serious assessment of another difference between the sexes. The following paragraphs are taken from an essay by Deborah Tannen, a professor at Georgetown University and a widely published author who writes on the subject of gender. As you read the paragraphs, see if you agree with her ideas.

> For women, as for girls, intimacy is the fabric of relationships, and talk is the thread from which it is woven. Little girls create and maintain friendships by exchanging secrets; similarly, women regard conversation as the cornerstone of friendship. So a woman expects her husband to be a new and improved version of a best friend. What is important is not the individual subjects that are discussed but the sense of closeness, of a life shared, that emerges when people tell their thoughts, feelings, and impressions.
>
> Bonds between boys can be as intense as bonds between girls, but they are based less on talking, more on doing things together. Since they don't assume talk is the cement that binds a relationship, men don't know what kind of talk women want, and they don't miss it when it isn't there.

Is it true that one can predict the behavior of most women and most men? Deborah Tannen believes that when it comes to close relationships, women want conversation while men are more interested in actually doing things together. Divide into groups and discuss what you think would be the predictable way a man would act and a woman would act in each of the following situations.

    A. Meeting for a family gathering

    B. Handling a disobedient teenager

    C. Dealing with a problem in a child's school

    D. Breaking up with a girlfriend or boyfriend

    E. Being stopped by the police

    F. Getting poor service in a restaurant

1. Does your group agree that women and men are, in general, predictable in their behavior?
2. Do you think culture plays a role?
3. To what extent does education play a role?
4. Can your group think of some other areas where behavior between men and women generally differs?

PORTFOLIO SUGGESTION

Keep a list of ideas generated by the class discussion. If you are required to write an essay contrasting typical male behavior with typical female behavior, you might consider the values, actions, goals, or priorities of the sexes. Because this topic has intrigued writers from many disciplines, you would also find this a rich subject for research. It is always interesting to find out if the research you uncover changes any of your current beliefs.

Writing an Essay Using Persuasion

32

CHAPTER OBJECTIVES

In this chapter, you will build an understanding of the different elements that make up the persuasive essay.

- analyzing a basic persuasive essay

- studying a list of guidelines for writing an effective persuasive essay

- comparing and discussing two arguments with opposing viewpoints

- reviewing a list of common transitions to help achieve coherence

- writing a persuasive essay on the topic *Laptops in the Classroom*

- considering additional topics for writing persuasive essays

What Is Persuasion?

From one point of view, all writing is persuasion because the main goal of any writer is to persuade a reader to see, think, or believe in a certain way. However, a more formal definition of persuasive writing exists. Anyone who has ever been a member of a high school debate team knows the techniques that an effective speaker or writer uses to present a case successfully. Learning how to recognize these techniques of persuasion and how to use them in your own writing is the subject of this chapter.

> An essay of **persuasion** presents evidence intended to convince the reader that the writer's position is valid. Evidence can include facts, statistics, testimony, and the support of recognized authorities. The writer may appeal to logic, emotion, and worthiness.

Analysis of a Basic Persuasive Essay

Study the following persuasive essay to focus on the different elements present in an effective argument.

DON'T CALL, DON'T TEXT, JUST DRIVE!

We live in a country where our freedoms are a point of pride. However, one person's exercise of a freedom should not be allowed to endanger the safety of others. This is particularly true in the case of people who talk and text-message while they are driving a vehicle. All states should enact strict laws, accompanied

(continued on next page)

by penalties, forbidding talking or text-messaging with a handheld cell phone while operating a vehicle.

In the past twenty years or so, the use of cell phones in the United States has exploded. In 1985, we had nearly 350,000 cell phone subscribers, but by 2011, more than 327 million people had cell phones. When the National Highway Traffic Safety Administration conducted a study, they found 10 percent of all drivers admitted to using cell phones while on the road during the day. Such widespread use of cell phones while driving has had lawmakers worried. What should they do about the growing national problem of distracted drivers?

According to Peter D. Loeb, professor at Rutgers University, cell phones are contributing to numerous vehicle fatalities. For example, in 2008, five teenagers were in a head-on collision in upstate New York. At first, it was rumored that the driver must have been drinking, but it was soon determined that the driver was distracted while text-messaging. Everyone in the car was killed. In another horrendous accident, a train operator in California was text-messaging a young friend and failed to observe a red light. Twenty-five people were killed and many others were seriously injured. Although not every accident results in fatalities, this risky behavior while driving is causing needless property damage and injury. Common sense tells us that state laws are needed to discourage cell phone usage while driving.

Opponents will say that banning the use of cell phones while driving is an invasion of privacy. They ask, "Will the authorities also regulate eating a sandwich or even talking to a passenger while driving?" They claim every driver does things while driving that could be considered distracting: turning on the radio, playing a CD, or looking at a map, just to name a few. Is the state going to ban all these activities, too? These opponents believe citizens must be educated to use good judgment instead of proposing more regulations. While we could wish that people would regulate themselves, we know this is not going to happen.

(continued on next page)

Sarah M Golonka/Tetra Images/AGE Fotostock

Most drivers are already in the habit of using their cell phones while driving. They are not going to change their habits unless they are forced to pay a fine.

Other critics of regulation argue that people should be able to make and receive calls because people often find themselves in serious situations that can be solved by using a cell phone. This sounds reasonable; however, in most cases, a driver can pull over to the side of the road to make or take a call. And if a driver is in an accident, it is more likely a nearby witness, not the driver, who makes the call. We all know that the majority of calls are simply for friendly conversation, and many of the people making these calls are teenagers who do not have the maturity to recognize the implications of being distracted at the wheel.

We can all agree that any activity that causes a person to take his or her eyes off the road is a serious risk for an accident. The state has a responsibility to protect the lives of all drivers on the road. Ideally, drivers themselves should accept responsibility for the safety of their fellow citizens, but the fact is most people are now using their cell phones while driving. Perhaps we cannot regulate against shaving or putting on makeup behind the wheel, but society should do what it can to save lives and property. At present, however, not every state has enacted laws for cell phone use while driving. Now it's time for all state governments to make regulations that carry stiff fines for those who disregard the law and endanger the safety of others.

ACTIVITY **1** **Analyzing the Writer's Argument**

1. In your own words, what is the issue being argued?

   _____

2. Underline the thesis statement.

3. Mark each sentence that presents a fact.

4. What are the sources for the writer's facts?

   _____

   _____

5. In your own words, why are these facts included?

   _____

   _____

6. How many examples in the form of anecdotes are given? _____

7. According to the writer, what is the opposition's point of view?

   _____

   _____

8. What are the reasons given by the writer for the necessity of a law regulating cell phone use?

   _____

   _____

9. Does the author provide a reasonable solution to the problem? Explain.

_____

10. Can you think of any other ways to strengthen the argument?

_____

_____

Guidelines for Writing a Persuasive Essay

Following are some basic guidelines for writing an effective persuasive essay.

1. **State a clear thesis.** Use words such as *must, ought,* or *should.* Study the following three sample thesis statements:

   The United States must reform its prison system.

   All states ought to have the same legal drinking age.

   We should not ban all handguns.

2. **Give evidence or reasons for your beliefs.** Your evidence is the heart of the essay. You must show the wisdom of your logic by providing the best evidence available. Your evidence may include personal observation, facts, statistics, expert opinion, and examples. You might even appeal to common sense.

3. **Use examples.** Well-chosen examples are among the best evidence for an argument. People can identify with a specific example from real life in a way that they cannot with an abstract idea. Without examples, essays of persuasion would be flat, lifeless, and unconvincing.

4. **Use opinions from recognized authorities to support your points.** One of the oldest methods of supporting an argument is to use one or more persons of authority to support your position. People will usually believe what well-known experts claim. However, be sure that your expert is someone who is respected in the area you are discussing. For example, if you are arguing that we must address the problem of climate change, your argument will be stronger if you quote a respected scientist who has studied the serious implications of climate change. A famous movie star giving the same information might be more glamorous and get more attention, but he or she would not be as great an authority as the scientist.

5. **Be careful to avoid faulty logic.**
   a. Do not appeal to fear or pity.
      Example: Children with parents who work don't do well in school.
   b. Do not make sweeping or false generalizations.
      Example: All women belong in the kitchen.
   c. Do not oversimplify with an either-or presentation.
      Example: A woman should either stay home and take care of her children or go to work and remain childless.
   d. Do not give misleading or irrelevant support to your argument.
      Example: Don't hire that man; he has six children.

6. **Answer your critics in advance.** When you point out beforehand what your opposition is likely to say in answer to your argument, you are writing from

a position of strength. You are letting your reader know that there is another side to the argument you are making. By pointing out this other side and then answering its objections in advance, you strengthen your own position.

7. **In your conclusion, point out the results, make predictions, or suggest a solution.** Here, you help your reader see what will happen if your argument is (or is not) believed or acted upon as you think it should be. You should be very specific and rational when you point out results, making sure that you avoid exaggeration. For example, if you are arguing that the purpose of college is to make students employable, it would be an exaggeration to say, "Unless students can find jobs after college, their time spent in college will have been a total waste."

Opposing Viewpoints: Should Career Counseling Be Mandatory?

With all of the employment problems that college graduates are now facing, many believe it is time for colleges to give students more realistic information and guidance to prepare them for the marketplace. The two writers that follow present their opposing views on this issue. Study their arguments, and answer each of the questions that follow.

A Debate: Should Career Counseling Be Mandatory in the First Year of College?

YES

We Cannot Let Careers Just Take Care of Themselves

As a freshman in the 1980s, I had little career counseling at my university. My trajectory was guided by an understanding—instilled at home—that using college to develop reading, writing, and critical thinking skills meant the career would take care of itself. From a career development perspective, the world I was preparing for was not unlike the one my parents had navigated. A college degree—any degree—opened the door to a world of opportunity.

Today everything has changed. Partly a function of a tight economy, there is a growing understanding that not all college degrees are equal. According to Georgetown University's Center on Education and the Workforce, a student's choice of major substantially affects employment prospects and earnings. This is complicated by an economy in which jobs now appear, morph, or vanish at breakneck speeds.

NO

We're Too Unformed at 18 to Get Tracked to Careers

When I was 18, I was certain of one thing: that I would never, ever teach. I wanted to be in the Army infantry (I wound up in the finance corps). I wanted to be an engineer blasting a Southern Pacific freight through the High Sierra (I wound up flying airplanes around Texas). Thankfully, a passing comment—"take a sociology course"—from a chummy professor in a starched oxford and sharp-looking tie changed my view of the world. Crazy? Not at all—just the 18-year-old mind in action. I didn't know who I was. How was I to be advised on a career?

Granted, there are those with destiny stamped upon their minds at a young age. But for most of us, we're just too unformed at 18 to make a sensible decision about a career, and that's just fine. While colleges must give students the skills to earn a good income, they should not be sending everyone down a job path shaped by the

(continued on next page)

Further, we have learned through our work with industry-college partnerships that employers seek not just the right degree, but students who are academically proficient and able to apply themselves in a professional setting. This is where mandatory career counseling for freshmen begins.

Career counselors equipped with the latest labor market intelligence and strong industry contacts can provide freshmen with real-time information about jobs and their correlations to each student's education, work experience, and interests. The counselors help these new students understand the specific skills and aptitudes employers seek. They also ensure students pursue appropriate internships and industry-recognized credentials that may be folded into their programs.

Consider the "app economy." Economist Michael Mandel notes that in 2007 there were zero jobs in this sector. Today, it accounts for nearly 500,000 jobs. Legions of workers are being hired as the programmers, designers, managers, and marketers of this burgeoning enterprise. Mandatory career counseling, if done well, could enable freshmen to learn about this new career and organize their college experiences accordingly.

Almost all jobs these days are undergoing changes like never before, and all freshmen and upperclassmen will need the ongoing support of career counselors.

—Julian L. Alssid

18-year-old brain. Students need the intellectual and social dexterity that only a wide range of courses can confer.

When I speak to freshmen at our annual orientation, I tell them not to worry about a major, that majors are artificial constructs and that few ever do what they actually studied. I tell them that after their first job, no employer will ever ask their GPA or major again. I assure them that people who smile, talk, and have good manners almost always do better in life than those who don't. I remind them they will likely change careers three times, that it is better to have the skills for all than the tools for one.

No one could have told me at 18 that college teaching would give my life such pleasure. A part of that 18-year-old boy is still happily within me, but he didn't know who he was. He didn't need mandatory advice; he needed to find his own direction. He needed to explore the world—and he did.

—Albin Cofone

ACTIVITY ② **Discussion Questions for the Debate: Should Career Counseling Be Mandatory in the First Year of College?**

Following the seven elements in the Guidelines for Writing a Persuasive Essay section, discuss the effectiveness of the two arguments.

1. Is each thesis clearly stated?
2. Evaluate the evidence given by each writer. Is the evidence convincing?
3. Have both writers provided examples? Mark them in the text.
4. Does either writer support the argument by giving expert opinions from authorities?
5. Discuss the logic of each argument. Can you find any weaknesses?
6. Does either writer pay attention to the opposing point of view?
7. Does each argument conclude with some type of suggestion, prediction, or solution?

Achieving Coherence

Like other methods of developing an essay, persuasion has its own special words that signal parts of the argument. The following chart can help you find transitional expressions that will move you from one part of your argument to the next.

TRANSITIONS COMMONLY USED TO SIGNAL THE PARTS OF A PERSUASIVE ESSAY

To signal the thesis of an argument

I agree (disagree) that . . .

I support (oppose) the idea that . . .

I am in favor (not in favor) of . . .

I propose . . .

. . . must (must not) be changed

. . . should (should not) be adopted

To signal a reason

The first reason is . . .	because
An additional reason is . . .	can be shown
Another reason is . . .	for (meaning *because*)
The most convincing piece of evidence is . . .	In the first place
	in view of
	just because

To admit an opponent's point of view

Most people assume that . . .

One would think that . . .

We have been told that . . .

Popular thought is that . . .

Some may claim . . .

The opposition would have you believe . . .

To signal a conclusion

We can conclude that . . .	as a result
This proves that . . .	consequently
This shows that . . .	so
This demonstrates that . . .	therefore
This suggests that . . .	thus
This leads to the conclusion that . . .	It follows that . . .

Opposing Viewpoints: Should Laptops Be Allowed in the Classroom?

Below is an essay by Professor Thom Curtis of the University of Hawaii arguing against the use of laptops in the classroom. Read the essay carefully, and then discuss the essay with your classmates. Use the Guidelines for Writing a Persuasive Essay to analyze the argument.

No, to Laptops in the Classroom

Last fall, I was called upon to teach a large section of our introductory sociology class for the first time in years. Almost immediately, I was struck by the walls of laptop screens stretching across the risers of the lecture hall. About half of the students were busily typing away.

My assumption that the students were using their machines to take notes was shattered a couple weeks later when during a break I walked to the top of the classroom and looked across the hall from the rear. On most of the students' screens were games, chats, email, and videos. I even sat down in an empty seat in the back row next to a student playing a video game. He was oblivious to my presence until other students sitting around us began to laugh.

Later, I talked with the class about my observations. I was regaled with stories about their abilities to multitask. Interestingly, none of the computerless students spoke up during the discussion. After class was a different story. Student after student approached me to report how distracting it was to have classmates all around them "multitasking" on games, chats, and music videos. They were having similar experiences in every class they were taking, and their levels of frustration were rising because teachers didn't seem to care.

My eyes were opened that day by what I saw from the rear of the lecture hall and the stories that I heard from frustrated students. I established a row in the front of the class for students who needed or desired to use laptops for taking notes and banned computers from the rest of the lecture hall. There were a few groans from students initially, but no substantive complaints after the first day. However, there are few things that I have done in class over the years that have earned more positive comments.

—Professor Thom Curtis

ACTIVITY ❸ **Writing a Persuasive Essay to Answer the Opposition**

Now, using all you have learned about writing a persuasive essay in this chapter, compose your own essay arguing in favor of laptops in the classroom.

Yes, to Laptops in the Classroom

_____

_____

_____

_____

_____

_____

_____

_____

_____

_____

_____

_____

_____

_____

_____

_____

_____

_____

_____

_____

_____

_____

_____

_____

_____

_____

_____

_____

_____

_____

Suggested Topics for Writing a Persuasive Essay

Essay topics

Argue for or against:

1. Digital textbooks to replace print textbooks
2. Legalization of medical marijuana
3. Banning certain books from public libraries
4. Educational opportunities for prison inmates
5. An age requirement for the use of Facebook
6. Single-parent adoption
7. Raising the minimum wage
8. Offensive song lyrics
9. Required courses in college
10. Laws against cyberbullying
11. Year-round public schools
12. Laws against selling supersized sugar drinks in fast-food restaurants and delis
13. Random drug testing in the workplace
14. Public high school dress codes
15. Mandatory attendance for college classes

WRITE FOR SUCCESS

Most areas of knowledge are not self-contained; they overlap and depend on each other. For example, if you study sociology, you will eventually need to understand statistics in order to comprehend the research in that field. Likewise, the field of writing overlaps with many other disciplines. A person's ability to write effectively will have a direct influence on that person's success in other college courses and in many career choices. Write a response that argues for the importance of learning to write well. Use examples from the list below or of your own choosing.

College courses	Job categories
a science lab	a job search
a history course	social work
a business course	teaching school

Working Together

Odd Andersen/AFP/Getty Images

°**congested**
blocked up with or too full of something

°**autonomous**
acting independently or having the freedom to do so

°**demonstrably**
clearly and undeniably

°**renowned**
known or talked about by many people

°**vying (present participle of *vie*)**
to compete with others in an attempt to get or win something

°**mandate**
to give an official order to do something

°**incremental**
occurring in especially small amounts or degrees

Analyzing a Newspaper Editorial

The following editorial, which appeared in the February 10, 2016 edition of *The Washington Times*, argues that while self-driving automobiles may soon be joining human drivers on the road, there are still some issues with the technology that need to be sorted out first. Read the piece out loud. Then divide into groups and discuss the questions that follow.

Self-Driven Cars Are on the Way

1   Machines with a mind of their own are the future, and self-driving automobiles will soon be sharing the road with cars and trucks with real drivers. Labor-saving devices are always welcome, and driving on roads in the congested° communities where most Americans live is certainly a chore. But motorists should keep their hands on the steering wheel until autonomous° vehicles are proved demonstrably° safer than human-piloted versions. Smart technology isn't always smart enough.

2   California is renowned° for its pursuit of trends that the rest of the nation strains to follow, but with the new selfie-mobiles California is proceeding with uncharacteristic caution. Google, based in Silicon Valley, leads the pack of software firms and automobile manufacturers vying° for a big slice of the driverless transportation pie, and is impatiently pushing state regulators to approve its computer-driven car with no steering wheel, no accelerator and no brake pedal. It's thrilling (but still scary) be at the mercy of a machine at the amusement park, but so far, not on the open road.

3   California is one of four states that has authorized the use of self-driving cars, and is completing the rules that would mandate° that trial models contain working steering wheels and pedals, and that a licensed driver sit behind the wheel — just in case. Caution gives Google hiccups. Google says if driver error on busy roads is to be eliminated, the place to start is with human drivers, with all their flaws and frailties. "We need to be careful about the assumption that having a person behind the wheel [will make driving safer]," says Chris Urmson, leader of Google's self-driving car project.

4   Major U.S. automobile companies like an incremental° approach, too. Ford is developing a "Ford Smart Mobility" program and General Motors has commissioned an "Autonomous and Technology Vehicle Development Team." Both are intended to supervise a careful transition from human- to computer-piloted car. Some self-driving features are available now, such as automatic braking and assisted parking. Still unresolved is how a self-guided model can cope with the unexpected, such as blowing trash or a police officer waving a car to the shoulder. Some tough ethical issues

(continued on next page)

°**nefarious**
evil or immoral

°**pilfered**
repeatedly stolen things in
small amounts

must be ironed out as well, such as whether a self-driven car that senses an approaching catastrophic crash will decide to sacrifice itself rather than the other car. Passenger protection shouldn't simply be a function of price.

5   Hackers will inevitably learn how to commandeer self-driving cars for nefarious° purposes. Rogue programmers who steal information and money from government and private institutions every day might find the pickings easy in a self-driven car. Nissan has used NASA technology to guide its self-driving test cars in California, and the hacker organization AnonSec says it has pilfered° 276 gigabytes of data from NASA's computer network. The group said it had taken over a $222 million Global Hawk military drone and tried — without success, fortunately — to send it nose first it into the Pacific Ocean.

6   Self-driven vehicles are only as safe as the software that controls them, and anyone with a computer knows that the idea of software perfection is a daydream. Software failure eventually strikes every user, whether behind the wheel or in front of a keyboard. It's far too soon for a motorist in a self-driven Belchfire 8 to climb into the backseat for a snooze and let the computer drive.

Questions for Group Discussion

1. What is the thesis of the editorial?
2. What supporting evidence for the thesis is given in the editorial?
3. Were any outside sources used to support the thesis? If so, mark these in the text.
4. Does the editorial say what will happen if nothing is done about the problem?
5. Does the editorial propose any solution to the problem?
6. Does the editorial seem reasonable to you?
7. Are you persuaded by the position the editorial takes? Why or why not?

Following the group discussion, your instructor may require each student to write his or her own analysis of the editorial using the above discussion as the basis for the analysis.

PORTFOLIO SUGGESTION

For many readers, the editorial page is the best part of the newspaper. On the editorial page, writers argue, passionately at times, about issues that are of great importance to society. Go to *refdesk.com* and scroll down the page for a list of newspapers. Pick a newspaper in your state and make a habit of reading the daily editorials. Print out editorials that interest you. If you subscribe to a newspaper, clip editorials that are about subjects that interest you. Reading newspaper editorials is an effective way of developing a sense for argumentative or persuasive writing. You can learn from editorials that are outrageous in their points of view, as well as from those that are logical and convincing. Keep these editorials in your portfolio for possible writing ideas.

Other College Writing: The Research Paper and the Essay Exam

33

How to Write and Document A Research Paper

NOTE: For two examples of college research papers, see Appendix A of the *Instructor's Resource Manual*.

Writing a well-researched and fully documented term paper has been called the single most useful skill a student can acquire in college. Because such writing calls for the integration of a number of sources to support the student's thesis, it is not an easy task. These integrated skills are explained in the pages that follow.

Getting Started

Setting Up a Work Schedule

As soon as a research paper is assigned, you should begin to plan your work schedule. Often an instructor will divide a research project into its parts with a deadline for each of these parts. This helps students to better manage their time and avoid feeling overwhelmed. If your instructor does not require these deadlines, you will need to set up your own schedule and stick to the deadlines you establish. Below is a sample work schedule that you can fill in with your own deadlines.

Work Schedule for a Research Paper

Research paper due date: _____

Deadline date for each of the following tasks:

_____   Choose the topic, being sure to narrow or expand the scope of the topic as necessary. (If possible, discuss with the instructor.)

_____   Find both print and electronic sources that could be useful; make a working bibliography; formulate your working thesis.

_____   Evaluate each source; download, copy, or take notes on material that is relevant. **(If taking notes, be sure to avoid plagiarism by properly quoting, summarizing, or paraphrasing the material.)**

_____   Develop the organization or outline for the paper (this would be another good time to discuss your plan with your instructor); write a first draft that integrates your research material.

_____   Revise and edit the first draft; write the final draft.

_____   Check the in-text citations and complete the works cited page.

_____   Do a final proofreading.

Be sure to allot the bulk of your time to the writing of the first draft and the revision and writing of the final draft. It is ideal to have a day or two at least between the writing of the first draft and the revision stage.

Choosing a Topic

If you are free to choose your own subject, give some thought to what truly interests you. The best papers usually grow out of a person's genuine interest in the material. Remember, you will be investing a great deal of your time to complete this assignment, so consider a topic that will be useful to you in some way, perhaps helping your understanding of an issue that you are studying in another course or an issue that is connected to your college major or future career plans.

Make sure you have your instructor's clear approval before you proceed with your research. Bring your instructor a proposed thesis statement along with any ideas you have jotted down so that you can have a productive conversation about your topic. Be mindful that you could discover early in the research process that your topic is unsuitable. For instance, a topic might be out of your comfort zone. The sources you find could be too technical and difficult to understand. If these issues arise, go to your instructor immediately and ask for help to change your focus. If you lose too much time by not making a needed change, you could easily become discouraged and find it hard to complete the assignment.

Gathering Sources

Most instructors encourage students to consult a variety of sources. You will want to start at your college library, where you might begin by reading some general material found in reference works to help you refine your topic. Then you will want to move to more specialized sources. Remember that the reference librarian is there to help you get started. Do not hesitate to ask for help.

Print

The library online catalog will direct you to reference works, books, and periodicals that are in the library's collections.

Library Website

College and local libraries subscribe to various databases. Here the reference information has been screened, cataloged, and indexed, unlike the material you might research on the Internet. A great number of resources will also be available here that are not on the open Web. These resources will include bibliographic sources, abstracts, full texts of articles, and other published materials. This is where you will want to focus your research. Ask your reference librarian to show you not only the list of databases that your library subscribes to but also which ones would be most useful for finding information on your topic.

Examples of Subscription Databases
Examples of Broad-Based Databases

These databases, which include articles from periodicals (journals, magazines, and newspapers), will cover a wide range of fields but not necessarily cover a wide range of periodicals in these fields.

> Academic Search Premier
> FirstSearch
> Academic OneFile
> Gale PowerSearch
> JSTOR
> LexisNexis Academic Universe
> Pro Quest

Examples of Single Discipline Databases

These databases will cover a wider range of periodicals in a particular discipline.

> ERIC (Education-related subjects)
> LION (Literature)
> Sociological Abstracts
> Historical Abstracts
> Education Search Complete
> Science Direct

NOTE: Some databases provide abstracts of articles. Others, like ERIC and Academic Search Premier (articles from more than 4,500 scholarly publications) are full text databases. Your research librarian will be able to direct you to those databases that are likely to be best for finding information on your particular topic.

Other Online Searches

Of course, you can also enter the Web using a public search engine. Keep in mind the following disadvantages.

1. The information is not always reliable. You will have to be much more careful about evaluating your sources.
2. A source you find on the Web one day may not be there the next day. The Web is constantly changing. You will need to document the date you accessed the information.
3. Search engines that depend on commercial sponsorship may place many of the product information sites first. You will need to avoid these long lists of irrelevant sites by typing in specific key terms in your search requests.
4. Search engines do not index exactly the same information. You should try at least three search engines in your search for appropriate information.

Examples of Search Engines
   Google
   Bing
   Yahoo!
   Ask
   AOLSearch

Managing Information from Sources

Today, many researchers, students and faculty members alike, find it easier to download or photocopy a great deal of their source material. By photocopying the title page and publication page, much of the needed bibliographical information will be secured. The passages that are relevant can then be marked or highlighted for possible use as a quote, paraphrase, or summary. In some cases, when you are unable to copy entire articles or books, you will want to use the traditional method of keeping information on note cards (either actual 3 × 5 index cards or a system of online note cards). Because you will be synthesizing material from many sources to make your own points, rearranging the order of material is often a common part of the process. Here, note cards have one distinct advantage: material can be easily arranged and rearranged as many times as necessary according to how your paper takes form.

SAMPLE NOTE CARD

Public perception of global warming   *3. Anderegg pg. 28*

"Studies have found that much of what Americans believe about global warming depends on how hot a summer they've been having or how cold the winter."

(explain how any one particular season does not represent a trend)

Keeping a Working Bibliography

Whether you organize your notes online or on 3 × 5 index cards, you need to keep accurate information on any sources that you might use in your paper. Keeping the proper information from the very beginning will save you future frustration and lost time when you must put together your works cited page. If you have your working bibliography written on note cards, it will be easy to arrange them in alphabetical order.

Core Elements You Need to Include in Your Working Bibliography

Element 1. Author (followed by a period)

- If there are more than two authors, use only the first author listed followed by a comma, and *et al.*
- For online sources, handles (@persiankiwi) and pseudonyms are acceptable.

Element 2. Title of Source (followed by a period)

- If the title is a full-length work (like a book), write it in italics. If it is a shorter piece of a work (such as an essay, article, or short story), use quotation marks.

Element 3. Title of Container (followed by a comma)

- In some cases, there are containers within containers. A database like Infotrac is a container for journals, which are themselves containers for articles.

Element 4. Other Contributors (followed by a comma)

- When present, spell out descriptors for roles: edited by, translated by, etc.

Element 5. Version (followed by a comma)

- Often left blank, this element includes edition, version, etc.

Element 6. Number (followed by a comma)

- Includes a scholarly journal's volume number, or season and episode number for TV episodes.

Element 7. Publisher (followed by a comma)

- For print books, new MLA guidelines recommend removing city names.

Element 8. Publication Date (followed by a comma)

- Dates for all resources should follow the same format.
- Include the time if it is available (relevant for tweets and online sources).

Element 9. Location (followed by a period)

- For print sources, use *p.* for a single page or *pp.* for multiple pages.
- For online sources, use the full URL unless a DOI (digital object identifier) is available.

Understanding Plagiarism

Paying careful attention when taking notes will help you avoid the problem of unintentional *plagiarism*. Whenever exact words, ideas, facts, or opinions from the works of other writers are used in a research paper and the sources are not specifically identified, the writer of the research paper is guilty of inappropriate use, known as *plagiarism*. When you are researching and writing reports and term papers, you must always be aware of the dangers of plagiarism. As long as you quote sources correctly and cite your sources properly, the integrity of your own work will be assured.

Plagiarism is the use of another person's work without acknowledging the source.

Most plagiarism is unintentional. Unintentional plagiarism is most often the result of carelessness during the research stage. The student's notes fail to report the exact source of the information used, or those notes do not indicate whether the words or sentences have been copied word for word, are paraphrased, or are summarized. Not keeping accurate notes at the research stage can lead to serious (and avoidable) problems at the writing stage. Careful note-taking is one of the keys to conducting successful research.

Some plagiarism is deliberate. This happens when a writer copies another person's work and presents it as his or her own, with no intention of acknowledging the real source. The public is rightly shocked when such dishonesty is exposed. Over the years, a number of news reports have revealed people in important positions who have plagiarized. At the university level, plagiarism is considered a very serious academic offense, one that often results in receiving a failing grade for a course and, in some cases, expulsion from a school.

For those students who are tempted to deliberately plagiarize an assignment, not because they are lazy or unwilling to do the work, but because they feel inadequate to the task, we would encourage going to their instructors from the start and asking for special help. Most colleges have writing labs that can lead students through the process of writing research papers.

Integrating Sources into the Research Paper

The following paragraphs appear in the book *Fatherless America: Confronting Our Most Urgent Social Problem,* by David Blankenhorn. A student doing research on the topic of fatherless children in America might come across this information and wish to use it in a research paper. The paragraphs from Blankenhorn's book will be used to demonstrate how this student can incorporate this source into a research paper.

> The United States is becoming an increasingly fatherless society. A generation ago, a child could reasonably expect to grow up with his or her father. Today, a child can reasonably expect not to. Fatherlessness is approaching a rough parity with fatherhood as a defining feature of childhood.
>
> This astonishing fact is reflected in many statistics, but here are the two most important: Tonight, about 40 percent of U.S. children will go to sleep in homes in which their fathers do not live. More than half of our children are likely to spend a significant portion of childhood living apart from their fathers. Never before in this country have so many children been voluntarily abandoned by their fathers. Never before have so many children grown up without knowing what it means to have a father.
>
> Fatherlessness is the most harmful demographic° trend of this generation. It is the leading cause of the decline in the well-being of children. It is also the engine driving our most urgent social problems, from crime to adolescent pregnancy to domestic violence. Yet, despite its scale and social consequences, fatherlessness is frequently ignored or denied.

°demographic
characteristic of a certain population

Avoiding Plagiarism: Using Direct and Indirect Quotation

A large part of writing a research paper is knowing how to incorporate the ideas of others into your text. This involves using a combination of carefully chosen direct and indirect quotations that will appear throughout the research paper. These quotations will lend authority to the points you are making. You must be selective, however, in using quotations. Students are sometimes tempted to include too many quotations or use quotations that are too long. Another common problem is the use of quotations that are not justified in the context of the material being presented. Unless every part of the quotation relates directly to the content of your paper, the quotation will seem out of place. Also, don't assume that your reader will see the relevance of a quotation. Always frame the quotation so that your readers will understand how the quotation relates to the point you are making.

> **Direct quotation** reproduces the exact words of another writer, using quotation marks.

The example below shows how a student could incorporate a *direct quotation* from the second paragraph of the Blankenhorn excerpt into a research paper.

> **According to David Blankenhorn, "tonight, about 40 percent of U.S. children will go to sleep in homes in which their fathers do not live."**

> **Indirect quotation** uses one's own words to report what another person has spoken or written.

The example below shows how the direct quotation above can be changed into an *indirect quotation*. Notice that the information is the same, but in the case of the indirect quotation, the writer uses his or her own words to express the ideas. No quotation marks are used.

> **David Blankenhorn claims that approximately 40 percent of American children live without fathers in their homes.**

Note: If a direct quotation is four or more lines long, it is usually set off by indenting the quotation and not using quotation marks.

TERMS USED TO INTRODUCE A QUOTE	
The author **claims**	As the author **says**
The author **states**	As the author **points out**
The author **explains**	As the author **reports**
According to the author	As the author **notes**
The author **adds**	

Avoiding Plagiarism: Paraphrasing

A second method of using the words or ideas of another writer is called *paraphrasing*. Use paraphrasing when you want to retain all the information a source offers, from a paragraph to a full page of material. When you paraphrase, you are required to pay close attention to your source because you must restate every idea contained in that source. Your paraphrase will be almost the same length as the original material. When you paraphrase, you cannot leave out any part of the original piece of writing, nor can you add any ideas of your own as you incorporate the material into your research paper. Paraphrasing demands a great deal of skill because a writer has to have extensive control of language to be able to restate ideas using different words and different sentence structures.

> **Paraphrasing** uses one's own words to restate every idea of a passage from another's work and results in a new passage that is almost the same length as the original.

Here is how the first paragraph in the original text by David Blankenhorn might have been incorporated into a research paper using *paraphrasing*.

> **As David Blankenhorn observes, our country is turning into a society without fathers. Twenty-five years ago, children could look forward to being raised by their fathers, but that is no longer true. We are reaching the point when childhood is just as accurately described as growing up without a father as growing up with a father.**

Note that the paraphrase has fifty-six words and the original has only forty-seven words. It is difficult to be as succinct as an experienced writer. Your own paraphrases may well be slightly longer than the originals.

Avoiding Plagiarism: Summarizing

A final method of incorporating the ideas of another writer into your research paper is *summarizing*. A summary includes only the main ideas of a published source; it is therefore a reduced version of the original. To write a summary, you will probably need to review the original material more than once to separate the main ideas from the details and specific examples. Although a summary should be significantly shorter than the text you are working from, you must not leave out any of that text's main ideas. Also, you may not add any ideas of your own. Writing successful summaries is a skill that is often used by writers as they research material for their own work. Extracting the main ideas from the works of others is at the heart of education itself.

> **Summarizing** uses one's own words to provide a condensed restatement of the main ideas of another person's work.

Below is a writer's *summary* of the first paragraph of the David Blankenhorn excerpt. Compare it with the paraphrase of the same material given in the Integrating Sources into the Research Paper section.

> **Unlike American children of a generation ago, today's children are as likely to grow up without a father as with one, which David Blankenhorn points out in his book on the matter.**

PRACTICE 1   **Using Note-Taking Techniques**

The third paragraph from the David Blankenhorn excerpt is reproduced below.

> Fatherlessness is the most harmful demographic trend of this generation. It is the leading cause of the decline in the well-being of children. It is also the engine driving our most urgent social problems, from crime to adolescent pregnancy to domestic violence. Yet, despite its scale and social consequences, fatherlessness is frequently ignored or denied.

Demonstrate your skill with note-taking techniques by using material from the paragraph to write direct and indirect quotations, a paraphrase, and a summary.

1. Show how you could incorporate a *direct quotation* of the first sentence into a research paper.

   _____

   _____

2. Show how you could incorporate an *indirect quotation* of the first sentence into a research paper.

   _____

   _____

Notice that certain key words from the original version will have to be retained.

3. Write a *paraphrase* of the paragraph.

   _____

   _____

   _____

   _____

   _____

   _____

4. Write a *summary* of the paragraph.

   _____

   _____

   _____

   _____

Documenting Sources Using MLA Guidelines

Whether you use direct quotation, indirect quotation, paraphrase, or summary, you must acknowledge your sources in a consistent format. This format can vary, depending on the style your instructor wants you to use. The most commonly accepted authorities are the Modern Language Association (MLA style) and the American Psychological Association (APA style). MLA style is often used in the humanities, and APA style is recommended for use in scientific writing. Because so many different combinations of sources and authorship are possible, you will need some guidelines for the style your instructor requires so that you can prepare the documentation properly.

In-Text Citations: Documentation within the Body of the Paper

Documentation is required in two places. The first place is in the body of the paper itself, directly after a quotation or use of a source. In-text citations are brief (usually the last name of the author followed by a page reference in parentheses), providing just enough information so that the reader can find the full documentation at the end of the paper.

Works Cited Page: Documentation at the End of the Paper

Full documentation must be provided at the end of the paper, on a page usually titled "Works Cited." In the past, the MLA style had specific directions for citing a source depending on its medium (such as how to cite a book, print article, or Website). The eighth edition of the MLA style guide has simplified its citation process into nine parts that are shared across most mediums. Note that most elements are separated by commas. Elements 1 and 2 have a period after them, and element 9 is followed by a period. If a work is being cited but one or more of the following elements do not apply, leave them blank.

The goal of responsible documentation is to create a works cited list that is **useful to readers** and makes the best "correct" choice when there is more than one "correct" way to document a source.

Keep these additional rules in mind:

1. Citations are given in alphabetical order, according to the author's last name.
2. Titles follow the standard rules. Titles of full-length works such as books are italicized or underlined, and titles of shorter works such as chapters, essays, short stories, and articles are placed within quotation marks.
3. If the citation takes more than one line, additional lines are indented five spaces.

Sample Entries for a Works Cited Page in MLA Style

Below are the simplified elements and examples for citation in the revised MLA style:

ELEMENT 1: Author

Write the name of the author followed by a period. If there are more than two authors, the revised MLA style now suggests that only the first author be listed followed by a comma, and then *et al.* (which means "and others").

Example:
```
Judt, Tony.                          (one author)
Pratchett, Terry, and Neil Gaiman.   (two authors)
Gerraro, Gary, et al.                (more than two authors)
```

If the author is an online handle or pseudonym, these can be used as the author name.

Example: @donnadear.

ELEMENT 2:
Source Title

This is the title of the work that you are drawing the information from. If the title is a full-length work (like a book), write it in italics or underline it. If it is a shorter piece of work (such as an essay, article, or short story), place it in quotation marks. This is also followed by a period.

Example: Judt, Tony. *Postwar.*
Davis, Lydia. "Marie Curie, So Honorable Woman."

ELEMENT 3:
Container Title

Many times we find titled pieces contained within another source. For instance, a student might quote from a specific section in book, or from a titled essay that was printed in a magazine. To properly cite the source, the student would include the title of the specific section or essay in the title element. Then the student would include the container title next, which would be the title of the book, magazine, or host site that it was found in. The container title is likely to be in italics. (Note that sites like *YouTube* and *Twitter* would be considered container titles.)

Example: Davis, Lydia. "Marie Curie, So Honorable Woman." *Samuel Johnson Is Indignant: Stories.*

Slaughter, Anne-Marie. "Why Women Still Can't Have It All." *The Atlantic.*

Ridgewell, Thomas. "How to YouTube." *YouTube.*

ELEMENT 4: Other
Contributors

After listing the author, title, and container, there might be a need to reference other contributors to the work, such as translators or editors. In the past, the MLA style abbreviated the description of the contributor's role. The current MLA style dictates that the role should now be spelled out.

Example: Kafka, Franz. *The Metamorphosis.* Translated by Stanley Corngold.

Abrams, M. H. *The Norton Anthology of English Literature.* Edited by Stephen Greenblatt et al.

ELEMENT 5:
Version

This is only relevant if quoting from a source that has different versions or editions. (However, if titles like "expanded edition" or "unabridged version" are not found, this element should be left empty on the works cited page.)

Example: Abrams, M. H. *The Norton Anthology of English Literature.* Edited by Stephen Greenblatt et al., 9th ed.

ELEMENT 6:
Number

If the source is part of a series of publications, the number of the series, volume, or issue should be noted. The MLA has revised the design in this element. Formerly, abbreviations like "vol." (volume) and "no." (number) were left out. The MLA now has these included in citation.

Example: O'Neill, Peggy, et al. "Creating the Framework for Success in Postsecondary Writing." *College English,* vol. 74, no. 6.

ELEMENT 7:
Publisher

Next to be listed is the publisher. MLA style now recommends removing the city from the publisher element as publishing companies are likely to have offices in multiple locations. For online sources, the publisher element may be omitted for some of the following reasons: the site is also a periodical, the site's name is the same as the publisher, or if the site is not actually involved in the production of the work (this would include sites like *YouTube*, which does not actually assist in creating the works it contains.)

Example: Ferraro, Gary, et al. *Cultural Anthropology: An Applied Perspective.* 10th ed., Cengage Learning.

NOTE: If there are actually two separate publishers working together, separate the names of the publishers with a forward slash.

ELEMENT 8:
Publication Date

Include the date of the source referenced. If a book has been republished, include the most current date unless the original publication date is applicable to the information being cited.

Example: O'Neill, Peggy, et al. "Creating the Framework for
Success in Postsecondary Writing." *College English*,
vol. 74, no. 6, 2012.

ELEMENT 9:
Location

When referencing a print source, include the page number. The revised MLA format now recommends using the abbreviation *p.* (page) or *pp.* (pages) when referring to page numbers. Note that the publisher, date, and pages are all separated by commas, not periods.

Example: Blankenhorn, David. "Fatherless Society." *Fatherless
America: Confronting Our Most Urgent Social Problem*,
Harper Collins, 1995, pp. 25-48.

If it is an online source being quoted, the direct URL should now be listed in place of the page number. The URL should come after the publication date (as would a page number for a book). The URL should be closed with a period and should not have angle brackets. It also does not need "http(s)://". However, if "www" is part of the address, it should be included.

Example: Forsyth, Mark. "10 Old English Words You Need to
Be Using." *Mental Floss*, 2015, mentalfloss.com
/article/53027/10-old-english-words-you-need-be-using.

Some articles are identified with a serial code called a DOI (Digital Object Identifier) that is used to identify specific electronic documents. If available, DOIs are preferred over URLs because, unlike URLs, DOIs do not change.

Below are additional samples of citations for miscellaneous materials (print or online).

These materials might include speeches, lectures, letters, interviews, radio programs, studies, reports, advertisements, pamphlets, charts, graphs, diagrams, conference presentations, music, works of art, and government documents.

Government document

United States Dept. of Agriculture. *How Many Calories Does
Physical Activity Use?* June 2011, www.choosemyplate.gov/
physical-activity-calories-burn.

A television or radio program

Salisbury, Mark. "Studying Abroad: Is It Really Worth It?" *Talk of the
Nation*, National Public Radio, WNYC, 9 Aug. 2012.

Work of art

Matisse, Henri. *Asia*. 1946, Oil on canvas, Kimbell Art Museum, Fort
Worth.

Music

Beethoven, Ludwig van. *Symphony no. 6 in F Major "Pastoral."* Berlin
Philharmonic Orchestra, conducted by Herbert von Karajan,
Deutsche Grammophon, 1977.

Should you need further information about documentation, a very good source is *The MLA Handbook for Writers of Research Papers* (eighth edition), published by the Modern Language Association of America (2016).

How to Take an Essay Exam: Writing Well under Pressure

The first rule for doing well on any test is to come to the test well rested and well prepared. Research has shown that reviewing notes and reading assignments systematically throughout the semester is much more effective than cramming for a test the night before. You'll be greatly rewarded if you learn to use your time efficiently and wisely.

Coming to the Exam Well Prepared

1. **Study the textbook chapters and your notes.** In your textbook, review headings and words in bold type, as well as information you have highlighted or underlined. Look for chapter reviews and summaries at the ends of chapters. If you have already made an outline, study that, too.

2. **Avoid having to face any surprises when the exam is distributed.** When the test is first announced in class, ask whether it will include material from the textbook in addition to material covered in class. Also, find out the format of the test: how many essay questions will there be and how many points will each question be worth? Ask how much time you will have to complete the test

3. **Form a study group if you can.** One way a study group can work is as follows: group members meet to draw up the major questions they believe are likely to be on the test. Each person is then assigned one of the questions. He or she is responsible for preparing all the information needed for answering one of those questions and presenting it to the group at their next meeting. The other students take notes and add whatever additional information they can. Members of the group can also quiz each other on the information that is to be covered by the exam.

4. **Prepare a study outline with or without a group.** If you are unable to be part of a study group, you should still try to predict what questions will be on the exam. Prepare an outline for study and then memorize your outline.

Remember that an essay test, unlike a multiple-choice test, requires more than simply recognizing information. In an essay exam, you must be able to recall ideas and specific details, and present them quickly in your own words. Thus, for an essay exam, some material needs to be memorized. Memorizing both concepts and factual information is quite a demanding task.

Analyzing a Prompt to Form a Strategy

The smart test taker does not begin to answer the first question immediately. Instead, he or she takes a few moments to look over the test and form a strategy for tackling it. The following pointers will help you become "test smart."

1. **When you receive the exam, read over each essay question twice.** How many points is each question worth? A well-written test will give you this information. How you budget your time should depend heavily on the weight of each question. If one essay question is worth fifty points, for example, you should

spend approximately half your time planning and answering that question. However, if the test consists of ten short essay questions and you have a class period of one hundred minutes, you should spend no more than ten minutes on each question and keep a careful watch on your time. Students often write too much for the first four or five questions and then panic because they have very little time left to answer the final questions.

2. **When you read an essay question, ask yourself what method of development is being asked for.** We all know stories of people who failed tests because they misunderstood the question. For example, if an exam question asks you to *compare* **or** *contrast*, you are being given a choice. If you are asked to *compare* **and** *contrast*, you are expected to do both.

3. **Use key words from the test question itself to compose your thesis statement.** In a test, the thesis statement should be the first sentence. Don't try to be too clever on a test. State your points as directly and clearly as possible.

4. **Answer the question by stating your basic point and then including as many specific details as you have time or knowledge to give.** The more specific names, dates, and places (all spelled correctly) you can provide, the more points will be added to your grade.

5. **If a question has more than one part, be sure you answer all the parts.** Check the question to be sure your answer covers all the parts.

Study the following question to determine exactly what is being asked for:

What were the social changes that contributed to the rise of the feminist movement in the 1960s in the United States? Be specific.

If the question were one of ten short essay questions on a ninety-minute final examination, the following answer would probably be adequate:

> The feminist movement grew out of many social changes happening in the 1960s in the United States. In 1961, the President's Commission on the Status of Women documented discrimination against women in the workforce. The result of the Commission's report was a growing public awareness, which soon led to the enactment of two pieces of legislation: the Equal Pay Act of 1963 and the Civil Rights Act of 1964. In addition, the development of the birth-control pill brought the discussion of sexuality out into the open. It also lowered the birthrate, leaving more women looking to the world of work. A high divorce rate, as well as delayed marriages, further contributed to more women being concerned with feminist issues. Finally, in 1966 the National Organization for Women was formed. It encouraged women to share their experiences with each other and to organize in an effort to lobby for legislative change.

Notice that the first sentence uses the key words from the question to state the thesis. The answer gives not one but four examples of the changes that were taking place in the 1960s. These examples are very specific, naming a report, legislation, and an organization, and giving dates whenever significant. Also, the examples are given in chronological order. Can you spot the transitional expressions the writer used to signal the movement from one example to the next?

Recognizing Frequently Used Terms

Sometimes terms in the question indicate which method of development the instructor is looking for in your answer.

Definition or analysis: A definition should give the precise meaning of a word or term. When you define something in an essay, you usually write an *extended definition* or an *extended analysis*, in which you explain the significance of the term in the context of your work.

Comparison/contrast: When you *compare* two people or things, you focus on the similarities between them. When you *contrast* two items, you point out the differences. Often you may find yourself using both comparison and contrast in an essay.

Narration: Narration is the telling of a story through the careful use of a sequence of events. The events are usually (but not always) presented in chronological order.

Summary: When you write a summary, you supply the main ideas of a longer piece of writing.

Discussion: The general term *discuss* is meant to encourage you to analyze a subject at length. Inviting students to discuss some aspect of a topic is a widely used method of constructing examination questions.

Classification: When you *classify* items of any kind, you place them into separate groups so that large amounts of material can be understood more easily.

Cause and effect: When you deal with causes, you answer the question *why*; when you deal with effects, you show *results* or *consequences*.

Process analysis: You are using process analysis when you give a step-by-step explanation of how something works or how something is (or was) done.

EXERCISE ① **Methods of Development**

All of the following college essay questions deal with the topic of computers. Use the previous list of terms to decide which method of development is being called for in each case.

1. Trace the development of the computer, beginning in 1937. Be sure to include all significant developments discussed in class.

   Method of development: _____

2. Choose two of the word-processing programs practiced in class and discuss the similarities and differences you encountered. In your opinion, what were the advantages and disadvantages of each?

   Method of development: _____

3. Explain the meaning of each of the following terms: *hard disk, memory, directory, menu,* and *software.*

   Method of development: _____

4. We have discussed many of the common business applications for the computer. Select ten applications and group them according to the functions they perform.

   Method of development: _____

5. Discuss the problems that have occurred in the typical office as a result of computer technology.

   Method of development: _____

EXERCISE ②   Methods of Development/Parts of a Question

Each of the following is an example of an essay question that could be asked in a college course. In the spaces provided after each question, indicate (a) which method of development (definition, comparison/contrast, narration, summary, discussion, classification, cause and effect, or process analysis) is indicated; and (b) how many parts there are to the question and what the parts consist of. This dictates how many parts will be in your answer.

1. What does the term *sociology* mean? Include in your answer at least four different meanings the term *sociology* has had since this area of study began.

   Method of development: _____

   The different parts of the question: _____

   _____

2. Compare and contrast the reasons the United States entered the Korean War with the reasons it entered the Vietnam War.

   Method of development: _____

   The different parts of the question: _____

   _____

3. Trace the history of our knowledge of the planet Jupiter from the time it was first discovered until the present day. Include in your answer at least one nineteenth-century discovery and three of the most recent discoveries that have been made about Jupiter through the use of unmanned space vehicles sent near that planet.

   Method of development: _____

   The different parts of the question: _____

   _____

4. In view of the dramatic increase in cases of contagious diseases, describe the types of precautions now required for medical personnel. What changes are likely to be required in the future?

   Method of development: _____

The different parts of the question: _____

_____

5. Explain the three effects of high temperatures on space vehicles as they reenter the earth's atmosphere.

   Method of development: _____

   The different parts of the question: _____

   _____

6. What was the complete process of restoring the Statue of Liberty to its original condition? Include in your answer six different aspects of the restoration, from the rebuilding of the inside supports to the treatment of the metal surface.

   Method of development: _____

   The different parts of the question: _____

   _____

7. Trace the history of the English language from its beginning to the present day. Divide the history of the language into at least three different parts, using Old English, Middle English, and Modern English as your main divisions.

   Method of development: _____

   The different parts of the question: _____

   _____

8. Discuss the events that led to World War II. Be sure to include the political and social problems of the time that directly and indirectly led to the war.

   Method of development: _____

   The different parts of the question: _____

   _____

9. Summarize the four theories that have been proposed as to why dinosaurs became extinct 65 million years ago.

   Method of development: _____

   The different parts of the question: _____

10. Define the term *monarchy* and discuss the relevance or irrelevance of this form of government in today's world.

    Method of development: _____

    The different parts of the question: _____

    _____

Composing a Thesis Statement

One of the most effective ways to begin an essay answer is to write a thesis statement. Your thesis statement should include the important parts of the question and should give a clear indication of the approach you intend to take as you construct your answer. By writing your opening sentence in this way, you give yourself a real advantage: as your professor begins to read your work, it will be clear what you are going to write about and how you intend to answer the question.

For example, suppose you decided to write a persuasive essay on the following issue:

> **Agree or disagree that doctors should be allowed to use germ-line gene therapy to alter a woman's egg, a man's sperm, or an embryo just a few days old to eliminate inherited diseases.**

An effective way to begin your essay would be the following thesis sentence:

> **A strong argument exists to support the view that doctors should be allowed to use germ-line therapy to alter the egg, the sperm, or the embryo if the purpose is to eliminate an inherited disease.**

The instructor would know that you clearly understand the test question and that you also have a plan for constructing the answer.

EXERCISE ❸   **Writing Thesis Statements**

Rewrite each of the following essay questions in thesis statement form. Read each question carefully and underline the word or phrase that indicates the method of development called for. An example has been done for you.

Essay question:	**How** does one learn another language?
Thesis statement:	**The process of learning another language is complicated but usually follows four distinct stages.**

1. Essay question: Discuss Thorstein Veblen's theory of the leisure class.

   Thesis statement: _____

   _____

2. Essay question: What are the effects of television violence on children?

   Thesis statement: _____

   _____

3. Essay question: Trace the development of portrait painting from the Middle Ages to today.

   Thesis statement: _____

   _____

4. Essay question: What are the major causes of the economic crisis facing African nations today?

   Thesis statement: _____

   _____

5. Essay question: What have been the most significant results of space exploration since the first moon landing?

   Thesis statement: _____

   _____

6. Essay question: What are the problems when a couple adopts a child from one culture and raises that child in another culture?

   Thesis statement: _____

   _____

7. Essay question: In what ways does the new Japan differ from the old Japan?

   Thesis statement: _____

   _____

8. Essay question: What four countries depend on tourism for the major part of their national income, and why is this so?

   Thesis statement: _____

   _____

   _____

9. Essay question: What factors should a college use when judging the merits of a particular student for admission?

   Thesis statement: _____

   _____

   _____

10. Essay question: Discuss the generally accepted definition of Alzheimer's disease, its sequence of characteristic symptoms, and the current methods of treatment.

    Thesis statement: _____

    _____

    _____

WRITE FOR SUCCESS

Many observers claim that basic honesty among the general public has declined since the 1950s when most people still left their homes unlocked. What examples of dishonesty and cheating have you observed? Write an argument addressed to your classmates describing the widespread lack of honesty and why it matters that they not cheat, plagiarize, or be otherwise dishonest in representing their work while in college or later in their chosen careers.

Working Together

Incorporating Sources: Using Direct and Indirect Quotation, Paraphrasing, and Summarizing

Many Americans believe the number of drunk drivers in the United States is a national disgrace. The following paragraph cites statistics given by the National Transportation Safety Board in a recent report:

> The National Transportation Safety Board (NTSB) has long been concerned about alcohol-impaired driving, which accounts for approximately one-third of all U.S. highway fatalities. In the past several decades, awareness of the dangers of alcohol-impaired driving has increased. Public and private entities focusing on this safety issue have changed social perceptions concerning alcohol-impaired driving; they have also achieved important legislative actions to help reduce it. Due to these efforts, the number of lives lost annually in alcohol-impaired-driver-related crashes declined 53 percent, from 21,113 in 1982 to 9,878 in 2011; and the percentage of highway fatalities resulting from alcohol-involved crashes is down from 48 percent in 1982 to about 31 percent today.

Working in Groups

You should answer each question on your own. Then, in a group with some of your classmates, discuss the answers and agree on a single response for each question. Your instructor may expect the results to be submitted at the end of the class session.

1. Write a sentence of your own in which you give a *direct quote* from the third sentence of the excerpt above.

    _____

    _____

    _____

2. Write a sentence of your own in which you give an *indirect quote* from the third sentence of the excerpt above.

    _____

    _____

    _____

    _____

3. Write a *summary* of the paragraph. Remember that when you do this, you will be reducing the paragraph to one or two sentences that focus on the main ideas.

_____

_____

_____

_____

4. Write a *paraphrase* of the last sentence.

_____

_____

_____

_____

PORTFOLIO SUGGESTION

-   Be careful to save all the copies of the articles and other materials you have used to write your research paper. You could be asked to refer to your sources again to make changes, or you might expand on your topic in the future.

-   Study your own research papers to see if you are overusing quotations because you lack the confidence to write your own paraphrases and summaries of the source material. It is true that if you do not understand the source material, you will find it impossible to write a paraphrase or a summary.

PART 6

Summarizing Short Texts Across the Disciplines

Meet the Challenge of Academic Work

Many skills are learned more easily by watching and working with an expert. If you learn to cook from your mother and father or from a master chef, you will probably be way ahead of someone who must learn to cook only from a book of recipes. College will be a combination of teachers and books. You will need to learn from both. Most academic work brings with it the challenge of reading large amounts of assigned material. With practice and with the help of your instructors, you can improve your reading and writing skills.

- When you are faced with a challenge, how do you generally respond?
- How can you use those same skills to meet the challenge of academic work?
- How can you put a plan in place to tackle, comprehend, and in some cases summarize your future reading assignments?

Why Does Academic Work Demand the Ability to Summarize?

It has often been said that unless you are able to put in your own words the ideas from a textbook or a lecture, you do not really understand those ideas. This ability to restate main ideas is one of the most important characteristics of the successful college student. When you listen to a lecture, you should not try to take down every word you hear. Instead, you need to recognize crucial concepts and take notes on the main ideas. When reading textbook material or an article, it is important to focus on understanding the main ideas. Finally, the writing of a research paper demands the ability to summarize source material. While it is true that research papers usually include a few carefully chosen direct quotations from printed and online sources, the greater part of the research paper must be written in your own words. Students are sometimes accused of plagiarism because they are not confident enough to transform the ideas from the original sources into their own words.

Because recognizing main ideas is such an integral aspect of college work, many schools are requiring students to demonstrate their ability to summarize a piece of writing. In many cases, final exams are now including written passages that must be summarized. For these reasons, Part 6 will first help you understand the skill of summarizing by using a model passage for study and practice. Then ten short passages, taken from a variety of disciplines, provide additional opportunity for practice. For each of these ten passages, you will need both to understand any challenging vocabulary and to recognize the difference between main ideas and supporting details. Finally, you must be able to restate these main ideas in your own words.

Working with a Model Selection

The following selection is taken from David Blankenhorn's book *Fatherless America: Confronting Our Most Urgent Social Problem.* The activities that accompany this selection will help you practice writing a summary. Begin by reading the passage and marking any words you do not know.

1   Like motherhood, fatherhood is made up of both a biological and a social dimension. Yet, across the world, mothers are far more successful than fathers at fusing° these dimensions into a coherent identity. Is the nursing mother playing a biological or a social role? Feeding or bonding? We can hardly separate the two, so seamlessly are they woven together. But fatherhood is a different matter. A father makes his sole biological contribution at the moment of conception, nine months before the infant enters the world. Because social paternity is linked only indirectly to biological paternity, a connection cannot be assumed. The phrase "to father a child" usually refers only to the act of insemination, not the responsibility for raising the child. What fathers contribute after conception is largely a matter of cultural devising.

°**fusing**

2   Moreover, despite their other virtues, men are not ideally suited to responsible fatherhood. Men are inclined to sexual promiscuity and paternal waywardness°. Anthropologically, fatherhood constitutes what might be termed a necessary problem. It is necessary because a child's well-being and societal success hinge largely on a high level of paternal investment: men's willingness to devote energy and resources to the care of their offspring. It is a problem because men frequently are unwilling or unable to make that vital investment.

°**waywardness**

3   Because fatherhood is universally problematic, cultures must mobilize to enforce the father role, guiding men with legal and extralegal pressures that require them to maintain a close alliance with their children's mother and invest in their children. Because men don't volunteer for fatherhood as much as they are conscripted into it by the surrounding culture, only an authoritative cultural commitment to fatherhood can fuse biological and social paternity into a coherent male identity. For exactly this reason, anthropologist Margaret Mead and others have observed that the supreme test of any civilization is whether it can socialize men by teaching them to nurture their offspring.

Understanding Vocabulary

To summarize a passage, it is first essential that you understand the ideas in the text. This means spending some time to make sure you understand all of the vocabulary words in the passage. The following basic techniques provide an overview to help you interact with and ultimately understand what you are reading. You will find even more detailed approaches in the "Strategies for the Active Reader" section of Part 7.

In some cases, the *context* of a word will lead you to its meaning; that is, by looking at the words and phrases that come before and/or after the word, you will be able very nearly to guess its meaning. At other times, you will have to consult a dictionary. The Blankenhorn selection contains several words that might prove challenging.

Understanding the meaning of words from context:

1   **We can hardly separate the two, so seamlessly are they woven together. (line 5)**

If two things are woven together so you cannot see where or how they were joined, we can guess that the word *seamlessly* (literally, *without any seam*) must mean something close to *perfectly*. If this is the word you choose, try reading the sentence putting in your synonym. (This could be a word or a phrase.)

2   **A father makes his sole biological contribution at the moment of conception, nine months before the infant enters the world. (line 7)**

We understand that *conception* means that moment when the sperm and egg unite. This is because the phrase that follows tells us the meaning: "nine months before the infant enters the world"; that is, when the child was conceived. For more coverage of context clues, see "Building Your Vocabulary" in Part 7.

Understanding the meaning of words by studying dictionary entries:

1   **. . . [M]others are far more successful than fathers at fusing these dimensions . . . (line 3)**

fuse (fyoo—z) v. fused, fusing, fuses. —tr. **1.** To liquefy or reduce to a plastic state by heating; melt. **2.** To mix (constituent elements) together by or as if by melting; blend. —intr. **1.** To become liquefied from heat. **2.** To become mixed or united by or as if by melting together. *"There was no separation between joy and sorrow; They fused into one."* (Henry Miller) See synonyms at **melt, mix.** —**fuse** n. a safety device that protects an electric circuit from excessive current, consisting of or containing a metal that melts when current exceeds a specific amperage, thereby opening the circuit.

Dictionary meaning that fits the context: blending or mixing

> **2 Men are inclined to sexual promiscuity and paternal waywardness. (line 14)**

way ward (wa 'ward) adj. **1.** given to or marked by willful, often perverse deviation from what is desired, expected, or required in order to gratify one's own impulses or inclinations. See Synonyms at **contrary, unruly. 2.** Swayed or prompted by caprice; unpredictable. [Middle English, short for *awaiward,* turned away, perverse]—**way 'wardly** adv.—**way 'wardness** n.

Dictionary meaning that fits the context: wildness

ACTIVITY **1** **Finding the Meaning of a Word**

Supply the meaning of the following words taken from the Blankenhorn selection:

Understanding the meaning of words from context:

> ... [A] child's well-being and societal success **hinge** largely on a high level of paternal investment: men's willingness to devote energy and resources to the care of their **offspring.** (lines 16 and 17)

a. Likely meaning of *hinge* _____

b. Likely meaning of *offspring* _____

> Because men don't volunteer for fatherhood as much as they are **conscripted** into it by the surrounding culture ... (line 23)

c. Likely meaning of *conscripted* _____

Understanding the meaning of words by studying dictionary entries:

a. *coherent* identity (line 3)
   Dictionary meaning that fits the context _____

b. *paternal* waywardness (line 13)
   Dictionary meaning that fits the context _____

c. *anthropologist* Margaret Mead (line 25)
   Dictionary meaning that fits the context _____
   _____

Finding the Main Ideas

When you are reading an important text, you will find it helpful if you mark or highlight the main ideas. If the author is careful to give each paragraph a topic sentence (a statement of the main idea), your job will be easier. Often, but not always, the topic sentence is the first sentence of the paragraph. Sometimes the topic sentence is only inferred. Remember, a main idea is different from a supporting detail.

ACTIVITY **2**   **Finding the Main Idea**

For each of the following three paragraphs from the Blankenhorn text, choose the answer that best expresses the main idea of that paragraph.

Paragraph 1

1. **Like motherhood, fatherhood is made up of both a biological and social dimension. Yet, across the world, mothers are far more successful than fathers at fusing these dimensions into a coherent identity. Is the nursing mother playing a biological or a social role? Feeding or bonding? We can hardly separate the two, so seamlessly are they woven together. But fatherhood is a different matter. A father makes his sole biological contribution at the moment of conception, nine months before the infant enters the world. Because social paternity is linked only indirectly to biological paternity, a connection cannot be assumed. The phrase "to father a child" usually refers only to the act of insemination, not the responsibility for raising the child. What fathers contribute after conception is largely a matter of cultural devising.**

Best expression of the main idea:

a. Fathers have different responsibilities toward their children, depending on the culture in which they live.

b. Mothers naturally bond both socially and biologically to their children.

c. Fathers are not as naturally bonded to their children as mothers are.

d. "To father a child" usually refers only to insemination.

Paragraph 2

2. **Moreover, despite their other virtues, men are not ideally suited to responsible fatherhood. Men are inclined to sexual promiscuity and paternal waywardness. Anthropologically, fatherhood constitutes what might be termed a necessary problem. It is necessary because a child's well-being and societal success hinge largely on a high level of paternal investment: men's willingness to devote energy and resource to the care of their offspring. It is a problem because men frequently are unwilling or unable to make that vital investment.**

Best expression of the main idea:

a. Children need their fathers for their sense of well-being.

b. Men are often sexually promiscuous.

c. It takes a lot of energy and money to raise a child.

d. Men are not naturally drawn to being responsible parents.

Paragraph 3

3. **Because fatherhood is universally problematic, cultures must mobilize to enforce the father role, guiding men with legal and extralegal pressures that require them to maintain a close alliance with their children's mother and invest in their children. Because men don't volunteer for fatherhood as much as they are conscripted into it by the surrounding culture, only an authoritative cultural commitment to fatherhood can fuse biological**

and social paternity into a coherent male identity. For exactly this reason, anthropologist Margaret Mead and others have observed that the supreme test of any civilization is whether it can socialize men by teaching them to nurture their offspring.

Best expression of the main idea:

a. Fathers often feel forced into caring for their children.

b. Cultures must find effective ways to encourage and even legally require men to take responsibility for their children.

c. The success of a culture depends on legally binding requirements.

d. Fathers should stay in communication with the mothers of their children.

The following ten reading selections are taken from disciplines you are likely to encounter throughout your college career. Practice writing a summary for each one as if you were using the ideas in a research paper or a term report.

1. Environmental Science: Chernobyl

G. Tyler Miller and Scott E. Spoolman

Nuclear energy is one of the most promising yet most dangerous sources of power in the world. A nuclear accident that took place years ago in Russia should teach us what can happen when such an energy source goes out of control.

1   *Chernobyl* is known around the globe as the site of the world's most serious nuclear power plant accident. On April 26, 1986, two simultaneous explosions in one of the four operating reactors in this nuclear power plant in Ukraine (then part of the Soviet Union) blew the massive roof off the reactor building. The reactor partially melted down and its graphite components caught fire and burned for 10 days. The initial explosion and the prolonged fires released a radioactive cloud that spread over much of Belarus, Russia, Ukraine, and Europe, and it eventually encircled the planet.

2   According to UN studies, the Chernobyl disaster was caused by a poor reactor design (not the type used in the United States or in most other parts of the world) and by human error, and it had serious consequences. By 2005, some 56 people had died prematurely from exposure to radiation released by the accident. The number of long-term premature deaths from the accident, primarily from exposure to radiation, range from 9,000 by World Health Organization estimates, to 212,000 as estimated by the Russian Academy of Medical Sciences, to nearly 1 million according to a 2010 study by Alexey Yablokov and two other Russian scientists, published by the New York Academy of Sciences.

3   After the accident, some 350,000 people had to abandon their homes because of contamination by radioactive fallout. In addition to fear about long-term health effects such as cancers, many of these victims continue to suffer from stress and depression. In parts of Ukraine, people still cannot drink the water or eat locally produced food. There are also higher rates of thyroid cancer, leukemia, and immune system abnormalities in children exposed to Chernobyl's radioactive fallout.

4   Chernobyl taught us that a major nuclear accident anywhere can have harmful effects that reverberate throughout much of the world.

2. Political Science: Liberals and Conservatives

Robert J. Brym and John Lie

When we vote for a political party, we do more than choose between a Democrat and a Republican; we are voting for values that are important to us. The following excerpt deals with the wider implications of our political choices.

1   Different categories of the population—rich and poor, blacks and whites, Californians and South Carolinians—tend to support different political parties. To understand why, we must first understand the difference between liberals and conservatives.

2   People who consider themselves liberal or "left-wing" tend to favor extensive government involvement in the economy and a strong "social safety net" of health and welfare benefits to help the less fortunate members of society. In contrast, people who think of themselves as conservative or "right-wing" favor a small role for government in the economy and a small welfare state. They believe that the economy will grow fastest if the state stays out of people's lives as much as possible.

3   Economic issues aside, liberals and conservatives also tend to differ on social or moral issues. Liberals are inclined to support equal rights for women and racial and sexual minorities. Conservatives are inclined to support more traditional social and moral values.

4   In general, people vote for parties that they think will bring them the most benefit. Because the Democrats are more liberal than the Republicans, low-income earners, African Americans, and Hispanic Americans tended to support Democrat Barack Obama in the 2008 presidential election, whereas high-income earners and non-Hispanic whites tended to support Republican John McCain. Few homosexuals and supporters of women's reproductive rights supported McCain; most supported Obama.

5   Which party wins a given election depends partly on *short-term factors*, including how charismatic the competing candidates are, the degree to which they inspire confidence, the state of the economy (voters tend to reject incumbents if the economy is in bad shape), and so on.

6   In addition, *long-term factors* influence election outcomes. For example, if segments of the population that tend to favor party A grow more quickly than do segments of the population that tend to favor party B, then party A will benefit. The rapid growth of the Latino population in the United States in recent decades has favored the Democrats, for instance. Another influential long-term factor is the degree to which different categories of the population

are politically organized. If a social class that tends to favor party B becomes more politically organized than does a social class that tends to favor party A, then party B will benefit; a long-term electoral advantage goes to the party that enjoys the support of more powerful lobbies, professional associations, and unions. Conversely, organizational weakness spells trouble. For instance, the declining strength of the union movement in the United States in recent decades has hurt the Democrats.

3. History: World War II and African Americans

Kevin Schultz

World War II was fought overseas, but some of the most important results of that conflict took place in our own country. The following selection demonstrates the connection between events taking place during the war and the growing civil rights struggle that would eventually sweep the entire nation.

Just as the wartime demand for labor created opportunities for women, it opened doors for African Americans. The movement to challenge racial bias in employment began in the early 1940s. Months before Pearl Harbor, A. Philip Randolph, leader of the Brotherhood of Sleeping Car Porters (an African American union), started the March on Washington Movement. Its goal was twofold: (1) to pressure the government to develop and enforce antidiscrimination measures in the industries that had lucrative defense contracts and (2) to end segregation in the military. President Roosevelt feared that Randolph's threat to bring more than 100,000 African Americans to march on the capital might provoke a race war. In response, the president issued Executive Order 8802, which gave Randolph half of what he demanded. Executive Order 8802 established the Fair Employment Practices Committee (FEPC), which required companies with federal contracts to make jobs available without regard to "race, creed, color, or national origin." Coupled with the demand for labor, the FEPC had some effect. In total, the percentage of African Americans in war production work rose from 3 percent to 9 percent during the war. Between 1942 and 1945, the number of African Americans in labor unions (traditionally the province of higher-skilled workers) doubled to more than 1 million. The average annual wage for African Americans quadrupled in the war years, from $457 to $1,976. Randolph's second demand, to integrate the armed services, would have to wait until after the war.

4. Health: Stress

Dianne Hales

Medical research is always making new discoveries. The following selection explains some of what recent research has revealed about the connection between stress and our physical health.

1   These days we've grown accustomed to warning labels advising us of the health risks of substances like alcohol and cigarettes. Medical researchers speculate that another component of twenty-first-century living also warrants a warning: stress. In recent years, an ever-growing number of studies has implicated stress as a culprit in a range of medical problems. While stress itself may not kill, it clearly undermines our ability to stay well.

2   While stress alone doesn't cause disease, it triggers molecular changes throughout the body that make us more susceptible to many illnesses. Severe emotional distress—whether caused by a divorce, the loss of a job, or caring for an ill child or parent—can have such a powerful effect on the DNA in body cells that it speeds up aging, adding the equivalent of a decade to biological age.

3   This occurs because of a shortening of structures called telomeres in the chromosomes of cells. An enzyme called telomerase maintains these structures but declines with age. Every time a cell divides, which is a continuous process, the telomeres shorten. The shorter your telomeres, the more likely you are to die.

4   Stress also triggers complex changes in the body's endocrine, or hormone-secreting, system. When you confront a stressor, the adrenal glands, two triangle-shaped glands that sit atop the kidneys, respond by producing stress hormones, including catecholamines, cortisol (hydrocortisone), and epinephrine (adrenaline), that speed up heart rate and raise blood pressure and prepare the body to deal with the threat.

5. Cultural Anthropology: Dietary Changes

Gary Ferraro

Cultural anthropologists study the different cultures of the world. They are interested in how these more than 5,000 distinctive cultures differ from one another. In the following selection, an anthropologist looks at what happens when the long-established diet of a particular group of people is altered.

1   The diets of indigenous peoples are admirably adapted to their nutritional needs and available food resources. Even though these diets may seem bizarre, absurd, and unpalatable to outsiders, they are unlikely to be improved by drastic modifications. Given the delicate balances and complexities involved in any subsistence system, change always involves risks, but for indigenous people the effects of dietary change have been catastrophic. . . .

2   Under normal conditions, food habits are remarkably resistant to change, and indeed people are unlikely to abandon their traditional diets voluntarily in favor of dependence on difficult-to-obtain exotic imports. In some cases it is true that imported foods may be identified with powerful outsiders and are therefore sought as symbols of greater prestige. This may lead to such absurdities as Amazonian Indians choosing to consume imported canned tuna fish when abundant high-quality fish is available in their own rivers. Another example of this situation occurs in tribes where mothers prefer to feed their infants expensive and nutritionally inadequate canned milk from unsanitary, but *high status*, baby bottles. The high status of these items is often promoted by clever traders and clever advertising campaigns.

3   Overall, the available data seem to indicate that the dietary changes that are linked to involvement in the world-market economy have tended to reduce rather than raise the nutritional levels of the affected peoples. Specifically, the vitamin, mineral, and protein components of their diets are often drastically reduced and replaced by enormous increases in starch and carbohydrates, often in the form of white flour and refined sugar.

628

6. English: My Grandfather and Poetry

Andy Waddell

Andy Waddell remembers as a child having to memorize Robert Frost's poem, "Stopping by Woods on a Snowy Evening." Although most of today's teachers do not require memorization of poetry, Waddell's approach is different. The following selection is taken from Waddell's essay "Why I Force My Students to Memorize Poetry."

1   When my grandfather was dying, my mother tried to distract him, from the pain of his suffering and from the indignity of the crowded public hospital where he would spend the last few days of his life, by asking him to recite a poem he'd learned in grade school. "I don't remember that," he barked. For my own part, I thought my mother was crazy. Besides having been out of grade school for 75 years, Grandpa suffered from arteriosclerosis, which had made him forgetful, a neighborhood wanderer, a man who couldn't always retrieve his grandson's name or what state he lived in.

2   "Sure you do, Dad," she said. "Half a league, half a league/Half a league onward." And to my amazement, Grandpa joined in. "All in the valley of Death/Rode the six hundred." Thirty, forty, fifty lines came rolling out of him. His voice deepened; the lines in his face relaxed. He was somewhere else.

3   The words were deep in his mind, close to the soul. As his brain shut down it had inexplicably chosen this to retain alive. Poem after poem, as well as the Gettysburg Address, the Preamble to the Constitution, the 23rd Psalm and many, many others, she coaxed out of him. These words, wedged in by rote so long before, were still active in his fading brain. Though now playing out the last scene of his strange and eventful history, this man who had lied about his age to get into the Great War, who had spent his working life pushing a mail cart, found that neither wasteful war nor sluttish time could ever dissever his soul from the souls of those writers, those poets whose words rolled round his head, whose cadences had entered his soul, had become a part of him.

7. Psychology: Birth Order

Jerry Burger

Do you ever wonder why many oldest siblings seem to share certain traits? Or why only children act the way they do? Some psychologists have studied the effects of birth order on personality. Even though many of their ideas have been discredited, it remains difficult to separate myth from fact.

1   Alfred Adler was the first psychologist to emphasize the role of birth order in shaping personality. That is, firstborn children in a family are said to be different in personality from middle-born children, who are different from last-borns. According to Adler, firstborn children receive excessive attention from their parents and tend to be spoiled. First-time parents can never take enough photos and seldom miss an opportunity to tell friends and relatives about the new arrival. However, this pampering is short-lived. With the arrival of the second child, the firstborn is "dethroned." Now attention must be shared with, if not given over to, the newest member of the family. As a result, the firstborn will likely feel less important and act out in negative ways. Adler suggested that among firstborns we often find "problem children, neurotics, criminals, drunkards, and perverts."

2   On the other hand, Adler's assessment of middle children—Adler himself was a middle child—was more positive. These children are never pampered. Even when they are the youngest there is always another sibling or two demanding much of the parents' time. Adler argued that middle children strive to be superior. The middle-borns are not quite as strong, not quite as fast, and not quite as smart as older brothers and sisters. It's as if they are always just a step behind. As a result, they are always looking at the person a little ahead of them in school or in the office, always putting in the extra effort to close the gap. As a result, Adler said, middle-born children are the highest achievers.

3   Although Adler believed firstborns made up the greatest number of difficult children, he felt last-borns had problems as well. Last-born children are pampered throughout their childhood by all members of the family. Older children often complain that their little brother or sister "gets away with murder," which would not have happened "when I was that age." However, Adler argued that this special treatment carries a price. A spoiled child is a very dependent child—a child without personal initiative. Last-born children also are likely to have strong feelings of inferiority because everyone around them is older and stronger. Before applying Adler's theory to the members of your own family, you should note that studies do not necessarily support Adler's ideas. Birth order often does not predict how people will score on personality tests, and results found in one study often fail to appear in another. Moreover, the structure and characteristics of modern families have changed since Adler's time. Adler's descriptions may fit some families, but there are many exceptions. In short, although Adler's ideas caused a great deal of research, most likely the impact of birth order on personality and intellectual development is far more complex than he suggested.

8. Education: Should We Control MOOCs?

Diana Kendall

Technology has had a huge impact in and out of the classroom. Diana Kendall describes one of the many new uses of technology and its impact on the landscape of teaching and learning.

1   If you are a student, can you imagine what it would be like to have 10,000 students in your class? If you are a professor, can you imagine what it would be like to teach 10,000 or more students at the same time?

2   These are questions that faculty and students are asking at some universities where MOOCs are taught. MOOCs, or massive open online courses, have become increasing popular, particularly after professors at universities like Stanford, Harvard, and MIT started using these types of courses. These schools have drawn hundreds of thousands of students to their online courses in computer science and similar fields.

3   Originally, almost all learning in colleges and universities took place in brick-and-mortar buildings with live professors and students. With the arrival of television and cable TV channels, instructional television allowed students to take courses without physically attending them. The introduction of the Internet and the dawning of the digital age opened higher education to anyone with access to a computer and an Internet connection. In the future, some people believe that the process of online education will go even further. The wider use of MOOCs will allow a large number of students to participate, especially with many MOOCs' open access.

4   The interactive user forums available with MOOCs make it possible for students to engage with the material. It will connect students and professors in a manner that does not require them to have face-to-face meetings. MOOCs are similar to an older teaching method, but today's MOOCs are unique in that many are taught by well-known professors in elite universities. Only now, they are allowing open access to the courses.

5   However, some question the role of MOOCs in the future of higher education. What should be the role of virtual teaching in higher education? Who should fund MOOCs? Should anyone regulate MOOCs? What state or federal agency will control how credit is granted to students who successfully complete MOOCs? How will students receive academic credit from universities where they are not officially enrolled? Can they use those credits to count toward graduation at another institution? From a practical standpoint, there are questions about how well students learn in MOOCs. Can students concentrate on video lectures for extended periods of time? Are these courses set up to help students engage with the materials and other students?

6   At least for now, it appears that MOOCs are moving forward. They are rapidly growing through organizations such as edX (led by Harvard), MIT, and Coursera (offered by Stanford, Princeton, the University of Pennsylvania, and the University of Michigan). Coursera had 62 universities signed up to participate in 2013. MOOCs have gained momentum because they take teaching, which has typically been a not-for-profit realm, and make it a profitable business for entrepreneurs. These entrepreneurs view MOOCs as cash cows that will help them increase their company's value. And if, in the process, they help educate students, that is a good thing too.

9. History: Walls

Charles Bowden

One would not ordinarily think of walls as a subject for a historical analysis, but nearly any object or concept can be traced through history with fascinating results.

1   A border wall seems to violate a deep sense of identity most Americans cherish. We see ourselves as a nation of immigrants with our own goddess, the Statue of Liberty, a symbol so potent that dissident Chinese students fabricated a version of it in 1989 in Tiananmen Square as the visual representation of their yearning for freedom.

2   Walls are curious statements of human needs. Sometimes they are built to keep restive populations from fleeing. The Berlin Wall was designed to keep citizens from escaping from communist East Germany. But most walls are for keeping people out. They all work for a while, until human appetites or sheer numbers overwhelm them. The Great Wall of China, built mostly after the mid-14th century, kept northern tribes at bay until the Manchu conquered China in the 17th century. Hadrian's Wall, standing about 15 feet high, 9 feet wide, and 73 miles long, kept the crazed tribes of what is now Scotland from running amok in Roman Britain—from a.d. 122 until it was overrun in 367. Then you have the Maginot Line, a series of connected forts built by France after World War I to keep the German army from invading. It was a success, except for one flaw: The troops of the Third Reich simply went around its northwestern end and invaded France through the Netherlands and Belgium. Now tourists visit its labyrinth of tunnels and underground barracks.

3   In 1859 a rancher named Thomas Austin released 24 rabbits in Australia because, he noted, "the introduction of a few rabbits could do little harm and might provide a touch of home, in addition to a spot of hunting." By that simple act, he launched one of the most extensive barriers ever erected by human beings: the rabbit fences of Australia, which eventually reached 2,023 miles. Within 35 years, the rabbits had overrun the continent, a place lacking sufficient and dedicated rabbit predators. For a century and a half, the Australian government has tried various solutions: imported fleas, poisons, trappers. Nothing has dented the new immigrants. The fences themselves failed almost instantly—rabbits expanded faster than the barriers could be built, careless people left gates open, holes appeared, and, of course, the rabbits simply dug under them.

4   In Naco [Arizona] all the walls of the world are present in one compact bundle. You have Hadrian's Wall or the Great Wall of China because the barrier is intended to keep people out. You have the Maginot Line because a 15-minute walk takes you to the end of the existing steel wall. You have the rabbit fences of Australia because people still come north illegally, as do the drugs.

5   Perhaps the closest thing to the wall going up on the U.S.-Mexico border is the separation wall being built by Israel in the West Bank. Like the new American wall, it is designed to control the movement of people, but it faces the problem of all walls—rockets can go over it, tunnels can go under it. It offends people, it comforts people, it fails to deliver security. And it keeps expanding.

10. Physics: Snowflakes

Kenneth Libbrecht

According to Kenneth Libbrecht, physics professor at the California Institute of Technology, the ordinary snowflake can only be understood by an extraordinary mix of physics, math, chemistry, and mystery.

1   The mystery of snowflakes is how they are fashioned into such complex and symmetrical shapes. Snowflakes are not made by machines, nor are they alive. There is no blueprint or genetic code that guides their construction. Snowflakes are simple bits of frozen water, flecks of ice that tumble down from the clouds. So how do they develop into such intricate six-branched structures? Where is the creative genius that designs the neverending variety of snow-crystal patterns?

2   Many people think snowflakes are made from frozen raindrops, but this is simply not true. Raindrops do sometimes freeze in midair as they fall, and this type of precipitation is called *sleet*. Sleet particles look like what they are—little drops of frozen water without any of the ornate patterning or symmetry seen in snowflakes.

3   You do not make a snowflake by freezing liquid water at all. A snowflake forms when water *vapor* in the air condenses directly into solid ice. As more vapor condenses onto a nascent snow crystal, the crystal grows and develops, and this is when its elaborate patterning emerges. To explain the mystery of snowflakes, we must look at how they grow.

4   In a snowflake, just an ordinary snowflake, we can find a fascinating story of the spontaneous creation of pattern and form. From nothing more than the simple act of water vapor condensing into ice, these amazing crystal structures appear—complex, symmetric, and in endlessly varying designs. Snow crystals are the product of a rich synthesis of physics, mathematics, and chemistry. They're even fun to catch on your tongue.

5   The scientific definition of a crystal is any material in which the atoms or molecules are lined up in a regular array. Ice is a crystal made of water molecules, and the normal form of ice is called *ice lh*, made of sheets of water molecules arranged into "puckered" hexagons. Hexagons, of course, have a six-fold symmetry, and this symmetry ultimately carries over into snow crystals.

PART 7

Blend Images – Andersen Ross/Getty Images

Further Readings for the College Writer

These selections show us professional writers at work, using the various methods of development studied in this textbook. A writer will sometimes use more than one method of development to construct a single piece of writing. For example, when Elaine Weiss defends her position on spousal abuse, she also uses elements of narration, details from her personal story, to support that position.

Each reading is introduced with a brief background note that provides a context for the piece and tells something about the author; marginal glosses are added to explain unfamiliar words or usages. Following each selection are two different sections. The first, "Questions for Critical Thinking," directs the reader to examine how each piece was constructed. The second section, "Writing in Response," invites student essays based on the themes found in each particular piece.

Before you approach the study of these readings, be sure to absorb the suggestions detailed in the following section, "Strategies for the Active Reader." Using these strategies in all of your college reading assignments will make you a more critical reader, one of the most important goals of an educated person.

Strategies for the Active Reader

This section will take you through the process of developing active reading strategies for print and digital resources. You will learn about previewing texts, summarizing readings, and understanding vocabulary. This process encourages you to preview, read, and then reread passages in order to thoroughly understand materials and to commit key points and themes to memory. Refer to the model selection, which provides a space for practicing and developing your own positive and unique reading habits. Developing and evolving your reading skills will help you read more quickly and effectively for both school and work assignments.

You may have noticed that technology is transforming at an ever faster rate; it is affecting both how we read and how we process information. In the past, a student's main source of knowledge was usually a print resource, but today's student will most likely read and interact with texts via a screen, such as a computer, smartphone, or e-reader. It is increasingly important for today's reader to develop flexible strategies to read actively because we spend so much time with a computer or handheld device. Many devices and the software that they run contain tools that allow the reader to comment, highlight, or otherwise mark important passages in the text. One of the strategies this chapter suggests is annotating, which focuses on careful readings of texts. When annotating a text, you underline key points, highlight significant portions, make brief comments, and use a dictionary. All of these approaches will aid your understanding and retention of the texts you are studying.

Becoming an active and involved reader is an important key to success in college and in your career. An active reader learns more efficiently, absorbing the contents of books and essays with greater awareness of their meaning and uses. Such awareness as a reader also leads to a greater ability to compose effective college essays and term papers. By closely examining examples of good writing, you will dramatically improve your own writing. When you make a notation on a thesis statement, highlight a topic sentence, or rewrite an intriguing detail, you are helping yourself recognize and later adopt the strongest components of what you read. Let's discuss some features of active reading that help students become better writers.

Previewing

Before you begin to read a selection, you should examine the title for key words that indicate what the article is about. Are there words in the title that should be noted? What questions will the writer likely raise? Read the introductory paragraph and the concluding paragraph, and then review the first sentences of the remaining paragraphs to gain a general understanding of the text's themes. Think about the last time you saw a movie preview: the clips from the movie do not give you the whole story, but they provide you with just enough of an idea of what the plot is about and make you interested enough to watch the full film. Previewing a text performs a similar function. As you review the paragraphs, analyze headings (usually in bold type) of the different parts of the selection. Be aware of boxed features (often found in textbook chapters) that give definitions of terms or other information in concise form. You might also find it helpful to read any end-of-chapter questions or summaries, as they will also help direct your reading. Find key words or terms in bold type in addition to any sentences that are printed in italics. Words, headings, or sentences are presented in this way to emphasize their importance. Observing these key features before reading the entire piece is one of the best ways to get an overview of the material you are about to read.

Annotating/Taking Notes

Why is marking up a book indispensable to reading? First, it keeps you awake. (And I don't mean merely conscious; I mean wide awake.) In the second place, reading, if it is active, is thinking, and thinking tends to express itself in words, spoken or written. The marked book is usually the thought-through book. Finally, writing helps you remember the thoughts you had, or the thoughts the author expressed.

MORTIMER ADLER

Once you have previewed the text, you are ready to begin a careful reading. Being an active reader means interacting with the text you are reading. This process involves some or all of the following activities:

- **Underlining key points.** Key points include the thesis, topic sentences, key words, definitions, and major divisions of the essay such as a discussion or results section.

- **Highlighting significant portions of the text.** Highlighting should be used to mark portions of the text that have enduring value to the topic you are studying or that you want to return to and remember. Some students make the mistake of highlighting too much material because they do not have enough experience distinguishing main ideas from less critical points. You may want to highlight an important quotation, the results of an experiment or test, or the key points of the text. Make a note—sometimes even a single word is sufficient—about why you highlighted the passage, so you can remember its importance later.

- **Making brief marginal comments.** Marginal comments, that is notes written in the margin of a text, might be as brief as a question mark to indicate a word or idea you don't understand, a check mark to indicate an important comment, or an exclamation point to emphasize a statement you find surprising. Sometimes you will want to make longer notations about the contents or the author's point of view. You may want to write the definition of a word that you do not understand or write a question next to an idea that sounds confusing. You might also find yourself disagreeing with the author, or you might prepare a response to an idea that does not match your own experience.

- **Writing a summary.** The summary could be as short as one sentence or as long as four or five, depending on the complexity of the ideas. Regardless of the length of the summary, it should help you remember what the paragraph discusses.

- **Using the dictionary.** If you cannot figure out the meaning of a word from its context or from a glossary that has been provided, you should look up the definition in a dictionary. In the "Understanding Vocabulary" section of Part 6, you saw how to use a dictionary to understand the meaning of words; however, dictionary entries contain a wealth of information in addition to the definition. Let's take the word *urban* as an example.

> ur·ban ('ər-bən)
> adjective
> 1. Of, relating to, or located in a city.
> 2. Characteristic of the city or city life.
> 17th century: Latin *urbanus*, from *urbs* city

- **Definition:** The word "urban" contains two definitions, so you would have to read both of them and any example sentences to figure out how it is being used in what you're reading. The word *urban* is used as an example for each of the parts of a dictionary entry.
- **Syllables:** Dictionaries use dots to separate syllables. *Urban* contains one dot that separates its two syllables—one on each side of the dot (ur·ban).
- **Phonology:** The apostrophe shows you where the word is accented and the letters represent how it actually sounds as opposed to how it is spelled ('ər-bən).
- **Part of Speech:** All dictionary entries include the part of speech that the word is categorized as: verb, noun, adjective, adverb, and so on.
- **Synonyms and Antonyms:** Sometimes, dictionaries provide synonyms and antonyms. In relation to the main word, synonyms are words that have a similar meaning, and antonyms are words that have an opposite meaning. Two synonyms for *urban* are *town* and *city*, and two antonyms are *rural* and *country*.
- **Origin:** Dictionaries often tell you the etymology of a word, that is to say a word's language origin. In the case of *urban*, it derives from the Latin word *urbanus* from the seventeenth century.

After reading a selection, you should be able to answer these basic questions:

1. What was the author's **purpose** in creating the piece of writing? Was it written to entertain, inform, or persuade?
2. What was the **main point or points** in the writing? What did the author **conclude**?
3. Who is the intended **audience** for the selection?
4. What is the **structure** of the selection? How many paragraphs make up the introduction? How has the author developed the points? Are the author's points **credible**, or do you question the author's integrity? What makes you question the author's integrity?
5. How does the author achieve **coherence**? For example, where does the author use transitions, repetition, and pronouns? Are the author's points difficult to follow?
6. Does the writer present both **facts** and **opinions**? Do you find yourself agreeing or disagreeing with the writer's **point of view**?

Building Your Vocabulary

Using Context Clues

Over the course of your college career, you will read hundreds of pages, and many of those pages will contain unfamiliar words. An online or paper dictionary can provide you with exact definitions, and some authors will even include a helpful glossary inside your textbook. However, you may not always have time to look up each new word. Fortunately, you can use context to figure out approximate definitions. *Context* refers to the words, phrases, and sentences surrounding a word. Often, there are clues available within a word's context to assist you in defining it. These useful hints are appropriately called **context clues**.

- **Definition Context Clues.** Sometimes, an author will provide the actual definition of the unfamiliar word within the sentence or surrounding sentences. He or she may use clue words and phrases in the context such as *is, means, refers to*, or *can be defined as*. If the author does not use specific language, he or she might instead place the definition of the new word between dashes, in parentheses, or between commas. Consider the following examples in which the vocabulary word appears in italic font, and the context clue appears in green font:

> The term *mobile* refers to an item that can be transported from place to place.
>
> In summer of 2012, NASA landed a rover—a machine operated remotely—on the surface of Mars.
>
> In 1993, the U.S. Air Force completed the nexus (network) of satellites known as the Global Positioning System.
>
> The goal of robotics engineers is to create machines that are indistinguishable from, or identical to, human beings.

- **Example Context Clues.** Instead of giving a definition, an author may provide examples to explain the meaning of a new word. If you are familiar with or understand the examples, you can determine the basic definition of the word. Look for phrases such as *for example, to illustrate, for one thing, such as*, and *for instance* to indicate the author's use of an example context clue. View the following examples in which the vocabulary word appears in italic font, and the context clue appears in purple font:

> The lab results suggested *minuscule* changes in the patient's blood profile. For example, the sugar levels had dropped only two points.

Since a change of "only two points" is insignificant, you can determine that *minuscule* means *very small*. The phrase "for example" indicates the example context clue.

> Many *aquatic* mammals, such as whales, dolphins, and harbor seals, must surface periodically in order to breathe.

If you know that whales, dolphins, and harbor seals live in the ocean, you can determine that aquatic means "living in water." The phrase "such as" indicates examples of the word.

- **Contrast Context Clues.** Often, instead of telling you what a word means, the author will tell you what it does *not* mean. He or she may include an antonym, or a word with the opposite definition, to help you figure out the approximate meaning of the unknown word. Look for words and phrases such as *on the other hand, while, even though, unlike, but*, and *however*. They often signal contrast clues. Study the following examples in which the vocabulary word appears in italic font, and the context clue appears in blue font:

  > The manager was *lackadaisical*, but his employees were all hardworking and ambitious.

  The word *but* suggests that the information that follows will contrast with the unfamiliar word. Therefore, you can determine that *lackadaisical* means the opposite of hardworking and ambitious. It means "lazy and passive."

  > While Willow spends money as fast as she can earn it, Tamara is *parsimonious*.

  The word *while* at the beginning of the sentence suggests that there will be a contrasting relationship. If Willow spends money quickly, Tamara must do the opposite. So, *parsimonious* must mean "frugal," or "careful with money."

- **General Knowledge Context Clues.** Of all the various types of context clues, general knowledge clues are the least obvious. They don't contain clue words or phrases, and they don't use special punctuation. Instead you have to rely on your own understanding of a situation or event to figure out the meaning of an unfamiliar word. Examine the following example, in which the vocabulary word appears in italic font:

  > Vu's luggage was *confiscated* because the baggage handlers found illegal imports hidden inside.

  Your existing knowledge of baggage-handling practices would lead you to define *confiscated* as "taken away." A person cannot bring illegal imports into the country.

  > Hilary's decision to study instead of going to a party with her friends was *prudent*. She got a perfect score on her test; her friends failed the exam.

  This scenario does not include any definitions, examples, or opposites. You must rely on your own knowledge to determine that *prudent* means "wise." If you want to succeed, it is wise to stay home and study for a test instead of partying.

An Annotated Text

Read a few paragraphs taken from an essay found in Part 7. Notice how the student has annotated the text.

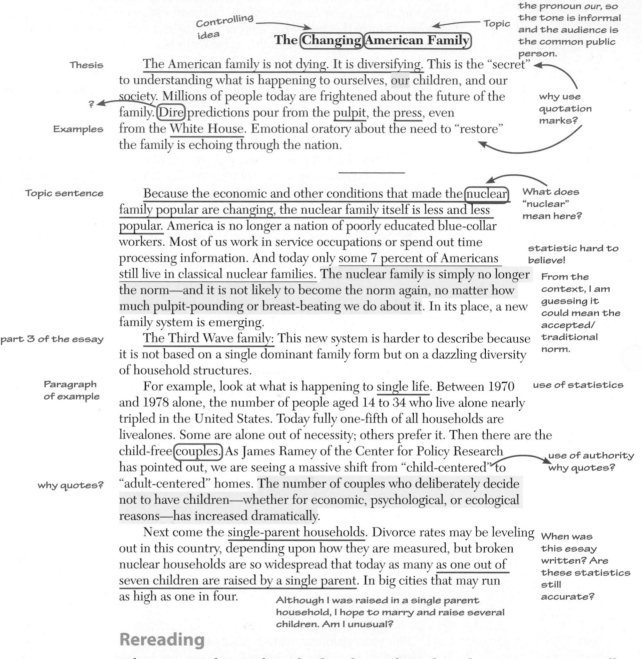

Controlling idea _____

The (Changing) (American Family)

_____ *Topic*

The author uses the pronoun our, *so the tone is informal and the audience is the common public person.*

Thesis   The American family is not dying. It is diversifying. This is the "secret" to understanding what is happening to ourselves, our children, and our

?   society. Millions of people today are frightened about the future of the family. (Dire) predictions pour from the pulpit, the press, even

Examples   from the White House. Emotional oratory about the need to "restore" the family is echoing through the nation.

why use quotation marks?

_____

Topic sentence   Because the economic and other conditions that made the (nuclear) family popular are changing, the nuclear family itself is less and less popular. America is no longer a nation of poorly educated blue-collar workers. Most of us work in service occupations or spend out time processing information. And today only some 7 percent of Americans still live in classical nuclear families. The nuclear family is simply no longer the norm—and it is not likely to become the norm again, no matter how much pulpit-pounding or breast-beating we do about it. In its place, a new family system is emerging.

What does "nuclear" mean here?

statistic hard to believe!

From the context, I am guessing it could mean the accepted/ traditional norm.

part 3 of the essay   The Third Wave family: This new system is harder to describe because it is not based on a single dominant family form but on a dazzling diversity of household structures.

Paragraph of example   For example, look at what is happening to single life. Between 1970 and 1978 alone, the number of people aged 14 to 34 who live alone nearly tripled in the United States. Today fully one-fifth of all households are livealones. Some are alone out of necessity; others prefer it. Then there are the child-free (couples.) As James Ramey of the Center for Policy Research

use of statistics

use of authority why quotes?

why quotes?   has pointed out, we are seeing a massive shift from "child-centered" to "adult-centered" homes. The number of couples who deliberately decide not to have children—whether for economic, psychological, or ecological reasons—has increased dramatically.

Next come the single-parent households. Divorce rates may be leveling out in this country, depending upon how they are measured, but broken nuclear households are so widespread that today as many as one out of seven children are raised by a single parent. In big cities that may run as high as one in four.

When was this essay written? Are these statistics still accurate?

Although I was raised in a single parent household, I hope to marry and raise several children. Am I unusual?

Rereading

When you read something for fun, for work, or for information, you generally only read it once. Think of the last article you read online; did you return to it? Probably not. Reading for school is very different. Based on the volume of reading that your instructors assign, you'll consider yourself lucky just to finish each text once. However, you should try to review the material, if possible, and revisit your annotations as well. For example, if you are studying difficult literary works or long chapters in a textbook, more than one reading may be needed before the meaning becomes clear, and you might have to make more annotations within the text depending on the difficulty of the content. Many of the same strategies suggested for previewing will aid you as you reread a given passage. One option is to make sure that you understand all of your annotations and notes. Another option is to review the post-reading questions; if you cannot answer those questions, rereading specific sections is an appropriate next step. You have a very important reason for making sure you are in control of what you read; it might appear on a test or otherwise affect your grade. No matter what your reasons are for wanting to master written material, required or otherwise, when you become a thoughtful reader, one of the great avenues to pleasure and meaning in life will open up before you.

Visiting Rites

Susan Musgrave

Susan Musgrave is the author of more than twenty books, including works of fiction, essay collections, and stories for children; she has also written a great many poems. Born in California to Canadian parents, she has traveled internationally, giving poetry readings and workshops. In addition, she has held writer-in-residence positions at more than one Canadian university. Since 1991, Musgrave has worked online with over a thousand students across Canada through the Writers in Electronic Residence Program. In the following essay, Susan Musgrave gives an open and honest account of a painful personal experience. In her hands, the grim reality of visiting her husband in prison takes on an almost poetic quality.

1   At first glance it looks like a fairy tale castle-hotel: parking lots shaded by endangered oaks, crewcut lawns, a stone wall running the length of the property. But when you look again you see it's a dungeon, with bars on every window and razor-wire surrounding the yard.

°the poet Lovelace
Richard Lovelace (1618–1657), British poet whose quoted words come from his lyric "To Althea, from Prison"

°incarnation
newly created reality

2   The poet Lovelace° may have been right when he wrote, "stone walls do not a prison make," but razor-wire doesn't leave a doubt.

3   Visitors call it Wilkie, as if they feel some affection for the joint, or because Vancouver Island Regional Correction Centre is too much of a mouthful. Built on Wilkinson Road near Victoria after the turn of the century, it was a mental hospital before its present incarnation.° Two gold-painted lions lie in repose on either side of the steps leading up to the prison doors. I hand over my driver's licence and sign in at the front desk as though committing myself, as if shock treatment might be a relief after everything I've been through in the last two days, since my husband was arrested for bank robbery.

°Birkenstocks
a brand of sandal

4   The newspapers say I am standing by my man. I'd rather be lying by him, I think, as I start to undress, taking off my wedding ring, my belt and sandals, before walking bare-soled through the metal detector. A guard inspects my Birkenstocks,° making sure I haven't concealed contraband—drugs, money, books—between the straps. I ask if I am allowed Kleenex—not that I plan to weep, but my motto has always been: if you want peace, prepare for war. The guard says he will "provide me with something."

°aesthetics
sense of good taste

°puce
a dark purple color

5   My visit is to take place "under glass." I enter the small Plexiglas and concrete booth, designed by someone who had the aesthetics° of the sensory-deprivation chamber in mind. The walls are off-cream, the trim around the windows a tinned-lima-bean green. All else is puce.°

6   It's familiar decor. Stephen and I were married in prison, in 1986, when he was serving a twenty-year sentence for bank robbery. He was paroled a few months after we took our vows, twelve years ago almost to this day. But prison is not an easy place to escape, even if they release you. STEVE LOVES SUSAN FOREVER is etched into the Plexiglas. While I wait for my Stephen with a

"ph," the guard brings me a roll of toilet paper and unwinds what he thinks I'll need. The $50,000 a year it costs to keep a man behind bars must not include the price of a box of Kleenex.

7   When the door to the prisoner's booth finally opens, the man I am supposed to be standing by is not the one standing before me. The guard picks up his telephone, I pick up mine. "He's refusing the visit," he says, point-blank.

8   I knew Stephen would be going through drug withdrawal, so I'm not surprised he can't keep our date. Part of me, though, feels betrayed. When we got married we vowed to be there for one another, in sickness and in health. The one-ply toilet paper, not meant for tears, is soon the size of a spitball in my fist.

9   I'm trying to leave when I am summoned to the office of the Director of Programs. He indicates a pile of papers on his desk and asks if I'm familiar with the "ion scanner." This device has detected microscopic particles of cocaine on my letters to Stephen; my driver's licence, too, is contaminated. Given that my husband has had a $1,000-a-day drug habit for the past six months, I expect my whole life is contaminated.

10   I ask why invisible drug particles could be a problem. "We don't want inmates in contact with individuals involved in drug-seeking activities," he explains. He will suspend my visits if I ever attempt to smuggle contraband to a prisoner. How could anyone smuggle anything through Plexiglas, over a phone? I ask. "Where there's a will, there's a way," he says.

11   Next time I visit, Stephen doesn't stand me up. I try to break the ice over the heavy telephone. "At least it's not long distance," I tell him. "It's not our dime."

°accentuating
emphasizing

12   Some previous visitor has severed the wires, and they have been repaired with electrician's tape. Our voices fade in and out, accentuating° the lonely long distance between us. Stephen says that just minutes before they fetched him for our visit, the wind slipped into his cell. He knew that meant I was near.

°stutters
makes repeated reflections

13   My hand reaches out to the glass, and I see the reflection of my hand rest itself on Stephen's hands. My reflection travels up his arm, stutters° over the track-marks, and then moves sadly on. I stroke his trembling face. Where there's a will, there's a way. A way to touch, even if it's this way.

14   I don't cry until the visit is almost over, and this time I have nothing to wipe my nose on except my T-shirt sleeve.

15   They lead Stephen away though the puce-coloured doors. I wait to be released, and to book my next visit. But when I begin to spell my name for the new guard on shift, she stops me. "I know who you are," she says. "You've been an inspiration to me all my life."

16   She has taken me by surprise. I hadn't allowed myself to see past the uniform.

17   "I used to write poetry—at university," she says. "We all did. But you didn't stop like the rest of us—we had to get jobs." Her voice drops to a whisper. "I admire everything you've ever done. Except for one thing."

18   I expect her to say, "Marrying a criminal."

°trite
overused and not
interesting

°domesticity
the life of the home

19   "You know those essays you used to write for the newspapers—about family life? Well, I thought they were trite.°" She doesn't think domesticity° a subject worthy of my inspirational words. As Stephen would say, everyone's a critic.

20   Some days I feel lost. Other days life continues without Stephen, though he is here in every grain of wood, every dustball behind the wood stove, every fixed or broken thing. Words are what I know, and I have freedom in my love. All of him washes over me, like the mystery of wind.

Questions for Critical Thinking

1.   Writers often take great care to compose an effective title. In this case, why is the use of the word "rites" such a good choice?

2.   In paragraph 2, the writer refers to a famous poem of the seventeenth century, "To Althea, from Prison" by Richard Lovelace. The poem contains the words "Stone walls do not a prison make/Nor iron bars a cage . . ." If stone and iron are indeed not the things that keep a person a prisoner, what things do keep a person "in prison"?

3.   Susan Musgrave makes real the agony of many people who have a loved one in prison. Make a list of several of the details of this narrative that give the essay its sad reality. One detail, the shedding of tears, can be traced in paragraphs 4, 6, 8, and 14.

4.   Narration achieves coherence by placing events in a time sequence. Divide the essay into parts according to the movement from one event to the next. Look for transitions of time that signal these movements.

5.   Narration should make a point. What do you think is the point of this essay? Select the sentence or sentences that reflect the author's point of view.

Writing in Response

1.   In paragraph 9, the writer tells us that, because her husband had a "$1,000-a-day drug habit," she expects her "whole life is contaminated." Nearly everyone has known a member of a family who has done something to make the rest of the family suffer. Write an essay that tells the story of that family's unhappy experience.

2.   Visiting a family member who has moved away may bring back happy or sad memories from the past. Write an essay that explores the experience of visiting someone who no longer lives nearby.

3.   The dreams we have for our lives are often far from the reality of how we must live in the present. Susan Musgrave is visiting a husband in jail, an experience no wife would wish for. Write an essay that uses narration to illustrate this truth that we cannot always be masters of our fate, or write an essay that uses narration to illustrate another truth—that we are masters of our fate.

4.   The author reports in paragraph 4 that she is being described as "standing by" her man. Write an essay that discusses the complex problems that come with standing by someone who has committed a crime or betrayed a trust. What part does forgiveness play in such a situation? When is loyalty self-destructive?

Summer Reading

Michael Dorris

Important events from childhood never fade from our minds. The late Native American novelist and essayist Michael Dorris (1945–1997) used his cultural background and his personal experience in many of his works. In the following essay, published in his book of collected writings, *Paper Trail*, the writer recalls a memorable summer during his adolescence when he was repaid a debt in an unexpected way. It was a repayment that profoundly changed his life.

1   When I was fourteen, I earned money in the summer by mowing lawns, and within a few weeks I had built up a regular clientele.° I got to know people by the flowers they planted that I had to remember not to cut down, by the things they lost in the grass or stuck in the ground on purpose. I reached the point with most of them when I knew in advance what complaint was about to be spoken, which particular request was most important. And I learned something about the measure of my neighbors by their preferred method of payment: by the job, by the month—or not at all.

°**clientele**
group of customers

2   Mr. Ballou fell into the last category, and he always had a reason why. On one day he had no change for a fifty, on another he was flat out of checks, on another, he was simply out when I knocked on his door. Still, except for the money part, he was a nice enough old guy, always waving or tipping his hat when he'd see me from a distance. I figured him for a thin retirement check, maybe a work-related injury that kept him from doing his own yard work. Sure, I kept a running total, but I didn't worry about the amount too much. Grass was grass, and the little that Mr. Ballou's property comprised didn't take long to trim.

3   Then, one late afternoon in mid-July, the hottest time of the year, I was walking by his house and he opened the door, motioned me to come inside. The hall was cool, shaded, and it took my eyes a minute to adjust to the muted° light.

°**muted**
soft

4   "I owe you," Mr. Ballou began, "but . . ."

5   I thought I'd save him the trouble of thinking up a new excuse. "No problem. Don't worry about it."

6   "The bank made a mistake in my account," he continued, ignoring my words. "It will be cleared up in a day or two. But in the meantime I thought perhaps you could choose one or two volumes for a down payment."

7   He gestured toward the walls and I saw that books were stacked everywhere. It was like a library, except with no order to the arrangement.

8   "Take your time," Mr. Ballou encouraged. "Read, borrow, keep. Find something you like. What do you read?"

9   "I don't know." And I didn't. I generally read what was in front of me, what I could snag from the paperback rack at the drugstore, what I found at the library, magazines, the back of cereal boxes, comics. The idea of consciously seeking out a special title was new to me, but, I realized, not without appeal—so I browsed through the piles of books.

10   "You actually read all of these?"

11   "This isn't much," Mr. Ballou said. "This is nothing, just what I've kept, the ones worth looking at a second time."

12   "Pick for me, then."

°appraisingly
with the intention of
making a judgment

13   He raised his eyebrows, cocked his head, regarded me appraisingly° as though measuring me for a suit. After a moment, he nodded, searched through a stack, and handed me a dark red hard-bound book, fairly thick.

14   *"The Last of the Just,"* I read. "By André Schwarz-Bart. What's it about?"

15   "You tell me," he said. "Next week."

°oblivion
total forgetfulness of the
world around

16   I started after supper, sitting outdoors on an uncomfortable kitchen chair. Within a few pages, the yard, the summer, disappeared, the bright oblivion° of adolescence temporarily lifted, and I was plunged into the aching tragedy of the Holocaust, the extraordinary clash of good, represented by one decent man, and evil. Translated from French, the language was elegant, simple, overwhelming. When the evening light finally failed I moved inside, read all through the night.

17   To this day, thirty years later, I vividly remember the experience. It was my first voluntary encounter with world literature, and I was stunned by the undiluted power a novel could contain. I lacked the vocabulary, however, to translate my feelings into words, so the next week, when Mr. Ballou asked, "Well?" I only replied, "It was good."

18   "Keep it, then," he said. "Shall I suggest another?"

19   I nodded, and was presented with the paperback edition of Margaret Mead's *Coming of Age in Samoa.*°

°Coming of Age in Samoa
groundbreaking 1925
study of adolescent
behavior in the South
Pacific

°intermission
a period between events

20   To make two long stories short, Mr. Ballou never paid me a dime for cutting his grass that year or the next, but for fifteen years I taught anthropology at Dartmouth College. Summer reading was not the innocent pastime I had assumed it to be, not a breezy, instantly forgettable escape in a hammock (though I've since enjoyed many of those, too). A book, if it arrives before you at the right moment, in the proper season, at a point of intermission° in the daily business of things, will change the course of all that follows.

Questions for Critical Thinking

1. The author uses narration as his method of developing ideas about the importance of reading. He orders the material by presenting a sequence of events. Summarize this narrative by listing the sequence of events. (Do not quote the conversations in the essay.)

2. Review paragraphs 2 through 6 of the essay and decide why Mr. Ballou could not (or would not) pay Michael Dorris. Do you think he did not have enough money, or was he unwilling to spend money on something other than books?

3. What were the author's reading habits before his encounter with Mr. Ballou? What do you think his reading habits were after this summer experience?

4. The second book Mr. Ballou gave the author was the anthropologist Margaret Mead's *Coming of Age in Samoa*, a book often assigned in college anthropology courses. In the next sentence, Michael Dorris tells us that "for fifteen years I taught anthropology at Dartmouth College." What connection does the writer want us to make?

5. When a person owes another person money, is it ever appropriate to repay the debt with something other than money—goods or services for example? When is it a good idea to settle a money debt in a nonmonetary way?

6. In the first paragraph, the writer tells us that some of his clients did not pay him at all, and in his last paragraph mentions that Mr. Ballou also never gave him money for mowing his lawn. Nevertheless, the writer did receive payment for his work. Explain this seeming contradiction.

Writing in Response

1. In this story, an adolescent has a summer job that changes his life. Write an essay in which you tell the story of yourself or someone else you know who had a part-time job while going to school. What happened? Were any lessons learned? You may want to use dialogue as part of your narration.

2. Write an essay in which you tell a story about a person in your neighborhood, a friend, or a relative. Remember that you will be relating a specific incident or a series of events to make a point. Your point might be what you learned from observing what happened to the person.

3. Michael Dorris concludes his essay by noting that if you come across a book "at the right moment," it could change the direction of your life. Write a narrative essay in which you tell the story of a life-changing event.

A Day at the Theme Park

W. Bruce Cameron

W. Bruce Cameron began an Internet-based humor column in 1995, and within a year, he was the most widely read humorist on the World Wide Web. Four years later, he began his newspaper columns for the Denver, Colorado, *Rocky Mountain News*. His pieces had such wide appeal that he expanded some of them into a book, *8 Simple Rules for Dating My Teenage Daughter*. The book quickly became a best seller and later became the basis of a television show, *8 Simple Rules*.

When W. Bruce Cameron writes about the problems that parents encounter while raising their children, he speaks from authority: he is the father of three teenagers, two girls and a boy. The following essay, which originally appeared in the *Rocky Mountain News*, is clearly based on the author's personal experience. While his humor makes us smile, the essay carries with it an element of truth about how parents will make great sacrifices for the sake of their children.

°**endearing**
appealing

°**utter**
complete

1   One of the most endearing° traits of children is their utter° trust that their parents provide them with all life's necessities, meaning food, shelter, and a weekend at a theme park.

2   A theme park is a sort of artificial vacation, a place where you can enjoy all your favorite pastimes at once, such as motion sickness and heat exhaustion. Adult tolerance for theme parks peaks at about an hour, which is how long it takes to walk from the parking lot to the front gate. You fork over an obscene amount of money to gain entrance to a theme park, though it costs nothing to leave (which is odd because you'd pay anything to escape). The two main activities in a theme park are (a) standing in line, and (b) sweating. The sun reflects off the concrete with a fiendish° lack of mercy. You're about to learn the boiling point of tennis shoes. Your hair is sunburned, and when a small child in front of you gestures with her hand she smacks you in the face with her cotton candy; now it feels like your cheeks are covered with carnivorous° sand.

°**fiendish**
cruel

°**carnivorous**
flesh-eating

°**DIA**
Denver International
Airport

3   The ride your children have selected for you is a corkscrewing, stomach compressing roller coaster built by the same folks who manufactured the baggage delivery system at DIA.° Apparently the theme of this particular park is "Nausea." You sit down and are strapped in so tightly you can feel your shoulders grinding against your pelvis. Once the ride begins you are thrown about with such violence it reminds you of your teenager's driving. When the ride is over your children want to get something to eat, but first the ride attendants have to pry your fingers off the safety bar. "Open your eyes, please sir," they keep shouting. They finally persuade you to let go, though it seems a bit discourteous of them to have used pepper spray. Staggering, you follow your children to the Hot Dog Palace for some breakfast.

4   Food at a theme park is so expensive it would be cheaper to just eat your own money. Your son's meal costs a day's pay and consists of items manufactured of corn syrup, which is sugar; sucrose, which is sugar; fructose, which is sugar;

and sugar, which is sugar. He also consumes large quantities of what in dog food would be called "meat byproducts." When, after a couple of rides, he announces that he feels like he is going to throw up, you're very alarmed. Having seen this meal once, you're in no mood to see it again.

°**pummeling**
a beating

5　　With the exception of that first pummeling,° you manage to stay off the rides all day, explaining to your children that it isn't good for you when your internal organs are forcibly rearranged. Now, though, they coax you back in line, promising a ride that doesn't twist, doesn't hang you upside down like a bat, doesn't cause your brain to flop around inside your skull; it just goes up and then comes back down. That's it, Dad, no big deal. What they don't tell you is HOW it comes back down. You're strapped into a seat and pulled gently up into acrophobia,° the city falling away from you. Okay, not so bad, and in the conversation you're having with God you explain that you're thankful for the wonderful view but would really like to get down now.

°**acrophobia**
fear of heights

6　　And that's just how you descend: NOW. Without warning, you plummet to the ground in an uncontrolled free fall. You must be moving faster than the speed of sound because when you open your mouth, nothing comes out. Your life passes before your eyes, and your one regret is that you will not have an opportunity to punish your children for bringing you to this hellish place. Brakes cut in and you slam to a stop. You gingerly touch your face to confirm it has fallen off. "Wasn't that fun, Dad?" your kids ask. "Why are you kissing the ground?"

7　　At the end of the day, you let your teenager drive home. (After the theme park, you are impervious° to fear.)

°**impervious**
unaffected

Questions for Critical Thinking

1. Is the purpose of this essay to inform, to persuade, or to entertain?

2. Explain what part of the one-sentence introduction is the topic.

3. What word could the writer have used for his controlling idea if he had wanted to reveal that controlling idea in the beginning of his essay?

4. Study the writer's two-sentence conclusion. What single word in that conclusion reveals the author's attitude toward theme parks and therefore gives us his controlling idea for the entire essay?

5. Choose a sensory image from each of the five body paragraphs (paragraphs 2–6) that you find especially humorous. Although humor is hard to analyze, try to explain why you were amused by each image you have chosen.

6. Underline the topic sentences of the body paragraphs.

Writing in Response

1. Many people have a dream to do something like go across the country on a motorcycle, visit Paris, or see the pyramids before they die. Write an essay that describes, either seriously or humorously, an activity that you want to do sometime during your lifetime.

2. In paragraph 2, the writer describes going to a theme park as "a sort of artificial vacation." Describe your idea of a "real" vacation.

3. We live in a permissive society. Write an essay that describes several situations in which a parent should say no.

4. Write an essay that describes a form of entertainment that you believe has become too expensive for the average person or family to enjoy.

5. Describe what you believe to be the best amusement or entertainment for children.

6. If you have ever enjoyed a visit to a theme park, describe the three best rides you experienced.

Gardenland

Michael Nava

Born of Mexican parents in Stockton, California, in 1954, Michael Nava grew up reading constantly. He was the first person in his family to attend college, where he excelled in literature and writing. Later, at Stanford University Law School, he began writing the first of his much-acclaimed seven-volume legal mystery series. Not many individuals have the distinction of being successful in two careers, but Nava works as a judicial attorney in the California Supreme Court while he also writes extensively to advocate for social justice. The following essay describes the neighborhood where he spent his childhood.

1   I grew up in a neighborhood of Sacramento called Gardenland, a poor community, almost entirely Mexican, where my maternal family, the Acunas, had lived since the 1920s. Sacramento's only distinction used to be that it was the state capital. Today, because it frequently appears on lists of the country's most livable cities, weary big-town urbanites° have turned it into a boomtown° rapidly becoming unlivable. But when I was a child, in the late fifties and early sixties, the only people who lived in Sacramento were the people who'd been born there.

2   Downtown the wide residential neighborhoods were lined with oaks shading turreted,° run-down Victorian mansions, some partitioned into apartments, others still of a piece, but all of them exuding a shadowy small-town melancholy. The commercial district was block after block of shabby brick buildings housing small businesses. The city's skyline was dominated by the gold-domed capitol, a confectioner's° spun-sugar dream of a building. It was set in a shady park whose grass seemed always to glisten magically, as if hidden under each blade of grass were an Easter egg.

3   Sacramento's only other landmarks of note were its two rivers, the American and the Sacramento. They came together in muddy confluence° beneath the slender iron joints of railroad bridges. Broad and shallow, the rivers passed as slowly as thought between the thick and tumble of their banks.

4   A system of levees° fed into the rivers. One of these tributaries° was called the Bannon Slough.° Gardenland was a series of streets carved out of farmland backed up against the slough. It flowed south, curving east behind a street called Columbus Avenue, creating Gardenland's southern and eastern boundaries. The northern boundary was a street called El Camino. Beyond El Camino was middle-class tract housing. To the west, beyond Bowman Street, were fields and then another neighborhood that may just as well have existed on another planet for all I knew of it.

5   What I knew were the nine streets of Gardenland: Columbus, Jefferson, Harding, Cleveland, El Camino, Peralta, Wilson, Haggin, and Bowman; an explorer, an odd lot of presidents, an unimaginative Spanish phrase, and three

°**urbanites**
city dwellers

°**boomtown**
a town experiencing uncontrolled growth

°**turreted**
with small towers

°**confectioner**
one who makes candies or sweets

°**confluence**
the meeting of two or more streams

°**levees**
raised banks to prevent flooding

°**tributaries**
small streams flowing into larger bodies of water

°**slough**
a stagnant bog

°inexplicable
impossible to explain

°haphazard
ruled by chance

°perusal
a quick reading or
reviewing of something

°utility
usefulness

°ramshackle
poorly constructed

°artifacts
objects of historical
interest

°millennial
of a thousand years

°celestial
heavenly

°virtually
nearly

inexplicable° proper names, one in Spanish, two in English. It was as if the streets had been named out of a haphazard° perusal° of a child's history text. There were two other significant facts about the streets in Gardenland; they all dead-ended into the levee and their names were not continued across El Camino Boulevard into the Anglo suburb, called Northgate. Gardenland's streets led, literally, nowhere.

6   Unlike El Camino, where little square houses sat on little square lots, Gardenland had not been subdivided to maximum utility.° Broad uncultivated fields stretched between and behind the ramshackle° houses. Someone's "front yard" might consist of a quarter acre of tall grass and the remnants of an almond orchard. The fields were littered with abandoned farming implements and the foundations of long-gone houses. For a dreamy boy like me, these artifacts° were magical. Finding my own world often harsh, I could imagine from these rusted pieces of metal and fragments of walls a world in which I would have been a prince.

7   But princes were hard to come by in Gardenland. Almost everyone was poor, and most residents continued to farm after a fashion, keeping vegetable gardens and flocks of chickens. There were neither sidewalks nor streetlights, and the roads, cheaply paved, were always crumbling and narrow as country lanes. At night, the streets and fields were lit by moonlight and the stars burned with millennial° intensity above the low roofs of our houses.

8   The best way to think of Gardenland is not as an American suburb at all, but rather as a Mexican village, transported perhaps from Guanajuato, where my grandmother's family originated, and set down lock, stock, and chicken coop in the middle of California.

9   My cousin Josephine Robles had divided her tiny house in half and ran a beauty shop from one side. Above her porch was a wooden sign that said in big blue letters GARDENLAND and, in smaller print below, beauty salon. Over the years the weather took its toll and the bottom half faded completely, leaving only the word GARDENLAND in that celestial° blue, like a road sign to a cut-rate Eden.

10   By the time I was born, in 1954, my family had lived in Gardenland for at least twenty-five years. Virtually° all I know of my grandfather's family, the Acunas, was that they were Yaqui Indians living in northern Mexico near the American border at Yuma, Arizona. My grandmother's family, the Trujillos, had come out of central Mexico in 1920, escaping the displacements caused by the Mexican Revolution of 1910. I have dim memories of my great-grandparents, Ygnacio and Phillipa Trujillo, doll-like, white-haired figures living in a big, dark two-story house in east Sacramento.

11   My grandparents settled on Haggin Avenue in a house they built themselves. My cousins, the Robles, lived two doors down. My family also eventually lived on Haggin Avenue, next door to my grandparents. Our house was the pastel plaster box that became standard suburban architecture in California in the fifties and sixties but it was the exception in Gardenland.

12   Most houses seemed to have begun as shacks to which rooms were added to accommodate expanding families. They were not built with privacy in mind but simply as shelter. We lived in a series of such houses until our final move to Haggin Avenue. In one of them, the living room was separated from the kitchen

by the narrow rectangular bedroom in which my brothers and sisters and I slept. Adults were always walking through it while we were trying to sleep. This made for jittery children, but no one had patience for our complaints. It was enough that we had a place to live.

13   By the standards of these places, my grandparents' house was luxurious. It was a four-bedroom, L-shaped building that they had built themselves. My grandmother put up the original three rooms while my grandfather was in the navy during World War II. My aunt Socorro told me that my grandmother measured the rooms by having her children lie head to toe across a plot of ground. She bought the cement for the foundations, mixed and troweled it, and even installed pipes for plumbing. Later, when my grandfather returned, they added a series of long, narrow rooms paneled in slats of dark-stained pine, solid and thick walled.

14   Massive, dusty couches upholstered in a heavy maroon fabric, oversize beds soft as sponges, and a leather-topped dining room table furnished the house. Like the rusted combines in the field, these things seemed magical in their antiquity. I would slip into the house while my grandparents were both at work and wander through it, opening drawers and inspecting whatever presented itself to my attention. It was in this fashion that I opened a little-used closet and found it full of men's clothes that obviously were not my grandfather's. Later I learned that they had belonged to my uncle Raymond who had been killed in a car accident. In a subsequent exploration I found pictures of his funeral, including a picture taken of him in his casket, a smooth-faced, dark-skinned, pretty boy of fifteen.

°petticoat
a woman's slip or underskirt

15   Another time, I found a voluminous red petticoat° in a cedar chest. Without much hesitation, I put it on and went into my grandmother's bedroom where I took out her face powder and lipstick. I applied these in the careful manner of my grandmother, transforming myself in the dressing mirror beneath the grim gaze of a crucified Christ. Looking back, I don't think I was trying to transform myself into a girl, but only emulating° the one adult in my family who loved me without condition. Because she was the soul of kindness, it never occurred to me, as a child, that my grandmother might be unhappy. Only looking back do I see it.

°emulating
imitating

16   She and my grandfather slept in separate rooms at opposite ends of their house. In the evening, my grandfather would sit on a couch in front of the television quietly drinking himself into a stupor while my grandmother did needlework at the kitchen table. They barely spoke. I would sit with my grandmother, looking at pictures in the *Encyclopedia Americana,* comfortable with the silence, which, to her, must have been a deafening indictment° of a failed marriage.

°indictment
condemnation

17   In my parents' house, the marriage of my mother and stepfather was as noisily unhappy as my grandparents' was quietly miserable. In each shabby house where we lived I would be awakened by their fights. I learned to turn myself into a stone, or become part of the bed or the walls so as to abate the terror I felt. No one ever spoke of it. There was only one house in which my family lived together peaceably but it only existed as a blueprint that had come somehow into my stepfather's possession.

18   In the evening, he would take it down from a shelf and unroll it on the kitchen table. Together we would study it, laying claim to rooms, planning

alterations. At the time, we lived in a tiny one-bedroom cinder-block house. My brother and I slept on a bunk bed in an alcove off the kitchen. At night, I could hear mice scampering across the cement floor, terrifying me when I woke up having to pee and pick my way through the darkness to the bathroom.

19   When we finally moved from the cinder-block house, it was to another, bigger version of that house rather than to the dream house of the blueprint. One night, my mother's screaming woke me. I hurried into the bedroom she and my stepfather occupied and found him beating her. When I tried to stop him, he threw me across the room. The next morning my mother told me he was sorry, but it was too late. Where I lived no longer mattered to me because I learned to live completely within myself in rooms of rage and grief. Now I think these rooms were not so different from the rooms we all occupied, my unhappy family and I.

20   Although not literally cut off from the outside world, Gardenland was little touched by it. We were tribal in our outlook and our practices. Anglos were generically called "paddies," whether or not they were Irish. All fair-skinned people were mysterious but also alike. Even TV, that great equalizer, only emphasized our isolation since we never saw anyone who looked remotely like us, or lived as we did, on any of the popular shows of the day. At school, the same homogeneity° prevailed. Until I was nine I attended a neighborhood grade school where virtually every other child was like me, dark eyed and dark skinned, answering to names like Juarez, Delgadillo, Robles, Martinez. My own name, Michael Angel, was but an Anglicized version of Miguel Angel, a name I shared with at least three other of my classmates.

°homogeneity
sameness

21   I had a remarkable amount of freedom as a child. As I said, we eventually lived on the same street as other members of my maternal family and I roamed their houses as unself-consciously as a Bedouin° child might move among the tents of his people. I ate in whatever house I found myself at mealtime and the meals were the same in each of my relatives' houses—rice, beans, lettuce and tomato salad, stewed or fried meat, tortillas, salsa. My grandparents did not lock their doors at night—who did? what was there to steal?—so that I could slip into their house quietly and make my bed on their sofa when my parents were fighting.

°Bedouin
an Arab nomad

22   But most of the time I spent outdoors, alone or with my friends. In spring, the field behind my house was overrun with thistles. We neighborhood kids put in long days cutting trails through them and hacking out clearings that became our forts. Tiring of the fields, we'd lurk° in abandoned houses, empty barns, and chicken coops. When all other amusements failed, there was always Bannon Slough, a muddy brown creek that flowed between thickly wooded banks. It was too filthy to swim in. Instead, in the steep shadows of bridges and railroad trestles we taught each other how to smoke and to swear.

°lurk
lie in wait, sneak about

23   Just as often I would be off by myself. Early on, I looked for ways to escape my family. I found it in the stillness of the grass and the slap of the slough's brown water against the shore. There I discovered my own capacity for stillness. Lying on the slope of the levee, I could hear my own breath in the wind and feel my skin in the warm blades of grass that pressed against my neck. In those moments, Gardenland *was* Eden, and I felt the wonder and loneliness of the first being.

24   For, like Adam, I was lonely. Being everyone's child, I was no one's child. I could disappear in the morning and stay out until dusk and my absence went

unnoticed. Children barely counted as humans in our tribe. We were more like livestock and our parents' main concern was that the head count at night matched the head count in the morning.

25   My loneliness became as much a part of me as my brown hair and the mole above my lip, something unremarkable. When I came out, I missed that sense of joining a community of others like me that so many of my friends describe. My habits of secrecy and loneliness were too deeply ingrained. I had become like my grandfather, who, in a rare moment of self-revelation, told me he was a "lone wolf"; the most unsociable of an unsociable tribe. Though I've changed as I've grown older, I still sometimes wonder if one reason I write is because I am filled with all the words I never spoke as a child.

26   Two things opened up for me the narrow passage through which I finally escaped Gardenland for good. The first was books. I learned to read early and, once started, could not get enough of books. In this affinity, I was neither encouraged nor discouraged by my family. Education beyond its most basic functions, learning how to read and write, to do sums, had absolutely no interest for them. My love of reading became simply another secret part of me.

27   There wasn't a library in Gardenland. Instead, a big white van pulled up to the corner of Wilson and El Camino, the city Bookmobile. Inside, patrons squeezed into a narrow passageway between tall shelves of books. The children's books occupied the bottom shelves. At the exit, a woman checked out books from a standing desk. The Bookmobile came once a week and I was a regular customer, always taking my limit of books.

28   Everything about the process pleased me. I was proud of my library card, a yellow piece of cardboard with my name typed on it, which I carried in a cowhide wallet that was otherwise empty. I liked taking books from the shelves, noting their heft° and volume, the kind of type, whether they were illustrated, and I studied the record of their circulation, the checkout dates stamped in blue on stiff white cards in paper pockets on the inside covers. I loved the books as much as I loved reading. To me, they were organic things, as alive in their way as I was.

°**heft**
weight

29   Like so many other bright children growing up in the inarticulate° world of the poor, books fueled my imagination, answered my questions, led me to new ones, and helped me conceive of a world in which I would not feel so set apart. Yet I do not believe that my brains alone, even aided by my bookish fantasies, would have been enough to escape Gardenland. For this, I needed the kind of courage that arises out of desperation.

°**inarticulate**
unable to express

30   I found this courage in my homosexuality. Early on, I acquired a taste for reading history, particularly ancient history. I suppose that pictures of ruined Greek cities reminded me of the crumbling, abandoned houses in the fields of Gardenland. But I was also fascinated by pictures of the nude male statues. There was something about the smooth, headless torsos, the irisless eyes of ephebes° that made me stop my idle flipping through pages and touch the paper where these things were depicted. By the time I was twelve I understood that my fascination was rooted in my sexual nature. One day, walking to school, clutching my books to my chest, girl-style, I heard myself say, "I'm a queer."

°**ephebes**
in ancient Greece, a young man between 18 and 20

31   It was absolutely clear to me that Gardenland could not accommodate this revelation. Gardenland provided the barest of existences for its people. What made it palatable° was the knowledge that everyone was about the same, united in ethnicity and poverty and passivity.

°**palatable**
acceptable

The only rituals were the rituals of family, and family was everything there. But I knew that I was not the same as everyone else. And I was certain that my family, already puzzled by my silent devotion to books, would reject me entirely if it became known exactly what thoughts occupied my silence.

°**unrequited**
unacknowledged

°**paradoxically**
seeming to be
contradictory

32   Had I been a different child I would have run away from home. Instead, I ran away without leaving home. I escaped to books, to sexual fantasy, to painful, unrequited° crushes on male classmates. No one ever knew. I turned myself into an outsider someone at the margins of a community that was itself outcast. Paradoxically,° by doing this, I learned the peasant virtues of my hometown, endurance and survival. As a member of yet another embattled community, those virtues I absorbed as a child continue to serve me.

Questions for Critical Thinking

1. Michael Nava's writing is a model for student writers. Consider the topic sentences of paragraphs 21, 22, 23, and 24. They are excellent examples of how he carefully structures his writing. In each of these paragraphs, underline the topic sentence. What do all the topic sentences have in common?

2. Effective description is always filled with words rich in meaning. Some of the nouns in paragraph 2 are *neighborhoods, mansions, melancholy, district, buildings, businesses, skyline, capitol, dream, park*, and *egg*. Find the adjectives that the author chose to describe these eleven nouns. Make a list of each noun phrase. How many adjectives were used?

3. In the last sentence of paragraph 5, Michael Nava claims, "Gardenland's streets led, literally, nowhere." Explain the difference between the terms *literally* and *figuratively*. Considering that Michael Nava would eventually leave his old neighborhood and seek a wider world, how do you interpret this sentence?

4. Descriptive writing at its best often uses simile (a comparison using *like* or *as*). In paragraphs 4 and 28, find the similes and explain how the comparisons work.

Writing in Response

1. Despite the negative details in paragraph 6, the writer can still say that "for a dreamy boy" like him, the items he lists were "magical." Write an essay, using examples from your own experience, showing how a person's imagination can transform even the most negative aspects of that person's surroundings.

2. Were you surprised to learn that the author is homosexual? Write an essay in which you first describe Michael Nava's attitude about his childhood in relationship to his homosexuality. Then provide an anecdote of your own that illustrates how what seems to be a burden as a child can turn out to be something positive. Explain this, keeping in mind the author's explanation of his own situation.

3. Write a descriptive essay of the neighborhood in which you grew up. Be sure to combine observations of the physical conditions along with your emotional reactions to those conditions.

4. In paragraph 15, Michael Nava remarks that it never occurred to him that his grandmother might have been unhappy. Only when he looked back did he realize this. Write an essay in which you look back with the fresh perspective you now have as an adult. Think of a person you knew in your childhood. How did you view that person then and how differently do you perceive that person now?

Black Men and Public Space

Brent Staples

After receiving a Ph.D. from the University of Chicago in psychology, Brent Staples earned a wide reputation as a journalist, essayist, and book reviewer. His powerful memoir *Parallel Time: Growing up in Black and White* remains outstanding for its combination of honesty and warmth. Staples is presently an editorial writer for *The New York Times*. The following essay was originally published in *Ms.* magazine.

°**discreet**
showing self-restraint

°**uninflammatory**
not arousing emotion

1   My first victim was a woman—white, well dressed, probably in her late twenties. I came upon her late one evening on a deserted street in Hyde Park, a relatively affluent neighborhood in an otherwise mean, impoverished section of Chicago. As I swung onto the avenue behind her, there seemed to be a discreet,° uninflammatory° distance between us. Not so. She cast back a worried glance. To her, the youngish black man—a broad six feet two inches with a beard and billowing hair, both hands shoved into the pockets of a bulky military jacket—seemed menacingly close. After a few more quick glimpses, she picked up her pace and was soon running in earnest. Within seconds she disappeared into a cross street.

°**unwieldy**
difficult to manage

°**quarry**
prey

°**wayfarers**
travelers

2   That was more than a decade ago. I was twenty-two years old, a graduate student newly arrived at the University of Chicago. It was in the echo of that terrified woman's footfalls that I first began to know the unwieldy° inheritance I'd come into—the ability to alter public space in ugly ways. It was clear that she thought herself the quarry° of a mugger, a rapist, or worse. Suffering a bout of insomnia, however, I was stalking sleep, not defenseless wayfarers.° As a softy who is scarcely able to take a knife to a raw chicken—let alone hold one to a person's throat—I was surprised, embarrassed, and dismayed all at once. Her flight made me feel like an accomplice in tyranny. It also made it clear that I was indistinguishable from the muggers who occasionally seeped into the area from the surrounding ghetto. That first encounter, and those that followed, signified that a vast, unnerving gulf lay between nighttime pedestrians—particularly women—and me. And I soon gathered that being perceived as dangerous is a hazard in itself. I only needed to turn a corner into a dicey situation, or crowd some frightened, armed person in a foyer somewhere, or make an errant move after being pulled over by a policeman. Where fear and weapons meet—and they often do in urban America—there is always the possibility of death.

°**elicit**
bring forth

3   In that first year, my first away from my hometown, I was to become thoroughly familiar with the language of fear. At dark, shadowy intersections, I could cross in front of a car stopped at a traffic light and elicit° the *thunk, thunk, thunk, thunk* of the driver—black, white, male, or female—hammering down the door locks. On less traveled streets after dark, I grew accustomed to but never comfortable with people crossing to the other side of the street rather than pass me. Then there were the standard unpleasantries with policemen, doormen, bouncers, cabdrivers, and others whose business it is to screen out troublesome individuals *before* there is any nastiness.

°**avid**
enthusiastic

°**taut**
tight, strained

°**warrenlike**
like a maze

°**bandolier**
a soldier's belt holding bullets, worn across the chest

°**hallucination**
a false perception

°**solace**
comfort in sorrow

°**lethality**
the capability of causing death

°**bravado**
a false confidence

°**perilous**
dangerous

°**ad hoc posse**
a group formed for a specific purpose

°**labyrinthine**
like a maze

4   I moved to New York nearly two years ago and I have remained an avid° night walker. In central Manhattan, the near-constant crowd cover minimizes tense one-on-one street encounters. Elsewhere—in SoHo, for example, where sidewalks are narrow and tightly spaced buildings shut out the sky—things can get very taut° indeed.

5   After dark, on the warrenlike° streets of Brooklyn where I live, I often see women who fear the worst from me. They seem to have set their faces on neutral, and with their purse straps strung across their chests bandolier-style,° they forge ahead as though bracing themselves against being tackled. I understand, of course, that the danger they perceive is not a hallucination.° Women are particularly vulnerable to street violence, and young black males are drastically overrepresented among the perpetrators of that violence. Yet these truths are no solace° against the kind of alienation that comes of being ever the suspect, a fearsome entity with whom pedestrians avoid making eye contact.

6   It is not altogether clear to me how I reached the ripe old age of twenty-two without being conscious of the lethality° nighttime pedestrians attributed to me. Perhaps it was because in Chester, Pennsylvania, the small, angry industrial town where I came of age in the 1960s, I was scarcely noticeable against a backdrop of gang warfare, street knifings, and murders. I grew up one of the good boys, had perhaps a half-dozen fistfights. In retrospect, my shyness of combat has clear sources.

7   As a boy, I saw countless tough guys locked away; I have since buried several, too. They were babies, really—a teenage cousin, a brother of twenty-two, a childhood friend in his mid-twenties—all gone down in episodes of bravado° played out in the streets. I came to doubt the virtues of intimidation early on. I chose, perhaps unconsciously, to remain a shadow—timid, but a survivor.

8   The fearsomeness mistakenly attributed to me in public places often has a perilous° flavor. The most frightening of these confusions occurred in the late 1970s and early 1980s, when I worked as a journalist in Chicago. One day, rushing into the office of a magazine I was writing for with a deadline story in hand, I was mistaken for a burglar. The office manager called security and, with an ad hoc posse,° pursued me through the labyrinthine° halls, nearly to my editor's door. I had no way of proving who I was. I could only move briskly toward the company of someone who knew me.

9   Another time I was on assignment for a local paper and killing time before an interview. I entered a jewelry store on the city's affluent Near North Side. The proprietor excused herself and returned with an enormous red Doberman pinscher straining at the end of a leash. She stood, the dog extended toward me, silent to my questions, her eyes bulging nearly out of her head. I took a cursory look around, nodded, and bade her good night.

10   Relatively speaking, however, I never fared as badly as another black male journalist. He went to nearby Waukegan, Illinois, a couple of summers ago to work on a story about a murderer who was born there. Mistaking the reporter for the killer, police officers hauled him from his car at gunpoint and but for his press credentials would probably have tried to book him. Such episodes are not uncommon. Black men trade tales like this all the time.

11   Over the years, I learned to smother the rage I felt at so often being taken for a criminal. Not to do so would surely have led to madness. I now take precautions to make myself less threatening. I move about with care, particularly

'wide berth
plenty of space

°skittish
jumpy from nerves

°congenial
friendly

°constitutionals
walks

late in the evening. I give a wide berth° to nervous people on subway platforms during the wee hours, particularly when I have exchanged business clothes for jeans. If I happen to be entering a building behind some people who appear skittish,° I may walk by, letting them clear the lobby before I return, so as not to seem to be following them. I have been calm and extremely congenial° on those rare occasions when I've been pulled over by the police.

12   And on late-evening constitutionals° I employ what has proved to be an excellent tension-reducing measure: I whistle melodies from Beethoven and Vivaldi and the more popular classical composers. Even steely New Yorkers hunching toward nighttime destinations seem to relax, and occasionally they even join in the tune. Virtually everybody seems to sense that a mugger wouldn't be warbling bright, sunny selections from Vivaldi's *Four Seasons*. It is my equivalent of the cowbell that hikers wear when they know they are in bear country.

Questions for Critical Thinking

1. An anecdote (a brief story that serves as an example) can be very effective when it answers some of the basic questions we would want to know: *who, what, where, when, why*, and *how*. The first paragraph of this essay is an anecdote. What are the writer's answers to these six basic questions?

2. How many other anecdotes are found in the essay? Name the paragraphs and answer the questions *who, what, where, when, why*, and *how* for each of the anecdotes.

3. Using your own words, compose a thesis for this essay.

4. In paragraph 2, the writer refers to his "unwieldly inheritance." What inheritance does he refer to? What is ironic about his use of the word *inheritance*?

5. In the third paragraph, several short examples are provided to strengthen the writer's point. How many examples does he give and what are they?

6. This essay first appeared, appropriately, in *Ms.* magazine. Brent Staples understands how the "victim" feels. Where in the essay does he show his empathy for the frightened individual?

7. The essay ends on a somewhat hopeful note. How has Staples learned to cope with and lessen the effects that his presence sometimes has on other people?

Writing in Response

1. This essay was published in 1986. Is it still relevant today? Write an essay in which you give examples from your own experience or from those you know that reveal the public mistrust or even fear of certain people. You may also research the details of some actual news events that would provide examples for your essay.

2. Write an essay of classification that explores a number of stereotypes.

3. It is always helpful to understand another person's perspective. Describe an incident that made you aware of another person's point of view.

4. In paragraph 7, the writer tells us that he "chose, perhaps unconsciously, to remain a shadow—timid, but a survivor." Write an essay that explores when it is best to remain in the background or when it is best to take a forceful stand.

Space Food

Scott M. Smith, Janis Davis-Street, Lisa Neasbitt, Sara R. Zwart (NASA)

The four-member author team—scientists and doctors who work closely with NASA—are all interested in questions of nutrition, health, medicine, and how the human body functions while in space. The efforts of the authors are concentrated on scientific experimentation as well as on education. Working together, they have made admirable progress in researching and teaching about the effects of outer space on the human body.

The following excerpt comes from a larger book called *Space Nutrition* and describes how food is chosen, prepared, and stored for space missions—an exercise in long-term planning, research, and execution. The scientists at NASA have many concerns and obstacles to overcome in feeding the astronauts who occupy a spacecraft.

° ISS
International Space Station, a habitable artificial satellite launched into orbit around the planet Earth in 1998

° astronaut
title awarded by NASA and other space agencies; from a Greek root, literally "star sailor"

°cosmonaut
title used by the Russian Space Agency; from a Greek root, literally "cosmos sailor"

°compressible
able to be pressed into a smaller shape, crushable

°Soyuz capsule
Russian spacecraft originally designed in the 1960s during the Soviet era

1   Space foods on the International Space Station are either rehydratable, thermostabilized, or in natural form. A rehydratable food is one that is dehydrated, meaning all of the water has been taken out. You might be familiar with some of these, like packets of hot cocoa mix or dried noodle soups. To eat one of these items, you must rehydrate it, meaning you must add the water back. Thermostabilized foods are heated to high temperatures and packaged in cans or closed pouches. Examples of thermostabilized foods are canned ravioli and soups. We also use some foods in their natural form, that is, just like they are in nature (or at the grocery store). A food in its natural form is in a vacuum-sealed package, meaning all of the air has been removed so that it stays fresh for a long time. These foods include nuts and dried fruit.

2   The ISS° crew members eat international foods, as the crew members are from many different countries. Right now, half of the space food items on board the ISS are American foods and half are Russian foods. Japanese, European, and Canadian food items are available also. The astronauts° and cosmonauts° have more than 300 food items to choose from.

3   Preparing food to eat in weightlessness is a challenge. Crumbs are not allowed, as they can float around the cabin and could float into someone's eye (or nose) or into instruments, or clog air vents. Also, the food must not float away while an astronaut is trying to eat it, so packages and foods are designed to make this less of a problem in space. Another challenge for food system developers is trash. Wrappers and empty packages must be compressible° to minimize the amount of trash on the spacecraft. The garbage truck doesn't stop by the International Space Station, and there are very few opportunities to get trash off the vehicle. In fact, trash is disposed of only when space vehicles such as the Space Shuttle, the Soyuz° capsules, and other cargo vehicles visit the ISS and then depart. This happens about once a month, and even these vehicles have limited amounts of space available, so trash must be as compact as possible. These are just a few of the challenges of developing space foods. The NASA Space Food Team does a great job of meeting these challenges, and of developing foods that the astronauts will like during their space missions.

4   Food storage is a big issue for space travelers. Until recently, the ISS had no freezers or refrigerators for food, so the food has had to be "shelf stable" and not likely to spoil for at least 6 to 12 months. Food for a Mars mission will need to be stable for up to 5 years. Recently, a small refrigerator-freezer known as MERLIN (Microgravity Experiment Research Locker/Incubator) was flown to the ISS. It can be used to store a small amount of fresh food and drinks. This is especially helpful for drinks, which up to now have been pretty much room temperature. Nothing beats a cold glass of juice!

5   Taste and texture—how the food feels in your mouth—are very important for space travelers. Many taste tests are conducted on Earth when new foods are being developed for space travelers. When adapting to space flight, some astronauts have reported that their tastes changed, and that in space they tended to like spicier foods. One of the reasons for this is related to congestion° that astronauts sometimes have, similar to when you have a cold and your nose is stuffy. Most of the ISS crew members say that this is troublesome only in the early days of flight, and that after a week or two, foods taste great.

°congestion
blockage of the nasal passages from inflamed blood vessels, also known as a stuffy nose

6   Before each mission, astronauts select their favorite foods from the available flight foods, and they taste the foods they have selected to make sure that they really do like them. The most popular space food is shrimp cocktail, in part because of the spicy sauce!

7   Other challenges in developing space foods are making sure that they are tasty, have good nutrient content, and can be easily prepared. Another big challenge, especially as we begin to think about sending humans to the moon and Mars, is shelf life (how long the foods will stay fresh). Even for an International Space Station flight, the foods have to be able to sit on the shelf (a shelf in the pantry, not in the refrigerator or freezer) and still be tasty for at least 9 months. It will be even longer for a Mars mission. Can you imagine going to the grocery store, filling your pantry with food—and not going back to the store for a year, or 2 or 3?

8   Food scientists in the Space Food Systems Laboratory at the Johnson Space Center have created another success story. They have developed special tortillas that taste good after almost a year. Tortillas in space work great for making sandwich roll-ups (a regular sandwich with two slices of bread would take three hands to make—otherwise one slice will float away!). The scientists keep these tortillas fresh with special packaging that includes an oxygen scavenger. An oxygen scavenger is a chemical that traps oxygen, and the lack of oxygen in the packaging prevents mold from growing.

9   Some space foods are irradiated. These foods are packaged and then exposed to a source of radiation that kills any mold or bacteria on the food, allowing it to be safe to eat for a long time. No radiation stays on the food. This is like when you go to the doctor to get an x-ray: once the x-ray is taken, there is no radiation on you.

Questions for Critical Thinking

1. This essay was written and distributed by the National Aeronautics and Space Administration (NASA). What makes NASA an authority on space nutrition?

2. What is the purpose of this essay?

3. What pattern of organization does the author use in paragraph 1? How can you tell?

4. In paragraph 3, the writers discuss the importance of trash disposal in space. How do astronauts' concerns about trash disposal compare to our concerns regarding this topic down here on Earth?

5. In paragraph 4, the writers reveal that one small refrigerator-freezer was recently installed in the International Space Station (ISS). Since refrigerator-freezers are extremely common appliances on Earth, why do you think it took so long for a single small one to make it to the space station?

Writing in Response

1. You've learned a lot about the kinds of food astronauts can and cannot eat in space. Write an essay detailing the benefits and drawbacks of a space diet.

2. Many of our earthly technologies were originally developed for space travel. Research this topic. Then write an essay detailing three everyday products that got their start in space and how they improve life on Earth.

3. In paragraph 9, the authors discuss how radiation is used to kill organisms on food in order to make it safe to eat. Compose an essay in which you discuss both the positive aspects and the negative aspects of radiation.

Fidelity

Scott Russell Sanders

Scott Russell Sanders, a Distinguished Professor of English at Indiana University, has written many books of fiction and nonfiction. In his work, he examines our place in the world of nature and the connection between culture and geography. In the following essay, he argues that community members need to be faithful to good works and to each other.

°**spare**
lean and trim

1   A cause needn't be grand, it needn't impress a crowd, to be worthy of our commitment. I knew a man, a lifelong Quaker, who visited prisoners in our county jail, week in and week out, for decades. He would write letters for them, carry messages for them, fetch them clothing or books. But mainly he just offered himself, a very tall and spare° and gentle man, with a full shock of white hair in his later years and a rumbling voice that never wasted a word. He didn't ask whether the prisoners were innocent or guilty of the charges that had landed them in jail. All that mattered was that they were in trouble. He didn't preach to them, didn't pick and choose between the likable and the nasty, didn't look for any return on his time. Nor did he call attention to his kindness; I had known him for several years before I found out about his visits to the jail. Why did he go spend time with outcasts, every week without fail, when he could have been golfing or shopping or watching TV? "I go," he told me once, "in case everyone else has given up on them. I never give up."

°**marooned**
cut off with little chance for quick escape

°**liable**
likely

°**flimsy**
lightweight and easily damaged

°**banking**
tilting to one side

°**whirl**
a rapid twirling

°**homing in**
directing toward

2   Never giving up is a trait we honor in athletes, in soldiers, in climbers marooned° by avalanches, in survivors of shipwreck, in patients recovering from severe injuries. If you struggle bravely against overwhelming odds, you're *liable*° to wind up on the evening news. A fireman rescues three children from a burning house, then goes back inside a fourth time to rescue the dog. A childless washerwoman in the deep South, who never dreamed of going to college herself, lives modestly and saves her pennies and in old age donates everything she's saved, over a hundred thousand dollars, for university scholarships. A pilot flies his flimsy° plane through a blizzard, searching for a pickup truck in which a woman is trapped; gliding and banking° through a whirl° of white, he catches signals from her cellular phone, ever so faint; the snow blinds him, the wind tosses him around, his fuel runs low, but he circles and circles, homing in° on that faint signal; then just before dark he spies the truck, radios the position to a helicopter crew, and the woman is saved. What kept him searching? "I hadn't found her yet," he tells the camera. "I don't quit so long as I have gas."

°**perseverance**
refusal to give up

3   Striking examples of perseverance° catch our eye, and rightly so. But in less flashy, less newsworthy forms, fidelity to a mission or a person or an occupation shows up in countless lives all around us, all the time. It shows up in parents who will not quit loving their son no matter how much trouble he causes, in parents who will not quit loving their daughter even after she dyes her hair purple and tattoos her belly and runs off with a rock band. It shows up in couples who choose to mend their marriages instead of filing for divorce. It shows up in farmers who stick to their land through droughts and hailstorms and floods.

°advocates
those who support a cause

°unsung people
people who are anonymous and unrecognized

It shows up in community organizers who struggle year after year for justice, in advocates° for the homeless and the elderly, in volunteers at the hospital or library or women's shelter or soup kitchen. It shows up in the unsung people° everywhere who do their jobs well, not because a supervisor is watching or because they are paid gobs of money but because they know their work matters.

4   When Jesse was in sixth grade, early in the school year, his teacher was diagnosed as having breast cancer. She gathered the children and told them frankly about the disease, about the surgery and therapy she would be undergoing, and about her hopes for recovery. Jesse came home deeply impressed that she had trusted them with her news. Before going to the hospital, she laid out lesson plans for the teacher who would be replacing her. Although she could have stayed home for the rest of the year on medical leave while the substitute handled her class, as soon as she healed from the mastectomy, she began going in to school one afternoon a week, then two, then a full day, then two days and three, to read with the children and talk with them and see how they were getting on. When a parent worried aloud that she might be risking her health for the sake of the children, the teacher scoffed, "Oh, heavens no! They're my best medicine." Besides, these children would only be in sixth grade once, and she meant to help them all she could while she had the chance. The therapy must have worked, because seven years later she's going strong. When Ruth and I see her around town, she always asks about Jesse. Is he still so funny, so bright, so excited about learning? Yes he is, we tell her, and she beams.

°unriddling
solving

5   I have a friend who builds houses Monday through Friday for people who can pay him and then builds other houses on Saturday, with Habitat for Humanity, for people who can't pay him. I have another friend who bought land that had been stripped of topsoil by bad farming, and who is slowly turning those battered acres into a wildlife sanctuary by halting erosion and spreading manure and planting trees. A neighbor of ours who comes from an immigrant family makes herself available night and day to international students and their families, unriddling° for them the puzzles of living in this new place. Other neighbors coach soccer teams, visit the sick, give rides to the housebound, go door to door raising funds for charity, tutor dropouts, teach adults to read; and they do these things not just for a month or a season but for years.

°board feet
a measure of lumber

°crusade
actions taken for a cause

°warbler
a small songbird

6   There's a man in our town who has been fighting the U.S. Forest Service for two decades, trying to persuade them to quit clear-cutting, quit selling timber at a loss, quit breaking their own rules in the Hoosier National Forest. All the while, those who make money from tearing up the woods call for more cutting, more road-building, more board feet.° This man makes no money from carrying on his crusade,° but he makes plenty of enemies, many of whom own chain saws and guns. He won't back down, though, because he loves the forest and loves the creatures that depend on the forest. Hearing him talk, you realize that he sees himself as one of those creatures, like any warbler° or fox.

7   I could multiply these examples a hundredfold without ever leaving my county. Most likely you could do the same in yours. Any community worth living in must have a web of people faithful to good work and to one another, or that community would fall apart.

Questions for Critical Thinking

1. The title of this essay is "Fidelity." We usually associate this word with marriage. How does the author use this term in the context of the essay? What other terms does the author use in the essay that are synonyms for his meaning of *fidelity*? Can you think of another word or phrase that would have also made a good title for this essay?

2. Review the essay and make a list of the everyday actions that are mentioned as examples of fidelity. How many examples does the author provide? Notice that some are just mentioned; others are given more context.

3. In paragraph 3, five sentences begin with the words, "It shows up in . . . ." Usually writing students are encouraged to avoid repetition in their work. Why would the author choose to begin five sentences with the same four words?

Writing in Response

1. In paragraph 6, Scott Russell Sanders relates an anecdote of a man who has been confronting the U.S. Forest Service in his attempts to stop clear-cutting. Although he admits that the man has made many enemies, Scott Russell Sanders implies that the man is doing something positive. Write an essay in which you show two sides of the argument, both against and in favor of clear-cutting. You may want to research some of the controversial issues surrounding this topic.

2. Write an essay that, like this essay, gives numerous examples of those in your own community who demonstrate what the author in his last paragraph refers to as "people faithful to good work and to one another."

3. Write a letter to a mayor or other local leader suggesting how the quality of life for the citizens of the community could be improved. Suggest what groups of volunteers could accomplish.

4. In our society, many disagree about how much financial support should be given to people in need. With limited budgets in so many cities and states, how much can we expect the government to provide for its people? Write an essay in which you give examples of what governments should do that individuals alone cannot accomplish.

5. Some wealthy people in our society have a sense of responsibility to give a portion of their money to needy causes. Research the Bill and Melinda Gates Foundation (or another philanthropic group) and write an essay giving examples of the different causes that the foundation (or other group) supports.

6. Sometimes a community-minded organization has its work supported not only by money but also by the fact that a well-known person is involved with that group. For example, Habitat for Humanity is closely associated with former president Jimmy Carter. Write an essay that gives examples of famous people who have become spokespersons for particular causes.

Slice of Life

Russell Baker

While Russell Baker may be best known for his sharp political and social commentaries, he is also well known as a humorist. After growing up in Baltimore, Maryland, during the Great Depression and then working in journalism for many years, his breakthrough came in 1962 when *The New York Times* gave him his "Observer" column. Until 1998, Russell Baker produced that column and numerous other essays, winning two Pulitzer Prizes for his work. Many readers have had a good laugh enjoying the following essay. They can identify with the problems facing a person who tries to make a holiday go smoothly.

°**sutures**
fine stitches to close surgical wounds

°**posterior**
the back side

°**skewered**
pierced by the knife

°**gingerly**
with great care

°**torso**
the body minus the head and limbs

°**execute**
perform

°**testy**
irritated

°**maneuver**
a strategic action

°**chassis**
frame or skeleton

°**Newton's Law**
principle stated by Isaac Newton (1642–1727), who discovered that every action has an equal and opposite reaction

1   How to carve a turkey:

2   Assemble the following tools—carving knife, stone for sharpening carving knife, hot water, soap, wash cloth, two bath towels, barbells, meat cleaver. If the house lacks a meat cleaver, an ax may be substituted. If it is, add bandages, sutures,° and iodine to above list.

3   Begin by moving the turkey from the roasting pan to a suitable carving area, This is done by inserting the carving knife into the posterior° stuffed area of the turkey and the knife-sharpening stone into the stuffed area under the neck.

4   Thus skewered,° the turkey may be lifted out of the hot grease with relative safety. Should the turkey drop to the floor, however, remove the knife and stone, roll the turkey gingerly° into the two bath towels, wrap them several times around it and lift the encased fowl to the carving place.

5   You are now ready to begin carving. Sharpen the knife on the stone and insert it where the thigh joins the torso.° If you do this correctly, which is improbable, the knife will almost immediately encounter a barrier of bone and gristle. This may very well be the joint. It could, however, be your thumb. If not, execute° a vigorous sawing motion until satisfied that the knife has been defeated. Withdraw the knife and ask someone nearby, in as testy° a manner as possible, why the knives at your house are not kept in better carving condition.

6   Exercise the biceps and forearms by lifting barbells until they are strong enough for you to tackle the leg joint with bare hands. Wrapping one hand firmly around the thigh, seize the turkey's torso in the other hand and scream. Run cold water over hands to relieve pain of burns.

7   Now, take a bath towel in each hand and repeat the above maneuver°. The entire leg should snap away from the chassis° with a distinct crack, and the rest of the turkey, obedient to Newton's Law° about equal and opposite reactions, should roll in the opposite direction, which means that if you are carving at the table the turkey will probably come to rest in someone's lap.

'sever
cut off

°sinewy
stringy and tough

8   Get the turkey out of the lap with as little fuss as possible, and concentrate on the leg. Use the meat cleaver to sever° the sinewy° leather which binds the thigh to the drumstick.

9   If using the alternate, ax method, this operation should be performed on a cement walk outside the house in order to preserve the table.

10 Repeat the above operation on the turkey's uncarved side. You now have two thighs and two drumsticks. Using the wash cloth, soap and hot water, bathe thoroughly and, if possible, go to a movie. Otherwise, look each person in the eye and say, "I don't suppose anyone wants white meat."

°compelled
forced or pressured

11 If compelled° to carve the breast anyhow, sharpen the knife on the stone again with sufficient awkwardness to tip over the gravy bowl on the person who started the stampede for white meat.

12 While everyone is rushing about to mop the gravy off her slacks, hack at the turkey breast until it starts crumbling off the carcass in ugly chunks.

13 The alternative method for carving white meat is to visit around the neighborhood until you find someone who has a good carving knife and borrow it, if you find one, which is unlikely.

14 This method enables you to watch the football game on neighbors' television sets and also creates the possibility that somebody back at your table will grow tired of waiting and do the carving herself.

°mutilations
damages beyond repair

15 In this case, upon returning home, cast a pained stare upon the mound of chopped white meat that has been hacked out by the family carving knife and refuse to do any more carving that day. No one who cares about the artistry of carving can be expected to work upon the mutilations° of amateurs, and it would be a betrayal of the carver's art to do so.

Questions for Critical Thinking

1. Not everyone brings the same sense of humor to written material. Did you find this essay humorous? Why or why not? How would you describe Russell Baker's humor?

2. Decide where in the essay you first realized the piece would be humorous. Mark that place.

3. What makes the title effective?

4. We have learned that one sentence is not an adequate paragraph. Why then has Russell Baker begun this essay with only one sentence in his first paragraph?

5. Go through the essay and mark every transitional word that signals movement from one step to the next.

6. Process writing can be directional or informational. Would you describe this essay as directional or informational?

7. Although this is intended as a humorous essay, Russell Baker has probably lived long enough and served turkey enough times to have seen most of the problems that he describes with exaggerated drama. Review the essay and make a list of the mishaps that often happen when people try to carve a turkey or do some other household chore.

Writing in Response

1. Write an essay in which you discuss a task you perform at holiday time. If you like, try your hand at humor.

2. Write a straightforward essay on how to carve a turkey (or how to prepare some other dish that calls for a special skill).

3. When a person lacks proper training to accomplish a particular task, the results can be disappointing. Write an essay in which you give several examples of processes that should be left to well-trained professionals. Point out the serious dangers of untrained persons attempting the tasks described in your essay.

4. Write a narrative essay telling of your attempt to perform a certain task for which you lacked the necessary skill. What was the final result?

How to Mark a Book

Mortimer Adler

Mortimer Adler (1902–2001) dropped out of his New York City high school when he was fifteen but later attended Columbia University. He failed to obtain his degree there, however, because he did not take the swimming test required for graduation. Despite this, he was given a teaching post at Columbia as an instructor in psychology, and in a few years he wrote a doctoral dissertation—the only student in the country to earn a Ph.D. without the benefit of even a high school diploma. In 1983, Columbia finally excused Adler from the swimming requirement and gave him his BA—sixty years after he should have graduated.

Adler firmly believed that everyone can find a good education by studying areas of knowledge that help people think clearly and exercise their free will, and throughout his life, Adler worked toward proving his theory. In 1946, while he was at the University of Chicago, Adler was instrumental in starting the Great Books Program, which brought adults together regularly to discuss classic works of literature and philosophy. To support this program, *Encyclopaedia Britannica* printed a set of fifty-four books. The idea behind the Great Books Program spread throughout the country, influencing the lives of many people for years.

1   You know you have to read "between the lines" to get the most out of anything. I want to persuade you to do something equally important in the course of your reading. I want to persuade you to "write between the lines." Unless you do, you are not likely to do the most efficient kind of reading.

°contend
assert

2   I contend,° quite bluntly,° that marking up a book is not an act of mutilation° but of love.

°bluntly
frankly

°mutilation
damage beyond repair

3   You shouldn't mark up a book which isn't yours. Librarians (or your friends) who lend you books expect you to keep them clean, and you should. If you decide that I am right about the usefulness of marking books, you will have to buy them. Most of the world's great books are available today, in reprint editions, at less than a dollar.

°prelude
an introductory action

4   There are two ways in which you can own a book. The first is the property right you establish by paying for it, just as you pay for clothes or furniture. But this act of purchase is only the prelude° to possession. Full ownership comes only when you have made it a part of yourself, and the best way to make yourself a part of it is by writing in it. An illustration may make the point clear. You buy a beefsteak and transfer it from the butcher's icebox to your own. But you do not own the beefsteak in the most important sense until you consume it and get it into your bloodstream. I am arguing that books, too, must be absorbed in your bloodstream to do you any good.

°reverence
deep respect

5   Confusion about what it means to *own* a book leads people to a false reverence° for paper, binding, and type—a respect for the physical thing—the craft of the printer rather than the genius of the author. They forget that it is possible for a man to acquire the idea, to possess the beauty, which a great book contains, without staking his claim by pasting his bookplate inside the cover.

Having a fine library doesn't prove that its owner has a mind enriched by books it proves nothing more than that he, his father, or his wife, was rich enough to buy them.

6   There are three kinds of book owners. The first has all the standard sets and best-sellers—unread, untouched. (This deluded° individual owns woodpulp and ink, not books.) The second has a great many books—a few of them read through, most of them dipped into, but all of them as clean and shiny as the day they were bought. (This person would probably like to make books his own, but is restrained by a false respect for their physical appearance.) The third has a few books or many—every one of them dog-eared and dilapidated,° shaken and loosened by continual use, marked and scribbled in from front to back. (This man owns books.)

7   Is it false respect, you may ask, to preserve intact and unblemished° a beautifully printed book, an elegantly bound edition? Of course not. I'd no more scribble all over a first edition of *Paradise Lost*° than I'd give my baby a set of crayons and an original Rembrandt!° I wouldn't mark up a painting or a statue. Its soul, so to speak, is inseparable from its body. And the beauty of a rare edition or of a richly manufactured volume is like that of a painting or a statue.

8   But the soul of a book *can* be separated from its body. A book is more like the score of a piece of music than it is like a painting. No great musician confuses a symphony with the printed sheets of music. Arturo Toscanini° reveres Brahms,° but Toscanini's score of the C-minor Symphony is so thoroughly marked up that no one but the maestro° himself can read it. The reason why a great conductor makes notations on his musical scores—marks them up again and again each time he returns to study them—is the reason why you should mark your books. If your respect for magnificent binding or typography gets in the way, buy yourself a cheap edition and pay your respects to the author.

9   Why is marking up a book indispensable° to reading? First, it keeps you awake. (And I don't mean merely conscious; I mean wide awake.) In the second place, reading, if it is active, is thinking, and thinking tends to express itself in words, spoken or written. The marked book is usually the thought-through book. Finally, writing helps you remember the thoughts you had, or the thoughts the author expressed. Let me develop these three points.

10   If reading is to accomplish anything more than passing time, it must be active. You can't let your eyes glide across the lines of a book and come up with an understanding of what you have read. Now an ordinary piece of light fiction, like say, *Gone With the Wind*,° doesn't require the most active kind of reading. The books you read for pleasure can be read in a state of relaxation, and nothing is lost. But a great book, rich in ideas and beauty, a book that raises and tries to answer great fundamental questions, demands the most active reading of which you are capable. You don't absorb the ideas of John Dewey° the way you absorb the crooning of Mr. Vallee.° You have to reach for them. That you cannot do while you're asleep.

11   If, when you've finished reading a book, the pages are filled with your notes, you know that you read actively. The most famous active reader of great books I know is President Hutchins, of the University of Chicago. He also has the hardest schedule of business activities of any man I know. He invariably° reads with a pencil, and sometimes, when he picks up a book and a pencil in

---

°deluded
deceived

°dilapidated
shabby

°unblemished
without a flaw

°*Paradise Lost*
epic poem by John Milton
(1608–1674)

°Rembrandt
Dutch painter (1606–1669)

°Toscanini
Italian conductor
(1867–1957)

°Brahms
German composer
(1833–1897)

°maestro
master musician

°indispensable
essential

°*Gone With the Wind*
novel about the American
Civil War

°John Dewey
American educator
(1859–1952)

°Mr. Vallee
Rudy Vallee, popular singer
(1901–1986)

°invariably
always

the evening, he finds himself, instead of making intelligent notes, drawing what he calls "caviar factories" on the margins. When that happens, he puts the book down. He knows he's too tired to read, and he's just wasting time.

12   But, you may ask, why is writing necessary? Well, the physical act of writing, with your own hand, brings words and sentences more sharply before your mind and preserves them better in your memory. To set down your reaction to important words and sentences you have read, and the questions they have raised in your mind, is to preserve those reactions and sharpen those questions.

13   Even if you wrote on a scratch pad, and threw the paper away when you had finished writing, your grasp of the book would be surer. But you don't have to throw the paper away. The margins (top and bottom, as well as side), the end-papers, the very space between the lines, are all available. They aren't sacred. And, best of all, your marks and notes become an integral° part of the book and stay there forever. You can pick up the book the following week or year, and there are all your points of agreement, disagreement, doubt, and inquiry. It's like resuming an interrupted conversation with the advantage of being able to pick up where you left off.

°**integral**
essential

14   And that is exactly what reading a book should be: a conversation between you and the author. Presumably he knows more about the subject than you do; naturally, you'll have the proper humility as you approach him. But don't let anybody tell you that a reader is supposed to be solely on the receiving end. Understanding is a two-way operation; learning doesn't consist in being an empty receptacle.° The learner has to question himself and question the teacher. He even has to argue with the teacher, once he understands what the teacher is saying. And marking a book is literally° an expression of your differences, or agreements of opinion, with the author.

°**receptacle**
a container

°**literally**
really, exactly

15   There are all kinds of devices° for marking a book intelligently and fruitfully.° Here's the way I do it:

°**devices**
techniques

°**fruitfully**
producing results

°**vertical**
up and down lines

1. *Underlining:* of major points, of important or forceful statements.

2. *Vertical° lines at the margin:* to emphasize a statement already underlined.

3. *Star, asterisk, or other doo-dad at the margin:* to be used sparingly, to emphasize the ten or twenty most important statements in the book. (You may want to fold the bottom corner of each page on which you use such marks. It won't hurt the sturdy paper on which most modern books are printed, and you will be able to take the book off the shelf at any time and, by opening it at the folded-corner page, refresh your recollection of the book.)

4. *Numbers in the margin:* to indicate the sequence of points the author makes in developing a single argument.

5. *Numbers of other pages in the margin:* to indicate where else in the book the author made points relevant to the point marked; to tie up the ideas in a book, which, though they may be separated by many pages, belong together.

6. *Circling of key words or phrases.*

7. *Writing in the margin, or at the top or bottom of the page, for the sake of:* recording questions (and perhaps answers) which a passage raised in your mind; reducing a complicated discussion to a simple statement; recording

the sequence of major points right through the books. I use the end-paper at the back of the book to make a personal index of the author's points in the order of their appearance.

16   The front end-papers are, to me, the most important. Some people reserve them for a fancy bookplate.° I reserve them for fancy thinking. After I have finished reading the book and making my personal index on the back end-papers, I turn to the front and try to outline the book, not page by page, or point by point (I've already done that at the back), but as an integrated structure, with a basic unity and an order of parts. This outline is, to me, the measure of my understanding of the work.

17   If you're a die-hard anti-book-marker, you may object that the margins, the space between the lines, and the end-papers don't give you room enough. All right. How about using a scratch pad slightly smaller than the page-size of the book—so that the edges of the sheets won't protrude? Make your index, outlines, and even your notes on the pad, and then insert these sheets permanently inside the front and back covers of the book.

18   Or, you may say that this business of marking books is going to slow up your reading. It probably will. That's one of the reasons for doing it. Most of us have been taken in by the notion that the speed of reading is a measure of our intelligence. There is no such thing as the right speed for intelligent reading. Some things should be read quickly and effortlessly, and some should be read slowly and even laboriously. The sign of intelligence in reading is in the ability to read different things differently according to their worth. In the case of good books, the point is not to see how many of them you can get through, but rather how many can get through you—how many you can make your own. A few friends are better than a thousand acquaintances. If this be your aim, as it should be, you will not be impatient if it takes more time and effort to read a great book than it does a newspaper.

19   You may have one final objection to marking books. You can't lend them to your friends because nobody else can read them without being distracted by your notes. Furthermore, you won't want to lend them because a marked copy is a kind of intellectual diary, and lending it is almost like giving your mind away.

20   If your friend wishes to read your *Plutarch's Lives,*° *Shakespeare,* or *The Federalist Papers,*° tell him gently but firmly to buy a copy. You will lend him your car or your coat—but your books are as much a part of you as your head or your heart.

°**bookplate**
a label placed in a book, with the owner's name

°***Plutarch's Lives***
famous biography of people from the ancient world

°***The Federalist Papers***
a series of articles published in 1787 urging the ratification of the U.S. Constitution

Questions for Critical Thinking

1.   Mortimer Adler begins his essay by quite clearly saying he will try to convince us that we should mark our books when we read. This, of course, means he is writing an argument. Yet the title is the typical title of a process analysis essay. Scan the essay to find where he gets to the process part of the essay. What paragraphs tell us how to mark a book?

2.   Where in the essay does Mortimer Adler use classification?

3.   Mortimer Adler uses a simile to make clear what he thinks a book is like. What is the simile? Explain the simile in your own words.

4. How would you define "active reading" using Mortimer Adler's viewpoint?

5. Mortimer Adler begins by making some disclaimer about marking up books. What are the cases in which a book should not be marked?

6. In paragraph 9, what are the three transitional words?

7. According to paragraph 12, what is the relationship between writing and memory?

8. In paragraph 14, Mortimer Adler claims that the reader or learner is not an "empty receptacle." Explain what he means by this.

9. Reread this essay. Using Mortimer Adler's advice, mark his essay.

Writing in Response

1. Our culture places a great deal of emphasis on owning things: fancy cars, beautiful jewelry, name-brand clothes. Mortimer Adler has a very different attitude about who owns a book. Explore his idea and expand it to look at other things. Who owns a college degree? Who owns a piece of property?

2. Using Mortimer Adler's ideas, write a guide for college students and give them advice on how to read a chapter in a textbook that they will be tested on.

3. Write an essay about your own reading habits or study habits. What is the process you follow when you do homework or study for an exam?

4. How important is it to have books in your home? Write an essay in which you give advice to someone about how to begin collecting books for a home library.

Neat People vs. Sloppy People

Suzanne Britt

Sometimes we learn the most about ourselves when our shortcomings are pointed out in a humorous way. The author of the following essay does just this, as she divides the human population into two basic groups. Suzanne Britt teaches English literature and writing at Meredith College in Raleigh, North Carolina. Her writing has been widely published—her essays and articles have appeared in periodicals such as *Newsweek* and *The New York Times*—and her books have been well received by readers of popular fiction and by students working in college writing classrooms. As you read the following essay, decide which of the two groups described by the author is the better one for you—or which group is the one you would like to join.

1   I've finally figured out the difference between neat people and sloppy people. The distinction is, as always, moral. Neat people are lazier and meaner than sloppy people.

2   Sloppy people, you see, are not really sloppy. Their sloppiness is merely the unfortunate consequence of their extreme moral rectitude.° Sloppy people carry in their mind's eye a heavenly vision, a precise plan, that is so stupendous, so perfect, it can't be achieved in this world or the next.

°**rectitude**
correctness

3   Sloppy people live in Never-Never Land. Someday is their *métier*.° Someday they are planning to alphabetize all their books and set up home catalogues. Someday they will go through their wardrobes and mark certain items for tentative mending and certain items for passing on to relatives of similar shape and size. Someday sloppy people will make family scrapbooks into which they will put newspaper clippings, postcards, locks of hair, and the dried corsage from their senior prom. Someday they will file everything on the surface of their desks, including the cash receipts from coffee purchases at the snack shop. Someday they will sit down and read all the back issues of *The New Yorker*.

°**métier**
French for "a person's specialty"

4   For all these noble reasons and more, sloppy people never get neat. They aim too high and wide. They save everything, planning someday to file, order, and straighten out the world. But while these ambitious plans take clearer and clearer shape in their heads, the books spill from the shelves onto the floor, the clothes pile up in the hamper and closet, the family mementos accumulate in every drawer, the surface of the desk is buried under mounds of paper and the unread magazines threaten to reach the ceiling.

5   Sloppy people can't bear to part with anything. They give loving attention to every detail. When sloppy people say they're going to tackle the surface of the desk, they really mean it. Not a paper will go unturned; not a rubber band will go unboxed. Four hours or two weeks into the excavation, the desk looks exactly the same, primarily because the sloppy person is meticulously creating new

piles of papers with new headings and scrupulously stopping to read all the old book catalogs before he throws them away. A neat person would just bulldoze the desk.

°**cavalier**
very informal and offhand

6   Neat people are bums and clods at heart. They have cavalier° attitudes toward possessions, including family heirlooms. Everything is just another dust-catcher to them. If anything collects dust, it's got to go and that's that. Neat people will toy with the idea of throwing the children out of the house just to cut down on the clutter.

7   Neat people don't care about process. They like results. What they want to do is get the whole thing over with so they can sit down and watch the rasslin' on TV. Neat people operate on two unvarying principles: Never handle any item twice, and throw everything away.

8   The only thing messy in a neat person's house is the trash can. The minute something comes to a neat person's hand, he will look at it, try to decide if it has immediate use and, finding none, throw it in the trash.

9   Neat people are especially vicious with mail. They never go through their mail unless they are standing directly over a trash can. If the trash can is beside the mailbox, even better. All ads, catalogs, pleas for charitable contributions, church bulletins and money-saving coupons go straight into the trash can without being opened. All letters from home, postcards from Europe, bills and paychecks are opened, immediately responded to, then dropped in the trash can. Neat people keep their receipts only for tax purposes. That's it. No sentimental salvaging of birthday cards or the last letter a dying relative ever wrote. Into the trash it goes.

10   Neat people place neatness above everything, even economics. They are incredibly wasteful. Neat people throw away several toys every time they walk through the den. I knew a neat person once who threw away a perfectly good dish drainer because it had mold on it. The drainer was too much trouble to wash. And neat people sell their furniture when they move. They will sell a La-Z-Boy recliner while you are reclining in it.

11   Neat people are no good to borrow from. Neat people buy everything in expensive little single portions. They get their flour and sugar in two-pound bags. They wouldn't consider clipping a coupon, saving a leftover, reusing plastic non-dairy whipped cream containers or rinsing off tin foil and draping it over the unmoldy dish drainer. You can never borrow a neat person's newspaper to see what's playing at the movies. Neat people have the paper all wadded up and in the trash by 7:05 a.m.

12   Neat people cut a clean swath through the organic as well as the inorganic world. People, animals, and things are all one to them. They are so insensitive. After they've finished with the pantry, the medicine cabinet, and the attic, they will throw out the red geranium (too many leaves), sell the dog (too many fleas), and send the children off to boarding school (too many scuffmarks on the hard-wood floors).

Questions for Critical Thinking

1. At what point in your reading of the essay did you become aware that this was a humorous piece of writing?

2. What explanation does Suzanne Britt give for a sloppy person's behavior? Do you agree with her?

3. In paragraph 3, what are the examples the writer lists when she presents the projects a sloppy person plans to do? Do these plans seem admirable to you?

4. Does the author use the block method or the point-by-point method to contrast sloppy people with neat people?

5. One of the reasons Suzanne Britt's writing is so appreciated is that readers recognize themselves in her essays. In paragraph 11, the author tells us that "neat people are no good to borrow from." What makes her supporting statements for this comment humorous?

6. Review the concluding paragraph of the essay. Do you know anyone who acts in the ways listed in that paragraph? By the time you have finished the essay, have you come to your own conclusion as to which category the writer herself belongs to?

Writing in Response

1. Write an essay that takes the opposite viewpoint from the one given by Suzanne Britt. Defend the neat person and criticize the sloppy person.

2. Describe two people you know who have very different approaches to being neat and organized. Explain what it is like to be with each of them.

3. How would you describe the household in which you grew up? In what ways were your family members very organized? In what areas were they disorganized? What are the problems of growing up in a household that is extreme in one way or another?

4. Write an essay in which you give advice to a young couple setting up a household. How would you advise them on being neat and organized?

5. Suzanne Britt claims that sloppy people cannot part with anything. Write an essay in which you analyze your own attitude about possessions. What are the things you have a hard time parting with? What things do you especially like to collect and save?

The Huge, Bee-Decapitating Hornet That Can't Survive Group Hugs

Matt Simon

Matt Simon is a science writer for *Wired* magazine. He authors the popular "Absurd Creature of the Week" column, where he delves into the biology and habits of unusual insects and animals from around the globe. In the following article, he puts a humorous twist on the behaviors of the Asian giant hornet, an insect that would (and probably should) terrify most readers.

°**decapitations**
beheadings, the chopping off of heads

°**mandibles**
jaws

°**marauders**
outlaws who attack and rob their victims

°**glut**
excessive supply, overabundance

°**formidable**
causing fear, intimidating

°**menaces**
threatens

°**ingenious**
clever and resourceful

°**apex predator**
an animal that is at the top of the food chain and has no natural predators of its own

°**incapacitating**
disabling

°**entomologist**
a scientist who studies insects

°**sans**
without (from French)

1   THIRTY ASIAN GIANT hornets, following a scent laid by their scout, descend on a hive of honey bees and get straight to the decapitations.° The hornets snag the tiny bees and pop their heads right off using their enormous mandibles.° Here a head, there a head. Desperately, the bees try to sting the hornets, yet they can't puncture the giants' armor.

2   Here a head, there a head—pop pop pop. One by one the bees fall, a single hornet taking down as many as 20 victims a minute. At that rate, the tiny band of marauders° can wipe out a colony of 30,000 bees in a few hours, a glut° of beheadings that makes the French Revolution look like Dance Dance Revolution.

3   The remarkable Asian giant hornet, Vespa mandarinia, grows to almost two inches in length and can sting through a rain jacket. And unlike a honey bee, it can sting repeatedly, its venom breaking down flesh and overloading kidneys. The hornet is formidable,° to say the least, but the native honey bees it menaces° have an ingenious° defense: They form a ball around the scout hornet and vibrate to cook the invader to death, keeping the colony's coordinates out of the hands of the scout's soldiers back at base.

4   The Asian giant hornet is in many ways a modern winged T. rex. It's an apex predator,° capable of taking down any other insect and incapacitating° any mammal dumb or unfortunate enough to disturb it. Should you come across one, don't move, as the good doctor Grant always said (OK fine, maybe he was wrong about that).

5   Just ask actual doctor Stephen Martin, an entomologist° at the University of Salford. Once while observing a nest, he and a colleague—sans° suits—displeased the hornets and got themselves attacked. "You close your eyes, you close your mouth, you grit your teeth, because it's quite frightening," he says. "The other guy just couldn't cope and he ran away, and he got stung several times. I was fine." If the hornets don't take you to be a threat, they'll leave you alone. No sense in wasting venom and risk getting squashed, after all.

°**divot**
dent

°**neurotoxins**
venoms or poisons that
harm the nerves

6　　　Get stung, though, and you'll want to go ahead and start considering a trip to the hospital. The hornet's venom breaks down flesh cells, leaving you with a divot,° while neurotoxins° glitch nerves, resulting in an intense, searing pain that one victim described as having a hot nail hammered into you. (Had he actually ever had a hot nail hammered into him? Seems like a really specific comparison.) Because of its size, the hornet can inject a whole lot of venom— you can end up with a teaspoon of the stuff in your system if a swarm jabs you 30 or 40 times. Catch enough stings and your kidneys will shut down, or even your heart if you have a weak ticker. If you happen to be allergic, it'll be anaphylactic shock° instead.

°**anaphylactic shock**
A life-threatening allergic
reaction wherein the throat
may swell and prevent
breathing. Swelling may
occur in other parts of the
body, and the sufferer may
develop hives and low
blood pressure.

7　　　What makes the Asian giant hornet particularly problematic is its size. Because this thing is so huge, so is its nest, which can weigh more than 20 pounds. That would snap a tree branch, so instead the hornet holes up in, well, holes in the ground—where unsuspecting humans can stroll too close. If you do, don't bother running. These things can fly at up to 15 miles per hour, and even faster if they've got a good tailwind.

8　　　While an Asian giant hornet can ruin your day, it can ruin a honey bee's life. But the native bee it menaces has evolved a rather unconventional way to fight back: group hugs.

°**pheromones**
chemicals released by
animals that affect the
behavior of other animals

9　　　Should a hornet scout find itself a beehive, the occupants won't rush out to intercept it. Instead, the bees will let the scout in to mark the location with pheromones° for its comrades to follow. It's a trap: On cue the workers swarm, forming a frantic, living ball around the intruder. The bees vibrate, revving up their body temperatures to begin cooking the hornet to death. All the while, carbon dioxide builds up inside the ball.

°**exploit**
to take unfair advantage of

10　　　The bees also exploit° a unique bit of insect anatomy: The hornet doesn't have a heart—literally and I suppose kind of figuratively when you think about it—and instead pumps blood with contractions of its body. "The bees just crowd it and crowd it and crowd it like a boa constrictor, so they prevent the hornet from being able to pump blood around its body," Martin says. This further raises the hornet's body temperature.

11　　　"So it's this combination of heating them, building up the carbon dioxide in the middle of it, and then restricting their blood flow by effectively squeezing them," Martin adds. The hornet scout eventually dies, taking with it the coordinates of the hive. It may have picked off a bee here and there in the struggle, and some of the workers themselves may have been crushed or asphyxiated,° but the hive is saved.

°**asphyxiated**
suffocated, deprived of air

°**countermeasure**
an action taken as a
response to another action

12　　　It's a remarkable countermeasure° that has evolved over millennia. That's time the introduced European honey bee ain't got. It hasn't stumbled upon the swarm countermeasure, so the hornet scout inevitably marks a European bee nest and returns with its friends. The marauders slaughter every adult, yet don't bother eating their relatively calorie-poor bodies. Instead, the hornets take the bee larvae back to their nest to feed to their own larvae, shuttling back and forth. The hornets will even post guards at the hive entrance to protect their booty overnight if they haven't finished looting in one day.

13　　　Beekeepers tending the European variety in China and Japan don't so much appreciate all this. Some attach special guards to their hives to keep the hornets out, while others take a rather more active approach, hiring people to volley the things with tennis or badminton rackets. (At least one overachieving beekeeper in Japan employs the enviable trap-plus-badminton-racket technique.) In wealthier Japan, beekeepers actually pay some brave soul to remove nearby hornet nests—apparently they've got solid health care over there or something.

14   The hornet's apparent attitude problem isn't exactly great for PR. "With hornets, people ask us often what use are they, they just sting us, they hurt us, we should just get rid of them all," Martin says. "We've got the bees, they make honey, they work really hard, they're really good."

°**pivotal**
extremely important

15   In reality, though, the Asian giant hornet serves a pivotal° function in the ecosystem. When it isn't terrorizing honey bees, it attacks things like caterpillars that can devastate crops. It's nature's very own high-powered pest controller.

16   And yes, that means if you throw rocks at their nests, you are indeed a pest and will be controlled. So don't do that. Unless you've got solid health care or something.

Questions for Critical Thinking

1. The overall pattern of organization used by the author is comparison/contrast. Interestingly, two (not one) comparisons are made. Identify these comparisons. Which of the two is more complex?

2. The author of this essay uses humor to describe what is actually a brutal and disturbing topic. What effect does this decision have on the essay? Do you agree or disagree with the author's choice?

3. In paragraph 2, the author describes the massacre of honey bees by Asian giant hornets as ". . . a glut of beheadings that makes the French Revolution look like Dance Dance Revolution." What does he mean by this comparison?

4. Review the reading, and make a list of transitional expressions (words and phrases) that signal a comparison or a contrast.

5. Though this essay's overall pattern of organization is comparison/contrast, the author departs from this pattern in paragraphs 9–11. What pattern of organization does he use in these paragraphs? How can you tell?

Writing in Response

1. Most comparison/contrast essays make a single comparison between two things; this essay makes two comparisons at once. Write an essay of your own in which you analyze the author's strategy. Comment on what effect you think his decision has on the essay.

2. Select two people, creatures, or products that share similarities. Then, write an essay comparing and contrasting them. If you feel up to it, try adding humor to your writing.

3. Write an essay in which you compare yourself with a character in literature (novels, nonfiction, graphic novels, comic books) or film (movies or television). Thoroughly explain how you are similar to and different from this character.

Why Marriages Fail

Anne Roiphe

Anne Roiphe is noted for her exploration of women's search for personal identity. Themes running through her fiction and nonfiction include feminism, marriage, family, and cultural identity. One commentator has referred to her writing as a "thoughtful and often provocative" analysis of history and of the forces that shape modern culture and society. Anne Roiphe's best-known novel is *Up the Sandbox!* She has also contributed to magazines such as *Redbook* and *Family Circle*. In the following essay, the writer examines one of the striking facts of our modern society, that is, the large number of marriages ending in divorce. As she explores this topic, we notice two impressive aspects of her writing: an analysis that is always clear and convincing, and a voice that is reasonable and calm.

°**obsolete**
no longer used

1   These days so many marriages end in divorce that our most sacred vows no longer ring with truth. "Happily ever after" and "Till death do us part" are expressions that seem on the way to becoming obsolete.° Why has it become so hard for couples to stay together? What goes wrong? What has happened to us that close to one-half of all marriages are destined for the divorce courts? How could we have created a society in which 42 percent of our children will grow up in single-parent homes? If statistics could only measure loneliness, regret, pain, loss of self-confidence and fear of the future, the numbers would be beyond quantifying.°

°**quantifying**
expressing an exact amount

°**infertility**
inability to conceive a child

°**stupefying**
astounding; astonishing

2   Even though each broken marriage is unique, we can still find the common perils, the common causes for marital despair. Each marriage has crisis points and each marriage tests endurance, the capacity for both intimacy and change. Outside pressures such as job loss, illness, infertility,° trouble with a child, care of aging parents and all the other plagues of life hit marriage the way hurricanes blast our shores. Some marriages survive these storms and others don't. Marriages fail, however, not simply because of the outside weather but because the inner climate becomes too hot or too cold, too turbulent or too stupefying.°

°**emeritus**
retired and keeping an honorary title

3   When we look at how we choose our partners and what expectations exist at the tender beginnings of romance, some of the reasons for disaster become quite clear. We all select with unconscious accuracy a mate who will recreate with us the emotional patterns of our first homes. Dr. Carl A. Whitaker, a marital therapist and emeritus° professor of psychiatry at the University of Wisconsin, explains, "From early childhood on, each of us carried models for marriage, femininity, masculinity, motherhood, fatherhood and all the other family roles." Each of us falls in love with a mate who has qualities of our parents, who will help us discover both the psychological happiness and miseries of our past lives. We may think we have found a man unlike Dad, but then he turns to drink or drugs, or loses his job over and over again or sits silently in front of the T.V. just the way Dad did. A man may choose a woman who doesn't like kids just like his mother or who gambles away the family life savings just like his mother. Or he may choose a slender wife who seems unlike his obese mother but then turns out to have other addictions that destroy mutual happiness.

°compulsively
unable to resist

°yearning
a deep desire

4   A man and a woman bring to their marriage bed a blended concoction of conscious and unconscious memories of their parents' lives together. The human way is to compulsively° repeat and recreate the patterns of the past. Sigmund Freud so well described the unhappy design that many of us get trapped in: the unmet needs of childhood, the angry feelings left over from frustrations long ago, the limits of trust and the recurrence of old fears. Once an individual senses this entrapment, there may follow a yearning° to escape, and the result could be a broken, splintered marriage.

5   Of course people can overcome the habits and attitudes that developed in childhood. We all have hidden strengths and amazing capacities for growth and creative change. Change, however, requires work—observing your part in a rotten pattern, bringing difficulties out into the open—and work runs counter to the basic myth of marriage: "When I wed this person all my problems will be over. I will have achieved success and I will become the center of life for this other person and this person will be my center, and we will mean everything to each other forever." This myth, which every marriage relies on, is soon exposed. The coming of children, the pulls and tugs of their demands on affection and time, place considerable strain on that basic myth of meaning everything to each other, of merging together and solving all of life's problems.

6   Concern and tension about money take each partner away from the other. Obligations to demanding parents or still-depended-upon parents create further strain. Couples today must also deal with all the cultural changes brought on in recent years by the women's movement and the sexual revolution. The altering of roles and the shifting of responsibilities have been extremely trying for many marriages.

°erode
to diminish; to make disappear

°euphoric
extremely happy

7   These and other realities of life erode° the visions of marital bliss the way sandstorms eat at rock and the ocean nibbles away at the dunes. Those euphoric,° grand feelings that accompany romantic love are really self-delusions, self-hypnotic dreams that enable us to forge a relationship. Real life, failure at work, disappointments, exhaustion, bad smells, bad colds and hard times all puncture the dream and leave us stranded with our mate, with our childhood patterns pushing us this way and that, with our unfulfilled expectations.

8   The struggle to survive in marriage requires adaptability, flexibility, genuine love and kindness and an imagination strong enough to feel what the other is feeling. Many marriages fall apart because either partner cannot imagine what the other wants or cannot communicate what he or she needs or feels. Anger builds until it erupts into a volcanic burst that buries the marriage in ash.

9   It is not hard to see, therefore, how essential communication is for a good marriage. A man and a woman must be able to tell each other how they feel and why they feel the way they do; otherwise they will impose on each other roles and actions that lead to further unhappiness. In some cases, the communication patterns of childhood—of not talking, of talking too much, of not listening, of distrust and anger, of withdrawal—spill into the marriage and prevent a healthy exchange of thoughts and feelings. The answer is to set up new patterns of communication and intimacy.

10   At the same time, however, we must see each other as individuals. "To achieve a balance between separateness and closeness is one of the major psychological tasks of all human beings at every stage of life," says Dr. Stuart Bartle, a psychiatrist at the New York University Medical Center.

11   If we sense from our mate a need for too much intimacy, we tend to push him or her away, fearing that we may lose our identities in the merging of marriage. One partner may suffocate the other partner in a childlike dependency.

°**clings**
holds on tightly

12   A good marriage means growing as a couple but also growing as individuals. This isn't easy. Richard gives up his interest in carpentry because his wife, Helen, is jealous of the time he spends away from her. Karen quits her choir group because her husband dislikes the friends she makes there. Each pair clings° to each other and is angry with each other as life closes in on them. This kind of marital balance is easily thrown as one or the other pulls away and divorce follows.

°**proverbial**
of or relating to proverbs, linked to a saying

13   Sometimes people pretend that a new partner will solve the old problems. Most often extramarital sex destroys a marriage because it allows an artificial split between the good and the bad—the good is projected on the new partner and the bad is dumped on the head of the old. Dishonesty, hiding and cheating create walls between men and women. Infidelity is just a symptom of trouble. It is a symbolic complaint, a weapon of revenge, as well as an unraveler of closeness. Infidelity is often that proverbial° last straw that sinks the camel to the ground.

14   All right—marriage has always been difficult. Why then are we seeing so many divorces at this time? Yes, our modern social fabric is thin, and yes the permissiveness of society has created unrealistic expectations and thrown the family into chaos. But divorce is so common because people today are unwilling to exercise the self-discipline that marriage requires. They expect easy joy, like the entertainment on TV, the thrill of a good party.

15   Marriage takes some kind of sacrifice, not dreadful self-sacrifice of the soul, but some level of compromise. Some of one's fantasies, some of one's legitimate desires have to be given up for the value of the marriage itself. "While all marital partners feel shackled at times, it is they who really choose to make the marital ties into confining chains or supporting bonds," says Dr. Whitaker. Marriage requires sexual, financial and emotional discipline. A man and a woman cannot follow every impulse, cannot allow themselves to stop growing or changing.

°**devastation**
shock; destruction

16   Divorce is not an evil act. Sometimes it provides salvation for people who have grown helplessly apart or were frozen in patterns of pain or mutual unhappiness. Divorce can be, despite its initial devastation,° like the first cut of the surgeon's knife, a step toward new health and a good life. On the other hand, if the partners can stay past the breaking up of the romantic myths into the development of real love and intimacy, they have achieved a work as amazing as the greatest cathedrals of the world. Marriages that do not fail but improve, that persist despite imperfections, are not only rare these days but offer a wondrous shelter in which the face of our mutual humanity can safely show itself.

Questions for Critical Thinking

1.   When an essay is concerned with answering the question *why*, we know the method of development is cause and effect. There are many ways to write an introductory paragraph; describe how Anne Roiphe chose to introduce her topic.

2. Certain transitional words in a piece of writing are used to help the reader understand how one idea connects to another. In paragraph 2, find two words that signal contrast, two words that signal cause, and one expression that signals to us that examples will follow.

3. Find at least two examples of the author's use of simile or metaphor.

4. Mark any place in the essay where the author uses an authority to support a point.

5. In paragraph 3, Anne Roiphe claims that "each of us falls in love with a mate who has the qualities of our parents." Do you agree or disagree with this claim? Do you have any counterevidence?

6. Summarize this essay by making a list of reasons why marriages fail, according to Anne Roiphe.

Writing in Response

1. Anne Roiphe provides a list of major problems that often occur in a person's life: loss of a job, serious illness, infertility, trouble with a child, or caring for an aging parent. Write an essay discussing how the occurrence of even one of these events can affect many of the relationships in a person's life.

2. Many couples go to therapists hoping to work out their problems. Write an essay in which you discuss the benefits of having a third person listen to a couple explaining their problems.

3. In your view, does going through hard times help or hurt a person's ability to sustain relationships? Write an essay answering this question by using your own experience and observations.

4. Many people believe that if they make a change (such as getting married, having a child, moving to another place) they will fix something that is broken in their lives. Write an essay in which you discuss the extent to which a major change can be a benefit for a person, and to what extent making a change will not really solve any of that person's problems.

5. The old expression "money comes between friends" can also be applied to family relationships. Write an essay in which you discuss how issues of money can have negative effects on people's relationships. How can money issues create several kinds of problems in people's lives?

If I Feel Uncomfortable I Must Be Doing Something Right

Elliot Begoun

Business writer Elliot Begoun is well known for his unconventional practices and often writes thought-provoking essays in order to encourage his readers to ask themselves challenging questions. It's not just his audience that he sometimes makes feel uncomfortable; he prides himself on stepping out of his own comfort zone. In this first-person essay, Begoun guides the reader through his experiences in trying new things and pushing himself to innovate and think creatively.

°**myriad**
a large number or varied in nature

°**mortified**
embarrassed

1   I am strange. To those who know me well, that statement can be applied to a myriad° of behaviors. But, what I am specifically referring to is this: I feel more comfortable speaking in front of a group of 3,000 strangers, than carrying on a personal conversation with just one. I have no issue negotiating a hard fought business deal, but would be mortified° sending my food back at a restaurant. I enjoy developing a complex strategic plan, but shutter when asked to make plans with another couple.

2   I have spent a lot of my life seeking shelter and refuge in my comfort zone. I resisted any situation that even remotely pushed me to its boundary, and certainly, anytime I found myself outside of it, I withdrew as quickly as possible. I spent years employing strategies that allowed me to remain right there in its safety. I staffed my departments to insulate me from discomfort and even had my wife and kids serve as buffers on a personal level. Looking back, I now recognize that I was doing myself such an incredible disservice.

3   Personal growth does not come from within your comfort zone. Rather, it is only found in those moments you find yourself feeling awkward, vulnerable or exposed. The more frequently you retreat from discomfort, the more closed you are to opportunity. I think back at the questions I didn't ask for fear of sounding foolish or the people I failed to introduce myself to because it felt awkward, and I wonder what growth I missed in those moments.

4   It is easier to insulate yourself as leader in an organization. For example, I always had people on my team who were great in social situations, so I did not have to be. For those questions I was uncomfortable asking, I had team members go seek out the answers and for the people I needed to know, I had introductions made for me.

5   When I started my own business, I knew that there would not be any insulation or buffer. If I was to succeed, I would have to boldly step out of that comfort zone, and frankly, I was terrified. It kept me up nights and I had some

doubt that I could. But, I was also highly motivated. I had wanted to do this my whole life, I had kids in college and a mortgage to worry about. So as they say, failure was not an option.

6   Sadly, it took this level of motivation and fear to finally get me to step off that 100 foot pole. But, as soon as I did, I started to experience life more fully, both professionally and personally. I found myself in situations I could have never dreamt being in. I've learned so much and have met so many great people. Almost everyday now, I come up against things that make me feel awkward, vulnerable and exposed. The biggest difference is that instead of retreating back to the safety of my comfort zone, I lean into that discomfort. I have recognized that when I feel uncomfortable, I am doing something right.

7   I share this personal story of discovery in the hope it will encourage you to step off that pole. Don't wait and waste time that could be spent experiencing new things. It is not nearly as scary as I convinced myself it would be. The stories I told myself about the things that could happen in those moments of discomfort have all proven false. Trust me, if you feel uncomfortable, you are doing something right and you will be living more fully.

Questions for Critical Thinking

1. What is Elliot Begoun's purpose for writing this essay?

2. What does the author state was his motivation for facing his fear?

3. What were the benefits of Elliot Begoun's facing his fear?

4. Does this essay contain a thesis statement? If so, which paragraph is it in?

Writing in Response

1. Describe a situation in which you were forced to face a fear. How did it turn out? Was it a positive or negative experience?

2. Write an essay about why it is important that we sometimes get out of our comfort zone. In what situations would this be beneficial? Why?

3. Based on your own life experiences, what is one piece of helpful advice you would give someone? Write an essay in which you give this advice.

The Perils of Being Too Nice

Jen Kim

Identity, personality, and relationships are all themes central to Jen Kim's writing. As a frequent contributor to *Psychology Today,* she has written many articles exploring her past, and she muses on what it means to be trying to fit into a changing world as well as detailing her own personal evolution over time.

1   When I was in high school, there was another Jennifer Kim in all of my classes.

2   She and I are still friends today, but during those painful and awkward years of adolescence, we simply became known as the "nice" (me) one or the "mean" one (her).

3   I suppose being called the nice one is better than being the "fat" one or the "stupid" one, but being the nice one had its own burdens.

°**differentiate**
tell the difference

4   When trying to differentiate° between us, classmates would look directly into my eyes and say, "Are you the nice one?"

5   I would shrug my shoulders, uncertain how to answer. It wasn't that the other Jennifer was particularly mean; she wasn't at all.

6   It was just that, I was too nice. Think Disney movie nice—to the point where it kind of makes you want to vomit.

7   As much as I'd like to admit that I was just a naturally delightful and kind person, I was not. In fact, I purposefully sought out to be overly nice and sweet to others.

8   During high school (and most of life), we just want to be accepted, and we're told that the best way to achieve this is by being nice to other people: *give compliments, share your food, buy them gifts, etc.*

9   So that's what I did—all the time. The strange thing was that even though I was doing nice favors for people, I still rarely felt like I was being genuinely accepted by anyone or building deeper friendships. Instead, I felt like I was losing not only my allowance, but also my sense of self.

°**sycophantic**
flattering, behaving in a way to gain advantage

10   To me, being the nice one meant being the sycophantic° one—devoid of personality or opinions. I found myself agreeing with other people more than offering up my own ideas.

11   And being too nice meant putting other people's needs and desires before mine. I saw myself bending over backwards for people who wouldn't dream of returning the favor.

12   Sure, I was always surrounded by people, but it eventually became difficult to be around them, because I felt like I had to constantly be "on" or live up to my "nice" label. Most times, I felt like the people I so desperately wanted to be liked by were the most inane° and boring people I'd ever met. And the depressing thing was I was trying to be just like them.

°inane
foolish

13   But I was still the nice Jennifer—confined only to adjectives such as: happy, smiling, generous, when truthfully, I didn't feel anything of those things.

14   Sometimes, I felt jealous of the other Jennifer, who could get away with any kind of behavior, because she wasn't always expected to be nice.

15   It was during college when I stopped the niceties. The other Jennifer went to a different college and, for the first time, I realized I didn't have to be so painfully nice.

16   And I wasn't. I wasn't mean, but I stopped going out of my way to do things for people I barely knew. It was hard to make friends at first, because I really wasn't sure who I was—I kept on trying to find a label that fit my personality (funny, smart, pretty, etc.) but none of them seemed right.

17   I spent most of my freshman year just wandering between groups of half-friends like a nomad trying to find a home.

18   Ten years later, I still don't have a label to define me. The closest one that comes to mind is: "weird" which is not great, but not terrible.

19   But, I find that it's still better than being nice.

Questions for Critical Thinking

1. What reason does Jen Kim give for wanting to be overly nice?

2. What were the effects of the writer's behavior? Were they positive or negative?

3. In which paragraph does Jen Kim give examples about what it means to be nice to people? What are the examples?

4. Jen Kim says that it was hard living up to the label of being "nice." What are some examples of labels that we place on others or ourselves that can potentially cause stress to the one being labeled?

5. What event prompted the writer to stop being the nice one?

Writing in Response

1. Many times we find ourselves in a setting where we are expected to act a certain way. Write about a situation in which you felt like you had to act in a way that did not feel natural to you.

2. In this essay, Jen Kim writes about the negative side of being too nice, but what about the positive side? Write about the positive effects of being nice to people.

3. Write your own cause-and-effect essay about a common label that people often give one another and the effects that it can have on the person.

Giving Students the Heroes They Need

Peter H. Gibbon

Peter H. Gibbon is a writer and inspirational speaker whose chosen topic is that of defining and analyzing heroism and the hero in our society today. Dr. Gibbon's book *A Call to Heroism: Renewing America's Vision of Greatness* deals with this topic in detail. In the following essay, Dr. Gibbon addresses the question of how to communicate to students a renewed sense of true heroism.

°**apathy**
lack of interest

°**nihilism**
absence of and scorn for any belief

1   Human beings are deeply divided, eternally torn between apathy° and activity, nihilism° and belief. We wage a daily battle between a higher and lower self. The *hero* stands for our higher self. To get through life and permit the higher self to prevail, we depend on public models of excellence, bravery, and goodness.

2   During the last 40 years in America, such models have been in short supply. Except among politicians and advertising firms, the word *hero* has been out of fashion since the late 1960s to describe past or present public figures. We are reluctant to use it this way, doubtful if any one person can hold up under the burden of such a word.

3   After the September 11 terrorist attacks, *hero* was resurrected to describe the firefighters and police officers who lost their lives in the World Trade Center, rescue workers who patiently picked their way through the rubble, passengers who thwarted terrorists on a hijacked airplane, and soldiers who left on planes and ships. In difficult times, we turn to the word *hero* to express our deepest sorrow, our highest aspiration,° and our most profound° admiration.

°**aspiration**
ambition; desire

°**profound**
deep

4   I have plugged *hero* into every available database; read hundreds of biographies and books on heroism; traveled the country talking to Americans about heroes; and interviewed educators, historians, journalists, ministers, politicians, scientists, and writers, asking questions that shaped my book, *A Call to Heroism:* How did we lose our public heroes? Why does it matter? Where do we go from here?

5   As a historian, I have been tracing the changing face of the American hero, researching what has happened to the presentation of heroes in history books, and analyzing ways revisionist historians have shaped teachers' attitudes, which in turn shape the way students respond.

6   The most rewarding part of this odyssey has been the five years I spent talking to students about heroes. Most of my audiences have been in high schools—from a thousand students sitting on gym bleachers to small classes in history and literature.

'jaded
worn out; wearied

7   In these talks, I challenge that they are too old, too jaded,° or too cynical for heroes. I quote Ralph Waldo Emerson, another true believer in heroes and a writer most students will know: "Go with mean people and you think life is mean" and "with the great, our thoughts and manners easily become great."

8   In spirited debate, they agree, disagree, challenge, and probe. "Is Malcolm X a hero? John Brown? Why is Hitler worse than Columbus?" They ask about celebrities, athletes, historical figures, politicians, and rescuers, and about personal heroes: parents, teachers, friends.

°synonymous
having the same meaning

°inclusive
comprehensive; including a wide range

9   For most of human history, *hero* has been synonymous° with *warrior.* Although we often link these words today, we do have an expanded, more inclusive° definition of *hero* than the Greeks. Modern dictionaries list three qualities in common after *hero:* extraordinary achievement, courage, and the idea (variously expressed) that the hero serves as a "model" or "example"—that heroism has a moral component.

°elusive
beyond one's grasp

°verity
truth

°temp'rance
moderation

°fickle
changeable

10   The moral component of heroism—and, I believe, the most important one—is elusive.° *The Oxford English Dictionary* cites "greatness of soul," which I believe to be a mysterious blend of powerful qualities summarized by Shakespeare in *Macbeth* as "king-becoming graces": "justice, verity,° temp'rance,° stableness, bounty, perseverance, mercy, lowliness, devotion, patience, courage, fortitude."

11   The greatest burden *hero* carries today is the expectation that a hero be perfect. In Greek mythology, even the gods have flaws. They are not perfect but rather hot-tempered, jealous, and fickle,° taking sides in human events and feuding among themselves.

12   In America today we define the person by the flaw: Thomas Jefferson is the president with the slave mistress, Einstein the scientist who mistreated his wife. We need a more subtle, complex definition of *hero,* one that acknowledges weaknesses as well as strengths, failures as well as successes—but still does not set the bar° too low.

°set the bar
set the standard

13   Some Americans reject the word *hero* outright and insist on *role model,* which is less grandiose, more human. I like author Jill Ker Conway's distinction: "Women should have heroines, not role models." Women, she said, are as physically brave and as daring as men, and the routine use of *role model* to describe outstanding women conceals their bravery and diminishes their heroism. Conway's distinction argues that *heroine* is a more powerful word than *role model* and that heroism is a reach for the extraordinary.

°subjective
based on individual perception, not facts

14   The definition of *hero* remains subjective.° What is extraordinary can be debated. Courage is in the eye of the beholder. Greatness of soul is elusive. How many and what kinds of flaws can one have and still be considered heroic?

15   Nevertheless, today we are reluctant to call past or present public figures heroic. The twentieth-century assumption of a hero as perfect has made many Americans turn away from the word—and the concept—altogether. The contemporary preference for *role model* and the shift from recognition of national to local heroes are part of the transformation of *hero* in the second half of the twentieth century.

16   There is something appealing about a society that admires a range of accomplishments and celebrates as many people as possible. But making *hero*

°**repudiation**
rejection or disowning

°**egalitarianism**
equality

°**disdainful**
scornful

more democratic can be carried to an extreme, stripping it of all sense of the extraordinary and leading to an ignorance of history, a repudiation° of genius, and an extreme egalitarianism° disdainful° of high culture and unappreciative of excellence.

17   We need role models and local heroes; but limiting our heroes to people we know restricts our aspirations. Public heroes—imperfect people of extraordinary achievement, courage, and greatness of soul whose reach is wider than ours—teach us to push beyond ourselves and our neighborhoods for excellence models, enlarging our imagination, teaching us to think big, and expanding our sense of the possible.

Questions for Critical Thinking

1.   The author begins the essay with an assessment of the human condition. State this condition in your own words. How does this lead to the subject of the essay: analyzing the term *hero* for today's youth?

2.   The author claims that in the last forty years, models of excellence, bravery, and goodness have been in short supply. If you agree, can you explain why this is so?

3.   What gives the author authority to write on this subject?

4.   To understand the meaning of a term in any depth, readers often need to see how a term has developed through history. How much of the essay is devoted to the historical use of the term?

5.   What is the difference between the terms *hero* and *role model*, as explained in this essay?

Writing in Response

1.   Write an essay that uses the Ralph Waldo Emerson quote as your thesis: "Go with mean people and you think life is mean" and "go with the great, our thoughts and manners easily become great." (*Mean* in this context means "small-minded.")

2.   In your opinion, how many and what kind of flaws can one have and still be considered heroic? Write an essay that provides three examples of people you consider heroes in spite of their flaws.

3.   In paragraph 8, Gibbon lists various people that one might consider heroic: "celebrities, athletes, historical figures, politicians, rescuers, . . . parents, teachers, friends." Choose a person to represent each of three of these categories. In an essay, explain how these three individuals fit your definition of hero. Be sure to consider the ideas presented by Peter Gibbon about the moral aspect of being a hero.

4.   Is it possible that some people who might be called heroes are simply people who love to take risks, not for any altruistic reasons but for the excitement it brings? Write an essay that gives several examples of people who do daring activities that are not necessarily heroic.

What Is This Thing Called Family?

Lee Herrick

Poet Lee Herrick has been published in many literary journals, including *Berkeley Poetry Review, Hawaii Pacific Review,* and the *Willow Review.* In 2000, he was nominated for a prestigious Pushcart Prize. Currently teaching at Fresno City College, he is the founding editor of the literary magazine called *In the Grove.* In the following essay, the poet explores the definition of family. He has experienced the special issues of living in a multicultural family. Born in South Korea in 1970, he was adopted when he was less than a year old and raised in California. His perspective may offer insight to all of us about what it means to be part of a family.

°**perspective**
a mental outlook

°**disdain**
contempt

°**quirks**
odd mannerisms

°**sibling rivalry**
competition among brothers and sisters

°**taunting**
making insulting comments

°**wary**
on guard; cautious

1   As a Korean adoptee raised by Caucasian parents, I have a unique perspective° on the notion of family. It is not defined by physical similarity. I look nothing like them. I am Asian and they are Caucasian, as is my sister (adopted as well, from Alameda). But the subtle similarities one acquires through family are inevitable—the sighs, the way one lifts her eyebrows in curiosity or disdain.° We joke about having each others' traits, but they are habits or quirks,° not the same shape of nose or chin.

2   My sister and I were raised in California's East Bay Area and later in the Central Valley. In the 1970s, the towns weren't as diverse as they are now. But we had great childhoods. We had a sibling rivalry° for the ages, but deep down there was a whole lot of love. I remember her defending me when racial slurs would come my way.

3   "He's Korean," Holly would say, when the other kids would tell me, "Go back to where you came from, Chinaman." She would intervene and change the subject when I was asked irritating questions like "What *are* you?" and "How can *she* be your sister?" I think of my sister like a defender, a protector. I also now realize that as much as she was defending me, she was defending herself and her right as an adoptee to have a brother who looked like me.

4   I remember an incident when I came home from grade school one day, sniffling and trying to conceal my tears after a day of particularly aggressive taunting—the subject at hand was my "flat face." It was hurtful and brought me to tears on the long walk home after the bus dropped me off. But it was also very strange to me because I was raised in a Caucasian family, so the boy taunting° me looked like my cousins . . . why was he so mean? It was also confusing because I didn't have an Asian accent, nor did I speak Korean or any other Asian language. My favorite baseball team was the Oakland A's, my favorite player Reggie Jackson. I loved *Star Wars*, Batman, and eventually Atari—all things 70s. I felt normal (whatever that is). Many well-intentioned people also told me, "you're so American!" or "you're not like other Asians I've met." To this day I am wary° of all these suspect declarations.

695

°inquisitive
questioning

5   I walked in the front door, Phil Donahue's inquisitive° lisp coming from the television. My mother noticed I had been crying. She bent down like a baseball catcher and took my face into her open hands, wiping my tears with her thumbs. "Oh, honey, what's *wrong*?" she asked.

6   I sniffed and wiped my nose with the back of my hand. "Nothing," I said.

7   "Honey, I'm your mom. You can tell me," she said.

8   "My face isn't flat, is it?" I asked, feeling the small mound of my nose on my face, proving it wasn't flat. I was still sniffling.

9   I can still remember the hurt look on her face, the sadness. I can't remember exactly what she said, but it was something about how some people are just ignorant and to let it "roll right off my back." I felt better that day, and time after time throughout my life as I encountered difficult times I would often repeat her mantra° in my head. She gave me something to use. Years later, as I was defining the term *idiot* in high school, acting out some of my anger, she would often be the one to spell out the conditions of my grounding. Of course, years later I came to appreciate the support (and discipline) she and my father gave me. Some things just take a while.

°mantra
a repeated verbal word or phrase

10   My father is a quiet man. I think of him as the model for giving of yourself as much as you can. Once, when I was fifteen or sixteen, at the height of my selfish teen years, he asked me if I wanted to help him volunteer serving hot dogs at the local Peach Fair.

11   "Do I get paid?" I asked, clearly not hearing the word *volunteer*.

12   "No," he said. He left, no doubt wondering what kind of person I was becoming.

°demeanor
the way a person behaves

°emulated
imitated

13   He is also the kindest, most soft-spoken, modest person I know. I have never heard him scream, not even when my sister and I were raising all kinds of hell as teenagers. Sure, he gets mad, but his calm demeanor° is a trait I have always admired (and probably never successfully emulated°).

14   Being a Korean adoptee has been wonderful but undoubtedly challenging. Anger, kindness, and forgiveness have all been a part of my life. To varying degrees I have to believe they are a part of all families. To say the least, being separated from one's birth mother is not easy to come to terms with, and it is complicated further by being in an interracial family. But that is what we are—a family.

15   I have come to believe that family goes far beyond a child's eyes looking like her mother and father's, or a child having the same mannerisms as her parents (which we do, in fact, have). It is more than a name or the number of bedrooms in a home. I have come to believe that family is about love and struggle and adapting. That there are many different types of family and that they evolve—2.5 kids and a white fence, single parent families, those involving incarceration,° illness (or a combination of all of these)—family is a wide term with plenty of room for interpretation.

°incarceration
imprisonment

16   Yes, I think about my birth parents from time to time, although I have not met them. But several years ago I returned to Seoul, the capital city where I was born. It felt like going home—no one staring at me because I was the only Asian

'**kimchi**
a spicy Korean dish

in a room, eating barbecued squid and kimchi° from the street vendor, shopping in Lotte World and the Namdaemun Market, seeing the ancient temples and modern skyscrapers downtown.

17   But while it felt like home, it really wasn't. Home is about family, the people who will stand up for you and say, "He's Korean." It is about people who comfort you and tell you that your face is not flat. It is *not* about perfection; it is about trying to be a good person (I realize this now when I am volunteering). It is about getting opportunities and support, discipline and the chance to fail and be responsible. No family member, no matter how present or absent, fills just one role. My sister is the protector but also an inspiration for kindness. My mother is a support system but also the creative force. My father is a role model but also a support system. They are all hilarious and have great work ethics. I can only hope just an ounce of this rubbed off on me.

18   I still find it interesting when children look just like their parents. Of course, biology dictates that likelihood, but not in my family. It is second nature that we don't look the same. Currently, my wife (part German-Irish, part Filipina) and I are adopting. We will soon welcome our daughter into our lives (and vice versa), aware of some of the many challenges of an international adoption, the beauty and hard work involved in family, and a foundation of unconditional love from which we should always begin.

Questions for Critical Thinking

1. Underline the thesis. What is the topic? What is the controlling idea?

2. Which paragraph gives the author's clearest definition of the term *family*?

3. The author provides several anecdotes, each one portraying the character of a different member of his family. Find each anecdote in the essay and explain how the anecdote reveals something important about that family member. How has that person influenced Lee Herrick's life?

4. Throughout the essay, the writer reports various examples of the ignorance shown by others when it comes to his racial background. Review the essay and trace these examples of ignorant thinking. In your view, which one strikes you as the worst?

5. In paragraph 9, the author tells us how words from his mother helped him get through a hard time and in fact became a mantra that helped him overcome some difficult experiences he had to endure later in life. What is a mantra? What are some examples of mantras that can be helpful in people's lives?

Writing in Response

1. What is your own definition of *family*? Give several examples of families you have known. In your opinion, what groupings could not be called families?

2. Lee Herrick admits about his sister and himself, "We had a sibling rivalry for the ages." Write an essay using extended definition to explore the meaning of the term *sibling rivalry*. Are there times when sibling rivalry can be constructive? When is sibling rivalry destructive?

3. What are the responsibilities family members should have for each other? Write an essay that presents several situations you have observed over the years, and give your expectations of how family members should treat each other.

4. What are the unique issues of the adopted child? Write an essay that gives several examples of the problems adopted children face. Conclude with advice about how these problems should be handled.

5. More than once in the essay, the writer looks back critically at different periods in his life. In paragraph 10, he refers to a period in his adolescence as "the height of my selfish teen years." Many of us look back to our adolescence with some sense of regret for moments of selfishness. Write an essay that explores the concept of selfishness. In what circumstances does one need to be "selfish"? What are some examples of the selfishness that is typical of adolescence?

The Ways We Lie

Stephanie Ericsson

Stephanie Ericsson is a writer who works in films and advertising. She has also produced nonfiction books such as *ShameFaced* and *Recovering Together*. Her book *Companion Through the Darkness* deals with the grief and complicated emotions people feel when their lives are changed through loss. In the following essay, the writer examines a subject familiar to everyone: the kinds of lies people tell.

1　The bank called today, and I told them my deposit was in the mail, even though I hadn't written a check yet. It'd been a rough day. The baby I'm pregnant with decided to do aerobics on my lungs for two hours, our three-year-old daughter painted the living-room couch with lipstick, the IRS put me on hold for an hour, and I was late to a business meeting because I was tired.

2　I told my client that the traffic had been bad. When my partner came home, his haggard° face told me his day hadn't gone any better than mine, so when he asked, "How was your day?" I said, "Oh, fine," knowing that one more straw might break his back. A friend called and wanted to take me to lunch. I said I was busy. Four lies in the course of a day, none of which I felt the least bit guilty about.

°**haggard**
worn and exhausted

3　We lie. We all do. We exaggerate, we minimize, we avoid confrontation, we spare people's feelings, we conveniently forget, we keep secrets, we justify lying to the big-guy institutions. Like most people, I indulge in small falsehoods and still think of myself as an honest person. Sure I lie, but it doesn't hurt anything. Or does it?

4　I once tried going a whole week without telling a lie, and it was paralyzing. I discovered that telling the truth all the time is nearly impossible. It means living with some serious consequences: The bank charges me $60 in overdraft fees, my partner keels over when I tell him about my travails, my client fires me for telling her I didn't feel like being on time, and my friend takes it personally when I say I'm not hungry. There must be some merit to lying.

5　But if I justify lying, what makes me any different from slick politicians or the corporate robbers who raided the S&L industry°? Saying it's okay to lie one way and not another is hedging.° I cannot seem to escape the voice deep inside me that tells me: When someone lies, someone loses.

°**S&L industry**
savings and loan industry

°**hedging**
avoiding

6　What far-reaching consequences will I, or others, pay as a result of my lie? Will someone's trust be destroyed? Will someone else pay *my* penance° because I ducked out? We must consider the *meaning of our actions*. Deception, lies, capital crimes, and misdemeanors° all carry meanings. *Webster's* definition of *lie* is specific:

°**penance**
consequence or penalty for a wrong

°**misdemeanors**
misdeeds

1: a false statement or action especially made with the intent to deceive;

2: anything that gives or is meant to give a false impression.

7   A definition like this implies that there are many, many ways to tell a lie. Here are just a few.

The White Lie

°arrogance
overbearing pride

8   The white lie assumes that the truth will cause more damage than a simple, harmless untruth. Telling a friend he looks great when he looks like hell can be based on a decision that the friend needs a compliment more than a frank opinion. But, in effect, it is the liar deciding what is best for the lied to. Ultimately, it is a vote of no confidence. It is an act of subtle arrogance° for anyone to decide what is best for someone else.

°pittance
a small amount

9   Yet not all circumstances are quite so cut and dried. Take, for instance, the sergeant in Vietnam who knew one of his men was killed in action but listed him as missing so that the man's family would receive indefinite compensation instead of the lump-sum pittance° the military gives widows and children. His intent was honorable. Yet for twenty years this family kept their hopes alive, unable to move on to a new life.

Facades

°façades
artificial fronts

10   We all put up façades° to one degree or another. When I put on a suit to go to see a client, I feel as though I am putting on another face, obeying the expectation that serious businesspeople wear suits rather than sweatpants. But I'm a writer. Normally, I get up, get the kid off to school, and sit at my computer in my pajamas until four in the afternoon. When I answer the phone, the caller thinks I'm wearing a suit (although the UPS man knows better).

°seduce
lure

°illusion
an erroneous perception of reality

°plethora
excess

11   But façades can be destructive because they are used to seduce° others into an illusion.° For instance, I recently realized that a former friend was a liar. He presented himself with all the right looks and the right words and offered lots of new consciousness theories, fabulous books to read, and fascinating insights. Then I did some business with him, and the time came for him to pay me. He turned out to be all talk and no walk. I heard a plethora° of reasonable excuses, including in-depth descriptions of the big break around the corner. In six months of work, I saw less than a hundred bucks. When I confronted him, he raised both eyebrows and tried to convince me that I'd heard him wrong, that he'd made no commitment to me. A simple investigation into his past revealed a crowded graveyard of disenchanted former friends.

Ignoring the Plain Facts

°ecclesiastical
church-related

°parish
a religious community attending one church

°pedophilia
sexual abuse of children

°diocese
church district, headed by a bishop

12   In the sixties, the Catholic Church in Massachusetts began hearing complaints that Father James Porter was sexually molesting children. Rather than relieving him of his duties, the ecclesiastical° authorities simply moved him from one parish° to another between 1960 and 1967, actually providing him with a fresh supply of unsuspecting families and innocent children to abuse. After treatment in 1967 for pedophilia,° he went back to work, this time in Minnesota. The new diocese° was aware of Father Porter's obsession with children, but they needed priests and recklessly believed treatment had cured him. More children were abused until he was relieved of his duties a year later. By his own admission, Porter may have abused as many as a hundred children.

13   Ignoring the facts may not in and of itself be a form of lying, but consider the context of this situation. If a lie is *a false action done with the intent to deceive,*

then the Catholic Church's conscious covering for Porter created irreparable consequences. The church became a coperpetrator with Porter.

Stereotypes and Clichés

°**stereotype**
oversimplified opinion

°**cliché**
overused expression

°**nanoseconds**
billionths of a second

14   Stereotype° and cliché° serve a purpose as a form of shorthand. Our need for vast amounts of information in nanoseconds° has made the stereotype vital to modern communication. Unfortunately, it often shuts down original thinking, giving those hungry for truth a candy bar of misinformation instead of a balanced meal. The stereotype explains a situation with just enough truth to seem unquestionable.

°**obliterated**
wiped out

15   All the *isms*—racism, sexism, ageism, et al.—are founded on and fueled by the stereotype and the cliché, which are lies of exaggeration, omission, and ignorance. They are always dangerous. They take a single tree and make it a landscape. They destroy curiosity. They close minds and separate people. The single mother on welfare is assumed to be cheating. Any black male could tell you how much of his identity is obliterated° daily by stereotypes. Fat people, ugly people, beautiful people, old people, large-breasted women, short men, the mentally ill, and the homeless all could tell you how much more they are like us than we want to think. I once admitted to a group of people that I had a mouth like a truck driver. Much to my surprise, a man stood up and said, "I'm a truck driver, and I never cuss." Needless to say, I was humbled.

Out-and-Out Lies

16   Of all the ways to lie, I like this one the best, probably because I get tired of trying to figure out the real meanings behind things. At least I can trust the bald-faced lie. I once asked my five-year-old nephew, "Who broke the fence?" (I had seen him do it.) He answered, "The murderers." Who could argue?

°**toy**
treat casually

°**refute**
prove false

°**sleight of hand**
trick performed quickly to avoid detection

17   At least when this sort of lie is told it can be easily confronted. As the person who is lied to, I know where I stand. The bald-faced lie doesn't toy° with my perceptions—it argues with them. It doesn't try to refashion reality, it tries to refute° it. *Read my lips* . . . No sleight of hand.° No guessing. If this were the only form of lying, there would be no such thing as floating anxiety or the adult-children of alcoholics movement.

°**pious**
devout

°**embellish**
add fictitious details

°**lubricate**
oil or grease

°**Martin Buber**
twentieth-century philosopher

°**shrouds**
covers

18   These are only a few of the ways we lie. Or are lied to. As I said earlier, it's not easy to entirely eliminate lies from our lives. No matter how pious° we may try to be, we will still embellish,° hedge, and omit to lubricate° the daily machinery of living. But there is a world of difference between telling functional lies and living a lie. Martin Buber° once said, "The lie is the spirit committing treason against itself." Our acceptance of lies becomes a cultural cancer that eventually shrouds° and reorders reality until moral garbage becomes as invisible to us as water is to a fish.

°**reticent**
keeping one's thoughts to oneself

19   How much do we tolerate before we become sick and tired of being sick and tired? When will we stand up and declare our *right* to trust? When do we stop accepting that the real truth is in the fine print? Whose lips do we read this year when we vote for president? When will we stop being so reticent° about making judgments? When do we stop turning over our personal power and responsibility to liars?

20   Maybe if I don't tell the bank the check's in the mail I'll be less tolerant of the lies told to me every day. A country song I once heard said it all for me: "You've got to stand for something or you'll fall for anything."

Questions for Critical Thinking

1. The title of this article is "The Ways We Lie." The author's use of the term "ways" indicates that this will be an essay of classification. What are some of the other terms that writers use to introduce the various categories in a classification?

2. In paragraph 2, the writer refers to an old saying, "the straw that breaks the camel's back." How could you express this idea in your own words?

3. In paragraph 5, the writer states, "When someone lies, someone loses." How would you interpret this saying?

4. Although Stephanie Ericsson does not write specifically about the pathological liar, how would you define such a person? Can you give examples of the kinds of crimes such people are likely to commit?

Writing in Response

1. In paragraph 3, the writer notes that "we exaggerate, we minimize, we avoid confrontation, we spare people's feelings, we conveniently forget, we keep secrets, we justify lying to the big-guy institutions." Think of an example from your own experience or observation that would illustrate each one. Would you call each of these examples a lie? Write an example essay in which each body paragraph is developed by using one of your examples.

2. Stephanie Ericsson has put lies into different categories. In paragraph 6, she suggests there are consequences to these lies. Write an essay in which you categorize the kinds of consequences that people pay for either telling lies or being the victims of lies.

3. Write a narrative that tells the story of how you or someone you know was lied to. What were the circumstances of the situation and what were the consequences?

4. Write an essay in which you give several examples of how telling the truth could lead to difficult situations.

The Changing American Family

Alvin and Heidi Toffler

No one denies that the American family has changed and will continue to evolve. Researchers Alvin and Heidi Toffler have concluded that not all of these changes are necessarily negative. As they share the results of their research, the Tofflers not only provide a broad historical review of some of the most striking changes the family has undergone but also classify families according to different types.

1   The American family is not dying. It is diversifying. This is the "secret" to understanding what is happening to ourselves, our children, and our society. Millions of people today are frightened about the future of the family. Dire° predictions pour from the pulpit, the press, even from the White House. Emotional oratory about the need to "restore" the family is echoing through the nation.

°**dire**
desperate; urgent; warning of disaster

2   Unfortunately, our attempts to strengthen family life are doomed unless we first understand what is happening. And all the evidence suggests we don't.

3   Despite misconceptions, the American family system is not falling apart because of immoral television programs or permissive child-rearing or because of some sinister conspiracy. If that were the problem, the solutions would be simpler.

4   To begin with, it is worth noticing that whatever is happening to family life is *not* just happening in the United States. Many of today's trends in divorce, re-marriage, new family styles, and attitudes toward children are present in Britain, France, Sweden, Germany, Canada, even in the Soviet Union and Eastern Europe. Something is happening to families in all these countries at once.

°**fracturing**
breaking up

5   What is happening is that the existing family system is fracturing°—and taking on a new, more diversified form—because of powerful pressures arising from revolutionary changes in energy, technology, work, economics, and communications. If permissiveness and immorality play a role, they are far less important than these other, larger pressures.

6   The whole world is changing rapidly, and it seems reasonable that you cannot have a revolution in all these fields without expecting a revolution in family life as well.

7   Human history has gone through successive phases—each characterized by a certain kind of family. In greatly simplified terms we can sketch these:

8   The First Wave family: Ten thousand years ago, the invention of agriculture launched the First Wave of change in history. As people shifted from hunting,

703

fishing, and foraging, the typical peasant-style family spread: a large household, with grandparents and children, uncles and aunts and sometimes nonblood relatives, as well as neighbors, boarders or others, all living together and—most important—working together as a production team in the fields.

9   This kind of "extended" family was found all over the world, from Japan to Eastern Europe to France to the American colonies. It is still the dominant type of family in the nonindustrial, agricultural countries today.

10   The Second Wave family: Three hundred years ago, the Industrial Revolution exploded in England and triggered the Second Wave of change.

11   The old style family which worked so well as a production team in the fields did not fit well in the new evolving world of factories and offices. The elderly couldn't keep up with the clattering machines. Children were too undisciplined to be really efficient factory hands. And the industrial economy needed workers who could move from city to city as jobs opened up or closed. That was hard to do with a big family.

12   Gradually, under these pressures, families became smaller, more streamlined, with the husband going out to work in a factory or office, the wife staying home, and the kids marching off to school. Old folks were farmed out to their own apartments or nursing homes. Young people moved into their own apartments as soon as they could afford it. The family adapted to the new conditions and the so-called "nuclear" family became the most popular model.

13   This is the type of family that most of today's evangelists, politicians, and others have in mind when they say we must "protect" the family or "restore" it. They act as though the nuclear family were the only acceptable form of family life.

14   Yet today, as society is struck by a new shock-wave of technological, economic, ecological, and energy changes, the family system is adapting once more, just as it did three hundred years ago.

15   Because the economic and other conditions that made the nuclear family popular are changing, the nuclear family itself is less and less popular. America is no longer a nation of poorly educated blue-collar workers. Most of us work in service occupations or spend our time processing information. And today only some 7 percent of Americans still live in classical nuclear families. The nuclear family is simply no longer the norm—and it is not likely to become the norm again, no matter how much pulpit-pounding or breast-beating we do about it. In its place, a new family system is emerging.

16   The Third Wave family: This new system is harder to describe because it is not based on a single dominant family form but on a dazzling diversity of household structures.

17   For example, look at what is happening to single life. Between 1970 and 1978 alone, the number of people aged 14 to 34 who live alone nearly tripled in the United States. Today fully one-fifth of all households are live-alones. Some are alone out of necessity, others prefer it. Then there are the child-free couples. As James Ramey of the Center for Policy Research has pointed out, we are seeing a massive shift from "child-centered" to "adult-centered" homes. The number of couples who deliberately decide not to have children—whether for economic, psychological, or ecological reasons—has increased dramatically.

18   Next come the single-parent households. Divorce rates may be leveling out in this country, depending upon how they are measured, but broken nuclear households are so widespread that today as many as one out of seven children are raised by a single parent. In big cities that may run as high as one in four.

19   In many countries at once, the single-parent household is becoming a key family form. Sweden gives one-parent households first crack at nursery and day-care facilities. Germany is building special blocks of apartments for them.

20   Then there is what we have called the "aggregate family." That's where two divorced people—each with kids—marry, and the kids from both sides come to know each other and form a kind of tribe. Often the kids get on better than the parents. It has been estimated that, before long, 25 percent of American kids may be part of such "aggregate families."

21   Trial marriages . . . single-sex households . . . communes . . . all can be found as people struggle to find alternatives to the nuclear model. Some of these will turn out to be workable alternatives; others will fall by the wayside.

22   We can also expect to see an increasing number of "electronic cottage" families—families in which one or both spouses work at home instead of commuting to the job. As the cost of gasoline skyrockets and the cost of computers and communication plummets, companies will increasingly supply their employees with simple work-at-home electronic equipment.

23   In such homes, we may well find husband and wife sharing the same work. Even children and old folks might pitch in, as they once did in the agricultural household. In our day, such "electronic cottage" families are as much an outgrowth of changes in energy, technology, and communications, as the nuclear family was a response to the factory system at the time of the Industrial Revolution.

24   In the new environment, nuclear households will no doubt continue to survive. For many people, they work. But this Second Wave family form will hardly dominate the future, as it did the recent past.

25   What we are seeing today, therefore, is not the death of the family, but the rapid emergence of a Third Wave family system based on many different types of family.

26   This historic shift to new, more varied and flexible family arrangements is rooted in and related to parallel changes now fast developing in other fields. In fact, we find the same push toward diversity at every level.

27   The energy system is diversifying, shifting from a near-total reliance on fossil fuels to new, alternative sources of energy. In the world of work, we see a similar trend: Older Second Wave industries engaged in mass production—turning out millions of identical items. Newer Third Wave industries, based on computers, numerical controls, and robots, custom-tailor their goods and turn them out in small runs. At the consumer level, we see an increasing variety of products.

28   The same shift toward diversity is even stronger in communications where the power of the great mass media is increasingly challenged by new "mini-media"—cable television, satellite-based networks, special-interest magazines. This shift toward diversity amounts to the demassification of the media.

29   In short, the whole structure of society is moving toward increased diversity It is hardly surprising that the family system is in tune with this shift. The recent startling changes in American family structure are part of this larger move from a mass society to one that offers a far greater variety of life choice.

30   Any attempt to go backward to a simpler system dominated by the nuclear family—or by any one model—will fail, just as our attempts to save the economy by "reindustrializing" have failed. For in both cases we are looking backward rather than forward.

31   To help families adapt to the new Third Wave society, with its diversified energy, production, communications, and politics, we should encourage innovations that permit employees to adjust their work hours to personal needs. We should favor "flex-time," part-time work arrangements, job-sharing. We should eliminate housing tax and credit regulations that discriminate against non-nuclear families. We need more imaginative day-care facilities.

32   An idea put forward by one businesswoman: a bank of word-processors and a nursery located in a suburban shopping center, so that busy housewives or husbands can put in an hour or two of paid work whenever it is convenient for them, and actually have their kids right there with them.

33   In short, anything that makes it easier to combine working and self-help, job-work with housework, easier to enter and leave the labor force, could smooth the transition for millions of people who are now caught, as it were, between the old, Second Wave family arrangements and the fast-emerging Third Wave family system.

°**wallowing**
surrendering to an
emotion

34   Rather than wallowing° in nostalgia and praising the "good old days"—which were never as good as they may seem in retrospect—we ought to be finding ways to make the new system more decent, responsible, morally satisfying, and humane. The first step is an understanding of the Third Wave.

Questions for Critical Thinking

1. The Tofflers argue that people should not be so upset about the changing American family. Find the paragraph where they begin using classification as a method of developing their argument.

2. Explain each of the three distinct categories, or "waves," described by the authors. Do you agree with this historical classification? Can you think of other ways to classify the family?

3. In paragraphs 16 through 24, find the nine types of families suggested for the Third Wave. Discuss the conditions of our modern world that make these "new" family groupings possible.

4. The Tofflers point out that only 7 percent of Americans still live in classic nuclear families. This fact frightens many people, even some who themselves are outside a nuclear family. What are some of the reasons for these fears? Do these reasons make you less optimistic than the Tofflers about the new family structures?

5. In paragraph 30, the writers point out that "[a]ny attempt to go backward to a simpler system dominated by the nuclear family . . . will fail" because that would mean looking backward instead of ahead. Do you agree or disagree? Why?

6. The Tofflers suggest we need to understand the Third Wave to make the new system "more decent, responsible, morally satisfying, and humane." What are some of their suggestions? Do you think American society is moving toward greater understanding of the Third Wave family? Discuss.

Writing in Response

1. An often-repeated saying is "the only thing you can be sure of in life is change." Most people have trouble adapting to change in their lives. Write an essay in which you classify the types of changes that can happen to a person during the course of a lifetime. You may want to include categories such as physical change, economic change, and social change. Be sure to provide good examples within each category.

2. Write an essay in which you classify the different types of relationships you have known. Explain what is unique about each type you select. Devote at least one well-developed paragraph to each category.

3. The Tofflers suggest that employers need to make innovations that will permit workers to adjust working hours to their personal needs. Write an essay in which you classify the kinds of innovations that could be made by employers to make life better for families. What is the likelihood that your suggestions will actually be put into effect? Why do you feel this way?

Ban Computers and Cell Phones from Classrooms

Ira Hyman, Ph.D.

Dr. Ira Hyman is a professor of psychology at Western Washington University. The author or coauthor of over twenty-five books, chapters, and articles, his research interests focus on human memory, and he has authored influential articles and led important experiments on this subject.

In his modest proposal to ban computers and cell phones from the classroom, Dr. Hyman defends his controversial opinion with hard data and quotes well-respected articles and studies. What do you think? Can Dr. Ira Hyman convince you too?

1   We should ban the use of computers and cell phones in classrooms. I know that is a radical statement and one that will generate controversy. But what else can we do?

2   Let me be clear that I love computers and I love my cell phone. I use computers for my work. I expect my students to use computers—for writing, research, data analysis, and almost everything else. Computers and cell phones are professional tools, and pretty fun toys. I know my students live on the internet. I seem to exist there as well and I frequently check email and various other accounts.

3   My concern is about using these tools in classroom settings. And I know the point of some classrooms is to teach with the computer. I do so when teaching my research methods and stats classes. But enough of the qualifications°—let me get to the argument.

°**qualifications**
something that limits a statement

4   In the traditional college classroom, computers and cell phones should be banned. There are two reasons for my suggested ban. The first reason is the most obvious. What is actually on that computer screen? Plenty of distractions become available when the computer or cell phone is activated. Students who are texting and surfing the web are students who are no longer engaged in the classroom. Cognitive° researchers have always known that although people can multitask, there are costs. The research on this topic is unequivocal.° This seems particularly true in the classroom. In the classroom, the primary task is learning. Being distracted by text messages or web surfing decreases learning.

°**cognitive**
relating to mental processes

°**unequivocal**
indisputable

5   For example, Kraushaar and Novak (2010) conducted a study of classroom learning over an entire academic term. The students used laptops and knew they would be monitored and tested. The students agreed to have spyware installed on their computers to track what they were doing. Even though the students knew they were being monitored, the students were frequently off-task. They used their computers for non-class activities about 40% of the time; checking email, surfing the web, using instant messaging. Time spent off-task predicted grades: the more someone was off-task, the poorer the grade. The students also woefully underestimated how much time they spent off-task.

°impair
damage or restrict

6   But what about the student who isn't surfing the web? What about the student who is using the computer for note taking? Would that be ok? This brings me to the second reason for the ban—Even when only used for note taking, computers impair° learning. In a recent study, Mueller and Oppenheimer (2014) had students watch a lesson and take notes. They either took notes with a computer or with pen and paper. The computer was not connected to the internet and the only available use was for note taking. But even in this completely limited situation, the students using a computer for note taking performed less well on a test than students using pen and paper for note taking. When allowed to go back and study their notes, the students who used a computer performed less well than those using pen and paper. Their approach to note taking did not aid learning and led to less useful studying later. Interesting, people wrote more when using the computer, but that didn't help. The problem is how people take notes. With pen and paper, people are selective and look to record the important points. With computers, people strive to take down everything; they aren't particularly selective. They aren't actively processing the information during learning. Their notes don't focus on the key aspects of the material. This means poor learning and less useful notes for studying later.

°primary
most important

7   So for two reasons, we should seriously limit computers and cell phones in the classroom. They distract from the primary° task and they result in less effective learning even when used appropriately.

8   Of course, sometimes the content of a class concerns using a computer. In that situation, we have to use computers in the classroom. But I suspect that in this situation a lot of multi-tasking happens. How can you keep their minds in the classroom when the world-wide web is at their fingertips?

9   By the way, I suspect we might find something similar if we looked at the effects of computers and cell phones on work meetings. How often have you seen people in meetings distracted by their cell phones? How often have you seen someone trying to get everything down and not actually thinking about the topic of discussion? If you want effective meetings, leave the cellphones outside. If you want effective classrooms, leave the cellphone turned off. Oh, and good luck getting people to follow this advice.

Questions for Critical Thinking

1.   How would you describe the author's tone in this essay?

2.   In your own words, explain Ira Hyman's explanation for why computers are not as useful as a pen and paper for note-taking.

3.   List some reasons why instructors should allow cell phones in the classroom.

4.   In which paragraph does the author summarize his article?

5.   In the study that the author cites in paragraph five, what was the relationship between how much time students spent off-task and their grade?

Writing in Response

1. Write a paragraph describing some other possible distractions in the classroom.

2. Good note-taking skills can be very important to a student's success in college. Write an essay that takes the reader through the process of note-taking.

3. Technology has in many cases become an integral part of modern education. Write an essay that gives examples of why technology is or is not important to education.

4. In paragraph 8, Ira Hyman asks, "How can you keep their minds in the classroom when the [World Wide Web] is at their fingertips?" Write an essay that describes some ways instructors can keep their students engaged in class. What should the instructor do or not do?

Why I Decided to Buy a Handgun

Trevor Hughes

Trevor Hughes, an author who writes for *USA Today* and whose journalism has led him to cover several mass shootings, describes his thought process as he makes what could be a life-changing decision.

1   After months of soul-searching, I've decided to buy a handgun.

2   It's not a decision to which I've come lightly. At least one co-worker came near to tears as she tried to dissuade° me. But after a horrendous° year of violence across the country, I'm left with the undeniable feeling that I ought to do something different. I'm no longer willing to wait for the government to protect me all of the time. As a former Vermonter and Boy Scout, I just can't escape the feeling that I need to take more responsibility for my own safety.

3   Here's the thing: more than almost anyone, I know the devastation handguns can cause. As a journalist who has covered many mass shootings, I've watched families ripped apart by death. I've seen entire communities shattered because some jerk who couldn't control himself decided to take out his anger on the world with a weapon.

4   I also know I'm not the only one struggling with this decision. Gun shops across our country are reporting a surge in sales. And it's a sad fact that gun sales go up after a shooting or a terrorist attack.

5   I have no illusions that I'm going to be the proverbial° good guy with a gun. And even worse, I know the statistics that show I'm at risk, as a middle-age white man living in Colorado, of using the gun to kill myself.

6   I recognize that my decision doesn't make the best logical sense. My head knows that. On the other hand, we humans are emotional creatures, and this decision helps me feel better. Perhaps there's just some comfort in feeling like I'm taking action, even if all the statistics tell me I might actually just be making the problem worse.

7   But.

8   What else should I do? Our politicians have demonstrated they aren't actually serious about reducing gun violence in America. I mean, while we accept that car crashes kill about 30,000 people annually, at least there's a serious effort underway to reduce that number. And at the same time, there does appear to be an actual belief around the world and in our own country that Americans are a soft target.

°dissuade
persuade against, talk somebody out of something

°horrendous
terrible

°proverbial
of or relating to proverbs, linked to a saying

711

9   I've never fired a handgun. And I hope to God I never fire mine in anger. The men and women we pay to carry guns and protect us rarely do it, and those that do often miss, or accidentally shoot their colleagues or innocent bystanders during the confusion of a gunbattle.

10   It's those innocent bystanders that have me worried. I've been in Aurora, in Roseburg, in Killeen. Time and time again, mass murderers have targeted groups that were unprepared to fight back. Soft targets. What a terrible phrase.

11   For me, like for many people I've talked to, San Bernardino was the tipping point. As someone who goes to lots of community meetings and rallies, I'm all too aware of how vulnerable we are. A holiday party? Your co-workers? (For me, it started with movie theaters.) I'm not a fan of waiting for the next attack from a religious terrorist.

12   That's got me thinking about that famous quote from Teddy Roosevelt: "Speak softly and carry a big stick."

13   You don't have to use that stick. In fact, plan on not using it. But if me carrying a concealed weapon—just like millions of my responsible neighbors in this country—deters someone from attacking my friends and neighbors, maybe that's worth it. You don't see terror attacks in this country on areas where there's lots of armed men and women. Instead, it's those soft targets that get hit. Maybe it's time we made sure our enemies, both foreign and domestic, understand that we shoot back.

14   I'm starting to feel like a soft target. I don't like feeling like a soft target. And once again, I'm left with this idea that an armed society ends up being a very polite society—and one that's highly resistant to attack.

Questions for Critical Thinking

1. What does Trevor Hughes state are his concerns with owning a handgun?

2. In paragraph 7, Trevor Hughes uses just one word: "But." This is technically a fragment sentence. Why would the author do this? What effect does it have in the essay?

3. In your own words, summarize one of the author's reasons for wanting to own a handgun.

4. What do you believe is Trevor Hughes's purpose for writing this essay?

5. Find one point in the essay that you strongly agree or disagree with. Briefly discuss why you agree or disagree.

Writing in Response

1. Gun control can be a very divisive issue, and usually everyone has formed an opinion about it at one time. Write an argumentative essay discussing your own opinion about the issue of gun control or gun ownership.

2. Trevor Hughes seems reluctant in his decision to purchase a handgun, but he feels like he is left with no choice. Write about a decision you were forced to make but were not completely happy with.

3. In paragraph 8, the author states that Americans are seen as a "soft target." Write an essay giving examples of other solutions that may help Americans from being seen as soft targets.

Why Don't These Women Just Leave?

Elaine Weiss

One of our society's most serious problems is spousal abuse. Elaine Weiss uses her own painful experience as an abused wife to discuss this problem in a direct and compelling way. Her essay argues against the commonly held belief that the problem could be solved if only the abused partner would simply leave the relationship. The writer does not support her argument with any outside facts or statistics, nor does she quote any experts on the matter. All she does is give us a clear and convincing personal history, one that is impossible to contradict.

°fabric
the underlying structure

°Carousel
a 1945 Broadway musical composed by Richard Rodgers

°Charles Boyer and Ingrid Bergman
screen actors who appeared together in the 1944 film drama *Gaslight*

°glib
offhand; slick

1   Last May, Neal and I celebrated our sixteenth wedding anniversary. This is his first marriage; my second. Ours is a fine, strong partnership, filled with shared interests, mutual respect, and ever-deepening intimacy. That's not the point of this story. This story is about my first marriage. But to tell the story of my first marriage is to take a risk—and I feel I have to start by establishing that I am capable of a good marriage.

2   I've spent nineteen years trying to make sense of my first marriage: the one that began in 1967 and ended when I left in 1976. I've spent nineteen years trying to unravel the tightly-woven threads of physical and verbal abuse that made up the fabric° of that marriage. I've spent nineteen years, and I may spend nineteen more. Why bother? Why not just be grateful that I found the strength to leave—that I didn't simply become a statistic in a "Domestic Violence" docudrama? Because, I still have nightmares, sometimes. Because, beautiful though *Carousel*° is, I can't watch Billy Bigelow hit Julie Jordan and watch her forgive him. Because when I see Charles Boyer° methodically driving Ingrid Bergman° slowly mad in *Gaslight*,° I cry, and then feel silly for overreacting. And because after O. J. Simpson's arrest, during the brief spasm of media interest in domestic violence, I overheard a woman in the beauty parlor proclaim, "You know, the women who let themselves be abused are just as sick as the men who abuse them. She should have walked out the very first time he raised a hand to her. That's what I would have done."

3   She should have . . . our glib° answer to women who are physically and emotionally abused. These days we're far too sophisticated to directly blame the woman for the man's behavior; we no longer say, "Well, if he beat her up, she must have done something to deserve it." Instead, we say, "She should have been more assertive." "She should have been more accommodating." "She should have left." "She should have gotten therapy." "She should have called the police."

4   So, as if the pain of the abusive relationship weren't enough, we tell women that this pain is their fault. They hear *she should*—never *he should*. They hear, "She should have stood up to him"—which, ideally, she should—but they never hear, "He should have stopped being abusive."

5   I know it's not as simple as that. I've read all the books and articles. I know that men who batter their partners are themselves in pain. I know that their behavior is a desperate attempt to make themselves feel in control. I know that many of them were once victims of abuse. I know they can't just stop—that they need professional help. And I sympathize—just as I sympathize with alcoholics and drug addicts. I'm no longer angry with my former husband (though this took me years to accomplish). But I am angry—hotly, fiercely angry—when I hear "Why don't these women just leave?"

6   To me, this question is as meaningless as asking the victim of a train wreck "Why didn't you just drive to work that morning?" Nevertheless, I'm going to tell you why I didn't leave; or, rather, why it took me eight years, seven months, and twenty-one days to leave. This is what I wish I had said to the woman in the beauty parlor.

7   I didn't leave . . . because abuse wasn't supposed to happen to people like me. I was only nineteen when I married, halfway through college, with little experience of the world. This was 1967; the term "spouse abuse" didn't exist: No one thought to join those two words, since no one accepted that it happened. Or, if it did, it happened only to impoverished, uneducated women married to men with names like Billy Bob, who turned into mean drunks on Saturday nights. It certainly didn't happen to nice Jewish girls from upper-middle-class families; they went to college, married nice boys, taught school for a while, and then started a family. This is what my friends and I were raised to believe, and this is how I thought the world worked. So when the abuse started, within a week of the wedding, I had no way to frame° what was happening.

°**frame**
to put into words

8   I didn't leave . . . because I thought it was my fault. My only experience of marriage was the seventeen years I had spent in my parents' home, and there I saw warmth, kindness, and love. If my marriage looked nothing like theirs, I assumed that I must be doing something wrong. My husband would become angry and throw me against a wall—then berate° me for "egging him on." Lying in bed that night, I would replay the scene, trying to pinpoint the exact moment where I had gone wrong. I always found it, too: "I should have laughed it off when he told me the dinner was disgusting." "I should have ignored it when he called me a 'fat dummy, too useless to live.'" "I shouldn't have cried when he announced that he wanted to have affairs with other women—and that if I didn't like it, I was being too possessive."

°**berate**
to scold angrily

9   I didn't leave . . . because I believed I could fix it. During our courtship, he was tender and affectionate. He told me I was the most wonderful girl in the world (in 1967 we were all "girls"—as were our mothers and grandmothers). So I held on to the image of the man who was once my loving boyfriend, and was now my menacing husband. He told me I had changed—that I was no longer the cute, bright girl he had married—and I imagined he must be right. Since rational people don't suddenly turn violent without provocation,° I must be provoking him. I thought that if I could just get it right, he would be nice to me again.

°**provocation**
something that causes a person to become angry

10   I didn't leave . . . because I told myself that I was overreacting. Yes, he would occasionally punch me in the stomach or choke me—but at least he never gave me a black eye or a broken arm. Yes, he would delight in pointing out an obese woman on the street and saying "Your ass is even bigger than hers"—but perhaps I did need to lose weight (I was then, as I am now, a size six). Yes, he would indicate another woman, tall, blond, buxom and leggy, and scold "Why

can't you look like that?"—but this was the 1960s, when the Beach Boys wished we all could be California Girls, and maybe a petite brunette couldn't hope to be seen as attractive. Yes, he would occasionally put a pillow over my face while I slept, then watch with detached interest as I woke up half-smothered—but I had to be imagining that, didn't I?

11   I didn't leave . . . because there was no support for women like me. There was no place I could tell my story and be told "It's not you—it's him. There's no way you can 'get it right,' because he desperately needs you to get it wrong." I convinced my husband to enter couple therapy, and tried to find the words to pin down my husband's actions. "If he goes through a door ahead of me, he gives it an extra push to let it swing back and hit me." "He tells me I'm so ugly that his new nickname for me is 'uggles.'" "I feel like I'm constantly walking on eggshells." The therapist's response was to insist that I had an obligation to stay in the marriage because my husband couldn't function without me. He also insisted that if I stopped being my father's Little Girl and became my husband's Adult Wife, my problems would be solved. Since this advice came from a professional, I assumed it had to be correct. We spent two years in weekly visits to this man, after which I was discharged with the admonition° to put my energy into supporting my husband.

°**admonition**
piece of cautionary advice

12   I didn't leave . . . because I grew accustomed to living a lie. He treated me well in public. To our friends, we were the perfect couple. Maintaining our outward loving appearance became an unspoken conspiracy between us. He called it "not airing our dirty linen in public," and I agreed. Of course I agreed. I was to blame for his behavior, and I couldn't manage to figure out how to be the sort of wife he cherished.° Which, he assured me, he surely would—if I could just learn how to make him happy. A wife who can't make her husband happy— why would I want that to become public knowledge? I agreed to the charade,° and I played my part well. Which probably explains why, when I finally left, he got to keep the friends; no one could see why I'd want to escape such a wonderful marriage.

°**cherished**
held dear

°**charade**
a pretense in which people act out parts

13   I didn't leave . . . and then one day I left. Why? It sounds so trivial in retrospect,° but it was triggered by an encounter with an unknown woman in New York City. This was in 1974, shortly after my husband and I moved to Manhattan. He had taken a job with a prestigious° corporate law firm and, after five years as a schoolteacher, I was beginning graduate school at Columbia University. One afternoon, as we stood on a street corner at a downtown crosswalk, I looked up to see a particularly lovely old building with a magnificent garden on its terraced roof. I pointed and said, "Isn't that building beautiful?" "Which one," sneered my husband, "you mean the one up there that looks exactly like every other building on the street?" A woman standing beside us turned abruptly. "She's right, you know. The building is beautiful—and you are a horse's ass." As the light changed and she stalked off, something shifted inside me. I finally realized that this man was never going to change, and that I deserved better. Within a year I announced that I was leaving.

°**in retrospect**
in looking back

°**prestigious**
having a high standing or reputation

14   Yes, of course it took more than this one encounter. My professors at Columbia told me I was a talented instructional designer, and encouraged me to enter the doctoral program. Fellow students became close friends. Many of them had never met my husband—I was more than half a couple. With professional and personal successes, I stopped caring about, hardly noticed, my husband's abuse. Ironically, the more I ignored him, the nicer he acted. The day I told him the marriage was over (my twenty-eighth birthday), he cried and

'idyllic
simple and carefree

begged me to stay. He told me how much he needed me. He said he couldn't imagine life without me. He swore he would change. He painted an idyllic° picture of the new life we would build. I barely heard him.

15   And so I left. I am one of the lucky ones. He didn't threaten me. He didn't physically try to stop me. He didn't stalk me. He didn't murder me. Some men do. I am one of the lucky ones. The impact on the rest of my life has been minimal. I didn't become homeless. I didn't turn to drugs or alcohol. I didn't enter into a series of abusive relationships. I didn't commit suicide. Some women do.

°anguish
agonizing mental pain

16   Instead, I went on to earn a doctorate, develop a successful consulting practice, and build a strong marriage. Life is good. But I still have nightmares, sometimes. I still walk out of movies that show acts of violence against women. And I still, and probably always will, feel anguish° when I hear someone ask "Why don't these women just leave?"

Questions for Critical Thinking

1. The author presents the opposing point of view to her own argument when she reports a conversation she once overheard in a beauty salon. Find the quote, underline it, and label it "opposing viewpoint" in the margin of the essay.

2. An author's thesis is usually found in the opening paragraph of a piece of writing, but that is not the case in this essay. Nevertheless, the writer's thesis is still very clear. We come to realize what that thesis is from the essay's contents, beginning with the title. Using your own words, write a sentence that will provide the thesis of this essay.

3. Why does the author begin her essay with a picture of her present marriage? What effect does this positive opening have on us as we read the rest of the essay?

4. In the first six paragraphs, the author presents the traditional thinking about women who find themselves in abusive relationships. What are some of those traditional ideas?

5. The heart of a persuasive essay is the evidence an author uses to support the essay's thesis. In this selection, which paragraphs present the evidence for the author's thesis? Find these paragraphs and underline the six reasons the writer gives for having stayed in her abusive relationship.

6. What are the words the author repeats as she introduces each new reason? What is the writer's reason for this repetition?

7. Paragraphs 11, 13, and 14 point out the roles that other people played in the author's struggle to understand her marriage. Explain the role of each of these people and the degree of influence each one had on the author's thinking.

8. What are all the elements that make this essay a convincing argument? Can you find any weak points in the writer's approach? Refer to the guidelines for writing a persuasive essay given in Chapter 32.

Writing in Response

1. Recall a relationship you remember well. Why did that relationship succeed or fail? Using the Weiss essay as your model, tell the story of that relationship. As you tell that story, make an argument to convince your reader about why that relationship did or did not work.

2. Write an essay in which you classify marriages according to their degree of success. Give each of your categories a heading. For instance, one category could be called "marriages doomed to failure."

3. In this essay, we learn that the image a family member presents in public may be very different from the reality the rest of the family experiences at home. Write an essay that describes someone you have observed whose actions at home are very different from that person's public image.

4. In paragraph 13 of the essay, Elaine Weiss presents a seemingly unimportant event that turns out to be an epiphany (an incident that is suddenly and profoundly revealing). Write your recollection of an experience you had or a moment in your own life that was an epiphany for you. Explain the effects of this moment of revelation on your life.

5. Many people seek the advice of counselors, therapists, and other experts to help them with their problems. In paragraph 11 of the essay, Elaine Weiss tells us that she received some unfortunate advice from a therapist, advice she assumed had to be correct because it came from a professional. Use your personal experience or experiences of others you know to make an argument for seeking help from experts. How can a person judge the advice of a professional?

6. Write a helpful letter to a friend who has been suffering in an abusive relationship. Advise that person what to do, and give the person a step-by-step plan to follow. (Use process as the letter's method of development.)

7. In paragraph 14, the author mentions the people who supported her during a difficult period in her life. Write an essay in which you discuss how the support of other people can be important when an individual is in distress. Your essay could be a narration of your personal experience, it could include classification of the types of individuals who can be helpful to people in need, or it could present an argument that many people need much more support than they are presently receiving.

Reference Guide for the ESOL Student

For many students in the United States today, English is not their first language. As a result, these students encounter obstacles to both spoken and written English. This appendix reviews some of the more common difficulties faced by these students.

Using the Articles *a*, *an*, and *the*

How Do You Know When to Use the Article *a* or *an* before a Noun?

Many languages do not use the articles *a*, *an*, and *the* before nouns. Remember that nouns are people, places, and objects. Use the article *an* before a noun beginning with a vowel sound. The vowels are *a, e, i, o,* and *u*. Use the article *a* before a noun that begins with a consonant letter sound. A consonant is any letter that is not a vowel.

- Most English nouns are **count nouns;** that is, they can be counted:

  one town   two towns
  one orange   two oranges

> Use *a* or *an* with single count nouns when the noun has not been specifically identified. (Perhaps the noun is being introduced for the first time to the reader.)
>
> **A town** in Georgia was struck by a tornado.
>
> **An orange** contains vitamin C.

- **Noncount nouns** cannot be easily counted:

  courage   homework   sugar

> Do *not* use *a* or *an* with noncount nouns.
>
> We admire people with *courage*.
>
> Do you have *homework* tonight?
>
> I like *sugar* in my coffee.

NOTE: Never add *-s* to make a noncount noun plural. Noncount nouns have no plural form.

- Learn to recognize common noncount nouns:

Abstract nouns:	beauty, courage, health, information, knowledge
Areas of study:	astronomy, biology, history, math, music
Diseases:	diabetes, measles, pneumonia
Games:	soccer, basketball, poker
Nouns that indicate a mass:	information, clothing, entertainment, equipment, furniture, homework, jewelry, luggage, machinery, mail, money, news, research, traffic
Food and drink:	flour, sugar, rice, salt, water, coffee, tea, milk, butter, oil
Natural substances:	air, blood, cotton, silk, coal, gasoline, ice, snow

- Some nouns can be countable or uncountable, depending on the context:

Count noun:	There is *a time* for work and *a time* for play.
Noncount noun:	*Time* is passing.
Count noun:	He found *a hair* on the lens of the camera.
Noncount noun:	She cuts *hair* for a living.

How Do You Know When to Use the Article *the* before a Noun?

Use *the* with both count and noncount nouns when the noun is specifically identified by its context. Do *not* use *the* if the noun has not been clearly identified or if the meaning carries the idea of *all* or *in general*.

Examples of nouns that are identified	Examples of nouns that are not identified or whose meaning carries the idea of *all* or *in general*
The city of Macon was struck by a tornado.	*A city in Georgia* was struck by a tornado.
The cities of Macon and Savannah were struck by tornadoes.	*Cities in Georgia* were struck by tornadoes.
The jacket with the hood is mine.	I would like *a jacket with a hood*.
The jackets with the hoods are new.	Jackets *with hoods* are popular.
The soldier spoke of *the courage that his platoon displayed* in the battle.	The soldier spoke of *courage*.

Most singular proper nouns do not take the article *the*.

I live on *Walnut Street* in *Buffalo, New York*.

The following categories of proper nouns do *not* take the article *the:*

Countries of one word:	Canada, Mexico
Continents:	Asia, Africa
States:	New Jersey, Arizona
Cities:	Miami, Detroit
Streets:	Elm Street, Rodeo Drive
Parks:	Central Park
Lakes:	Lake Michigan
Persons:	Mayor Fernandez, Captain Cook
Days of the week:	Monday, Tuesday
Months of the year:	January, February

There are many exceptions to this rule, so it is important to learn the following list of categories of nouns that *do* require the article *the*.

The following categories of proper nouns take the article *the*.

Most bodies of water, including oceans, seas, canals, gulfs, and rivers:

the Indian Ocean, the Panama Canal, the Ohio River

Deserts and mountain ranges:

the Sonoma Desert, the Rocky Mountains

Countries whose names suggest plural units:

the United States, the United Arab Emirates, the Philippines

Geographical regions and areas:

the Middle East, the Mississippi Delta, the Northwest Territory

Historical periods and events:

the Great Depression, the French Revolution, the Civil War

Most buildings, bridges, hotels, and highways:

the Sears Tower, the Golden Gate Bridge, the Marriott Hotel, the Dixie Highway

Groups:

the National Education Association, the National Basketball Association, the Red Cross

What Are the Other Determiners besides *a, an,* and *the*?

Determiners are those adjectives that identify and quantify nouns. In a series of adjectives before a noun, these determiners always come first.
For count nouns, you can choose from the following determiners:

Singular:	a, one, each, every, this, that
Plural:	the, these, those, few, a few, many, more, most, some, several, any, two, three, and so on

Following are some examples:

I have *one book* to read.

I have *many books* to read.

For noncount nouns, you can choose from different determiners:

the, this, that, some, little, a little, much, more, any

Following are some examples:

I have *much homework* to do.

Notice you cannot use specific numbers.

Incorrect: I have *five homeworks* to do.

Correct: I have *some homework* to do.

or

Correct: I have *five homework assignments* to do.

(Adding the count noun *assignment* allows you to use the number *five* and a plural noun.)

English Word Order

Word Order for Adjectives

When more than one adjective is used to modify a noun, use the determiner before the first noun:

Determiner:	a, each, the, this (see previous list)
Judgment:	friendly, stunning
Size:	tiny, petite
Shape:	round, slender
Age:	young, elderly
Color:	yellow, green
Nationality:	Korean, Nigerian
Material:	wax, wood

Following are some examples:

I found *a* beautiful, antique, silver bracelet.

She purchased *two* large, oval, linen tablecloths.

Word Order for Adverbs

Adverbs showing frequency (*always, often, usually, sometimes, never*) come after forms of the verb *be*, but before other verbs.

My aunt *is usually* on time.

My aunt *usually brings* us candy.

Word Order for Negation

Not is placed after the first helping verb. When there is no helping verb, insert a form of the verb *do* before *not*.

Statement:	The patient *has been taking* the medicine.
Negation:	The patient *has not been taking* the medicine.
Statement:	The patient *takes* the medicine every day.
Negation:	The patient *does not take* the medicine every day.

The Idiomatic Use of Prepositions

Learning to choose the correct preposition comes mostly from reading and listening to the natural use of prepositions. Some expressions should be carefully studied. Learn these uses of prepositions for expressing time.

Use *on* for a specific day or date	Use *in* for a period of time	Use *at* for a specific time
on Thursday	in the morning	at 12 noon
on Friday	in the afternoon	at 3 a.m.
on August 25, 2016	in the evening	at dawn
	in 2013	at dusk
	in the summer	at night
	in August	
	in six hours	

Special Problems with English Verbs

The Five Forms of English Verbs

Most English verbs have five forms. One exception is the verb *to be*, which has eight forms.

	Regular	Irregular	Verb *be*
Base form (used for first person, second person, and third-person plural)	walk	go	be (am, are)
-s form (present third-person singular)	walks	goes	is
-ing form (present participle)	walking	going	being
Past tense form	walked	went	was, were
Past participle form	walked	gone	been

The Meanings of English Helping Verbs

Of the twenty-three helping verbs (including forms of *do, have,* and *be*), nine are called **modals.** These modals function only as helping verbs. They do not have the five forms of the main verbs. They are used to form tenses and to add shades of meaning to the main verb. Be sure you know these meanings. Notice that in some cases, a modal may have an alternate expression that has the same meaning such as *can, must,* and *should*.

English Helping Verbs

	HELPING VERB	MEANING	EXAMPLE
1.	can	ability	I *can* paint this room.
	is able to (another option for *can*)		I *am able to* paint this room.
2.	could (after a past tense)	ability	He said I *could* paint this room.
3.	will	intention	I *will* paint this room.
4.	shall	usually used for questions	*Shall* I paint this room?
5.	would	intention (after a past tense verb)	I promised him that I *would* paint this room.
6.	may	permission	*May* I paint this room?
7.	might	possibility	I *might* paint this room if you buy the paint.
8.	must	necessity	I *must* paint this room before we move in.
	have to (another option for *must*)		I *have to* paint this room before we move in.
	must	probability	He *must* be running late; he has not shown up yet to help me paint the room.
9.	should	advisability	The room is shabby; I *should* paint it.
	ought to (another option for *should*)		The room is shabby; I *ought to* paint it.
	should	expectation	He *should* arrive soon with the paint.
	ought to (another option for should)		He *ought to* arrive soon with the paint.

Verbs That Do Not Occur in the Continuous Form

The continuous form, which is verbs ending in *-ing*, indicates an ongoing activity:

> **Continuous form:**   The chef is *learning* to make pastry.

Some English verbs cannot occur in the continuous form, even though they indicate an ongoing activity. These verbs are called **stative verbs and should take on the present tense ending.**

> **Incorrect:**   The chef is understanding today's demonstration.
>
> **Correct:**   The chef *understands* today's demonstration.
>
> **Incorrect:**   He is knowing how to make pie crust.
>
> **Correct:**   He *knows* how to make pie crust.

Do not use the continuous form with stative verbs.

Verbs with Stative Meanings

STATE OF BEING	MENTAL ACTIVITY	SENSORY PERCEPTION	MEASUREMENT	RELATIONSHIP	EMOTION
be	believe	appear	cost	belong	desire
	doubt	feel	equal	contain	dislike
	know	hear	measure	entail	hate
	remember	see	weigh	have	like
	think	seem		own	love
	understand	smell			want
		taste			

Note that in some cases, a verb may have both a stative meaning and an active meaning. A verb with a stative meaning suggests a present state of being, while a verb with an active meaning ends with *-ing* to suggest that an action is being done at that present moment.

Stative verb: The child *weighs* sixty pounds.

but

Active verb: The grocer is *weighing* the fruit.

The Verb Forms *been* and *being*

Although *been* and *being* may sound similar in speech, when writing them, there is an important difference. Use *been* when a past participle is needed. *Been* will follow *has, have,* or *had.*

Active voice: The actress *has been studying* her part.

Passive voice: The part *has been studied* by the actress.

Use *being* when a present participle is needed. *Being* will follow some form of the helping verb *be (am, is, are, was, were).*

Active voice: The scientists *are* being observant.

Passive voice: The experiment *is being observed* by the scientist.

Idiomatic Expressions Using *do* or *make*

Following are some of the many natural expressions using *do* or *make. Note that the verbs do* and *make* cannot be used interchangeably. Even though they both express an action, they are completely different actions. The verb *do* expresses that something must be done or completed. The verb *make* expresses that something needs to be made or created.

do the wash	*make* the bed
do the dishes	*make* a pie, cake, meal
do your homework	*make* a decision
do a job	*make* a mistake
do the shopping	*make* a deal
do the laundry	*make* progress
do someone a favor	*make* a speech
do your hair	*make* a living

Verb-Preposition Combinations

The uses and meanings of prepositions in the English language are very difficult to master. When they are part of two-word and three-word combinations with verbs, the prepositions are called **particles,** and the combinations are called **phrasal verbs.** Some of these particles may be separated from the verb, and others may not be separated. Since there is no clear rule, each one must be learned the same way you would learn a new vocabulary word. Below are a few common verb-preposition combinations.

Separable phrasal verbs

ask out (invite on a date)	He *asked out* the older girl. He *asked* the older girl *out*.
call off (cancel)	Let's *call off* the party. Let's *call* the party *off*.
call up (telephone)	The office manager *called up* the applicant. The office manager *called* the applicant *up*.
clear up (solve)	Can you *clear up* this problem? Can you *clear* this problem *up*?
fill out (complete)	Please *fill out* these forms. Please *fill* these forms *out*.
get back (recover)	The student *got back* the test results. The student *got* the test results *back*.
leave out (omit)	Don't *leave out* any answers. Don't *leave* any answers *out*.
look over (review)	*Look over* this paper for any errors. *Look* this paper *over* for any errors.
look up (research, check)	*Look up* the Web site on the Internet. *Look* the Web site *up* on the Internet.
make up (create, invent, lie)	Do you think he *made up* the story? Do you think he *made* the story *up*?
turn down (refuse)	She *turned down* our generous offer. She *turned* our generous offer *down*.
turn off (switch off)	*Turn off* the light. *Turn* the light *off*.

Nonseparable phrasal verbs

call on (visit; choose)	Doctors used to *call on* patients in their homes. The teacher *called on* me for the answer.
check in on (visit)	Joshua *checks in on* his elderly mother at least twice a week.
get away with (escape consequences of)	Our dog always tries to *get away with* something when we are out.

get along with (be on terms with)	The new employee *gets along with* all her good coworkers.
get over (recover from)	We took a long time to *get over* the loss of our pet.
get at (hint, suggest)	What do you think the editorial was *getting at?*
go over (review)	Please *go over* the chapter before taking the test.
let up (diminish in force)	The storm will soon *let up.*
look into (investigate)	The federal agents will *look into* the case.
run into (meet)	I always *run into* someone I know at the supermarket.
run out of (become used up)	The printer will soon *run out of* paper.
speak up (talk in a louder voice)	Please *speak up* so that I can hear you.
turn up (appear)	Has your lost mitten *turned up* yet?
wear out (become unusable through long use)	He *wore out* five pairs of jeans this season.

Verbs Followed by Gerunds or Infinitives

Some verbs may be followed by gerunds (an *-ing* form of the verb), while others are followed by infinitives (the *to* plus the base form of the verb). Still, others may be followed by either a gerund or an infinitive. Because this is a challenging aspect of becoming fluent in English, begin by learning the most commonly used expressions. Then gradually increase your correct usage of these many expressions. Look for them as you read, and try to incorporate them into your speaking and writing.

Verbs followed by gerunds

admit	deny	finish	postpone
appreciate	discuss	imagine	practice
avoid	eat	keep	risk
consider	enjoy	miss	suggest

I suggest *going* on a cruise.

I *quit eating* junk food.

Verbs followed by infinitives

agree	decide	mean	promise
ask	expect	need	refuse
beg	have	offer	want
choose	hope	plan	
claim	manage	pretend	

I *hope to visit* you by the end of the summer.

Verbs followed by either gerunds or infinitives

begin	hate	remember	try
continue	like	start	
forget	love	stop	

Stuart *began reading* at age four.

or

Stuart *began to read* at age four.

ESOL Word Confusions

When Do You Use *no* and When Do You Use *not*?

Use *no* before a noun. *No* is an adjective.

I have *no food* in the house.

Use *not* before a verb, adverb, or adjective. *Not* is an adverb.

I am *not going.*

They were *not very* satisfied.

We are *not unhappy.*

What is the Difference between *a few* and *few* and between *a little* and *little*?

Use *a few* and *a little* to mean *some:*

With count nouns:	We have *a few cans* on the shelf, maybe five or six.
With noncount nouns:	We have *a little money* in the bank.

Use *few* and *little* to mean *not many* or *not much:*

With count nouns:	We have *few cans* left, two or three at most.
With noncount nouns:	We have *little money* in the bank.

What Is the Difference between *on* and *in*?

Use the preposition *on* when you want to say that something is on top of something else. Use the preposition *in* when you want to say that something is in or inside something else.

Examples of on	*Examples of in*
I am on the road.	You are in the building.
She is on the couch.	Clean the dishes that are in the sink.
Stand on the stool.	Sit in this chair.
Set the papers on the desk.	The dog is in the house.

Other ESOL Concerns Addressed
in *The Writer's Workplace*

active voice	Chapter 12
agreement (pronoun/antecedent)	Chapter 9
agreement (subject/verb)	Chapter 4
capitalization	Chapter 13
case	Chapter 9
clauses	Chapters 6 and 7
collective nouns	Chapter 4
comma	Chapter 13
direct and indirect quotation	Chapters 13 and 33
look-alikes/sound-alikes	Chapter 15
negatives (double)	Chapter 10
parallel structure	Chapter 10
passive voice	Chapter 12
phrases	Chapters 3 and 5
pronouns	Chapter 9 and Appendix B
punctuation	Chapter 13
relative clauses	Chapter 7
spelling rules	Appendix D
transitional expressions	Chapters 18, 19, 21, 22, 23, 24, 26 and Appendix E
verbs	Chapters 3, 11, and 12
-ed on past tense	Chapter 3
irregular	Chapter 11 and Appendix C
lie/lay; rise/raise; sit/set	Chapter 15
present and past participles	Chapter 5
-s for the present tense	Chapter 3
who/whom	Chapter 9

Parts of Speech

Words can be divided into categories called **parts of speech.** Understanding these categories will help you work with language more easily, especially when it comes to revising your own writing.

Nouns

A **noun** is a word that names a person, place, or thing.

Common nouns	Proper nouns
officer	Michael Johnson
station	Grand Central Station
magazine	*Newsweek*

Nouns are said to be **concrete** if they name things you can see or touch.

    window   paper   river

Nouns are said to be **abstract** if they name things you cannot see or touch. These words may express concepts, ideas, or qualities.

    marriage   democracy   honesty

To find out whether a word is a noun, it may help to ask one or more of these questions:

- Can I make the word plural? (Most nouns have a plural form.)
- Can I put the article *the* in front of the word?
- Is the word used as the subject or object of the sentence?

Pronouns

A **pronoun** is a word that takes the place of a noun. Like a noun, a pronoun can be a subject or an object in a sentence. It can also be used to show possession.

Pronouns can be divided into eight classes. Four of these are given in the following chart: *personal pronouns, relative pronouns, demonstrative pronouns, and indefinite pronouns.*

CLASSES OF PRONOUNS

PERSONAL PRONOUNS

	Subjective		Objective		Possessive	
	Singular	**Plural**	**Singular**	**Plural**	**Singular**	**Plural**
1st Person	I	we	me	us	my (mine)	our (ours)
2nd Person	you	you	you	you	your (yours)	your (yours)
3rd Person	he she it	they	him her it	them	his (his) her (hers) its (its)	their (theirs)

RELATIVE PRONOUNS
(CAN INTRODUCE NOUN CLAUSES AND ADJECTIVE CLAUSES)

who   what   whose   which   that   what   whoever   whichever   whatever

DEMONSTRATIVE PRONOUNS
(CAN POINT OUT THE ANTECEDENT)

this   these   that   those

INDEFINITE PRONOUNS
Singular

another	someone	everyone	no one	each	much
anyone	somebody	everybody	nobody	either	one
anybody	something	everything	nothing	neither	such
anything					

Plural

both   few   many   several

Singular or Plural
(depending on meaning)

all   any   more   most   none   some

Adjectives

An **adjective** is a word that modifies, describes, or limits a noun or a pronoun. Adjectives usually come directly before the nouns they modify, but they can also appear later in the sentence.

Here the adjective comes directly in front of the noun it modifies:

The *unusual* package was placed on my desk.

Here the adjective occurs later but refers back to the noun it modifies:

The package felt *cold*.

Verbs

A **verb** is a word that shows action or expresses a state of being. It can change form to show the time (past, present, or future) of that action or state of being.

Verbs can be divided into three classes: action verbs, linking verbs, and helping verbs.

Action Verbs

An **action verb** tells us what the subject is doing and tells us when the action occurs.

In this sentence, the action takes place in the present:

The athlete *runs* five miles every morning.

In this sentence, the action takes place in the past:

The crowd *cheered* for the oldest runner.

Linking Verbs

A **linking verb** joins the subject of a sentence to one or more words that describe or identify the subject.

Here the linking verb *was* identifies *he* with the noun *dancer:*

He *was* a dancer in his twenties.

Here the linking verb *seemed* describes *she* as *disappointed:*

She *seemed* disappointed with her job.

COMMON LINKING VERBS			
act	become	look	sound
appear	feel	remain	taste
be (am, is, are, was, were,	get	seem	turn
has been, have been, had been)	grow	smell	

Helping Verbs (Also Called Auxiliaries)

A **helping verb** combines with the main verb to form a verb phrase. It always comes before the main verb.

The helping verb could show the *tense* of the verb:

It *will* rain tomorrow.

The helping verb could show the *passive voice:*

The new civic center *has been* finished.

The helping verb could give a *special meaning* to the verb:

Barry Manilow *may be* singing here tonight.

COMMON HELPING VERBS

		Forms of *be*		Forms of *have*	Forms of *do*
can	shall	being	are	has	does
could	should	been	was	have	do
may	will	am	were	had	did
might	would	is			
must					

Adverbs

An **adverb** is a word that modifies a verb, an adjective, or another adverb. It often ends in -*ly*, but a better test is to ask yourself if the word answers one of the questions *how*, *when*, or *where*.

The adverb could modify a *verb:*

The student walked *happily* into the classroom.

The adverb could modify an *adjective:*

It will be *very* cold tomorrow.

The adverb could modify another *adverb:*

Winter has come *too* early.

Learn to recognize the common adverbs in the following list.

COMMON ADVERBS

Adverbs of frequency		Adverbs of degree	
always	often	even	only
ever	seldom	extremely	quite
never	sometimes	just	surely
		more	too
		much	very

Prepositions

A **preposition** is a word that may be used to relate a noun or pronoun to some other word in the sentence. The preposition with its noun or pronoun and any modifiers is called a **prepositional phrase**.

The letter is *from* my father.

The envelope is addressed *to* my sister.

Read through the following list of prepositions several times so that you will be able to recognize them. Your instructor may ask you to memorize them.

COMMON PREPOSITIONS

about	behind	except	onto	toward
above	below	for	out	under
across	beneath	from	outside	underneath
after	beside	in	over	unlike
against	between	inside	past	until
along	beyond	into	regarding	up
among	by	like	since	upon
around	concerning	near	through	with
as	despite	of	throughout	within
at	down	off	till	without
before	during	on	to	

Conjunctions

A **conjunction** is a word that joins or connects words, phrases, or clauses.

A conjunction may connect *two words:*

Sooner *or* later, you will have to pay.

A conjunction may connect *two phrases:*

The story was on the radio *and* in the newspaper.

A conjunction may connect *two clauses:*

Dinner was late *because* I had to work overtime.

CONJUNCTIONS

COORDINATING CONJUNCTIONS	SUBORDINATING CONJUNCTIONS		CORRELATIVE CONJUNCTIONS
and yet	after	if, even if	either … or
but so	although	in order that	neither … nor
or	as, as if, as though	provided that	both … and
nor	as long as	rather than	not only … but also
for (meaning *because*)	because	since	
	before	so that	
	even though	that	
	how	though	
		unless	
		until	
		when, whenever	
		where, wherever	
		whether	
		while	

ADVERBIAL CONJUNCTIONS
(also known as conjunctive adverbs)

To add an idea:	furthermore	*To show an alternative:*	otherwise
	moreover		instead
	likewise		
	in addition	*To show likeness:*	on the other hand
	also		
	besides	*To show emphasis:*	likewise
			similarly
To contrast:	however		
	nevertheless	*To show time:*	indeed
	nonetheless		in fact
	consequently		meanwhile
To show results:	therefore		
	accordingly		
	hence		
	thus		

Interjections

An **interjection** is a word that expresses a strong feeling and is not connected grammatically to any other part of the sentence.

Oh, I forgot my keys.

Well, **that means I'll have to sit here all day.**

Studying the Context

Because one word may function differently or have different forms or meanings in different sentences, you must often study the context in which the word is found in order to be certain of its part of speech. In the following sentence, *for* functions as a preposition:

The parent makes sacrifices *for* the good of the children.

But in this next sentence, *for* functions as a conjunction, meaning *because:*

The parent worked two jobs, *for* her child needed a good education.

Irregular Verbs

Following is an alphabetical listing of the principal parts of common irregular verbs.

Base form	Past tense	Past participle
arise	arose	arisen
bear	bore	borne
beat	beat	beat, beaten
become	became	become
begin	began	begun
bend	bent	bent
bet	bet	bet
bind	bound	bound
bite	bit	bitten, bit
bleed	bled	bled
blow	blew	blown
break	broke	broken
breed	bred	bred
bring	brought	brought
build	built	built
burst	burst	burst
buy	bought	bought
cast	cast	cast
catch	caught	caught
choose	chose	chosen
cling	clung	clung
come	came	come
cost	cost	cost
creep	crept	crept
cut	cut	cut
deal	dealt	dealt
dig	dug	dug
dive	dived, dove	dived
do	did	done
draw	drew	drawn

Base form	Past tense	Past participle
drink	drank	drunk
drive	drove	driven
eat	ate	eaten
fall	fell	fallen
feed	fed	fed
feel	felt	felt
fight	fought	fought
find	found	found
fit	fit	fit
flee	fled	fled
fling	flung	flung
fly	flew	flown
forbid	forbade, forbad	forbidden
forget	forgot	forgotten
forgive	forgave	forgiven
freeze	froze	frozen
get	got	gotten
give	gave	given
go	went	gone
grind	ground	ground
grow	grew	grown
hang	hung, hanged*	hung, hanged
have	had	had
hear	heard	heard
hide	hid	hidden
hit	hit	hit
hold	held	held
hurt	hurt	hurt
keep	kept	kept
kneel	knelt	knelt
know	knew	known
lay (to put)	laid	laid
lead	led	led
leave	left	left
lend	lent	lent
let	let	let
lie (to recline)	lay	lain

*See the dictionary to clarify usage.

Base form	Past tense	Past participle
lose	lost	lost
make	made	made
mean	meant	meant
meet	met	met
mistake	mistook	mistaken
pay	paid	paid
plead	pleaded, pled	pleaded, pled
prove	proved	proved, proven
put	put	put
quit	quit	quit
read	read*	read*
ride	rode	ridden
ring	rang	rung
rise	rose	risen
run	ran	run
say	said	said
see	saw	seen
seek	sought	sought
sell	sold	sold
send	sent	sent
set	set	set
sew	sewed	sewn, sewed
shake	shook	shaken
shave	shaved	shaved, shaven
shed	shed	shed
shine	shone	shone
shoot	shot	shot
show	showed	shown, showed
shrink	shrank, shrunk	shrunk, shrunken
shut	shut	shut
sing	sang	sung
sink	sank	sunk
sit	sat	sat
slay	slew	slain
sleep	slept	slept
slide	slid	slid
sling	slung	slung

*Pronunciation changes in past and past participle forms.

Base form	Past tense	Past participle
slink	slunk	slunk
slit	slit	slit
sow	sowed	sown, sowed
speak	spoke	spoken
speed	sped, speeded	sped, speeded
spend	spent	spent
spin	spun	spun
spit	spat	spat
split	split	split
spread	spread	spread
spring	sprang	sprung
stand	stood	stood
steal	stole	stolen
stick	stuck	stuck
sting	stung	stung
stink	stank, stunk	stunk
stride	strode	stridden
strike	struck	struck
string	strung	strung
swear	swore	sworn
sweep	swept	swept
swim	swam	swum
swing	swung	swung
take	took	taken
teach	taught	taught
tear	tore	torn
tell	told	told
think	thought	thought
throw	threw	thrown
wake	woke, waked	woken, waked
wear	wore	worn
weave	wove	woven
weep	wept	wept
wet	wet	wet
win	won	won
wind	wound	wound
wring	wrung	wrung
write	wrote	written

Spelling

Forming the Plurals of Nouns

Almost all nouns can be made plural by simply adding **s** to the singular form:

girl	girl**s**
dinner	dinner**s**

However, each of the following groups of words has its own special rules for forming the plural.

1. **Words ending in -y.** For words ending in **-y** preceded by a *consonant,* change the *y* to *i* and add *es.*

la**dy**	lad**ies**
ceremo**ny**	ceremon**ies**

Words ending in *-y* preceded by a *vowel* form their plurals in the regular way, by just adding **s.**

day	day**s**
monk**ey**	monkey**s**
vall**ey**	valley**s**

2. **Words ending in -o.** Most words ending in *-o* preceded by a *consonant* add **es** to form the plural.

hero	hero**es**
pota**to**	potato**es**
ec**ho**	echo**es**

However, musical terms or names of musical instruments add only **s.**

pian**o**	piano**s**
sol**o**	solo**s**
sopran**o**	soprano**s**

Words ending in *-o* preceded by a *vowel* add **s.**

patio	patio**s**
radio	radio**s**
rodeo	rodeo**s**

Some words ending in -o may form their plural with **s** or **es.**

memento	memento**s**	or	mento**es**
pinto	pinto**s**	or	pinto**es**
zero	zero**s**	or	zero**es**

If you are uncertain about the plural ending of a word ending in -o, it is best to consult a dictionary. The dictionary gives all the endings of irregular plurals. If no plural form is given, you know the word forms its plural in the regular way, by adding only **s.**

3. **Words ending in -ch, -sh, -s, -x, and -z.** For words ending in -ch, -sh, -s, -x, and -z, add **es.**

witch**es**	dress**es**	buzz**es**
dish**es**	tax**es**	

4. **Words ending in -fe or -f.** For some words ending in -fe or -f, change the f to v and add **es.** You can hear the change from the f sound to the v sound in the plural.

wife	wi**ves**
leaf	lea**ves**

For other words ending in -fe or -f, keep the f and just add **s.**

sheriff	sheriff**s**
belief	belief**s**

Again, you can hear that the f sound is kept in the plural. Some words can form their plural either way. If so, the dictionary will give the preferred way first.

5. **Foreign words.** Some words borrowed from other languages use the plurals from those other languages.

cris**is**	cris**es**
phenomen**on**	phenomen**a**
alumn**us** (masc.)	alumn**i**
alumn**a** (fem.)	alumn**ae**
alg**a**	alg**ae**

6. **Compound nouns.** Plurals of compound nouns are formed by putting s on the end of the main word.

brother-in-law	brother**s**-in-law
passer-by	passer**s**-by

7. **Irregular plurals.** Some nouns in English have irregular plurals.

child	children
deer	deer
foot	feet
goose	geese
man, woman	men, women
moose	moose
mouse	mice
ox	oxen
sheep	sheep
tooth	teeth

Adding Endings to Words Ending in –Y

1. When a *y* at the end of a word is preceded by a consonant, change *y* to *i* and add the ending. (After you have studied the examples, write the other words on the blanks.)

Word		Ending		New word
carry	+	er	=	carr**ier**
merry	+	ment	=	merr**iment**
funny	+	er	=	_____
lovely	+	ness	=	_____
vary	+	es	=	_____

Exceptions: Do not change the *y* to *i* if the ending starts with *i*. In English, we seldom have two *i*'s together.

study	+	ing	=	stud**ying** (not *studiing*)
ready	+	ing	=	_____

Some long words drop the *y* when the ending is added. You can hear that the *y* syllable is missing when you pronounce the word correctly.

military	+	ism	=	militarism
accomp*any*	+	*ist*	=	_____

2. When a *y* at the end of a word is preceded by a vowel, do *not* change the *y* when adding the ending. Simply add the ending.

surv**ey**	+	s	=	surv**eys**
enj**oy**	+	ment	=	_____

Learning to Spell *Ie* or *Ei* Words

Use this rhyme to help you remember how to spell most *ie* and *ei* words:

i before *e*

except after *c*

or when sounded like *a*

as in **neighbor** or **weigh.**

i before *e* (*ie* is much more common than *ei*):

bel*ie*ve	fr*ie*nd	y*ie*ld
ch*ie*f	shr*ie*k	

except after *c*:

*cei*ling	con*cei*ve	re*cei*ve
con*cei*t	re*cei*pt	

or when sounded like *a* as in *neighbor* or *weigh:*

b**ei**ge   r**ei**ns   v**ei**n

eight   sl**ei**gh

Once you have learned the rhyme, concentrate on learning the following groups of words, which are exceptions to the rhyme.

Exceptions to the *ie/ei* rule

ie	ei	ei	ei	ei
ancient	caffeine	leisure	either	counterfeit
conscience	codeine	seize	neither	Fahrenheit
efficient	protein	seizure	sheik	foreign
sufficient			stein	height
			their	
			weird	

When Should the Final Consonant of a Word Be Doubled?

When you add an ending that begins with a vowel (*-ed, -er, -est, -ing*) to a word, how do you know whether you should double the final consonant of that word? The answer to this question involves a complicated spelling rule. However, the rule is well worth learning because once you know it, you will suddenly be able to spell scores of words correctly.

In the examples below, can you explain why the word *trap* doubles its *p* but the word *turn* does not double its *n?*

The final p doubles: trap + ing = tra**pp**ing

The final n does not double: turn + ing = tur**n**ing

Because the last three letters (*rap*) in the word *trap* are a consonant-vowel-consonant combination, you double the final consonant in this one-syllable word (when adding an ending that begins with a vowel). Since the last three letters (*urn*) in the word *turn* are a vowel-consonant-consonant combination, you do not double the final consonant in this one-syllable word (when adding an ending that begins with a vowel).

> Double the final consonant of a one-syllable word when adding an ending that begins with a vowel only if the last three letters of the word end with a consonant-vowel-consonant combination.

PRACTICE   Study the list of words that follows. For each of these one-syllable words, decide whether to double the final consonant when adding an ending that begins with a vowel.

One-syllable word	Consonant-vowel-consonant combination?	Double?	Word with -ing ending
1. drag	_____	_____	_____
2. drain	_____	_____	_____
3. slip	_____	_____	_____

4. crack   _____   _____   _____

5. broil   _____   _____   _____

6. win   _____   _____   _____

NOTE: In words with *qu*, like *quit* or *quiz*, think of the *qu* as a consonant: *quit* + *ing* = qui*tt*ing. The *u* does have a consonant *w* sound.

For words of more than one syllable, the rule has one more condition: If the first syllable in the newly formed word is accented, do not double the final consonant.

Thus,

pre fer´ + ed = pre ferred´

(The new word *preferred* maintains the accent on the second syllable, so the final *r* is doubled.) However,

pre fer´ + ence = pref´ er ence

(In the new word *preference,* the accent is on the first syllable, so the final consonant *r* is not doubled.)

Is it One Word or Two?

Deciding whether certain words should be joined to form compound words is difficult. To avoid confusion, study the following three groups of words.

These words are always written as one word:

another	good-bye,	playroom
bathroom	*or* good-by	roommate
bedroom	grandmother	schoolteacher
bookkeeper	nearby	southeast, northwest, and so on
cannot	nevertheless	yourself
downstairs	newspaper	

These words are always written as two words:

a lot	dining room	high school	no one
all right	good night	living room	

The following words may be written as one or two words depending on their use. After you have studied the spellings and definitions, write the proper words on the blanks in the sample sentences.

all ready (pron, adj):   **completely prepared**

already (adv):   **previously; before**

He was _____ there by the time I arrived.

I have _____ read that book.

We were _____ for the New Year's Eve party.

all together (pron, adj):   in a group

altogether (adv):   completely

Our family was _____ at Thanksgiving.

I am _____ too upset to concentrate.

Have you gathered your papers _____?

all ways (adj, noun):   every road or path

always (adv):   on every occasion

Be sure to check _____ before you cross that intersection.

_____ look both ways before you cross that intersection.

She _____ figures out the homework.

any one (adj, pron):   one person or thing in a specific group

anyone (indefinite pron):   any person at all

Did _____ ever find my gloves?

She will talk to _____ who will listen to her.

I would choose _____ of those sweaters if I had the money.

every one (adj, pron):   every person or thing in a specific group

everyone (indefinite pron):   all of the people

_____ of the books we wanted was out of stock.

_____ was so disappointed.

_____ of the workers disapproved of the new rules.

may be (verb):   might be

maybe (adv):   perhaps

The news broadcast said that there _____ a storm tomorrow.

If it's bad, _____ I won't go to work.

_____ my car won't start.

Spelling Commonly Mispronounced Words

Several common English words are often mispronounced or pronounced in such a way that the result is incorrect spelling. Below are sixty common words that are often misspelled. As you study them, be careful to spell each of the underlined syllables correctly.

1. **Remember the *a* in each underlined syllable:**

acciden**tall**y	ex**traor**dinary	mini**a**ture	temper**a**ment
basi**call**y	inciden**tall**y	sep**a**rate	temper**a**ture
bound**ar**y	liter**a**ture		

2. Remember the *e* in each underlined syllable:

consid**era**ble	fun**er**al	math**e**matics	scen**ery**
dif**fer**ence	int**er**esting	nu**mer**ous	

3. Notice, however, that the words below in column 1, which end in *-er*, drop the *e* when they change to the new form in column 2.

disas**ter**	laund**er**	ent**r**ance	laun**dry**
ent**er**	monst**er**	hind**r**ance	monst**rous**
hind**er**	rememb**er**	hun**gry**	remem**br**ance
hung**er**	disas**trous**		

4. Remember the *i* in each underlined syllable:

as**pi**rin	fam**i**ly	sim**i**lar

5. Remember the *o* in each underlined syllable:

choc**o**late	hu**mor**ous
envi**ron**ment	lab**o**ratory
fa**vor**ite	soph**o**more

6. Remember the *u* in each underlined syllable:

lux**u**ry	ac**cu**racy

7. Remember the *y* in each underlined syllable:

stu**dy**ing	car**ry**ing

8. Remember the underlined consonant in each of the following words:

b	**g**
proba**b**ly	reco**g**nize
c	**n**
ar**c**tic	gover**n**ment
d	**r**
can**d**idate	Feb**r**uary
han**d**kerchief	lib**r**ary
suppose**d** to	su**r**prise
use**d** to	

t

authentic   promptly
identical   quantity
partner

9. Do not add an extra *e* after the *th:*

athlete   athletic

10. Do not transpose the underlined letters:

tragedy
persuade   prefer
perform   prescription

Spelling Two Hundred Tough Words

Word List 1: Silent Letters

b	**l**	**s**
clim**b**	co**l**onel	ai**s**le
crum**b**	**n**	debri**s**
de**b**t	autum**n**	i**s**land
dou**b**t	colum**n**	**t**
c	condem**n**	depo**t**
indi**c**t	**p**	lis**t**en
d	**p**neumonia	mor**t**gage
knowle**d**ge	**p**sychology	**w**
We**d**nesday		ans**w**er
h		
ex**h**ibit		
r**h**etoric		
r**h**ythm		
sc**h**edule		

Word List 2: Double Letters

accidenta**ll**y	co**mm**i**tt**ee	po**ss**e**ss**ion	su**gg**est
acco**mm**odate	exa**gg**erate	prefe**rr**ed	su**mm**arize
acro**ss**	fina**ll**y	questio**nn**aire	tomo**rr**ow
a**nn**ual	guarant**ee**	reco**mm**end	wri**tt**en (but wri**t**ing)
a**pp**arently	nece**ss**ary	su**cc**eed	
a**rr**angement	o**cc**asiona**ll**y	su**cc**e**ss**	

Word List 3: *-able* or *-ible*

-able. Usually, when you begin with a complete word, the ending is *-able*.

acceptable   agreeable

These words keep the *e* when the ending is added:

knowledgeable   noticeable
manageable   peaceable

These words drop the *e* when the ending is added:

conceivable   imaginable
desirable   indispensable

-ible. Usually, if you start with a root that is not a word, the ending is *-ible*.

audible	illegible	possible
compatible	incredible	susceptible
eligible	permissible	tangible
feasible	plausible	

Word List 4: *de-* or *di-*

de-		**di-**	
decide	despise	dilemma	dispense
decision	despite	dilute	dispute
delinquent	despondent	discipline	dissent
descend	destructive	discuss	divide
describe	develop	disease	divine
despair	device	disguise	division
despicable			

Word List 5: The *-er* Sound

Most words ending with the *-er* sound are spelled with *-er,* like the words *prisoner, customer,* and *hunger.* Words that are exceptions to this should be learned carefully.

-ar	**-or**	**-ur**
beggar	actor	murmur
burglar	author	
calendar	bachelor	**-yr**
cellar	doctor	martyr
dollar	emperor	
grammar	governor	
pillar	humor	
polar	labor	
similar	motor	
vulgar	neighbor	
	professor	
	sailor	
	scissors	

Word List 6: -ance or -ence

Most words with the -ence sound at the end are spelled -ence. Here are a few examples:

audience   intelligence
correspondence   presence
excellence   reference
existence

Learn these exceptions:

-ance		-ense	-eance
allowance	guidance	license	vengeance
ambulance	ignorance		
appearance	nuisance		
assistance	observance		
attendance	resistance		
balance	significance		
dominance	tolerance		

Word List 7: Problems with s, c, z, x, and k

absence	concede	exceed	prejudice
alcohol	consensus	exercise	recede
analyze	criticize	fascinate	sincerely
auxiliary	ecstasy	magazine	supersede
awkward	emphasize	medicine	vacillate
biscuit	especially	muscle	vicious
complexion			

Word List 8: Twenty-Five Demons

acquire	corroborate	judgment	privilege
argument	courageous	lightning	ridiculous
benefit	extremely	ninety	secretary
cafeteria	frightening	ninth	truly
category	grateful	occurred	until
cemetery	inoculate	occurrence	village
conquer			

Transitions

Transitions are words or phrases that take the reader from one idea to another. Here are some of the most commonly used transitional expressions. They are especially useful when you want to make the connections between ideas clear to your readers.

Transitions for description—to show place

above, on top of	to the left, to the right
beneath, under	beside, near, close by, at hand, next to
ahead, in front of,	across from, nearby,
in the distance	in the neighborhood
behind, in back of	between, in the middle, in the center
toward, away from	

Transitions for narration—to show a shift in time

recently	suddenly	then
previously	immediately	next, the next day
earlier	meanwhile	several weeks later
in the past	at the same time	the following month
a few days ago	within a few minutes	finally
a hundred years ago	soon, soon afterward	eventually
now, by now	later, later on	in the end
at once	after a little while	

Transitions to show examples

for example	a case in point is. . .	specifically
another example is. . .	one such case	for instance
to illustrate	a typical case	such as
an illustration of this is. . .	consider the case of. . .	

Transitions for process

the first step	while you are. . .	the last step
in the beginning	as you are. . .	the final step
to start with	next	finally
to begin with	then	at last
first of all	the second step	eventually
	after you have. . .	

Transitions for comparison

again	like
Also	likewise
as well as	moreover
both	the same
equally	similar to
furthermore	similarly
just as	so
just like	too

Transitions for contrast

although	nevertheless
and	on the contrary
but	on the other hand
despite	otherwise
different from	still
even though	though
except for	unlike
however	whereas
in contrast with	yet
instead	

Transitions for cause

because
caused by
results from
the reason is that
since

Transitions for effect

accordingly
as a result, resulted in
consequently
for this reason
so, so that
then, therefore, thus

Terms that signal classification

divisions, divided into
categories, categorized by
types, kinds
groups, groupings, grouped into
areas, fields

Phrases that signal definition

is defined as
is understood to be
means that
is sometimes thought to be
signifies that

Transitions for persuasion

To signal the thesis:
I agree (disagree)
I (do not) support
I am (not) in favor of
. . .should (not) be changed
. . .should (not) be adopted
I propose

To signal a reason:
a convincing piece of evidence
an additional reason
because
in view of this fact

To admit an opponent's viewpoint:

while it is true

although there are those who. . .

the opposition would have you believe. . .

of course,

some may claim

we have been told that. . .

popular thought is that. . .

most people assume that. . .

To signal a conclusion:

therefore

consequently

as a result

RHETORICAL TABLE OF CONTENTS

CHAPTER 1: Gathering Ideas for Writing

ACTIVITY 5: Preparing Questions for an Interview (page 15)

1. What is a typical day at work like?
2. What is the range of salaries that a person could expect to earn as a lawyer?
3. What are the different areas of law practice, and how did you choose which one you wanted to pursue?
4. What is the most interesting case you have ever had?
5. What are some of your greatest challenges, and how do you handle them?

CHAPTER 2: Recognizing the Elements of Good Writing

ACTIVITY 1: Providing Examples for Different Approaches to a Subject (page 22, sample answers)

1. *A personal story:* the story of my unusual part-time job.
2. *Effects:* the hidden costs of having a job while going to school.
3. *How to do something:* how to succeed in school while holding a job.
4. *Comparison/contrast:* the contrast between students who hold a job while going to school and students who can devote all their time to school.
5. *Persuasion:* three good reasons why you should not work while you are going to school.

ACTIVITY 2: Understanding Purpose in Writing

1. *Purpose*: Information
2. *Purpose*: entertainment
3. *Purpose*: persuasion
4. *Purpose*: information
5. *Purpose*: persuasion

ACTIVITY 3: Identifying an Audience and a Purpose (page 24, sample answers)

1. *Audience:* first-time users of online banking; *Purpose:* information.
2. *Audience:* creative non-fiction class; *Purpose:* entertainment.

3. *Audience:* city or state government; *Purpose:* persuasion.
4. *Audience:* Chair of an academic department; *Purpose:* persuasion.
5. *Audience:* Students in Fashion 101 or users of a build-your-own blog website; *purpose:* information.

CHAPTER 3: Finding Subjects and Verbs in Simple Sentences

Practice 1 (page 36)

1. gym   2. coach   3. He   4. athletes   5. People

Practice 2 (page 37)

1. morning, June   2. flowers, grass   3. people, village, square   4. lottery, Mr. Sommers   5. man, time, energy, activities

Practice 3 (pages 37)

1. They   2. It   3. They   4. She   5. We
6. Nobody *or* No one

Practice 4 (pages 38)

1. The, confident
2. Her, long, strenuous (*her* is a possessive pronoun used as an adjective)
3. Several, the, finish
4. a, terrible, one
5. A, disappointing, the

Note: A, an, and *the* are usually called *articles* or *noun determiners.*

Practice 5 (pages 39)

1. Exercise, thoughtful nutrition
2. Mothers, fathers
3. factors, factors

Practice 6 (pages 39)

1. child: *concrete common noun*
2. Helen Keller: *concrete proper noun*
3. She: *personal pronoun*
4. park: *concrete common noun*
5. leaves: *concrete common noun*

6. thought: *abstract common noun*
7. parents, teacher: *compound subject; concrete common nouns*
8. Everyone: *indefinite pronoun*
9. time: *abstract common noun*
10. Who: *relative pronoun*

EXERCISE 1: Finding the Subject of a Sentence (page 40)

1. train   2. Steven Laye   3. She   4. Decorations
5. man   6. pathway   7. Buses, cars   8. People
9. Lights   10. Enthusiasm

EXERCISE 2: Finding the Subject of a Sentence (page 40)

1. Road   2. Child   3. She   4. Deer   5. Clouds
6. Family   7. Someone   8. Aunt   9. Man
10. Message

EXERCISE 5: Recognizing Prepositions (page 43)

1. down   2. under   3. toward   4. among
5. for   6. through   7. over   8. at   9. until
10. despite

EXERCISE 7: Finding Subjects in Sentences with Prepositional Phrases (page 44)

1. Jane would grow up in high-waisted floor-length dresses, with fans, bonnets, and parasols.
2. In that era, she wrote many humorous stories about social issues before her death in 1817.
3. In spite of the popularity of her stories, this author remained anonymous and relatively unknown at death.
4. Over 200 years later, artists remember Jane's appeal through movies and books.
5. In 1995, the instant movie classic *Clueless* came out in theaters.
6. Beneath the modern glamor of cell phones, malls, and short skirts, this movie portrayed Austen's character from 1815: the naïve matchmaker, *Emma*.
7. Throughout America and England, audiences enjoyed *Bridget Jones's Diary*, as a book in 1996 and then a movie in 2001.

8. Without Jane's *Pride and Prejudice* in 1813, Bridget Jones's complicated relationship with Mr. Darcy would not have existed.
9. On February 5, 2016, the movie *Pride and Prejudice and Zombies* was released as another contemporary twist on Jane's timeless work.
10. From beyond the grave, the Regency era author Jane Austen influences pop culture in the modern world.

Practice 7: (page 45)

1. Alex Harkavy, a high school senior, has an auditory-processing disorder.
2. Marcia Rubinstein, an educational consultant, can help him find the right college.
3. For instance, Landmark, a college in Putney, Vermont, specializes in programs for students with learning disabilities.
4. A federal law, the Americans with Disabilities Act, was enacted in 1990.
5. Now many colleges, both public and private ones, offer support for learning-disabled students.
6. One particular guidebook, *Peterson's Colleges with Programs for Students with Learning Disabilities or Attention Deficit Disorders*, is especially helpful.

Practice 8 (page 46)

1. Here in America the sale of human organs for transplant is against the law.
2. Unfortunately, there is a disturbing illegal market in the sale of these organs.
3. Where do some people desperately look for kidneys?
4. Why are so many donors exploited and unprotected?
5. Get involved. (you)
6. Work toward a solution to this tragic social problem. (you)

EXERCISE 8: Finding Subjects in Simple Sentences (page 46)

1. students   2. freshman   3. plenty   4. iPad
5. flight   6. passengers   7. people   8. flyers
9. freshman   10. classmate

Practice 9: (page 48)

1. is   2. has   3. comes

EXERCISE 11: Finding Action Verbs (page 49)

1. Some hug
2. divers dive
3. stylists are paid
4. bride could hire
5. Some steal
6. One warmed
7. tester enjoys
8. cleaners are needed
9. Tasters check
10. One will interest

EXERCISE 13: Finding Linking Verbs (page 51)

1. My dream last night was wonderful.
2. I had been transformed.
3. I looked young again.
4. The house was empty and quiet.
5. In a sunlit kitchen with a book in hand, I appeared relaxed and happy.
6. In the morning light, the kitchen felt cozy.
7. It seemed safe.
8. The brewing coffee smelled delicious.
9. The bacon, my usual Sunday morning treat, never tasted better.
10. In this dream, life felt satisfying.

EXERCISE 15: Finding Helping Verbs (page 54)

1. Graduation from high school does not signal the end of one's learning.
2. In today's world, workers must adjust to many changes in the workplace.
3. They will need to understand new technologies.
4. Can they recognize the difference between facts and opinions in news articles?
5. All citizens would benefit from annual refresher courses in their fields.
6. Everyone should read a daily newspaper.
7. Senior citizens might take courses at local community colleges.
8. Also, they could keep their minds active with crossword puzzles and other games.
9. Have people learned to try new recipes from television cooking programs?
10. Do we take responsibility for keeping our minds curious and engaged?

EXERCISE 17: Identifying Parts of Speech (page 55)

1. b   2. a   3. a   4. f   5. d   6. c   7. f   8. e   9. d   10. c

CHAPTER 4: Making Subjects and Verbs Agree

Practice 1 (page 62)

1. barks   2. wakes   3. become   4. deserve
5. throw

Practice 2 (Page 63)

1. doesn't   2. were   3. doesn't   4. Were
5. doesn't

EXERCISE 1: Making the Subject and Verb Agree (page 63)

1. writers present
2. They nominate
3. writer lives
4. She doesn't
5. we see
6. She wears
7. books center
8. book is
9. She was
10. We don't

EXERCISE 4: Agreement with Hidden Subjects (page 65)

1. words hidden
2. individual was called
3. Wonder-wench could flatter (or) offend
4. you can (never) forget
5. Golden retriever might be
6. (you) stare
7. person could become
8. you would like
9. Definition means
10. English speakers resurrect

EXERCISE 6: Agreement with Collective Nouns
(pages 67)

1. crew is
2. union accuses
3. group files
4. team are
5. public voice
6. crowd grows
7. audience interrupt
8. jury hears
9. group have
10. crowd sit

EXERCISE 8: Agreement with Indefinite Pronouns
(page 69)

1. Many were
2. They feature
3. Each was
4. All was
5. Most were
6. Few deny
7. Each was
8. One was
9. nothing was
10. Much is

EXERCISE 10: Subject-Verb Agreement with Compound Subjects (page 71)

1. Macaroni and cheese is
2. meal (and) others have
3. mother (and) father enjoy
4. habits (or) routine needs
5. salad (or) vegetable is
6. Adults (and) children do
7. pizzas (and) sodas are
8. lack (or) eating causes
9. chips (nor) popcorn is
10. apple (or) carrot sticks make

CHAPTER 5: Understanding Fragments and Phrases

EXERCISE 1: Putting a Conversation into Complete Sentences (pages 80–81)

1. What else would you like to have in the house?
2. I don't want anything except more wine.
3. I bet we have one hour before the storm hits.
4. It looks like it's going to be bad.
5. Let's hope there are no blackout this time.
6. What about candles? Do we have any?
7. We don't have any.
8. You can find some at the store on the corner.
9. Are you ready to go?
10. Just let me grab my coat

EXERCISE 3: Correcting Fragments That Belong to Other Sentences (page 84)

1. Fishing is one of the oldest sports in the world and **can be one of the most relaxing.** A person with a simple wooden pole and line can have as much fun as a sportsman **with expensive equipment. For busy executives, overworked teachers, and even presidents of nations**, fishing can be a good way to escape from the stress of demanding jobs.

2. The first electric car was built in 1887. It was sold commercially **six years later.** At the turn of the century, people had great faith in new technology. In fact, three hundred electric taxicabs were operating in New York City by 1900. However, electric cars soon lost their popularity. The new gasoline engine became more widely used. **With our concern over pollution**, perhaps electric cars will become desirable once again.

3. Maya dropped out of college two years ago. She had found it hard to read the textbooks **and other assignments.** Her mind wandered. She had never read very much for personal enjoyment **except maybe a magazine now and then.** Books had always seemed boring. She preferred to talk with her friends. She got a job instead working in a restaurant **for two years.** Now Maya, **having saved enough money to return to the local community college**, is back in school. She is ready **to put her mind on her coursework.** She has decided to major in hospitality. To get a degree, she will need to learn much better study habits.

Practice 1 (page 86)

1. INF 2. PP 3. INF 4. INF 5. PP

Practice 2 (page 87)

1. P 2. G 3. G 4. P 5. P

EXERCISE 5: Identifying Phrases (page 88)

1. participle phrase
2. prepositional phrase
3. prepositional phrase
4. verb phrase

5. group of prepositional phrases
6. noun phrase
7. infinitive phrase
8. gerund phrase
9. verb phrase
10. prepositional phrase

EXERCISE 11: Correcting the Fragment That Contains a Participle (pages 92–93, sample answers)

The zombie staggered forward in the cramped country cemetery. It tripped over and disturbed tombstones and graves that had not been visited in years. A gravedigger working the night shift became aware of unnatural moans growing louder in the distance. The worker looked out at the cemetery with his mouth open in disbelief.

EXERCISE 13: Correcting Fragments (pages 93–94, sample answers)

1. Early morning is a time of peace in my neighborhood.
2. The gray mist covers up all but the faint outlines of nearby houses.
3. I can barely make out the shapes of cars in the streets and driveways.
4. Often, I sit and look out the window.
5. Holding a steaming cup of coffee, I slowly wake up.
6. The only sound to be heard is the rumbling of a truck.
7. It is passing by on the highway a quarter mile away.
8. Children are all tucked in their beds.
9. No barking dogs can be heard.
10. I love to sit by the window in this soft, silent dream world.

CHAPTER 6: Combining Sentences using Coordination

Practice 1 (page 102)

1. The audience listened, for this was a man with an international reputation.
2. She could have told about all his successes, but instead she spoke about his disappointments.

3. Her words were electric, so the crowd was attentive.
4. I should have brought a recorder, or at least I should have taken notes.

EXERCISE 1: Combining Sentences Using Coordinating Conjunctions (pages 103–104)

1. *contrast:* but
2. *add:* and
3. *result:* so
4. *add, both clauses are in the negative:* nor
5. *reason:* for
6. *result:* so
7. *contrast:* but
8. *choice:* or
9. *contrast:* but
10. *choice:* or

Practice 2 (page 108)

1. The restaurant is always too crowded on Saturdays; nevertheless, it serves the best food in town.
2. The land was not for sale; however, the house could be rented.
3. The lawsuit cost the company several million dollars; consequently, the company went out of business a short time later.
4. The doctor told him to lose weight; furthermore, she instructed him to stop smoking.

EXERCISE 4: Combining Sentences Using Adverbial Conjunctions (pages 108–109)

1. *emphasis:* in fact
2. *emample:* for example
3. *contrast:* nonetheless
4. *adds an idea:* also
5. *emphasis:* indeed
6. *contrast:* however
7. *adds an idea:* in addition
8. *alternative:* instead
9. *alternative:* on the other hand
10. *time:* meanwhile

EXERCISE 7: Combining Sentences Using the Semicolon (page 112)

1. Some people are afraid of public speaking; some fear it more than death.
2. It was dark; she couldn't find the light switch.
3. The resort had restaurants and a gym; the beach was lined with palm trees and blue lounge chairs.
4. The trains were running late; subway riders had to push their way into the train car.
5. Lisbeth worked hard for two years in her entry-level position before receiving a big promotion.
6. He decided to simplify his lifestyle in the city; his family was impressed.
7. She always spoke to everyone with respect; they all admired her.
8. The story touched my heart; I read it twice.
9. Many young adults today expect a lot in exchange for very little time and effort.
10. The instructor introduced new approaches in the course; sincere students were open to trying them.

CHAPTER 7: Combining Sentences using Subordination

EXERCISE 1: Identifying Dependent and Independent Clauses (pages 122)

1. IC 2. DC 3. DC 4. IC 5. IC 6. DC
7. DC 8. IC 9. IC 10. DC

Practice 1 (page 124)

1. DC 2. PP 3. PP 4. DC 5. PP 6. DC

Practice 2 (page 126)

1. a. Soraya went out to celebrate after she won the floor routine competition.
   b. After she won the floor routine competition, Soraya went out to celebrate
2. a. The family was excited when Carla returned from Venezuela this spring.
   b. When Carla returned from Venezuela this spring, the family was excited.

EXERCISE 4: Combining Sentences Using Subordination (pages 126–127, sample answers)

1. While she was eating breakfast, the results of the election came over the radio.
2. This year the town council voted in favor of the plan whereas last year they voted against the identical plan.
3. I will see Shonda Rhymes tonight because she is speaking at the university.
4. The worker hoped for a promotion even though not one person in the department had received a promotion last year.
5. Because the worker hoped for a promotion, he did all his work accurately and on time.

Practice 3 (pages 129–130)

1. The chemistry lab that I attend is two hours long.
2. The student assistant who is standing by the door is very knowledgeable.
3. The equipment that was purchased last year will make possible some important new research.

Practice 4 (page 131)

1. no commas
2. no commas
3. Her biology course, which met four times a week for two hours each session, was extremely demanding.
4. no commas
5. My own poetry, which has improved over the semester, has brought me much satisfaction.

EXERCISE 8: Combining Sentences Using Relative Pronouns (pages 132–133)

1. Stress, which we experience every day, can do a great deal of harm.
2. People whose jobs are demanding often use food to help them cope. (no commas)
3. The practice of eating to cope with stress, which usually goes back to childhood, is often automatic.
4. Some foods that people turn to in times of stress can actually increase tension. (no commas)
5. Sweet foods, which are popular with people who need a lift, are actually not energy boosters.
6. Another substance that people use to get an energy boost is caffeine. (no commas)

7. One of the biggest mistakes is using alcohol, which is really a depressant, to feel calm and relaxed.

8. People who want to feel a sense of calm should eat three light meals a day and two small snacks. (no commas)

9. Sufficient protein, which maintains an adequate energy level, is needed throughout the day.

10. A person should eat regularly to avoid binges, which put on pounds and drain one's energy.

CHAPTER 8: Correcting Fragments and Run-Ons

EXERCISE 1: Recognizing Fragments (page 145)

1. b   2. c   3. a   4. c   5. d   6. c   7. a
8. d   9. b   10. d

Practice 1 (page 148, sample answers)

Answers will vary.

1. *Coordination*: Chronic procrastinators are those people who put things off at school or at work; **in addition**, they may also avoid obligations to their family members at home.

2. correct as is

3. *Subordination*: **Sometimes** a person sometimes feels inadequate or overwhelmed by a task, he or she keeps putting off what has to be done.

4. *Coordination*: Believe it or not, the average worker, according to recent research, wastes two hours a day on nonwork activities; this adds to the cost of doing business.

5. *Two sentences*: One way to deal with the tendency to procrastinate is to break up a complicated task into its smaller parts. Another way is to reward oneself for accomplishing a task that seems too difficult or unpleasant.

EXERCISE 4: Recognizing and Correcting Run-Ons (page 148, sample answer)

I had this dream the other night. My sister and I were at a pool, which had seats all around it like a stadium. I can't remember if people were watching us or not. My sister suddenly fell into the pool, so I jumped in and swam to the bottom to save her. Then, these weird arms appeared and tried to keep her down. Finally, I got her free, but just as we were about to swim to the surface, someone was putting boards over the top of the pool so we couldn't get out. That's where my dream ended.

CHAPTER 9: Choosing Correct Pronouns

Practice 1: (pages 158–159)

1. I   2. me   3. me

Practice 2: (page 160)

1. he   2. me

Practice 3: (pages 161–162)

1. whom   2. who   3. whoever   4. who   5. who

EXERCISE 3: Choosing the Correct Pronoun Using *Who/Whom* (page 162)

1. who   2. whom   3. who   4. Whom   5. who's
6. whom   7. who   8. whose   9. who   10. whom

EXERCISE 5: Choosing Correct Pronoun Forms (page 163)

1. she   2. me   3. whoever   4. she   5. who
6. Who   7. they   8. whom   9. him   10. I

Practice 4: (pages 165–166, sample answers)

1. Everyone should bring suggestions to the meeting.

2. These sorts of clothes are popular now.

3. These sorts students didn't know what they were eating.

4. If the bird watchers hope to see anything, they must get up early.

5. This type of book appeals to me.

Practice 5: (pages 166–167, sample answers)

1. I enjoy math exams because I can show what I know.

2. When I took geometry, I discovered that frequent review of past assignments helped make the course seem easy.

3. People always need to practice their skills.

4. Math games can be fun for a student if he or she has a spirit of curiosity.

5. When studying math, you must remember that you have to "use it or lose it."

Practice 6: (page 167, sample answers)

1. The biologist asked the director to bring back the biologist's microscope.
2. The report says that both the atmosphere and oceans have gotten warmer since the 1950s.
3. At the laboratory, the scientists said that the research had run into serious difficulties.
4. The testing equipment, which was accidentally dropped onto the aquarium, was badly damaged.
5. I don't watch the 10 o'clock news anymore because the programs have become too slick.

EXERCISE 7: Making Pronouns and Antecedents Agree (pages 168–169)

1. Vanessa asked her friend to take Vanessa's video off the site.
2. Before deciding on a treatment, a person must think about the side effects involved.
3. When the student received the award, his or her name was misspelled on it.
4. People used to think that drilling holes in one's head would help with seizures and migraines.
5. Everybody was looking forward to his or her winter break.
6. Each of the contestants chose songs from his or her childhood.
7. You need to wear gloves because the weather report said the temperature will drop tonight.
8. These kinds of videos are disturbing.
9. The lady said we had to leave the movie theater.
10. Those types of people need to think before posting things.

CHAPTER 10: Working with Adjectives, Adverbs, and Parallel Structure

Practice 1: (pages 178–179)

1. Unique type: *adverb modifies verb* known
2. mild form: *adjective modifies noun* form
3. more severe: *adverb modifies adjective* severe
4. very high: *adverb modifies adjective* high
5. occur regularly: *adverb modifies verb* occur
6. anxious people: *adjective modifies noun* people
7. starchy foods: *adjective modifies noun* foods
8. helpful walk: *adjective modifies noun* walk

EXERCISE 1: Adjectives and Adverbs Used in Comparisons (pages 181–182)

1. easier 2. tallest 3. more easily 4. better
5. most famous 6. most helpful 7. more slowly
8. worst 9. worse 10. most delicious

Practice 2: (page 184)

1. quickly 2. really 3. awful 4. good 5. well

EXERCISE 3: Revising Misplaced Modifiers (page 187)

1. I gave the puppy with the white paws to my sister.
2. I am looking for the missing keys to the filing cabinets.
3. We decided to buy better sleeping bags before the camping trip.
4. The pilot always put passenger safety first.
5. They need to go home immediately after the party .
6. Watching the faces of the judges, the dance contestants waited eagerly.
7. The jeweler wanted to design a special charm bracelet for his new customer.
8. I took my daughter, who loved a day off from school, to my office.
9. The accountant almost forgot to tell his client about the change in the law.
10. Take only one tablet every day.

EXERCISE 4: Revising Dangling Modifiers (page 188)

1. Wearing his tuxedo, Victor fed the pit bull.
2. While she scrolled through Instagram, the photo caught her eye.
3. Hoping to see the news, I turned on the television set at seven o'clock.
4. Although I ran up the stairs, the train had already left for Philadelphia.
5. After she danced around the room, the temperature felt much warmer.
6. I thought my son, dressed in a Dracula costume, looked perfect for Halloween.
7. She saw three spiders hanging from the ceiling in her bedroom.
8. After I wiped down the window, the hummingbird flew away.
9. We listened to the neighbor's dog howling all evening without a stop.
10. After I had painted my room all afternoon, my cat demanded her dinner.

Practice 3: (page 190, sample answers)

1. A person should never (or shouldn't ever) go out with something cooking on the stove.
2. You have neither a bike nor a car. or You haven't either a bike or a car.
3. I don't want anything. or I want nothing.
4. I will never (or won't ever) break my promise.
5. I can't (or can hardly) wait until summer.

Practice 4: (page 191)

1. dirty
2. sewing her own clothes
3. willingly explain the lesson more than once

EXERCISE 6: Revising Sentences for Parallel Structure (page 192)

1. bitterly cold   2. to watch television
3. a dedicated father   4. dark   5. graceful
6. sunny   7. to work out at the gym
8. fill out my calendar   9. was showcased
10. and finally at him

CHAPTER 11: Mastering Irregular Verb Forms

Practice 1: (page 204)

1. became   2. cost   3. hit   4. spread   5. quit

Practice 2: (pages 205–206)

1. bought   2. spent   3. bled   4. kept
5. thought   6. sought   7. fought   8. taught
9. led   10. sent

Practice 3: (page 205)

1. began   2. rose   3. sung   4. grew   5. flown
6. known   7. rode   8. sprung   9. written
10. shown

EXERCISE 1: Practicing Irregular Verb Forms (page 206)

1. began   2. written   3. knew   4. bet
5. hit   6. threw   7. kept   8. come
9. shrunk   10. hidden

EXERCISE 4: Practicing More Irregular Verb Forms (page 208)

1. mistaken   2. broken   3. taken   4. shaken
5. saw   6. wrung   7. gone   8. burst
9. forgiven   10. eaten

CHAPTER 12: Using Verb Tenses Correctly

Practice 1: (page 217)

1. went   2. have gone   3. has studied
4. took   5. has been

Practice 2: (page 218)

1. has fascinated   2. has become, have watched
3. have replaced, had existed   4. had lived
5. has built

EXERCISE 1: Practicing with Sequence of Tenses (page 219)

1. have stopped   2. would have   3. will buy
4. had never been   5. liked   6. will soon be
7. are   8. knew   9. would go   10. had gone

EXERCISE 3: Correcting Unnecessary Shifts in Verb Tense (pages 221–222)

1. will take   2. was   3. doesn't   4. came
5. doesn't   6. continues   7. has   8. came
9. prefers   10. arrived

EXERCISE 6: Forming Active Voice and Passive Voice (pages 224–225)

1. *Active voice:* The child dialed the wrong number.
2. *Active voice:* My grandmother very carefully crocheted the sweater.
3. *Passive voice:* Cherry Creek was struck by a tornado last spring.
4. *Passive voice:* The leaves were blown across the yard (by the wind).
5. *Active voice:* In the seventies, many fashionable young men and women wore platform shoes.

Practice 3: (page 226)

1. When President Roosevelt died in 1945, the law required that Vice President Truman take over immediately.

2. It was essential that President Truman act quickly and decisively.

3. Truman must have wished that he were able to avoid using the atomic bomb to bring an end to World War II.

4. He felt it was necessary that the United States help Europe recover from the destruction of World War II.

5. President Truman always insisted that other countries be economically strong.

CHAPTER 13: Learning the Rules for Capitalization and Punctuation

EXERCISE 1: Capitalization (page 236)

1. We   2. Winter Solstice
3. General Motors   4. Old Testament
5. Louisiana Purchase, France   6. Southwest
7. Automobile Workers Union, President Obama
8. Dominican   9. Game of Thrones and The Voice
10. Judge Johnson

Practice 1: (page 238)

1. On October 8, 2015, the city of Flint, Michigan, announced that its water source would switch back to Detroit's water system.

2. Problems with the water supply of the United States, Europe, Canada, and other parts of the world are growing.

3. Water is colorless, tasteless, odorless, and free of calories.

4. You will use—on an average day—twenty-four gallons of water for flushing, thirty-two gallons for bathing and washing clothes, and twenty-five gallons for other uses.

5. It took 120 gallons of water to create the eggs you ate for breakfast, 3,500 gallons for the steak you might eat for dinner, and more than 60,000 gallons to produce the steel used to make your car.

Practice 2: (page 239)

1. The most overused bodies of water are our rivers, but they continue to serve us daily.

2. American cities often developed next to rivers, and industries followed soon after in the same locations.

3. The people of the Industrial Age can try to clean the water they have used, or they can watch pollution take over.

4. The Great Lakes are showing signs of renewal, yet the struggle against pollution there must continue.

5. Many people have not yet been educated about the dangers to our water supply, nor are all our legislators fully aware of the problem.

Practice 3: (page 240)

1. To many people from the East, the plans to supply more water to the western states seem unnecessary.

2. However, people in the West know that they have no future without a good water supply.

3. When they entered Salt Lake Valley in 1847, the Mormons found dry soil that needed water before crops could be grown.

4. Confidently, the new settlers dug ditches that brought the needed water.

5. Learning from the past, modern farmers are trying to cooperate with nature.

Practice 4: (page 241)

1. Some parts of our country, I believe, do not have ample supplies of water.

2. The rocky soil of Virginia, for example, cannot absorb much rainwater.

3. Johnstown, Pennsylvania, a town of twenty-one thousand, is situated in one of the most flood-prone valleys of America.

4. It is not, therefore, a very safe place to live.

5. The Colorado, which is one of our longest rivers, gives up most of its water to farmers and cities before it reaches the sea.

Practice 5: (page 241)

1. Dear, your tea is ready now.
2. I wonder, Jason, if the game has been canceled.
3. Dad, could I borrow five dollars?
4. I insist, sir, on speaking with the manager.
5. Kim, is that you?

Practice 6: (page 242)

1. 4,876,454   2. 87,602   3. 156,439,600
4. 187,000   5. 10,000,000,000,000

Practice 7: (page 242)

1. "I won't," he insisted, "be a part of your scheme."
2. He mumbled, "I plead the Fifth Amendment."
3. "I was told," the defendant explained, "to answer every question."
4. "The court case," the judge announced, "will be televised."
5. "The jury," said Al Tarvin of the press, "was handpicked."

Practice 8: (page 242)

1. Kicking, the child was carried off to bed.
2. To John, Russell Baker is the best columnist.
3. When you can, come and visit us.
4. We surveyed the students in the class; out of the twenty, seven were married.
5. Some types of skin cancers can kill, doctors say.

EXERCISE 4: Using the Comma Correctly (page 243)

1. In Miami, Florida, a valedictorian gets ready to give a speech in front of a full auditorium of about 4,000 friends and family.
2. Even though she is nervous, she has properly prepared.
3. The determined youth did research, in fact, on how to manage her anxiety.
4. Her findings, which were taken from a study on communication apprehension, explained that heart rates during public speaking reveal four different styles of nervousness.
5. The styles were identified as the Average, the Insensitive, the Confrontational, and the Inflexible.
6. The people with the average heart rate reaction have the expected amount of adrenaline pumping, and they feel generally positive about public speaking.
7. Those identified as having an insensitive nervousness style are much less apprehensive about speaking in public, have a much lower heart rate, and usually have a lot of experience in front of an audience.
8. The people with a confrontational reaction to public speaking have a very high heart rate in the moments right before they speak, but after they start, the rate relaxes to average.
9. The inflexible have the highest heart rate of all, and this incredible anxiety can be used to enhance their performance or diminish it.

10. The valedictorian in Florida steps to the podium, takes a deep breath, and says "Congratulations, graduates."

EXERCISE 7: Using the Apostrophe (page 246)

1. sun's   2. press's   3. room's
4. Anthony and Maria's   5. nobody's
6. his   7. Queen Elizabeth's reign   8. That's
9. boys'   10. book's

Practice 9: (pages 248–249)

1. "The Gift of the Magi" is one of the short stories in O. Henry's book *The Four Million*.
2. Franklin Delano Roosevelt said, "We have nothing to fear but fear itself."
3. No quotation marks with indirect speech
4. The term "reggae" refers to a popular musical style originating in Jamaica.
5. She read the article "Can Empathy Be Taught?" in a recent issue of *Academe*.

Practice 10: (page 249)

1. One of the best ways to remember a vacation is to take numerous photos; one of the best ways to recall the contents of a book is to take notes.
2. The problem of street crime must be solved; otherwise, the number of vigilantes will increase.
3. The committee was made up of Kevin Corey, a writer; Anita Poindexter, a professor; and Jorge Rodriguez, a politician.
4. The bank president was very cordial; however, he would not approve the loan.
5. The retailer wants higher profits; the customer wants lower cost.

Practice 11: (page 251)

1. Three vocalists performed in Los Angeles recently: Ariana Grande, Adele, and Sam Smith.
2. The official has one major flaw in his personality: greed.
3. No colon
4. The college offers four courses in English literature: Romantic Poetry, Shakespeare's Plays, The British Short Story, and The Modern Novel.
5. No colon

Practice 12: (page 251)

1. Herbert Simon is—and I don't think this is an exaggeration—a genius.
2. George Eliot (her real name was Mary Ann Evans) wrote *Silas Marner.*
3. You should—in fact, I insist—see a doctor.
4. Unemployment brings with it a number of other problems (see the study by Brody, 2010).
5. Mass media (television, radio, movies, magazines, and newspapers) are able to transmit information over a wide range and to a large number of people.

EXERCISE 10: Other Marks of Punctuation (page 252)

1. To measure crime, sociologists have used three different techniques: official statistics, victimization surveys, and self-report studies.
2. "The Bells" is one of the best-loved poems of Edgar Allan Poe.
3. The lake has one major disadvantage to swimmers this summer: weeds.
4. E. B. White wrote numerous essays for adults; however, he also wrote some very popular books for children.
5. Tuberculosis (also known as consumption) has once again become a serious health issue.
6. The Victorian Period (1837–1901) saw a rapid expansion of industry.
7. He promised me—I know he promised—that he would come to my graduation.
8. Do you know what the French expression "déjà vu" means?
9. She wanted to go to the movies; he wanted to watch a movie at home.
10. She has the qualifications needed for the job: a teaching degree, a pleasant personality, two years' experience, and a love of children.

CHAPTER 14: Choosing Words that Work

EXERCISE 1: Using Words Rich in Meaning (page 264)

Confident:

1. e 2. d 3. b 4. a 5. c

Eating:

1. d 2. f 3. a 4. e 5. b 6. c

EXERCISE 3: Denotation/Connotation (page 266, sample answers)

1. mansion 2. trudge 3. straggler 4. junk
5. ancient 6. scars 7. chat 8. ragged
9. muttering 10. relaxing

EXERCISE 6: Revising Wordy Sentences (pages 269–270, sample answers)

1. The deadline for your project is May 18, *or* Your project is due a week from this Friday.
2. The thought of the exam is stressful for her.
3. The best place to study is our library.
4. Some people believe that astrology is a science.
5. We all need better organizational skills.
6. Mike is very handy mechanically.
7. She is wrapping a present.
8. The concert might be canceled due to rain.
9. The causes for unemployment are complex.
10. The box was oblong.

EXERCISE 8: Recognizing Language Inappropriate for Formal Writing (page 273)

1. *beating around the bush:* failing to get to the point
2. *chill out:* calm down; relax
3. *dude:* man
4. *businessmen:* businesspeople
5. *come clean:* confess /speak honestly
6. *downer:* disappointment
7. *guts:* courage; determination
8. *a dump:* a mess / disorganized
9. *guys:* scientists / assistants / researchers
10. *crash:* rest/ go to sleep

CHAPTER 15: Paying Attention to Look-Alikes and Sound-Alikes

GROUP I: (pages 281–284)

oral, aural; capital, capitol; cloth, clothes, close; course, coarse; complement, compliment; forward, foreword; past, passed, past; peace, piece; plain, plane; presence, presents

EXERCISE 1: Group I Words (pages 284–285)

1. aural, oral
2. piece, peace
3. capital, capital
4. cloth, clothes, close
5. course, coarse
6. complement, compliment
7. forward, foreword
8. past, passed
9. plain, plane
10. presents, presents

GROUP II: (pages 286–288)

principal, principal, principle; reign, rain; site, sight, cite; stationary, stationery; two, to, too; vain, vein; waist, waste; whether, weather; whole, holes; write, right, rite

EXERCISE 3: Group II Words (pages 288–287)

1. principal, principle
2. rein, reign
3. cite, sight
4. stationery, stationary
5. two, to, too
6. vain, vein
7. waste, waist
8. weather, whether
9. whole, hole
10. right, rite

GROUP III: (page 290)

it's, its; they're, there, their; where, were, we're; whose, who's; your, you're

EXERCISE 5: Group III Words (page 291)

1. It's, its
2. its, it's
3. they're, their, there
4. they're, their, there
5. We're, were, where
6. Where, we're
7. Whose, who's
8. Who's, whose

9. you're, your
10. your, you're

GROUP IV: (pages 292–294)

accept, except; advise, advice; affect, effect; breath, breathe; choose, chose; conscience, conscious, conscientious; custom, costume; council, counsel, consul; desert, dessert; diner, dinner, diners

EXERCISE 7: Group IV Words (page 294)

1. accept, except
2. advice, advise
3. affect, effect
4. breathe, breath
5. choose, chose
6. conscious, conscience
7. customs, costumes
8. council, counsel
9. desert, dessert
10. dinner, diner

GROUP V: (pages 295–298)

emigrate, immigrate, emigrants, immigrants; further, farther; loose, lose; personal, personnel; quite, quiet, quit; receipt, recipe; special, especially; than, then; thought, thorough, though, threw, through; used to, used, use

EXERCISE 9: Group V Words (page 298)

1. emigrated   2. farther   3. loose
4. personnel   5. quiet   6. receipt
7. special   8. than   9. through, though
10. used

Practice 1 (page 300, sample answers)

1. laid the package
2. raised his son
3. set the groceries
4. laying down the new floor
5. lay out my clothes
6. raises many questions
7. set the timer
8. laid down the law
9. setting the table

10. raised a substantial amount of money

Practice 2 (page 301)

1. rising 2. lie 3. sitting 4. lay 5. rose
6. lying 7. sat 8. risen 9. lain 10. sat

EXERCISE 11: Group VI Words (page 302)

1. laid 2. sitting 3. sit 4. raised 5. rose
6. rose 7. raised 8. lie 9. lying 10. laid

CHAPTER 16: Working With Paragraphs: Topic Sentences and Controlling Ideas

EXERCISE 2: Finding the Topic Sentence of a Paragraph (pages 311–313)

1. This situation was one of the worst I had ever been in.
2. Today, the hospital nurse has one of the hardest jobs of all.
3. A person's life at any given time incorporates both external and internal aspects.
4. We are the great "Let's junk it" society!
5. In order to shop wisely, several basic rules should be kept in mind.

EXERCISE 5: Distinguishing a Topic Sentence from a Title (pages 316–317)

1. T 2. T 3. TS 4. T 5. TS
6. T 7. T 8. TS 9. T 10. TS

EXERCISE 8: Finding the Topic in a Topic Sentence (page 318)

1. Remodeling an old house
2. two-part topic: college work and high school work
3. A well-made suit
4. Growing up near a museum
5. My favorite room in the house
6. The huge trade imbalance of the United States
7. One of the disadvantages of skiing
8. Spanking
9. An attractive wardrobe
10. the first year

EXERCISE 11: Finding the Controlling Idea (pages 320–321)

1. *Topic:* vigorous exercise; *controlling idea:* a good way to reduce the effects of stress on the body
2. *Two-part topic:* Buffalo and Toronto; *controlling idea:* differ
3. *Topic:* television violence; *controlling idea:* causes aggressive behavior
4. *Topic:* athletic scholarships available to women; *controlling idea:* increasing
5. *Topic:* caffeine; *controlling idea:* several adverse effects on the body
6. *Topic:* Serena Williams and her sister Venus; *controlling idea:* dominated the world of women's tennis
7. *Topic:* training a cat to do tricks; *controlling idea:* takes great patience
8. *Topic:* babysitting for a family with four preschool children; *controlling idea:* exhausting
9. *Topic:* the hours between five and seven in the morning; *controlling idea:* productive
10. *Topic:* the foggy night; *controlling idea:* spooky

CHAPTER 17: Working with Paragraphs: Supporting Details

Practice 1 (page 331)

Topic sentence: Certainly we all need to know how to care for a cold most effectively.

Examples of how to care for a cold that people already know: People know they should get lots of rest and drink plenty of fluids. *Examples of information people may not know:* They should not take antibiotics, aspirin, or Tylenol. *Studies with mixed results:* Studies have not proved that Vitamin C or Echinacea are effective. *Mineral supplements:* Supplements with zinc have been proven effective in shortening the length and seriousness of a cold.

EXERCISE 1: Finding the Topic Sentence and Supporting Details (pages 331–332)

Paragraph 1

Topic sentence: Diabetes, a disease of the pancreas, falls into two types.

Type I: This type, called juvenile diabetes, affects younger people who must inject themselves with insulin two or three times a day.

Type II: This type usually affects adults over 35 and is connected to overweight, poor diet, lack of exercise, and ethnicity.

Paragraph 2

Topic sentence: As time passed, the Gonzalez family became a melting-pot success story by anyone's measure.

First example: One of Uncle Sergio's and Aunt Catin's children became a college instructor.

Second example: Another son rose to be an official in the Nixon and Reagan administration.

Third example: Another child became a South Bronx social worker.

Fourth example: The author, John Gonzalez, became a journalist.

Fifth example: The author's sister became a public school teacher and later a college instructor.

Sixth example: One cousin became a doctor.

Seventh example: Another cousin became a psychiatric social worker.

Eighth example: Another cousin became a police officer.

EXERCISE 4: Distinguishing a Supporting Detail from a Restatement of the Main Idea
(pages 336–337)

1. a. SD,   b. R,   c. SD,   d. SD
2. a. SD,   b. SD,   c. R,   d. SD
3. a. R,   b. SD,   c. SD,   d. SD
4. a. SD,   b. SD,   c. R,   d. SD
5. a. SD,   b. SD,   c. SD,   d. R

CHAPTER 18: Developing Paragraphs: Illustration

EXERCISE 1: The Sources for Illustrations
(pages 347–348)

1. survey
2. hypothetical example
3. example from personal experience
4. examples from outside research

EXERCISE 4: Analyzing Paragraphs That Use Examples (page 350)

1. *The topic sentence in one's own words:* As a lover of junk, I have a happily messed-up life.
2. 17
3. (Students underline all 17 examples.)
4. yes (the word *list,* line 3)
5. Like the junk itself, the examples have no obvious order.

CHAPTER 19: Developing Paragraphs: Narration

EXERCISE 4: Placing Details in Order of Time Sequence (pages 366–367)

3, 1, 4, 2, 5

EXERCISE 7: Working with Transitions
(pages 369–370, sample answers)

The author's choice of transitions:

1. A few months ago
2. Then
3. A few weeks later
4. Twenty-four hours later
5. the next three months
6. Today
7. from time to time

CHAPTER 20: Developing Paragraphs: Description

EXERCISE 1: Selecting the Dominant Impression
(pages 383–384, sample answers)

1. well-stocked
2. greasy
3. out of date
4. vandalized
5. garish
6. eccentric
7. littered
8. cramped
9. posh
10. restored

EXERCISE 3: Revising Vague Dominant Impressions
(page 385, sample answers)

1. a brilliant blue
2. cool
3. rejuvenating
4. destructive
5. clean and bright
6. bustling
7. rich and decadent
8. his happy self again
9. comfortable
10. satisfying for now

Practice 1 (page 387)

1. *Sound:* loud humming; *touch:* cool; *sight:* large refrigerator case, milk, cream, soda, beer
2. *Smell:* onion, caraway seed, pumpernickel
3. *Sight, smell, and taste:* cheese, smoked meat

EXERCISE 6: Recognizing Sensory Images
(page 387–388)

Touch and bodily feelings: hungrier than he had been in the morning; dipping head in milk; covering his eyes; drew his head back in disappointment; pain in his tender left side; difficult to eat
Taste: milk with bread; did not taste nice; normally his favorite drink; unable to eat; turning almost against his will
Smell: something to eat; sweetened milk

EXERCISE 12: Using Spatial Order   (pages 392–393)

1. 3, 1, 5, 4, 2
2. 4, 5, 2, 1, 3
3. 2, 3, 1, 4

CHAPTER 21: Developing Paragraphs: Process Analysis

EXERCISE 1: Is the Process Complete?   (page 407)

Missing steps in the recipe for the Swedish spice cake: a list of ingredients, directions for separating the eggs yolks from the egg whites (saving the egg whites until later), temperature of the oven, how long to bake the cake

EXERCISE 4: Ordering in Logical Sequence
(page 409)

4, 8, 7, 10, 1, 3, 6, 9, 5, 2

CHAPTER 22: Developing Paragraphs: Comparison/Contrast

EXERCISE 1: Evaluating the Two-Part Topic
(pages 422–423)

Answers could vary depending on explanation.
1. too broad   2. suitable   3. suitable   4. suitable
5. too broad or suitable, depending on explanation
6. suitable   7. too broad or suitable, depending on explanation   8. suitable   9. too broad
10. too broad or suitable, depending on explanation

EXERCISE 4: Recognizing the Two Approaches to Ordering Material   (pages 427–428)

1. Block, differences
2. Block, similarities
3. Block, differences
4. Point-by-point, similarities

EXERCISE 7: Using Transitions in Comparisons and Contrasts   (pages 430–431, sample answers)

1. Dr. Rappole has an excellent bedside manner, but Dr. Connolly is very withdrawn.
2. The first apartment had almost no furniture, was badly in need of painting, and felt dark and cheerless; likewise, the second apartment was equally bare, felt totally neglected, and looked out onto a brick wall.
3. In the United States, interest in soccer has become apparent only in recent years; however, in Brazil, soccer has always been immensely popular.
4. Unlike the French Revolution, *which relied heavily on the common people*, the Russian Revolution was dominated by an elite group of thinkers.
5. Whereas Sandro is carefree and fun loving, with more interest in theater than math, his sister Noreen takes math more seriously and wants to become an engineer.

CHAPTER 23: Developing Paragraphs: Cause and Effect

EXERCISE 1: Finding Causes and Effects in Paragraphs (pages 445–446)

Causes of headaches:

1. nervous tension
2. dietary factors
   a. dependency on caffeine
   b. salt allergy
   c. low blood sugar
3. environmental factors—chemicals
   a. polishes
   b. waxes
   c. bug killers
   d. paint

Effects of headaches:

1. nausea
2. interrupted sleep, which can worsen the physical and emotional state
3. reliance on drugs with negative side effects
4. reduced productivity on the job, even absences
5. interruption of family life

EXERCISE 3: Looking for the Causal Relationship (page 448)

1. U 2. C 3. U 4. C 5. C
6. U 7. C 8. U 9. C 10. U

CHAPTER 24: Developing Paragraphs: Definition and Analysis

EXERCISE 1: Defining by Class (page 466)

1. Mythology is one form of a culture's literature.
2. Nylon is a strong, resilient, synthetic material.
3. An amoeba is a protozoan.
4. A tricycle is a vehicle.
5. Cabbage is a plant.
6. Democracy is a form of government.
7. Asbestos is a fibrous mineral.
8. A piccolo is a musical instrument.
9. Poetry is a division of literature.
10. A university is an institution of learning.

CHAPTER 26: Moving from the Paragraph to the Essay

Practice 1 (page 494)

1. F 2. TH 3. TH 4. T 5. F

EXERCISE 1: Recognizing a Thesis Statement (pages 494–495)

1. F 2. TH 3. F 4. F 5. T
6. F 7. F 8. TH 9. TH 10. T

EXERCISE 6: The Thesis Statement: Adding the Strategy of Development (page 499)

1. The effects of gambling are disastrous.

   Strategy of Development: cause and effects

2. Learning how to do your own tax return can be frustrating.

   Strategy of Development: process

3. The sight of our neighborhood park is dismaying.

   Strategy of Development: description

4. The meaning of the term patriotism is often controversial.

   Strategy of Development: definition

5. Student loans fall into several categories.

   Strategy of Development: classification

EXERCISE 9: Identifying Common Introductory Patterns (pages 502–503)

1. 3. (begins with the definition of the concept to be discussed)
2. 7. (begins with a number of descriptive images leading to the thesis)
3. 1. (begins with farm work, a general subject, then narrows down to cidering, the specific topic of the essay)

EXERCISE 12: Finding Transitional Expressions (pages 508–509)

Transitional expressions: In the past, Sometimes, many times, For one thing, For another, For example, Naturally, Then, after a short while, Of course, Finally

Pronouns: They (world problems), they're (world problems), it (land), it (land), all this (reasons for backing one side or another), we (United States), their (Somalia), we (United States), our (United States), their (Soviet Union), its (the superpower), its (the superpower), their (both sides), their (both sides), no one (neither the United States or the Soviet Union), they both (Ethiopia and Somalia), both (United States and Soviet Union), we (United States), itself (Somalia), ourselves (United States), our (United States)

Repeated terms: appear/disappear/reappear, reasons geopolitical/geopolitically, supported, ally, bases, ties, moved into, both sides

CHAPTER 33: Other College Writing: The Research Paper and the Essay Exam

EXERCISE 1: Methods of Development
(pages 609–610)

1. summary   2. comparison/contrast
3. definition   4. classification   5. cause and effect

INDEX